EUROPE
1914

60°   30°   15°

Reykjavik ● ICELAND

FAEROE ISLANDS

SHETLAND ISLANDS

Bergen

HEBRIDES

ORKNEY ISLANDS

NORTH SEA

Glasgow ●
● Edinburgh

Belfast ●

IRELAND **Dublin** ★
● Liverpool

Cork ●

GREAT BRITAIN

NETHERLANDS

London ★ Amsterdam ●

Southhampton ●

Colo

Brussels ★

B

Cherbourg ● **BELGIUM** Frank

Brest ● **LUXEMBOURG** ★

Paris ★ *Seine River* Strasbourg

Nantes ● *Loire River*

FRANCE

Dijon ● B

SWITZERL

Clermont-Ferrand ● Geneva ●

Lyon ● Turi

Bordeaux ● Ge

ATLANTIC OCEAN

Santander ●

Rhône River

Marseille ● **Mona**

Porto ●

Douro River

SPAIN

PORTUGAL *Tagus River*

Madrid ★ Barcelona ●

Lisbon ★ *CORSI*

Valencia ● *BALEARIC ISLANDS*

Guadalquivir River *MAJORCA* *SARDIN*

Sevilla ●

MADEIRA

Cadiz ●

Tangier ● Gibraltar ●

Algers ★ Tu

Rabat ★ Oran ●

Casablanca ● **SPANISH MOROCCO**

CANARY ISLANDS

IFNI

MOROCCO **TUNIS**

ALGERIA

SPANISH SAHARA

RIO DE ORO

45°

30°

~~When Eisenhower was elected~~

- 1960's Vietnam War:
- Suez ~~War~~ Crisis

post WWII — *WW II*

Europe focuses on European unity
now moves to European common market
① *coal + steel commission → European*
market → common currency

Tenth Edition

CONTEMPORARY EUROPE

A HISTORY

know Iron curtain — division between
democratic + communist Europe
theme after WWII : unity in Europe
democratic independence
in western Europe to 1989; dependence
of communism in Eastern Europe
"velvet Revolution" 1989? collapse of comm.
in Chezchoslovakia
—905 Czech broken up and disintegrated

1945-49 western Europe period of reconstruction

JAMES WILKINSON
Harvard University

H. STUART HUGHES

PEARSON

Prentice
Hall

Upper Saddle River, New Jersey 07458

EXAM UP TO COLLAPSE OF COMMUNISM

Library of Congress Cataloging-in-Publication Data
Wilkinson, James D.,
  Contemporary Europe : a history / James Wilkinson, H. Stuart Hughes.—
10th ed.
    p. cm.
    Includes bibliographical references and index.
    ISBN 0–13–184176–9
  1. Europe—History—20th century. 2. World War, 1914–1918—Europe.
3. World War, 1939–1945—Europe. 4. National socialism—Europe. 5.
Communism—Europe. 6. Post-communism—Europe. 7. World politics—20th
century. 8. European federation. I. Hughes, H. Stuart (Henry Stuart),
1916–II. Title.
D424 .W54 2004
940.5—dc22

                                            2003016516

Editorial Director: Charlyce Jones Owen
Senior Acquisitions Editor: Charles Cavaliere
Managing Editor: Joanne Riker
Production Liaison: Fran Russello
Marketing Director: Beth Gillette Mejia
Production Editor: Bruce Hobart
Marketing Manager: Heather Shelstad
Manufacturing Buyer: Tricia Kenny
Cover Design: Bruce Kenselaar
Photo Researcher: Melinda Alexander
Image Permission Coordinator: Michelina Viscusi
Composition/Full-Service Project Management: Pine Tree Composition
Printer/Binder: Phoenix Book Tech
Cover Printer: Phoenix Color Corp.

Pearson Education Ltd., London
Pearson Education Singapore, Pte. Ltd
Pearson Education, Canada, Ltd
Pearson Education—Japan
Pearson Education Australia PTY, Limited

Pearson Education North Asia Ltd
Pearson Educación de Mexico, S.A. de C.V.
Pearson Education Malaysia, Pte. Ltd
Pearson Education, Upper Saddle River, New Jersey

10 9 8 7 6 5

0-13-184176-9

For Prassede

Contents

5 Technology and Society: Between Old and New 126

6 The Years of Stability, 1924–1929 147

7 The High Culture of the 1920s 170

8 The Great Depression, 1929–1935   193

9 The Fascist Regimes   212

10 The Stalinist System 242

11 European Civilization in Crisis 261

12 The Road to Catastrophe, 1935–1939 278

13   The Second World War   303

Index   601

Maps

Preface

In preparing the tenth edition of this book, I have once again attempted to respect both the structure and the tone of earlier editions and to make additions and emendations in such a manner as to retain the harmony of the whole.

Those features that gave *Contemporary Europe* a distinctive character in its earlier editions—its treatment of Europe as a single unit, including Eastern Europe and the Mediterranean nations as well as the West; its use of political history as a unifying structure; its extended treatment of cultural developments—have been retained. With the end of the Cold War and the growing European membership of both NATO and the European Union, such an integrated approach seems even more pertinent than before.

The principal changes in this tenth edition are an expanded final chapter, now including the five years from 1997 through 2002; less extensive revisions of earlier chapters, especially those dealing with the Cold War; and a thoroughgoing revision of the bibliographies at the end of each chapter to take account of recent scholarship. To accommodate the new text while still keeping the length of the book as a whole within the overall limit of 600 pages, I have further reduced the narrative devoted to military events in Chapters 2 and 13.

The personal perspective that I bring to the task of revision has been shaped by a half dozen years of residence (and dozens of shorter trips) in both Western and Eastern Europe since 1962, during which I witnessed some of the events described here. For their hospitality and help in deciphering current events, I am especially indebted to Gabriella Bagnato, Laurence Coutrot, Jacques Lautman, Ida Calabi Limentani, Dominique Moïsi, Diana Pinto, Wolff-Dietrich Webler, and Mechta Scholz-Webler, among others. The following reviewers provided invaluable insight: Dr. John Powell, Cliona Murphy, Chris Waters, and Charles E. Endress. Melissa Stockdale offered essential bibliographic advice. Prassede, to whom the book is dedicated, knows how much she has contributed in support and editorial insight both to this and to past revisions.

After the euphoric hopes of 1989, the challenges of dealing with political and economic reconstruction in Eastern Europe and meeting the ambitious goals of the

European Union have sobered many Europeans. The events of September 11, 2001 have further highlighted the vulnerability of industrialized nations to terrorism, and brought the challenge of coordinating Europe's response with that of the United States. At the same time the pressures of a global economy are forcing a reexamination of the price Europeans are willing to pay for the lessening of their economic and cultural autonomy. Despite these challenges, however, it is clear that the Europe as a whole is moving toward progressively greater integration—of which the successful launch of the euro in January 2002 is but one example—another measure of the old continent's capacity for renewal.

James Wilkinson

EUROPE IN 1914

The funeral procession of Britain's King Edward VII in 1911. (*Courtesy Getty Images, Inc./Hulton Archive Photos*)

I. THE UNIQUENESS OF EUROPE

At the beginning of the twentieth century, Europe was the center of the world. Nearly all Europeans—and most non-Europeans as well—assumed that this tiny continent would continue to play its customary leading role in global affairs, as it had during the preceding four centuries. Europe's technological advances, economic resources, military might, political influence, and cultural achievements alike gave the continent a measure of prestige and importance unmatched by other regions of the world. Few suspected that the end of its global supremacy already loomed. As we now know, the outbreak of World War I in 1914 marked the beginning of the end of Europe's preeminence.

Yet it would be wrong to see the past ninety years of European history simply as a decline from the heights of 1914. For one thing, Europe's loss of power was relative, not absolute. Forced increasingly to share the world stage with competitors such as the United States and Japan, the continent nonetheless retained a strong political and economic influence. At the start of the new milennium, three of the five permanent members of the United Nations Security Council, four of the eight acknowledged world nuclear powers, and five of the so-called Group of Eight (G-8) leading industrial nations remained European. Though European empires had given way to independent states in Asia and Africa, Europe's political institutions and cultural legacy still marked former colonies as diverse as India, Senegal, and Singapore.

Europe's relative decline also had the paradoxical effect of bringing the New World into more direct contact with the Old. Twice during the twentieth century—in the First and Second World Wars—Americans intervened militarily in what began as a European conflict; American troops remain in Europe today. The Cold War reinforced the American commitment to resist Soviet expansion in a weakened Europe. As the demise of Soviet Union led to a new configuration of Eastern Europe in the 1990s, the United States role in Europe underwent change as well. Yet in many ways, the United States and Canada remained as tightly linked to Europe as before. Meanwhile, Europeans began to seek a new identity. Their former claims to world supremacy gone, they settled into a more modest role that would have seemed unimaginable a century earlier.

The European Heritage

"A little cape on the Asiatic continent"—that was how Europe appeared to the French poet Paul Valéry in 1919. Struck by the disparity between the region's modest geographical dimensions and its enormous influence on world history, Valéry asked what it was that had given Europe its preeminence. Why had the Europeans alone succeeded in achieving almost universal domination throughout the world in the decades before the First World War?

The most obvious answer lay in Europe's technological superiority. Of all the great world civilizations, only modern Europe had created a sustained dynamic of technical change. The Chinese, the peoples of India, the ancient Romans, and the Arabs alike were satisfied with a modest improvement in the technological achievements of their ancestors. Modern Europeans, in contrast, had not only discovered the "scientific method" of rational inquiry and precise observation, but in addition prized the technological improvements fed by science. The result was a society that welcomed and rewarded innovation, that prided itself on growth, and that had outstripped all others in accumulating both military might and economic power. The armed forces that European nations could send into combat were the world's most powerful both in size and in technical sophistication. Compared with the combined military might of other nations, such as the United States and Japan, Europe possessed an overwhelming advantage. The only threat to its military superiority lay in the Continent's internal rivalries; Europe alone was strong enough to defeat Europe.

Creating modern technology and its military applications required wealth. Here again, Europeans occupied a position of enviable strength. Modern capitalism, like modern technology—with all its complex financial and industrial devices—was a creation of the European spirit. Over the centuries, Europeans had learned how to mobilize their financial resources for investment and profit. Small wonder, then, that Europe in 1914 was the center of a world market—a worldwide system of banking and trade—with overseas investments that dwarfed those of its only major competitor, the United States. European capital financed railroads, plantations, and factories abroad. Interest paid on these loans, in turn, further swelled bank assets in London, Paris, and Berlin. Fully 83 percent of the foreign investments in all countries in 1914 was of European origin. The colonial empires of France and Britain increased the European share in world commerce to a still greater degree (see Chapter 1, V). The system was anchored by the convertability of Europe's major currencies into gold. The so-called gold standard was a monument to Europe's financial importance and to the strength of its leading currency, the British pound.

Yet another claim to uniqueness—though one that remained imperfectly realized in 1914—was Europe's role as the birthplace of democracy. The ancient Greeks of Athens had pioneered this form of shared political power; Britain, with the Magna Carta and the House of Commons, showed how democracy and monarchy could be combined through the institution of a parliament. But the most spectacular European affirmation of the democratic impulse was the French Revolution of 1789, which, despite the violence and despotism to which it soon gave way, expressed a determination to expand the rights of citizenship to a broad segment of the populace. Throughout the nineteenth century, the number of European experiments in democracy increased, until democratic institutions appeared destined to become the characteristic norm.

There remained yet another source of European self-confidence: a distinctive cultural tradition. When pressed to define what set their culture apart from that of other peoples, most Europeans in 1914 would have replied that they were the preeminent bearers of "civilization." By this they meant those aspects of culture that bridged the diverse heritages of their Latin, Germanic, and Slavic forebears. "Civilization" they equated first of all with the level of material comfort made possible by their technological progress. Many Europeans had come to expect an abundant diet, competent medical care, decent housing, public transportation, and (starting around 1880) electric lighting as a matter of course. Though not all shared in this abundance, a core of European countries running from England through France, Holland, Germany, and northern Italy had achieved a standard of living by 1914 that set Europe apart.

The bustle of horse-drawn traffic around the Bank of England in London, the world's financial capital, around 1910. *(Courtesy H. Armstrong Roberts)*

But European definitions of "civilization" extended beyond material well-being. Europeans took pride in their national systems of education (especially their great universities), their high rates of literacy, and their museums and concert halls, which became showplaces for European achievements in the arts. "Civilization" was a concept they also associated with the Christian faith, which, though variously celebrated throughout Europe, still distinguished the Continent's religion from African, Moslem, and Far Eastern creeds. (The important Jewish contribution to European culture was frequently and unjustly overlooked.) Finally, "civilization" denoted such progressive features of public life as the rule of law, an orderly society, and the absence of abuses such as slavery and officially sanctioned torture.

In all these areas, Europeans, when they paused to consider the problem at all, considered themselves in a position of enviable superiority to those in the less fortunate regions of the globe. Although the Germans, the French, the British, and the Russians were constantly at odds over the relative merits of their own, separate cultural traditions, all agreed on one fundamental point—the superiority of things European. At the end of the nineteenth century, they believed that Europe would remain the engine of world progress. Each recent decade had seen the Continent become still wealthier and more powerful. Why should this happy process end?

The most perceptive observers detected a threat in the rivalries that divided Europeans among themselves. But far more Europeans considered their quarrels with other countries healthy and "life giving." It never occurred to most that the very competitive spirit that had spurred Europeans to attain the heights of progress might now be about to cast them into ruin.

The Rise of the Nation-State

European cultural rivalries found their corresponding political expression in the concept of the nation-state. Until recently, Europeans (and Americans as well) have assumed that the normal form of political organization was a fairly large territorial unit, inhabited by a people who considered themselves culturally and linguistically homogeneous. The dominance of this political model has obscured its comparatively recent origin and the large variety of alternative possibilities that were gradually eliminated through the course of time.

The nation-state was a European invention. Chronologically, it followed two other characteristic European political systems—feudalism and absolute monarchy—which had evolved during the thousand years that separated the end of the Roman Empire from the dawn of the modern age. All three represented attempts to organize resources in order to enable ruling elites wield power more effectively. Feudalism, the earliest of the three, was a system of governing created for a warrior aristocracy. In return for a pledge of loyalty to the king, feudal lords received lands sufficient to maintain themselves and their armed retainers, who in turn pledged loyalty to them. The king theoretically retained control over the whole edifice; in practice, however, the divisions and subdivisions into which royal power was fragmented weakened the crown at the expense of the nobility and a powerful Catholic church.

Feudalism created great legal inequalities, as well as economic and political decentralization. Lords reigned over their small territories with little interference from the crown, and society became rigidly stratified, with a small landed elite ruling over a large mass of illiterate peasants. It was largely in an attempt to recover some of the power which they had delegated to their nobles that rulers in England and France began to create the bureaucratic system that eventually transformed feudal monarchies into modern nation-states. Gradually, ambitious monarchs enlarged the territory that they controlled directly, and at the same time employed officials to administer it who answered to them rather than to the feudal lords. Central administration, in turn, helped to create a sense of common belonging—first through legal norms, as in the English common law, then through common identification with the crown as a symbol of national unity.

From absolute monarchy it was but a short step to the nation-state. Its origin lay in Western Europe. As the early modern kings brought more and more territory under their control, it became conceivable that an entire ethnic group might find itself united in a single territorial unit. First, England, France, and Spain organized themselves around a common ethnic core in the period between the fifteenth and the eighteenth centuries. Other ethnic groups might be included within the nation, but these were accorded the lower status of "national minorities." In the nineteenth century, Germany and Italy overcame their more stubborn disunity and emerged as nation-states as well. By the twentieth century, the nation-state had become the norm throughout Western Europe. In the central and eastern parts of the Continent, the multinational Austro-Hungarian and Russian empires remained as relics of the past. But these empires, too, were subject to nationalist pressures from within.

As the twentieth century began, the nation-state claimed exclusive and total allegiance from its citizens. These claims were resisted by some Europeans who maintained their loyalty to older regional or dynastic ties. In Germany and Italy especially—the newcomers to the family of nation-states—a Bavarian or a Venetian might feel little allegiance to faraway rulers who governed from Berlin or Rome. Yet the persistence of these local ties made the calls for national integration all the more strident. It was precisely because recent nation-states recognized the fragile basis of their unity that they strove to strengthen a fledgling national consciousness.

Prewar European Society

Europe on the eve of the First World War was not only a continent at the height of its power; it was also a continent marked by deep social divisions within each nation-state. The nineteenth-century British prime minister Benjamin Disraeli had written of the "two nations" that coexisted uneasily within Britain's borders: the privileged and the poor. But this simple and dramatic opposition ignored a far more complex social reality. In fact, one could distinguish in prewar Europe among at least four distinct social groups, whose relative strength varied as one moved from the industrialized West to the more agrarian East. Besides the wealthy aristocrat and the destitute worker living at opposite extremes of the social spectrum, there existed a large and varied middle class as well as a shrinking number of peasant farmers in most countries of Western and Central Europe. In the East, the middle class remained small and the working class even smaller; the great majority of the total population were peasants on the land.

At the apex of Europe's social structure stood the royal houses and the aristocracy—a caste that had only partially adjusted itself to the modern concept of the nation-state. Europe's aristocracy was prenational in origin, and in some respects remained international until the First World War. The leading noble families—like the royal families themselves—had uncles and cousins scattered throughout Europe, and still possessed an international language—French—in which they could converse. State occasions like the coronation of King Edward VII of England in 1901 thus took on the aura of family reunions—for Edward was uncle both to the German emperor, William II, and to Alexandra, wife of Tsar Nicholas II of Russia.

Late nineteenth-century European society was frankly aristocratic. The old nobility, constantly reinforced by promotions from the upper middle class, was far from a spent force. Although feudal privileges were a thing of the past (in legal terms, except in Russia, all citizens were equal), the less tangible prestige of high status remained. Nearly everywhere the nobility held vast tracts of land, and in many places still exerted an informal dominance over the whole political and social life of the countryside and played a leading role in government. The German chancellor was invariably an important nobleman, and as late as the 1890s, both the Conservative and the Liberal parties in Britain furnished a peer as prime minister. At the top of the government hierarchy, cabinet ministers were more likely to be upper middle class than aristocratic in origin, but just below the top, the nobility were entrenched. They were strong at the royal courts, in the elite corps of the civil service, in the upper houses of parliament, and, more particularly, as diplomats and army officers, positions that they almost monopolized in some countries. Even in republican France, a large proportion of the ambassadors and military chiefs were of noble origin.

The more public-spirited aristocrats and the leading members of the upper middle class together constituted the "notables" of the national or local communities. The prosperous middle class—business and professional people—tended to dominate the lower houses of parliament and to manage domestic affairs, as opposed to the aristocratic role in military and foreign affairs. Many of them were linked to the nobility through business or marriage. Indeed, in countries like Britain and Germany an informal alliance existed between the two. This understanding was based on the tacit agreement that the aristocrats would hold command over the more showy and impressive manifestations of the national life, while the bourgeoisie stood modestly to the rear, possessing the reality of power but content to restrict themselves to practical affairs and to the direction of the economy.

In the early twentieth century, Europeans with money and position enjoyed their privileges openly and saw no reason to apologize for them; a democratic simplicity of manner had not yet become the style. Wealth and its accompaniments were what most clearly set apart aristocracy and upper bourgeoisie alike from the rest of the population—this and access to a superior education. In Western Europe the best schools might often be run by the state—indeed, on the Continent such was usually the case—but they were elitist in character nonetheless. The "public" schools of England, the *lycées* of France, the *Gymnasia* of Germany were in fact if not in theory the preserves of the privileged classes. Here the sons of the wealthy and well born, plus a scattering of talented recruits from the lower orders, received the classical education that was almost universally supposed to fit them for the positions of responsibility they would later occupy. Such an education was heavily weighted toward literature and rhetoric; it was weak in science, economics, and technology. But it produced future leaders who spoke and wrote with ease, fluency, and correctness, who understood one another's literary allusions, and who carried themselves with a confidence deriving from a sense of superior talent. This solidarity in manners and education, perhaps even more than their wealth, made the leaders of Europe's upper classes formidable antagonists when the spokesmen of democracy and the trade unions began to challenge their ascendancy.

Beneath the aristocracy and the upper middle class were the hard-working but far less wealthy members of the lower middle class. They included self-employed tradesmen, shopkeepers, and skilled artisans, as well as the growing number of clerks, salespeople, and employees who staffed government offices, insurance firms, or department stores. The lower middle class prized its hard-won status—expressed in sober dress, a carefully furnished front parlor reserved for guests, and "genteel" pastimes—all the more because of a precarious economic situation that left its members vulnerable to sliding once more into the ranks of the poor. Clinging to "respectability" on an income often little higher than that of the factory workers they despised, the mass of lower-class men and women

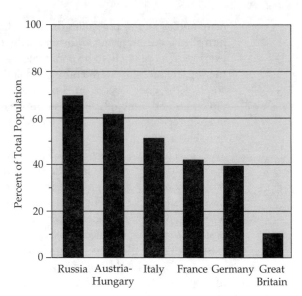

FIGURE 1.1 Share of the population dependent on agriculture in several European countries in 1900. Note the contrast between Russia, whose industrialization had barely begun, and England, which had been an industrial power for over a century.

was especially vulnerable to the economic tremors that would disrupt the lives of all too many in the decades to come.

Europe in 1914 was an increasingly urban continent, with more large cities and a larger urban population than any other. This fact reflected a profound demographic shift during the preceding century, when hundreds of thousands of country dwellers moved off the land into the new industrial centers of the British midlands or the German Ruhr area in search of factory jobs. Huddled together in tenements or factory barracks, toiling long hours, often for derisory wages, these new city residents both drove the engine of European prosperity and were its principal victims. The specter of social unrest which Disraeli had warned against in his portrait of "two nations" seemed to fade, however, as the century neared its close. Gradually rising wages, coupled with growing political power, lifted the workers from misery to a low but tolerable living standard in many urban centers. Left behind in this change, however, were thousands of slum dwellers too ill or too crippled to work—the shadowy mass of beggars and vagabonds that had become a permanent army of the destitute, camped within the precincts of the city, unable or unwilling to depart.

Despite Europe's rapid urban growth, a traveler in 1914 would have found vast tracts of countryside untouched by industry as he journeyed east from the Ruhr toward the borders of Russia. There were, to be sure, predominantly agricultural areas in the West as well, such as Ireland and central France. But whereas agriculture in these areas was becoming more mechanized and more commercial, in other parts of Europe an older, more labor-intensive system of farming persisted, which had survived little changed from feudal times. Here the great mass of the population were peasants, scattered in villages or grouped in large estates, living according to the rhythm of the seasons, as generations of their forebears had done before them. Much as city dwellers might romanticize the life of sturdy, uncorrupted peasants, theirs was a hard and often brutal existence, marked by periodic hunger and the constant threat of disease. Both in Eastern and in Southern Europe, millions of peasants formed a great reservoir of rural laborers whose conservatism stood in sharp contrast to the changing urban scene. The transformation of this peasant class into an active political force through both military conscription and industrialization during the first decades of the twentieth century was to prove a factor of enormous consequence for Europe as a whole (see Figure 1.1).

The Perils Ahead

By 1914, it should have been apparent that the world would not much longer continue to pay economic and cultural tribute to Europe. But most Europeans gave only passing heed to the two brief and surprising wars that had marked the turn of the century—the conflict of 1898, in which the United States had emerged as a world power by depriving Spain of its last relics of Caribbean and Pacific dominion, and the war of 1904, in which imperial Russia had been decisively beaten by a resurgent Japan.

A few European diplomats realized the significance of these events, but the majority were too absorbed in the intricacies of their own alliance systems. These diplomats had been guided throughout most of the nineteenth century by the tenuous but still very real notion of a "Concert of Europe"—a general European interest that was to be safeguarded by periodic congresses of representatives of the Great Powers. By 1914, the idea of a Concert of Europe was all but dead. The German capital of Berlin in the year 1878 had witnessed the last time that the foreign ministers of the powers assembled to reach decisions that concerned the entire European community.

By the first years of the twentieth century, European statesmen worried over domestic discontent more than they heeded the danger of a Europe-wide conflict. Cultural critics of the European scene similarly found their attention drawn to what they perceived as the failings of their unique and wonderful civilization—its materialism, cold rationality, and lack of inspiring vision—rather than to its strengths. Both practical politicians and intellectual observers failed for the most part to appreciate how vulnerable a world whose strengths they took for granted had now become. The significance of these attitudes is apparent in the record of the two vast and infinitely destructive wars in which the Europeans all but committed cultural and political suicide.

II. THE PROMISE OF THE NEW ERA

In the first decade of the twentieth century, disquiet concerning the threat of social change or cultural decline was more than balanced by a prevailing mood of optimism in the more "advanced" countries of Western and Central Europe. Indeed, the expectations of the average individual had never been so high. For the past century humankind—particularly in Europe—seemed to have been advancing steadily. And as they peered into the coming era, Europeans tended to project this past progress into an indefinite future. On the basis of the record of the last hundred years—in which the dominant notes had been peace, prosperity, and the democratization of political and social life—there seemed no reason to imagine that movement would not continue in the same direction forever.

Technology and Science

The great Paris Exposition of 1900 was the climax of a quarter century of such displays and fittingly ushered in the new century. These expositions had been primarily devoted to the triumphs of modern science and technology—achievements of which Europeans were most proud and that formed the basis for their own optimism about the future.

In most countries of Western and Central Europe, the nineteenth century had been the era of what is called in very general terms the Industrial Revolution. Sometime during the years between 1800 and 1900, great nations like France, Germany, and Italy, and smaller ones like Belgium and Sweden, had equipped themselves with the machinery of a modern industrial society. Faithfully copying English accomplishments of the latter part of the preceding century, they had built factories and roads and notably improved their agricultural methods. Machine production had characterized this initial phase of the Industrial Revolution; first textile and later iron and steel production had been the pace-setters of mechanization. And in the second and third quarters of the nineteenth century, the railroad and the steamship had similarly revolutionized land and water transport.

These extraordinary economic changes brought about a vast growth of cities that in turn produced far-reaching social and political alterations. Three aspects of the Industrial Revolution of the nineteenth century deserve comment. First, these social and economic changes did not affect all areas and classes of the European population. Although they transformed old cities and created new ones, they left much of the country-side nearly undisturbed. They profoundly altered the character of the urban middle class and brought into being a whole new class of factory workers, but they affected the peasantry much less markedly. In Southern and Eastern Europe particularly, by far the larger part of the population still lived in a pre-industrial world scarcely touched by the breath of modernity. People in the country and in small towns shared only to a slight extent in the new cult of material progress; they remained conservative and traditionalist, skeptical of the novel ideas bred in the cities. The significance of this contrast between rural and urban ways of life, and the fact that they could exist simultaneously and side by side, will recur again and again in the analysis of the social and ideological conflicts of the twenti-eth century.

Second, the new century was bringing with it another and even more far-reaching industrial revolution. The age of coal and iron was about to give way to the age of electricity, light metals and plastics, and the internal combustion engine. By 1900, electric lights and telephones were becoming widespread; the automobile had just been in-vented; the airplane, the radio, and the motion picture were shortly to make their appearance. The Industrial Revolution of the nineteenth century had been a grimy, sooty affair; Europeans thought of William Blake's "dark Satanic mills," a picture of dirt and ugliness. The new industrial age promised to be cleaner, brighter, tidier. Already the vast differences between owners and workers that had marked the society of the mid–nineteenth century were diminishing; in clothing, in cleanliness—even in physique—the gap between them was narrowing. Here also, Europeans could find reason for optimism about the future.

Finally, the triumphs of European technology in the nineteenth century had greatly enhanced the popular prestige of science and scientific or pseudoscientific expla-nations. The Industrial Revolution and its sequels were the outcome of applied scientific knowledge; the inventors had linked the world of abstract science with the world of business. In the last decades of the nineteenth century, Europeans had become science minded. By 1900, people of ordinary education had discarded a large number of their traditional beliefs; for the explanations of the universe and of human affairs that religion or folk wisdom offered, they had substituted the neater and clearer explanations of modern science. Or at least they thought so. They thought that to reason scientifically meant to seek a single, simple "cause" for every phenomenon and to prefer a materialist or determinist explanation to one that stressed mystery or the "spirit." Frenchmen or Germans of 1900 who prided themselves on their "scientific" thinking had a rather inaccurate notion of what science actually was.

At the very least, this idea of science was out of date—it reflected the certainties of an earlier scientific age. The paradox of the popular scientific beliefs of the first part of the twentieth century was that they bore so little relation to the actual thinking of the more advanced scientists of the era. Just at the time that the older and simpler explanations were winning the allegiance of the general public, they were losing the faith of the scientists themselves. The new men and women of science were beginning a radical revision of their earlier ideas, particularly in physics; here the notion of plural and even contradictory explanations produced the most perplexing results (see Chapter 7, I). The vast changes in scientific thinking that have taken place in our time offer not the least of the reasons for referring to the past three quarters of a century as a time of almost constant revolution.

Human Welfare

Never before in human history had average citizens lived so well as they did in the more advanced countries of the Western world at the opening of the twentieth century. Poverty and disease still existed, of course. But the enormous progress already made in eliminating them aroused hopes that these, like so many other scourges that had once plagued humanity, might eventually become no more than an evil memory.

In reviewing the century just past, Europeans could point to accomplishments that would have staggered the imagination of earlier ages. Most vestiges of serfdom and feudal dependence had been abolished. Nearly everywhere—with the notable exception of Russia—administrative and police methods had become far more humane and less arbitrary; torture, for one thing, was universally condemned, if not universally eradicated. The right if arrested to a trial and to legal counsel was also widely accepted, if not always honored in practice. Similarly, medicine and hygiene had made more progress in one century than in all the rest of human history. Surgery and anesthetics had been vastly improved; no longer were hospitals chambers of horrors that one entered only to suffer, sicken, and die. A Frenchman and a German—Louis Pasteur and Joseph Lister—had presented overwhelming scientific evidence that infection was caused by germs and could be controlled through cleanliness and antiseptics. Infant mortality had been cut to a fraction of its earlier toll; at the same time the span of human life was being steadily extended. The population of Europe continued to grow in the decades after 1900, not because the birthrate remained high (it was falling) but because doctors and public health officials each year succeeded in saving tens of thousands of additional lives.

In brief, the humanitarian hopes of the philosophers and publicists of the eighteenth century had, in the century following, begun to become reality. And along with this new respect for human life went a new consciousness of the importance of health and physical well-being. By 1900, city people throughout Europe were trying to get outdoors; the twentieth-century cult of sport and the open air had already begun. Hiking clubs sprang up in many urban centers, and the bicycle, whose popularity reached the level of mania in the years before the First World War, offered an affordable means of escape for weekend picnics in the country as well as a new form of sport.

Interior decoration and social manners reflected the change. The heavy, overstuffed, ornate furniture of the mid–nineteenth century gave way to lighter and simpler styles. The Arts and Crafts movement in England championed a return to unadorned interiors with the argument that houses and their furnishings should be more "honest," while on the Continent the partisans of art nouveau called for an artistic style based on graceful, organic shapes—another repudiation of pretentiousness in fashion. Social conventions, too, were beginning to lose their stiffness and formality. The new weekend cycling excursions, for example, often included members of both sexes (unchaperoned) in what seemed to their elders a daring breach of conventionality. The first signs of the twentieth-century revolt against Victorian middle-class morality were clearly in evidence.

These social and intellectual changes were most completely summed up in the spread of literacy. By 1900, the countries of Northern and Western Europe were sending almost their whole populations to school. Britain and France, Germany and Switzerland, Scandinavia and the Low Countries had virtually wiped out the enormous handicap of illiteracy. Italy and Austria-Hungary lagged behind, but here too a universally literate population had become a practical possibility for the near future. Only on the periphery of Europe—in Spain and Portugal, the Balkan countries, and the vast exception of tsarist Russia—was illiteracy still accepted as normal. These were also the countries that had made small progress toward political democracy. The coupling of the two deficiencies was obvious—literacy was the prerequisite to the democratic forms of political life that were confidently riding the wave of the future.

Women and the Family

One area in which progress was less easy to discern was the position of women. From our present perspective, it is difficult to remember just how disadvantaged was the situation of European women a century ago. Few enjoyed voting rights at the local level; with the lone exception of Norway, no state permitted women to vote in national elections (though not all men were eligible voters either). In most of Europe, married women were legally minors; they could not own or dispose of property, bring a lawsuit, or open a bank account without their husbands' consent. Their opportunities for higher education were restricted, and their wages remained approximately half those of men. The number of women who worked after they married was low—10 percent in Britain by the turn of the century, 12 percent in Germany. The majority were expected to be subservient to their husbands and to devote their energies to child rearing and work in the home.

In the realm of women's work, the nineteenth century had actually seen a regression from patterns prevalent in the eighteenth. Whereas both peasant and city-dwelling women had often worked alongside men in an earlier age—sharing their labor in the fields or their duties in city shops—Victorian codes of behavior decreed that, at least for prosperous families, the woman's place was in the home. Middle-class husbands in the nineteenth century looked upon it as a mark of success that they could support their families by themselves, saving their wives from the need to work. Thus, the nineteenth century saw the growth of an ideal that Virginia Woolf later termed "the angel of the household"—the woman devoted to husband and children, guardian of the warmth and security of home, more interested in devising next week's dinner menus or darning her husband's socks than in politics or finance.

The latter half of the century saw a gradual improvement in some of the worst features of women's legal, educational, and political status. Furthest advanced in this process was Britain, which as early as 1857 had made divorce available to women on the grounds of cruelty or desertion by the husband, and which by 1914 had improved the quality of women's schooling and allowed some women (the older and more prosperous) to vote in local elections. Paradoxically, it was this promise of change in Britain that served to embolden the supporters of an unrestricted right to vote to wage the suffragette campaign during the years 1909 to 1914. Under the direction of Mrs. Emmeline Pankhurst and her two daughters, Sylvia and Christabel, the suffragettes resorted to acts of civil disobedience and destruction of property in an attempt to win attention for their cause. Their tactics did not succeed in wresting votes for women from a reluctant British Parliament, but they did force male politicians to conclude that not all women welcomed their legal minority and confinement in the home.

In the rest of Europe—with the exception of the Scandinavian countries—the prospect of votes for women was far more distant, and the scattered women's movements, far more tame. Yet even here, advances were occurring in the realm of education and legal rights. As usual, it was middle-class women who took the lead in urging reform; they could more readily afford the time and expense than their working-class sisters.

A change that touched women from all social strata, however, was the gradual reduction in the size of families. Between 1890 and 1930, the birthrate in Northern and Western Europe slowed to half its previous level. France, where smaller families had already become the norm in the early nineteenth century, led the way. England, Scandinavia, and Germany followed France's lead after 1870. As the process of industrialization moved across Europe after 1900, similar patterns emerged further east. Not only did women have fewer children, they married earlier and lived longer; as a consequence, their children were grown and independent by the time these women reached middle age. Here was the start of a demographic revolution that was to have profound effects on European women's lives after 1914, making it increasingly possible for them to devote their time and energies to activities other than the traditional role of "angel of the household."

The combination of a lower birthrate and a lower death rate meant that Europe's population gradually stabilized. During the nineteenth century, medical advances had meant that more children survived infancy, thus adding to the population pressures that brought millions of immigrants from Southern and Eastern Europe to the shores of the United States, South America, and Australia in search of a better life. But as the birthrate fell and families became smaller after 1914, the population increase slowed until births and deaths were approximately equal. European demographers, noting this trend, worried that the Continent had lost its "vitality" and would soon be overtaken by other societies producing more numerous offspring. But, in fact, the slowing of population growth, which freed women from spending all their time as mothers, stemmed in large part from a desire to preserve a high standard of living for the next generation. With the advent of smaller families, the share of wealth for each individual increased.

The Peace Movement

By 1914, Europe had gone so long without a major war that the very idea was becoming a dim memory. For more than forty years—the longest such span to date in modern history—the Great Powers had been at peace with one another. Since the War of 1870 between France and Germany, conflicts had been limited to engagements in the Balkans and to overseas struggles such as the Spanish-American War, the Russo-Japanese War, and the Boer War of 1899–1902, in which Britain had defeated the South African republics of the Orange Free State and Transvaal.

In the major nations of Western and Central Europe, a whole generation had come of age without knowledge of warfare among equals. The long freedom from intra-European conflict had produced the illusion that it would never recur. People began to argue that mankind had become too civilized for such barbarian pursuits. More concretely, this sentiment—and general humanitarian feeling as well—had manifested itself in the growth of organized pacifism. The pacifist movement had steadily gained adherents since the last decades of the nineteenth century. France and Britain, Switzerland and Scandinavia all had vigorous propagandists for peace; Germany alone was a significant exception.

The pacifists did not rest their case on humanitarian grounds alone. They also argued that under modern conditions war simply did not pay. Moreover, they found that the organization of the business world itself precluded war between the Great Powers. In the early years of the twentieth century, vast interlocking cartels had been organized throughout the Western world. In banking and shipping, in textiles and chemicals and tobacco, the international cartelists had strung almost invisible nets binding the economies of potentially enemy states. War would not occur, the argument ran, because the directors of the cartels would not allow it. And the cartelists themselves, under heavy attack for their monopolistic position, found it to their interest to encourage such illusions.

Yet all the agitation for peace had produced but minuscule achievement. Two international conferences had assembled, but these had accomplished very little. The Hague Conference of 1899, called at the initiative of tsarist Russia (which was beginning to feel the strain of the arms race), had immediately run into uncompromising German resistance to any real disarmament. The conference succeeded only in adding a few new provisos to the traditional rules of war and in setting up a panel of judges to which the nations might resort for arbitration, if they so desired. Another Hague conference, eight years later, accomplished still less.

It is fitting that a discussion of the promise of the new century should end with the "pipe dream of peace." For here the gap between promise and performance, between aspiration and reality, was widest and produced the greatest subsequent disillusionment.

The gospel of pacifism: French Socialist political leader Jean Jaurès (1859–1914) delivers an impassioned speech to a political rally in 1913. (*Courtesy Roger-Viollet, Getty Images, Inc./Hulton Archive Photos*)

III. THE IDEOLOGIES OF PROGRESS

The overall view of the world embodied in the early twentieth-century confidence about the future may be called an *ideology of progress*. The nineteenth century had been the first great age of ideology, and it was in this period that the word first came into general use.

Ideology and Conservatism

Ideology lies somewhere between abstract political and social philosophy on the one hand, and the practical activities of parties and pressure groups on the other. Indeed, it provides the link between the two. An ideology is a general concept of the actual or ideal nature of society that gives meaning and direction to the lives of large groups of people.

In one aspect, it is a theory of history, charting the "inevitable" course of human affairs and assuring its adherents that the future lies with them. It is no accident that it was the historically minded nineteenth century that first began to think in this fashion. From another standpoint, ideology is linked to class, rationalizing and endorsing the aspirations of one social class and attacking those of its perceived enemies. Finally, it may be viewed as a secular cult with its own saints and martyrs, its own creed, and its own system of missionary work, propaganda, and indoctrination.

The French Revolution of 1789 marked the beginning of the age of ideology. In breaking the cake of custom, it called all traditional arrangements into question and opened the way to competing definitions of what constituted a proper society. Similarly—and rather paradoxially—it produced for the first time a conscious ideology of conservatism. Under the old regime, conservatism had been spontaneous and implicit; as the expression of things as they were, it did not need justification or a coherent political ideology. After the revolutionary era of 1789–1815, the situation changed. The conservatives, restored to power after the fall of Napoleon, were no longer so secure. They needed to explain and to justify their attempted return to the past. The Revolution, by attacking conservatism, had in fact created a conservative ideology in response to its own claims.

By 1900, conservatism seemed to be declining nearly everywhere. Even many conservatives felt that their days were numbered. The first half of the nineteenth century had been more promising for them. For a generation after 1815, the alliance of "throne and altar" had held firm; the religious justification of conservative rule had kept the mass of European populations in check. But the Revolution of 1848—renewing and extending to the rest of Western and Central Europe the French tradition of 1789—ended all that. Despite the defeat of the revolutionary movements and the return of the conservatives to power, the victory of reaction was an illusion. In the next half century, conservatism steadily retreated; from decade to decade, progressive-minded leaders conquered quietly and without bloodshed one after another of the positions that their fathers had tried to overwhelm in one great rush as they manned the barricades of 1848.

By 1900, the conservatives had become defeatists. They saw their own political labors as little more than delaying actions, doomed to be submerged in longer or shorter time by the rising flood of democracy. They had lost confidence in their own traditionalist and mystical ideology, which, in an age of science, no longer sufficed. The ideologists of progress had set the new rules of political debate, rules that at least purported to be logical and scientific, and the conservatives were supinely allowing themselves to enmeshed in subtleties that at heart they detested.

European conservatism would not recover its nerve and self-confidence until it learned how to break the rules of the game—and with this knowledge gained at least another generation of grace.

Liberalism

Conservatism constituted the Right of the European political spectrum—so called because the conservative deputies had become accustomed in the course of the nineteenth century to seat themselves on the right of the semicircular halls in which Euorpean parliaments usually met. In the center and on the left sat the apologists of progress: liberals, radicals, and socialists.

Liberalism by 1900 was roughly equivalent to the political center. In nineteenth-century Europe this term meant something far different from what it does in America today. In the United States, to be liberal means to be considerably to the left of center—something more than a democrat, with a definite predilection for the welfare state. In nineteenth-century Europe, liberalism was a predemocratic faith and usually distrustful of full democracy. It had no smell of socialism about it; instead it was a doctrine of political moderation.

For European liberals the three key terms were *freedom, law,* and *representative institutions.* Their first and most passionate belief was in the freedom of the individual. Such principles as freedom of speech, of the press, of assembly, and of religion, embodied in the first ten amendments to the United States Constitution, regularly formed the pre-ambles to European constitutions drafted under liberal auspices. Other articles of these constitutions confirmed the further principles that liberal agitation had won from reluc-tant sovereigns: a guarantee of the regular processes of law, including the equality of citi-zens before the courts, and the powers of the parliamentary chambers, which claimed exclusive responsibility for legislation and taxation and which were gradually to wrest ex-ecutive authority from the monarch himself.

To liberals, these principles of liberty, law, and representation were the sum of progressive aims. They were interested in going no further in the direction of change and reform. Democracy rather frightened them. The characteristic liberal leader was a man of wealth and education, a member of the upper middle class or, even more typically, an en-lightened aristocrat. Liberals usually did not wish to deprive the king of all his power or reduce him to the mere figurehead that he is in contemporary European monarchies. They saw hereditary monarchy as a stabilizing force and felt that the king, as head of state, should retain a certain amount of independent initiative, particularly in the field of foreign affairs. Another conservative safeguard favored by liberals was an upper house of parliament—a senate or house of peers, either hereditary or appointed by the king. For the elected lower house—the chamber of deputies or house of commons—liberals advo-cated a restricted suffrage; they thought it monstrous for the ignorant masses to have an equal vote with men of property and education. The constitutional arrangements that conformed most closely to their ideas were those of Britain after the Reform Act of 1832 or the July Monarchy in France after the Revolution of 1830.

European liberals were usually frank elitists. They were convinced of the virtues of their own class, and although they were often forced to compromise with democracy, they believed that little good could come of it. Like the conservatives, they were eventu-ally reduced to delaying tactics; by the end of the nineteenth century, European liberals were finding it impossible to halt the unrush of reform as they confronted an ever wider electorate. At the same time, however, their philosophy of skepticism and mistrust had hidden strengths that the future would reveal.

Radicalism

Pure electoral democracy of the type represented for more than a century by both Ameri-can political parties lies halfway between European liberalism and the political ideology known as *radicalism.* Actually, few European leaders of the moderate Left called themselves democrats. Democracy was a utopian abstraction rather than the watchword of an organized political movement. In Europe, the democratic forces tended to group themselves to the left of center under the banner of radicalism—something more militant and intolerant than simple faith in majority rule.

Here again, differing terminology confuses the issue. To an American, the radical means a firebrand, very likely a revolutionary of some sort. To a European, *radicalism* means a political allegiance rooted in the struggles of the nineteenth century. Today, radicalism is rather tame; a century ago, however, it was a fighting faith, for the introduction of democracy into Euorpe was far more difficult than it had been in the United States. Europe had too many relics of the past—privileged bodies of all sorts, which the liberals were generally ready to leave intact or to reform but slightly. Hence the European radical was something more than a democrat—that is, something besides a citizen who advocated an equal vote for every man (but not for every woman!) and the abolition of all remaining vestiges of class distinctions. He was also, at least in Catholic countries, an anticlerical. He believed that the church had far too much power in public life and that stringent measures were required to curb the overweening pretensions of the priests.

In general, then, European radicals were more "advanced" than the liberals. The tide of the future seemed to be running in their favor, and by the first decade of the twentieth century, they were riding the crest of the wave. In one respect, however, they were often untrue to broader democratic values. They believed passionately in equality, but their devotion to liberty was less certain. In their attitude toward organized religion, they were frequently intolerant of their enemies, real or imagined. European democracy was not to assume its final form until it had fused the liberal love of freedom with the radical insistence on political equality.

The characteristic European radical was a member of the lower middle class or of the middle bourgeoisie—a small businessman, a landholding peasant, a lawyer, or a doctor. Although on occasion he used inflammatory language, he was in no sense a revolutionary. He thought of himself as a "little man," economically independent, and in every moral and intellectual respect the equal of the great. His vision of the good society was a shopkeepers' paradise in which small enterprises held the field against monopolists on the one hand and the forces of collectivism on the other. Thus, like most Americans, the radicals of Europe disliked the very idea of discussing politics in terms of class conflict. Such talk seemed to violate the basic principle of the equality of the citizen. But more and more European politics *was* being talked about in these terms, and this would be even more true after the First World War.

Socialism

As liberalism tended to be the political faith of the upper bourgeoisie, and radicalism characterized the lower middle classes, so the urban workers had rallied to socialism as the doctrine that best expressed their own needs. This *proletariat*, as Karl Marx called it, was the creation of the Industrial Revolution of the nineteenth century; its problems were unprecedented in history, and the solution proposed for them was also new.

Socialism was a collectivist doctrine. In its simplest form, its goal was to take away from the "capitalists" the ownership of basic industry—the "means of production," in Marx's phrase—and to turn it over to the community as a whole. Thus real equality, as opposed to the "sham" equality of democratic doctrine, would be installed. In thus dismissing as a deception the technical equality before the law characteristic of European parliamentary states, the socialists were far from total error. Class inequalities were very real in the Europe of of 1914. Even in countries that called themselves democracies, industrial and agricultural workers labored under all sorts of economic and psychological handicaps. Nor was it the most democratic nations that had gone farthest to remedy these abuses. The pioneer in social legislation had in fact been semiautocratic Germany, with aristocratic Britain next. Farthest behind lagged the two great democracies, France and the United States. In 1914, neither had any substantial body of legislation regulating wages and hours or providing for insurance against the misfortunes of factory labor.

When socialist doctrines first appeared in Europe—just before the middle of the nineteenth century—Marxism was only one of the many forms in which these ideas expressed themselves. Gradually, however, the teaching of Karl Marx won an unmistakable ascendancy; it far surpassed its competitors in its intellectual coherence and "scientific" form. When Marx died in 1883, the new socialist parties of Europe honored him as their prophet and considered him their mentor even when they flouted his advice.

Indeed, these parties generally behaved very differently from the pattern Marx had sketched. The founder of modern socialism had conceived of such parties as fighting nuclei of workers directed by socially conscious intellectuals. He had not been sure that violent revolution would be necessary to overthrow the citadels of capitalism—his writings are unclear on this point—but he suspected that force would be required, and he urged the proletariat not to "shrink" from violence. Marx based his conviction of an inevitable final showdown on his "law of increasing misery." He believed the rich would grow richer and the poor, poorer. Capital would be concentrated in fewer and fewer hands while more and more free artisans, shopkeepers, and peasants would be forced down to the status of proletarians.

In the last quarter of the nineteenth century, the law of increasing misery failed to operate. Indeed, the condition of the European working classes improved rather than deteriorated. Only the consciousness of the evils of industrial society and resentment against them actually increased. At the same time, the realistic chances of revolutionary activity seemed greatly reduced. The period from 1848 to 1871 had been full of wars and revolutionary tumults. The succeeding era of peace between the powers was also one of peace at home. Between the bloody suppression of the Paris Commune in 1871 and the Russian Revolution of 1905, there were no revolutionary outbreaks in the major European countries. Armies and police forces had been notably strengthened and made more efficient; the more cool-headed socialist leaders recognized that the barricade and street fighting of 1848 was no longer possible. Moreover, most of these people had ceased to be revolutionists at heart; they had been caught up in the pervading mood of confidence in long-term progress. They had become gradualists, believing in the slow reform of industrial conditions through legal, democratic means.

In addition to its emphasis on class struggle, European socialism was profoundly international. Marx and the other founders of the movement had taught their followers to hate armaments, war, and military service; the official doctrine was that proletarians had more in common with the workers of another land than with the capitalists of their own. Marx himself had accordingly organized an international association of workingmen that maintained a precarious existence from 1864 to 1876, when it finally succumbed to its own internal divisions. This small and fragile organization is known in socialist history as the First International. The Second International, formed in 1889, was far more robust. A federation of the socialist parties of Europe, its delegate congresses paralleled in unofficial form the state diplomacy of the Great Powers.

The congresses of the International resounded with peaceful protestations from delegates of potentially enemy nations. Indeed, its activities offer a final explanation for the widespread illusion that war would not occur. But the actual accomplishments of the Second International were almost as insubstantial as those of the Hague conferences. The one resolution with teeth in it—a pledge to call a general strike to forestall future threats of war—never won a majority, for the average European socialist leader was in truth a solid citizen, with a stake in the existing order of society. He was far less revolutionary and far more patriotic than he professed to be. It should have surprised no one when in August 1914, the socialist parties of Europe declared support in overwhelming majority for their counties' war efforts.

IV. THE TRIUMPH OF PARLIAMENTARY DEMOCRACY

By 1914, parliamentary government had become the European norm. Deviations were ascribed either to the special conditions of small countries or to a backwardness that must eventually succumb to the forces of progress.

Parliamentary Government in Practice

The United States is the only major democracy that has not operated under the parliamentary system. Its "presidential" constitution provides for a strict separation of powers: Executive authority is vested solely in the president, Congress restricts itself to legislative functions, and the president remains in office even when his party loses its majority in Congress. This type of constitution has had little appeal in Europe. In 1914, the only state that operated even approximately on a presidential basis was the federal state of Switzerland—oldest and smallest of the three European republics then in existence.

Elsewhere, separation of powers did not exist. According to the parliamentary model that had developed in the eighteenth century in Great Britain and in the early nineteenth century in France, the effective executive was in fact a committee of the legislature or parliament. The theoretical head of state—the king or (in France) the president—had gradually become a figurehead. Besides performing ceremonial functions, his chief duty was to appoint a prime minister who, along with the colleagues whom he gathered about him to constitute a cabinet or ministry, actually managed the business of state. The king or president could use a certain amount of discretion in naming the prime minister. Sometimes the choice was obvious; at other times leadership was unclear and it might be necessary to try out alternate combinations. But the chief criterion was always the same: Could the proposed prime minister command a majority in the House of Commons or Chambers of Deputies? If he failed to do so, or if he lost his majority, he and his cabinet must resign. Thus the ministry—or "government," as the French put it—would fall, a far less catastrophic event than it seemed to American readers of the daily newspapers.

This procedure had grown up randomly as precedents gradually became established. It was nowhere codified in written constitutions (Britain did not even have a written constitution), and in practice it took two rather different forms. In Britain, where political life was dominated by two or three relatively stable parties, the cabinet rather than Parliament held the whip; as leaders of the majority party in the House of Commons, the prime minister and his colleagues kept a firm hand on their followers and were seldom overthrown by an adverse vote. On the Continent, more particularly in France and Italy, the situation was reversed. Here parliaments were supreme. Since parties were numerous and ill disciplined, the ministry—which usually represented more than one party—could never be sure of its majority. Because it stood at the mercy of the defection of even a small group of supporters, its tenure was usually brief. In France, for example, the maximum term was three years; the average, much shorter.

The Progress of Democracy

In 1900, no major European country—with the possible exception of France—could be considered a democracy in any effective sense. Fourteen years later, when the war broke out, at least three had virtually completed the evolution from aristocratic to democratic rule.

The years 1900 to 1914 were the golden age of European democratic progress. In this period, electoral democracy triumphed in country after country. France had enjoyed universal manhood suffrage since the Revolution of 1848; it had been a republic since 1870, at least in name, when France's defeat in the Franco-Prussian War forced the abdication of Emperor Napoleon III. In 1875, France's new National Assembly approved a republican constitution which guaranteed the vote to all adult males (women were forced to wait for the same right until 1946). But not until the early years of the twentieth century did French democracy become a militant reality. The injustice done to a single army officer of Jewish origin—the celebrated Captain Dreyfus—eventually mobilized the forces of French republicanism in a vigorous assault on political reaction and the church. The elections of 1902 and 1906 were liberal landslides. And in 1905 the liberal-minded majority in the French parliament brought to a climax a half decade of legislative warfare against church influence in education and politics by severing all connection between the Catholic clergy and the French state.

In Britain, periodic extensions of the suffrage in the half century from 1832 to 1885 had given most adult males the vote. But here, as in France, it took another generation for this democratization to sink into the national consciousness and alter the voting habits of the average citizen. In 1900, the House of Commons was still aristocratic in composition—still the "best club in Europe." Its attention was directed toward imperial and foreign affairs, and it had a crushing Tory majority. Six years later, all this was reversed: The Liberals—more particularly their radical wing—scored a stunning electoral triumph and proceeded to democratize with a vengeance. Under Lloyd George's eloquent leadership, reform followed reform in dizzying succession: social legislation, income and inheritance taxes, and, finally, drastic limitations on the powers of the hereditary House of Lords. By the outbreak of the war, England, like France, in all important respects could be considered a democracy.

A third great power, Italy, crossed the democratic watershed in the same period. Italy had only recently achieved unification in the struggles of national reassertion, or *Risorgimento*, which lasted from 1859 until Rome was finally annexed—leaving only the Vatican still under papal control—in 1870. The country's first steps toward democracy were timid, reflecting politicians' doubts about just how much popular support the new political institutions enjoyed. A monarchy like Britain, but in other political respects more closely resembling France, Italy had had a highly restricted suffrage based on property qualifications. Though parliamentary in form, the nation was not yet democratic in practice. But forty years after unification, Italy's political system seemed sufficiently secure to move further toward true democracy. The election of 1913 swept away these restrictions. The vast majority of Italian men, some still illiterate, were able to vote for the first time. Although few contemporaries realized it, Italy had entered a period of revolutionary change that was to continue, in one form or another, for more than a generation.

The smaller countries of Northern and Western Europe by 1914 had also evolved toward the parliamentary democratic model. Unlike Switzerland—the cradle of European republicanism—all of them were monarchies. The Low Countries—Belgium and the Netherlands—and the three Scandinavian nations of Norway, Sweden, and Denmark had the reputation of being well-run and peace-orientated states. On the whole, their populations were more prosperous, better educated, and more democratic in manners than the citizenry of the major European nations. In Sweden and the Netherlands, traces of aristocratic privilege lingered, but these were little more than picturesque variations on the dominant tone of triumphant democracy.

The Exceptions

Europe as a whole, however, offered far graver and more threatening exceptions. In the countries of the Iberian Peninsula, democracy was scarcely even an aspiration. Economically and educationally backward, Spain and Portugal vegetated outside the mainstream of European events and influences. The former was in theory a constitutional monarchy; the latter became a republic in 1910. But in both countries real power was held by corrupt and selfish cliques of army officers and landholders.

A similar situation prevailed in the newer but equally backward states of the Balkan Peninsula—Greece, Bulgaria, Serbia, Montenegro, and Romania. Unlike Spain and Portugal, the Balkan countries were not isolated from the major pressures of European international politics. Instead they were the clients and potential enemies of great powers. The three eastern empires—Germany, Austria-Hungary, and Russia—were deeply embroiled in the Balkan rivalries.

These three empires, as opposed to the three democratized powers of the West, still stood firm for imperial prerogative and class rule. For a century they had been the citadels of European conservatism. All had evolved to some extent in a parliamentary democratic direction, but in 1914 they still lived under curious, hybrid institutions that hovered in a limbo between autocracy and constitutionalism.

On the surface, Germany looked much like a Western democracy. The constitution with which Bismarck had crowned German unification in 1871 after its victorious war with France bore a deceptive resemblance to the Western norm. Its chancellor seemed to perform the role of prime minister; its Reichstag tried to behave like a chamber of deputies. True, the Reichstag was elected by universal manhood suffrage. But its legislative authority was incomplete, it had virtually no control over the army budget, and the chancellor was not responsible to it—that is, he was not obliged to resign if he lost his Reichstag majority. With all its faults, however, the imperial constitution was less defective from the democratic standpoint than the constitution of the federal state of Prussia. It was also less significant. Prussia, which was larger and more populous than all the other German states combined, was the wheel within the wheel that ran the whole machine. Its king was the German emperor; its prime minister was usually imperial chancellor also. It ran the army and most of the internal administration of the whole country. Prussia's constitution was frankly aristocratic. Through a complex system of three-class voting, its parliament (or Diet) was dominated by a permanent conservative majority, devoted to its king-emperor and to the military values that he exemplified.

Nor was Austria-Hungary the parliamentary state it seemed. Although the constitutions under which it lived conformed more closely to the Western European norm than did the institutions of Germany, the problem of national minorities in the Austro-Hungarian empire dominated everything else and made a mockery of the constitutional arrangements existing on paper. The Compromise of 1867 with the Hungarians had split the old Austrian empire into two separate countries linked by a common sovereign and by common ministries for finance, war, and foreign affairs. Both halves of the empire had parliamentary constitutions, and there was even a rudimentary joint parliament consisting of "delegations" to which the three joint ministries reported. But in each half, the ruling nationality was outnumbered by the sum of its national minorities; these latter grew more militant each year, and normal operation of parliamentary institutions became impossible. In the western or "Austrian" half of the country—a collection of separate provinces with no traditional name—the German Austrians ruled with a slipshod tolerance. In 1906 they had introduced universal manhood suffrage, thus producing an influx of minority deputies, particularly from the politically experienced and well-educated Czechs, whose obstructionism paralyzed the functioning of parliament.

In the eastern half—the kingdom of Hungary—no such behavior was tolerated. As opposed to the loosely joined assemblage of territories that made up "Austria," Hungary was a closely knit state, with a thousand-year tradition of its own. And the Hungarians (or Magyars) did not mean to grant any other nationality the parity with the German Austrians that they had so recently won for themselves. In Hungary, voting was public and based on a high property qualification; electoral districts were ruthlessly gerrymandered. The Hungarian aristocracy thus kept a firm grip on power and held to a minimum the number of minority representatives who reached the halls of parliament in Budapest.

Finally, there was Russia. In name, the Russian empire was still an autocracy. But it had changed more in the first decade of the new century than any other of the Great Powers of Europe. The revolution of 1905 had produced a constitution and a parliament (or Duma). This body was chosen by a complex system of indirect voting, and its powers were narrowly limited, but it still represented an epoch-making innovation for a country that as late as 1900 had possessed no semblance of a constitution. The emperor and his chief ministers still exercised power with few checks or limits; as they would discover in World War I, the price for such unlimited power was that they could also be held directly responsible for the country's misfortunes. A growing middle class and the start of industralization (financed largely through French and British investments) coexisted uneasily with an aristocracy and imperial house still wedded to Russia's feudal past. In the early twentieth century, Russia was commonly held to be the enigma of Europe—a half-awakened giant with enormous and rather frightening potentialities for the future.

V.   THE DANGER SIGNALS

As the second decade of the twentieth century opened, it was understandable that European democrats should dismiss as mere anachronisms the vestiges of autocratic and aristocratic rule in the three empires of the east. These should be shrugged off as relics of a vanishing past. But the same progressive-minded citizens were less justified in their neglect of certain newer symptoms of undemocratic behavior that had about them the aura of a most disconcerting modernity.

Imperialism at Home and Abroad

In 1885, on returning to the British foreign ministry, which he had relinquished five years earlier, the Marquess of Salisbury told his fellow peers: "I do not exactly know the cause of this sudden revolution. But there it is. It is a great force—a great civilizing, Christianizing force." He was referring to the sudden scramble for colonial dominion that in half a decade divided the greater part of the African continent among the European powers.

Thus began the era of high imperialism that extended for a single generation from the 1880s to the First World War. In this period, the Europeans in one final spurt completed their domination over the rest of the world—through direct colonial possession in the case of Africa and the Pacific, through indirect economic and diplomatic pressures in Asia and the Near East. What is most surprising in retrospect is how recently all this occurred, and how shortly thereafter followed the present-day movement for colonial liberation.

With Japan rapidly modernizing itself and India firmly in British hands, the Ottoman Empire and China remained as the most enticing objects for European exploitation. In both areas, the Great Powers had wrested from weak, bewildered emperors economic concessions and extraterritorial privileges that drastically curtailed the rulers' sovereignty. But in words, at least, the two great empires of the Near East and Far East remained independent. In Africa, such diplomatic niceties were superfluous. Here the Europeans divided vast stretches of territory among themselves, either as colonies or as "protectorates" in which the local ruler was left a shadow authority. Most of the continent went to Britain and France. The British dominated the south and east, the French the north and west, including nearly the whole Sahara Desert. The Germans and Italians, latecomers to the colonial game, picked up relatively unprofitable lands, while the Belgians—favored by the astuteness of their businessman king—acquired the enormous potential riches of the Congo. This latter dominion was relinquished in 1960, leaving the two territories that Portugal had taken over in an earlier age as the most durable of European possessions on the African continent until they, too, at last achieved independence in 1974.

By 1902, when the white settlers of the Boer republics succumbed to the overwhelming power of the British Empire, only four areas in all Africa remained even technically independent: the Arab-speaking country of Morocco in the far northwest, which the French were already coveting; the similarly Arab land of Egypt, which was "occupied" and dominated by the British; the eastern mountain empire of Ethiopia, which had repulsed the Italians in 1896; and finally, the small west coast republic of Liberia, whose independence was supervised by American rubber interests.

So far as Europeans at home were concerned, three aspects of this new wave of imperialist activity were of decisive importance for the future. First, as Lenin, among others, was to emphasize, the colonies helped to keep the fat on the European economy; they contributed heavily toward a standard of living that Europe could not have achieved on its own. Second, colonial rule was a standing reproach to the democratic professions of the Europeans; however they might try, the colonial powers could not square the prevailing radical ideology with their domination over nonwhite peoples.

The issue was, of course, most acute for France and Britain, for these were the greatest colonial powers and the most democratic of the major nations of Europe. Both

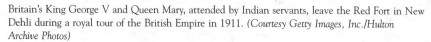

Britain's King George V and Queen Mary, attended by Indian servants, leave the Red Fort in New Dehli during a royal tour of the British Empire in 1911. (*Courtesy Getty Images, Inc./Hulton Archive Photos*)

made brave efforts to find a scheme of reconciliation, and both failed. The British formula of a self-governing dominion worked in Canada and Australia, where whites soon outnumbered the aborigines. But when in 1910 it was applied to South Africa—in a generous gesture of reconciliation with the Boers—the results were far less satisfactory, although another generation had to pass before this was generally recognized. For in South Africa, as in the rest of the continent south of the Sahara, the blacks far outnumbered the whites, and there was no foreseeable possibility that further white settlement would ever substantially alter this situation. To the black masses, self-government for white settlers was no solution at all.

The French formula initially seemed more promising. The French did not draw a color line and aimed at complete assimilation; they offered the chance to become equals, *as Frenchmen,* to the "elites" among the blacks south of the Sahara and among the Arab-speaking peoples to the north. These chosen individuals were to receive a full French education and to become French in speech and sentiment. In numerous cases, the technique worked admirably. Many Africans did in fact find acceptance in French society and did come to behave like Frenchmen. But assimilation applied only to a select minority; here again, the black masses remained unaffected. After the Second World War, when the masses began to awaken, the assimilated elites had no alternative but to move with the new current and to proclaim themselves African rather than French in their allegiance.

Finally, the late nineteenth-century wave of high imperialism enormously encouraged sentiments of national and racial superiority already latent in the European populations. Ruling tens of millions of blacks was a heady business, and it naturally attracted the more adventurous and ruthless spirits. Cecil Rhodes—the founder of modern South Africa—offered a model for empire building, and Rudyard Kipling rationalized the process in popular verse. Here a note of irony or of national guilt sounded under the confident proclamations about taking up "the white man's burden": The British conscience was periodically troubled by the brutal treatment of the natives that imperial rule entailed. Other Europeans were less squeamish. From 1904 to 1908, the Germans waged a war of near extermination in their colony of Southwest Africa. In the Congo, before its formal annexation to Belgium in 1908, King Leopold II's business colleagues literally worked hundreds of thousands of natives to death in the newly developed mines and plantations.

Such conduct blatantly contradicted the central democratic principle that "all men are created equal." But few democratic-minded Europeans at the turn of the century made the obvious comparisons; they followed a double standard—one kind of behavior for home, another for the colonies. This at least was true in Western Europe. In Central and Eastern Europe the new emphasis on racial superiority took a more virulent form. The three great empires of the east shared only partially in the final wave of imperial expansion: Austria-Hungary acquired no colonies at all; Germany arrived in Africa too late; Russia confined its expansion to the vast stretches of Siberia, Central Asia, and the Caucasus, which were contiguous to the Russian landmass, and whose nomad or Moslem populations could hence be dominated directly from the center. In these three empires there was no such sharp cleavage as in the West between democracy and colonial practice, between conduct at home and conduct abroad. The German and Russian ruling classes were not democratic in sentiment, and they were quite accustomed to ruthless behavior in ruling their own national minorities.

Thus a continental, home-grown imperialist ideology expressed itself in Pan-Slavism and, still more characteristically, in Pan-Germanism. The "pan" movements were true to current fashion in teaching the superiority of one's own linguistic group, but they went beyond this in calling for the union of vast masses of people. Uniting all the Slavs (under Russian leadership), or uniting all Germans wherever they might be, in Germany, in Austria, or in the numerous German-speaking clusters scattered through Eastern Europe, would shatter existing boundary lines; in the three empires of the east, German and Slav lived inextricably entangled. To preach the superiority of one meant to demand the subjugation of the other. Pan-Slavism and Pan-Germanism were intolerant, explosive, destructive forces. The former eventually succumbed—like so much else in Russia—to the Revolution of 1917. But Pan-Germanism went on to inspire the youthful Adolf Hitler and to provide Nazism with the rudiments of an ideology and with some of the most fanatical of its recruits.

Popular Militarism

To the middle-class mind, war and military service have traditionally been hateful. The military ethic is the very negation of the bourgeois virtues of rationality, toleration, and peace. Similarly, for socialists, war, fully as much as capitalism, was a curse to be wiped out forever. The ideologies of progress, then, were clearly antimilitary. Their triumph seemed to imply the destruction of militarism as one more relic of a barbarous past.

Yet paradoxically, during the first decade and a half of the twentieth century and alongside the rising tide of pacifism, war and military service suddenly became popular. One of the first signs of the change came in Britain during the Boer War; Liberal party speakers denouncing this imperialist conflict found themselves shouted down by angry crowds. A few years later, the naval-building race with Germany aroused similar popular enthusiasm; the British sporting instinct was stung by the threat of being overtaken by an upstart competitor, and German nationalists, spurred on by their emperor, responded with massive support of the navy's program for challenging the traditional mistress of the seas.

Of all the ramifying conflicts that contributed to the origins of the First World War, the Anglo-German naval race seems the one that might most easily have been avoided. Germany did not need a big navy on any rational ground, for it was basically a land power, guarded by the finest army in the world. Nor did even the most sanguine of Germany's naval propagandists claim that its fleet could reach parity with Britain's in any reasonably near future. When Admiral Tirpitz launched Germany's new building program in 1897, his purpose was to create a fleet that would annoy the British and make them hesitate about going to war; in his own words, his navy would make war too great a "risk." Thus, during the seventeen years preceding the outbreak of world conflict, the naval race embittered relations between Britain and Germany without fundamentally changing the balance of military power.

In Germany, the navy was a bourgeois affair. Far more than the army, which remained an aristocratic preserve, the German fleet drew its officers from the prosperous middle class. Hence it offered an ideal means for canalizing the new martial enthusiasm of the bourgeoisie. Elsewhere in Europe, middle-class nationalists began to rally to similar causes as the second decade of the century opened. In France, they supported the three-year army law of 1913—a desperate effort to keep up with Germany's growing population by adding another year to the term of military service. In Italy, they found an outlet for their enthusiasm in the successful campaign for the conquest of Tripoli in 1911.

Italy, more than any other country, dramatically suggests the new prestige of the martial life. And it also typifies the way in which early twentieth-century militarism was a movement of youth, closely linked with "irrationalist" innovations in literature and the fine arts. In Italy, as elsewhere, young people were bored. They knew too much of peace and nothing of war. They were tired of the policy of caution which their country had followed, except for a brief era of imperial adventure in the late 1880s and early 1890s. To be sure, that policy had preserved the weakest of the Great Powers from harm. But Italy's impatient youth had nothing but scorn for such prudent considerations. They were deaf to the counsels of the wise old statesman Giovanni Giolitti; they listened rather to their poets: to the "futurist" Filippo Marinetti, and to Gabriele D'Annunzio, who was to lead the interventionist campaign of 1915. Their creed (the words are Marinetti's) was direct and simple: "We want to glorify war, the world's only hygiene—militarism, deed, destroyer of anarchisms, the beautiful ideas that are death-bringing, and the contempt of woman."

The New Left

If the European Left was traditionally devoted to peace, it also had potentialities that paralleled the new cult of violence among the spokesmen of the Right. There was, for example, the Jacobin tradition—the memory of revolutionary France, a nation in arms against a host of invaders and ruthlessly resorting to terror at home to curb suspected traitors in its midst. This memory never failed to mobilize a substantial segment of the French political left in support of military measures. It suggests why the old radical Georges Clemenceau could eventually prove so tough a war leader.

Farther to the left, and also drawing on revolutionary memories, was the new movement known as *syndicalism*. Syndicalism, which was particularly strong in France and Italy, was an ideology of direct action. It preached the doctrine of the revolutionary general strike that would deliver the mines and factories of Europe into the workers' own hands. And in so doing it taught the working class to distrust its self-constituted spokesmen, the socialist parliamentarians and intellectuals. Indeed, in its tone and manner it expressed a deep-seated anti-intellectualism: It felt no need for a coherent philosophy of economics or politics. In this respect it broke far more sharply than had Marxism with the main tradition of European public life.

The great days of syndicalism came during the first decade of the twentieth century. Then French society in particular was shaken by a series of tumultuous strikes that took on an almost revolutionary character. After 1910, the movement—which had always been characterized by an anarchical lack of central direction—began to break up. Workers grew discouraged as it became apparent that all the syndicalist agitation had accomplished nothing.

During the war and in the postwar years, the former syndicalists went in two contrasting directions. One group joined Benito Mussolini and his fascist emulators—thus swelling the forces of irrationalism and direct action inspired by the advocates of imperial glory and popular militarism. The other element went to the newly founded Communist parties.

Only after the Bolshevik Revolution of 1917 did communism became an organized reality in European politics. Yet on the eve of the war, the makings of future Communist parties already existed in European socialism. For more than a decade before 1914, Lenin and his intellectual associates had consulted an outspoken left minority within the Second International. Lenin, like the syndicalists, believed in ruthlessness and the revolutionary recourse to violence. Like them, he was disgusted with the parliamentary caution of the dominant figures within European socialism. But he expressed these views with an intellectual coherence and penetration that left the syndicates far behind. Where they had failed, Lenin was to succeed.

VI.   The Origins of the World Conflict

The First World War was produced by the confluence of two explosive pressures—the aspirations of the national minorities in Central and Eastern Europe and the dynamic of the rival alliance systems among the Great Powers. These two pressures met with disastrous consequences. Diplomacy could not contain the resulting rush of nationalist fervor, which swept away prudence and reason on all sides. If Austria played a key role in kindling national minority passions through its mishandling of relations with Serbia, it was the rise of Germany as a major power since 1870 that proved the chief destabilizing factor in the diplomatic balance among European nations. Germany both feared its neighbors—France, England, and Russia—and felt thwarted in its hopes for further expansion. By 1914 it was spoiling for a fight.

What allowed the crisis to escalate, with catastrophic results, was a failure on the part of Europe's political and military leaders to recognize the fragility of the diplomatic balance that had assured peace for the past four decades. No one, it is safe to say, desired the First World War. But decades of peace left leaders unable to imagine the true cost of war. Because people could not conceive of a disaster of these dimensions, too few took steps to avert it, while some actively sought to encourage it for their own ends, until all were overwhelmed by destructive forces they might well have mastered with more wisdom and greater will.

The Nationalities Problem

Understanding the nationalities problem in Europe requires that we resist the pull of familiar terminology. To an American ear, the word "nationalism" generally has a positive ring. It implies the love of one's country, respect for its laws and customs, and pride in its achievements. Americans tend to use the term as a synonym for "patriotism," and to believe that national feeling provides an essential glue which holds a country together.

Thus it is often difficult for Americans to grasp the intensely destructive role that nationalism has played in Europe. It is even more difficult to understand that these nationalist hatreds were rooted in ethnic or religious, rather than in racial differences. Living in a country of far greater ethnic and racial diversity, Americans tend to assume that the lines of cleavage that separate one group from another will be racial. Yet a shared racial background has not prevented repeated and bloody quarrels among Europeans. In a sense, Europe has been the scene of a centuries-long civil war among people who are racially identical and ethnically similar. The French and the Germans, for example, took opposite sides in both world wars, and thereby slaughtered millions of each other's citizens.

What made the nationalities problem especially acute in Europe was that most populations were ethnically mixed. Patterns of settlement occurring over many centuries had not resulted in a clear ethnic map with easily defined boundaries. Instead, Europe resembled a patchwork, with groups of quite different language or culture living side by side. As the wave of nationalism swept across Europe in the nineteenth century and these groups began to demand cultural and even political autonomy, it was impossible to give one "core" group control without immediately alarming and offending national minorities that coexisted within the same territory. Thus, in addition to the clash between nation-states, there was also rising internal friction within nation-states as well.

In 1914, the question of these national minorities was almost exclusively an Eastern European concern. In the West, most boundaries were of longer standing and followed recognized lines of national allegiance. In Germany, the overwhelming majority of the inhabitants spoke German and felt themselves to be German (its Polish population constituted the outstanding exception). Even in the Russian empire, the Great Russian nationality formed the central core of the state and easily dominated the others. For Russia, the chief problem lay in its western borderlands, where the Finns, the peoples of the small Baltic states, and, most important, the Poles all had long-standing complaints of one sort or another against rule from St. Petersburg.

Of the three eastern empires, Austria-Hungary had by far the most serious minority problems. In fact, the Dual Monarchy was often referred to less as a nation than as a mere conglomeration of nationalities. No fewer than ten distinct linguistic and ethnic groups lived together in uneasy union under the Monarchy. Two—the Germans and the Magyars—dominated; the remaining eight resented that domination with increasing intensity as the nineteenth century progressed. The growth of nationalism among these subject peoples threatened some day to rend the whole Austro-Hungarian empire asunder.

Most troubling to the Austrian rulers were the three Slavic peoples within the borders of the Empire. Of these the Poles, part of whose territory Austria had annexed in the eighteenth century, fared best. Worried that Polish nationalists might upset the status quo, Austria followed a calculated policy of giving its own Poles the position of a favored minority within the state. Austrian policy dealt otherwise with two other branches of European Slavdom, however. The Czechs and the South Slavs looked to Russia for deliverance, and they had it in their power to paralyze the empire. The Czechs of Bohemia and Moravia had long ago lost their separate national existence; like the Poles, they lived on hopes and historical memories. The South Slavs, though culturally less advanced than the Czechs, were closer to independence. Part in and part out of the Austro-Hungarian Empire, they were in a position that naturally aroused maximum awareness of every national injustice.

In 1903 the Serbian monarchy had reverted to the ambitious and Russian-oriented Karageorgevich dynasty. An aggressive anti-Austrian policy was the result. The Serbian leaders longed to have their country assume for the South Slavs the role that nineteenth-century Prussia had played for the Germans and Piedmont for the Italians—the core around which unity would be achieved. To fellow Serbs just cross the border, and to the Croats and Slovenes farther west, Serbia promised the liberation of *all* the South Slavs within the confines of the Austro-Hungarian Empire. This pledge had taken on greater urgency since 1908 when, to the intense indignation of the Serbs, Austria annexed the South Slav provinces of Bosnia and Herzegovina, which had been technically still under Turkish suzerainty.

In 1912 and 1913, the small nations of this area went to war, first to deprive Turkey of nearly all its remaining European territory and subsequently to quarrel over the spoils. The Turks had been the oppressors of the Balkan peoples for more than five hundred years; the Balkan drive for national liberation, which began in the early nineteenth century, was completed in the First Balkan War of 1912–1913. But independence settled nothing. No Balkan nation was satisfied with its boundaries of 1913. Each had fellow nationals living within its neighbor's borders. Serbia—the most ambitious of the lot—stood in a particularly difficult position, with a Bulgarian minority inside its borders while it looked north and west in an attitude of unreserved hostility toward the Austro-Hungarian oppressors of its "blood brothers." It was obvious to any astute observer of the Balkan scene that the settlement of 1913 was no more than an uneasy truce.

The Alliance System

Although the Concert of Europe had all but disappeared, the system of European alliances worked reasonably smoothly in the period from 1870 to 1890. Britain continued in its traditional detachment; the French nursed their grievance over the loss of Alsace-Lorraine; and Austria-Hungary and Italy moved into a defensive alliance with Germany. The new German Empire held the center of the stage. Its chancellor, Prince Bismarck, kept insisting that Germany was now a satisfied power. By reassuring Russia and isolating France, he held apart the two powers that could possibly threaten the status quo in Central Europe.

With Bismarck's dismissal by the young Emperor William II in 1890, international relations moved into a graver phase. Within four years, Russia and France had signed a military agreement. By 1900, the German alliance with Italy had virtually become a dead letter. The British, alarmed by their isolation among the Great Powers that the Boer War had revealed, reached a "cordial understanding" with France in 1904. In 1907, the new alliance system was completed when Britain and Russia achieved a similar settlement of past differences.

In theory, then, the Great Powers stood three against three: A Triple Alliance—Germany, Austria-Hungary, and Italy—faced a looser Triple Entente—Britain, France, and Russia. In reality, the situation was rather less neat. Germany and Austria could no longer count on Italy. Within the rival coalition, only France and Russia were bound by a true alliance. Moreover, during the period 1890 to 1907, the balance had turned heavily against Germany. Although the Germans were probably the strongest single nation in

MAP 1.1 The European alliance system on the eve of the First World War.

the world—as their war record was to prove—they felt "encircled" by the united hostility of the French and the Russians, with whom they shared borders in the west and east (see Map 1.1). In this situation, they felt bound to support Austria as the sole ally that remained loyal to them. Without Bismarck's restraining influence, they also felt more ready to risk a minor conflict in the Balkans on the assumption that it could easily be contained.

Even if the war could not be kept localized in the Balkans, however, German leaders were ready to risk a wider conflict in order to preserve and enhance Germany's dominant role on the Continent. To many, that role—to which Germany had acceded in 1870 after its defeat of France—now seemed in jeopardy. German industrial leaders had become convinced that, despite its rapid and impressive industrialization of the past three decades, their nation was falling behind in the race with England, France, and the United States to dominate global markets. At the same time, the German military command voiced alarm at the increasing armed strength of France and Russia, which had become military allies in 1894. Persuaded that Germany was becoming increasingly vulnerable to both economic and military pressure, influential pressure groups around Chancellor Bethmann Hollweg argued for a preventative war that would ensure German superiority in Europe by eliminating its rivals before they could impose their will and humble Germany in turn.

The Outbreak of War

The assassination at Sarajevo on June 28 rudely shook the statesmen of Europe. In view of the tense relations between Serbia and Austria-Hungary in 1914, no one in Europe should have been surprised that the fuse that set off the great explosion was lighted there. Far from being—as journalists phrased it—an "obscure corner" of Europe, the capital of Bosnia was as likely a place as any for the great war to begin. The heir to the Austro-Hungarian throne, the Archduke Francis Ferdinand, might have known that he took his life in his hands when he ventured to pay a state visit there. No act was better calculated to stir Serbian resentment; it was natural that the assassin should be a young Bosnian heated to fever by Serbian propaganda.

From this point on, events unrolled with an iron logic. Serbia had only an indirect complicity in the assassination. Although its prime minister knew in a general way what was afoot, the slayers of the archduke were in no sense the agents of the Serbian government that the Austrians claimed they were. Moreover, when the Austrians followed up the assassination with a severe ultimatum, the Serbs agreed to nearly all their terms. They drew the line only at the unprecedented demand that Austro-Hungarian officials participate, *within Serbian territory*, in the investigation of the crime. It was the Austrians, rather, who bore responsibility for the ensuring conflict in that they purposely made their requirements unacceptable in order to settle once and for all—by war if necessary—the threat to the integrity of their empire posed by Balkan nationalism. They hoped that a show of force would teach their upstart neighbors to the south not to meddle in Austria's internal affairs.

Germany, however, bore a yet heavier responsibility for the outbreak of hostilities. German leaders deliberately precipitated a war they could have prevented had they but chosen to restrain their weaker Austrian ally. Instead, they issued the Austrians a "blank check" by promising unlimited support to the nation that they correctly regarded as their only reliable ally and by pressing the Austrians to act quickly against Serbia so as to split apart the Triple Entente, while at the same time sabotaging British efforts at mediation. Papers surviving from the German government deliberations of July 1914 suggest that Chancellor Bethmann Hollweg believed that a limited war would help to ensure the German Empire's military supremacy on the Continent and win it additional colonies (at Belgium's expense), as befitted its status as a growing world power. In effect, Germany fell victim to the grandiose dreams of *Weltpolitik*. An expansionist foreign policy led its leaders to gamble on a successful challenge to the diplomatic status quo, with catastrophic results.

The original Austro-German policy was predicated on the assumption that the war could be "localized." What made it a Europe-wide conflict was the entirely predictable Russian decision to support the Serbs. This brought the whole alliance system into play. For if Russia went to the aid of Serbia against Austria-Hungary, it had also to be prepared to face the German empire. Still worse, the Russian military machine was slow

War fever in 1914: German volunteers march off to fight with hats raised and
a burst of song. (*Courtesy Sueddeutscher Verlag/Bilderdienst*)

and cumbersome, and if the country was to mobilize at all, technical considerations
obliged it to do so fully and against *both* its potential enemies. Thus when the Russians
were ostensibly doing nothing more than offering to protect their Serbian "brothers"
against Austria-Hungary, it looked in Berlin as though they were also threatening Germany itself.

In the frenzied weeks between the assassination and the outbreak of the conflict,
it was the Russians who began the process of escalation by mobilizing prematurely. But
the Germans, too, found that they could not mobilize against one foe alone; their military plans decreed that a threat from Russia should be answered by attacks against both
the tsar's forces and against their French allies. Yet to launch a successful offensive
against France required the Germans to invade neutral Belgium in order to sweep down
on Paris from the north. Hence there arose the seeming illogical result that a threat from
Russia caused the Germans to mass troops on the Belgian border, all the time assuming
(erroneously) that Britain would simply stand aside if the German troops received the
order to attack.

In this succession of events, French responsibility was minimal. It has been argued that the French did not act with sufficient energy to restrain their Russian allies. In
reality, they were kept in the dark about what the Russians were doing: The latter de-

ceived them about the extent of the mobilization until it was a *fait accompli*. The French government accepted the fact of war with resolution and confidence, but it did nothing to bring war about. Indeed, it took up arms not so much in fidelity to its Russian ally as in defense of a European equilibrium that appeared threatened by German hegemony.

The British, too, reacted primarily to the German threat, in compliance with their long-standing policy to prevent the English Channel ports from being seized by a hostile power. It is true that they kept the Germans guessing up to the very last whether they would intervene—thus encouraging the war party within the Reich—and did not disclose their secret military commitments to France. Nonetheless, though more energetic sabre rattling might have sobered the German high command into rethinking their invasion plans, the British cannot be held responsible for Berlin's decision to attack.

Thus the melancholy sequence unfolded: Austria-Hungary threatened Serbia, Russia supported Serbia, Germany supported Austria, France supported Russia, Britain supported France. Italy alone remained aloof. On August 4, 1914, the armies started to move. The First World War had begun.

READINGS

For a general interpretation of the changed position of Europe in the twentieth century, see James Joll, *Europe Since 1870: An International History* (rev. ed. 1990), Norman Stone, *Europe Transformed 1878–1919** (1983) and J. M. Roberts, *Europe 1880–1945,** 2nd ed. (1989). A reminder of the forces of continuity can be found in Arno J. Mayer, *The Persistence of the Old Regime: Europe to the Great War** (1981). The best general history of the prewar decades is Eric Hobsbawm, *The Age of Empire, 1875–1914** (1987). Hobsbawm's *The Age of Extremes: A History of the World, 1914–1991** (1994) is a remarkably successful attempt to chart the major themes of this century in a single volume. Mark Mazower, *Dark Continent: Europe's Twentieth Century** (1998), offers a salutory reminder that antidemocratic forces enjoyed widespread support in Europe, and that the defeat of fascism and communism were by no means foreordained. Two valuable older works are Carlton J. H. Hayes, *A Generation of Materialism, 1871–1900* (1941; reprint ed. 1983), and Oron J. Hale, *The Great Illusion, 1900–1914** (1971). On the two least privileged groups in European society—the workers and peasants—see Charles, Louise, and Richard Tilly, *The Rebellious Century 1830–1930** (1975), and T. Shannon, ed., *Peasants and Peasant Societies* (1971). Eugen Weber stresses the variety of the peasant experience within a single country in *Peasants into Frenchmen* (1976). A view of the opposite end of the social scale is offered in David Cannadine's detailed and fascinating *The Decline and Fall of the British Aristocracy** (1990).

Among the introductory works devoted to the history of individual countries, for Britain, see Peter Clarke, *Hope and Glory: Britain, 1900–1990* (1996); Paul Johnson, ed., *Twentieth Century Britain: Economic, Social, and Cultural Change** (1994); and the

---

*Books marked with an asterisk are available in paperback.

classic account of British society on the eve of World War I, George Dangerfield's *The Strange Death of Liberal England** (1934). For France, Gordon Wright, *France in Modern Times: From the Enlightenment to the Present,** 5th ed. (1995), is a judiciously balanced account that includes an extensive bibliography, while Charles Sowerwine, *France Since 1870: Culture, Politics and Society** (2001), is especially good on the period after World War II. Theodore Zeldin, *France, 1848–1945,** 4 vols. (1973–1977) presents a rich panorama of French society, topically arranged and teeming with detail, though with little analysis.

For Germany, Gordon A. Craig, *Germany 1866–1945** (1978) and *The Germans** (1982), offer the best general introduction; see also Volker R. Berghahn, *Modern Germany: Society, Economy, and Politics in the 20th Century** (1983), and Alexander Gerschenkron's masterful study, *Bread and Democracy in Germany** (1943, reprint edition with an introduction by Charles Maier, 1989). A critical but comprehensive survey of Italian history in the modern era can be found in Denis Mack Smith, *Italy: A Modern History,** rev. ed. (1969); see also Christopher Seton-Watson, *Italy from Liberalism to Fascism, 1870–1925* (1967). For Spain, see Raymond Carr, *Modern Spain, 1875–1980** (1981), and for the Hapsburg Empire, both C. A. Macartney, *The House of Austria: The Later Phase, 1790–1918* (1978), and Alan Sked, *The Decline and Fall of the Hapsburg Empire, 1815–1918* (1989). Russia's path into the twentieth century is recounted in Geoffrey Hosking, *Russia: People and Empire** (1997), Richard Pipes, *Russia Under the Old Regime** (1974), and Nichilas V. Riasanovsky, *A History of Russia,* 6th ed. (2002). The complex modern history of the Balkan region is ably surveyed in Stevan K. Pavlowitch, *A History of the Balkans, 1804–1945** (1999) and Misha Glenny, *The Balkans: Nationalism, War, and the Great Powers, 1804–1999** (1999). See also Joseph Held, ed., *The Columbia History of Eastern Europe in the Twentieth Century* (1992), whose ten contributors cover developments in the region in separate chapters, and the fine one-volume synthesis *Eastern Europe in the Twentieth Century** (1994) by R. J. Crampton.

On women and the family at the start of the century, see the fundamental study of Louise Tilly and Joan W. Scott, *Women, Work and Family* (1978). Michelle Perrot, ed., *A History of Private Life, vol. 4: From the Fires of Revolution to the Great War** (1990) explores the domestic sphere during a time of rapid change. Women's attempts to win a broader role for themselves in society are treated in comparative perspective in Richard J. Evans, *The Feminists: Women's Emancipation Movements in Europe, America and Australia 1840–1920* (1977). An account of the British suffragette movement by one of the principal participants is Christobel Pankhurst, *Unshackled: The Story of How We Won the Vote* (1959). Also of interest is June Purvis, *Emmeline Pankhurst: A Biography* (2002).

For the origins and perversions of nationalism, see Elie Kedourie, *Nationalism,** 3d ed. (1969), Hannah Arendt, *The Origins of Totalitarianism** (1951, 1958), and the rich anthology *Becoming National: A Reader,** eds. Geoff Eley and Ronald Grigor Suny (1996). Benedict Anderson, *Imagined Communities: Reflections on the Origin and Spread of Nationalism,** rev. ed. (1991) stresses both the contingent character of national identity and its New World roots within a broad comparative perspective. George Lichtheim, *Imperialism* (1971) and Wolfgang J. Mommsen, *Theories of Imperialism* (1980) explore the links between Europe's national rivalries and its frenetic expansion of colonial control in the late nineteenth century, while Liah Greenfeld, *Nationalism: Five Roads to Modernity** (1992) details the different character assumed by nationalism in Britain, the United States, France, Germany, and Russia.

The best general account of the diplomacy of the half century preceding the outbreak remains A. J. P. Taylor, *The Struggle for Mastery in Europe, 1848–1918* (1954). William R. Keylor, *The Twentieth-Century World: An International History,** 4th ed. (2001) provides a valuable survey of international relations on the eve of the war, emphasizing Germany's ambitions to play a larger role in world affairs. Jonathan Steinberg, *Yesterday's Deterrent: Tirpitz and the Birth of the German Battle Fleet* (1965) examines the naval arms race that helped to precipitate the world war, as does Volker Berghahn, *Germany and the Approach of War in 1914* (1973). The shortcomings of the alliance system are detailed in George F. Kennan's *The Decline of Bismarck's European Order: Franco-Russian Relations, 1875–1890** (1979) and *The Fateful Alliance: France, Russia, and the Coming of the First World War** (1984). Paul Kennedy, *The Rise and Fall of the Great Powers** (1987), places the rivalry among European nations in a comparative context. For a clear and thoughtful overview of the crisis leading to the war itself, see James Joll, *The Origins of the First World War** (rev. ed. 1992), which can be usefully supplemented by Samuel R. Williamson, Jr., *The Origins of a Tragedy** (1981) and the same author's *Austria-Hungary and the Origins of the First World War** (1991), as well as the relevant chapters in David Kaiser's impressive comparative study *Politics and War: European Conflict from Philip II to Hitler* (1990).

A major feature of the debate of the war's origins during the past two decades has been a return to the argument that Germany deliberately provoked the war in its quest to become a world power. This interpretation, advanced by Germany's enemies during the war and then gradually discredited in the years after World War I, was revived by the German historian Fritz Fischer in his *Germany's Aims in the First World War** (1967) and expanded in his *War of Illusions: Germany's Policies from 1911 to 1914* (1975). The controversy that Fischer unleashed is detailed in John A. Moses, *The Politics of Illusion: The Fischer Controversy in German Historiography* (1975), while Fischer's provocative thesis is weighed and refined in David Kaiser, "Germany and the Origins of World War I," *Journal of Modern History*, 55 (September 1983). For an assessment of the recurring shifts in the controversy of the war's origins from war's end to the present, see J. W. Langdon, *July 1914: The Long Debate: 1918–1990* (1991).

The war preparations of other belligerents are examined in Zara S. Steiner and Keith Neilson, *Britain and the Origins of the First World War,** 2nd ed. (2003); John F. V. Krieger, *France and the Origins of the First World War* (1984); R. J. B. Bosworth, *Italy, the Least of the Great Powers: Italian Foreign Policy Before the First War* (1980); and D. C. B. Lieven, *Russia and the Origins of the First World War* (1984); as well as in Paul M. Kennedy, ed., *The War Plans of the Great Powers, 1880–1914* (1979).

2

THE FIRST WORLD
WAR

British troops attempt to free a tank—first introduced into combat in the final months of the war—bogged down in the mud of northern France. (*Courtesy Brown Brothers*)

I. THE CHARACTER OF THE CONFLICT

[handwritten margin note: epoch - period of time in history or a persons life]

To the generation of the 1920s and 1930s, the First World War was the overwhelming catastrophe that dominated their epoch. A generation later, after the Second World War had been fought, the earlier conflict seemed dwarfed by its successor. It receded into the background, apparently less important and less interesting than the war that followed twenty years later. With the further passage of time, however, the perspective has altered. The First World War now appears fully as important as the Second—indeed, in certain respects, even more decisive in its effects.

It was the first of the world conflicts that fundamentally altered the character of European society. It was the first war that made it impossible to reconstruct the European community on the old basis. This war "stacked the cards for the future"; it created a situation in which domestic and international stability could not be maintained, and further war eventually became unavoidable.

The Early Illusions: The Strength of the Powers

When the war started in August 1914, nearly all Europeans were convinced that it would be brief. The general staffs had made their plans on that basis, and civilians had agreed that the delicate economic arrangements of an advanced industrial society could not stand the strain of a protracted conflict. Among other things, the nations would run out of cash. Almost no one foresaw that a bankrupt power could go on fighting merely by printing more and more paper money. Similarly, with respect to human resources, even the wildest imaginings of contemporaries did not grasp the millions of casualties that the reality of war was to produce. Again, it seemed unthinkable that the privileged sons of an advanced society should be called on to suffer far more and far longer than their ancestors of ruder ages. As one German officer put it, "No one would have dared at the beginning of the war to expect from the soldier what he afterward had to endure for years as a constant necessity."[*]

The illusion of a brief war was, of course, matched by the corresponding illusion of a quick victory. Each side believed it had the secret of sure success; neither realized how evenly the two coalitions were matched. Since the strength of the powers varied from department to department within the military establishment, it was impossible to compute what each factor would weigh in the final reckoning. How did one balance Russian manpower against German technical excellence? Or British dominance of the seas against the continental communications system of the Central Powers?

To a superficial observer, the Entente powers—Britain, France, and Russia—might appear the stronger. Russia was by far the most populous of the powers. Britain was mistress of the seas, with all the resources of the empire to draw on, the arbiter of world trade, outclassed only by the United States and Germany in industrial equipment. France, with the second-best army in the world, enjoyed a happy balance between indus-

---

[*]Quoted in Alfred Vagts, *A History of Militarism: Civilian and Military*, rev. ed. (New York: Meridian Books, 1959), 283.

try and agriculture that gave it a unique position of self-sufficiency among the European powers. But the advantages of the Entente were more apparent than real; they were potential rather than fully available at the outbreak of hostilities. The strength of the Entente was scattered through the extremities of Europe and into all the corners of the globe, and its fighting effort rested on far-stretched and perilous lines of communication. Everything depended on whether Britain could continue to supply itself with food and raw materials from abroad, on whether a steady flow of equipment from the West would prove adequate to maintain the primitive economy of the Russian Empire.

At the start, then, the military fortunes of the Entente powers depended primarily on France. Distance and bureaucratic inefficiency made the Russian army the slowest to mobilize of all the major land forces—hence the Russian decision to act even before war became inevitable. Russia's army, like the country, was vast, but it was poorly led, ill equipped, and only feebly supported by the home government; its peasant soldiers could scarcely comprehend the technical job of the modern soldier nor did they know why they were ordered to fight. Britain had a well-trained professional army, but it was only a small elite force; nearly two years were needed to bring the country's manpower to bear on the decisive battlefields. France was thus left to face the German onslaught virtually alone. To the French themselves, however, this prospect was not as depressing as it appears in retrospect. Although they knew that the Germans would eventually outnumber them,

The enthusiasm with which the war was greeted during its first months is still evident on the faces of these volunteers massed in front of a British recruiting office early in 1915. (*Courtesy Getty Images, Inc./Hulton Archive Photos*)

they were convinced that they were their enemies' equals in military technique and superiors in offensive "doctrine." Moreover, they were justly proud of their 75-millimeter gun, which was, in fact, the best field piece in existence. The French did not appreciate their inferiority to the Germans in machine guns and heavy artillery—weapons that were to prove decisive in the first weeks of the conflict.

On the side of the Central Powers, Germany and Austria-Hungary, the strength was almost entirely Germany, while the source of weakness almost always lay with Austria. In this respect, the Dual Monarchy resembled Russia; it looked stronger than it was. In technical efficiency, it lay somewhere between backward Russia and the three heavily industrialized powers, Germany, Britain, and France. Indeed, at some points in the war on the Eastern Front, the military decision seemed to depend largely on which was more inefficient and demoralized, Austria or Russia. But in addition, the Austro-Hungarian Empire suffered from a special weakness—perhaps half its army, drawn from the discontented nationalities, could not be fully relied on. Slavic units seemed so likely to desert to their Russian "brothers" that the Austrian command hesitated to send them to the Eastern Front.

By the middle of the war, the Central Powers had achieved a unity of command that the Entente was to attain only in 1918, as Austria-Hungary became more and more a junior partner, subjected to German overall direction. The Central Powers had a second military advantage as well. They constituted a compact land mass; they enjoyed excellent "internal" lines of communication and hence could readily shift troops from one front to another. But to speak of this solid continental situation is also to suggest a position of peril. Although Austria was self-sufficient in food, Germany was almost as dependent as Britain on imports from overseas. And at the start of the war—that is, until the submarines really began to take a toll—Britain was in a better position than Germany to starve out its enemy. Furthermore, the Central Powers' "internal" situation meant a two-front war—a war in which Germany must bear the burden on both fronts. On both of these—even, at first, in France—the Germans would be outnumbered; hence the essence of German strategy was to knock out the enemy to the west before the enemy to the east could fully mobilize.

Moreover, although Germany had gone further than any other power in the technical perfecting of its armed forces, it still did not fully utilize its potential resources. The aristocratic survivals in German society were a heavy drag on its efficiency as an industrial state. Field commands were thus often given to crown princes or important noblemen whose qualifications for such posts were mediocre. Both Germany and France—in contrast to Britain's tradition of a small professional army—in theory demanded military service of every able-bodied male citizen. In practice, however, France called up a larger proportion of those eligible to serve—thereby partially balancing the disparity in population between the two countries, which was about three to two in Germany's favor. The French showed little prejudice in the appointment of reserve officers to command their fighting masses in wartime. In France, almost any man with a higher education could become a reserve officer, and promotion from the ranks was not impossible. In Germany, Jews and men of humble origin or advanced political opinions were systematically excluded from the corps of reserve officers, and the promotion of an enlisted man was nearly unknown. Aristocratic prejudice thus erected an intangible but very real barrier to the indefinite expansion of Germany's armed forces and helps explain why, in the opening weeks of the war, France was able to field two more fighting divisions than the invading enemy.

Beyond merely technical considerations, French democracy was an asset that became increasingly apparent as the war dragged on. Not only in a military sense, but also in the wider context of national morale, the anachronisms and inequities within German society exerted a profoundly depressing effect. Once Russia had left the war—and President Wilson had redefined the conflict as a war for democracy—it became clear that nearly all the psychological advantage lay on the side of Entente.

The Failure of Strategy and of Military Technique

The wars of Napoleon, Bismarck's "lightning" wars from 1864 to 1870—even the Second World War—showed generals in control of the weapons at their disposal and competent to carry out the operations they had planned. The First World War was quite different. It demonstrated a failure of strategy and of military technique on a gigantic and unprecedented scale. In its bungling, infinitely wasteful character, it was more like the American Civil War than like its predecessors or successor among European conflicts. And, like the Civil War, it soon became a war of attrition that, after four long years of slaughter and discouragement, finally came to an end only because one side ran out of men and materiel, overwhelmed by the numerical and industrial superiority of its adversary.

Here is Winston Churchill's retrospective verdict: "Events passed very largely outside the scope of conscious choice. Governments and individuals conformed to the rhythm of the tragedy, and swayed and staggered forward in helpless violence, slaughtering and squandering on ever-increasing scales." By the end of 1914, the campaign in the west had become a war of position—a hopeless deadlock in which, despite the loss of hundreds of thousands of lives, the front did not shift in either direction by more than ten miles in three years. The failure of the military mind was patent. Although official propaganda made frenzied efforts to conceal it, by 1917, this failure had become clear to nearly everybody. Only in 1918, when the end was already in sight, did the generals begin to show that they were learning the new realities of their profession.

The great surprise, of course, was trench warfare. The defense had proved so much stronger than the attack that the war had turned into a colossal siege. But this new turn in strategy should not have been totally unexpected: It had been predicted as early as 1902, in an article published in a Swiss military journal. In the Russo-Japanese War, the campaign in Manchuria had bogged down in just this fashion. But the European military refused to heed these portents of the future. They dismissed the conflict of 1904 as a squalid Asiatic struggle and clung to their illusions about a war of movement.

The French, rather than the Germans, were the more deceived. During the early years of the century, their staff training fell into the hands of a group of "young Turks" who put their faith in an offensive of unbridled fury. The most important of the group was Colonel Ferdinand Foch—later to redeem his reputation as supreme Allied commander at the end of the war. Foch and his colleagues taught what was less a military than a mystical doctrine. It could be summed up in one word—*attack*—always and everywhere. As one of these enthusiasts declared, "The victorious army will be the one which, scornful of reserves and fortresses, will first jump at the throat of the enemy and will at once obtain the moral superiority that forces . . . events. . . . It is necessary that the concept of the offensive penetrate the soul of our nation."

This was the doctrine behind the French war plan for a rapid advance through Lorraine into central Germany. The plan failed utterly. Not until—as Foch put it—the French military leaders had forgotten what they had taught and learned before 1914 did they reach a true understanding of what they were about. The German war plan was less feckless. Indeed, it almost succeeded. But once it too had failed, the German generals, like the French, had to buckle down to the painful business of relearning their profession from scratch.

Psychological Shocks and the Attrition of Morale

The illusion of a short war vanished, and with it the thoughtless enthusiasm with which so many of the combatants on both sides first went into battle. The reality was infinitely more grim and less glamorous than anyone had imagined. A vast disillusionment ensued—a psychological revulsion that gripped millions of men in uniform.

This was particularly true in France, which had the misfortune of being the main theater of combat. Moreover, France—along with little Serbia—suffered the highest rate of casualties in proportion to the nation's total available manpower. True to their doctrine of the "furious" offensive that would sweep all before it, the French generals squandered lives on a reckless scale. The desperate position of an army fighting deep within its own frontiers seemed to justify such waste, and in the first sixteen months of combat, France suffered roughly half of its total war casualties. Two-thirds of a million men were killed—a total without precedent in history. The next three years were less bloody, but by this time an attitude of infinite grief and hopelessness had settled on the nation.

During the first year of the war, nearly half the families of France received one of the dreadful telegrams which in clipped, patriotic prose announced the death of a husband or son. The conflict had run only a quarter of its course, and already the whole nation seemed in mourning. The French themselves, of course, had no idea how long the war would go on. In their matter-of-fact, logical fashion they made their computations: Reckoning from what they knew of the toll of lives, they concluded that eventually *every* husband or son in the trenches would be either killed or mutilated.

The case of France is the clearest and most dramatic, but nearly as great a tragedy occurred in Germany, where the end rather than the start of the war brought casualty lists that the nation could no longer endure. Even Britain, after its new army went into battle in 1916, suffered only slightly less than the major adversaries on the continent. Everywhere, the loss of human life on an unimagined scale inflicted a psychological shock that was also without precedent. It produced a vast crisis of confidence, shaking men's minds to their depths and calling into question all the optimistic assumptions with which the century had opened. It spared nothing—leaders, governments, society itself. To quote Churchill once more, "Injuries were wrought to the structure of human society which a century will not efface."*

*Winston S. Churchill, *The World Crisis, 1911–1918*, I (New York: Charles Scribner's Sons, 1923), 1–2.

In the end, Britain and France held firm; their institutions and way of life stood the test. But they were victors, and victory helped to ease the strain. Vanquished Germany, on the other hand, plunged into years of social and political turmoil. Austria-Hungary disintegrated. And Russia turned to communism. Nor is it without significance that Russia had squandered lives most recklessly of all. With infinite cynicism, the Russian generals calculated that their endless supply of men would compensate for a disgraceful shortage of arms and materiel. In certain battles on the Eastern Front, it was literally true that as one Russian soldier fell, an unarmed comrade picked up his rifle and stumbled on. These stolid peasant soldiers, their officers thought, would endure anything. They did not envision a day when the long-suffering peasants would simply drop their rifles and start walking home, to claim as their own the factories and farms of Russia.

II. THE WESTERN FRONT

From the Schlieffen Plan to the First Battle of the Marne

The basic German plan of attack had been devised in 1905 by the military chief of staff, Count Alfred von Schlieffen. It called for a vast sweeping movement through Belgium that would corner the French army to the east of Paris and end the war in the west at one stroke. To be sure, this plan violated the neutrality of Belgium, which had been guaranteed by the Great Powers shortly after that country had won its independence in 1830, and thus entailed the danger (which in fact occurred) of bringing Britain into the war on the side of Germany's enemies. In the German military mind, however, this risk was more than balanced by the advantages of surprise that the Schlieffen Plan possessed. Germany's only hope, the generals calculated, lay in knocking France out before the Russian mass began to move. Only then could the nightmare of a war on two fronts be avoided. And in order to destroy the French armies quickly, it was essential to bypass the strong forts on the northeastern frontier and to advance through the more lightly defended northwest.

Schlieffen's bold concept, then, was to strip down to skeleton forces not only the troops defending Germany against Russia but also the left wing (the southern flank) of his attack against France. In both cases he ran a risk—he exposed East Prussia to Russian invasion and the area from Alsace to Frankfurt to invasion by the French. And although these risks bothered him, he failed to give the emperor and chancellor adequate warning of them. Everything depended, he thought, on maintaining overwhelming pressure on the right wing of his main attack. His dying warning was supposed to have been, "Make the right wing strong."

It fell to Schlieffen's successor, Helmuth von Moltke the younger, to test the plan in action. And it failed the test. The reasons for this failure—including modifications ordered by Moltke once war had begun—have been much debated. But even had the plan been carried out to the letter, it was far too optimistic in its assessment of German strength and enemy weakness to succeed. As one historian noted in retrospect, "The

Germans underestimated their opponents and paid the penalty for doing so."* Among their miscalculations, the Germans underestimated the Belgians, who they assumed would not resist the superior German forces seeking to cross their territory. But the Belgians fought back from the shelter of the fortresses that guarded their land; forced to reduce these strongholds to submission, the German armies lost precious time. When the greatest of the forts, Liège, finally fell on August 18, the Schlieffen Plan was a full four days behind schedule.

The delay created by Belgian resistance allowed a British force under Sir John French to cross the Channel and come to the aid of the French armies defending the north against the German advance. That advance continued—a million and a half men, organized in seven armies—but French troops, bolstered by the seasoned professional soldiers in the British lines, inflicted heavy casualties on Moltke's troops. At this point, worried by the deteriorating condition of its forces, the German command made the fateful decision to alter the Schlieffen Plan and strike to the east of Paris rather than to its west, as Schlieffen had originally intended. Paris was full of reserve troops, waiting to defend the capital. Apprised of the enemy's new position, the French commander-in-chief, Joseph Joffre, now seized the opportunity to send these forces out of Paris against the unprotected German left flank. Summoning every vehicle in Paris that he could lay his hands on—including a collection of motorized taxicabs—Joffre sent his troops on September 6 to meet the enemy at the river Marne.

The success of the French counterattack wavered in the balance for two days. At some points the situation looked desperate, but French morale was high—the soldiers knew that their country's fate depended on them—and many German units were worn out by their long advance. Around the Battle of the Marne a host of legends has gathered. Along with the defense of Verdun, it is the proudest memory in the French annals of the war. Typical is the telegram that the dashing Foch, by then an army commander, sent to his chief: "My left is giving way, my right is falling back . . . I am ordering a general offensive, a decisive attack by the center."

By September 9 the German armies were in full retreat, pursued by the French and British. For four days they reeled back. Then, on September 13, they called a halt along the Aisne, the best defensive line in Northern France. Joffre had won a great victory. Moltke had resigned his command in disgrace; the Schlieffen Plan lay in shambles. But just as the Germans had failed to destroy him, so Joffre had failed to throw the invaders out of his country. The two sides were at a deadlock. It was now clear that the war would continue at least until the following year.

"The Race for the Sea" and the Stabilization of the Front

October and early November were occupied by the series of battles misleadingly referred to as "the race for the sea." It was rather a series of local engagements, following the German stand on the Aisne, in which each army in turn tried to outflank the other. The

*Gordon A. Craig, *Germany, 1945–1966* (New York: Oxford University Press, 1978), 343.

result was a steady extension of the line toward the west. Finally the armies reached the sea—the English Channel—which brought all flanking operations to an end.

At all costs, the British and French wanted to hold the Channel ports, for these alone could ensure direct communications between the two allies, particularly after the great Belgian seaport of Antwerp fell to the Germans on October 9. The British resolve to hold on to the whole French seacoast stretched the fighting front in a northerly arc through Flanders—the most depressing terrain of all those over which the armies were to fight for the next four years. South of Flanders it ran through the chalk uplands of Artois, then past Vimy Ridge, which the Germans held, to the city of Arras, which remained in French hands. From Arras to Noyon it continued almost due south across pleasant, open farm country. At Noyon it changed its course, now running west to east until it reached Verdun. Noyon, only 60 miles from Paris, was the closest point to the capital the Germans held. Each day on the front page of his own newspaper the old, indomitable Clemenceau—radically dissatisfied with the whole conduct of the war—ran the banner headline, "THE GERMANS ARE AT NOYON," never letting his fellow citizens forget for one moment the peril in which their nation stood.

From Noyon the line ran along the Aisne until it reached Reims and the chalk region of Champagne. Then came Verdun, the great fortress, standing out as a bold French salient, and southeast of it a similar German salient at Saint-Mihiel. At Verdun began the quiet sectors of the line, which extended south and east to the Swiss frontier. Although this portion accounted for nearly half the whole front, it was only lightly held on both sides. The terrain was woody and rugged, traversing the Vosges Mountains in the south, and there seems to have been a tacit agreement that it was unsuitable for large-scale operations.

Even here, however, the opposing armies were installed in regular trenches (see Map 2.1). Ever since the Germans had dug in along the Aisne in mid-September, each attack or repulse had eventually been reduced to static trench warfare. The result was the colossal novelty of an almost unbroken line of improvised fortifications extending for more than 300 miles. Sometimes the two lines ran as much as five miles apart; sometimes they were so close that the opposing troops were within shouting distance of each other. Indeed at Christmas in this first winter of the war, a spontaneous, informal truce was declared in certain sectors, and the soldiers advanced without fear into no-man's-land to fraternize and exchange gifts. The following year no such scenes occurred, for the drabness and horror of life in the trenches had dulled men's souls—the boredom broken only by the sudden danger of a sniper's bullet, the anxious waiting before an attack, the cold, the mud, wet and swollen feet, and the dread moment of fear as the order came to go "Over the top!".

The Germans at least had the illusion of victory as they stood deep within the enemy's frontiers. But more and more, they were troubled about the purpose of the war. The French did not need to ask themselves such questions, for theirs was the simple imperative of holding fast and of liberating the territory that the enemy had occupied. This amounted to almost one-tenth of France, including a large part of its major industry, four-fifths of its coal, and nine-tenths of its iron resources. The year 1915 was dominated by the illusion that the moment of liberating occupied France was at hand.

MAP 2.1 The First World War: The Western Front.

The Year 1915: The War of Attrition

The central reality of trench warfare was simple: The defense had nearly all the advantages. The trenches had originally been crude and makeshift, but during the winter of 1914–1915 they became increasingly complex, as barbed wire and communication trenches were added and protected dugouts installed to the rear. Fieldworks such as these could survive a terrible pounding from the artillery. Once the barrage lifted and the attackers went over the top, opposing machine gunners could quickly get back into position and mercilessly strafe the advancing columns.

These lessons sank into the German mind more quickly than into the French and British. The Germans had a new chief of staff, the young and attractive Erich von Falkenhayn, who had replaced the ailing Moltke, completely shattered by his failure on the Marne. Falkenhayn himself wanted to make a major effort in the west, and indeed in April and May of the new year he launched a massive offensive against the British bastion of Ypres, which barely failed of success. In this battle—for the first time in the war—the Germans used poison gas, but they used it in insufficient quantity and wasted its surprise effect.

After his failure before Ypres, Falkenhayn was obliged to yield to the overwhelming pressure exerted by the German eastern command, the redoubtable team of Hindenburg and Ludendorff. He had to give up offensive plans against France for the rest of the year and concentrate on trying to knock out the Russians. Thus the military initiative in the west passed to the French and British. The French, of course, were still the dominant partners in the alliance. The British had ready the first contingents of their new volunteer army, but the bulk of it would not go into action until 1916. Until then, the French strategic view prevailed.

Joffre and his colleagues had still not cast off all their earlier illusions. They still believed in massed frontal attack, to which they now added the notion of an artillery preparation exceeding anything previously known in history. The French were justly proud of their artillery tradition, and in the long winter of waiting, their guns, like their men, had been dug in and all possible targets registered with deadly accuracy. Joffre at least no longer believed that one great attack would end the war. In its stead he planned a succession of partial attacks, which would gradually wear down the enemy. This the French called the "war of attrition."

In line with this altered strategy, Joffre devised a series of offensives that ran from May through the autumn. The first, in Artois, was an initial success. It achieved a breakthrough of three miles, and for a few hours victory seemed to be in sight. But then the Germans closed the gap, and when the fighting finally died down at the end of June, the French came to the sickening realization that they had lost 400,000 men and gained nothing. The same thing happened in September, when the main blow fell to the east in Champagne. This time the French did not dare reveal their losses (which totaled around 145,000). And the year ended with the front almost unchanged.

Everywhere the story had been the same. The artillery preparation had been massive (in Artois the French calculated that eighteen shells would fall on every yard of the front line), but such long preparation had eliminated the possibility of tactical surprise and had given the Germans the chance to mass their reserves where they would be most useful. Usually there was a breakthrough at some point. But then the attackers found themselves advancing over unfamiliar terrain, where the defenders knew every available shelter or strong point. Eventually the Germans would seal off the hole in the line, and the French would continue to hammer away, unable to cut losses by admitting their failure. Finally, they would be left with no more than a tiny salient, which simply lengthened their own line and made it harder to defend.

The ghastly truth was gradually becoming clear to a few Frenchmen. One deputy brutally summed up the events of 1915: "The war of attrition is working against us."

The Preparations for 1916

Thus, as the third campaigning season of the war opened, the Central Powers were apparently in a far better position than the Entente. They had won brilliant victories over the Russians. The extension of the conflict to new theaters had on balance proved to their advantage. The time had come for the Germans to turn west again and inflict a mortal wound on the French. And for the decisive blow, Falkenhayn and his advisers—with an astute regard for French psychology—chose the great symbolic fortress of Verdun.

III. THE WIDENING OF THE CONFLICT

The Eastern Front: Tannenberg to Vilna

The war on the Eastern Front always differed from the war in the west (see Map 2.2). Although at times the forces engaged on each side were nearly as great in the east as in France, the fighting in Austria and Russia never reached the same level of intensity nor did it so fire the imagination of contemporaries. For one thing, it was more like an old-fashioned war. True, both sides regularly dug trenches, but these were neither as continuous nor as fully developed as on the Western Front. Similarly, the general level of materiel and troop training—at least among the Austrians and Russians—was lower and the morale of the soldiers poorer. The armies in the east were subject to sudden and surprising waves of depression or confidence, while the front mirrored the mood of the soldiers, ranging back and forth over hundreds of miles. In erratic succession, victory followed discouragement, and the decisive blow that was always expected never materialized.

The vast plains of Poland and Russia devoured men and dwarfed the efforts of the generals. As Napoleon had discovered in 1812 and Hitler was to learn in 1941, in these great fields and marshes and forests victory could never be complete. No matter how much Russia might be knocked about, the results could not decide the war as a whole. The real decision—as the Germans gradually learned to their sorrow—could come only in France, where the front was apparently immovable. Once the Germans had failed on the Marne, then they were left with no realistic prospect of defeating their enemies: They could only fight the war to a draw. Thus they had lost a four-year conflict in its first six weeks. Condemned to fight on two fronts, they could do nothing but pursue the will-o'-the-wisp of victory through the endless stretches of Russia. After three years of fighting, Russia did indeed finally collapse. But by then it was too late. The number of Germany's enemies had become overwhelming and the nation's reserves of manpower were close to exhaustion.

The war in the east began, as expected, with a Russian invasion of Germany's most exposed territory, East Prussia. Something like panic followed, and desperate measures seemed called for. In this hour of peril, Germany found inspired leadership. Quietly and undramatically, in a north German railroad station, the ablest team of commanders that the war was to produce shook hands and began their celebrated collaboration—Field

MAP 2.2 The First World War: The Eastern Front.

Marshal Paul von Hindenburg, already old, enormous in bulk, taciturn, and with an iron integrity that inspired confidence wherever he went; and his chief of staff, General Erich Ludendorff, sharp, hard-driving, an organizer of genius. When they first met, they were both unknown to the public; a week later they won the victory that made them figures of legend for the duration of the war.

The elements of the victory of Tannenberg had already been prepared when Hindenburg and Ludendorff arrived on the spot. The Russians had blundered, and the fashion in which this blunder came about explains a great deal of what was wrong with the whole Russian conduct of the war. Their commander, Samsonov, had led his army in reckless fashion too far into enemy country. Its supply train was improvised, its soldiers weary, unfed, and demoralized. By August 26, Samsonov's forces were scattered over a sixty-mile front in a dangerously exposed position. As a result, Hindenburg and Luden-dorff had three days of grace in which to concentrate their forces, and they did it with extraordinary skill. By the end of the month they had Samsonov in a trap. The exhausted Russians surrendered in droves—120,000 out of an army of 200,000—while their commander stole away in the darkness and put a bullet through his head.

Coming, as it did, one week before the Battle of the Marne, Tannenberg gave the Germans a welcome consolation. As a purely *military* triumph, Hindenburg's victory was more complete than Joffre's, and it was followed by the liberation of East Prussia, as Rennenkampf's reserve army was pursued deep into Lithuania. The year 1915 saw still greater victories of the Central Powers over the Russians. The field commander was August von Mackensen, a handsome, ruthless figure, who had the art of charming even the touchy Austrians. He soon became famous as master of the lightning attack that surprised and utterly destroyed the enemy. With a new army of eight divisions transferred from the Western Front, Mackensen was instructed to attack to the south.

He succeeded brilliantly. On May 1, a perfect spring day, the artillery barrage opened with stunning effect, and the attack began. Two weeks later the Germans had advanced 95 miles. By June, the Russians were out of Galicia. Then the advance slowed and it was not until August 4 that Warsaw fell; but the Germans and Austrians continued to push on. The Russians were in appalling straits. Morale was extremely bad, and the half-armed, underfed, and ragged soldiers continued to surrender by the tens of thousands.

At this moment of crisis, the tsar himself assumed personal command. It was only a symbolic gesture—its military significance was nil—but it was one in the relentless series of errors that finally led to the fall of the Romanov dynasty. It was not this gesture that gave the Russians a respite, but the slowing down of the German armies as their communications lines became too far extended. Their last great victory was the capture of the Lithuanian city of Vilna in mid-September. By that time, the Russians had retreated so deeply into their own country that it was impossible to pursue them farther. The Central Powers had pushed back the whole front on an average of 200 miles. All Poland was in their hands—a possession nearly as perplexing and embarrassing as Belgium. Outnumbered by almost half a million, they had captured more than twice that number and inflicted an equal toll of additional casualties. Nowhere in the course of the war was the military record of either side to be more brilliant. The Germans had won great victories—but *victory* itself, complete and decisive, still eluded them.

The Entrance of Italy

Just after the great spring offensive of 1915 took off against the Russians, the unfortunate Austrians were forced to confront another enemy. On May 23, Italy declared war.

The Italians had originally decided to remain neutral. This seemed the most prudent course. Technically they were still in alliance with the Central Powers. More realistic considerations, however, inclined them toward the Entente, for it was Austria that held the "unredeemed" lands along the Adriatic for which Italian patriots longed.

The bulk of the Italian people—to the extent that they were politically conscious at all—undoubtedly favored a neutral course. Such was the view of the chief Catholic leaders, of the Socialists, and of the motley majority in the Chamber of

Deputies that looked to Giolitti for guidance. But the master of Italian politics was temporarily out of power. The more conservative and nationalist Antonio Salandra was serving as prime minister; in charge of foreign affairs was Sidney Sonnino, who was part English. Both responded wholeheartedly to the pressure for intervention on the side of the Entente—a pressure relentlessly exerted by the royal court, the nationalists, army and navy leaders, even a minority of democrats with emotional ties to England and France.

Giolitti believed that Austria would pay a good price to keep Italy neutral, and events confirmed his opinion. Grudgingly, and only after persistent German prodding, the Austro-Hungarian government promised to turn over to Italy not *all* the empire's territory inhabited by Italians but at least the largest area and the one about which Italians cared most—the Trentino; and it agreed to local autonomy for the seaport of Trieste. But the final Austrian offer arrived to late. Salandra and Sonnino had come to a far more favorable agreement with the British and French. The secret Treaty of London of April 26 promised Italy additional stretches of Austro-Hungarian territory—which had a large population of *non-Italians*—plus further acquisitions to be made at the expense of Turkey.

In return, the Treaty of London stipulated that Italy should declare war within a month. But how was this to be done? How was intervention to be managed when a majority of the deputies had expressed themselves against it? Salandra, the generals, and the king were relieved from their embarrassment by a series of street demonstrations that overawed the deputies. With the nationalist poet D'Annunzio leading the agitation, the frightened chamber was forced to vote for war.

Actually, Italian intervention did not alter the course of the war very much. Although it forced the Austrians to divert a number of divisions from the Eastern Front, it did not seriously threaten the Austro-Hungarian state. In eleven successive battles on the mountainous Isonzo front, the Italians never succeeded in advancing more than twelve miles. Not until the autumn of 1917 did the Italian theater suddenly become of crucial importance.

Balkan Involvements: Turkey, Bulgaria, Romania, Greece

In November 1914, Turkey declared war on the side of the Central Powers. This was only to be expected, in view of the predominant influence that Germany had exerted over Turkish economic and military policy in the immediate prewar years. The involvement of the other Balkan countries, however, was less certain. It came later in the war, and only as a result of the same sort of bargaining and realistic calculation that had gone on in the case of Italy.

In September 1915, the Bulgarians signed a military alliance with Germany and Austria providing for extensive territorial gains at Serbia's expense. Here again the decision was logical in terms of Bulgaria's fierce antagonism toward Serbia and of Bulgaria's humiliation in the Second Balkan War. But still the Bulgarians wanted to wait until they were sure that the Serbians would be unable to retaliate. By the autumn of 1915, the Central Powers were at last ready for their knockout blow. Once again the Germans felt obliged to wrest strategic direction from their faltering Austrian allies. Mackensen—fresh from his victories over the Russians—directed the campaign and carried out his assignment with his customary speed and thoroughness.

In early October, the armies of the three allied nations converged mercilessly on Serbia. The Serbians fought desperately, but they were overwhelmed by numbers. In six weeks, the campaign was over, and the terrible westward retreat over the mountains began. In mid-November came a heavy snowfall, in which tens of thousands of soldiers and civilian refugees froze or died of typhus. Fewer than 100,000 of the Serbian army finally fought their way through to the Adriatic. Here they were rescued by the British and Italian navies and transported to safety on the island of Corfu. Serbia, like Belgium, had simply been swallowed up in battle. But its sufferings under occupation were to be far more intense. Of all the belligerents on either side, Serbia endured the heaviest casualties, both military and civilian.

A year later it was Romania's turn. The year 1916 had begun with a deceptive series of Entente successes. The French held off the Germans at Verdun, the British staged their first great offensive along the Somme, and the Russians suddenly came to life and struck back at their enemies with astonishing results. In June and July, under the command of a new and talented general named Alexei Brusilov, the Russian armies advanced all along the line. In the end, however, Brusilov gained nothing. Victory eluded him, as it had Hindenburg and Ludendorff and Mackensen the year before. Brusilov lost more than a million men; another million quietly deserted. The spirit of the Russian armies was broken.

The Romanians, however, anxiously searching the skies for portents, did not realize this. All they saw was that a propitious moment had arrived to enter the war on the side of the Entente. And their choice—like Bulgaria's—was comparatively easy. The major goal of Romanian expansion was Transylvania, which formed part of Hungary. On August 28, 1916, Romania declared war. But this calculated decision came a couple of months too late; Germany had already surmounted the threat from Brusilov and contained the British pressure along the Somme. Hence it meant nothing that the Romanians advanced almost unopposed fifty miles into Transylvania. Their success was completely illusory; the formidable Mackensen was already plotting their destruction. Three armies converged on the hapless Romanians. By the end of the year they had lost three-quarters of their country and were all but out of the war.

The final Balkan intervention—that by Greece—is a complex affair, and one that does no credit to Entente diplomacy. In Greece, as contrasted to Bulgaria or Romania, the national leaders were hopelessly divided: King Constantine, whose wife was German, inclined toward the Central Powers; his prime minister, Eleutherios Venizelos, was ardently pro-Entente. Venizelos had a clearer view of the national interest, for the lands that the Greeks had marked out for future annexation belonged to Germany's new allies, to Turkey and, to a lesser extent, to Bulgaria. Moreover, the Entente powers, whose navies dominated the Mediterranean, were in a far better position than Germany and Austria to bring pressure on the wavering Greeks.

For two full years, Britain and France gradually nudged Greece into the war—first, by establishing a vast fortified camp around Salonika on Greek soil; second, by supporting Venizelos in his intrigues against the king. Finally there came a military showdown. An Anglo-French navy appeared off the coast near Athens. Entente agents stirred up a minor civil war. By early 1917, King Constantine had been forced to abdicate, and Greece had formally joined the Entente.

The Dardanelles Expedition

The Greek involvement in the war forms part of a larger pattern of Entente action against the Turkish Empire, which had begun in earnest in early 1915. At that time, with the front in France stabilized, a number of the more imaginative British and French leaders—among them Winston Churchill, the youthful first lord of the admiralty—had begun to argue for diversionary operations against the Turks. Why continue to butt one's head against a stone wall, they reasoned. Why go on with these costly assaults in France that accomplished nothing? It was far better to swing around the flank—to attack the Central Powers where they were weakest, in what Churchill, a quarter century later, was to describe as the "soft underbelly of Europe."

The major stumbling block of the 1915 expedition against the Turks was that no clear decision was ever taken either for or against this diversionary strategy. Instead, the British and French high commands consented grudgingly to an expedition that was to prove totally inadequate for its task. Originally, it was planned to seize the Gallipoli peninsula alongside the Dardanelles and thereby dominate the focal points of the Turkish state, Constantinople and the straits joining the Black Sea to the Mediterranean. At first, the planners believed that a naval squadron could do the job alone. Later they added ground forces, notably Dominion troops from Australia and New Zealand. But at no time did they provide what was required for a really decisive blow.

When the invading force scrambled ashore on April 25, it found little initial opposition. Success seemed assured. But then Turkish resistance hardened and the attackers were pinned to the ground. The same thing happened three and a half months later, when reinforcements were sent and new landings attempted. By this time it was August, and the British Empire troops were suffering from heat, lack of water, flies, and dysentery. The coming of autumn added further hardships. By December there was nothing to do but evacuate the exhausted British soldiers. This operation, at least, was highly successful: Losses were light, and that achievement gave a bleak consolation to a disappointed British public.

There was another eastern area in which the British began to operate in the year 1915: the Arab world. Where they had failed at Gallipoli, here—in a much wider sphere—they were to succeed brilliantly. First in Mesopotamia, later in Palestine, finally among the Arab nomads, where the almost legendary Colonel T. E. Lawrence stirred up something resembling a holy war, the British pushed ahead and worked on Arab sympathies. In the end, they succeeded in freeing the entire Arab world from Turkish rule. The Ottoman Empire, like the Austrian, simply dissolved.

The War at Sea: Jutland

In the decade and a half preceding the outbreak of the war, the Germans had tried to challenge the British mastery of the seas. This effort failed. Far from making war too much of a "risk" for Britain, the German naval-building program, by embittering relations between the two powers, led them closer to the brink.

In the years of intense naval competition, the British aim had been to keep at least a three-to-two lead over the Germans in the total number of ships in service and to exceed them in technical efficiency. In the first respect, they substantially succeeded. But in technical excellence, the Germans frequently triumphed. This was particularly true of battle cruisers, submarines, and lighter craft of all sorts.

The latter threat, however, took two years to become apparent. In the early phases of the war, the British clearly had the upper hand. They confined the main units of the German navy to its home bases, and they set about systematically rounding up the German overseas colonies and the German cruisers and raiding ships that were preying on commerce. By the end of 1914, this task was essentially accomplished. Throughout the seven seas, the only remaining challengers to British mastery were the navies of the United States and Japan.

Yet a real threat persisted: Fast units of the German fleet could always break out and do extensive damage. Once, at the end of 1914, they raided the peaceful seaside resort of Scarborough. Four times in all, the German battle cruisers sailed forth, looking for a fight. The fifth foray, on the last day of May 1916, led to the one great naval battle of the war. For a day and a night, in the North Sea off Jutland, the two navies met in a confused and blundering fight. At first, the battle cruisers alone were engaged. Toward evening, the main fleets of battleships suddenly and rather surprisingly made contact. At this point, the Germans realized their peril. With the heavy guns of the British battle fleet bearing down upon them, they turned and made for home. Darkness favoring them, they escaped almost untouched.

To this day debate has raged as to who "won" the Battle of Jutland. From the standpoint of seamanship and gunnery, the honors belong to the Germans. They shot more accurately, and they sank nearly twice the tonnage the British did. More particularly, their battle cruisers proved distinctly superior. In fact, the defects revealed in British battle-cruiser construction were the greatest lesson of the whole battle: At least two of them had blown up in combat because of internal defects—at which the bluff battle-cruiser commander, Sir David Beatty, had cried out in bewilderment, "There seems to be something wrong with our damned ships today!"

In a wider sense, however, the British were the victors. Britain's ultimate fate depended on its navy and Sir John Jellicoe, the British commander in chief, was thus, as contemporaries put it, the only man "who could lose the war in an afternoon." Far from doing that, he saved his fleet, and he chased the Germans home. They were never to emerge in such force again. After Jutland, the German fleet moldered in port, and the nation turned to put its whole reliance on the new and deadly weapon of the submarine.

IV. THE ECONOMICS OF WARFARE

The war began, as the British expressed it, in an atmosphere of "business as usual." Economic life would go on just as before, and only the fighting men would suffer directly from the war's upsets. These illusions lasted only a few weeks. By the end of 1914, it was already apparent that this war would be different from all its predecessors in the way it caught whole civilian populations in its grip. In the end it would prove to be Europe's first "total war."

Blockade versus Submarine

Both Germany and Britain, as the two most highly industrialized of the great European powers, depended on overseas imports of raw materials and, more particularly, of food. Hence it was logical that each should try to starve the other out.

The British method was blockade, which they had used a hundred years earlier against Napoleon, with only mediocre results. The law of the seas had since been codified by international agreement: The Declaration of Paris of 1856 gave legal force only to an *effective blockade*—a close control over the enemy's ports by ships stationed just off-shore—and guaranteed the rights of neutrals to carry goods to all belligerents, except for specific categories of armaments defined as contraband. Beginning in 1914, the British violated both these provisions: Properly apprehensive of Germany's mine fields and shore defenses, they maintained a remote, rather than a close, blockade and systematically in-terfered with neutral commerce.

The first violation concerned only the Germans and hence caused no particular trouble. The second violation, however, antagonized a host of neutral nations, among them the United States. The British contended that the 1856 list of contraband articles bore no relation to the realities of modern warfare, since it excluded such essentials as rubber, cotton, oil, and copper. They drew up their own list, therefore, and enforced it as thoroughly as they could. As the United States slowly moved away from neutrality, it be-came apparent that the U.S. government regarded the British violations of the laws of war as no more than vexatious: They hindered trade, but they did not entail loss of life. It was far different with the chief weapon of German economic warfare, the submarine.

"Necessity knows no law," the German chancellor had declared, in justifying to the Reichstag the invasion of Belgium. He might have said the same of submarine war-fare. It was ruthless, it was cruel—but after the British blockade began, it offered almost the only means available for a beleaguered continental power to strike at its maritime ad-versary. As the war progressed, it became more and more the practice for submarines to sink a ship on sight without bothering to inquire whether it was an enemy vessel or a neutral that might or might not be carrying contraband. Naturally, the neutrals were outraged.

Two limitations on submarine warfare, however, had curtailed its ravages in the earlier phases of the conflict. First, the Germans began using their new weapon too soon. In 1914, they could keep only six or seven submarines at sea at one time; hence they gave the British ample warning of what was to come. The latter were quick to work out coun-termeasures. For the first two years of the war, such devices as patrols and mines kept the total of tonnage sunk within bearable limits. Not until the autumn of 1916 did losses of merchantmen take a sudden spurt that threatened the very survival of Britain.

By that time, the American declaration of war was only a few months away. This suggests the second factor that had limited the submarine menace—the vigorous protests of President Woodrow Wilson as spokesman for the leading neutral power. The sinking of the *Lusitania* in May 1915 had sent a wave of indignation throughout the

United States. This great British liner had been torpedoed without warning off the coast of Ireland, and more than a thousand lives had been lost, including a hundred Americans. As a result of the *Lusitania* tragedy and its sequels, Wilson finally wrested from the German government a pledge that, in the future, merchant ships would not be sunk without warning. But the German promise contained an escape clause: The Imperial Government reserved to itself "complete liberty of decision" in the event that the United States should not exert equally successful pressure on the British to stick to the rules of war. In early 1917, the Germans availed themselves of this "liberty of decision"—with results that were to prove fatal for the final outcome of the conflict.

The Home Fronts

As the war ground on into a second year and then a third, the lives of civilians at home became steadily grayer and more drab. The inexorable casualty lists brought gloom and despair into millions of homes. By the end of 1916, the tally published in British papers reached the level of 4,000 dead or wounded each day. Life became more regimented as shortages of both goods and manpower grew ever more severe. The war had now become one of attrition—one in which the organization of material resources counted more heavily than individual bravery on the battlefront. Far from being a contradiction, the term "home front" expressed an important reality: The war could be won or lost according to how well each nation mobilized its economy and steeled its noncombatant citizens to support the military effort.

Economic regimentation attained various degrees of severity among the belligerents, reflecting their relative wealth or poverty. Of the major Western powers, France went through the war with the least government-imposed control. The French prided themselves on their balance between industry and agriculture and on the country's near self-sufficiency in foodstuffs. France did, of course, suffer from an acute shortage of military manpower, and a large part of its industrial resources lay in the northeast sector of the country occupied by the enemy. But the French tended to work out these problems—as they financed their war—by improvising. Britain and, later, the United States supplied the French with a steady stream of weapons and munitions, while the labor of women, foreigners, and prisoners of war helped fill the manpower gaps created by the absence of so many soldiers at the front. But even in France, agricultural production declined by nearly half from 1913 to 1917, with the result that such staples as meat and sugar were rationed.

Other countries were forced to make more massive adjustments in the allocation of manpower to nourish their defense industries. Where the industrial base was weak—as in Russia and Italy—there were simply not enough workers to produce armaments and still continue to supply consumer goods. In Russia, war industries occupied 24 percent of the industrial working class in 1914; by 1917 that figure had risen to a staggering 76 percent. In Italy, the comparable figures were 20 percent in 1914 and 64 percent by the war's end. The combination of limited resources and pressing need led governments to impose centralized control on the economy. By 1916 all belligerent countries had introduced rationing and some system of price restraints.

It was Germany that set the model for these government controls and supplied the example that was later to be followed by virtually all the belligerents in the Second World War. The Germans had started the war in surprisingly poor economic shape. In strictly military terms they were the best prepared of the Great Powers, but they had neglected to take the most elementary economic precautions. They had done almost no stockpiling, for example, and as the British blockade began to take effect, shortages appeared almost everywhere. The reason for their lack of preparedness was the mistaken conviction that the war would be short; here again, as with the Schlieffen Plan, the Germans showed themselves overconfident.

Once alerted to their danger, however, the Germans responded with vigor and imagination. As "Organizer of German Trade and Industry," the chancellor appointed the talented and visionary industrialist Walther Rathenau. Rathenau's "war socialism," as unorthodox as his own personality, brought good results. He began to organize the various branches of economic enterprise into compulsory cartels under mixed state and private control; his successors in office ruthlessly eliminated uneconomic small businesses and set up a system of block cooperative purchasing from neutrals. The result was a concentration of German industry into a small number of mammoth enterprises, such as the chemical giant I. G. Farben, founded in 1916, whose economic weight would be felt during the coming Weimar and Nazi periods. Manpower controls were simultaneously imposed in Germany, culminating at the end of 1916 in the Auxiliary Labor Law, which, at least in theory, mobilized for war service all German males between the ages of seventeen and sixty.

Attempts to put Europe's economy under government control naturally affected the position of organized labor as well. Paradoxically, however, the war strengthened rather than weakened the bargaining power of unions in all the Western belligerents. Before the war, labor unions had been legal but vigorously opposed by employers in Germany, France, and Britain, who refused to share power and were not above employing armed thugs to break strikes and hamper union organizing efforts. In 1914, however, the patriotic swell that prompted socialist parties to forsake their internationalist principles in favor of the defense of the fatherland did much to win middle-class opinion to the side of the unions, no longer seen (in Kaiser Wilhelm II's phrase) as "comrades without a country." Then, too, the desperate shortage of skilled workers in munitions industries meant that organized labor had a strong bargaining position in its struggles with management. A strike, by halting the flow of munitions, could spell defeat on the battlefield. In return for promises not to strike while the war continued, unions in Britain, Germany, and France received both improved wages and representation on the government boards created to manage the war economy. Though these provisions were to be challenged during the 1920s, they marked a significant advance for the labor movement in Europe.

The ideal invoked by war propagandists in each belligerent country was a partnership between the home and the military fronts—an equitable sharing of dangers and burdens by the entire nation. This, after all, was one of the principal reasons many Europeans had hailed the coming of war in 1914. To them it seemed a cause that would force rich and poor within each country to compose their differences in order to confront a greater enemy without. In reality, however, such a partnership was undermined by many inequalities, some unavoidable, some the product of deceit and collusion. Skilled workers, for example, were more valuable to the nation's war effort on the factory assembly line than in the trenches, and were thus frequently exempted from military service. Peasants, whose farm labor could be performed by others, were not so lucky, and perished at the front in disproportionately high numbers. Sparing industrial workers was at least a rational policy, given the country's war needs. Less easy to justify were the profits made by entrepreneurs who secured war contracts for products ranging from uniforms to cannons, and for whom each further month of conflict meant good business. The wealth of some war profiteers caused great resentment among the many who were suffering privation due to rationing and war losses.

To counter these threats to national unity, governments resorted to a variety of measures that restricted civil liberties while the war lasted. Not only was war news censored—a precaution at which few at first took offense—but criticism of the war effort could be prosecuted as treasonous. In Britain, the government went so far as to curtail the hours when liquor could be served in pubs, alleging that munitions workers would produce shoddy goods if allowed too much beer at lunchtime. In France, the former premier, Joseph Caillaux, spent two years in prison awaiting trial for having suggested that the French would best be served by a compromise peace. As the war continued, what had begun as spontaneous enthusiasm now had to be kept alive by artificial means. Recruiting

On the home front, German women take the place of male workers drafted for army service in a weapons factory. (*Courtesy H. Armstrong Roberts*)

posters and advertisements for war bonds reached a broad public with a calculated appeal to the emotions. In an atmosphere of patriotic fervor heated by government propaganda, many felt it prudent to do as they were told and keep dissenting opinions to themselves.

V. THE END OF OLD EUROPE

The Bloodletting of 1916: Verdun and the Somme

Falkenhayn had chosen well in picking Verdun for the site of the great offensive that would induce France to sue for peace. In itself, Verdun possessed no particular military significance; it jutted out from the French line as an awkward salient whose loss might even have been an advantage. Joffre, with arrogant self-confidence, had systematically neglected its defenses, but once the Germans began their attack, he saw no alternative but to hold on at all costs. The defense of Verdun became a symbol. Once more, as on the Marne, the French command, trained in offensive doctrine yet unable to advance, awakened an intense national response through its desperate resolve to retreat no farther.

On February 21, the German attack opened. Its commander was the imperial crown prince, whose victory was intended to buttress an already threatened dynasty. The attack had been preceded by the greatest bombardment yet known in human history, as two million shells rained on Verdun and its outer ring of forts. Four days later, the Germans took the first of these, Douaumont, the key to the city on the northeast, and the fall of Verdun itself seemed at hand.

Its savior, however, was already on his way to take command. Henri-Philippe Pétain had merely been an elderly colonel when the war broke out; but as he proved himself in combat, he had risen rapidly until at age sixty-two he found the assignment that exactly suited his temperament. As calm and reserved as Joffre, Pétain displayed far more human warmth, and did not suffer from the old French illusions about the merits of offense. It was in defense, rather, that he was at his best. Here he could bring into play his systematic powers of organization and his ability to inspire affection and confidence among his men. Perhaps because he had remained a relatively junior officer for so long, Pétain was able to empathize with the common soldier to a far greater degree than most officers in the French high command. That empathy gave him a decided advantage in handling troops made rebellious by the endless carnage at the front.

Pétain's success at Verdun was chiefly due to these two talents: his organization of supply and his considerate treatment of his soldiers. The supply problem he solved by improvising a substitute for the railroad that had been cut. The "sacred road," as the French called it, was reserved solely for military traffic and kept in constant repair as a steady stream of trucks, regularly spaced, plied day and night up to the fortress and back. This procedure, which was to become standard in the Second World War, was a novelty in the First. As for his men, Pétain tried to spare them in every possible way. As opposed to the German insistence on keeping their units in the line until they literally dropped of exhaustion, Pétain set a two-weeks' maximum for front-line duty. He made possible this system of rotation by drawing in reserves from all other sectors of the front until he had more than half a million men at his disposal. Thus the defenders were able to hold on. Week after week they suffered and died in shellholes and improvised trenches; week after week they stopped successive waves of German attackers. By April 10, when Pétain issued the famous order "Courage! On les aura,"* both he and his soldiers knew that Verdun would be held.

Then, in July, the British opened their greatest offensive of the war. The planned attack along the Somme brought the supreme moment that the British had been awaiting for two years. Their new army, launched for the first time en masse, was now to prove its mettle under a new commander, Sir Douglas Haig, who had succeeded Sir John French in December 1915. The Somme offensive had originally been planned as a joint Franco-British effort, but the defense of Verdun both delayed it and reduced the contingent that the French could supply. Thus when the time came, Joffre could put only twelve divisions into the line, and the Somme became mainly a British show. As such, it reflected the Anglo-Saxon emphasis on meticulous preparation and weight of materiel. The outcome was to prove that these alone could not ensure success.

On July 1, after a full week's artillery bombardment, the attack opened on a 25-mile front. From the start nearly everything went wrong. The shells that had pummeled the German lines for seven days had not reached their real target: the German machine-gun crews hidden in dugouts excavated 40 feet below the surface. As the heavily laden British soldiers stumbled across the no-man's-land that separated them from the enemy trenches, the Germans raced up from their dugouts to the parapets above and raked the attacking troops with an incessant, deadly fire that slaughtered wave after wave.

By the end of the first day, the failure was manifest. The British had lost nearly 60,000 men, including more than half the officers engaged—the worst rate of casualties on either side in the entire war. At Verdun casualties had been about even—each side lost 350,000 men. The Germans, intending to bleed their enemies white, had done the same to themselves. The Somme had added half a million German casualties, 410,000 British, 190,000 French. Human imagination could not grasp such a fearful toll. And for nothing: At the end of the year, the front ran only a few miles from where it had stood at the beginning.

These terrible facts at last began to sink into the minds of the men at the front. On neither side was morale the same after 1916. The British knew that the flower of their new army had been sacrificed in one reckless gamble. Before Verdun, the Germans had begun to surrender in large numbers for the first time; the Somme had convinced them that they were materially outclassed by their enemies. Even the French, inspired though they were by the defense of the great fortress, realized that the victory was not worth the cost. France would never again be able to make such an effort: The new recruits were different from their elders, already tired and defeatist before they had even seen battle.

*"Courage! We'll get them!"

Verdun and the Somme marked the climax of the war. The year 1917 was to usher in a new war—and a new Europe.

The "Turnip Winter" and Its Consequences

The spirit of the men at the front had been broken. The ordeal of the civilians was to follow. During the bitter winter of 1916–1917, morale at home snapped. As misery settled over every household, people began to ask themselves, at first in whispers, then more openly, whether it was worth going on, whether there was not some way to stop this cruel bloodshed before European civilization perished utterly.

Germany suffered most. An early frost had spoiled the potato harvest; people grew thin on a diet of turnips and synthetics; the canals froze; transport was choked; coal ran short; cold and drabness and hopelessness blighted men's souls. The French ate better

A British soldier shelters in a trench under German fire during the Battle of the Somme, oblivious to the dead comrades around him. (*Courtesy Imperial War Museum, London*)

and were warmer—but they were mourning the losses they could never replace. The British now knew what war really was. The Italians were in a state of smouldering discontent. The Austrians and Russians were at their last gasp.

Gradually it was borne in upon men's minds that Europe would never again be the same. Too many had died; too much that was gentle and rare had been destroyed. Everywhere the elite had been ruthlessly cut down. In theory, losses should have been distributed evenly through all classes of the population—except in Britain, which did not introduce conscription until the beginning of 1916—since universal military service was the rule. In practice it worked out otherwise. The aristocracy and the young men of education were by far the hardest hit. In Britain the reason was obvious: Such people had been the first to volunteer. Yet even in the other countries, elite units were thrown into combat first; boys from upper-class families volunteered while still under age, and the proportion of losses among officers was higher than among enlisted men. Everywhere, then, the European aristocracy went under, stubbornly, blindly, through a pathetic combination of heroism and ineptitude in command.

With it went into limbo the whole tone of life that the aristocracy had tried to set. After 1916, although nobilities continued to exist, their parts were played out; they were leaders and exemplars no longer. The old elegance had gone; the other classes no longer cared to imitate courtly manners. To the "lost generation," the old precepts rang hollow and meaningless. With half their number dead or maimed, the rest felt burned out and adrift, no longer sure of the significance of their own lives or of the society in which they lived.

In one sense, then, the great change that first became noticeable during the winter of 1916–1917 strengthened the democratic currents that had already been running so strongly in Europe in the years just preceding the outbreak of the conflict. Mass suffering at home and in the trenches made the First World War the first great democratic war. A common slaughter, a common drabness effectively leveled all classes. But this was democracy in its most primitive and negative meaning. In their more refined and subtle manifestations, democratic values suffered almost as much as did those of the aristocracy. The new equality of suffering not only leveled the classes, it also further embittered relations between them, as the remaining injustices and anomalies stood out ever more starkly. And as democratization advanced, disillusionment followed. The parliamentary governments of Britain, France, and Italy all proved themselves incompetent in directing the war, and they shamelessly lied to their people in an effort to cover up their mistakes.

This deception, more than anything else, was responsible for what had been called the wartime "decadence of democracy." Governments everywhere enforced censorship in both a stupid and a capricious fashion. Still worse, they tried to "organize enthusiasm"—to drum up excitement and jubilation for the ghastly failures of their generals—to conceal losses and to falsify communiqués. All these things sickened the men at the front, from whom the truth could not be hidden. Particularly in France, the fighting men were outraged by the patriotic "brain-stuffing" that went on behind the lines. It was no wonder that a British journalist, for four years unable to report what his own eyes had seen, entitled his postwar book of wartime experience *Now It Can Be Told.*

The campaign of 1917 opened on a changed Europe—a fact that became almost immediately evident on the battlefields.

Ludendorff versus Nivelle

As a result of the failures of 1916, both sides changed their high commands. At the end of August—when the fortunes of the Central Powers seemed at their lowest—the Eastern Front team of Hindenburg and Ludendorff replaced Falkenhayn. Four months later, Joffre, who had been so recklessly confident about Verdun, was also eased out. For the "hero of the Marne," the last two years of his command had been an anticlimax and a disappointment. But he was a national symbol nonetheless, and a face-saving device was found by reviving for him the old title of Marshal of France, which had never before been awarded under the Republic.

Joffre's successor was General Robert Nivelle. Young, eloquent, and far more congenial to parliamentarians than the aloof and dictatorial Joffre, Nivelle appeared to be a man of infinite promise. He had distinguished himself in the later phases of the defense of Verdun, where he had replaced Pétain in local command and mounted two brief offensives that were models of careful preparation and economy in manpower. Yet scarcely had the French and British governments agreed to Nivelle's plans when they began to be shaken by doubts. Nivelle himself seemed to have lost confidence: He became fussy and irritable, and his planning was less careful. One by one, things went wrong. Nivelle talked too openly about his projects: The Germans captured a full plan of the coming offensive. The rain fell ceaselessly. Finally, and most important, only a month before the attack was to open, Ludendorff foiled his adversary by new dispositions, which meant that the great blow would fall largely in a void.

When Hindenburg had assumed command the previous summer, with Ludendorff, his one-man brain trust, in the newly established office of first quartermaster-general, both immediately saw that Germany's military effort was dangerously overextended. In 1916, as in 1914, the German army had been obliged to fight major battles on at least three fronts. This could not happen again: Germany, only slightly more slowly than France, was reaching the end of its manpower reserves. In 1917, then, Hindenburg and Ludendorff resolved to concentrate on knocking Russia out of the war while restricting operations in the west to the most economical defense possible.

In carrying out this decision, they resorted to a stratagem that Nivelle had dismissed as impossible. They drew back their army in France an average of twenty-five miles to a new and shorter line that could be held with thirteen fewer divisions. All through the winter the Siegfried (or Hindenburg) Line was prepared with characteristic German thoroughness. Then, in early March, the carefully phased withdrawal began. The French and British were caught almost completely by surprise. Suddenly between them and the enemy there stretched a wide zone of desolation, systematically laid waste by the retreating Germans.

When the French went over the top in Champagne on April 16, they found an enemy better entrenched and farther away than they had expected. Once again, as had happened so often in the past, the first day was enough to predict nearly total failure.

Nivelle had promised to break off immediately if this should happen, but now, faced with the reality, he fell into the old trap: Refusing to admit defeat, he continued to hammer away. This time, however, his soldiers had had enough. They had been deceived too often; the bitterness of nearly three years of futile losses finally overflowed. Unit after unit refused to go over the top. By May, a large part of the French army was in a state of mutiny. Obviously Nivelle had to go. And the choice of his successor was equally obvious—Pétain, the "hero of Verdun," the only general in France who could possibly face the storm and restore confidence to a demoralized army.

The Longing for Peace

By the summer of 1917, the British and the Germans had joined the French in longing for the war to end. Peace without victory, peace without annexations or indemnities, became the slogans of this new, or reawakened, revulsion against the ceaseless slaughter. The French mutinies of the spring had not been an isolated phenomenon. They gave tangible evidence of a war weariness and even defeatism that were rapidly spreading among French civilians and were openly voiced by a number of Socialist or Radical Socialist parliamentarians. Similar sentiments found expression in England on the left wing of the Labour party and in an open letter published in the *Daily Telegraph* by the Conservative elder statesman Lord Lansdowne. Finally, in Germany, the advocates of a peace of compromise temporarily obtained a majority in the Reichstag and sought to impose their will on the Imperial Government. The Peace Resolution of July 1917 called in what sounded like unmistakable terms for a settlement that would leave neither side the victor.

The diplomats were equally active. In late 1916 and early 1917, all sorts of intermediaries, official or semiofficial, were scurrying about Europe, trying to establish contact between the belligerents. In December 1916, President Wilson made a final effort to get the warring powers to formulate clear aims on which negotiation could begin; from February to June of the next year, the young Austrian emperor, convinced that only an early peace could save his throne, entered into secret contact with the French and British governments; in August, the Pope, who had constantly pleaded for peace and was particularly concerned about preserving Catholic Austria, made his last and supreme effort to induce the powers to come to terms. None of these attempts even remotely approached success. All would-be peacemakers received evasive or ambiguous responses. By the autumn of 1917, it was clear that the war would go on. A whole year of flagging war sentiment and nearly constant efforts for peace had come to nothing; the belligerents girded for renewed combat.

The peace "offensive" failed because of its hopeless lack of coordination. Neither side was ever ready to talk when the other was. When one coalition faltered, the other plucked up hope. Indeed, any hint of willingness to make peace was interpreted by the enemy as a sign of weakness and a reason to go on fighting all the harder. After more than two years of war, each belligerent had settled into ineradicable distrust of its enemies, and the vicious circle was impossible to break. Moreover, the warring coalitions either failed to specify their war aims or insisted on territorial changes that their enemies could never have accepted. Thus the Germans refused to give an unambiguous pledge to

„Ihr Menschen, hört auf — ich kann nicht mehr!"

The war weariness that gripped Europe in 1917 is evident in this political cartoon from the German satirical weekly *Stimplicissimus* of June 19, 1917. It depicts an exhausted Death on the battlefield pleading: "Cease, mankind—I can bear it no longer!"

restore the full independence of Belgium, and the French and British added to their war aims a demand for the liberation of the subject nationalities of Austria-Hungary.

Perhaps the clearest case in point was the failure of the Reichstag's Peace Resolution of July 1917. In its demand for a peace without annexations, the Reichstag undoubtedly voiced the longings of the great majority of the German people. But the Reichstag lacked real power, and what power it did have, it did not know how to use. It forced the resignation of the chancellor over the peace issue, but then it acquiesced in a successor who, on this issue, was worse than his predecessor. When the new chancellor declared that he accepted the Peace Resolution, "as he understood it," he meant that he was not accepting it at all. And in this he reflected the views of the true ruler of Germany, Ludendorff, who in the past year had established an effective dictatorship, both military and civilian. Ludendorff was dead set against democracy, and he was dead set against a peace of compromise. Indeed, until only six weeks before the end of the war,

Ludendorff stubbornly exemplified and held out for the irreducible program of the German ruling classes: large annexations in both east and west, unrestricted submarine warfare, and uncompromising resistance to democratization at home.

Thus the Peace Resolution was effectively buried. And, as a final irony, when autumn brought a new turn in Germany's favor, even its sponsors forgot the resolution and fell back into their annexationist dreams.

VI. THE YEAR OF DECISION

The New War: Russia and the United States

The spring of 1917 saw two events that were to change the whole character of the war, breaking the deadlock and bringing renewed hope of victory to both camps: The first was Russia's defection from the Entente and the second was the entrance of the United States on the French and British side. The military implications of neither of these events were properly realized at the time; they even temporarily intensified the drift toward a negotiated peace. Only in the autumn did the military potentialities of the new situation become fully apparent. Only then did it become clear that the final period of the war was opening and that in this climatic phase each side in turn would have a chance to win.

The first Russian Revolution of March 1917 gave brief comfort to the French and British, for there seemed to be hope that under its new democratic government the Russian people would fight more enthusiastically than before. But the morale of the Russian army had sunk too low to be revitalized by a sudden injection of democracy. After one last summer's effort, the nation's military resources collapsed. Even before the second revolution, in November, the Russian army was in full dissolution (see Chapter 3, III).

The American declaration on April 6 had brought into the war a new and potentially stronger ally to compensate for the loss of Russia. President Wilson's decision to ask Congress to go to war was not a simple act; it took him a long time to reach that resolve. Various factors had to be weighed, including ties of democratic sentiment that linked the country to the British and French and the more tangible but probably less influential ties of massive wartime loans. The immediate and precipitating cause of Wilson's decision, however, was a still more tangible act on the part of the Germans. In January 1917, Ludendorff and the other military chiefs induced the emperor and the chancellor to resort to unlimited submarine warfare.

This also had been a desperately debated decision, and the German civilian authorities held out against it until the last. What finally persuaded them was the military men's assurance that even if the submarines did bring the United States into the war, American troops would never be able to reach Europe in time and in sufficient numbers to affect the outcome. Here, of course, the Germans were disastrously mistaken. But even the Allies—as the French and British now began to be called—were almost equally skeptical about the American contribution. It would take at least a year to materialize, and in the meantime the defenders of France would have to face the German storm alone.

The Lloyd George and Clemenceau Governments

In girding for the expected crisis, the British and French had the advantage of new and stronger leadership. Within eleven months of each other, both the Allies changed prime ministers, bringing to power the leaders who would put their characteristic stamp both on the final war effort and on the making of the peace.

Britain had started the war under the Liberal government of Herbert H. Asquith, which had already been in power six years. It had long outlived its original reforming mandate, and was driven by internal dissensions. More important, its leader was not fitted by temperament or experience to mobilize the energies of a nation at war. Tolerant, judicious, and urbane, Asquith hated war and the uncivilized behavior that went with it. Only grudgingly would he consent to even the most obvious emergency measures. Hence, as it became apparent that the war would be a long one, authority passed by successive stages to Asquith's most energetic subordinate, an eloquent Welshman with a radical past, David Lloyd George. First, in May 1915, when the government was enlarged to include the Conservatives, Lloyd George became minister of munitions. A year later he took over as secretary of state for war. Finally, at the end of 1916 and at age fifty-three, he replaced Asquith as prime minister.

Lloyd George proved the effective war leader that Asquith had never been by breaking all the rules. As one of his first acts as prime minister, he dissolved the large, unwieldy cabinet that Asquith had assembled in favor of a tiny war cabinet of just five individuals. Thereafter, Lloyd George and his cabinet colleagues ran the war while consulting Parliament as little as possible. Their improvisatory style, personal and often capricious, offended many politicians. But it also brought results. In a time of war, the British voters proved more than willing to trust the strong figure who had succeeded the indecisive Asquith, and turned a blind eye to the fact that Parliament was no longer in charge.

France had gone into the conflict under the leadership of the moderate left government of René Viviani. In the first flush of war enthusiasm, the ministry had been enlarged into a "Sacred Union" of all the parties, and it was with this formula, under a succession of chiefs, that France had stumbled along during the next three years. In the spring and summer of 1917, however, the crisis of defeatism tore the Sacred Union wide apart. If the war was to continue at all, the conservatives and superpatriots could govern no more in coalition with the Socialists and left moderates. France had to make a choice; it could no longer get along on improvisations. Again the choice was obvious—Georges Clemenceau, the old Jacobin patriot, the implacable critic of his country's war effort.

Clemenceau was seventy-six when he assumed command of his country's war fortunes. But age had done nothing to diminish his intensity. Clemenceau the patriarch embodied France's fierce determination to prevail in a war that now hung in the balance. Over the course of his long public life, he had pursued a successful dual career as politician and journalist—both of which gave broad scope to his gift of passionate oratory. Clemenceau was best on the attack. His biting speeches and outspoken editorials had helped to marshal support for Captain Dreyfus, and had later stirred French patriots to resist the Germans. Now "the Tiger," as he was known, prepared to enter combat once again.

The Lloyd George and Clemenceau governments had much in common. Both were led by former radicals who had ceased to be such; both were semidictatorial and impatient with opposition; and both frankly rested on conservative and military support. In this respect, they revealed how different the final year of the war was from its earlier phases. During the first two years of the fighting, the great Western European democracies had enjoyed a true national unity. In the third year of the war, they had undergone a profound crisis of conscience. The last year ostensibly saw the restoration of the earlier unity, but this was more apparent than real. Part of the nation remained outside the consensus: The political Left hovered in limbo, skeptical and disaffected. The new "unity" actually cloaked the dominance of the leaders of old-fashioned nationalism. This leadership knew precisely what it wanted: victory and the attainment of ambitious national aims.

Caporetto, Cambrai, Brest-Litovsk

The last months of 1917 were marked by three events that set the stage for the final campaigns of the war: the battles of Caporetto and Cambrai and the armistice on the Eastern Front leading to the Treaty of Brest-Litovsk.

For two and a half years the Italian and Austrian armies, both riddled with discontent, lay gripped in weary stalemate in impossible mountain terrain. Time after time the Italians had hammered away along the Isonzo River northwest of Trieste without achieving any substantial result. Then on October 24, 1917, the unexpected happened. The Austrians, reinforced by picked German units and favored by low-hanging clouds, advanced in a massive attack that overwhelmed the Italian mountain positions. Retreat turned into rout as tens of thousands of deserters swept along with them in blind panic the troops to the rear. Then, when it had left the enemy far behind, the vast flood of men slowed down and grew good-humored: An army of 400,000, sick of war, was simply going home. Under these circumstances, with discipline almost gone, it is amazing that the Italian command was able to save the situation at all. For two weeks, they stemmed the retreat as best they could, in the vain hope of making a stand at each successive river line. Finally, on the Piave, only twenty miles short of Venice, the line held. The crisis was over.

Caporetto, as the great defeat was called, taught the Western Allies an essential lesson. Up to this time, disappointed by the Italian war effort, the French and British had scorned the Isonzo front as unworthy of their attention. Now they began to realize that a disaster on one front was bound to have repercussions elsewhere. The war was all of a piece; a failure in one sector, no matter how minor, could have grave effects on the alliance as a whole. Hence, after the brutal awakening of Caporetto, the French and British quickly despatched help to their hard-pressed ally and took the first steps toward the unified command that they were to achieve the following spring.

Meantime, in Flanders, the British were preparing an attack that was to establish a novel pattern for the final phase of the war. On November 20, before Cambrai, the newly invented tank first appeared in mass formation. This offensive weapon helped ensure a substantial breakthrough at Cambrai. The British success was merely local—but it gave a foretaste of what would happen when the Allies regained the initiative and could at length bring to bear on the Germans their crushing numerical superiority. Both sides had thus learned how to break the trench stalemate and to fight a war of movement. The Germans were to strike first. But Ludendorff could not move until he had finally accomplished what he had attempted in vain in 1915—the elimination of Russia from the war.

After the March revolution the Russians made one last military effort. Under the stimulus of Alexander Kerensky, minister of war in the provisional government, they pulled together a force of 200,000 men to attack the Austrians in Galicia. The attack ended in rout. It was now the German's turn to advance and, almost without resistance, they cut deep into Russia. By August their drive toward Petrograd* had reached the outskirts of Riga. Throughout the early autumn Ludendorff kept up a merciless pressure: He was in a hurry to begin shifting his troops to the west. On November 7, the Bolsheviks seized power. One of their first acts was to sue for peace.

With the eastern armistice concluded on December 15, the peace negotiations at Brest-Litovsk began. When the Germans presented their terms, even the hardened Bolsheviks caught their breath: Germany demanded the annexation, open or masked, of all Russia's western provinces. The Bolshevik negotiators struggled helplessly for better terms. In February, they even broke off the negotiations entirely. The German reply was to take up arms and to advance to within a hundred miles of Petrograd. Faced with this brutal reality, the Soviet negotiators finally accepted Lenin's reasoning that Russia had no recourse but peace at any price.

The final terms of the Treaty of Brest-Litovsk, signed on March 3, 1918, were even harsher than those originally presented. Germany now acquired one quarter of Russia's vast territory, almost half of its population, and three quarters of its coal and iron resources—more than the Nazis were able to conquer even at the height of their invasion during World War II (see Chapter 13, III). The Baltic lands of Estonia, Latvia, and Lithuania; the rich breadbasket of the Ukraine; and the oil-rich Causacus region all fell under German control at Brest-Litovsk. Less than a year after having voted for peace without annexations in the Peace Resolution of July, 1917, the Reichstag ratified the treaty by an overwhelming majority. In light of later German protests against the far milder terms of the Treaty of Versailles (see Chapter 4, IV), it is well to remember this eagerness to profit from Russian weakness at the moment of seeming German victory.

Meantime, a constant stream of German military trains had been traversing the Reich from east to west. By early March, when the troop transfers from Russia were completed, the Germans had an overall superiority of 10 percent and far more fresh divisions than their adversaries on the Western Front.

The Allied March to Victory

Ludendorff had decided to risk everything on one last gamble. Beating down the moderates who argued that Germany should take advantage of its favorable military position to reach a compromise peace, he persuaded Hindenburg and the emperor to make a final drive for victory in France. No one had any illusions as to what the decision meant. By summer, Germany would have no reserves left. Failure would mean total defeat. Ludendorff was staking all his country had on a desperate wager that he could beat France and Britain before American help could arrive.

He came very close to doing it. For four months Ludendorff kept up a constant series of attacks, with dizzying effect. Five separate German offensives managed to drive

*As St. Petersburg was renamed, in more Slavic fashion, after Russia declared war on Germany.

the Allies back forty miles. These losses threatened to weaken the Allies further by inflaming the suspicions that the French and British nourished of each other's willingness to fight. Faced with an almost complete breakdown of mutual confidence and frightened by Ludendorff's success, the civilian leaders of both countries at length decided on extreme measures. They agreed to appoint as supreme commander of Allied forces Clemenceau's military adviser, Foch, the most brilliant of France's soldiers.

At first—for all his dash and confidence—the new Allied commander-in-chief could do little more than parry Ludendorff's repeated blows. By the end of May, the Germans were again at the Marne, only thirty-seven miles from Paris, and the disheartening process of evacuating the capital began once more. This time, however, Paris was in no real danger. Although the French did not know it, Ludendorff was already reaching the end of his resources. His advance halted for six weeks while he tried to resupply and reinforce his tired troops. When Ludendorff finally struck along the Marne west of Reims in mid-July, Foch was ready for him. The Germans briefly crossed the river, but that was all. On July 18, Foch ordered a counterattack; nine American divisions took part. The second Battle of the Marne, like the first battle four years earlier, was a great Allied victory. From this time on, Foch never lost the initiative. On August 8, "the black day of the German army," the whole front began to roll back toward the German border. The outcome of the war was no longer in doubt. The only question was when the fighting would end. Nearly everybody, even on the Allied side, thought it would continue into 1919; no one quite realized how close the Germans were to collapse.

Some credit for the early victory, however, must also be conceded to General Foch's leadership. The electric little Frenchman, who had been straining at the leash during three long years of combat, now at last had found the assignment that suited his talents—as Joffre had found it on the Marne, or Pétain at Verdun. With the Germans on the run, the doctrine of the attack finally came into its own. Foch's strategy was to keep the enemy off balance—to maintain unrelenting pressure until the whole front reeled back under the accumulated shock. By mid-September, the Allies had forced the Germans back to the Hindenburg Line. From here Foch mounted a great pincer movement: The British were to advance over the old battlefields of Flanders—now a mass of desolation—while the Americans were to attack farther east through the Argonne Forest. Both these attacks stalled. Foch was bitterly disappointed as the inexperienced Americans, despite their reckless courage, bogged down in difficulties of transport and supply. But the advance ground slowly on. By early October, the British were taking town after town in Flanders, and the Americans were regaining momentum.

On September 29, Ludendorff's nerve broke. Only an immediate armistice, he told his incredulous emperor, could save Germany now. Five days later, the liberal Prince Max of Baden was appointed chancellor, and the long-delayed democratization of the Reich began.

In late October, the Italians at length pulled themselves together and took revenge for Caporetto. Crossing the Piave in force, they defeated the Austrians at Vittorio Veneto. Then came total breakdown. The Austro-Hungarian army dissolved into its component parts, as the different national units struggled to board trains for home, and even the Hungarian minister of war ordered his own troops to lay down their arms. On November 3, Austria signed an armistice. Southern Germany lay open to invasion.

In this desperate situation, the Germans on the Western Front could not hold out for long. By the end of October, although they still stood on French soil, they had only one reserve division left, and overall they were outnumbered by 40 percent. In less than three months they had lost almost 300,000 prisoners; the remains of thirty-two divisions had simply been broken up.

At home, morale had already cracked. Memories of the "turnip winter" of 1916–1917 returned to haunt its survivors, and revolutionary defeatism swept the country. On November 3, the German fleet at Kiel mutinied. Refusing to put out to sea on one last great raid, the crews seized control of their ships and of Kiel itself. From here the mutiny spread to the other seaports of northern Germany. Four days later, revolution broke out in Bavaria, which was directly exposed to invasion from the south. On November 8, a German armistice commission met Foch for the first time. The ninth saw the emperor's abdication and the proclamation of a German republic. On the tenth, the emperor fled to the Netherlands. Meantime the German delegation had accepted Foch's armistice terms. On the eleventh hour of the eleventh day of the eleventh month, 1918, the First World War came to an end.

The Balance Sheet

The First World War had been a "total war"—a conflict whose destructive effects exceeded the ability of most contemporaries to comprehend them. Altogether, between eight and ten million men had been killed in the four and a quarter years of conflict. Germany lost nearly two million, Russia a million and three quarters, France almost a million and a half, the British Empire just under a million. Italian deaths were less than half a million; American, just over 100,000. About 20 million in all had been wounded—seven million of these permanently disabled—some by mustard gas and shrapnel, others reduced to the condition of psychological paralysis popularly termed "shell shock." The dead were for the most part young; their loss continued to be felt well after the war as birthrates dipped and agriculture and industry alike struggled to make up for the absence of so many energetic and talented workers, felled in the prime of life.

Yet these statistics, frightening though they were, did not tell the full story of the war's destructiveness. The land, too, had suffered. A great swath of France lay devastated—some of it, apparently, so blasted that it could never be put under cultivation again. Factories and farm towns in the richest industrial region of the country had been left in ruins. Treasures of learning and architecture—the university library of Louvain in Belgium, with its medieval manuscripts, and the ancient town hall of Ypres—had likewise been destroyed. They could never be replaced.

The war continued to wreak its destruction on the living well after the armistice. In Germany and Austria, the Allied blockade had taken a fearful toll: Vienna, Berlin, and countless other cities were reaching the last extremities of hunger. In Central and Eastern Europe, millions of civilians were dead or dying from malnutrition and diseases that their weakened bodies could not resist. Influenza, typhus, and cholera epidemics raged everywhere. The estimated loss of life in what have been termed "war-induced diseases" exceeded five million outside of Russia; in Russia, the three-year civil war provoked an even higher toll (see Chapter 3, IV).

Jubilant British soldiers at the front learn of the German surrender from their commanding officer in November 1918. (*Courtesy H. Armstrong Roberts*)

One of the most profound effects of the war—but also the most difficult to calculate—was on the psyche of the men and women who had witnessed this catastrophe of wanton self-destruction. Throughout the Continent, even among the "victors," citizens could not escape the question of whether the war should have been fought at all. The sense of European superiority over the rest of the world that had characterized the decades preceding the First World War became increasingly difficult to sustain. How could the world's most "civilized" continent have fallen victim to such an orgy of self-destruction? The gulf between the war's high-flown rhetoric and the bloody reality of the trenches was most apparent, of course, to the survivors who returned to civilian life with a burden of cynicism and disillusionment captured in Robert Graves's *Good-bye to All That* (1929):

> England looked strange to us returned soldiers. We could not understand the war madness that ran about everywhere, looking for a pseudo-military outlet. The civilians talked a foreign language; and it was newspaper language. I found serious conversation with my parents all but impossible.*

*Robert Graves, *Good-Bye to All That* (New York: Octagon Books, 1980), 228.

The disillusionment with a political order responsible for such senseless carnage helped to undermine long-established dynasties and prepared the way for radical changes in the map of Europe. Three empires—the Turkish, the Austro-Hungarian, and the Russian—succumbed by war's end to the pressures for change brought on by inept leadership and (in the case of Turkey and Austria-Hungary) outright defeat. In Germany, Italy, and Hungary, revolutions flared briefly as well. But it was in Russia that the combination of war-weariness and faith in a new political order to end the war produced the most dramatic outcome. There, a byproduct of the First World War—one with far-reaching consequences—had been the Bolshevik Revolution of November 1917.

READINGS

For an overview of the war and its effects, see Bernadotte Schmitt and Harold C. Bedeler, *The World in the Crucible, 1914–1918** (1984), with an extensive bibliography, and Marc Ferro, *The Great War, 1914–1918** (1973), which is especially good on the war's social impact. Hew Strachan, *The First World War*, Vol. I: *To Arms** (2001) is the first of a promised massive three-volume work that covers virtually all aspects of the war. The best purely military study is John Keegan, *The First World War* (1998). A longer account, which has become a classic, is Winston S. Churchill, *The World Crisis, 1911–1918*, 6 vols. (1923–1927; one vol. abridgement, 1931). The way the powers blundered into the conflict and why their diplomatic efforts failed are surveyed in David Stevenson, *The First World War and International Politics* (1988). Marc Bloch, *Memoirs of War, 1914–15** (1980, reprint ed. 1988) combines a perceptive eyewitness account of the early months of the war with a rich selection of contemporary photographs. A masterful evocation of the Battle of the Somme as seen from the soldier's perspective is offered by John Keegan in *The Face of Battle** (1976).

For the economics of the war, see Gerd Hardach, *The First World War, 1914–1918** (1977), and Gerald Feldman's two studies, *Army, Industry, and Labor in Germany, 1914–1918* (1966) and *Iron and Steel in the German Inflation, 1916–1923* (1977), whose observations concerning Germany suggest the problems confronted by the other powers as well. The interplay between economic management and technology is explored in the concluding chapters of William H. McNiell's *The Pursuit of Power: Technology, Armed Force, and Society** (1982).

For the internal politics of the major belligerents, see Jere C. King, *Generals and Politicians* (1951; repr. 1971) on France; on Britain, see the relevant chapters of Samuel H. Beer, *Modern British Politics: Parties and Pressure Groups in the Collectivist Age** (1982), and Paul Quinn, *British Strategy and Politics, 1914–1918* (1965). On Italy, see John A. Thayer, *Italy and the Great War: Politics and Culture, 1870–1914* (1964); and on Germany, see Hans W. Gatzke, *Germany's Drive to the West* (1950). John W. Wheeler-Bennett, *Brest Litovsk: The Forgotten Peace, March 1918,** rev. ed. (1971) details the military and diplomatic calculations which induced Russia to leave the war. Arthur Marwick offers a vivid,

*Books available in paperback are marked with an asterisk.

though somewhat impressionistic, account of the war's social effects within Britain in *The Deluge: British Society and the First World War,** 2nd ed. (1991), while Jürgen Kocka explores changes in German society from a sociologist's perspective in *Facing Total War: German Society, 1914–1918* (trans. 1984). Marwick, *Women at War, 1914–1918* (1977) explores the war's impact on gender roles.

Robert Wohl details the intellectual climate that led youth to see the war as a change to promote Europe's spiritual renewal in *The Generation of 1914** (1979). One government's attempt to enroll culture on the side of its armies is explored in Martha Hanna, *The Mobilization of Intellect: French Scholars and Writers During the Great War* (1996). Paul Fussell's *The Great War and Modern Memory** (1975) evokes with haunting literary skill the emotional legacy of the conflict, more particularly in Britain. Britain during and after the war is also the focus of Samuel Hynes, *A War Imagined: The First World War and English Culture* (1992). Robert Graves, *Goodbye to All That** (rev. ed., 1960) is the disabused autobiography of a British survivor. George L. Mosse, *Fallen Soldiers: Reshaping the Memory of the World Wars* (1990) explores the cult of the war dead and its political uses after 1918. Among the many war novels written by contemporaries, the sense of loss and anger at the soldiers' needless sacrifices are conveyed with special force in Richard Aldington, *Death of a Hero* (1929), Erich Maria Remarque, *All Quiet on the Western Front** (1928), and Henri Barbusse, *Under Fire** (1917). A troubling but powerful account of a German officer's delight in combat is Ernst Jünger's war diary, *Storm of Steel* (1929). Vera Brittain, in *Testament of Youth** (1933), balances these accounts of battle with a moving description of life on the British home front, while Pat Barker, in *Regeneration** (1991), tells the story of shell-shocked soldiers (including the poet Siegfried Sassoon) in a British sanatarium, and the inner conflict faced by the psychiatrist who must heal them so they can fight again.

THE RUSSIAN REVOLUTION AND ITS CONSEQUENCES

The last surviving photograph of the deposed Tsar Nicholas II, taken shortly before his execution by Bolshevik troops in July, 1918. *(Courtesy Brown Brothers)*

I. IDEOLOGY AND THE WAR

At its start, the First World War was neither an ideological struggle nor in a real sense a world conflict. It was an old-fashioned European quarrel—the last and greatest of a succession of such quarrels dating back nearly three centuries to the Thirty Years War. Essentially it was fought for national, imperial aims. In the origins of the conflict, ideological goals figured scarcely at all. At the start, at least, the men in the trenches had little sense of fighting to preserve a specific form of government or even a more vaguely realized "way of life." They thought almost solely in national terms. The French and British, for example, felt very simply that they were defending their countries rather than fighting to preserve or extend an abstract principle like democracy. It was only a minority of Italian democrats who, before the United States entered the war, saw the conflict as a struggle of Western democratic society against autocracy and, in consequence, argued that their country should go to the aid of nations whose institutions resembled its own.

This lack of ideology was only natural. The warring coalitions were separated by no clear difference of political principle. The two great democracies, it is true, were fighting alongside each other. But they were also in alliance with tsarist Russia, the most reactionary of the powers. Hence, at the start of the war, the Entente had no real ideological cohesion. Its adversaries, however, were the more closely linked by ideological ties: Both Germany and Austria-Hungary were qualified autocracies or semiparliamentary states. In the ideological spectrum, the Entente occupied the two extremes, and the Central Powers lay somewhere in between. If Russian autocracy could be thought of as canceling out Anglo-French democracy, then there was little to choose between the two coalitions. Indeed certain Germans even argued that it was *they* rather than their adversaries who were fighting for democracy. The German Social Democrats, for example, soothed their Marxist consciences with the claim that by defending their country against Russia, they were keeping "Asiatic" despotism out of Central Europe and thus preserving Germany for the democracy that was bound to come.

In the crucial year 1917, all this changed. With the entrance of the United States, the conflict in truth became a *world* war. And with the first Russian Revolution, only a month before, the Entente attained an enviable ideological unity. Now that Italy and America had been added to the coalition—and Russia had cast off its exhausted despotism—five great democracies were ranged in one camp. For a few brief months, this illusion persisted. President Wilson shared it. In his war message to Congress he clearly linked the recent revolution in Russia with the new course on which his own country was embarking. "Does not every American," he asked, "feel that assurance has been added to our hope for the future peace of the world by the wonderful and heartening things that have been happening within the last few weeks in Russia?"

The Bolshevik Revolution destroyed these hopes. Once more the Entente was ideologically driven asunder, as Russia under its new leaders deserted the coalition and proclaimed a novel international role of its own. The brief idyl of Russo-American cooperation was at an end. Ideological competition took its place. Just as the war had been converted into an ideological struggle in 1917 by the two great semi-European powers—Russia and the United States—so the final year of the conflict was to be dominated by the competition between them for the allegiance of the European masses.

The International Opposition

At the start of the war, the Socialist parties of Europe forgot their internationalism and rallied to support their countries' war efforts. In France, in Britain, in Germany, the Socialists fell into line almost without a murmur. Everywhere a truce between political parties prevailed. What in France was called the Sacred Union, in Germany took the ancient name of *Burgfrieden*—the peace within a beleaguered fortress. For the first time, moreover, Socialist ministers in France and Britain entered the government and shared in the direction of the war effort.

This decision did not pass unquestioned. Everywhere there remained a pacifist minority, which was either silenced through party discipline or exiled from party councils. But for the first two years of the war, Socialists of this opinion were impotent. The tide of patriotic unity was running too strongly against them. In Italy alone, the Socialist party was to maintain a consistent antiwar stand: First it opposed intervention, and subsequently, after Italy had joined the Entente, it took a position of passive nonsupport of its country's war effort.

By the end of 1916, this attitude was beginning to win favor elsewhere. Socialists and pacifist moderates were coming to have second thoughts about the war. Not only did the bloody stalemate on the Western Front seem to make a mockery of the patriotic slogans under which the war was being fought; the Socialists also began to realize that they had made a bad bargain by consenting to serve in coalition governments. They had found that their ministers possessed little real power: They served chiefly as window dressing, to keep labor at home in line while the conduct of the war remained in conservative and nationalist hands. More particularly, they had almost no influence on the formulation of war aims. Hence what had begun as a minority protest within European socialism had become, by 1917, something of a mass movement. Through a series of international congresses, the antiwar Socialists had established a modest but increasingly effective organizational framework. By mid-1917, the notion of "peace without victory" was gaining popularity everywhere.

Wilson versus Lenin

The phrase "peace without victory" was originally Wilson's. The American president was associated in people's minds with the idea of a settlement in which there would be neither victors nor vanquished. But this was while the United States was still neutral. The U.S. declaration of war changed all that: It brought subtle but decisive alterations in the tone of Wilson's utterances. His appeal was still for a peace of justice, but it was now based on the presupposition of Entente victory. The war must be fought to a finish. International justice was not to be reached through a compromise settlement; it would be *imposed* by the victors on the vanquished.

The need to continue the war limited the force of Wilson's idealistic appeal—except where it could be harnessed to the propaganda of subject nationalities struggling for independence. Wilson was unable to keep Russia in the war. He could do little to reinvigorate the war-weary in Britain and France. The Italian masses continued as disaffected as before. Furthermore, Wilson now had a competitor who offered what he did and more—a peace of justice, but an immediate peace and one arrived at through social revolution. This was V. I. Lenin, the Bolshevik leader and, since November 1917, the master of the Russian state. The competition between the two was not lost on contemporaries. A Swiss writer observed, "It is certain that mankind must make up its mind either for Wilson or for Lenin."*

Lenin, as a revolutionist living in exile in Switzerland, a tiny left minority within international socialism kept pressing for an end of caution and an unequivocal cessation of hostilities. Once back in Russia—helped on his way by the Germans, who correctly foresaw that he would undermine the country's war effort—Lenin was able to put these precepts into practice. Almost the first act of the Bolshevik government was to issue, on the day after its assumption of power, a "Peace Decree" that called on the warring nations to lay down their arms.

To understand this appeal, it is necessary to trace the succession of events in Russia that had brought Lenin and his companions to power.

II. PREREVOLUTIONARY RUSSIA

In 1900, Russia was the only true autocracy left in Europe (see Chapter 1, III). The authority of the state did not rest, as in Western Europe, on parliamentary institutions but on a complex, routinized bureaucracy and a potent secret police. Yet it would be wrong to imply that Russia had made no political progress during the previous century. The contrary was true—despite periodic checks and reactions, there had been a slow but steady liberalization. The serfs were freed just after the middle of the century, and the period immediately following saw the installation of a new judicial system and the establishment of representative institutions on the local level.

At the Imperial Court, however, scarcely anything had changed. Tsar Nicholas II, who ascended the throne in 1894, lived in a world of illusions. Both weak-willed and stubborn, he was surrounded by reactionary advisers and dominated by his superstitious German wife. Into the sickly, hothouse atmosphere of the court, it was impossible for the breath of reality to penetrate.

The Revolution of 1905

Suddenly, revolution broke this unnatural calm. Touched off by the defeat of Russia in the war of 1904 with Japan, a series of strikes and popular outbreaks in the major cities forced the tsar at last to pay some regard to his people's complaints. This brief revolution revealed how much Russia had changed in the past decade. Industrialization had come swiftly. A systematic policy of state aid to the arms industry had brought the results that

*Quoted in Arno J. Mayer, *Political Origins of the New Diplomacy 1917–1918* (New Haven, Conn.: Yale University Press, 1959), 393.

might have been anticipated—large concentrations of "proletarians," sometimes working more than eleven hours a day, and living in the wretched conditions that throughout Europe had uniformly accompanied the first stages of the Industrial Revolution.

Although this new industrial working class had borne the brunt of the revolutionary fighting, it was middle-class liberals who primarily profited from the concessions with which the tsar had calmed the storm. The October Manifesto of 1905 had promised true parliamentary government, with universal manhood suffrage, ministerial responsibility, and a full array of individual liberties. But the actual constitution—or "Fundamental Laws"—of the following May was less liberal. Ministerial responsibility was dropped, and a year later a system of indirect voting replaced equal universal suffrage. As it finally worked out, the parliament, or Duma, was a fairly tame, conservative body, in which the poorer classes of the population were most inadequately represented.

The Policy of Stolypin

In the period from 1907 to 1911, however, the Duma was able to achieve a few constructive results. More specifically, it turned its attention to the gap that was now opening between city and countryside in Russian society. The cities were rapidly being modernized; the country remained in its primitive state, hardly touched by change. Indeed, in certain respects the emancipation of the serfs in 1861 had brought a retrogression to an earlier agrarian order. Specifically, it had extended a traditional institution, the *mir*—a peasant commune controlling the village land and periodically reassigning it among the individual families. A large landowner, if he happened to be enlightened, could modernize his estate and make it an economic enterprise. A community of freed serfs was trapped in the old routines and old methods of cultivation.

Now the Duma majority, which followed the lead of the vigorous, somber prime minister, Peter Stolypin, proposed to modernize Russian agriculture by permitting individual peasants to leave the *mir* and establish their own farms. Stolypin hoped in this fashion to build up a class of self-reliant landholding peasants who would support the Russian state much as a similar class had proved to be a prop to the French Republic. Hence, he systematically favored the peasants who wanted to contract out of the *mir*; in the decade 1907 to 1917, more than two million households availed themselves of this opportunity.

The social effects of Stolypin's agrarian reform have been much debated. Some declare that it produced excellent results and that if Russia had only had a decade or so more of peace, it would have developed into a modern democracy. Others stress that this policy increased social antagonisms in the countryside by widening the gap between rich and poor. One thing is certain, however: As the Bolsheviks were eventually to discover, small-scale peasant farming was no answer to Russia's needs; only a system of large-scale cultivation could provide an adequate food supply for the newly swollen population of the cities.

With Stolypin's assassination in 1911, the era of reform came to an end. The three years preceding the outbreak of war were a period of drift and of an ominous false calm.

The Revolutionary Parties: Social Revolutionaries and Bolsheviks

The leading parties in the Duma were the moderate Octobrists, who accepted the reforms of 1905–1906, and the more progressive-minded Constitutional Democrats, or Cadets. Both were respectable middle-class parties; the distinction between them corresponded roughly to the Western European cleavage between liberals and moderates.

Both, however, lacked adequate contact with reality, for they thought in terms that were only partially applicable to Russia's actual situation. They had the attitudes of nineteenth-century Western European reformers and were convinced that the institutions that had proved their worth in Britain or France would work equally well in Russia. But Russia in the period just preceding the war was still very different from Western Europe: Most of its population lived in pre–nineteenth-century conditions; the rest was being hustled into the twentieth century at a dizzying pace. In this respect, Russia in 1917 resembled the countries of Asia following the Second World War. There was the old traditionalist order on the one hand; on the other, the new order of forced industrialization based on monopoly and state favors. Between the two, free-enterprise capitalism scarcely existed. This, of course, was the form of economy that had provided the basis for Western European liberalism and radicalism in the nineteenth century. Without it, the corresponding parties in Russia lacked adequate support. The deeper longings of the Russian people were expressed in the traditional, mystical worship of "Holy Russia" and the tsar, and in newer doctrines of social overturn and revolutionary violence.

The Social Revolutionaries constituted the strongest party in Russia in 1917. They were distinctively Russian—they had no Western European counterpart. Their formal organization dated only from 1901, but their origins extended deep into the nineteenth century—to the terrorists of the 1880s, and beyond them, to the *narodniki*, the idealistic intellectuals of the previous decade, who hoped that by "going to the people," they might share and improve the lot of the peasants. The Social Revolutionaries spoke for the rural masses. This association was a source both of strength and of incoherence. As a peasant party, they had by far the largest potential following in Russia, but their peasant affiliation also accounted for their tumultuousness and lack of a clear program. In these failings, the Social Revolutionaries accurately reflected the political inexperience of their constituents. Perhaps the only coherent proposal they made was summed up in the slogan "the land to the peasants." This apparently simple goal was susceptible to the most varying interpretations, and the consequent misunderstanding between the right and the left wings of the Social Revolutionaries was to prove decisive in the weeks immediately following the Bolshevik seizure of power.

The other revolutionary party, the Social Democrats, was split by the far deeper division that by 1917 had made them in effect two separate parties. The Russian Social Democrats were an offshoot of the Marxist socialism of Western and Central Europe. In theory, they were just another European Socialist party; in fact, however, they were very different from their Western counterparts. Three peculiarities of the Russian situation had given them a highly eccentric character.

First, since late nineteenth century, Russia was a police autocracy rather than a constitutional state; it was difficult for the Russian Social Democrats to evolve toward democratic, legalist methods as most of the Western European parties either had done or were about to do. With the electoral road to power cut off, their very situation condemned them to conspiracy and subversion. They renounced assassination as a weapon—they thought it childish—but although they castigated the Social Revolutionaries as terrorists, they shared with them a propensity for constant and feverish plotting.

Second, until the late 1890s, Russia had almost no industrial proletariat. In the seedtime of Marxist ideas in Russia, the prerequisites for a working-class movement were almost entirely lacking. At its inception, Russian Social Democracy was an affair of the intellectuals, who were quite free to spin complex webs of theory, untroubled by a mass base or a responsible trade-union movement.

In about 1900, this situation changed radically. An urban working class appeared, and alongside it the social evils that go with rapid industrialization. But the new Russian working class also was somewhat different from the corresponding social category in the West. It had no strong craft or artisan tradition to give it a conservative bent. Rather, it consisted of uprooted peasants, whose patterns of thinking inclined them more toward inarticulate protest and revolutionary violence than toward disciplined trade-union activity.

Along with his new social situation appeared the third great anomaly of the Russian scene: the towering figure of Lenin. Vladimir Ilyich Ulyanov—to use his real name rather than his revolutionary pen name—was something new in the world, a man of education and immense self-discipline (his revolutionary comrades called him "Herr Doktor," inspired by his teutonic tidiness), capable of cruelty, deceit, and utter ruthlessness in pursuit of his revolutionary goals. The son of an ennobled director of schools, Lenin had passed a serious, scholarly, idealistic youth. Shocked by the death of his elder brother, who had been hanged for terrorist activities, he had turned to Marxist studies and to revolutionary propaganda. As nearly always occurred in such cases, he had been caught by the police and exiled to a desolate place in Siberia. He passed his three years there in study, in writing, in plotting. He was only thirty when he emerged in 1900, but he was already a seasoned revolutionist, prepared to challenge the older leaders of the party in a ruthless struggle for power.

Three years later, Lenin nearly succeeded. At the 1903 congress of the Russian Social Democratic party, held abroad, first in Brussels and subsequently in London, Lenin temporarily won over a majority to his point of view. He and his followers forced through a party constitution providing for a tight, disciplined organization. From this point on the Leninists within the Russian Social Democratic party called themselves Bolsheviks—from the Russian word for "majority." Their opponents naturally came to be called the Mensheviks—the "minority." Actually the position of the two factions was soon reversed. Lenin's opponents regained their predominance, and they kept it right down to the outbreak of the war. But Lenin, with his characteristic tenacity, refused to give up the Bolshevik label: He fully appreciated the psychological advantage that the term "majority" gave him.

In reality, Lenin cared almost nothing for majorities. His mind was severely practical. Although he was a master of the subtleties of Marxist theory, he was interested in such abstractions only when they could be used to further his own program. And this program was very simple: to build up in Russia a Marxist party that would be radically different from the tolerant, legalist Socialist parties of the West—a new type of party dedicated solely to revolution. Lenin knew that economic conditions in Russia contradicted all Marxist principles. In terms of orthodox theory, his own country, whose industrialization was just beginning, was not "ripe" for a socialist revolution. But that did not trouble him. He was convinced that by organizing around himself a tight core of professional, trained revolutionists who would look to him alone for guidance, he could eventually succeed.

And so he bullied and browbeat his party comrades into submission, dominating them, as one complained, by literally *living* the revolution twenty-four hours a day. Nearly all these followers were intellectuals: No one else had time or desire to lead the stern existence that Lenin demanded of them. But for such people, the Bolshevik way of life often had a deep appeal. It accorded with the social idealism and self-dedication that had been characteristic of the Russian intelligentsia during the whole latter half of the past century.

By 1914, however, Lenin's faction had fallen on evil days. By his insistence on iron discipline, he had in effect split the party into its two constituent parts. In Russia itself—both in the Duma and in the trade unions—the Mensheviks were by far the stronger of the two; already legalist by inclination, they were rapidly turning themselves into a regular Social Democratic party on the Western model. In contrast, the Bolsheviks were almost powerless. They had become the laughingstock of the Duma when their chief spokesman there was discovered to be a police agent; they were literally reduced to highway robbery to obtain funds; and only a few leaders remained who were neither in exile nor alienated by Lenin's autocratic control—among them the faithful but intellectually limited Georgian who had just chosen the revolutionary nickname of Stalin. Lenin himself was in Switzerland, consumed by frustration at his own impotence. At home, he was still almost unknown. If a popular hero did exist, it was not Lenin but Leon Trotsky—a dynamic, driving, imaginative figure who refused to join either the Bolshevik or the Menshevik faction. As a very young man, the eloquent Trotsky had become the popular tribune of the Revolution of 1905, in which Lenin had played scarcely any part.

One of the reasons for Lenin's triumph in November 1917 was to be his dramatic alliance with Trotsky. But that could come about only after the miseries of war had reduced Russia to a state in which even a tiny revolutionary faction like the Bolsheviks had a chance for success, if only it were sufficiently determined in its bid for power.

Russia at War

Russia succumbed to war-weariness earlier than any of the other belligerent powers. The country's primitive economy could not support a long war: Even food ran short as the transport system proved completely inadequate. Under the best and most efficient of governments, Russia would have had a bitter struggle to survive. Under the government it had, the country's war effort was doomed from the start.

In the supply of war materials, corruption and profiteering were commonplace. At court, pro-German sentiments were openly paraded: The tsarina herself encouraged them. And she in turn fell under the spell of a disreputable faith healer, Gregory Rasputin, whose influence with the imperial family became a public scandal. In December 1916, a group of conservative nobles murdered Rasputin, but his death made no more

Lenin (1870–1924) addressing Red Army troops at a May Day celebration in 1920.
(*Courtesy Brown Brothers*)

real change than had the tsar's action of the previous year in assuming military command. Apparently, nothing could stop the drift toward economic and psychological collapse.

The failure of Brusilov's offensive in the summer of 1916 destroyed what was left of military morale. The terrible winter of 1916–1917 did the rest. By the spring of 1917, the Russian people had had enough.

III. FROM THE MARCH TO THE NOVEMBER REVOLUTION

The first of the two Russian revolutions of 1917—the March revolution—was both incoherent and incomplete. Its basic causes were war-weariness and distrust of the pro-German faction in the government and the imperial court. More immediately, what toppled the tsarist regime was a series of almost spontaneous strikes and riots in Petrograd, climaxed by a mutiny of the troops garrisoning the capital. In these events, the revolutionary parties played almost no part. If any group had guided and canalized the agitation, it had been the constitutional parties in the Duma, the Octobrists and the Cadets. Hence, it was logical that these should predominate in the provisional government formed on March 12.

Four days later, with a double abdication by the tsar and his brother, the Romanov dynasty disappeared at last after three centuries of unbroken rule. Russia thus ceased to be a monarchy; its future regime was left open, pending the election of a constituent assembly. Abroad, most people in the Entente camp agreed with President Wilson; they assumed that Russia was now firmly set on a liberal, constitutional course—that it had become a middle-class democracy like its great Western allies. But this was far from the truth. The March revolution had settled nothing.

The Provisional Government and the Soviets

For eight months, the provisional government struggled to rule Russia. At the end of that time it was overthrown by the Bolsheviks with absurd ease. The explanation of this failure is simple—the provisional government had not done the two things for which the people were clamoring: It had not taken Russia out of the war, and it had not satisfied the land hunger of the peasantry.

Lenin, with his relentless logic, had grasped almost from the start that these would be the two crucial issues. On his return from exile in April, he immediately set about to exploit the difficulties with which the provisional government was contending. He did not wait a moment. The very night of his arrival at the Finland station in Petrograd, he explained to the cheering throng that greeted him the substance of his "April Theses": immediate peace, the nationalization of the land, and all power to the soviets of workers' deputies.

These soviets were the great novelty of the Russian revolutions. Their name was the Russian word for "council," and that is what they were—informal bodies speaking for the urban workers, and in some localities, for the peasants and soldiers also. They had originated—almost spontaneously—in the tumults of 1905 and had left behind them a popular revolutionary memory. Hence, it was natural that they should be revived in 1917. This time, however, their role was much extended. Shortly after the March revolution, the chief of them, the Petrograd Soviet, began to act as a shadow government, paralleling and challenging the acts of the provisional government itself.

Within the soviets, the Bolsheviks were only a minority—both the Mensheviks and the Social Revolutionaries were stronger. But Lenin correctly surmised that this situation might be only temporary. If the Bolsheviks offered a program with sufficient revolutionary appeal, they could gradually infiltrate the soviets and gain control over them. Thus they would finally have in their hands the sort of weapon they had always lacked before: truly popular bodies that would capture the imagination of the urban masses. Lenin, therefore, set out to win over the majority in the local soviets. He outflanked the Social Revolutionaries by stealing their agrarian program: land for the peasants. He astounded and disconcerted the Mensheviks, and even his own followers, by calling for a second, or proletarian, revolution. Before Lenin's arrival, Russian Marxists of both varieties had been following a cautious, orthodox course. They had accepted the "bourgeois" revolution that had already occurred and had agreed to wait for the long-term ripening of economic conditions before launching a second revolution. This, Lenin sharply told them, would not do. The second revolution must come at once.

Above all, Lenin outmaneuvered everybody on the issue of peace. He alone declared in unequivocal terms that the Russian army should lay down its arms immediately.

Bolshevik revolutionists are mowed down by machine gun fire on the Nevsky Prospekt in Petrograd during the July uprising of 1917. *(Courtesy Corbis-Bettmann)*

With this demand, he hit the provisional government at its weakest point. For with each month that passed, it became more evident that the country would not follow its new leaders in their policy of continuing the war on the side of the Entente.

By May, the war issue had already caused a shift in the provisional government toward the left. The outstanding figure in the old ministry—Professor Paul Milyukov, leader of the Cadets and minister of foreign affairs—was obliged to resign. Milyukov had been the chief spokesman for the policy of loyalty to the Entente, and his departure clearly signified the failure of this course. The new government included two Social Revolutionaries and two Mensheviks. Initially this seemed to give them an advantage over their Bolshevik rivals, but events proved just the opposite: The two more moderate left parties steadily lost ground through their involvement in the continued unpopularity of the provisional government.

This was particularly true of the leading figure in the reorganized ministry, the right-wing Social Revolutionary Alexander Kerensky. Kerensky was even younger than Lenin and Trotsky and, like them, a dynamic organizer and forceful orator. But, as minister of war and later prime minister, he had the misfortune to represent in the popular mind the policy of continuing the war, and it was this association that eventually destroyed him. The new ministry had tried to moderate the war policy as much as it could—it had declared for a peace without annexations or indemnities. But in the summer of 1917 it was proving impossible to get the warring nations to agree on such a solution. All peace efforts had failed, or were about to fail. Kerensky was vainly trying to steer a compromise course between Milyukov's loyalty to the Allies and Lenin's demand for a separate peace with the Central Powers.

Thus, with the failure in early July of Kerensky's last despairing offensive on the Galician front, the provisional government began a slow decline. Ten days later, the Bolsheviks—reinforced by the adhesion of Trotsky, whose revolutionary militancy now coincided almost exactly with Lenin's program—made their first major show of force. It came too early. The provisional government crushed it, and Lenin was obliged to take refuge in Finland. In the succeeding weeks, however, Kerensky's difficulties increased: His government could reach no decision on the crucial question of land reform, and the peasants in consequence began to take matters into their own hands. Still worse, a right-wing military conspiracy forced Kerensky to turn to the Bolsheviks for support. In the field, the armies were breaking up as the soldiers drifted back to their homes; in the factories and in the Petrograd garrison, Bolshevik propaganda was steadily winning converts.

By October, the Bolsheviks had a majority in the Petrograd Soviet. Trotsky was elected its new chairman. The time had come, Lenin decided, for the supreme bid for power.

The Bolshevik Revolution

The revolution was almost bloodless. In late October, the Bolshevik leaders had organized themselves as a "military-revolutionary committee" to coordinate preparations for the rising. On the appointed day—the early morning of November 7—the revolutionary forces of soldiers, sailors, and Red Guards carried out their assignments with speed and precision. Seizing the key points of the capital city, they imprisoned or drove to flight the members of the provisional government. By afternoon, Lenin was able to announce victory to a meeting of the Petrograd Soviet. In the evening, the second All-Russian Congress of Soviets—with whose meeting the revolution had been timed to coincide—received full power from the Petrograd Soviet, which it delegated in turn to the local soviets of workers', soldiers', and peasants' deputies.

Before adjourning, the congress did two further things. It issued its basic orders, the Peace Decree, already mentioned, and the Decree on the Land, to satisfy at last the clamor of the peasantry; and it appointed a Council of People's Commissars to govern the state.

Thus informally did the new de facto constitution of Russia come into effect. In theory, Lenin had done what he had promised: He had won all power for the soviets—the shadow government had become the real government. In fact, something rather different had occurred. The Bolshevik leaders, in their new guise of people's commissars, had seized power for themselves. They subsequently accepted certain left-wing Social Revolutionaries as associates, but final authority continued to rest with Lenin, Trotsky, and their party colleagues. The party dictatorship had been established that would rule Russia for decades. In no sense could the Bolsheviks be said to speak for the Russian

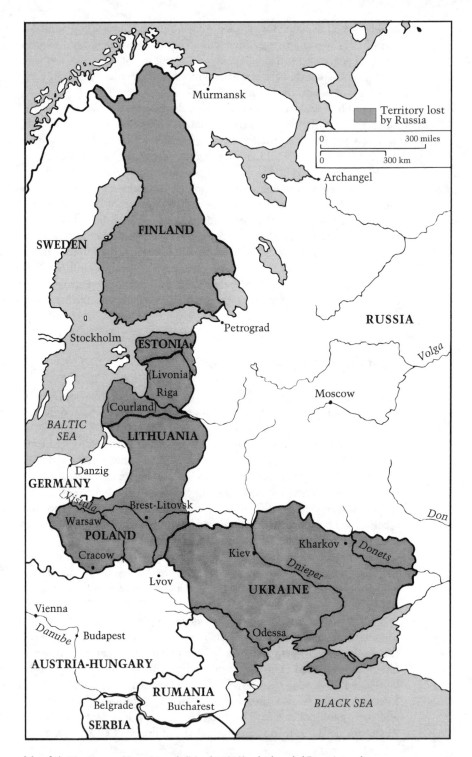

MAP 3.1 The Treaty of Brest-Litovsk (March, 1918), which ended Russia's involvement in World War I, allowed Lenin to make good on his promise of peace, but ceded
vast parts of Western Russia to Germany. The treaty was nullified eight months later
when Germany surrendered to the Allies in November, 1918.

people. Although they had won a majority in the Petrograd Soviet, in the local soviets they were still outnumbered. This was to become abundantly clear with the long-deferred elections to the Constituent Assembly.

The election of an assembly to draw up a new constitution was a customary liberal-democratic device in countries that had just undergone a revolution. It had occurred at least three times in France, and throughout Western Europe it had provided the traditional method for giving legal sanction to a revolutionary change of regime. Hence it was natural that the provisional government—whose inspiration was liberal-democratic and Western—should have followed this same procedure. But it had postponed calling the elections, and the date it finally set fell two and a half weeks after the Bolshevik seizure of power. Thus the elections were held in a setting quite different from that in which they had been planned. They were held under an authority that was no longer liberal-democratic, but rather represented a disciplined, fanatical minority that openly scorned the principle of majority rule.

The elections produced, as might have been expected, a clear majority for the Social Revolutionaries. The Bolsheviks obtained slightly less than a quarter of the seats. The Mensheviks and the Cadets figured scarcely at all. These results obviously embarrassed the new rulers of the Russian state. The popular verdict was difficult to explain away. But Lenin, always fertile in expedients, found a suitable subterfuge. The Social Revolutionaries, he explained, no longer existed as a party. By throwing in their lot with the Bolsheviks, the left-wing Social Revolutionaries had in effect dissolved their party. "The people," Lenin triumphantly concluded, "voted for a party which no longer existed."

When the assembly met in mid-January, then, its proceedings unfolded in a world of unreality. It elected a president and engaged in a desultory debate. But as soon as the Bolshevik deputies found themselves outvoted, they simply walked out, followed after a little while by the left-wing Social Revolutionaries. At this point, the Bolshevik high command decided to shut down the assembly. "The sailor in command of the military guard . . . announced to the president of the assembly that he had received instructions to close the meeting 'because the guard is tired.'"*

Thus ended the brief and foredoomed experiment in Western constitutional government. The third All-Russian Congress of Soviets, which the Bolsheviks were now able to dominate, assumed the functions of the Constituent Assembly. The Bolshevik dictatorship had come to stay.

IV. THE CIVIL WAR

Lenin's power, however, was not to be consolidated for more than three years. From December 1917 until November 1920, the Bolshevik regime was engaged in a life-and-death struggle for its very existence.

At first, the new revolution encountered a stunned acceptance. People had suffered too much to be prepared to take up arms once again; and the transfer of power to

*Edward Hallett Carr, *The Bolshevik Revolution 1917–1923*, I (New York: Macmillan, 1950), 112, 119.

the local soviets frequently did not mean much of a change, since in the larger cities, these had already been exercising a de facto authority. In the more remote districts, moreover, the change of regime in Petrograd made scarcely any difference. Communications had so deteriorated that the central government was physically unable to make its will prevail. Many country people continued to live their lives almost as if nothing had happened.

In no sense, then, did Russia leap from capitalism to socialism overnight. On the contrary, the new rulers of the country were perplexed about what to do with their power. In putting socialism into practice, they had almost no precepts to guide them. Marx had scorned this sort of planning as "utopian," and even the more practical-minded Lenin had focused his attention so exclusively on how to seize power that he had hardly had time to think about what should be done with the power once it was in revolutionary hands. The first acts of the new Council of People's Commissars bore all the marks of haste and improvisation.

Peace and land reform were the first and easiest matters to deal with. The two original decrees of the All-Russian Congress of Soviets had already established the broad outlines of future settlement. With the Central Powers, Lenin and his colleagues eventually signed the humiliating and ruinous Treaty of Brest-Litovsk (see Map 3.1). As far as the land was concerned, the original decree, by abolishing private property, in effect invited the peasants to seize it from their landlords—thus ratifying a process that had actually been going on for several weeks. A subsequent decree of February 1918 tidied up this procedure by reserving title to the state. But the peasants had actual possession of the land, and they simply divided it up among themselves. The method of partition varied from area to area. Where the Social Revolutionaries predominated in the local soviets, the criterion tended to be capacity to work the land—which favored the more prosperous peasants; in Bolshevik areas, it tended to be the number of mouths to feed in each family, a procedure obviously devised to win favor with the poor and the landless.

As far as other branches of the economy went, the Bolsheviks were hesitant in the extreme. In general, they seem to have assumed that major enterprises would continue under their old management, with no more than a general supervision to ensure that they were run in the people's interest. Only when certain branches of industry proved recalcitrant did the government resort to nationalization. In these cases, the Bolshevik leaders soon got themselves into further difficulties, for it was not clear whether the factories in question should be run by the workers themselves—which seemed the more popular course—or by professional managers—which was obviously more efficient. Not until June 1918, and under the threat of massive German penetration of the Russian economy, did the Council of People's Commissars finally decree the nationalization of basic industry.

The Generals in Arms: Allied Intervention

In the meantime, a number of tsarist military leaders had taken arms against the new regime. To the south—in the Ukraine and in the Caucasus—the revolt was led at the start by General Kaledin and subsequently by General Denikin and Baron Wrangel; in White Russia and the Baltic region, General Yudenich threatened Petrograd; and in

Siberia, Admiral Kolchak, the most persistent of the insurgent military chiefs, proclaimed himself "Supreme Ruler of Russia" and eventually succeeded in dominating most of the country east of the Ural Mountains.

For three years, the Bolshevik government strove desperately to ward off these multiple threats. Time after time, it seemed that the new regime was about to succumb, for no sooner was one general beaten in one part of the country than another raised the standard of revolt many hundreds of miles away. Month after month, the battles ebbed and flowed in a crazy tangle of local engagements. At the height of the civil war, the authority of the central government extended no farther than old Muscovy, the region surrounding the major cities of Moscow and Petrograd. Still the Soviet regime managed to hold on. In November 1920, with the final defeat of Baron Wrangel, the Bolsheviks had won the civil war.

What accounts for this surprising victory by a regime that seemed to have almost nothing in its favor? How is the Bolshevik success to be explained? First, by the genius of Trotsky. As commissar of war, the dynamic revolutionary leader transformed himself into a military figure; by skillfully combining the enthusiasm of proletarian volunteers with the indispensable technical knowledge of former tsarist officers, Trotsky created a new Red Army. Second, the lack of coordination among the insurgent generals worked in the Bolsheviks' favor. Each was thoroughly independent and jealous of the authority of his rivals; moreover, all of them were operating at long distances from each other on the periphery of the vast Russian landmass, while the Red Army, through its control of the center of the country, had the advantage of internal lines of communication.

In addition to these technical considerations, the Bolsheviks had the intangible asset of appearing to be on the "people's" side. The balance of popular appeal had initially been more equal—a number of the insurgent chiefs had taken a moderate stand and had promised to restore the constitutional liberties that the Bolsheviks had violated. But as fighting continued and atrocities multiplied on both sides, hatred and bitterness produced an impassable gulf between them. The generals and the "White" armies they commanded became associated in the public mind with a restoration of the old regime. In the areas they controlled, they behaved at least as despotically as the Bolsheviks. The decisive factor, however, was the conviction among the peasants that a White victory would mean abrogation of the revolutionary land settlement.

Finally, the White generals were also associated with foreign intervention—with the Germans in the Baltic States, with the British and French in the northern ports, and with the Japanese and Americans around Vladivostok on the Pacific. The German armies had lingered on after the Peace of Brest-Litovsk to exploit their newly formed dependent states. The Japanese were fishing in troubled waters in the hope of territorial gain. The British and French purpose in Russia was less clear. The protection of military supplies was the official explanation, but it was also apparent that ideological considerations were involved. The Western Allied governments detested the Bolshevik regime and wanted to help overthrow it. They gave both material aid and moral encouragement to the White generals, but they went about it in a blundering and hesitant fashion. The Anglo-French expeditionary force in Russia was not on a sufficient scale to accomplish anything; it was withdrawn in the autumn of 1919 after the Labour Party in Parliament had exposed its absurdities. Yet it had stayed long enough to give the Russians a permanent distaste for foreign armies and for those who associated with them, and it had cast the Bolsheviks in the novel and paradoxical role of patriotic defenders of the motherland.

Dictatorship, Terror, War, Communism

The experience of civil war immeasurably strengthened the trend toward party dictatorship. On December 20, 1917, a week and a half after the fighting began, the Council of People's Commissars set up a special body called the Cheka (later renamed GPU) to combat "counterrevolution and sabotage." Thus was founded the secret police that was to play so prominent a role in subsequent Soviet history. The following July, the left-wing Social Revolutionaries followed their right-wing party colleagues into the limbo that had swallowed up the Mensheviks and the constitutional parties. On a charge of terrorist and treasonable activities, the leaders of the left-wing Social Revolutionaries were arrested and their newspapers suppressed. This act ended the fiction of a coalition government. The same Congress of Soviets that had suppressed the Social Revolutionaries concluded its labors by approving a constitution which in effect sanctioned the rule of a single party, whose committees paralleled and gradually came to dominate the regular organs of the state.

A week later, the tsar and his family were executed, and in the month of August, Lenin himself gave orders for "an unsparing mass terror." Thereafter, although a few oases of liberty remained, opponents of the regime lived in a precarious and harassed existence and left the country in wave after wave. The necessities of civil war greatly accelerated the process of collectivization and dictatorial control. This was particularly true for labor and the peasantry. Urban workers were subjected to a "militarization" policy that enrolled them in labor battalions. The peasants had to submit to forced requisitions by workers' detachments and "committees of the poor." Only by such drastic means were the Bolsheviks about to keep the economy functioning at all and to provide the cities and the Red Army with a minimum ration of food.

Such were the desperate expedients of what came to be called *war communism*. In bloody and brutal fashion, war communism may have accomplished something—it may have staved off the very worst. But it was no better than a jumble of emergency improvisations executed often with extreme cruelty. It bore as little resemblance to socialist theory as it did to laissez-faire capitalism. When the smoke of the civil war had cleared, Lenin and his colleagues found themselves obliged to reformulate their economic policies almost from scratch.

If Russia had been exhausted in 1917, at the end of 1920 it was prostrate. The three years of civil war had been still worse than the corresponding period of international war. Wide stretches of the land lay desolate; communications were disrupted everywhere. Industrial production had fallen to only 16 percent of its 1912 level. Still worse, the prerequisites for recovery were lacking: The larger cities had lost more than a third of their population as urban workers dispersed to the countryside in search of food. Regular trade had almost ceased to exist: What exchange of goods there was largely depended on "bagmen" who, like the peddlers of old, went between farm and town carrying on their backs the precious goods that brought exorbitant prices. The official channels of trade were empty: Since industrial products scarcely existed, the peasants saw no point in bringing their crops to market. Meanwhile, tens of thousands of disbanded soldiers were roving the countryside in search of food. The Russian economy was caught in a series of vicious circles from which no escape seemed possible. Both the people and the government were too crushed and weary to find any way out of the morass.

Two events of 1921 revealed the urgent need for drastic action. In March there was a mutiny of the sailors of the Kronstadt naval base near Petrograd. The very units whose aid had been so important in the success of the November revolution now turned against the regime they had helped to install; among their grievances figured a plea for a more understanding treatment of the peasantry and calls for a "Third Revolution" that would finally transfer power to peasants' and workers' soviets rather than leaving it in the hands of the Communist party. On Lenin's orders, the mutiny was savagely repressed. Then that spring and summer, for the second successive year, there was a drought in the Volga Basin. The wheat crop failed; starvation took a dreadful toll. For the next two years eastern and southern Russia lay in the grip of a great famine in which 3 million people perished (see Figure 3.1).

It gradually became clear that the peasant was the key to the situation. The peasantry—whom Marxist theory had always neglected—was the only force that could possibly break through the vicious circle. As Lenin put it to the tenth congress of his own party, "Only an agreement with the peasantry can save the socialist revolution in Russia."

The Pacification: NEP and the Nationalities Settlement

Thus the core of the New Economic Policy (NEP), which Lenin launched in March 1921, was an effort to conciliate the peasantry. It aimed to start the economy moving by providing inducements for the peasants to bring their crops to market. And the only way to achieve this end that the Bolshevik leaders could see was restoring many aspects of a

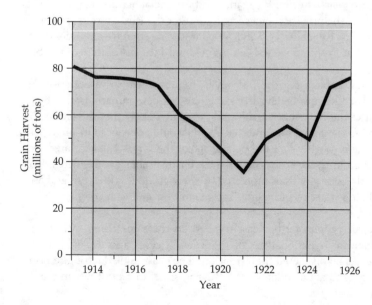

FIGURE 3.1   The Russian grain harvest during the years 1913–1926. Note the sharp drop during the years of the civil war from 1918 to 1921—a period far more destructive for Russian agriculture than the First World War. By 1926 grain production had still not returned to the level of 1913.

capitalist economy. The peasants not only received the right to dispose of their surplus crops as they chose, but the Fundamental Law of May 1922 also gave them security in land tenure. Both private property in land and the old village community, or *mir*—plus a number of mixed or intermediate types of tenure—received official sanction; in addition, peasants were permitted to sell or lease their land and to hire labor to work it, just as they desired.

Similarly, in the commercial field, private enterprise won official recognition. What a later generation was to call the *black market* now became a legal market. The disreputable "bagmen" of the civil war period transformed themselves into "Nepmen," who soon grew prosperous and respectable as they started trade flowing again. In industry, small private enterprise enjoyed an equal freedom; recovery started earlier here than in the large industries, which remained nationalized. Even in the field of finance, capitalist principles prevailed, as the foundation of a new state bank, or Gosbank, restored orthodoxy in financial practice, and the issue of a new unit of currency brought a galloping inflation to an end.

The retreat from socialism seemed complete. But the Bolshevik rulers of Russia had not changed their purpose: They had merely improvised once more to meet a desperate emergency. Lenin assured his party followers that it was sometimes necessary to take one step back in order to advance two steps forward. Furthermore, the economic structure of the revolution had not been completely dismantled. What Lenin called the "commanding heights" of the economy—heavy industry, the transport system, foreign trade—remained in state hands. Socialism was still no more than a distant mirage. But the *prerequisites* for a socialist policy had been retained. The implications of this situation of socialism held in reserve were not to become apparent until seven years after the institution of NEP, when Lenin's successor, now politically and economically secure, launched a decade of heroic and brutal effort to transform the Russian economy from top to bottom, and thus at last to make the real and decisive break with the past.

In July 1923, two years after NEP began, another official action completed the pacification of the country: the provision of a constitution for the Russian state, renamed the Union of Soviet Socialist Republics (USSR). With it, the internal nationalities question found the solution that in substance was maintained until the dissolution of the Soviet Union in 1991.

The nationalities problem put the Bolsheviks in a most embarrassing position. In theory, Lenin and his colleagues believed in complete self-determination for subject peoples. Immediately after the November revolution, it seemed likely that the nationalities would be left free to go their own way and that Russia would be reduced in size to the two-thirds of its area where roughly half the people spoke the Great Russian language. And this in fact happened in the western borderlands. First as subject states dependent on Germany, subsequently as new nations protected by the victorious Allies, Finland and Poland and the three Baltic states of Lithuania, Latvia, and Estonia won complete independence.

But when subject peoples farther east tried to do the same thing—when the Ukrainians and the three main nationalities of the Transcaucasus also declared themselves free—the Bolsheviks reconsidered their position. They cast aside doctrinaire principles and began to think and act as rulers of the Russian state. In fact, if not in public profession, they set about reconquering the formerly subject peoples. The victory of the Red Army over the Whites in the civil war was also a victory of the Great Russians over all the minor nationalities.

For two years thereafter, the relation of these non-Russian territories to the central government remained unclear. Obviously it was impossible to restore the old situation of bureaucratic or quasi-colonial control. Yet the grant of full autonomy to non-Russians would mean a renewed threat of secession. In this dilemma, Lenin—disregarding the advice of his specialist on nationality problems, the russified Georgian Stalin—produced an astute solution: a federal state. On paper, its constitution resembled that of the United States or Switzerland. A Council of Nationalities, in which the constituent republics had equal representation, balanced the Council of the Union, in which representation was based on population. In reality, however, the new Soviet constitution stood closer to that of imperial Germany. In the Soviet Union, as in the German Reich, one single state had more weight than all the others put together.

This dominant state, of course, was the Russian Soviet Federated Socialist Republic (RSFSR), which included most of European Russia and Siberia too. Its capital was the same as that of the Union—since 1918, the old metropolis of Moscow. Its government departments and leading personnel tended to overlap and blend with the corresponding administrative organs and individuals in the Union. Furthermore, the Russian Republic was itself a federation within a federation. Its smaller nationalities were not set up as constituent states of the Soviet Union; they enjoyed more limited rights as autonomous republics or areas within the RSFSR. When the Soviet Union was founded, only three major republics were granted even technical parity with the Russian Republic—the Transcaucasian, the White Russian, and the Ukrainian.

Of these, the last was by far the most important. The largest of the former subject nationalities, indeed the second most numerous of all the Slavic peoples, the 30 million Ukrainians offered the great riddle of Eastern Europe. Were they a true nationality and so deserving of independent status? Or were they simply an intermediate people, caught between the Poles and the Russians, under whose successive rule they had passed their whole modern history? The Ukraine was far from being a clear national unit. Its language closely resembled Great Russian. Its urban working class was largely of Great Russian origin. The dominant political sentiment among its peasantry frequently seemed to be nothing more than a murderous hatred of its vast Jewish minority. Only its educated bourgeoisie had been much affected by the nationalist teaching of its professors. Thus the Bolsheviks could offer all sorts of explanations for denying independence to the Ukraine. Beyond these national considerations, however, the new rulers of Russia found compelling realistic reasons for keeping the Ukraine at all costs: As the richest area of the Union in agricultural and industrial resources, it seemed essential to the very survival of the Soviet state.

The settlement of 1923 proved far from satisfactory to millions of Ukrainians. Elsewhere in the Union—in the formerly colonial areas of the Transcaucasus and Central Asia—Soviet rule could bring visibly beneficial effects in the form of modernization and social equality. The Ukraine, however, as an area that was *already* among the most advanced, stood to gain little from the new regime. Hence it was natural that the Ukraine should be the focus of discontent among the nationalities during the whole interwar era.

The 1923 constitution—like so many Soviet institutions of this period—was still subject to change. But like the other post–civil war acts of settlement, it served to give the Bolshevik regime a breathing space, a pause for consolidation in a Europe where revolutionary hopes had been disappointed everywhere and which was now hardening into an attitude of unreserved hostility toward the whole Soviet experiment.

V. THE INTERNATIONAL FAILURE

The Bolshevik leaders had never imagined that at the end of six years in power they would find themselves isolated in a hostile world. They had assumed that the revolution would spread to other parts of Europe. Moreover, they took it as axiomatic that unless the revolution triumphed in at least one of the advanced industrial states of Western and Central Europe, it could not possibly survive in Russia. Their expectations proved wrong on two counts: The revolution failed to spread to the countries that were "ripe" for it, and it entrenched itself in Russia, where it should theoretically have been unable to survive at all.

These are facts that tend to be forgotten today. Communism has come to be thought of almost exclusively as an ideology of Russian origin. So closely are Bolshevism and communism associated with Russia that it no longer seems strange for the two to have come together, and it is difficult to imagine how their history could possibly have been different.

Had the Bolshevik Revolution never occurred, communism would still almost certainly have come into existence both as an ideology and as an international movement. The name "communist" had long been in common use on the left wing of international Social Democracy; as a fighting label, it evoked memories of Marx's original *Manifesto* published in 1848. After Marx's death in 1883, his legacy and the future direction of the communist movement was disputed between moderates and radicals. The differences between the dominant Right and the revolutionary Left within the Second International, founded in 1889, were already so great that a secession of the minority might well have occurred even without the experience of the First World War and the Russian Revolution. The "inevitabilist" moderates on the Right argued that there was no need for revolutionary political movements, but that they should create a legal, democratic party and await capitalism's self-destruction; with the end of capitalism, they would assume the mantle of power legally and peacefully. The "activist" radicals on the Left countered with the argument that, while the fall of capitalism might be inevitable, its pace could be hastened through revolutionary action.

It was this left wing that throughout Western and Central Europe rallied to the support of the Bolshevik experiment and sought to imitate it elsewhere. It was this faction that reconstituted itself as international communism. But the fact that Russia was the only country in which the revolution was successful gave the whole movement a new orientation. By making Russian dominance almost inevitable, it changed the character of communism, placing on it the stamp that it bore for seventy years until the early 1990s.

The Third International

The wartime revival of international socialism at first seemed to play into the hands of the Bolshevik leaders. The wave of war-weariness that was everywhere driving Socialists toward the left apparently put Lenin in an excellent strategic position. By a systematic appeal to the yearning for peace, the Bolsheviks hoped to lead the European masses toward general revolution and social overturn. In this fashion, they believed, the axis of the movement would be displaced farther west, where it would come to rest at last on a secure proletarian base. Thus it would lose its eccentric Russian character and settle down where it belonged—in the advanced industrial society of Western and Central Europe.

In this international viewpoint, in this subordination of Russian interests to the revolutionary needs of Europe as a whole, the original Bolshevik leaders were quite sincere. By experience and sympathy, they were internationalists. They had lived long years of exile abroad, they knew foreign languages, they were intimately acquainted with their ideological partners in other countries. Among them, Stalin alone—a most significant exception—was provincially Russian and had scarcely traveled. The rest would almost certainly have concurred in shifting the headquarters of the revolutionary forces farther west—perhaps to Berlin—if circumstances had permitted; they would have been happy to shed their specifically Russian character and join with their German comrades in leading a truly international movement.

It was in this spirit that the Third International, or Comintern, was founded. At the outbreak of the war, the old Second International had collapsed; its constituent elements had gone their separate ways as patriotic Socialist parties. Nor was it possible to revive it at the war's end. The differences of attitude toward the Bolshevik Revolution that had developed in the meantime had become too great to be bridged. At a final meeting of the Second International held in the Swiss capital, Berne, early in 1919, radicals called for "revolution as in Russia, socialization of property as in Russia, application of Marxism as in Russia." They were still a minority; but they were determined to break away. Hence only those European Socialists already sympathetic with the Bolshevik experiment gathered in Moscow in March 1919 to constitute themselves as a new International.

The crucial question was already clear: Would individuals and groups who were merely sympathizers be allowed to join, or would all be obliged to submit to the rigid discipline that Lenin had already imposed on his own party? The issue hung in the balance throughout the first year of the Comintern's existence. And its final solution had a disastrous effect on a revolutionary movement that, in the meantime, had been encountering unexpected resistance nearly everywhere.

Revolutionary Stirrings: The German and Hungarian Revolutions

When the war ended in November 1918, most of Europe seemed ready for revolution. The sufferings of the mobilized workers and peasants in the trenches had made it appear only fair that the common people of the warring countries should never return to their old situation of social and economic discrimination. Factory workers had gained new confidence from high wages and their indispensability to the war effort; the example of the Bolshevik success had inflamed imaginations everywhere. At the very least, European labor was militant and on the march. At the most, the active leaders of the proletariat were prepared to bring down the whole structure of capitalist society.

The great nations of the West—Britain and France—that had the two advantages of being already political democracies and of emerging victorious from the war, were least shaken by social unrest. In these countries, the postwar disturbances did not extend beyond strikes and political demonstrations. But even here, especially in the French general strike of May 1, 1919 (a significant date for socialists), worker discontent had revolutionary overtones and was marked by frequent manifestations of sympathy with the Soviet Union. The British Labour party, moderate and socialist at heart, kept its distance from the Bolsheviks; but individual unions were less cautious. British dockers, for example, refused to load ships carrying supplies to the anti-Bolshevik forces engaged in the civil war there. Some measure of the "international solidarity" on which Lenin counted was certainly evident in France and Britain during the years 1919 and 1920.

Italy came much closer to revolution. As a people who were just beginning the experiment of political democracy and whose war record had been far from brilliant, the Italians had countless reasons for postwar dissatisfaction. In the elections of 1919—the first under universal male suffrage—Italian socialism emerged as the strongest party in the country. But this was socialism of a curious sort; it was neither moderate and legalist, nor did it resemble Lenin's communism. It called itself *maximalism*—meaning that it stood for a maximum program of immediate socialization. Yet it was unwilling to do anything concrete and realistic to bring this great change about. Lacking discipline and a clear sense of direction, it simply *talked* revolution. Italian maximalism offered the classic case of a movement that, although sympathetic to the Bolsheviks, nevertheless found it impossible to follow Lenin's revolutionary precepts. The most it could achieve was a dramatic but ineffective occupation of the northern Italian factories in the autumn of 1920. From this point on, its decline began. For the next two years, revolutionary enthusiasm in Italy was steadily on the wane.

Central Europe, of course, offered the greatest revolutionary opportunities and those that concerned the Bolsheviks most. At the end of 1918, the German Reich and the Austro-Hungarian domains showed all the indications of readiness for revolution: defeat, hunger, sickness of war, and burning social resentment. Austria-Hungary felt the added humiliation of enforced partition and the clash of nationalisms within a formerly multiethnic state. The old order had failed utterly; the new order still had not appeared. It seems no mere coincidence that the two areas where Bolshevism did have a brief success were both in Central Europe: Hungary, where a soviet republic under Béla Kun survived for four months in the spring and summer of 1919; and the southern German state of Bavaria, where a similar regime led an even more fleeting existence.

As in Russia, the Bolshevik revolution in Hungary followed an earlier, moderate revolution that failed. The Hungarian Kerensky was Count Miháilyi Károlyi, an aristocrat from one of the richest families in Hungary whose social conscience led him to break with his past. Under Károlyi's brief government, some attempts were made to stem hunger, house refugees and demobilized troops, and revive the economy. But these social problems, grave as they were, paled before the threat to the territorial integrity of Hungary itself. Though World War I had ended with the German surrender at Compiègne, Hungarian lands continued to be under assault by Czechs in the west, Croatians and Serbs in the south, and Romanians to the east. This threat assured Károlyi some measure of domestic support. Despite his failure to solve any of Hungary's pressing social problems, hope remained that he might at least prevent a wholesale dismemberment of the country by its rapacious neighbors. But when the French sanctioned Romanian claims to much of eastern Hungary in March, 1919, Károlyi's last claim to public support evaporated and the government fell.

In his place emerged the communist Béla Kun, imprisoned by the Károlyi government for political agitation, but now given power in the hopes that he could rally Soviet military support for embattled Hungary. Kun and his self-styled "people's commissars" peppered Hungary with revolutionary decrees touching everything from a new currency to the conversion of churches into movie theaters. Yet the short-lived regime demonstrated the difficulties that left-wing forces had in converting popular discontent with the old order into support for the new. The minister of the interior, Tibor Szamuelly, attempted to forestall counterrevolution from the right by instituting a "Red Terror" that alienated many potential supporters of the Kun government among the middle class. Kun's decision to nationalize the country's great landed estates rather than distribute these lands to the peasantry, who had farmed them for generations, turned the peasants against the regime as well. A decision to attack Romanian troops, who had occupied Hungarian territory in July 1919, was the last straw. Kun's left-wing government proved no more effective at defending Hungarian soil than its more moderate predecessor.

Kun's successor was a conservative military officer—Admiral Miklós Horthy. In November 1919, Horthy rode to power with the blessing of the military, the old aristocracy, and the new, fascist right. With Horthy installed as regent, this radical right-wing faction, led by Gyula Gömbös, spearheaded a "White Terror" that claimed many left-wing and Jewish victims during the years 1919–1921 before a moderate conservative government returned to power. Within the short space of two years, the political pendulum had swung wildly from left of center to the far Left to the far Right. Now, for the balance of the decade, radicalism of both Right and Left declined or was suppressed in Hungary in the name of conservative consensus.

But these were minor victories and minor defeats for the revolution as a whole. Berlin was the real target; here the fate of Bolshevism in Central Europe—and with it the future of communism as an international movement—was to be decided.

Although Germany was declared a republic two days before the war came to an end, the German revolution bore a curious and artificial character. The real changeover to parliamentary institutions had come a month earlier under the chancellorship of the liberal Prince Max of Baden. Prince Max, called to power in Germany's supreme crisis when Ludendorff's nerve failed, took the essential steps toward democracy. He made his own ministry responsible to the Reichstag, and he introduced legislation for equalizing the Prussian voting system. With these goals accomplished or about to be accomplished, there seemed to be no urgency about going on to declare Germany a republic. There was no great popular pressure for such a move. The pressure came, rather, from President Wilson, who refused to agree to an armistice as long as the emperor was on the throne.

The monarchy still might have been saved, however, under a younger member of the house of Hohenzollern. The declaration of a republic was finally prompted by the fear of left-wing demonstrations in Berlin. With leftist agitators shouting for a soviet republic, it seemed safer to the moderate Social Democratic ministers who were trying to ride the storm to declare Germany an ordinary constitutional republic. And this is what Germany actually became. After five years of repeated social disorders, the German Reich settled into the framework of middle-class democracy. The next six years, from 1924 to 1930, gave Germany a brief period of equilibrium under institutions modeled on those of Britain and France.

Again and again, however, in the years from 1919 to 1923, the German Communists had attempted to seize power. The first effort came only two months after the end of the war, in January 1919, in the form of an immense demonstration in the streets of Berlin. In the reprisals that followed, there perished the most talented leader of the German Left, Rosa Luxemburg, whose vision of communism was far freer and more spontaneous than Lenin's, and who, ironically enough, had advised against a revolutionary rising. The last effort came in the autumn of 1923, in Saxony and Hamburg, just a month before Hitler was to make his first bid for power. Between the two major attempts, there had been an almost continual series of minor revolutionary episodes, but these had gradually changed in character. At first they were genuinely popular risings, almost without official party direction, in which left-wing Independent Social Democrats stood shoulder to shoulder with regular Communists. As the years passed, such movements became more and more contrived and conspiratorial; spontaneity passed out of them, as the Independent Social Democrats and other free spirits fell away. At the end, a narrow party bureaucracy was trying, without success, to direct the whole revolutionary effort under Moscow's supervision.

This great change of temper and tactics shows better than anything else what happened in the years 1919 to 1923 to international communism as a whole. The final failure of the revolution in Germany, the Bolsheviks saw, meant its wider failure as an international movement. This defeat was partly their own fault; it was partly the result of circumstances over which they had no control. The mistakes of the Communist leaders and the changed circumstances of the years after 1920 blasted all revolutionary hopes for a full decade of European history.

The Reasons for the Failure

In the summer of 1920, the second congress of the Comintern took the fateful decision that had been debated during the whole year past. It decided to impose "iron discipline" on its constituent parties. The Twenty-One Conditions required for affiliation to the Third International demanded more than disciplined obedience; they also specified that the party in question must expel its "reformists" and engage in illegal agitation.

These were conditions that no democratic-minded Socialist could accept. Now all European leftists had to make their choice—either for or against the Leninist doctrine, Bolshevik, Soviet, or Communist, however it might be called. As a result every European Socialist party split. The majority stuck to legalist, democratic principles and kept the old party names of Socialist, Social Democratic, or Labor. The minority established themselves as Communist parties and affiliated with the Third International. Only the Italian Maximalists tried to straddle the issue—professing their sympathy with Bolshevism while at the same time refusing to accept the Twenty-One Conditions. In the end, they, too, regretfully decided that they could not join the Comintern.

In the meantime, economic conditions had suddenly turned against the working class. The two years immediately following the war were a period of boom and labor shortage in which organized workers felt themselves strong and confident in pressing their demands. At the end of 1920, the situation changed. A sharp depression threw hundreds of thousands out of work. With unemployment and a labor surplus now threatening, European labor lost its militancy. Simultaneously, its more conservative leaders, who had been overwhelmed in the immediate postwar period, began to regain their old control.

This was true of the trade-union leadership, which had vainly tried to check the irresponsibility and tumultuousness of its followers in 1919 and 1920. It was also true of the Socialist parties. These not only survived the secession of the Communists; they even temporarily profited by it, since they emerged from the crisis with new cohesion and clarity of purpose. Moreover, they were gaining additional constituents to replace the ones they had lost. Middle-class recruits flocked to them in large numbers, for in the perspective of 1921 and 1922, the record of the European Socialists was very reassuring. In the war they had steered between the two extremes of chauvinism and defeatism; they had behaved like patriots without being deceived by the propaganda of the superpatriots. And, as a postwar policy, they were trying to combine resistance to Communist revolution with steady insistence on social reform and a profound belief in international reconciliation.

Thus, by 1921 the Socialist parties were emerging as a great force for order and stabilization in Western and Central Europe. Socialism, more than anything else, was holding the discontented workers in line. All intermediate positions had disappeared: A European leftist must now be either a Socialist or a Communist, and the distinction between them was crystal clear. The former internationalist Socialists had had to make their choice. There was no longer any room for halfway stations.*

In the Communist camp, a Muscovite discipline reigned. With the final failure of the revolution in Germany and the death of Lenin three months later, the international spirit vanished from the Comintern. It was thereafter to be run in Russian interests, as a new and eccentric arm of Soviet foreign policy. How could a non-Russian Communist object? Was it not the first duty of every Communist, whatever his nationality, to preserve the revolution in the one country where it had triumphed? Thus international communism succumbed to bureaucratic control from Moscow. The life went out of it. Its leadership became routine and unimaginative. Not until the 1930s—in the new situation of fascism and the Great Depression—was communism to regain its ideological flexibility and its ability to inspire party members and large numbers of sympathizers alike.

To moderate and conservative Europeans, the distinction between Socialists and Communists was of little consequence. Long after the revolutionary tide receded, the fear of the Left that it had prompted gave the Right a potent weapon in gaining support. The final and unintended consequence of the creation of the Third International was an

*In 1920, the chief of these intermediate parties, the German Independent Social Democrats, broke up, part going to the Social Democrats and part to the Communists.

ideological crusade launched against it by the disciples of fascism. Fear of revolution proved stronger than allegiance to the liberal tenets of parliamentary democracy, free speech, or individual liberty; in the name of anti-Bolshevism, all were to fall under siege by the end of the decade.

READINGS

For the ideological aspects of the First World War and the propaganda duel between Wilson and Lenin, see Arno Mayer, *Political Origins of the New Diplomacy, 1917–1918* (1959).

Introductions to Russia on the eve of revolution are contained in Hans Rogger, *Russia in the Age of Modernization and Revolution, 1881–1917** (1983), and in Geoffrey Hosking, *Russia: People and Empire* (1997). For an illuminating portrait of Russia's last ruler, see Anatol Lieven, *Nicholas II: Twilight of the Empire** (1994). Melissa Stockdale, *Paul Miliukov and the Quest for a Liberal Russia, 1880–1918* (1996) examines alternative paths to reform through the life of a major historian and critic of Bolshevik politics. For the major protagonists in the revolution, Bertram D. Wolfe's *Three Who Made a Revolution** (1948) still gives one of the best accounts of the complex personal relationships among Lenin, Trotsky, and Stalin; it can be usefully supplemented with Adam B. Ulam, *The Bolsheviks** (1965).

Dmitri Volkogonov's *Lenin: A New Biography* (1994) is a pathbreaking, critical study of Lenin's life and career based on access to hitherto secret archives. (The author, a former Soviet general who would later become a dissident, was chair of the Russian Archives Declassifying Commission from 1991 until his death in 1995.) Robert Service, *Lenin, A Biography** (2002) is excellent on Lenin's early thought and writings, while Robert C. Tucker, in *Stalin as Revolutionary, 1879–1929** (1973), chronicles the future dictator's formative years. Volkogonov has also written a biography of Leon Trotsky—*Trotsky: The Eternal Revolutionary* (1996)—which stresses both the single-minded pursuit of revolution and the political blindness which ultimately undid Revolution's chief ideologist. Isaac Deutscher offers a portrait of Trotsky written from the sympathetic perspective of a disciple in his trilogy *The Prophet Armed** (1954), *The Prophet Unarmed** (1959), and *The Prophet Outcast** (1963).

On the revolution itself, see Sheila Fitzpatrick, *The Russian Revolution, 1917–1932** (1982); Orlando Figes, *A People's Tragedy: A History of the Russian Revolution** (1996); Richard Pipes, *The Russian Revolution** (1990); Robert V. Daniels, *Red October: The Bolshevik Revolution of 1917,** rev. ed. (1984); and the older but still standard account of Edward Hallett Carr, *The Bolshevik Revolution*, 3 vols. (1950–1953), the latter favorable to Lenin and his colleagues. For an eyewitness account, also favorably biased but deservedly a classic, see John Reed, *Ten Days That Shook the World** (1919).

A sizeable literature explores the social and cultural aspects of the Russian revolution. See especially Donald Raleigh, *The Workers' Revolution in Russia, 1917: The View from Below** (1987). Teodor Shanin examines the aims of the peasants in *The Awkward Class* (1972), while David Mandel explores the role of the working class in *The Petrograd*

*Books marked by an asterisk are available in paperback.

Workers and the Fall of the Old Regime (1984). Marc Ferro, *October 1917: The Social History of the Russian Revolution* (trans. 1980) provides an overview of the revolution's social impact, while Anna Horsbrugh-Porter, ed., *Memories of Revolution** (1993) provides eyewitness accounts by a broad cross-section of Russian women.

Opposition to the Bolsheviks from their former supporters on the Left is described in Paul Avrich, *Kronstadt 1921** (1970, rev. ed. 1991) and Vladimir Brovkin, *Behind the Front Lines in the Russian Civil War** (2001). Jane Burbank chronicles the attempt of Russian intellectuals to salvage their faith in revolution while condemning the new regime in *Intelligentsia and Revolution: Russian Views of Bolshevism, 1917–1922** (1987). The Bolshevik response to opposition is examined in George Leggett, *The Cheka: Lenin's Political Police** (1981). On the civil war, see Evan Mawdsley, *The Russian Civil War** (2001) and the collection of essays in Diane P. Koenker, William G. Rosenberg, and Ronald Grigor Suny, eds., *Party, State and Society in the Russian Civil War** (1989). Some sense of the chaos and uncertainty of this period is conveyed in Ivan Bunin, *Cursed Days: A Diary of the Revolution* (1998) and Boris Pasternak's classic novel, *Doctor Zhivago** (1958). The canonization of their leader by the victors is admirably analyzed in Nina Tumarkin, *Lenin Lives! The Lenin Cult in Soviet Russia** (1983).

The spreading effects of the revolution, particularly in Central Europe, are traced in Charles L. Bertrand, ed., *Revolutionary Situations in Europe, 1917–22* (1977), and F. L. Carsten, *Revolution in Central Europe* (1972). For a brilliant interpretation of why the Bolsheviks failed outside Russia, see Joseph A. Schumpeter, *Capitalism, Socialism, and Democracy*, 3d ed. (1950).

THE SETTLEMENT
OF 1919–1923

The Big Four at Versailles, 1919. From left to right: David Lloyd George of Great Britain, Vittorio Emmanuele Orlando of Italy, Georges Clemenceau of France, and Woodrow Wilson of the United States. *(Courtesy Brown Brothers)*

I. THE WILSONIAN VISION

Nationalism and the War

Nationalism was a force that European Marxists had always underestimated. Lenin, in his appeals to the peasants and workers in the trenches to lay down their arms, ruled out the possibility that the proletarians in uniform might actually believe in the justice of their respective national causes. But in 1917 and 1918, nationalism in Europe was far from dead. One indication of its tenacity had been the response of the Socialist parties to the original declarations of war. Another was the fact that even in the bitter year 1917, the armies of the Western and Central European belligerents—drained though they were by defeatism and war weariness—had fought on. And the final year of the war—the year of the Allied march to victory—seemed to vindicate nationalist war leaders like Lloyd George and Clemenceau, who had urged their people to hold out to the last. When the war ended, nationalists of one sort or other were ruling both the victorious nations of the West and the new or enlarged states that were springing up in East Central Europe. Their control—and the substantial popular support they enjoyed—suggests a final and decisive reason for the failure of Lenin's international revolutionary hopes in the years 1919 through 1923.

Paradoxically enough, Woodrow Wilson himself contributed mightily to this strengthening of national sentiment in the final year of the war. In his ideological competition with Lenin, the American president suffered because he did not promise immediate peace. This was indeed a handicap as long as the defeatist spirit of 1917 persisted, but when the morale of the warring peoples had been remobilized for the final effort of 1918, the handicap began to turn into an advantage. Once it was clear that tangible national gains might be won from victory, Leninism began to lose its appeal. Furthermore, it soon became apparent that Lenin could not carry out what he had promised. He could continue to urge immediate peace, but he could do nothing to win it; he could preach the liberation of subject nationalities, but he could not help in their struggle for freedom. This became evident after the Treaty of Brest-Litovsk revealed the weakness of the Bolshevik regime and its humiliating subjection to German armed force.

Wilson, in contrast, had behind him the enormous resources of the United States, whose potential gradually unfolded with the progress of American mobilization in the latter half of 1917 and the first months of 1918. By March of 1918—when Brest-Litovsk was exposing the extent of Lenin's weakness—Wilson was just coming into his full strength. American troops were pouring ashore in France by the tens of thousands, and a bottomless reservoir of additional strength lay behind them. Lenin had nothing of the sort to help him. The Bolshevik leader's only weapon was revolutionary subversion; Wilson could bring into play the unlimited resources of the strongest nation on earth. This lesson was not lost on the nationalist leaders of East Central Europe, the spokesman of the Poles and the Czechs, the Rumanians and the Yugoslavs, whose ambitions were to prove decisive for the character of the peace settlement reached in 1919.

Nationalists, realistically calculating their chances in the last year of the war, correctly concluded that they would gain most from Wilsonianism. And so they rallied to it—at least in words. In fact, however, they altered the Wilsonian appeal, gradually molding it and interpreting it in directions that the president had never intended. In the end, they converted it into something far more crudely nationalist than it had originally been. Thus Wilson became the prisoner of the forces of old-fashioned nationalism he had earlier opposed. This was to be the final irony of the peace settlement of 1919.

Wilson's Aims: The Fourteen Points

The American declaration of war changed Wilson's aim from "peace without victory" to a peace imposed by the victors on the vanquished. The president himself was not entirely aware of how great the shift actually was. He did not fully appreciate the contrast between his earlier, almost pacifist pronouncements and the ringing appeal he delivered on April 6, 1918, to mark the first anniversary of American intervention: "Force, Force to the utmost, Force without stint or limit, the righteous and triumphant Force which shall make Right the law of the world, and cast every selfish dominion down in the dust."

Three months earlier Wilson had issued his Fourteen Points to clarify his own aims and, if possible, to rally sentiment in the Allied nations behind them. The timing of the declaration was significant, for, once again, the ideological competition with Lenin was the crucial consideration. From the negotiations at Brest-Litovsk, the Bolshevik leaders had been issuing pronouncements calculated to rouse the hopes of subject peoples everywhere. Wilson's answer was to draw up a formal list of war aims that would prove to all the world that the Western Allies were willing to go as far as Lenin in their search for a peace of justice. The Fourteen Points address "was not an idealistic program of peace aims made in a political vacuum but primarily a tactical move in psychological warfare, made up in a pragmatic fashion from varied sources and suggestions."*

Nearly all Wilson's points deal with political, military, or territorial issues. Besides laying down such general aims as freedom of the seas, disarmament, and an international association to guarantee the peace, the American president made a number of concrete proposals for settling the nationalities question: Belgium, Serbia, and Rumania were to be restored; France was to regain Alsace-Lorraine; Italy was to have its frontiers adjusted "along clearly recognizable lines of nationality"; an independent Poland was to be set up, "with free and secure access to the sea"; and finally, "the peoples of Austria-Hungary, whose place among the nations we wish to see safeguarded and assured, should be accorded the freest opportunity of autonomous development."

The only economic proposal in the whole list was a vague statement on the removal of trade barriers. Nor did Wilson seem in any way to recognize that national questions were often intertwined with social issues of bewildering complexity. He showed no awareness of the situation—so frequent in East Central Europe—in which the landlord class was of one nationality and the peasantry of another. The possibility that the land hunger of the peasants might be a deeper longing than the desire for national self-determination likewise escaped him. In brief, he failed to understand that much of Europe did not have the type of society that could support the democratic settlement he advocated. He seemed not to know that through most of the wide belt of territory lying

*Victor S. Mamatey, *The United States and East Central Europe, 1914–1918* (Princeton, N.J.: Princeton University Press, 1957), 172.

between Germany to the west and Russia to the east, democracy had never existed and was still a completely unfamiliar way of life.

In Wilson's vision, the self-determination of peoples offered the key to international peace and progress, for self-determination suggested two things: redrawing boundaries in a fair and just fashion and democratization *within* the new boundaries thus established. Once each people was in control of its own destinies, Wilson believed, the way to international concord would be open. This faith was not unfamiliar to Europeans. It had been held by most radical thinkers in the middle of the nineteenth century. But the faith had waned since then. The extremes to which popular nationalism had proceeded in the quarter century before the outbreak of the war aroused doubt whether democracy and nationalism always went together, or, if they did, whether this was necessarily good. A tempered skepticism had replaced the earlier trust in the democratic virtue of national feeling.

But Wilson was not a European. He was a political scientist, a professor, a former president of Princeton, and an intellectual, but he was insufficiently familiar with Europe's history and the complexity of its problems. Indeed, he expressed impatience with all these complications and made a virtue of his ignorance. The American delegation, he told one of its members, would be "the only disinterested people at the Peace Conference" because they were the only ones without territorial claims. In this sense Wilson tried to play the role of an honest broker, balancing the demands of the victorious French, British, and Italians on the one hand and the defeated Germans and Austrians on the other, with little success. It is not true, as his detractors have asserted, that Wilson was merely a dour Puritan, rigid and inflexible. Actually, he proved himself both a seasoned politician and a reasonable negotiator—skills without which he could scarcely have won election to the White House. But he failed to understand the underlying economic and social problems threatening Europe's fragile postwar peace. In his exclusive trust in merely political solutions, his neglect of economic and social issues, his lack of a historical sense, and in his addiction to simple (and thus superficial) formulas, Wilson was true to the purest of the ideologies of progress. It was as the last great exponents of nineteenth-century idealism that Wilson was to try to impose on his hesitant allies his own version of a just and lasting peace.

Wilson had tried to elevate the First World War to a higher moral plane when, in an effort to justify American intervention in 1917, he termed it a "war to make the world safe for democracy." But this was not how most Europeans saw it. In their view, it was primarily a war to make the world safe for themselves. Nationalism and the defense of national interests (including expanding the nation's frontiers) proved the predominant motives of the First World War. Much of the literature produced by war veterans revolved around nationalism, and much of that dealt with the theme of disillusionment. The war they had been led to expect—short, glorious, a noble crusade for their homeland—turned out to be long, bloody, and sordid. This was not a literature of inspiration and uplift, but rather an indictment of deception and betrayal.

II. THE LIBERATION OF EAST CENTRAL EUROPE

Point Ten of the Fourteen Points, the one dealing with "the peoples of Austria-Hungary," had a calculated ambiguity. It could be read either as reassuring the two dominant nationalities, the German-speaking Austrians and the Hungarians, that the Allies did not intend to destroy their respective positions, or as supporting the claims of the subject peoples in their struggle for liberation. And this evidently was precisely what Wilson intended. As late as January 1918, when he announced the Fourteen Points, he had not yet decided what to do about the Austro-Hungarian Empire. He could not fail to take a stand for fairer treatment of the subject nationalities, but he had yet to be convinced that this meant full independence and, with it, the breakup of the empire as a political unit.

As a cautious transition phrase, then, Wilson offered "autonomous development." If it meant anything, it signified no more than self-government *within* the empire. But this was not at all what the leaders of the nationalities themselves desired. They would settle for nothing less than full independence. One of the great, if largely subterranean, dramas of the year 1918 was the fashion in which these leaders gradually won the American president to their point of view by facing him with a series of accomplished facts. Wilson has often been accused of willfully breaking up Austria-Hungary at the Peace Conference of Paris. Nothing could be further from the truth. Months before the Peace Conference met, the Austro-Hungarian Empire had *already* broken up, as the leaders of the subject nationalities took matters into their own hands and boldly pushed them to the final solution.

The Role of the Czechs

As the best educated, the most democratically minded, and the most advanced economically of the subject nationalities, the Czechs held the key to the situation. They were also the only ones who could destroy the whole empire. The other nationalities—the Poles, the Rumanians, the South Slavs, and the Italians—merely formed parts of larger groups the majority of whom dwelt outside Austria-Hungary. These nationalities looked beyond the borders of the empire for deliverance. The Czechs alone—and the neighboring and less developed Slovaks, whose language closely resembled theirs—lay entirely within the imperial frontiers. The border nationalities could be peeled off one by one, and still the central Danubian core of the empire would remain intact. Should the Czechs go, however, all would be lost: The Hungarians would then have no reason for staying with the German-speaking Austrians, and the empire would simply dissolve.

In retrospect, it seems that the Austrian statesmen should have done everything in their power to conciliate the Czechs before it was too late. At the start of the war, "Trialism," as it was called, might have succeeded: If the empire had been converted from a dual into a "trial" monarchy by giving the Czech land of Bohemia the same parity with "Austria" that Hungary had earlier received, the empire might have been saved. But the Austrians seem never to have considered this solution seriously. And while they delayed, there emerged new and talented Czech leaders who drove single-mindedly toward their goal of full independence.

This was a final distinction between the Czechs and the other nationalities—the eminence and skill of their leadership. As the war continued, the Czech propagandists in exile came to recognize as their undisputed chief the scholarly, serene Thomas G. Masaryk. Faithfully seconding him was the more lively and intriguing Eduard Beneš. Together Masaryk and Beneš made the most effective team of national spokesmen in all Europe. Beneš knew every trick of propaganda; Masaryk could speak the lofty, philosophical language that Wilson admired. On May 30, 1918, during a highly successful visit of Masaryk to the United States, the Czechs in exile drew up a charter of independence at Pittsburgh. Two and a half months later the British granted them recognition, and in September, ten weeks before the end of the war, the Americans followed suit. Czechoslovakia had become an independent nation.

The Allied Promises; The Pact of Rome

The independence of Czechoslovakia climaxed a series of concessions by the Western Allies that had been gradually mounting for more than three years. First the British and French had promised the Italians their "unredeemed" lands within the Austrian Empire in order to get them into the war. Then the Allies made similar pledges to the Serbs in order to keep them fighting. Finally, the Allies held out the bait of Transylvania to the Rumanians, which the latter grabbed for, with the disastrous results already described.

Meantime, it had become apparent that Poland would be reconstituted. Initially the Russians proposed to set it up as a dependent state. Then the Germans actually did so, and held Poland in their grasp until the very end of the war. Polish leaders were long divided over whether they should look to the Entente or to Germany for their freedom. Three things eventually decided them: Their "independent" status under German control was proving to be a farce; it was becoming apparent that the Allies would win the war; and Wilson's Thirteenth Point, with its phrase about "free and secure access to the sea," seemed to promise the Poles nearly everything they desired.

It was still necessary, however, to convince the American president that the Austro-Hungarian Empire should be broken up. The process began in March 1918, when the Serbian leaders wrested from Wilson permission to tell their parliament—convened in the island refuge of Corfu—that he and his Allies "would meet Serbo-Croat national aspirations as far as possible." It was accelerated the next month by the signature of the so-called Pact of Rome. In this document, the representatives of Austria's subject nationalities, meeting in the Italian capital, pledged solidarity with each other in the common struggle for independence. Then in May came Masaryk's visit to the United States, as the Czech propaganda offensive began to gain momentum. By the summer of 1918, it was becoming obvious that Wilson was rapidly being won over and that soon nothing would stand in the way of realizing the nationalities' maximum program.

The Dissolution of Austria-Hungary

On October 16, 1918, the Austrian emperor issued a manifesto promising to reorganize his dominions as a federal state. The concession came far too late. It satisfied neither Wilson nor the subject nationalities. It merely hastened the process of dissolution.

By the end of the month, it was becoming obvious that even the Hungarians had lost faith in the empire. The other nationalities quietly drew their own conclusions. On October 28, a Czech National Committee in Prague began functioning as a separate government. The Croatian Diet declared its independence the next day. Meantime, the war came to an end, as the disintegration of the empire continued unchecked. The vanquished Rumanians—who had succeeded in reentering the conflict just in time—took over Transylvania on the first of December. And on the same day, the prince-regent of Serbia proclaimed the union of his country with the lands inhabited by the Croats and Slovenes. A South Slav or Yugoslav state had at last become a reality. But its birth had been far from effortless. Until the very last, the Croats and Slovenes of Austria-Hungary had tried to obtain assurances of equality from the Serbs, which the latter had stubbornly refused to give. Here again the outlines of future conflict were clear: The whole foundation of the Yugoslav state rested on an assumption of Serbian supremacy that the sister peoples were reluctant to accept. Seventy years later, in 1989, the tensions inherent within the Yugoslav state would finally spell its end.

Thus occurred the liberation of East Central Europe. The last nine months of the year 1918, which had seen so many other dramatic events, also witnessed the creation of a continuous belt of small independent nations separating Germany from Russia. The Peace Conference could do no more than ratify a settlement for East Central Europe whose major outlines had already been determined on the spot.

III. THE PEACE CONFERENCE OF 1919

The Armistice

On November 7, 1918, the German Reichstag deputy Matthias Erzberger set out on a forlorn mission. In a modest convoy of three automobiles, protected only by a large white flag, he crossed the line between the retreating Germans and the victorious Allies in search of Marshal Foch and an armistice to end the war. It was unprecedented for a civilian rather than a soldier to be given such an assignment. But it was typical of the way in which the German command—ever since Ludendorff's collapse six weeks before—had been trying to shirk responsibility for its defeat. And if a civilian had to do the job, Erzberger was the logical man to go. As the author of the Peace Resolution of July 1917, he was already identified in the public mind with a compromise settlement. Nor was he afraid of the unpopularity that his armistice mission might bring down upon him. He gladly accepted unpopular assignments—indeed, he almost seemed to seek them out. (And for this he perished by an assassin's bullet three years later.)

The fashion in which the 1918 Armistice came about was the origin of the famous "Stab-in-the-Back" legend—the legend that the civilians and the home front had betrayed the German Army while it was still undefeated. And the terms of the Armistice seemed to bear out the legend. Erzberger had hoped that he would be able to negotiate with Foch, but when he actually met the Allied commander-in-chief in his railroad-car headquarters in the Forest of Compiègne, Foch simply asked his deputy to read off an already-prepared list of terms. These were designed to make it impossible for Germany to resume the struggle. They provided for a massive surrender of warships, guns, airplanes, and rolling stock; for the evacuation of the left bank of the Rhine and of bridgeheads opposite its major cities; and for the annulment of the Treaty of Brest-Litovsk, with the relinquishment of Germany's territorial gains to the east. Erzberger obtained a few modifications in the final Armistice that came into effect on November 11, but in essence the Armistice foreshadowed what the peace treaty was to be—a victors' settlement imposed on the vanquished.

One other thing rankled in German memories. Throughout the winter while the Peace Conference was in progress, the Allies were apparently maintaining their blockade of the Reich. Starvation and suffering continued, and the Germans accused their late enemies of holding the whip of hunger over them. They did not know, however, that it was not the Allies but German shipowners who were delaying the arrival of food by refusing to donate their vessels for humanitarian purposes. Owing to their stubbornness, it was not until April that relief shipments began to arrive. Thus, far from offering further evidence of Allied harshness, the continued hunger in Germany "only proved the weakness of the German government in the face of the German shipping lobby."*

Personalities and Organization: The Big Three

Paris was the natural choice for the site of the Peace Conference. As the capital of the nation that had borne the heaviest burden in the war, it seemed to deserve that honor, and the French insisted on it. The choice of the French capital seriously handicapped Wilson in his efforts to arrive at a peace based on justice and distorted the character of the peace treaties, leaving upon them an imprint of triumph and revenge.

Another fateful circumstance was Wilson's decision to attend the conference in person. This was entirely unprecedented. No American president had ever left the country before; never since has the chief executive been away for so long a time. But Wilson was convinced that he alone could persuade the Allies to make the sort of peace he envisioned. In the final months of the war, he had won the grudging consent of his Allies to accepting the Fourteen Points as the basis for negotiations. And it was on this understanding that the Germans agreed to end the war. But Wilson well knew that the French and British—and, still more, the Italians—were far from prepared to let the central principle of national self-determination govern all the decisions of the conference. All three—and the smaller Allies as well—had their own national aims that they were completely unwilling to sacrifice to the wider goal of a just peace.

Wilson had redefined the war as a war for democracy. But this was not the war's original character, and the nationalist leaders who were governing the Allied Powers, great and small, at the end of the conflict, did not naturally think in these terms. They had humored Wilson's ideological eccentricities, since they could not afford to offend the United States: American aid was indispensable to their survival. Once the war was safely won, however, they felt free to return to their traditional nationalistic views.

*Klaus Epstein, *Matthias Erzberger and the Dilemma of German Democracy* (Princeton, N.J.: Princeton University Press, 1959), 294.

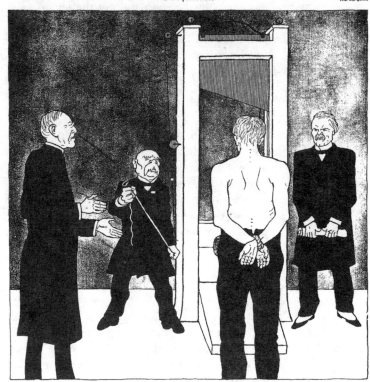

Versailles (Th. Th. Heine)

A bitter German view of reparations: Wilson, Clemenceau, and Lloyd George confront Germany, portrayed as a condemned prisoner facing the guillotine. Wilson declares: "You, too, have the right to self-determination; would you like to have us pick your pockets before or after your execution?"

„Auch Sie haben noch ein Selbstbestimmungsrecht: wünschen Sie, daß Ihnen die Taschen vor oder nach dem Tode ausgeleert werden?"

Thus, inevitably, the conference was to be marked by conflict between the old-style nationalism of the European leaders and the new-style nationalism of President Wilson. And the American president could see no alternative but to go himself to Paris to fight for the peace in which he believed. More particularly, he wanted to fight for the League of Nations, the new association of states that he intended to make an integral part of the peace treaties. The League was Wilson's favorite scheme. He gave it priority in the peace negotiations, and for its sake he was prepared to make sacrifices on what he regarded as minor points.

Here also lay a danger for the future. The French in particular were willing to accept the League since it offered no threat to them and could even be turned to the uses of French security. With tongue in cheek, they could concur in what was still a mere abstraction, trading their consent to it for Wilson's agreement to some of their more realistic national aims. And there was still another danger: The League—with the limitations on national sovereignty that it implied—offered the best ammunition to Wilson's enemies at home, the Republican nationalists who had just won the midterm election of 1918. The point on which the president insisted most was the one that they liked least. Europeans, unfamiliar as they were with the workings of American politics, did not realize the weakness of Wilson's position in 1919. They regarded him as still the leader of his country. They did not understand that Wilson, having lost his majority in Congress, was in a position that, in a European parliamentary state, would have brought about his immediate resignation.

Finally, Wilson's decision to attend dictated much of the organization and procedure of the conference. It meant, for one thing, that there was a constant time pressure. The American president could not be away from Washington too long—indeed, in the middle of the conference he returned to the United States for a full month—and this made it urgent to get on with the work. It also doomed the original plan of quickly drafting a preliminary treaty and then drawing up a final treaty with more deliberation—a plan that was scrapped in favor of pushing through a single document. It also meant that nearly all the work of the conference had to be delegated to smaller groups and that Wilson could not possibly follow in detail the progress of each one of them.

The Peace Conference opened in plenary session on January 18, 1919. This was a pure formality; after that the full meetings of the conference became less and less important. The real work was done in specialized committees. Here the usual diplomatic horse trading went on; here the representatives of the smaller powers, denied the forum of a full meeting, pleaded their special cases, with a vast array of historical data and statistics, nearly all of it shamelessly slanted. The French and British usually appointed experienced diplomats to these committees; Wilson, however, brought with him a large delegation of professors, and their presence on the committees and behind the scenes offered one of the great novelties of the conference. In addition, there was the president's personal adviser and friend Colonel Edward M. House, who was more of a diplomat than his chief and far more inclined to compromise on crucial issues.

Above the "experts" and diplomats towered the real masters of the conference: the heads of government and foreign ministers of the Great Powers. It was at their secret meetings that the final decisions were hammered out. They originally met as a Council of Ten, which included not only the French and British and Americans but also the Italians and even the Japanese, who had entered the war simply to acquire former German colonies. Later the Japanese and the foreign ministers tended to drop out, as the inner circle was reduced to the "Big Four": Wilson, Clemenceau, Lloyd George, and the Italian, Orlando. Finally, when the Italian delegation left the conference in vexation, the Big Three alone remained. Their deliberations dominated the rest of the proceedings and produced most of the legend and controversy that the Peace Conference left behind it.

In the private meetings of the Big Three, Wilson faced formidable antagonists. Lloyd George was willing to go with him part of the way. But the mercurial little Welshman was slippery and unpredictable, and he was seldom at liberty to follow his natural inclinations toward a democratic peace. Time after time he showed himself to be the prisoner of his own supporters, the British Tory nationalists and the prime ministers of the overseas dominions, who, like the Japanese, were bent on colonial gains. He had, moreover, just won an election—the "Khaki Election" of December 1918—by using demagogic slogans about a punitive peace. Yet Lloyd George was an easy person to deal with, in comparison with Clemenceau. The French prime minister knew just what he wanted, he stood on home ground, and he refused to budge from his bedrock demands. With half a century of political experience behind him, Clemenceau judged men and

Jubilant soldiers and sailors celebrate the armistice of November, 1918 in the streets of Paris; note the American flag, carried to honor America's contribution to the Allied war effort. (*Courtesy Getty Images, Inc./Hulton Archive Photos*)

events in realistic fashion; he could have been called a cynic were it not for his burning French patriotism. Clemenceau's desire was simple: security from German invasion. He had experienced two invasions in his lifetime and he did not want his country to endure a third. Hence he was skeptical of Wilson's schemes and willing to accept only those that could be made to serve French security interests. And should Clemenceau ever be tempted to forget these interests, Marshal Foch was always behind him, pleading as a soldier with single-minded stubbornness for the ancient French goal of "natural" and defensible frontiers.

This, then, was the balance of policies and personalities as the Peace Conference opened.

The Order of Business: The League, the Colonies, the Rhineland, Reparations

Wilson had given priority in his own mind to the establishment of a League of Nations, and it was with this goal that the conference began its labors. It was not hard to reach unanimous agreement to set up such a body and to appoint a committee to draft its constitution. But the decision to go ahead with the League catapulted the conference into one of its most vexatious problems—the disposition of the former German colonies. Here the opposing viewpoints met head on: The Japanese and the prime ministers of the British dominions wanted outright annexation, whereas Wilson insisted on a trusteeship or "mandate" arrangement.

In view of the fact that Japan and the dominions were already in possession of the spoils, Wilson did not come off too badly. The powers finally agreed on a three-stage mandate system. True, the lowest category of these—Class C—which applied to former German Southwest Africa and to the islands of the Pacific that had been conquered by Japan, Australia, and New Zealand, was no more than veiled annexation. But Class B—covering most of the African colonies—provided for real supervision by the League to assure that the natives' welfare was respected. Class A—applicable to the Arab lands formerly under Turkish rule—envisaged a fairly rapid evolution toward independence. Five present-day nations of the Near East, in fact, grew out of Class A mandates, and three of the Class B areas in Africa, Cameroon, Tanganyika (present-day Tanzania), and Togo, achieved independence in the 1960s.

With this comparatively simple problem out of the way, Wilson was free to turn his attention to the central issue of France's claims on Germany. But his fighting spirit had already been weakened by the colonial struggle, and just as the debate with the French was reaching its climax, he was compelled to return home. During Wilson's absence from mid-February to mid-March, the conference seemed to be marking time. Actually, two very important things occurred. In the first place, after conferring with Senate leaders, Wilson became convinced that it would be necessary to reduce the supranational features of the League in order to obtain American acceptance. On his return to Paris, the president was obliged to have the Covenant of the League altered to give explicit recognition to the Monroe Doctrine; this shift weakened his position by seeming to cast him, too, in the role of pleader for selfish national goals. The second notable change was a stiffening in the attitude of the French. With Wilson away, the more conciliatory Colonel House had conceded a number of important points; when the president returned, he found it impossible to win back all the ground he had lost.

There resulted the first great explosion of the conference—a rupture of relations between Wilson and Clemenceau, as the American president took to his bed with influenza and ordered his ship to stand by for immediate departure. But after two weeks of crisis, House reconciled the two. Once more, the decisions eventually reached were a compromise. The French gave up Foch's favorite scheme of separating the Rhineland from Germany to form a buffer state, and they consented to reduce the demands of their client nation, Poland, on Germany's eastern frontiers. In return, though, Wilson had to agree to the military occupation of the Rhineland for fifteen years, and to an undertaking on the part of the United States and Britain to come to the aid of France "in the event of any unprovoked movement of aggression against her . . . by Germany."

The American president also gave his consent to what was undoubtedly the worst feature of the whole settlement—the provisions on reparations. Earlier Wilson had insisted that Germany should be made to pay only *reparations* in the narrower sense—that is, compensation for the direct war destruction the German armies had wrought. He had refused to countenance an *indemnity* to cover the cost to the Allies of waging the war. But on this issue Lloyd George—bound by his pledges to the British electorate—joined Clemenceau. He insisted that the Germans must pay the whole bill. And such was the decision of the conference.

In deference to Wilson's views, the sums demanded were defined only as *reparations*, but their size and the categories of payments included in them clearly indicated that this concession to the American view was only verbal and that Clemenceau and Lloyd George had put indemnities into the final treaty. The French and British leaders, moreover, steadfastly refused to grant the two points on which the American experts insisted—either a fixed sum of money, or a fixed number of years for payment. As one American financial expert in Wilson's delegation put it, some French and British participants at the conference "wanted to collect more than Germany had agreed to pay or could pay; and others wanted to take all her capital, destroy her, and then collect a large reparations bill." As the bill for reparations finally emerged from the conference, it was indeed both vague and astronomical. And the Big Three had added—without at all realizing the repercussions it would produce—the clause that was to infuriate the Germans most of all: the demand that Germany accept full "responsibility" (or "guilt," as it came to be called) "for causing all the loss and damage" incident to the war.

The Secret Treaties and the Adriatic Explosion

Wilson asserted that before his arrival in Paris he knew nothing of the secret treaties between his allies—and more particularly the Treaty of London, by which the French and British had brought Italy into the war. It would have been more accurate to say that he was resolved to ignore the secret treaties, which the Bolsheviks had published to all the world, and that the American press had aided him in this resolve by keeping strictly silent about them.

Thus when the Peace Conference finally came to discuss the Italian claims, Wilson insisted that he was not bound by the Treaty of London or by its successor, the still more generous Treaty of Saint Jean de Maurienne. For this firm attitude, the American president had several justifications that had not applied in the case of the French demands on Germany. Italy's mediocre contribution to victory did not seem to deserve much of a reward. Furthermore, the Italian claims were not simply at the expense of a defeated foe, as France's had been, but conflicted with those of a new friend, the recently founded state of Yugoslavia. Finally, the Italian leaders overplayed their hand—they not only insisted on their full pound of flesh; they added to it the Adriatic seaport of Fiume, which had not been specified in the original treaties.

Wilson was prepared to grant the Italian claims against Austria alone—the city of Trieste and the South Tyrol (or Trentino and Alto Adige) right up to the Brenner Pass, which meant that a quarter of a million German-speaking Austrians would be included within the new Italian frontiers. But he was unwilling to do the like with the Adriatic lands inhabited by Croats and Slovenes. At this, the Italian delegates, Vittorio Orlando and Baron Sidney Sonnino, set up a great cry of betrayal and stamped out of the conference. But Orlando and Sonnino gained nothing by sulky withdrawal. They finally found themselves obliged to return to Paris and to pick up the broken threads of negotiation. Wilson still held firm. Continuing to support the Yugoslavs, he would not yield on the Adriatic shore, except in the case of two small strips with a considerable Italian population. When the Peace Conference adjourned in June, the question of Fiume remained undecided.

IV. The Peace of Paris

The settlement that emerged from the Peace Conference is called the Peace of Paris. The individual treaties that constitute it bear the names of the localities near Paris where they were signed.

The Treaty of Versailles

Dwarfing all the others, of course, and frequently confused with the whole settlement, was the Treaty of Versailles with Germany. On June 28, 1919, it was signed with great ceremony in the Hall of Mirrors in the palace of Louis XIV—the same hall in which, forty-eight years earlier, the victorious Germans had founded their new empire. This time the Germans were simply handed the treaty on a take-it-or-leave-it basis. As in the case of the Armistice, they had hoped to be able to negotiate on specific terms, but they found themselves faced instead with what they called a *Diktat*. When the news reached home, a wave of indignation swept the country; German patriots clamored for refusal to ratify the treaty. For a few days the constitutional assembly meeting at Weimar toyed with the same idea. In the end counsels of prudence prevailed: Germany obviously could not renew the war. The ministry resigned, the deputies protested, a suitable subterfuge had to be found to obtain a majority for ratification. But the terms of the treaty stood, virtually as the Big Three had originally drafted them.

Although the Treaty of Versailles was undoubtedly harsh, it was not as severe as the Treaty of Brest-Litovsk, which the Germans had imposed fifteen months earlier on the vanquished Russians. (See Chapter 2, VI.) It left the Reich intact—Wilson had successfully resisted all notions of dismemberment—but seriously reduced in area. Both in the west and in the east its frontiers were contracted. In the west, Alsace-Lorraine returned to France, which also received the right to exploit for fifteen years the industrially rich Saar Basin. Two small strips of land went to Belgium, and northern Schleswig to the Danes. In the east, the reconstituted state of Poland bit deeply into Germany's borders. Indeed, the so-called Polish Corridor—giving the new nation that "free and secure access to the sea," which Wilson had promised—completely cut off East Prussia from the rest of Germany. The only solace granted to German feelings was the separation of the German-speaking seaport of Danzig from the rest of the Corridor as a free city under the supervision of the League of Nations.

The military terms of the treaty were even more severe. In addition to the fifteen-year occupation of the left bank of the Rhine and the demilitarization of a zone thirty miles wide on the right bank, the Allies sought in all possible ways to prevent Germany from ever again becoming a major military power. They forbade it to build offensive weapons, such as airplanes and submarines, and they limited the German army to a small professional force of 100,000 men. They imposed an equally drastic ceiling on the navy and added the provision that Germany surrender by far the larger part of its merchant fleet. The costs of occupation were, of course, to be borne by the Germans themselves.

Finally, there were the reparations clauses. In the definitive text of the treaty, the total sum to be paid still remained unspecified. All the Germans knew was that in the next two years they must somehow turn over five billion dollars; at the end of that time, they would learn the final bill. And should they ever question why they were paying these vast sums, there was always Article 231, the famous "war guilt" clause of the treaty, to remind them.

The Minor Treaties: Saint-Germain, Trianon, Neuilly, Sèvres

The settlements with Germany's allies followed the general pattern of the Treaty of Versailles (see Map 4.1). They too provided for territorial losses, military restrictions, and reparations payments. In each case, however, there were significant local differences.

Austria and Hungary, now left destitute as small and separate states, signed their own separate treaties. The Treaty of Saint-Germain with Austria dealt with a state that did not want to be a nation at all. With its empire gone, "Austria" had lost its meaning. It now consisted of no more than its old Alpine and Danubian provinces, which had a German-speaking population. These people could see no other recourse than to merge with their neighbors of similar speech by joining the German Reich. But this solution the Allies forbade. They obliged the German Austrians to go their way alone. They added to the Austrian sense of injury, moreover, by leaving within the boundaries of the new state of Czechoslovakia three million German-speaking Bohemians and Moravians. The vast majority of these Sudeten Germans, as they were later called, never reconciled themselves to the rule of a Slavic people whom they considered their cultural inferiors.

In a territorial sense, the Treaty of Trianon with Hungary was the harshest of all, for by conceding the maximum claims of Czechoslovakia, Romania, and Yugoslavia, it deprived the historic kingdom of Hungary of more than two thirds of its area and left one third of all ethnic Hungarians outside its borders. No plebiscites were permitted to determine the wishes of this displaced population. As a British official remarked, harshly but candidly, to a Hungarian representative in Paris at the time, Allied leaders "had more important things to worry about than the fate of ten million people in Hungary." Thus the country was stripped of much of its resources and left to its fate. During the whole interwar period, the Treaty of Trianon occupied the foreground of the Hungarian national consciousness. Flags were flown permanently at half mast and "No, no, never" became the patriotic slogan—the refusal to accept for one moment the shame of the most humiliating peace treaty of modern times.

The Treaty of Neuilly with Bulgaria was mild in comparison. It gave Bulgaria's Aegean seacoast to Greece and smaller portions of territory to Yugoslavia and Romania, thus reducing the country still further from its already contracted borders of 1913. The final peace settlement—the Treaty of Sèvres with Turkey—ratified the liberation of the Arab states, the more important of which simply exchanged one foreign master for another by becoming Class A mandates of Britain and France. This loss the Turks were willing to accept, but when the Allies tried to carry out the terms of their secret treaties by carving up Asia Minor itself—the homeland of the Turkish people—nationalist sentiment rebelled. By the time the sultan, after long delays, finally accepted the treaty in August 1920, the Turkish nationalists were already in arms against it. From the moment of its signature, the Treaty of Sèvres was a dead letter.

MAP 4.1 The postwar territorial settlement.

A Critique

The settlement of 1919 has occasioned more debate than almost any other issue of contemporary European history. It has been attacked as a great betrayal of all that Wilson stood for and defended as the best that could be obtained under the circumstances, including by far the fairest delimitation of frontiers that Europe had ever known. Both contentions are justified, for each depends on where one lays the emphasis and on which of the specific terms of the treaties one chooses to focus.

Even a generous historian, however, must make at least one major criticism: The reparations imposed on Germany were both unjust and impossible to collect, and the "war guilt" statement that sought to justify them was a radical distortion of the actual origins of the conflict. This is what the great British economist John Maynard Keynes argued in his masterly polemic *The Economic Consequences of the Peace*, in which he poured out all the pent-up wrath of an expert whose advice had been flouted. The reparations clauses in turn suggest one cardinal fault of the treaties as a whole—their neglect of the economic aspects of settlement and their almost exclusive concentration on national and territorial questions. Thus in their haste to accept the liberation of East Central Europe, the peacemakers of 1919 did not pay sufficient attention to what they were doing to the economy of the area. They forgot that the Austro-Hungarian Empire, despite all its faults, had given economic unity to the Danube Basin, and that if the empire must end, something must be found to replace it. The demise of the Austro-Hungarian Empire now left Germany the dominant economic power in the region.

It should also be added that although the boundaries drawn in 1919 conformed more closely to the linguistic frontiers of Europe than any before or since, in case of doubt the peacemakers almost invariably resolved the conflict in favor of the victors or their newly created allies. And doubtful cases were legion in East Central Europe, where different nationalities frequently lived inextricably entangled. In certain disputed regions, Wilson had insisted on plebiscites, for example in northern Schleswig and in Upper Silesia. But Wilson well knew that in a number of critical areas, such as the South Tyrol and the border rim of Bohemia, he and his colleagues had directly violated the wishes of the inhabitants. For these major injustices—and for all the others that the passage of time might reveal—he relied on the machinery of the new League of Nations as the ultimate corrective.

The greatest disappointment of the whole peace settlement was the failure of the League to fill the place in international affairs for which the American president had intended it. And this was less the fault of the Europeans than of Wilson's own countrymen. In March 1920, the American Senate refused to ratify the Treaty of Versailles, largely because of the Covenant of the League of Nations, which, as Wilson had insisted, formed an integral part of it. He had already had the Covenant substantially modified, and he refused to accept the further amendments that might have saved the treaty as a whole.

With the United States out of the League and withdrawn into the new isolation of the 1920s, Britain and, more particularly, France were left to carry out the terms of a treaty in which they had never really believed. Moreover, the failure of American ratification also removed the guarantee of aid against potential German aggression with which Wilson and Lloyd George had tried to allay Clemenceau's fears. While the British hesitated, the French quite simply went about converting the peace settlement into what they had wanted from the start. They used the machinery of the League of Nations to protect French security; they made military alliances with the new or newly enlarged nations of East Central Europe; and they held the whip of reparations collections over a prostrate Germany.

Yet in their efforts to prevent a second world war, the framers of the peace settlement ironically made that war more likely by creating a power vacuum in Eastern Europe that none of its guarantors could fill. Despite their promises to the so-called successor states of the Austro-Hungarian Empire, neither the French nor the British were able to offer them real protection should Germany or the Soviet Union challenge the new postwar order. The First World War had been triggered by an incident in Serbia, at the fringes of the continent; the next conflict would likely arise in the new area of potential instability created in the East.

As finally drafted, the Treaty of Versailles had fallen between two stools—it was neither a peace of iron nor a peace of reconciliation. It was neither severe enough to hold down the Germans forever, as the French had desired, nor sufficiently generous to reconcile the vanquished to their new situation. The same was true of the way in which the terms of the treaty were applied. In the early 1920s, when the French tried to enforce the letter of the Versailles settlement, they received insufficient support from the British; after 1924, when the French shifted over to reconciliation, it was too late to eradicate the resentment that had already become fixed in German minds. Such was the final tragedy of the Treaty of Versailles.

V. THE FINAL LIQUIDATION OF THE WAR

The Peace of Paris brought the First World War to its official end, but it did not bring stability to Europe. Numerous areas of conflict remained, and local wars and disturbances continued for four more years. Not until the end of 1923 did the Continent reach a new and precarious equilibrium.

The Local Wars: Poland, Turkey, and the Adriatic

The final adjustment of Poland's frontiers involved both formal warfare and sporadic local fighting that continued for nearly three years after the Treaty of Versailles was signed. In Upper Silesia, a plebiscite held in March 1921 returned a vote of three to two in Germany's favor. At this, the Poles took up arms, German irregular forces responded in kind, and the League of Nations was obliged to step in. A partition of the area resulted: Most of it went to Germany, but the major industrial and mining resources were awarded to Poland.

Meanwhile, the Poles had embroiled themselves in a far more serious conflict with their great neighbor to the east. Poland's eastern frontier had remained unspecified in the settlement of 1919, to which, of course, Bolshevik Russia was not a partner. The Poles themselves demanded a restoration of the eighteenth-century boundaries of the state, including nearly all the Ukraine and White Russia. The Allies, on the other hand, proposed a boundary several hundred miles to the west—called the Curzon Line, after the British foreign secretary who devised it—which ran fairly close to the linguistic frontier. But such a frontier was impossible to establish with any accuracy. In these borderlands, Poles blended imperceptibly into Ukrainians; the landlords tended to be of the former nationality, the peasants of the latter. The Polish government refused to accept the Curzon Line and, in April 1920, attacked Soviet Russia to enforce its claims. This local war in turn became part of the civil war and foreign intervention that were currently wracking the Soviet state. At first the Poles succeeded in occupying most of the Ukraine, but then the Red Army turned on them and advanced nearly to Warsaw. Only the most stubborn resistance, plus the promise of French military aid, saved the Polish capital.

It was now obvious that neither side could impose its will on the other. In the Treaty of Riga of March 1921, the warring powers resorted to a device that was to become standard after the Second World War: They divided the disputed area along the line at which military operations had come to an end. The result satisfied no one. Neither Poland nor Russia recognized the frontier of 1921 as final. And the same was true of the Germans, who never, even in the most hopeful days of international reconciliation, were prepared to accept their boundary to the east.

The interwar position of Poland was now established—as a client state of France, exposed to the merciless enmity of its neighbors to the east and to the west. Should French help ever falter, the Poles were doomed. As early as 1922, with the final delimitation of Poland's frontiers, the double threat to its existence that eventually precipitated the Second World War was already fully evident.

Similarly in Turkey, the settlement reached at Paris proved only temporary; the Treaty of Sèvres never came into effect. The nationalist leader Mustapha Kemal (subsequently called Atatürk) refused to accept its provisions. A new Turkish regime, he argued, should not be shackled by the mistakes of the moribund Ottoman Empire. He therefore attacked the Greeks, who had already landed in Asia Minor to take over the lands that the Allies had awarded them; he fought off their further advances, driving them back to the Aegean; and he deposed the sultan, whose authority in the meantime had virtually ceased to exist. Thus the wartime Allies, hopelessly divided in their attitude toward resurgent Turkey, were obliged to draft a new settlement. The Treaty of Lausanne, in July 1923, restored Turkish authority over all Asia Minor and the area around Constantinople.

With the Treaty of Lausanne and the proclamation of a republic that same year, Turkey completed its postwar metamorphosis. It was no longer a decrepit empire, struggling to maintain a hated dominion over far-flung regions of alien speech. It had become a compact national state, bent on rapid modernization and adaptation to Western norms. Atatürk and his Nationalist followers brought in universal suffrage, a parliament, and president as head of state, with strict separation between church and state. They urged Turkish women to put aside the veil, and forbade polygamy; Western dress was encouraged, the Roman alphabet adopted, and the legal system revised in accordance with Swiss law. At the same time, however, the exchange of populations between Turkey and Greece—with each country expelling hundreds of thousands of citizens belonging to the opposing ethnic group—further embittered relations between Turkey and its nearest Western neighbor.

Finally, there remained the supremely vexing problem of the city of Fiume and the Dalmation shore. The Italian government tacitly renounced the latter but kept up a futile annexationist propaganda for the seaport itself. After the question had hung fire for three months, the nationalist poet D'Annunzio, enraged by the indecision of his government, decided to take over Fiume himself, with the aid of a strange crew of war veterans and adventurers. For more than a year he governed it in eccentric and dictatorial fashion. At the end of 1920, the Italian government, by then in less nationalist hands, came to an amicable agreement with Yugoslavia for establishing Fiume, like Danzig, as a free city, and proceeded to expel D'Annunzio from its administration. But this agreement in turn was in effect for only fifteen months before it was overthrown by a Fascist coup. And when Mussolini himself came to power, he formally annexed Fiume to Italy.

Germany: Reparations and the Ruhr

Of all the undecided questions that disturbed Europe during the four years following the signature of the peace treaties, the problem of Germany itself was naturally the most important. And the central feature of this problem was the collection of reparations.

At first it seemed as if postwar Germany was settling into a peaceful democratic course. The elections to the constituent assembly, held in January 1919, gave a crushing majority to the three parties that had sponsored the Peace Resolution of 1917—the

Renegade German soldiers occupy government buildings in Berlin during the Kapp Putsch, 1923. (*Courtesy Bundesarchiv, Koblenz*)

Catholic Center, the Democrats, and the Social Democrats. The constitution that resulted from their labors was in the Western democratic mold. But this constitution had been in effect for less than a year when a new period of troubles began. In March 1920, a rightist coup—the Kapp Putsch—temporarily won control of Berlin, and a few days later the Communists took up arms in the Ruhr.

Threatened as it was from both the right and the left, the government also had to contend with the problem of reparations. After a series of conferences between the Allies and Germany failed to arrive at agreement on the amount and manner of payment, the French took matters into their own hands; in March 1921, they occupied three industrial cities in the Ruhr Valley. Thus coerced, the Germans accepted the Allied reparations bill—finally fixed in May at 33 billion dollars—and proceeded to pay as best they could.

For a year and a half, a coalition government under a Center chancellor struggled to fulfill the reparations terms of the treaty. By the end of 1922, the Germans would bear no more. The government's reluctance to impose restraints on the business community was already inducing a severe inflation of the mark, and the Allies refused to renew a moratorium that had eased the strain for a few months. In December, Germany defaulted. The next month the French and Belgians—this time totally unsupported by the British—proceeded to occupy the entire Ruhr.

The 1923 occupation of the Ruhr marked both the climax and the end of the postwar time of troubles. Initially it awakened a wave of patriotic revulsion. Rallying behind a new ministry of nonparty experts and industrialists, the German people resorted to passive resistance. Railroad workers, government officials, and factory hands alike refused to cooperate with the French occupiers, hoping thereby to bring Germany's most heavily industrialized area to a standstill. The French in turn tried to coerce the Germans by operating the Ruhr mines and railroads for their own benefit. French soldiers arrested and imprisoned the strikers.

Hoping to deprive the French of the Ruhr's riches, Germans suddenly discovered that they themselves could ill afford the loss. Strikes and mass arrests in the Ruhr created a ripple effect of unemployment throughout the country. Over four fifths of the nation's coal, for example, came from the Ruhr coal mines, which now stood idle. It began to dawn on a growing number of Germans that shooting oneself in the economic foot, even for patriotic motives, might be too high a price to pay for continuing to reist French occupation. The French, meanwhile, found the costs of occupation mounting, though they managed to extract little of value from the industries they now controlled.

In the end, both the French and German governments were forced to retreat over the Ruhr crisis. Coercion did not pay, and passive resistance brought on more evils than the occupation itself. The German state almost dissolved, as Communists, nationalist fanatics, and separatists working for the French contended with each other in a confused, many-sided civil war. In more than one area, starvation threatened. And to support the hundreds of thousands whom passive resistance had thrown out of work, the German government printed paper money faster and faster as the mark went into the wildest inflation that the world had yet seen.

By late summer, both sides were sick of the struggle. In September, a new German ministry under Gustav Stresemann called off passive resistance. At the same time the French were coming around to a more realistic assessment of their reparations claims. As the year 1923 drew to a close, the era of postwar stabilization was already in sight.

READINGS

Pierre Renouvin, in *War and Aftermath, 1914–1929* (1968), sketches a general portrait of European diplomacy during and after the war, as does William R. Keylor (see readings for Chapter 1). The effect of Wilson's policies on the dissolution of the Austro-Hungarian Empire is traced in Sked (see readings for Chapter 1), Z. A. B. Zeman, *The Break-up of the Hapsburg Empire, 1914–1918* (1961; reprint ed., 1971), and in Victor S. Mamatey, *The United States and East Central Europe, 1914–1918* (1957). An older account, inspired by both national patriotism and a Europe-wide cultural experience, is Thomas Garrigue Masaryk, *The Making of State* (1927), by the founder of Czechoslovakia.

The finest overall account of the Paris peace conference, combining impressive scholarship with a superb narrative, is Margaret MacMillan, *Paris 1919* (2001). Harold Nicolson's *Peacemaking 1919*, new ed. (1945) is the sprightly and revealing diary of a participant. Arthur Walworth, *Wilson and His Peacemakers: American Diplomacy and the Paris Peace Conference, 1919* (1986) stresses the American perspective. In his *Politics and Diplomacy of Peacemaking* (1967), Arno J. Mayer argues that the Bolshevik menace dominated the conference behind the scenes, while Piotr S. Wandycz, in *France and Her Eastern Allies, 1919–1925* (1962), traces the alliance system that resulted from this fear. Efraim and Inari Karsh, *Empires of the Sand: The Struggle for Mastery in the Middle East, 1789–1923** (1999), stresses the indigenous causes for the breakup of the Ottoman Empire and downplays European responsibility for ensuing instability in the region.

For a spirited and scholarly account of the Germany in the last phases of the war and the negotiation of the armistice itself, see Klaus Epstein, *Matthias Erzberger and the Dilemma of German Democracy* (1959; reprint ed., 1971). A more popular but worthwhile study is Richard M. Watt, *The Kings Depart: The Tragedy of Germany—Versailles and the German Revolution* (1968). Other studies of the negotiations from the point of view of the separate participants include René Albrecht-Carrié, *Italy at the Paris Conference* (1938; reprint ed., 1966); Ivo J. Lederer, *Yugoslavia at the Paris Peace Conference* (1964); and Sally Marks, *Innocent Abroad: Belgium at the Paris Peace Conference of 1919* (1981).

The classic denunciation of the economics of the treaties is John Maynard Keynes, *The Economic Consequences of the Peace* (1920), to which should be added the reply by a French economist, Etienne Mantoux, *The Carthaginian Peace, or the Economic Consequences of Mr. Keynes* (1946; reprint ed., 1978). Mark Trachtenberg, *Reparations in World Politics: France and European Economic Diplomacy, 1916–1923* (1980) provides an excellent modern summation of the issues.

*Volumes marked with an asterisk are available in paperback.

TECHNOLOGY
AND SOCIETY: BETWEEN
OLD AND NEW

A British family and friends pose proudly beside their new automobiles during an excursion to the country in the 1920s. The freedom brought by motor transport and the expansion of leisure time made such pleasures increasingly common in the decade following World War I. *(Courtesy H. Armstrong Roberts)*

The first years of the twentieth century brought with them a second industrial revolution that was to substitute for the nineteenth-century dominance of coal and iron a cleaner, lighter, and speedier technology typified by the automobile and the airplane, synthetic products, and the radio. The earlier technology—with its connotations of dirt and heavy labor—had separated European society into two sharply differentiated classes of proletarians and owners, those who performed the drudgery of industrial production as against those who managed them and lived on the proceeds of their toil. Under the aegis of the new technology, this division would become less clear-cut. The primacy of heavy industry was to be challenged by lighter and more specialized products, and production itself was to lose its old exclusive importance, as management and distribution absorbed more and more time and personnel. In this new technological and industrial situation, clerks and technicians would begin to take the place of factory hands and heavy labor; a blurring of class lines would naturally follow. And the result would be a de facto democratization of life far more real and deep than anything that the radical political leaders of the previous century had been able to bring about. The new society of abundance was also to be a society of greater equality.

Yet this change came about neither rapidly nor smoothly. Too many of the old attitudes toward class distinctions and the place of women in society remained for the transition to be easy. The war itself, while it forced massive population shifts and spurred advances in technology, also fostered a postwar feeling of deep nostalgia for the prewar years. Many survivors hoped that the war would prove to be merely a parenthesis which, now safely closed, would permit the return to a settled, stratified, deferential society unthreatened by change. Thus they vigorously resisted the pace at which Europe was being transformed into something new. From the vantage point of the 1920s, it often seemed that the comfortable familiarity of "the way it was before the war" was a loss that nothing could replace. The inability of Europeans to come to terms with the new society—in contrast with their frank acceptance of change after the Second World War—was to be a major source of domestic tension during the interwar period.

I. THE NEW TECHNOLOGY

The Pace of Change

The experience of the First World War greatly accelerated the changes, both social and technological, that were already evident in the immediate prewar era. The necessities of combat and of economic mobilization acted as a spur to invention and to boldness in the exploitation of unorthodox methods. The army itself—with its regimentation, training in the use of new weapons, and enforced health measures such as mass innoculation—imposed new, uniform patterns of thought and action on recruits drawn from widely disparate backgrounds. For the many peasant soldiers conscripted into the French, German, and Russian armies, the war experience tore them from familiar surroundings and thrust them into unexpected roles. The language they were expected to comprehend and to speak while in uniform was not the dialect of their native villages but a standard national tongue that many at first found unfamiliar and difficult. The reading skills needed to decipher written orders, the mechanical skills required to repair damaged trucks and guns, the mathematical skills necessary for artillery placement and accuracy of aim—all these were learned of necessity by young men who had had scant formal schooling before. The army thus became in time the "school of the nation."

On the home front, too, the factories needed to supply munitions and materiel were often places where new skills and attitudes were learned during the war years, especially by the many women workers replacing men called to active service. Change in old habits was possible: This in itself became one of the chief lessons taught both in the trenches and on the factory floor. Those who had tasted such changes often found it difficult to content themselves with traditional forms of rural or domestic life once the war ended.

The most obvious area where technology raced ahead during the war concerned innovations that could aid the national military effort. Military requirements for aerial reconnaissance first brought the airplane into its own, where it proved far superior to the cavalry traditionally used to probe enemy defenses. The British blockade stimulated the development of synthetic products, such as chemical nitrates, in Germany. The case of the automobile was similar. At the outbreak of the conflict, horse-drawn vehicles predominated in the streets and on the highways of Europe; by the end of the war, the reverse was true. The armies had gone into battle almost wholly dependent on horse transport; when the fighting ended, although the artillery was still horse drawn, the success of trucks and tanks and motorized ambulances had convinced even the most conservative that the future lay with the internal combustion engine. The first Battle of the Marne had been won in part thanks to the fleet of taxicabs mobilized to ferry French soldiers from Paris to the nearby battlefield; more impressive in terms of a sustained effort was the resupply mission undertaken by thousands of trucks along the *voie sacrée* at Verdun after the Germans had cut the rail lines. In both cases, motorized transport brought victory.

The same speeding-up of development was apparent in the case of technical innovations that had found a less direct application to war needs—electric power and radio, for example, and the newly invented motion picture. The 1920s saw the decisive shift to electricity in field after field. By the end of the decade, an urban building without electricity was considered disgracefully old-fashioned, and the electrification of the countryside had become a major goal of all nations that wished to be in the technological vanguard. Even Lenin—hampered as he was by the backward condition of Russian society—had proclaimed rural electrification as one of the first tasks of the new regime. When once asked to define what Bolshevism stood for, he replied, "Electrification and soviets!"

Motion pictures and radio, forms of entertainment that before 1914 had been only rare and exciting novelties, were already commonplace by the mid-1920s. Going to motion pictures had become the usual form of cheap entertainment in all except the smallest towns and villages; no prosperous home was now without its radio set. By the end of the decade another innovation—the talking motion picture—began to transform still further the range and character of mass entertainment.

Two other means of communication whose development had been speeded by the war left their mark on the 1920s: the illustrated tabloid press, and the gramophone. Both owed their invention to Americans. Popular journalism featuring banner headlines, simple text, and lavish use of pictorial material had been pioneered in the United States by William Randolph Hearst in the 1890s; Thomas Edison had earlier invented the gramophone in 1877. During the First World War, the propaganda potential of an illustrated daily newspaper had not escaped European governments eager to intensify the war effort on the home front. Here Britain took the lead, with papers such as the *Daily Express* and the *Daily Mail* offering their readers extensive photo coverage of the war. During the next decade the development of lighter cameras, the telephoto lens, and flashbulbs further spurred news photography to the point that even the staid *Times* of London published its first picture page in 1922.

By making music independent of the vaudeville stage or the concert hall, the gramophone likewise found a mass audience in the 1920s. Troops had listened to patriotic songs such as the British "It's a Long Way to Tipperary" in the trenches during the war, where the music helped to lessen the boredom of life behind the lines, as it did on the home front. With the return of peace, the popularity of recorded music soared. Even before motion pictures reached small towns, gramophones played scratchy recordings of everything from popular dance tunes to Enrico Caruso's interpretation of Verdi arias. Jazz orchestras and opera alike suddenly reached a far larger and more diverse audience than ever before.

These inventions had their most dramatic impact on rural living after the war. No longer were country dwellers so isolated—so cut off, as they formerly had been, by a wall of mutual incomprehension—from the ways of the great cities. In the 1920s both new forms of entertainment and new means of communication began to bring the peasantry into unprecedentedly close contact with the metropolis. Rural bus lines linked villages that even the smallest railways had never touched, and year after year the telephone network was extended to ever more remote communities.

These new means of communication also began to reach out across national and continental frontiers. If Europeans were slower than Americans to improve and extend their highways—a country like France, for instance, already had a fine road network, well-fitted to the first generation of the automobile—they moved faster in developing commercial aviation. As early as 1919, two British pilots made the first transatlantic flight. Only a few years later, regular commercial service was inaugurated between major European cities. When American flying was still largely limited to military uses and carrying the mails, air travel was becoming a normal mode of transport for Europeans. From 1920—when the Dutch instituted a regular air service between Amsterdam and London—each year saw the opening of some new line linking the European capitals. By the end of the decade, Europeans were inaugurating more remote services to their Asian and African colonies. Only on the eve of the Second World War, however, were Europe and the United States—which had been connected by telephone since 1927—to be linked by a regular air service.

In the United States, the exploitation of the new methods of communication and transport was usually left to private enterprise; competition and independent initiative were the rule. In Europe, on the contrary, the government almost always stepped in, either to run the new service itself or to enforce a monopoly. Radio broadcasting, on the model of the BBC, founded in 1922, was thus nearly invariably monopolized by the state, and commercial aviation was farmed out to individual companies on a noncompetitive basis.

What was noteworthy about technological innovation in the decade following the First World War was not simply the rapidity with which change occurred, but the pervasiveness of its effects. In part, this was because one did not need to be wealthy to enjoy these new inventions. The daily newspaper, moving pictures, and rural bus service were within the reach of most; gramophones, wireless sets, telephone service, even the automobile declined rapidly in price during the 1920s as mass production introduced lower prices through economies of scale.

Equally important for the broad impact of the new technology, however, was its accessibility to the uneducated. By substituting pictures for text, tabloid journalism communicated its message even to those whose reading skills were rudimentary; moving pictures, especially after the advent of sound, demanded no reading skills whatever. Telephones allowed subscribers to communicate without writing. And whereas one needed musical training to play the piano or cornet, a gramophone allowed anyone to "play" Tchaikovsky or Scott Joplin merely by placing a needle in a groove. The result was a widespread democratization of culture—a process whose effects are still being felt today.

The Rationalization of Production

In the field of production and technology, "rationalization" became the slogan of the decade. From one standpoint, this effort also reflected the war experience, since military exigencies had dictated a search for more efficient solutions and the postwar reconstruction of war-devastated plants and mines had given free scope for innovation. From another standpoint, the drive for rationalization offered further evidence of America's new prestige and influence. For the models of efficiency that the Europeans copied usually derived from the United States—the chain-belt method of mass production first perfected by Henry Ford; the standardization of parts and supplies, which substituted skilled repairmen for old-fashioned artisans; the "scientific" reorganization of work in the factory, usually called "Taylorization," after Frederick Winslow Taylor, its American inventor; and the exploitation of novel machinery, such as the electric furnace, which reduced the cost of producing light metals like aluminum to a fraction of its former level. In nearly all these techniques and in the wide variety of new products that accompanied them—rayon, plastics, nitrates, and special types of building cement, to cite only a few—the United States had taken the lead.

A similar rationalization, but at a much slower pace, was also occurring in the countryside. Here, too, the war accelerated developments already in progress. The peasantry, second only to the aristocracy, had suffered the heaviest war losses. At the end of the fighting, a real shortage of rural manpower began to appear for the first time in history in such countries as Britain, France, and Germany, and with it a pressure to consolidate holdings, to introduce farm machinery, even to abandon the cultivation of marginal land. Moreover, the peasants now had the money to make such improvements, for the food shortages of the war and immediate postwar periods had resulted in high prices for farm goods, and in many areas, small farmers were able to wipe out almost entirely their traditional burden of debt. Meantime, the long-term drift of young people to the cities continued—reinforced, in the postwar years, by the psychological shocks of the conflict itself and the growth of new and attractive types of white-collar employment.

But changes such as these came at a most uneven pace. The agricultural countries of Southern and Eastern Europe were at first almost untouched by them. Even in the industrialized nations, the process of rationalization affected certain sectors of the economy heavily, while scarcely disturbing the established routines of sectors closely adjacent. In France, for example, the main work of modernization was confined to the areas devastated by the recent war, such as the textile plants of the north and northeast. In Britain, a dangerous gap opened between the newer industries like electricity, chemicals, automobiles, and aircraft, where equipment was up to date and methods of production rationalized, and the older industries based on coal and iron and textiles, which languished in nineteenth-century inefficiency. Even Germany—the European leader in the propaganda for rationalization—carried the work forward in a disorderly fashion. The great inflation of 1923 enormously stimulated the concentration and cartelization of industry. But not all these new combines could demonstrate their economic rationality. If this rationality were true of "vertical" concentrations, such as the steel trust, the Vereinigte Stahlwerke, founded in 1926, or the great chemical combine I. G. Farben, no argument of utility or efficiency could be made for "horizontal" combinations, like that of the trust-monger Hugo Stinnes, which sprawled octopus-like over the economy, sweeping up such diverse enterprises as chemicals, textiles, forests, and shipping lines along its way.

Furthermore, clear-sighted Europeans well knew that in the race for rationalization they no longer had all the advantages on their side. In this sort of competition, the countries of the New World, more particularly the United States, had a scope for innovation and mass production that Europe could not match. The European market was too small and its economic horizons too narrow—and these handicaps were intensified by a sharp postwar resurgence of economic nationalism. Thus even the countries in the European vanguard were moving forward only within the *European* frame of reference; in the *world* competition, they were falling behind. Germany—to take the outstanding case—by 1928 had recovered its place as second only to the United States in overall industrial production. Despite the loss of the resources of Upper Silesia and the Saar, it had increased its productive capacity by 40 percent of the prewar figure. But its *share* of world production, which had been 17 percent in 1909, had fallen to just over 11 percent at the end of the 1920s.

Yet it was not merely the unavoidable limitations of the European economy that restricted the process of rationalization and the passage to a new type of society. The economic and social effects of the war itself were also at work. For although some of these had acted to speed the pace of change, more of them, as the 1920s wore on, revealed themselves to be both depressing and conservative in their long-range implications.

II. THE SOCIAL AND ECONOMIC EFFECTS OF THE WAR

Population Movements: Refugees and Emigration

The First World War, hardly less than its successor, churned up and dislocated the civilian populations of Europe. Only in the countries of the West did the mass of the people remain untroubled. In Central and Eastern Europe, social revolution and the postwar redrawing of boundaries set millions moving. It is impossible to know how many families, at one time or another, were on the road, driven from their homes by hunger, political terror, or the longing to remain with their fellow nationals.

The Bolshevik Revolution produced the most dramatic migrations. By the end of the civil war, perhaps as many as a million and three quarter Russians had left their country, scattering widely throughout the rest of Europe. A small percentage subsequently returned—but the vast majority remained abroad, the older ones consumed with homesickness and never assimilating with their new environment, the younger gradually merging into the population around them. Paris was the greatest center for this influx and reflected in the arts and in the theater the stimulating innovations that the refugees from Russia brought with them.

In Central Europe, the defeated powers found themselves forced to absorb a mass of refugees who refused to accept the new allegiances imposed by the boundaries of 1919. In the post-Versailles years, Germany experienced a foretaste of a problem it was to face on a far, far greater scale after 1945—the incorporation into a nation with diminished territory of hundreds of thousands whose homes now lay beyond its borders. The vast majority of these—nearly three quarters of a million—came from the lands awarded to Poland, but there were also more than 100,000 Germans who had settled in Alsace-Lorraine after 1871 and now declined to live under French rule. The absorption of this additional population proved comparatively painless: A great industrial state like Germany was accustomed to internal migrations, and a few years after the war its economic expansion was able to take up the slack. But in the case of small and agrarian Hungary, an added population of 400,000 from its border regions imposed a severe strain. The presence of this undigested mass of discontented refugees suggests a further reason why the Hungarians never accepted their new boundaries as defined in the Treaty of Trianon.

The Greeks and the Turks eventually agreed to a massive exchange of populations. Although this device was copied elsewhere on a smaller scale, it was not able to regularize all the anomalies of citizenship that the war had produced. Many postwar refugees—unwanted in their new homes—never succeeded in achieving secure legal status. Thus the 1920s produced that new and pathetic symbol of contemporary society, the "stateless person," the refugee without a passport, the scarcely tolerated dweller in a foreign land who could be expelled at any moment by the whim of some dictator or petty bureaucrat.

Such were the direct effects of the war and the postwar settlement. Among the indirect effects, the restriction of emigration to the United States was probably the most important. The American quota laws of 1921 and 1924 abruptly halted a process that had become a normal part of Europe's population rhythm. Over the course of centuries, Europeans had become accustomed to seeing the adventurous and the unwanted among them emigrate overseas. More particularly, in poor peasant areas emigration had acted as an essential safety valve on the pressure of population. As this pressure mounted with each passing decade of the nineteenth century, the small streams of overseas migrants grew to a mighty torrent. In 1913, about two million Europeans left for overseas, the greater part of them bound for the United States; subsequently, with the lifting of wartime restrictions on transport, 800,000 more poured into the United States alone.

At this point, the American Congress took alarm. The result was the quota system, which in its final form fixed the number of annual arrivals at 2 percent of the total residents of each national origin in the United States in 1890. By setting this as the governing date, the law of 1924 favored the countries of older emigration while choking off immigration from Southern and Eastern Europe—for only in the quarter century before the war had arrivals from these areas reached large proportions. Thus the American quota system worked almost diametrically contrary to Europe's needs: Poor lands like Italy and Poland, from which literally millions would have liked to emigrate, found immigration into the United States almost completely stopped; the richer lands of the West—notably Great Britain—which, enjoyed ample quotas, did not fill their totals.

There remained, of course, the other major areas of overseas settlement—South America and the British dominions. In the decade of the 1920s, Argentina received just under a million and a half immigrants, and Brazil, 840,000. But more than half of these, dissatisfied with their new conditions of living, returned to Europe, and the million-odd that remained were only a fraction of those that the United States would have been able to absorb in the same period. Nor did the British dominions provide an adequate substitute—for these, like the United States, had begun to restrict immigration in order to favor people of Anglo-Saxon or northern European origin.

Thus postwar Europe was largely left to cope with its population problem unaided. Fortunately, one land of traditional immigration had increased rather than reduced its readiness to receive strangers from beyond its borders. This was France—the only great country of Europe that before the war had been notably underpopulated, and whose war losses left it with a severe shortage of personnel. In the 1920s, France's population was stable and even declining; its birthrate was failing to keep up with its deaths. Had it not been for the more than a million and a half foreign workers whom France received in the years from 1920 to 1928—most of them from Italy, Poland, Switzerland, and Belgium—the country would have been less populous at the outbreak of the Second World War in 1939 than it had been when it faced the First World War a generation earlier. And even in its situation of demographic stability, France found its military manpower decreasing, as the average age of its people steadily rose.

Between 1913 and 1928, the population of Europe—despite the losses of the war—grew from 498 to 534 million, a net gain of 36 million. But this gain was very unevenly distributed: Germany experienced substantial increases, but Britain and France grew scarcely at all; the largest share of the increase came in the poor peasant areas of Italy and East Central Europe. These lands, however, could not cope with their growing populations. Unable to industrialize adequately and with emigration largely cut off, they let their surplus people remain on the farms—with depressing effects on rural wages, the standard of living, and the whole morale of the countryside.

In the nineteenth century, the growth of population had acted to spur economic initiative. In countries like Britain, France, and Germany, the new industries of the cities had drained off the rural excess and mobilized it for production. After 1920, on the contrary, both population stability and population gain seemed to act as social and economic depressants. In the former situation—which was characteristic of the advanced industrial societies of the West, with the notable exception of Germany—a stable population became associated with economic stagnation. In a situation of growth—characteristic of the south and east—the new population could find no suitable employment. Here once again, although the possibilities of progress were present, Europe became snarled in a complex web of short-run difficulties, from which, for the better part of a generation, it could find no escape.

Boom and Bust, 1917–1922

By the midpoint of the First World War, abnormal economic conditions in nations mobilized for combat had begun to change substantially the standard of living and the relative position of classes within the European population. Initially, factory workers had suffered, since wages failed to keep pace with mounting costs. By 1917, however, these discrepancies had largely disappeared. In that year, the French cost-of-living index (with 1914 as 100) stood at 180, and wages at 170. On paper, then, there was still a slight gap between the two. But family income had now pulled ahead, since overtime pay had become usual and more members of working-class families had found jobs. Thus, family take-home pay, including overtime hours and the wages of wives and daughters, was far higher, in real terms, at the end of the war than it had been at the start.

The effect of this change, if it had continued—as it was in fact to do after the Second World War—would have been to reinforce the democratic currents within European society. It had already stimulated the confidence of the working classes in the months immediately following the Armistice. But the postwar boom came to a very rapid end. As soon as the immediate needs of reconstruction and the accumulated backlog of nonmilitary orders had been filled, a short but severe depression set in. The end of 1920 found all the Western nations contending with the same problems: sagging currencies, stagnating production, and massive unemployment.

By 1922 recovery had begun. But it was to be slow and hesitant, and the confident rhythm of the immediate postwar years was never to be regained—as was reflected in the timorousness of European trade-union and Socialist leadership in the years of apparent stability. In rather different fashion, the same tone prevailed among the salaried middle class. One of the threatening and depressing features of the society of the 1920s was that both the working classes and the white-collar workers were nursing profound economic grievances.

For the salaried middle class, the war had brought little but hardship. Like the workers, people in this group had suffered severely from the price rise in the early part of the conflict but, in contrast to industrial labor, they found no compensation in the later years. Clerical and professional salaries continued to lag behind steadily mounting prices. In France, the pay of civil servants rose scarcely 50 percent during the war, while the cost of living almost doubled. But this was not all. Even lower middle-class people, unlike the workers, usually had savings in addition to their salaries. And savings were still more dangerously undermined than were wages and salaries by the economic dislocations of the war.

All the governments except the British had financed their military effort in reckless and haphazard fashion—mostly by printing paper money. With the coming of peace, the bill had to be paid somehow. In the immediate postwar years, governments shifted and tacked and tried to avoid facing up to the inevitable. For a while—at least in the victor countries—the illusion persisted that reparations from Germany would solve the problem. By 1923 this illusion had vanished. One after another the nations of Europe defaulted on their obligations—a few, like Soviet Russia, by simply refusing to recognize the debts incurred by the previous regime, but most by a currency inflation of varying proportions. In Britain alone inflation was minimal; by the mid-1920s the pound had been restored to its prewar relation to the dollar. In France and Italy, on the other hand, three quarters of the previous value of money was wiped out. And in the defeated nations—Austria, Hungary, and Germany—the old currency ceased to exist as the economy plunged into an inflationary crisis that shook European society more profoundly than any other series of events in the entire decade.

The German Inflation of 1923

This vast social crisis brought about a "proletarization" of the middle class. When the French marched into the Ruhr in early 1923, they precipitated a sweeping change in the relationship of Germany's social classes that had been in the making ever since the war ended. The crisis of 1923 shattered traditional German society. It constituted the real German revolution, dividing old from new in a far more profound fashion than had the brief and largely superficial political revolution of 1918.

By the summer of 1923 the mark had become practically worthless (see Figure 5.1). A whole suitcase full of paper money was sometimes needed to settle a small debt, and even this cumbersome fashion of payment soon proved impracticable, as the value of money fell almost from hour to hour. Finally, only payment in kind made sense. Durable goods of intrinsic value stood at a premium; people rushed to buy whatever seemed likely to survive the inflation intact. Under such conditions the regular functioning of the economy became impossible. With advance planning out of the question, trade and production were reduced to the most primitive forms of barter and muddling through from day to day.

In November, the new Stresemann government stabilized the mark at the rate of one trillion old units of currency to one of the new. It was obviously the only thing to be done, but its effects were devastating. Such a drastic reconversion had no precedent in

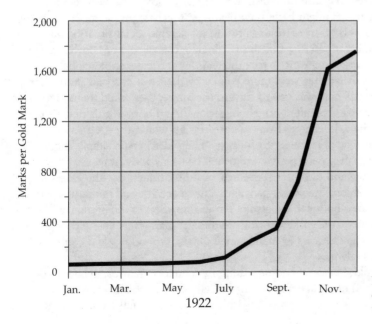

FIGURE 5.1   German inflation. In the course of 1922 alone, the mark lost more than 97 percent of its value.

history; never since the invention of the modern financial system had the face value of money vanished so utterly. In effect, all promises to pay of whatever sort—bank notes, pensions, savings, mortgages, and bonds—had been wiped out completely. Those who had skimped and saved and trusted in their governments and in the future were left without a penny.

Had everyone suffered equally, these losses might have been easier to bear. In fact, however, the German population was divided into those who suffered desperately, those who suffered a little, and those who suffered not at all or even profited by the inflation. In the last category were the major industrialists and stock owners in the more solid industrial concerns. As holders of real rather than paper values, these people rode through the inflation untouched and were in a position to buy up the enterprises of their weaker competitors who had been unable to withstand the financial storm. The inflation of 1923 thus strengthened the tendency toward the concentration of industrial holdings that already characterized the German economy. In the category of moderate sufferers were most industrial workers. Few of these had substantial savings, and most of them were able to return to their previous standard of living once industry began to pay stable wages again. But even they incurred less obvious losses, the results of which were to become apparent only years later. Among the side effects of the inflation were the abolition of the eight-hour day—which had ranked as one of German labor's major postwar gains—and the almost total loss of trade-union treasuries. Together, these two changes helped intensify that mood of defeat which had settled upon European labor after 1920 and which, a decade later, was to be responsible for the apathy and disunion of the German working classes in the face of the Nazi menace.

The greatest sufferers were the lower middle class. In economic terms, the inflation had "proletarized" a large part of them—had reduced them to a level as low (or even lower) than that of the industrial workers. In psychological terms, however, the effect was rather different. Indeed, had the proletarization of the middle class been emotional as well as financial, the results might have been healthier, for these people might then have been united with the workers in protest against an intolerable social situation and in resistance to the oncoming of fascism. But this the middle class would not do. They nursed their grievances in isolation, refusing to face the realities of their economic plight.

The truth was that they were more pained by their loss of social status than by their financial disaster. Whom was one to trust in the future, they asked themselves, now that their government had defaulted on its obligations? And how, in this new situation, could they cling to their differences from the proletariat, which they felt so deeply but which they no longer had the money to support? The older people simply shook their heads in bewilderment; the young people went their own way without regard for their elders. Hence both young and old were consumed with dissatisfaction—the elders in passive and pessimistic fashion, the young people in a more activist and militant mood that led them to seek out new political leadership. An examination of the origins of German fascism shows that some of the earliest recruits to the Nazi party were young people of the lower middle class, former officers or men trained for the professions who could find no proper outlet for their talents.

Young and old, however, had one thing in common: their passionate nationalism. The old liberal and rational explanations had failed them; the newer Marxist explanations they rejected with scorn. They saw only the nation to fall back on, and in its hour of defeat they identified the national humiliation with their own. The result was what psychologists call *projection*: "Instead of being aware of the economic and social fate of the old middle class, its members consciously thought of their fate in terms of the nation. The national defeat and the Treaty of Versailles became the symbols to which the actual frustration—the social one—was shifted."*

The Limits to Recovery and the Narrowing of Economic Horizons

By 1924 European society and the European economy seemed to be over the hump. Or, to put it at the very latest, by 1926, when France stabilized its currency and Britain mastered the general strike, things seemed as if they had returned to normal.

In France, the most impressive achievement was the reconstruction of the country's devastated cities and farms. The First World War had been fought in France's most heavily industrialized region. At the end of the war, France found itself with nearly a million destroyed buildings; 9,000 factories were similarly blasted; most of its coal and iron mines were wrecked or flooded; 6,000 bridges were gone; and 1,000 miles of railway lines were put out of use. These losses at first seemed almost as irreplaceable as that of the million and a half young men who had been killed, but, in fact, the French were able to repair their physical damage rather quickly. In this task they were signally aided by the reacquisition of Alsace and Lorraine. The former territory had a well-developed textile industry. The latter possessed some of the finest iron deposits in the world. With the return of Lorraine to France, the country jumped to first place among the iron-producing nations of Europe.

Toward its citizens whose property had been destroyed, the French state behaved with extraordinary generosity. It compensated them not just for the damage they had suffered; it also paid for the complete replacement of their assets, plus suitable improvements and modernization. The results were highly satisfactory from a technical standpoint and made a notable contribution to the postwar rationalization of production, but in architectural terms most of the new building was undistinguished, and its financing was lamentable. The French had hoped that reparations from Germany would cover the bill in full; in the end these accounted for only 40 percent of the total. The rest was paid for through inflation—with social and political results that disillusioned and depressed a whole generation of Frenchmen (see Chapter 6, II).

Across the Rhine, German industry—with the threat of French seizure no longer hanging over it—resumed its customary brisk pace. In the late 1920s, French patriots regularly lamented the fashion in which the defeated enemy was not suffering sufficiently for past sins and was apparently prospering rather more than the victor nations. But German prosperity was more apparent than real. It was entirely dependent on foreign loans—particularly from the United States. Even in the "good" year 1927, the country had a foreign trade deficit of nearly a billion dollars. And this prosperity also proved far more beneficial to the great cartels than it did to the public at large. By the end of the

*Erich Fromm, *Escape from Freedom* (New York: Holt, Rinehart & Winston, 1941), 216.

1920s, such combines as the Vereinigte Stahlwerke and I. G. Farben effectively dominated the German economy. The former grouped together more than half the country's steel-producing capacity—a capacity equivalent to that of the whole of Great Britain. The latter, with its 300,000 employees, ranked as the largest trust in the world.

By 1925, the national incomes of the major countries of Western and Central Europe had returned to their prewar level. During the next four years, this figure rose an average of 30 percent. In the conditions of the late 1920s, however, increases of such an order were insufficient; they could not keep up with world competition. For in this crucial half decade, the newest powers like the United States and Japan were pulling ahead.

Here again, there is a direct relation between the war and a European economic recovery that could not generate a self-sustained advance. In four years of conflict, Europe had consumed its economic fat; it had eaten up its savings. No longer could it produce a large surplus of funds for investment overseas. French overseas holdings were only half what they had been in 1913; Britain, which had invested 160 million pounds abroad in the seven years preceding the war, invested only 45 million pounds overseas between 1920 and 1927. With this reduction of foreign investments went a corresponding loss of revenue from trade and transshipment. During the war years, the producing nations of Asia and the Americas grew accustomed to dealing with each other directly, rather than resorting to the British or French as middlemen. They began the generation-long process of breaking loose from European financial and commercial dominance. In the 1920s, the total volume of world trade in manufactured products—which had tripled between 1870 and 1913—remained practically stationary; *European* trade had sensibly diminished.

In those same prewar decades, the rate of growth of European industrial production had averaged more than 3 percent annually; in the 1920s, it hovered just over 1 percent. Once again, the mental attitude of societies just emerging from the world conflict was responsible. Rather than enlarging the horizons of political leaders and businessmen—as it was to do after 1945—the war experience seemed to have narrowed them; in the 1920s the economic directors of the Western European nations could think of nothing better than to revert to old routines. Thus in Britain, both the government and the Bank of England ranked it as a great triumph when in 1925 the country succeeded in returning to the prewar gold standard. They failed to see that this restoration of financial orthodoxy was a hollow victory that hurt rather than improved Britain's economic situation. By overvaluing the pound in relation to other currencies, thereby raising the price of British goods, the return to gold increased the difficulties with which the country's foreign trade was already contending.

In short, by the mid-1920s, the pattern of postwar recovery in the major European nations was already established in a partial and unsatisfactory fashion. Germany seemed to be prospering—but this prosperity was frantic and uneven in its distribution. France and Britain, on the other hand, were threatened with industrial stagnation. In both countries, the older industries were settling into chronic depression. This was particularly true in Britain, which, as the oldest industrial power, had the highest percentage of obsolete equipment. Long before the onset of the Great Depression of the 1930s, British industry was already depressed and running on part time; its total volume of exports rose to only three quarters of what it had been before the war. Throughout the decade, whole areas of the country in the Midlands, Lancashire, and South Wales remained in a state of permanent depression, and the "depressed areas" became a standing reproach to British political leaders of all parties. Here, another new and threatening phenomenon was concentrated—the permanent army of unemployed, which even in the best years never fell below one million, and in most depressed branches of the economy, such as coal mining and textiles, averaged around 16 percent of the working force. The unemployed and their families eked out a miserable existence on what came to be called the "dole"—the extended insurance payments instituted in the depression year of 1921 and subsequently enlarged into a permanent system.

Stagnation in industry found its parallel in stagnation on the farms. By 1925, the good postwar years of European agriculture were over. Now that they had paid off their debts and improved their holdings, landowners and peasants found themselves once again face to face with their old difficulties. In the late 1920s, with the stabilization of the European currencies, interest rates rose and prices fell. Farmers were caught in the familiar squeeze; overproduction threatened, as the prices of staple crops fell on the world market. In country after country, the agricultural population turned to their government for help. The help, when it came, was grudging and insufficient—not sufficient to finance the renewal of an agrarian rationalization program on a planned and massive scale, but just enough to keep afloat a rural population whose political influence far outbalanced its real economic weight.

Such, in sum, was the character of economic policy in the 1920s: patching up, muddling through, insisting on financial orthodoxy whatever the price, hoping against hope that something would break through the stagnation of commerce, the reduced rhythm of industry, and the permanent depression on the farms. By the mid-1920s, the wiser European economic observers had realized that the Continent would never return to "normal," but they could conceive of no alternatives. The renewal of systematic economic thinking and planning had to wait for the Great Depression of the 1930s to sweep away the smugness and illusions of the previous decade.

III. THE NEW SOCIETY

Nevertheless, the society of the 1920s was significantly different from what it had been before the war. It was less tradition bound; it was more democratic; and the relics of the past were regarded as anachronisms by many, rather than as patterns of life to be admired and imitated.

The New White-Collar Class

By the 1920s, the center of gravity of European society had definitely shifted from the countryside to the city. Even France, the most agrarian of the advanced nations, had experienced a major change. The prewar percentage of its working population, which had been slightly under one-half, fell to just over one third in 1931. But this new population of the cities was rather different from what Karl Marx had anticipated. It no longer consisted primarily of "proletarians." In fact, the urban working class, as defined in the nineteenth-century sense, grew scarcely at all after 1900. It remained stationary—for although industry expanded, the productivity of the labor force was also increased, as new and more efficient machines were introduced, and the same work could be done by fewer workers.

What grew, rather, was the new white-collar class. People in this group—who rejected the Marxian scheme of things—reinforced the more conservative and prosperous members of the old working class, who were also turning away from doctrinaire socialism. White-collar workers and the higher ranks of industrial labor swelled the tide of middle-class democratization. In dress, in manners, in thought, they behaved as bourgeois rather than as proletarians. This was only natural; their jobs as managers, office personnel, technicians, and sales staff demanded a comparatively high standard of literacy. They worked behind a desk or a counter, not on the factory floor. Their growing numbers also reflected the increasing role that government was playing in the lives of Europeans of all classes—as that role grew, so did the size of the bureaucracy. In England, where the proportion of white-collar workers was the highest, this group numbered 19 percent of the labor force in 1910, and 24 percent by 1930; in Germany, the figure doubled during this twenty-year period, rising from 9 percent in 1910 to 18 percent in 1930. Thereafter, the growth continued, though less rapidly, until well after the Second World War.

Although class distinctions remained apparent in virtually all of Europe after the First World War, the gap between the classes had perceptibly narrowed. For the first time, something approaching a middle-class style of life had begun to be the norm in the more advanced countries of Central and Western Europe. This leveling effect was not due to the growth of the white-collar class alone. Those on the upper end of the economic scale showed a new reserve in displaying their wealth after the enforced regimentation of the war years. Even for the rich, the war had simplified life: Clothing became less elaborate, servants rare, and entertaining less opulent. The rich, moreover, were no longer the same persons. Many had been impoverished by inflation and high taxes, and their places had been taken by speculators and war profiteers, whose outlook was more plebeian.

To this new social mobility—to this blurring of class lines in the cities—the postwar style of life notably contributed. Manners had become more relaxed, and with them the traditional code of sexual behavior. Almost before anyone was aware of what had happened, Europe had been caught up in the jazz age. Old-fashioned moralists shook their heads as respectable women began to smoke in public and young people demanded and won a freedom that their elders had never known. Symbolic of this new emancipation was the "flapper girl," wearing short hair, short skirts, and provocatively red lipstick. Gone were the confining corsets and many-layered dresses of the prewar era; in a literal sense, young women in the 1920s moved through life without the weight and constraints of the past.

Democratization in fashion was further aided by the increasing availability of inexpensive, ready-made clothing sold to the general public in department stores. Not only was the cut of the clothes aggressively stylish; new synthetic materials allowed customers to create the illusion of an expensive wardrobe for only a modest sum. Chief among these synthetics was rayon—discovered in the 1890s but mass produced only during the First World War. Similar in appearance to silk but costing only a fraction of its price, rayon allowed even a shop girl to dress with something approaching elegance. As more young, single women entered the work force as salaried employees, the number of those with both the disposable income and an interest in dressing smartly rose, which in turn encouraged a further expansion of ready-made apparel. Postwar social changes and changes in taste and merchandising were thus mutually reinforcing.

Were these changes positive? European of the old school condemned them as materialistic, selfish, and immoral. They worried about the "Americanization" of the Continent—threatened by an invasion of jazz, commercial advertising, and silent comedies from Hollywood. But America, though often the source of the new culture, was not to blame for the culture's popularity. A tremendous desire for novelty and entertainment after the privations of the war years existed in Europe, especially among the young. If mass culture was indeed threatening Europe, it was because a sizeable proportion of the European public welcomed the novelty and escapism that it promised them.

Leisure-Time Pursuits

Both the new white-collar class and the old working class benefited from a phenomenon that was to mark the interwar period decisively: the expansion of leisure time. At its origin lay the legislation introduced by several countries immediately after the war to reduce the length of the workday from ten to eight hours. The figure of ten hours already represented progress over the twelve-hour day common in the mid-nineteenth century. But by 1918, this progress seemed meager indeed. As a reward for their patriotic cooperation in the war effort, the labor unions in France and Germany had been promised still further reductions in the workday once the war ended. Their gain benefited not just blue-collar labor, but all salaried employees.

The result was an unprecedented amount of free time at the disposal of a growing segment of the population—those who were neither agricultural workers nor self-employed, but who earned an hourly or weekly wage. Of course, this free time could be spent simply resting at home or loafing about with friends. Yet many sought not simply rest, but entertainment. The new demand for leisure entertainment explains in turn the rapid expansion of the moving picture industry and the sale of recorded music during the 1920s. Another hallmark of the period was the growth of professional spectator sports. Before the war, cycling events such as the Tour de France (begun in 1903) had already attracted huge crowds of spectators in both cities and towns. Now in Western and Central Europe even larger crowds paid good money to see professionals engaged in team sports such as rugby and—the most popular European sport of all—soccer.

The growth of public interest in paid sporting events also reveals the process of democratization at work. Before 1914, a strict hierarchy governed which sports were considered "proper" for which class. Rugby, associated with elite British schools and universities, was considered the proper sport for the upper class. After the First World War, however, it ceased to be identified with the higher social strata alone. By 1930, professional teams offered social (and financial) advancement for talented athletes from the working classes. Only tennis, golf, and polo remained as "upper-class" sports—principally because of the expense they still entailed.

The new white-collar class at its leisure: a beach scene in England in 1935.
(*Courtesy H. Armstrong Roberts*)

Municipal Services

Though the effects of the wartime economy continued to restrict public consumption until the mid-1920s, ordinary citizens in Central and Western Europe on the whole lived better than they had before the war. This improvement in living standards reflected not only the surge in white-collar jobs and the growth of leisure activities, but also an increased willingness of state and local government to provide for the needs of its citizens. Cities had, of course, invested in services as diverse as streetcars and public housing before the war. Now, however, partly as a result of the controls imposed during wartime, a consensus emerged that government needed to do more.

The link between wartime and postwar attitudes concerning services to be provided for the citizen can most clearly be seen in the realm of housing. The British government had announced during the war that it would sponsor a program to build "homes fit for heroes" once peace was at hand; that promise led to the Housing and Town Planning Act of 1919. The Act directed local authorities to take a census of their housing needs and pledged the government to make good on any financial losses incurred in the building program to follow. Germany took the lead in public housing after 1924 with ambitious projects in Berlin, Stuttgart, and Frankfurt done in an uncompromisingly modern style (see Chapter 7, V). Almost half of the new residential units built in Germany from 1924 until 1931 were built with government assistance, financed through a Housing Rent Tax introduced in 1924. France and Sweden also invested massively in new housing, while the city of Vienna, faced with an acute shortage of affordable low-income housing after the war, responded with projects such as the Karl-Marx-Hof.

The idea that government had an obligation to improve the lot of the common citizen extended to public facilities such as sports gymnasiums, libraries, and museums. With the increasing urbanization of Europe, medical experts began to warn that city life posed health threats to the young unless the opportunity for regular physical exercise could be provided them. These warnings led to the construction of both outdoor and indoor sports facilities in a number of European cities during the 1920s. One of the most popular was the covered swimming pool—available year round for a sport that, while not as competitive as soccer or track, offered greater possibilities for purely recreational and health use.

During the 1920s a new spirit gradually altered the relations between museums and the public. Rather than temples of art set aside for connoisseurs, museums now became teaching institutions, reaching out to include citizens whose backgrounds might not incline them to art appreciation. Georg Swarzenski, director of the Frankfurt Städel Museum since 1906, was one of several museum heads who inaugurated a rich series of gallery talks and pamphlets for visitors after the war in an attempt to broaden the appeal of art.

The Emancipation of Women

With the lowering of class barriers and the broad access to leisure activities came a third and no less important form of democratization: the entry of women into professional and political life. Here again, the First World War dramatically accelerated changes already underway before 1914. Through the wartime labor force shortage, European women made more progress toward economic equality in the four years of the conflict than they had in the entire previous generation of feminist agitation. Now a whole range of industrial and professional jobs was open to them that before the war had been strictly reserved to men. Women lawyers, women physicians—even women members of parliament and cabinet ministers—began to appear. Lady Astor inaugurated the trend in 1919, when by entering as an elected member of the British House of Commons she became the first European woman to take her seat in a national political body.

Before the war, only Norway had instituted women's suffrage; Denmark followed suit in 1915. With the war's end, women's suffrage became a reality in two larger countries as well. Germany took the lead; in the republican constitution of 1919, women received the vote on an equal basis with men. Britain advanced more hesitantly. In 1918 an act of Parliament extended the suffrage to older and more prosperous women, but not until ten years later were all women entitled to vote on the same basis as men. France and Italy made no similar moves. Another generation had to pass before the Latin coun-

English suffragettes picket the House of Commons in London in 1924.
(*Courtesy Corbis-Bettmann*)

tries were ready for women's suffrage. Here, far more than in the nations to the north, the vestiges of women's traditional inferiority of status lingered. Those who looked optimistically toward the future did not realize that the forces of social conservatism were far from beaten, that in several countries, authoritarian regimes would soon come to power and set back the cause of women's rights for at least a generation.

Technological advances aided the cause of women's emancipation by reducing the time and effort spent in homemaking. The electric stove, electric lights, and (most revolutionary of all) the electric vacuum cleaner all promised to free women from traditional domestic chores. The Werkbund Exhibition, held in the German city of Stuttgart in 1927 to highlight the advantages of the new architecture (see Chapter 7, V), also featured a specific appeal to women, who, its organizers believed, would see the advantages of clean, uncluttered interiors requiring minimal upkeep. Here, as in the arena of voting rights, the war accelerated a break with the past.

In one respect, however, the First World War reinforced a more traditional view of women as wives and mothers. The deaths of millions of young soldiers during the conflict prompted fears of a further decrease in population through a lower birthrate after the war, especially among patriots fearful that army strength would suffer without a continuing supply of fresh recruits. France, whose population increase was already the lowest in Europe (aside from Ireland) before the war, took the lead in 1920 by passing national legislation forbidding any advocacy of birth control or abortion. The law was not rigorously enforced, however, with barely 350 cases a year going to court in a country of 40 million inhabitants. A more positive means toward the same end was the child or family allowance—first introduced by Belgium in 1930, followed by France two years later—which assured each family a regular subsidy from the state for each new child.

Thus we should not see the 1920s as a period of complete emancipation for women. Here, as in other fields, change and nostalgia for old, familiar patterns were in conflict. Many women themselves seemed unsure of whether they wished fully to take up the new opportunities offered them or remain in roles that, though often demeaning, seemed secure. Women's groups in Germany, for example, greeted the new rights to vote of 1919 more as a burden than as a welcome innovation. The fact that some German women made use of their right to vote for Adolf Hitler and the Nazi party in the late 1920s and early 1930s—a party that publicly proclaimed that a woman's proper place was in the home as a helper to her husband and caretaker for her children—suggests that the relations between old and new expectations were complex. In a society where working women could neither count on day care for their children nor equal pay with their male colleagues, and where the traditional values of the family remained strong, women could find persuasive reasons to return to the home. Not until the 1960s would Europe see a truly far-reaching change in women's roles, marked by more pervasive social support and by changes in women's self-perception as well as legal status.

READINGS

For a general introduction to the interwar period, see the relevant chapters in E. J. Hobsbawm, *The Age of Extremes: A History of the World, 1914–1991** (1994), as well as the older study of Raymond J. Sontag, *A Broken World, 1919–1939** (1971). For an overview of the economy, see Derek H. Aldcroft, *From Versailles to Wall Street, 1919–29** (1977); Gilbert Ziebura, *World Economy and World Politics, 1924–1931: From Reconstruction to Collapse* (trans. 1990); and David S. Landes, *The Unbound Prometheus: Technological Change and Industrial Development in Western Europe from 1750 to the Present** (1969). The spectrum economic and social changes is explored in Gerold Ambrosius and William H. Hubbard, *A Social and Economic History of Twentieth-Century Europe** (1989). Eugene Michel Kulischer's *Europe on the Move: War and Population Changes, 1917–1947*

*Books marked with an asterisk are available in paperback.

(1948) is still the standard work on the major alterations in Europe's population during the interwar period.

The specific problems of the individual European countries are dealt with in the following: for Britain, Sean Glynn and Alan Booth, *Modern Britain: An Economic and Social History** (1996), John Stevenson, *British Society, 1914–1945** (1984), D. H. Aldcroft, *The British Economy, Vol. I: The Years of Turmoil, 1920–1951* (1986), and the classic and irreverent account by Robert Graves and Alan Hodge, *The Long Week-End** (1940); for France, Tom Kemp, *The French Economy 1913–1939: The History of a Decline* (1972); and for Germany, Richard Bessel and E. J. Feuchtwanger, eds., *Social Change and Political Development in Weimar Germany* (1981), and the previously mentioned study by Alexander Gerschenkron, *Bread and Democracy in Germany** (1943).

The campaign for rationalization in the workplace and its effects on leisure are surveyed in Gary Cross, *The Quest for Time: The Reduction of Work in Britain and France, 1840–1940* (1989). For the effects of leisure time on popular entertainments, see Michael R. Marrus, ed., *The Emergence of Leisure* (1974). D. L. LeMahieu examines the relations between radio and state-sponsored culture in Britain in A *Culture for Democracy: Mass Communication and the Cultivated Mind in Britain Between the Wars* (1988), while Raymond Williams deals with the democratization of education and the media in *The Long Revolution* (1961). A study of the culture of sport and its commercialization in a country where the phenomenon appeared early is Richard Holt, *Sport and Society in Modern France* (1981).

6

THE YEARS
OF STABILITY, 1924–1929

Dr. Gustav Stresemann of Germany makes his first speech at a League of Nations conference in Geneva in 1924, marking Germany's diplomatic reconciliation with its former adversaries. *(Courtesy Brown Brothers)*

During the twenty-year span between the First World War and the Second, no more than six years could be considered in any sense "normal." This was the period of apparent stabilization that separated the liquidation of the Ruhr crisis at the end of 1923 from the onset of the Great Depression at the beginning of 1930.

The five previous years had been the era in which the military sequels to the war gradually disappeared and the revolutionary threat was checked. In the second half of the 1920s, peace finally became a reality, and the stabilization of society provided a basis for at least short-term planning, as opposed to the previous tendency to improvise from month to month and to live by temporary expedients. On the international scene, voluntary pacts replaced settlements imposed by force, as the League of Nations acquired prestige and influence. On the domestic front, conservative government became the rule. This was the classic era of ministries led by businessmen or by political figures in sympathy with the business point of view. In general, these governments remained in the parliamentary democratic mold; indeed, one salient characteristic of the period was the apparent consolidation of democratic practices. But curiously enough, even the countries living under authoritarian regimes—Fascist Italy and Soviet Russia—in this era turned a relatively conservative face to the outside world, reserving their more dynamic activities for the next decade. In Italy, the first ten years of Fascist rule were a period of caution in foreign affairs; in the Soviet Union, Lenin's successor, Stalin, marked time during his first half-decade of power (see Chapters 9 and 10).

The late 1920s were also characterized by a restoration of financial orthodoxy and of prewar practices in industrial production. In this sense, as in government at home and in foreign relations, the era showed a return to "normal." What marked its economic prosperity likewise proved true of its politics and its international relations: The return to good times was more apparent than real. Just under the surface lurked threatening forces that needed only a suitable opportunity to break out again. At the end of the decade, the Great Depression was to reveal how illusory was the optimism of the late 1920s and how shaky were the foundations of economic prosperity and international concord on which it rested.

I. THE SPIRIT OF LOCARNO

History texts fifty years ago gave much attention to the international conferences of the 1920s. They recounted in full detail the cast of characters and agenda of each of them and their record of failure or accomplishment. Today these matters can be dealt with more briefly. In present perspective, the inconclusiveness of these conferences looms larger than their achievements. With the hindsight acquired through the experience of fascism and communism on the march, the Second World War, and the Cold War that followed it, the progress made in the 1920s toward a lasting peace seems small indeed.

Yet if these years were mostly barren of diplomatic results, they were decisive in changing the character of diplomacy itself. They closed the era of international relations in the old sense and ushered in the new era of mass democracy in foreign affairs which has continued until our own day. The social and political changes of the years immediately preceding the war had weakened the diplomatic monopoly of the old aristocracy and, with it, the sense of what it meant to be a "good European." This process was enormously accelerated by the course of the war. Both the intensification of national passions that the conflict aroused and Wilson's insistence on a new type of diplomacy responsive to the popular will had worked in a similar direction.

Wilson had pleaded for "open covenants openly arrived at." His condemnation of secret treaties, such as the one that had brought Italy into the war, permanently discredited these transactions with the European public. But the new diplomacy that replaced it was in many respects less effective in keeping the peace. It was more open, true, but it was also more amateurish and slipshod in its methods. The preference now went to conferences among heads of government or foreign ministers rather than to long and patient negotiations between professional diplomats. And the results—although fully exposed to the public—were frequently inconclusive and confusing. For the ordinary newspaper reader, and even for members of parliaments themselves, it was often next to impossible to learn precisely what a given international conference had accomplished—more particularly since the participants did everything in their power to make their achievements seem greater than they actually were.

In the 1920s, only the less dangerous faults of the new diplomacy were manifest—its carelessness and its tendency to work through amateur negotiators and informants over the heads of those who had been trained for the job. It was not until the 1930s that the more sinister aspects of the postwar situation became apparent. It was only then that the fascist dictators completely subverted the new diplomacy to give it once again the worst features of the old. In the hands of a Hitler, the traditional procedures of international relations became meaningless; diplomacy was reduced to a subservient instrument of military preparation and economic and psychological pressure. The decisive influence in foreign affairs passed to the war planners and the commercial strategists—the specialists in armaments and the subtler weapons of economic penetration. This final transformation of the new diplomacy has remained characteristic of international relations down to the present day.

The Phase of Liquidation: The Dawes Plan and the Changed Position of France

In the first postwar years, the foreign ministers of the powers seemed to be in continuous session. Their agenda was almost always the same—the problem of German reparations. This phase in international affairs ended with the French occupation of the Ruhr. The Ruhr crisis, lacerating though it was, marked at least two steps forward in the settlement of the reparations question. First, by substituting the reality of force for the unreality of negotiating with a defeated enemy who had no bargaining power, the French action opened the way to a more honest confrontation of the issue; second, by showing the futility of both coercion and passive resistance, it brought both sides to a more accurate assessment of where each stood, and with that came a new readiness to compromise.

In September 1923, the German government ended its passive resistance to the Ruhr occupation. Two months later, the French agreed to have the reparations question studied by two international committees. From the resulting deliberations there emerged the plan that for the first time put reparations on a practicable basis—the Dawes Plan of April 1924, named after the chairman of the committee which drafted it, Charles G. Dawes, who the following autumn was to be elected vice president of the United States.

The Dawes Plan, which came into effect in the summer of 1924, started Germany's annual reparations payments at 250 million dollars, with the provision that they were to be gradually increased over the next five years. By the end of that time they were to be more than doubled. In addition, the plan provided for a foreign loan, amounting to nearly as much as the first annual reparations installment, which was intended to support the newly stabilized mark and start money flowing for future reparations payments. More than half of this loan was subscribed for by American financiers, who thereby set the pattern of German dependence on American capital that was to characterize this half-decade of illusory prosperity.

Although contemporaries did not fully realize it, the year 1924 witnessed a major alteration in France's international position. It marked the end of the Indian summer of French greatness for which the unique conditions of the immediate postwar years had provided the setting. France—once the "great nation" without peer both by patriotic claim and by the reality of its strength and resources—had long ceased to be the arbiter of Europe. The German victory in the Franco-Prussian War of 1870 had demoted it from first to second position among the continental European nations. In the global rating of the powers, it ranked behind both Britain and the United States, whose immediately mobilizable strength was less than that of France, but whose ultimate economic potential was greater. Thus at the outbreak of the First World War, France stood no higher than fourth among the world powers. Paradoxically, even its eventual victory confirmed this diminished role. Whereas France could not possibly have survived and won without the aid of its Allies—and it emerged from the war irremediably drained of its best human resources—Germany was able to hold off a mighty coalition for four years almost unaided and to recover its economic and human strength far more rapidly than its victorious foe.

The settlement of 1919 produced a power vacuum in Europe. One great power—Austria-Hungary—had ceased to exist; two others—Germany and Russia—were in a state of disgrace and international quarantine; a fourth—the United States—had withdrawn from the European scene. Meanwhile, a fifth power, Great Britain, was vacillating between rigor and leniency in its attitude toward its former enemy. This left France alone to police Europe and enforce the peace. The four years of 1919–1923 were years of a restored French hegemony merely because no other power was prepared to challenge a position of leadership that had passed to France almost by default.

The Ruhr occupation revealed that even under these optimum conditions, France was not strong enough to do the job alone. With the British reluctant to follow, the French were obliged to fall back on alliances with the smaller nations of East Central Europe—primarily with Poland, but also with the three states that were linked by gains made at Hungary's expense, Czechoslovakia, Rumania, and Yugoslavia, which came to be called the Little Entente. Yet the strength of all these four together did not remotely approach that of a great power. The apparent solidity of the Little Entente derived almost entirely from the temporary weakness of Germany and Russia. Under the new conditions of the middle and late 1920s, France had no recourse other than resorting to the League of Nations to see what could be made of its novel machinery for eliminating international discord and enforcing the peace.

The Phase of Hope: The League and Locarno

As devised by the peacemakers of 1919, the organs of the League of Nations struck a careful balance between the principle of equality among sovereign states and the realities of great-power predominance. The authority of the League was thus divided between the Assembly—in which every member nation had an equal vote—and the Council, on which Britain, France, Italy, and Japan had permanent seats, and four smaller powers (later increased to six), chosen for a fixed term of years by the Assembly, served as temporary members. The membership of the League originally consisted solely of the signatories of the Treaty of Versailles, but since other nations could be admitted by a two-thirds vote of the Assembly, the League was gradually enlarged to include nearly all the sovereign states of the globe except the two quarantined powers, Soviet Russia and Germany, and the United States, which had chosen not to join.

The League's Council and Assembly met in the Swiss city of Geneva, and it was there that it had its Secretariat—a body that was able to do much effective work of a technical nature in the interwar period. Beyond such quiet labors as regulating passports and international communications and controlling the traffic in drugs, the main business of the League was to keep the peace. And the effectiveness with which it could do so largely depended on how seriously its membership took their obligations to bring before it all important matters at issue and to abide by the League's decision on them.

From the very beginning there were at least two reasons for skepticism. First, the League's machinery for enforcing its decisions lacked "teeth." It depended on a unanimous vote of the Assembly and on the willingness of the membership to apply Article 10 of the Covenant—the key provision of the whole document—by which each individual member undertook to "respect and preserve as against external aggression the territorial integrity and existing political independence" of the others. Thus the recommendation by the Council and subsequent vote by the Assembly of what came to be called "sanctions" against an aggressor constituted both a doubtful and a cumbersome process. Second, the sphere of the League's day-to-day influence was almost entirely restricted to Europe. With the United States and Soviet Russia out, and Japan uninterested, effective leadership within the League devolved on the former European Allies, Britain, France, and Italy. It is significant that during the only period in which the League was able to make its influence felt at all—the second half of the 1920s—it concentrated on European problems, finding a temporary basis of agreement between the victors and vanquished Germany.

The changed atmosphere that began to manifest itself in 1924 was particularly associated with the fortunate coincidence that France and Germany almost simultaneously found foreign ministers of an unusually conciliatory turn of mind, both of whom remained in office uninterruptedly for six years. On the surface, the two were extremely different human beings. The Frenchman, Aristide Briand, was a man of humble origin, a former Socialist turned conservative, already seven times prime minister and a master of the parliamentary art, with a quarter century of political experience behind him—a supple, insinuating debater, who had developed to a fine point the talent for veiling precise meanings in ambiguous but alluring phraseology. Only one thing about him was clear: However often Briand might be accused of hypocrisy and deceit, the genuineness of his devotion to peace was beyond doubt.

His German counterpart, Gustav Stresemann, was a man of sterner stuff. A businessman and the son of a prosperous beerhouse owner, Stresemann had ranked during the war as a leading nationalist and annexationist among Germany's parliamentary liberals. The defeat of 1918 shook him out of his illusions and started him on the slow process of revising his earlier beliefs. Emotionally shattered by the national catastrophe, Stresemann passed the next five years in the political wilderness, gradually working out a new and practical policy that would combine the fulfillment of Germany's treaty obligations with systematic pressure for their revision. Thus, in 1923, in his country's hour of crisis, Stresemann stood out as the one man capable of giving a clear lead. The rest were either discredited or dead. After three months as chancellor in the summer and autumn of 1923, Stresemann never again headed the German government. But from that time on until his death in 1929, Stresemann's presence at the foreign ministry was considered indispensable to all cabinets, whatever their political complexion.

Yet for all the atmosphere of cordiality that surrounded their frequent and rather vague conversations, neither Briand nor Stresemann ever conceded very much. Each remained acutely aware of his country's national interests and of the line beyond which he would never consent to retreat. Their most substantial achievement—indeed, almost the only substantial achievement in international affairs of the whole decade—was the negotiation of the Locarno Treaty and the entrance of Germany into the League of Nations that followed it. And this was more the regularizing of an existing situation than a bold departure along the new path first blazed by the creation of the League itself.

Following an effort by the short-lived British Labour government of 1924 to put teeth into the League Covenant through a provision for compulsory arbitration—known to history as the Geneva Protocol—Stresemann came forward with a more modest idea. His original proposal of February 1925 for a Rhineland mutual guarantee pact was welcomed by Briand, who began his long tenure in the French foreign ministry two months later and who added to Stresemann's scheme the condition that Germany should enter the League of Nations. The following autumn, after months of quiet negotiation, the foreign ministers were ready for a dramatic display of international concord. In early October 1925, at the Italian Swiss lakeside resort of Locarno, the statesmen of Europe spent ten idyllic and informal days that were marked by such unconventional diplomatic spectacles as Briand rowing Stresemann around in a small boat. By December, the treaties that resulted from these happy hours were ready for signature in London.

The Locarno agreements included a main treaty guaranteeing the Franco-German and the German-Belgian frontiers—to which, besides the three principal powers involved, Great Britain and Italy adhered as guarantors—and a series of bilateral arbitration treaties. The agreements were followed, as Briand had proposed, by Germany's admission to the League in March 1926, with its great-power status recognized by a permanent seat on the Council. The general jubilation engendered by the "spirit of Locarno" tended to make people forget what the agreements had omitted. Although the Germans had signed treaties of arbitration with Poland and Czechoslovakia, they had not specifically accepted their frontiers with these two states. No "eastern Locarno" completed the agreements applying to the west alone, since neither Poland nor Czechoslovakia were prepared to yield even a fraction of the territories they had so recently acquired. As the post-Locarno years passed, it became obvious that the relaxation of tension and new sense of security along the Rhine had no counterpart in East Central Europe, where old hatreds raged as bitterly as before.

The Phase of Illusion: The Young Plan and Disarmament

Thus, in the international field, the era of stability produced its best effects very early. The period after 1926 was to be an anticlimax, marked only by disappointment and illusory success.

After five years of operation, the Dawes Plan had revealed certain technical defects, more particularly in the transfer of reparations payments from one country to another. The Young Plan of June 1929—named, as its predecessor, after an American financier, Owen D. Young—established a more efficient machinery for making these payments, scaled them down still further, set a final 59-year limit to them, and ended international control over their delivery. To contemporaries, it appeared that the Young Plan had dealt definitively with this vexing matter and that reparations would trouble the statesmen of Europe no more. They could hardly guess that only three years later, faced with a resurgent Germany caught in a desperate economic depression, some of the same statesmen would be forced to deal with reparations once again and, in effect, to bury them forever.

As early as 1929 the German public was behaving less passively than it had five years earlier when the Dawes Plan was inaugurated. The Young Plan unleashed within the Reich a storm of opposition to accepting the new arrangements. Nearly all the rightist and nationalist groups banded together in a vicious campaign of abuse against Stresemann—a campaign that quite literally killed him, since he wore himself out in combating his enemies' lying propaganda. Stresemann's death, coming in the same month as the great Wall Street stock market crash, gave an ominous foretaste of what lay ahead.

The decade closed with disarmament occupying the center of the international stage. In 1927, a conference of the three largest naval powers—Britain, the United States, and Japan—was unable to reach any sort of agreement. Three years later, a larger conference, this time including France and Italy, finally achieved some modest gains—most of which, however, were canceled out by an "escalator clause" to which the powers were permitted to resort if they considered that their national needs demanded it. At the end of 1930, when the preparatory commission of the League of Nations for general disarmament completed its labors, it was quite apparent that the draft convention it had adopted had no consensus behind it and that the major disarmament conference scheduled for fourteen months later could produce only the most profound disagreements.

Meanwhile the statesmen hovered between trepidation and hope. The Young Plan ranked as a success, and the Germans had received their reward for accepting it: an early evacuation of the Rhineland by the occupying forces. But this single encouraging achievement was far outweighed by what appeared on the negative side of the balance—the weakening of Briand's influence, the death of Stresemann and the revival of German nationalism, the American Great Depression and its threatened repercussions in Europe, and the snail's pace of disarmament. All these signified the renewal of the general

European crisis—economic, social, and political—that had been held at bay for six years and that now in country after country was returning in full force on the domestic front.

II. THE CONSERVATIVE GOVERNMENTS

In domestic affairs as in foreign policy, the second half of the 1920s was characterized for each of the powers by the personality of a single statesman who put his stamp upon the period. In Britain, it was Stanley Baldwin; in France, it was Raymond Poincaré; in Germany, Gustav Stresemann incarnated the hopes of his countrymen both for domestic stability and for international peace.

A further generalization is in order: The internationalist outlook of the second half of the decade had sprung from the parliamentary left. It found its first and clearest expression in the policy of short-lived governments led by statesmen with moderate leftist views—who fell from power because of domestic rather than foreign issues—and its most enthusiastic supporters continued to be on the left. But the conservatives subsequently took over the new internationalism from its original proponents. Indeed, successful manipulation of peace sentiment in the late 1920s by the parliamentary right was a principal reason for the conservatives' long tenure of power.

British Prologue: From the Irish Settlement to the First Labour Government

Lloyd George's coalition government had emerged from the war with high prestige and an apparently justified confidence in its ability to carry on almost indefinitely. Its first act was to confirm its mandate by the election of December 1918. Its calculation proved well founded—by playing on patriotic themes and the hope of substantial gains from reparations, it crushed both Labour and the independent wing of the Liberals and brought back to the House of Commons a majority that outnumbered its combined opponents by nearly four to one.

Thus the prospect for the 1920s was a scarcely veiled single-party rule; the Conservatives would allow Lloyd George to continue as prime minister as long as they themselves held the realities of power; and both the coalition Liberals and the parliamentary opposition would be reduced to impotence. With the Liberals divided in their loyalties to Lloyd George, the traditional second party of British politics had gone into a decline that no subsequent change of fortune could arrest. Labour had taken its place as the chief opposition party—but with fewer than sixty seats in the House of Commons, the British Socialists were far from ready to challenge the overwhelming predominance of the Conservatives.

That this situation did not last—that the coalition was to be replaced first by a purely Conservative government, and second, and more fleetingly, by Labour itself—was the result of an accumulation of unforeseen difficulties and mistakes. There were the economic depression of 1921 and British hesitations in international affairs. Above and beyond these, there was the revolt of Ireland.

Since the seventeenth century, Ireland had existed as a semicolonial dependency of Great Britain. Although the majority of its population was separated by religion and tradition from that of its larger island neighbor, the country had been ruled by a thin stratum of Protestant gentry of English sympathies. In the late nineteenth century, however, after repeated extensions of the suffrage, the Catholic majority finally came into its own; it began to send to the House of Commons a solid phalanx of members single-mindedly pledged to the cause of Irish home rule and prepared to obstruct all other parliamentary business in order to achieve their aims. Thus, from the 1880s on, the Liberals had good reason to take up the Irish cause; in this case, ideological devotion to the principle of freedom was reinforced by need for Irish votes. After three decades of futile effort to get a home rule bill through Parliament, the Liberals finally succeeded just on the eve of the First World War.

But the home rule bill of 1914 never came into effect. The one part of Ireland with a Protestant majority—the northeastern region known as Ulster—threatened to defend by force its union with Britain, and in this resistance it enjoyed the support of an influential segment both of the Conservatives and of the army. What the Liberal government would have done if the general European conflict had not supervened is far from clear. The army was mutinous, civil war was threatening, and Asquith was trying to work out a compromise that would avoid coercing Ulster into accepting home rule. The overriding necessities of wartime decided the issue. The government merely shelved the Irish question for the duration. For the next four years, Ireland lived in ominous calm, broken by an abortive rebellion on Easter 1916, for which fourteen nationalist leaders paid with their lives.

In the election of 1918, however, Irish politics suddenly revived—and with a new virulence occasioned by the four years of waiting. Instead of the comparatively mild "home rulers" of the prewar period, Ireland now sent to Parliament more than seventy members of the new party called Sinn Fein ("Ourselves Alone"), who were no longer satisfied with mere autonomy and were pledged to a program of complete independence. These people refused to take their seats at Westminster. Instead, they established themselves as an Irish parliament—the Dail Eireann—meeting at Dublin, and in January 1919, they formally declared Ireland an independent nation.

Lloyd George's government took its time about dealing with this act of open rebellion. Only gradually did it drift into war with the Sinn Fein. But by the autumn of 1919, when the British decided upon full repression, they acted in the most inept fashion possible. They did not send in the regular army to subjugate Ireland in a quick campaign. They merely reinforced the regular Irish constabulary by recruiting a special force of volunteers—the notorious "Black and Tans"—whose discipline was lax and whose methods were unnecessarily cruel.

For more than a year, two irregular armies fought a strange and undeclared war in the city streets and rural byways of Ireland. Both sides were ruthless—the Irish volunteers no less than their British counterparts. Although most of the population went calmly about its ordinary tasks, no one could be sure that violence would not suddenly erupt in the form of ambushes, bomb explosions, arson, torture, or the seizure of hostages. It was a brutal and sickening struggle, made no better by the increasingly blunt fashion in which a large segment of British public opinion began to question the justice and expediency of the whole policy of repression. Nor did the passage of another home rule bill do any good—the Dail Eireann refused to accept it and continued to issue its orders as the clandestine government of Ireland.

By the summer of 1921, the pressure on the British authorities to reach a settlement had become overwhelming. Lloyd George summoned the Sinn Fein leaders from their political shadow world to meet with him in London and discuss a compromise. By a regular treaty signed between the Irish representatives and the British government, most of Ireland, under the name of the Irish Free State, became a self-governing dominion on the model of Canada or Australia. Ulster was granted special status: The six Protestant counties of the northeast, which had accepted the home rule act of 1920, were set up as an autonomous region of the United Kingdom, called Northern Ireland, which was both to have a parliament of its own and to continue to send members to the British Parliament at Westminister.

The treaty of December 1921 did not give the Irish Free State formal independence. But it gave the substance, and for moderate-minded Irish citizens, that was enough. A narrow majority in the Dail accepted the treaty and prepared to put the new institutions into effect, but the irreconcilable nationalist minority, under Eamon de Valera, refused to submit and declared for a continuation of the struggle with Britain. The British, however, would have no more of it; they were sick of fighting. It was left to the new government of the Irish Free State to wage another and still more cruel civil war for an additional year until in the spring of 1923, de Valera and his irreconcilables were finally overwhelmed.

Barbed wire being laid in Dublin in 1921 in preparation for the British occupation of the city. (*Courtesy Corbis-Bettmann*)

It is hard to say who won the Irish struggle. Temporarily it was the moderate nationalists who had accepted the compromise of 1921. But by 1927, de Valera had returned to the political arena; five years later he was president and undisputed spokesman of his country. Indeed, after the Second World War, Ireland declared itself a republic and severed its remaining links with the British Commonwealth. The nationalist triumph seemed complete. Yet to this day the Ulster problem remains unresolved—the six counties of the northeast, despite protracted and occasionally violent opposition by their own Catholic minority, answered with equal violence by the Protestants—have kept their special status as an integral part of the United Kingdom along with England, Scotland, and Wales (see Chapter 22, I).

The tragic struggle in Ireland notably undermined the authority of Lloyd George's coalition government. So did the economic depression of the early 1920s and the disputes with France over foreign policy. In the autumn of 1922, the more aggressive Tories decided to cast aside Lloyd George and persuaded the elderly and respected Scotsman Andrew Bonar Law to lead a purely Conservative government. This new Tory ministry immediately went to the country to confirm its mandate; in the parliamentary elections of November 1922, it emerged triumphant, with a substantial majority over all the other parties and factions combined.

Both wings of the Liberals had continued their decline. But Labour had returned in force, more than doubling its previous parliamentary representation. This new strength and militancy on the part of Labour was to become still more evident six months later, when Bonar Law's ill health necessitated a change of prime minister. The Conservative leaders and the king passed over the outstanding candidate, Lord Curzon—thereby establishing the constitutional precedent that under the new conditions of democracy a peer was no longer suitable to lead the government—and picked instead the comparatively obscure Stanley Baldwin.

Baldwin's first tenure of office was unexpectedly brief. Rashly staking his own and his party's reputation on the untried plank of tariff protection, he called for another election. This time, the Liberals closed ranks and united behind Asquith; Labour continued to gain confidence; and both opposition parties raised havoc with the Tories' new protectionist stand. When the votes were counted, the Conservative party, though still the strongest in the House of Commons, had lost its majority and had unmistakably been repudiated by the electorate.

After the election of December 1923, Asquith faced a difficult choice. Although his party was still the weakest of the three, it had made a substantial recovery, and it occupied a strategic position between its two larger rivals. The Liberals might have agreed to a coalition either with the Conservatives or with Labour; in either case the new government would have had a solid majority. Asquith chose to do neither. True to the spirit of tolerance and fair play with which he was almost excessively endowed, he declared that Labour, as the second party and the stronger of those that had successfully opposed protection, should be given a chance to govern alone. His decision amounted to political suicide for the Liberals; never again were they to come within striking distance of power. And for Labour it was a curious and not altogether welcome gift, for it meant that the first Socialist government in Western European history was to conduct its risky experiment under the most unfavorable conditions possible.

Britain: The Baldwin Era, 1924–1929

The first Labour government was a flimsy structure from the beginning. Without a parliamentary majority, it could exist only on Liberal sufferance. Even organizing it proved extremely difficult. There were literally not enough Labour leaders in Parliament with sufficient experience and standing to man a full cabinet, and the new prime minister, Ramsay MacDonald, felt obliged to call on a scattering of former Liberals and independents to complete his ranks. Thus the ministry began tamely—and in this it reflected the personality of its leader, who was far more cautious than his public style suggested.

A Scotsman of humble origin, Ramsay MacDonald appeared a born leader. He was handsome, he was eloquent, his whole manner suggested an innate superiority to other men. But on closer acquaintance his followers discovered in him both vanity and hesitation, and in his noble, poetic language a lamentable absence of clear thought. In his ten months of office, from January to November 1924, MacDonald tried to do little more than reassure the country that Labour was not so bad as people had feared. Only in the international field did he take decisive action, with the diplomatic recognition of Soviet Russia and the launching of the policy of conciliation with Germany. Meanwhile the Tories waited for a suitable opportunity to bring him down.

This came earlier than they had any right to expect. The matter was trivial—the government's failure to prosecute a Communist editor for publishing seditious articles—but it gave the Conservatives exactly the issue they needed to harass the prime minister. The Tories pressed the case relentlessly; MacDonald was inept in replying. He finally made it a matter of confidence, and with the Liberals now voting against him, the first Labour government went down to ignominious defeat.

In the ensuing election, the Conservatives again exploited the "red" danger to the full. The timely discovery, just before polling day, of a letter—probably forged—from the Russian Zinoviev of the Third International to his loyal followers in Britain gave the public the impression that Labor was somehow tainted with communism or, at the very least, was insufficiently alert to the Bolshevik menace. The Tories would probably have won the election of 1924 without the aid of the Zinoviev letter, for the Labour government had been a disappointment, but the discovery of this strange document certainly helped. From the third election in as many years, the Conservatives emerged with the biggest majority of the whole decade; Labour lost a quarter of its seats; and the Liberals received a crushing blow from which they never recovered.

So Baldwin returned—this time for five years—and proceeded to give the country the "sane, commonsense Government" that he had promised. Like MacDonald, Stanley Baldwin was a cautious mediocrity; his language was vague and moralizing, and he hated to make up his mind. But he was far more successful than MacDonald in inspiring public confidence. He wore his tweeds and smoked his pipe and looked the simple but astute north-country businessman that he was. Above all he seemed "safe"—and this was evidently what a majority of Englishmen wanted after a full decade of upsets and adventures.

Thus he gave the country a carefully measured dose of basic conservatism and occasional innovation. Most of the time he relied simply on the old English virtue of "muddling through." But in the international field—after quickly withdrawing the hand of friendship that Labour had tentatively held out to the Soviet Union—he was happy to see his foreign minister, Austen Chamberlain, working in harmony with Briand and

Stresemann in the League of Nations. Similarly at home, he gave Chamberlain's half brother, Neville, the minister of health, free rein to undertake a program of pensions for widows, orphans, and the aged, and local government reform that ranked as the only great constructive achievements of the entire half-decade.

The Conservative mandate to govern remained unquestioned for almost five years. But as the decade of the 1920s ended, it became increasingly apparent that all was not well in Britain. Baldwin did nothing substantial about the interlocking problems of industrial and commercial stagnation, of the depressed areas, and of permanent unemployment. He postponed action from year to year, hoping that things would somehow take a turn for the better, and in the one major case of social unrest that occurred during his long tenure of power—the general strike of 1926—he behaved in a fashion that intensified the bitterness of class feeling.

The strike had its origins in the languishing coal industry. The government in July 1925 had conceded to the miners' demand that a royal commission be appointed to inquire into their grievances. Yet when the commission made its report the following March, it satisfied neither side. The mine owners, with tacit government support, thereupon shut down the pits and defied the trade unions to do their worst. In response, the unions called a general strike, which lasted for nine days in early May. Its scope was unprecedented—two and a half million workers were out. Equally unprecedented were the enthusiasm and efficiency with which the government mobilized volunteers from the propertied classes to run the essential services. Oxford and Cambridge students unloaded ships; there was even the story of a peer at the throttle of a train, who, when rebuked for reaching the station ahead of schedule, replied that he had only just discovered how to stop the engine. Nobody lost his life in the strike; still, there was sporadic local violence and great intensity of feeling.

This was particularly true of the way in which the strike came to an end. After two days of frantic negotiations, trade-union leaders capitulated without gaining a single one of the miners' demands. The latter naturally felt betrayed; they continued their own strike, desperately and hopelessly, for six months after the general strike ended. Then—as if the bitterness of labor's failure was not already enough—the Baldwin government pushed through Parliament the Trade Disputes Act of 1927, which banned sympathetic strikes and severely limited labor's bargaining power. In this undisguised piece of class legislation lay the remote origins of a revulsion of feeling that, two years later, was to end Baldwin's long period of rule and sweep the Labour party into power once more.

France: The Poincaré Era, 1926–1929

In France the decade of the 1920s was marked by a double political failure, first by the Right and then by the Left, until in 1926 the country at last attained a precarious equilibrium.

The French parliamentary elections of 1919, like those in Britain a year earlier, produced a conservative and nationalist majority. Indeed the "Horizon-Blue Chamber," as it was called, from the number of war veterans in blue uniforms who sat in it, was the most conservative that France had known since the turn of the century. But the victorious coalition of parties—the Bloc National—did not know how to exploit its success. It repudiated old Clemenceau because he had yielded to Wilson on the Rhineland, and under leaders of lesser stature it embarked on the ill-fated policy of coercing Germany and asserting French hegemony throughout Europe.

The Ruhr failure of 1923 ended this phase of postwar French history. The government's resort to military action had frightened many people at home—conjuring up as it did the specter of renewed warfare—and the resulting wave of pacifist feeling reinforced the general discontent over the high cost of living and carried the Left into power. The Cartel des Gauches that defeated the Bloc National in the election of 1924 consisted of an alliance between the Radicals (since the early 1900s the strongest party in France) and the Socialists, who were just recovering from the secession of their Communist wing. These two could get along admirably when it came to electoral campaigning; for such purposes the old slogans of anticlericalism and "republican" solidarity gave excellent service. But when it came to governing, the two parties were almost immediately at odds.

The ministry led by Edouard Herriot in 1924 was, like its leader, primarily from the Radical party; it had no Socialists in it, but it depended on them for its support. The chief issues it faced were financial—inflation and the related problems of reparations and war debts to the United States. On matters such as these, the laissez-faire Radicals and the quasi–Marxist Socialists were poles apart. In addition, Herriot, like most French statesmen, was more rhetorician than student of economics. He had only the vaguest notions about financial policy, and his attitude toward the country's economic plight was lax and irresponsible. For a full decade, France had been living beyond its means. Its war financing through inflationary practices and public debt had been the worst of any major belligerent. By 1919, its circulation of banknotes had increased more than sixfold, while taxation had not raised sufficient funds to cover even normal peacetime expenditures; and to all this it had added the enormous expense of reconstructing the devastated areas.

For five years the deputies had played politics as usual with problems of an unprecedented gravity. Then, in 1924, with the previous year's disappointment on reparations, the accumulated errors of a half decade cascaded on the hapless Herriot. Inflation continued unchecked, and the government seemed powerless to stop it. After less than a year in office, Herriot gave up the struggle. His two successors did no better. By the summer of 1926 the franc had fallen to two cents—a tenth of its prewar value—and heroic measures seemed called for.

Once again, as in 1917, France found the right leader. Raymond Poincaré stepped in to form a national union ministry, in which he had made a place for six former premiers. Poincaré was not a popular man—but his firmness and rectitude could awaken confidence after twelve years of financial facility. Even Poincaré's faults—his coldness and his narrowness of vision—might rank as assets in this sort of crisis. Moreover, he had learned from earlier disappointment; as wartime president of the Republic, he had felt eclipsed by the more appealing Clemenceau, and as prime minister during the Ruhr invasion he had experienced the realistic limits to nationalist agitation and solutions of force.

It was a temperate and chastened Poincaré, then, who took up the task of "saving the franc." He did nothing very extraordinary to bring this about; he simply behaved like the scrupulous and systematic lawyer that he was, tightening up the administration here and improving the collection of taxes there until the franc held firm and even began to mount on the foreign exchanges. In 1928, it was finally stabilized at twenty to the dollar, the rate it was to maintain for most of the interwar period. The French realized that at last they had a "serious" government, one that meant what it said. Indeed, in their gratitude that something at least had been rescued from the financial wreck, many people almost forgot that they had lost three-quarters of their savings. They reacted in a notably different fashion from the Germans, who were overwhelmed with bitterness by their losses.

With this achievement behind him, Poincaré was solidly installed in power. He retained the premiership for three years—an interwar record—and the basically conservative coalition he led won without difficulty the election of 1928. Confidence in the French economy was based on more than the now-stable franc. French industry had in fact rebounded since the bust of 1919–1920 in spectacular fashion. Steel production had tripled from three million tons in 1920 to 9.7 million tons in 1929, while automobile output rose sixfold from 40,000 to 254,000 cars during the same period. France's large agricultural sector—still employing half the working population—while not efficient, managed to supply the nation's food needs to a far greater extent than British farmers could in Britain.

Yet Poincaré's success, like Baldwin's, was only transitory. Both leaders profited from a unique period of tranquility that was soon to come to an end. France was far more closely tied to the international financial market and trading community than its leaders had supposed. Thus when the weak link in the Western European economy—Germany—finally snapped in 1929, a few months after Poincaré's retirement, a new time of troubles for all was close at hand.

Germany: The Stresemann Era, 1923–1929

When Stresemann assumed power in the desperate summer of 1923, Germany was almost out of leaders. Public sentiment had turned against the Social Democrats, whose attitude toward the country's late enemies did not seem sufficiently patriotic, and the two outstanding figures among the leadership of the middle-class democratic parties, Matthias Erzberger and Walther Rathenau, had been murdered by nationalist fanatics.

Stresemann's three months of power marked the turning point for the republican regime that had been established at Weimar four years earlier. It ended the era of constant uncertainty, in which people scarcely knew from month to month under what sort of authority they were going to live. Through a resort to martial law and firm action against both types of extremists that were threatening the state—the Communists in Saxony and Hitler's National Socialists in Bavaria—Stresemann, like Poincaré three years later, proved the seriousness of his intentions and his resolve that middle-class democracy in Germany should become a reality at last. And this is exactly what happened. When in November Stresemann retired as chancellor—to continue for the next six years as foreign minister—the Weimar constitution had finally come to function in an approximately "normal" fashion.

Germany's republican constitution was the most complete and carefully drafted that Europe had yet seen. It was a lawyer's masterpiece that seemed to cover every possible contingency. In its provisions for women's suffrage and a popular referendum on major issues, it went beyond the constitutions of Britain and France. In most respects, however, it either imitated the common practice of Europe's parliamentary states or

Gustav Stresemann, chancellor (1923) and foreign minister (1923–1929) of Germany, symbol of the years of stability during the Weimar Republic. (*Courtesy Brown Brothers*)

continued, in modified and democratized form, the institutions of the old imperial regime. Even traces remained of the old authority of the emperor himself, for the presidency that had replaced the imperial office was rather stronger than the corresponding position in France or in Britain. By the famous Article 48 of the Weimar constitution, the president was empowered to take emergency action in periods of grave national danger.

By 1924, the great majority of the German electorate had at least passively accepted the new republican institutions. It was significant that in the two Reichstag elections of that year, the nationalist party had its first real success at the polls, and that early in the following year it gave tangible evidence of its "domestication" by consenting to serve in the government. Still more symptomatic were the results of the presidential election held in the spring of 1925. On the death of the first president, the Social Democrat and former saddlemaker Friedrich Ebert, a plurality of the nation's voters picked old Field Marshal von Hindenburg, the hero of the nationalist Right, who proceeded to carry out his functions in punctilious accordance with his constitutional oath.

By the middle of the decade, then, German democracy seemed to be firmly established. To the new and rather surprising economic prosperity, there was now added a cessation of domestic strife, a pacification of spirit that made the violence of the previous half decade—the constant street fights and assassinations—seem only an evil memory. Even in the best years of the Weimar regime, however, this democratic consensus was neither as complete nor as solid as it seemed to be. For all its apparent stability, the party system never functioned properly. With six major parties in the field, coalition government was inevitable, and the task of forming such coalitions was still further complicated by the primacy of foreign affairs and the consequent necessity of keeping Stresemann—who alone commanded confidence abroad—in the foreign office, although his own party ranked as the least important of the six. Under these conditions, authority tended to pass from the Reichstag and the ministers to the party machines that made and unmade governments at their own discretion or, alternatively, to the civil servants who alone could ensure continuity of policy.

Thus there came to be something flat and uninspiring about Weimar democracy. A creeping paralysis and decay began to affect the parties most intimately associated with it. First the Democrats started to lose votes. In the election of 1928 this party—which typified better than any other the moderate middle-class democracy of the 1920s—made a poor showing from which it never recovered. Then the Center lost its democratic moorings. Since the death of Matthias Erzberger, it had lacked decisive leadership, and it gradually drifted into a situation of ideological confusion. As a Catholic party, it appealed to all types of voters, from socialist-minded trade unionists to conservative landowners and businessmen, and its centrist situation in the ideological spectrum made it an indispensable partner in all coalitions, whether of the Right or of the Left. No government ever lacked Center ministers, and the Center provided the chancellor more frequently than any other party. But this political bigamy was bad for the Center. No clear policy line was possible when the same ministers served first in a government of the Right and then in one of the Left.

If the Center was thus engaged in a perpetual balancing act, the other great party on which the regime rested, the Social Democrats, was succumbing to weariness and ossification. The Social Democrats and the trade unions were hard hit by the inflation of 1923. In subsequent years, they reknit their cadres and tried to carry on as before. But the life seemed to have gone out of them. Both the party and the unions found their leadership aging and becoming more bureaucratized and the young people less and less interested in their activities. In the election of 1928, the Social Democrats made a surprising recovery, and for the first time since 1920 they were able to enforce their claim to the chancellorship. But this victory availed them nothing; they no longer knew how to devise and carry out an imaginative social program.

This same election produced other and more threatening symptoms of approaching change. Two million voters cast their ballots for small parties and independent candidates that appealed to discontents and resentments of all sorts, more particularly those of the peasantry. Still worse, the Nationalists came under new leadership. The industrialist and superpropagandist Alfred Hugenberg forced his way into control of the party, brushing aside the three-year-old policy of moderation to form an alliance with Hitler's struggling National Socialists—an alliance that was to vent its full venom in the following year when it waged the campaign against the Young Plan, which cost Stresemann his life.

By 1928, the forces of nationalism and reaction, which had been in abeyance for a mere three or four years, began to come to life again. Only on the surface and in the great cities had Germany changed. Deeper down and throughout the countryside, the old imperial mentality lingered on. A decade later, the superficiality and incompleteness of the Revolution of 1918 had become painfully apparent. The consequences of all that the builders of German democracy had left undone now returned to plague them: They had not broken up the great estates of the Prussian nobility; they had not purged the judiciary and the civil service; they had not altered the composition and prestige of the officers' corps. In all these places, reaction remained entrenched. Landowners concealed the veterans of extremist bands as farm workers; judges acquitted nationalist terrorists or handed down ridiculously short sentences; civil servants sabotaged the reforming measures of their ministerial chiefs; the army—made still more aristocratic and tight-knit by the restrictions imposed in the Treaty of Versailles—pursued with impunity its goal of clandestine rearmament, reporting not to the chancellor but to President von Hindenburg himself, who cast a cloak of respectability over its illicit activities.

In brief, even before the death of Stresemann and the onset of the Great Depression, German democracy was beginning to reveal its fragility. Like Stresemann's own policy of "fulfilling" the terms of the Versailles Treaty, German democracy had an air of the synthetic and provisional. Indeed, in the minds of many nationalists, the republic and Versailles were almost interchangeable ideas. The same assembly that drafted the republican constitution had also accepted the humiliation of the treaty, and the two documents betrayed the irremediable taint of antipatriotism. The reconciliation of 1925–1928 had been transitory and largely unreal. The nationalist Right had never actually abandoned its nostalgia for the past.

III. THE LURKING NEMESIS

What has just been said about Germany applies to a lesser extent to the other countries of Western and Central Europe. Each of these, and all together, contained depressing or explosive forces that the prosperity and peace—domestic and foreign—of the "good years" after 1924 barely succeeded in concealing.

The War Debts–Reparations Nexus

In the minds of businessmen, economists, and occasionally even diplomats, the dominating preoccupation of the era was the precariousness of the new-found prosperity. Statesmen and the public usually took it for granted. More farsighted economic thinkers questioned its permanence. For the prosperity of the late 1920s rested on a fragile base— and this was particularly the case in Germany, whose state of health, whether economic or psychological, should have been the crucial consideration for Europeans during the whole interwar period.

To all outward appearance, Germany was booming. Not only was industry expanding; the German municipalities were also adding to their public services, improving city transport, laying out parks and recreation centers, and constructing hospitals, schools, and workers' housing. Many of these buildings were being designed in the new "International Style," which, with its simple masses and clean lines, began to give the cities of Germany an aspect of tidy and efficient modernity (see Chapter 7, IV). Defeated Germany, as the French complained, was becoming the showplace of Europe, while victorious France was growing shabbier; almost no architectural imagination had gone into the reconstruction of the devastated areas, which for the most part were ugly and conventional, and elsewhere construction lagged, as French housing slipped into a state of backwardness that was to last for another thirty years.

But the German building boom was expensive, and it was financed in slipshod fashion by excessive issue of municipal bonds. These found ready takers in the United States, which also invested heavily on German industrial expansion. Thus in the 1920s, as in the period after the Second World War, German prosperity was overwhelmingly dependent on American financial aid. But there were two important differences: In the years after 1924, the help came from American private capital rather than from the government, and it was usually in the form of short-term loans rather than of grants extending over a number of years. Hence it was inordinately sensitive to fluctuations in the U.S. economy. The maintenance of German prosperity was impossible unless the postwar boom continued in the United States.

There was a further difference between the two postwar periods. In the 1920s, the United States was not alone, as it was to be after 1945, in its position of economic benefactor. Germany was also involved, through its reparations payments to France, Britain, and a number of lesser powers. These in turn were obliged to pay back to the United States the sums they had borrowed during the war. The question of war debts engendered continual bitterness; for an entire decade it dominated and poisoned relations between France and the United States. The Republican administrations in the United States held the French to the letter of their bond and brushed aside the argument that the Americans, who had lost so few lives in the common cause, might at least recognize

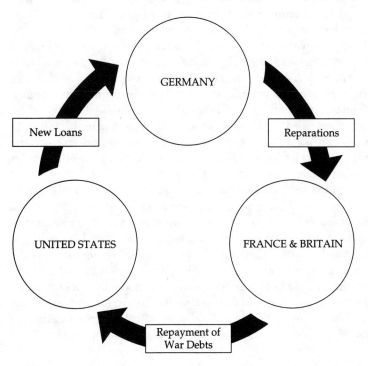

FIGURE 6.1 The war debts-reparation problem. American loans financed German reparations, which in turn provided France and Britain with the money needed to repay their wartime debts to the United States. This circular movement of capital could easily be upset—as it was by the Wall Street crash of 1929, which halted loans to Germany and led Germany to default on reparations to France and Britain.

the enormous contribution in blood that the French had made, by exercising a corresponding generosity in releasing them from their debts.

The French answered stubbornness with stubbornness. Should Germany ever default on reparations, they claimed, then they, the French, could no longer pay their war debts. Thus the two problems became one, as reparations and war debts were associated in a tight nexus, to which the United States alone held the key. The result was a most curious triangle of transatlantic payments—the Americans lent money to Germany, Germany paid it out to France in the form of reparations, and finally it returned to the United States again as payment of war debts (see Figure 6.1). Everything ultimately rested on American capital. One sign of weakness on Wall Street, and the whole fragile structure would come tumbling down.

The Weakening of Colonial Authority

If the war debts–reparations problem primarily concerned the two former enemies, France and Germany, a second area of interwar weakness, the colonial question, involved France in a common difficulty with its recent ally and rival colonial power, Great Britain.

From one standpoint, 1919 marked the apogee of European colonialism. With the breakup of the Ottoman Empire and the assignment of most of its Arab-speaking areas as mandates to Britain and France, the Europeans had brought under their control an unprecedented extent of territory. At the same time, however, the reaction against colonialism was already beginning. The Wilsonian innovation of mandates had implied it, and almost constant unrest in some of the more advanced areas of Asia and Africa proved that the lesson of self-determination that Wilson had preached in Europe was finding eager converts in the Europeans' colonies and dependent states.

France's troubles lay in the Arab world. In Morocco, which had never been completely pacified after its acquisition in 1912, revolt flared among the tribesmen of the Riff mountains. In the mid-1920s, the French and the Spanish (who held a smaller Moroccan protectorate over the Mediterranean coast area) were obliged to fight a regular military campaign of subjugation until they finally captured the rebel leader Abd el-Krim. A similar situation prevailed in the new mandate of Syria, where the insurgent Druses resisted for nearly two years. Here once again the French were driven to drastic measures—only after they had twice bombarded Damascus could they recover control of the Syrian capital and put the Druse leaders to flight.

The British sore point was India—the largest and most populous colonial area in the world. The postwar era started badly with the Amritsar massacre. In April 1919, a local military commander ordered his soldiers to fire on an unarmed crowd gathered for a Hindu festival for a full ten minutes, with a resulting loss of nearly four hundred lives. Amritsar was not an isolated incident; it marked the beginning of the alienation of the Indian elite, who increasingly sided with the nationalist Congress party (founded before the war), and accepted the teachings of civil disobedience and nonviolent resistance incarnated in the compelling personality of Mahatma Gandhi. To Gandhi and his followers, British reliance on force to maintain control of India showed the true weakness of their colonial masters. When London continued to impose the wartime suspension of civil liberties after 1918, Gandhi countered by calling for a nationwide boycott of British goods and a refusal to obey the "Black Acts" suspending civil rights. His well-publicized fasts and his march to the sea in 1930 in defiance of the government's salt monopoly made the British look ridiculous. To these subtle acts of rebellion the colonial power could find no better reply than a crude resort to mass arrests.

By 1935 Gandhi's propaganda had won a substantial success. The Government of India Act of that year, by providing for native ministries in the Indian provinces, obviously offered a preparation for full independence. And the framework for India's continued association with Britain had also been made ready with the evolution of the Empire into a Commonwealth of sovereign states. Here the decisive act was the Statute of Westminster of 1931, which completed the transformation of the overseas dominions—Canada, Australia, New Zealand, South Africa, and the Irish Free State—into independent nations, linked to Great Britain only by the symbol of a common crown and by sentimental ties of long association. Through this act—and the settlement with Ireland that had preceded it—the British showed that for all their ineptness in India, they were a full generation ahead of the French in their conceptions of colonial development.

The Decay of Liberalism
and the Authoritarian Undercurrent

The colonial question was particularly embarrassing to liberal and radical parties. Conservatives could frankly assert the superiority of European rule, but the ideologists of progress found it impossible to square the realities of colonial government with the democratic principles they advocated at home.

The colonial dilemma was only one manifestation of the obsolescence of liberalism, which became increasingly apparent as the decade of the 1920s wore on. That obsolescence was evident in the dwindling of the German Democrats, in the incapacity of the French Radicals to deal with the financial crisis, in the electoral decline of the British Liberals. Parties such as these seemed unable to cope with current problems. The solutions they offered were too literary and rhetorical, too vague, too moralistic—in short, too old-fashioned. Although high-minded and tolerant, their leaders had neither the technical competence nor the toughness of soul needed to deal with the economic stringencies and crude realities of power that were coming to dominate the postwar era.

Conservative, business-oriented leaders—men like Stresemann or Baldwin or the two Chamberlains or Poincaré—could at least make some show of coping with such problems. A military figure or "strong man" could stage an even more plausible performance. And however modest a figure they might cut, "strong men" were never long absent from the scene in the middle and late 1920s.

The first of these "strong men" to appear on the postwar political stage was the future Italian dictator, Benito Mussolini. In October 1922, after threatening to march on Rome with his bands of black-shirted Fascists—ostensibly to deliver the Italian capital from the threat of a "Bolshevist" insurrection—Mussolini succeeded in having himself named Italian prime minister by the frightened king. Yet once in power, he moved cautiously. For nearly two years he governed with a semblance of parliamentary legality and respect for such liberal tenets as press freedom and the multiparty system. Many Italians, unsure of Mussolini's intentions but grateful for the stability he had brought to a country in chaos, assumed that he would simply impose strong government within the framework of existing Italian institutions. But beginning in 1924, after fraudulent elections had given his Fascist party a crushing majority in parliament, Mussolini showed his true hand. He progressively subverted what was left of Italian liberties and replaced the republic with a "corporatist" state of which he was now the uncontested leader (see Chapter 9, I).

Mussolini was not alone. In 1923, General Primo de Rivera seized power in Spain. Three years later, Marshal Pilsudski set up a similar military dictatorship in Poland—thereby establishing a pattern that each of the new democracies of East Central Europe was to follow, until only Czechoslovakia remained in the parliamentary mold. In Eastern Europe the usual formula became a veiled dictatorship in which the monarch himself played the leading role. In 1929 King Alexander of Yugoslavia took over the realities of power—as King Carol was to do after his triumphant return to Romania in 1930, and King Boris in Bulgaria later in the same decade. These royal dictatorships were not full-fledged fascist regimes; they maintained the form, if not the substance, of parliamentary government. But they prepared for a fascist mentality in East Central Europe by the practices they encouraged or tolerated—police brutality, the training of young people for systematic violence, anti-Semitism, the persecution of national minorities, and the tacit alliance of the wealthier classes with military adventurers.

Meantime the Portuguese had established what came to be the longest-lived of European dictatorships. In 1926 a military coup had overthrown the country's republican regime. Two years later, Antonio de Oliveira Salazar had taken office as minister of finance and the strongest figure in the government. In 1930 a single party was founded on a quasi-fascist model, and in 1932 Salazar became prime minister and the unquestioned ruler of his country—a post which he was to occupy without interruption during the succeeding three and a half decades of tumult and overturn in European political history. Thus, by 1930, quite openly in East Central Europe, and just under the surface in the democratic West, rightist authoritarianism was quietly prospering. Mussolini was at the height of his popularity at home, and an increasing number of people abroad, more particularly in Germany, were talking about imitating him.

To date the new authoritarianism had shown a reassuring face. In most respects it seemed to reinforce, rather than to undermine, the prevailing temper of sober conservatism. But what would happen if it should discard moderation and if its destructive and "demonic" aspects rose to dominance? Here Germany obviously held the key—and it was troubling to observe that German clandestine rearmament had become more brazen and that Soviet Russia, in accordance with an understanding originally reached at Rapallo in 1922, was providing factories and training areas for the German armed forces in return for German technical education. This was the last and worst of the secret nightmares of the 1920s. The Soviet-German understanding, which Locarno had weakened but not destroyed, might one day flower into a true alliance before which the democracies of Western Europe would find themselves adrift and powerless.

READINGS

Jon Jacobson, in *Locarno Diplomacy* (1972), gives a sober assessment of the Locarno Agreement's limited effects in reducing European tensions. An older but still useful account of interwar diplomacy is the collaborative volume edited by Gordon A. Craig and Felix Gilbert, *The Diplomats: 1919–1939** (1953). Judith M. Hughes, in *To the Maginot Line: The Politics of French Military Preparations in the 1920s* (1971), critiques in thoroughgoing fashion the conventional assumptions about French diplomacy and military policy. The pressures exerted by the world of finance on international relations in the 1920s are illuminated in Stephen A. Schuker, *The End of French Predominance in Europe: The Financial Crisis of 1924 and the Adoption of the Dawes Plan* (1976) and Dan P. Silverman, *Reconstructing Europe After the Great War* (1982).

For an introduction to domestic politics during this period, in addition to Sontag (see readings for Chapter 5), there is the fine comparative study of Charles S. Maier, *Recasting Bourgeois Europe: Stabilization in France, Germany, and Italy in the Decade After World War I** (1974). For the vicissitudes of Weimar politics, see Arthur Rosenberg's *A History of the German Republic* (1936); Erich Eyck's *A History of the Weimar Republic,** 2 vols. (1962–1963); and the more recent work by A. J. Nicholls, *Weimar and the Rise of Hitler,** 2d ed. (1980). Jonathan Wright, *Gustav Stresemann, Weimar's Greatest Statesman* (2002) makes a strong case for the thesis in its subtitle. Anton Kaes, Martin Jay, and Edward Dimendberg, eds., *The Weimar Republic Sourcebook** (1994) is especially strong on social and cultural history. For Britain, besides Mowat and Stevenson (see readings for Chapter 5) there are A. J. P. Taylor, *English History, 1915–1945** (1965) and Max Beloff, *Wars and Welfare: Britain, 1914–1945* (1967). Ross McKibben's *The Evolution of the Labour Party, 1910–1924** (1974) traces the road that led to the first Labor government. On France, see Philippe Bernard and Henri Dubief, *The Decline of the Third Republic, 1914–1938** (1985), as well as the relevant chapters in David Thomson's *Democracy in France Since 1870,** 5th ed. (1969), which is excellent on long-term trends.

On the Irish struggle for independence, see the relevant chapters in R. F. Foster, *Modern Ireland, 1660–1972** (1988), and Peter de Rosa, *The Rebels: The Irish Rising of 1916** (1990), a journalistic but vivid account of the Easter rebellion. On the issue of Northern Ireland, see Nicholas Mansergh, *The Unresolved Question: the Anglo-Irish Settlement and Its Undoing, 1912–1972* (1991). The transformation of Irish politics into literary myth and patriotic identity is chronicled in Declan Kiberd's richly suggestive *Inventing Ireland: The Literature of the Modern Nation* (1996).

On the rise of Fascism in Italy, in addition to Maier, see Elizabeth Wiskemann, *Fascism in Italy** (1969) and Adrian Lyttleton, *The Seizure of Power: Fascism in Italy, 1919–1929** (1973). Stanley G. Payne, *A History of Fascism, 1914–1945** (1995), examines the decay of liberalism and the appeal of right-wing solutions in interwar Europe, as does Walter Laqueur and George Mosse, eds., *International Fascism, 1920–1945** (1966), which first appeared as an issue of the *Journal of Contemporary History*.

*Books marked with an asterisk are available in paperback.

THE HIGH CULTURE
OF THE 1920s

Albert Einstein (1879–1955) writes an equation for the density of the Milky Way during a visit to Pasadena, California in 1931. (*Courtesy AP/Wide World Photos*)

I. THE CULTURAL SETTING

A Decade of Innovation

In politics and economics, the 1920s were predominantly years of conservatism and caution; in cultural life, however, these years were marked by bold innovation. In this decade, the "modern temper" finally triumphed, altering the character of science and the arts for a full generation. Yet the change was far from uniform. In each cultural area, words like "modern" or "contemporary" carried very different meanings. In physics, they meant relativity, plural explanations, and indeterminacy; in social thought, they suggested both a cult of the irrational and a meticulous concern for precise meanings; in literature, they conveyed bold explorations of the inner world of thought and feeling; in the fine arts and music, they signified a revolt against sentimentality and an inclination toward sharp tones and hard outlines. But in every instance, twentieth-century styles displayed a common scorn toward the preceding century. The cultural innovators rejected the lessons of their grandfathers and self-consciously chose new idioms of expression.

Toward the generation of their fathers, however, they frequently showed more respect. Actually, the cultural innovations of the 1920s were not as startling as they seemed to the contemporary public. Many—perhaps most—of them were the logical outgrowths of changes that occurred a generation earlier. The twentieth-century revolution in physics had its origins in the 1890s, as did Freud's theory of psychoanalysis and Schoenberg's twelve-tone scale. Indeed, in the last two instances, the innovators themselves found in the 1920s the wider audience that they had earlier been unable to reach. Such experiences were common in the immediate postwar years: Ideas or modes of expression that before the war had appeared to be revolutionary or impossibly difficult now began to attract the attention and to win the allegiance of the general educated public. The war itself was thus not the cause of the wave of cultural innovation that preceded it, but it did contribute to an increased receptiveness toward cultural novelty. The social and psychological shocks that four years of struggle had inflicted disturbed established patterns of thought and expression and prepared for new ways of looking at the universe. Again and again in the postwar years, it was asserted that Europe's traditional culture had failed—that the leisurely cultural traditions of the European upper bourgeoisie no longer sufficed to express the new realities of life and that something sharper and more vital must be created to take its place. The result was a cultural and scientific outpouring of a richness that no other single decade in the century can match.

The Major Centers

In novelty of expression, defeated Germany took the lead. This was perhaps natural since German society was so much more gravely disturbed by the war and its aftermath than were the societies of France or Britain. In Germany, the former ruling classes—and the culture they embodied—had abdicated their authority. The prewar Reich had exuded an atmosphere of stuffiness and self-satisfaction; in postwar Germany, the cultural temper was raffish, tormented, and revolutionary. For a number of years, the young insurgents had the arts almost entirely to themselves, and even when life became somewhat more stable, the cultural atmosphere of Weimar Germany remained incomparably lively and diverse. Only in the quieter university towns did intellectual activity continue much as before. Towns such as Göttingen and Tübingen kept their previous eminence, as did the artistic and literary center of Munich. But the great novelty was the sudden emergence of Berlin—modern, untrammeled by tradition, and the largest city on the European continent—as the most experimental and daring center of all.

Paris, however, still eclipsed Berlin in range of cultural activity. The city on the Seine remained what it had been for centuries: the literary and artistic capital of Europe. Indeed, in certain respects Paris increased its earlier lead. In the field of painting it had no rival. The school of Paris drew into its orbit not only the most varied talents from all parts of France but also the eager and ambitious who poured in from Spain and Italy, from Russia and America. In the ballet, in the theater, in the novel, Paris enjoyed a preeminence that was reinforced by the talents of foreigners. The Russian ballet and the American expatriate novelists like Ernest Hemingway suggest how postwar conditions intensified artists' long-established tendency to seek in Paris the ideal city for cultural creation.

In different ways, then, Berlin and Paris both profited because other centers had apparently become less hospitable to talent. American writers fled to France in revulsion against postwar conventionality and "materialism" in their own country. Austrians and Hungarians, who had become accustomed to life in great capital cities, felt cramped and stifled within the narrow confines to which the settlement of 1919 had reduced their national communities. Tens of thousands of educated Russians fled from Bolshevik tyranny, as did a smaller number of Italians after the establishment of the Fascist dictatorship. Thus the 1920s saw the beginnings of that uprooting of European intellectuals which was to become almost a mass movement in the next two decades.

Two further changes occurred. In England, the decade of the 1920s was characterized by an extraordinary deprovincializing of cultural life. No longer did Britain seem as separated from the Continent as it had once been; no longer were the British themselves so satisfied with their traditional island ways. Now they were much more ready to learn from the French and the Germans, the Russians and the Austrians. Here again the experience of four years of fighting in a continental war doubtless contributed to the change of attitude. Before 1914, the "Bloomsbury Circle," for example, had been a group of very young writers without much influence; now it set the intellectual fashions by quiet but persuasive propaganda for French painting, the Russian ballet, and Viennese psychoanalysis. The Bloomsbury group had grown up in the intense intellectual atmosphere of Cambridge—and the 1920s were also to be the period in which the preeminence of Cambridge in physics and philosophy won nearly universal recognition. The 1920s likewise saw music—a form of art that Britain for two centuries had chiefly regarded as an alien importation from the Continent—at length achieving a new status, as major native composers awakened the interest of an alert and educated public.

II. The Progress of Natural Science

The Revolution in Physics

In the early twentieth century, physics stood out as the dominant natural science—displacing biology and geology, which had held a similar position in the age of Darwin. In both cases the reasons for preeminence were the same. In the late nineteenth century, the biological sciences provided the metaphors and ways of thought—positive, determinist, material—that were congenial to the wider intellectual temper and seemed most readily applicable in other fields. In the twentieth century, the more abstract and indeterminate language of physics appealed to a society that was questioning nearly all the old certainties. Furthermore, a spurt of progress resembling that which biology had made in the second half of the nineteenth century was to give physics a special prestige in the first third of the century following.

At its earliest, the twentieth-century revolution in physics can be dated from 1895, when Professor Wilhelm Konrad Röntgen of Munich discovered X-rays. Thus began the atomic age, as one revelation followed another in quick succession. A year after Röntgen's discovery, Henri Becquerel's experiments with uranium opened the way to an analysis of radioactivity, on which Pierre Curie and his wife, Marie, were soon to be working, and in the next year, the identification of the electron as a negatively charged particle suggested an approach to explaining this whole series of new phenomena.

Initially, the explanations were presented in terms that combined the old Newtonian principles of motion with the nineteenth-century concept of electricity. Thus the physicists of the first decade of the twentieth century viewed electricity as the common property of all matter and pictured the atom as a miniature Newtonian solar system, in which the positively charged nucleus held in dynamic tension negatively charged electrons—varying in number from one in the case of hydrogen to ninety-two in the case of uranium—that were circling in orbits around it. In this fashion, a physicist like Lord Rutherford (working first in Montreal and Manchester, subsequently in Cambridge) in 1903 was able to ascribe radioactivity to an explosive disintegration of atoms of great weight—that is, those that had a large number of electrons in orbit—and seven years later to make the basic discovery that identified the nucleus of the atom with its positive charge.

Many previously unfamiliar phenomena fitted conveniently into the new explanatory scheme. On the border between physics and chemistry, it enabled scientists to bring to virtual completion the periodic table of the elements by locating several theoretically possible elements that earlier had escaped detection. Meantime, however, two further threats to intellectual consistency had appeared. In different forms, the discoveries of Albert Einstein and Max Planck overturned the newly devised scheme of explanation and opened the major phase in the physical revolution that is still going on.

Einstein's work bore only tangentially on atomic theory, since it dealt chiefly with mechanics and astrophysics. As early as 1905, he had suggested that the notion of space and time as absolutes had to be abandoned, that these categories should properly be viewed as always relative to the person measuring them. During the First World War,

Einstein extended his theory to encompass the phenomenon of gravitation. His general theory of relativity postulated that the properties of both time and space are affected by a gravitational field. The stronger the gravitation, the slower the time and the more "curved" the surrounding space. Like a magnet that attracts iron filings placed near it and rearranges them in a predictable pattern, Einstein argued, a large mass such as a star exerts a measurable influence on the space-time continuum in its immediate vicinity. During the solar eclipse of 1919, Einstein's calculation of the deflection of light by the sun's gravity was confirmed by simultaneous astronomical observations from points on both shores of the South Atlantic.

Even for atomic physics, however, the implications of Einstein's theory of relativity were already clear. The hard, solid "matter" of traditional science—which men like Rutherford had dissolved into electricity—needed to be redefined further in terms that made its particles no more than a "series of events in space-time." These conclusions were confirmed by the more directly relevant theories of Max Planck, who, independent of Einstein, had almost simultaneously arrived at equally revolutionary conclusions.

Planck originally devised his "quantum theory" in 1900 to take account of certain jumps and discontinuities that he had observed in radiation phenomena. According to his new explanation, radiation did not come in continuous waves but rather in definite units or *quanta*. Indeed it was in terms of quanta, Planck argued, that energy, in general, and changes of atomic structure, in particular, should be viewed. At the start, physicists did not quite realize how novel this theory was, and the efforts of Niels Bohr of Copenhagen to fit Planck's quanta into the "solar system" explanation of the atom seemed initially successful. In 1913, Bohr, working in Rutherford's laboratory, devised a way of combining the English physicist's theory of orbits with a concept of a series of "jumps" of electrons from one orbit to another.

This reconciliatory theory held the field for twelve years. Then in 1925 began the final phase of the revolution in physics, when it was discovered that Bohr's explanations did not account for all the phenomena observed in the hydrogen spectrum. Only in the more abstract language of differential equations could new explanations be devised that treated light as having certain properties of a wave as well as those of a series of particles. In terms of classical mechanics, unitary theory had broken down completely. Sometimes one spoke of particles, sometimes of waves. Physicists chose between the two on a pragmatic basis as one theory rather than the other seemed to fit particular experimental facts. Bohr himself, driven to revise his own earlier theories, spoke of a new philosophical concept, which he termed "complementarity" and which allowed for the simultaneous existence of two seemingly incompatible states. Rather than being mutually exclusive, the concepts of light as particles and of light as waves could be seen to coexist, however uneasily, on a higher logical plane.

Physics was fast moving toward the very limits of what could be known with certainty. In 1927, Bohr's younger German colleague, Werner Heisenberg, arrived at the formulation of an *indeterminacy principle*, for which he was to receive the Nobel Prize. Subatomic particles, Heisenberg argued, could have either their position or their velocity plotted with reasonable accuracy. But it was impossible to have a complete knowledge of both at once. The more precisely one determined the position, the less precisely one could ascertain the velocity, and vice versa. The best that could be done was to assign limits to our ignorance through a mathematical equation that showed what could not be known. Given this irreducible uncertainty, Heisenberg argued, particles such as electrons should be treated with the tools of statistics—their exact position and velocity described in terms of probability. This conclusion Einstein refused to accept. At a meeting of physicists held in Belgium in 1930, he insisted that Heisenberg's "indeterminacy" was merely a temporary setback on the road to more certain knowledge of the universe. To reduce the physical world to the merely probable was an idea that he found repellent. "God," he asserted, "does not throw dice." Thus the greatest pioneer of twentieth-century physics found the revolutionary conclusions of his colleagues uncomfortable, though subsequent research has supported Heisenberg, not his brilliant critic.

However bewildering abstract scientific theory might appear around 1930, on the level of practical applications, scientists were advancing from triumph to triumph. Two milestones of the year 1919 inaugurated the period of applied atomic physics: the invention of the mass spectroscope, which made possible the identification of more than two hundred stable isotopes (that is, variant forms of the basic atoms), and Rutherford's initial experiment with controlled atomic transformations. During further experiments of the latter sort, physicists discovered a whole new series of constituent particles of the atom comparable to electrons—positrons, protons, neutrons, and the like—until, by 1944, seven in all had been identified. The most far-reaching of these discoveries was the identification of the neutron by Sir James Chadwick in 1932. It was with these particles, which carried no charge and hence could pass freely through the atoms in their paths, that the physicists began the intense bombardment of basic matter which was to culminate during the Second World War in the awesome discovery of the atomic bomb.

Yet in the organization of scientific research, economic and social factors began to exert an increasingly important influence. In the past, the isolated scientist or physician could produce useful and even epoch-making results with the simple equipment of his own home laboratory. By the 1920s, however, only a well-furnished laboratory or research institute could contribute to the growth of scientific knowledge. With this change, the problem of the organization and financing of research took on a new urgency. In such respects, a large and wealthy society like that of the United States enjoyed obvious advantages; a command economy, such as the Soviet Union, held potential assets for the future. Thus even as early as the 1920s, men of science in the three countries that together had accounted for most of the scientific progress of the nineteenth century—Britain, Germany, and France—were beginning to wonder whether the economy and the way of life that had yielded such marvelous results a generation or two earlier would prove capable of dealing with the unfamiliar and pressing demands of twentieth-century mass society.

III. SOCIAL SCIENCE AND PHILOSOPHY

The "Old Masters": Freud, Croce, Weber, Durkheim

In social thought, the decade of the 1920s can be regarded in two contrasting fashions. On the one hand, it was an era of consolidation, in which an earlier revolution in ways of looking at society began to find wide acceptance and to extend into new areas of knowledge. On the other hand, it was marked by a philosophical revolution of its own, which drastically altered the earlier vocabulary of intellectual exchange, creating a cleavage between English and continental thinking that was never satisfactorily bridged.

At the end of the First World War, a generation of unusually original social thinkers was passing from the scene or turning its intellectual activity in new directions. In Austria, the most influential figure of the whole half century—Sigmund Freud—had virtually completed the outlines of his psychoanalytic theory. In Italy, Benedetto Croce had attained a position of unquestioned philosophical leadership. The volumes of his *Philosophy of the Spirit* (1902–1909), in which Croce defined the criteria of aesthetics and historical study, were achieving the position of classic formulations that they retained for the whole interwar period. In Germany and France, Max Weber and Émile Durkheim had put the study of sociology on a more empirical and objective basis, by deriving from specific and manageable problems the principles for the scientific study of society that the nineteenth-century fathers of sociology had tried in vain to formulate at one blow.

Durkheim died during the war; Weber, a year and a half after its close. Freud and Croce lived on for another generation, broadening the scope of their thinking and directing it into novel and unsuspected channels. But the effect on younger contemporaries was the same—alive or dead, the "old masters" continued to dominate the field, and the study of human society remained fixed in the paths that these had marked out for it in the prewar years.

Psychology: Behaviorism, Gestalt Theory, and the Heirs of Freud

Without doubt, the greatest single change that distinguished the intellectual atmosphere of the 1920s from that of the period before 1914 was psychology's leap into the center of attention. Here again, however, the way had been prepared in the prewar era. The social thought of the decade and a half preceding the outbreak of the war had been markedly subjective in character. In nearly all the major writings of this period, the common element had been an emphasis on unconscious mental processes, on criticism of one's own thinking, and on the doubtful character of knowledge about society. The war experience had further encouraged this tendency toward subjectivity and self-doubt. When all stable values had been thrown into question, the human psyche emerged as the one fixed point in an indeterminate universe.

The Freudian theory of psychoanalysis most clearly exemplified the new trend, but its preeminence did not pass unquestioned. The laboratory study of experimental psychology continued on its patient, cautious way, scarcely troubled by the philosophical quarrels of the Freudians and their foes. These latter included the Behaviorists, who followed the American J. B. Watson in stressing the relationship of internal feelings to the observable activities and the physiological structure of the individual—as opposed to the psychoanalytic practice of deducing unconscious thought and emotion from dreams, random remarks, and slips in speech. Behaviorism—in Europe at least—had only a passing influence; a more serious intellectual challenge to the teachings of Freud came from the German Gestalt school. These theorists, who were speculative philosophers rather than clinicians, held that the way to understand an individual mind was through the painstaking delineation of its whole form (*Gestalt*) in an effort to grasp all the subtle connections linking the complexities and apparent contradictions that constituted a single, unique emotional life.

Nevertheless, it was Freud and his school who aroused the liveliest interest. The great Viennese psychiatrist was a little more than sixty and apparently at the height of his powers when the war came to an end. Four years later, however, he was stricken by a cancer of the mouth, which necessitated operation after operation and which finally killed him in 1939, just after the outbreak of the second world conflict. This constant battle with illness severely limited Freud's ability to work—but he continued with stoical resolution in the two main areas of his earlier activity, the clinical practice of psychoanalysis and the publication of books and articles on psychological theory.

Most of Freud's time was devoted to clinical psychiatry, which he had revolutionized a generation earlier with his novel technique of free association. More and more, however, those who lay on the couch in his office and sought his help were not regular patients but fledgling psychiatrists who had come to Vienna to be trained in psychoanalytic method. In the half decade before the war, psychoanalysis had become an international movement, and although the four years of the conflict checked this development, its growth was resumed after 1918 on a still larger scale. Besides Vienna, which remained the general headquarters, Berlin, Budapest, London, and New York were main centers of psychoanalytic teaching and practice. Paris, Rome, and the Latin and Catholic countries

Sigmund Freud (1856–1939), founder of the school of psychoanalysis. (*Courtesy Brown Brothers*)

in general showed themselves much less receptive to Freudian ideas. It was in the German- and the English-speaking worlds that psychoanalysis became firmly established in the 1920s.

The foundation of new psychoanalytic institutes and the maintenance of contact among them necessitated a great deal of consultation and correspondence on the part of the founder himself. Freud also continued with his theoretical writing, but it began to change in character. The main structure of his theory, which he had begun in 1899, with his *Interpretation of Dreams*, was now finished. In contrast to the volumes that presented and explained the central ideas and the method of psychoanalysis, Freud's later writings were shorter and more speculative, and they showed greater concern for the social and historical implications of his theories. The most influential of these, *Civilization and Its Discontents* (1930), dealt with the restriction of instinctual expression that Freud found inevitable in civilized societies and forecast the inhuman behavior to which the authoritarian states of Europe would very shortly resort. The measured pessimism in this little book was echoed in two brief studies of religion: *The Future of an Illusion* (1927), in which Freud voiced his confidence in a humanist and atheist morality, and *Moses and Monotheism* (1939), his last work, in which he traced the tragic history of the Jews (his own ancestors) to their creation of the concept of a single deity.

Meantime the psychoanalytic movement continued to be shaken by internal splits and struggles that were themselves of an almost religious intensity. Just before the first war there had been two notable defections from the Freudian camp. One of these, led by Alfred Adler of Vienna, had tried to turn psychoanalysis away from its basic emphasis on the unconscious emotions of the individual and to direct it toward questions of conscious participation in group life. Adler's teaching offered a curious combination of stress on the will—a Nietzschean inheritance—and of socialist ideals of Marxist origin. In the 1920s its influence did not extend very far, and Adler's own death in 1937 robbed it of its chief. The real importance of ideas of this sort was to be apparent only a decade later, when the Second World War focused attention once again on the relation between individual psychology and the organization of society.

A more serious challenge came from the Swiss Carl G. Jung, who had once ranked as Freud's heir apparent. In the years following the war, Jung diverged further and further from the teachings of his original master. Through his study of Oriental philosophy and religion, the Swiss psychiatrist concluded that there existed a vast "collective unconscious" in which the same myth symbols kept repeating themselves in widely separated places and ages. By tapping the resources of these great "archetypes," Jung argued, people could reach a higher understanding of their emotional difficulties. Hence, although he did not profess a specific faith of his own, Jung urged on his patients and on his readers the therapeutic value of a return to religion. In this emphasis on the usefulness of faith—which contrasted so sharply with Freud's atheism—Jung made a notable contribution to the wider movement of return to religion in the postwar epoch.

Sociology and Anthropology

During the war and immediate postwar years, Max Weber wrote the books that were to rank as the basic documents of contemporary sociology. In his studies of the relation between religion and economic activity, and in his work of synthesis, *Wirtschaft und*

Gesellschaft (Economics and Society), Weber tried to apply what he had earlier defined as the "ideal-type" method. This procedure involved the conscious and even arbitrary selection of certain typical or salient features of social and historical phenomena so as to "idealize" them and thus make them comparable to one another.

In 1919 and 1920, Weber's influence was at its height. After two decades of withdrawal from teaching—made necessary by a severe psychic depression—he had accepted a university chair in Munich. The Bavarian capital was an extremely lively place in these years; a brief phase of left-wing Socialist and Communist rule had been followed by a longer period of nationalist reaction. Extremism of all sorts was flourishing; indeed, the same persons often engaged in both political and artistic experimentation. For all these contrasting tendencies, Weber had understanding and even sympathy. His mind was a tissue of contradictions held in tense equilibrium—he was a fervent nationalist and a doctrinaire democrat, a freethinker and a man fascinated by religion, an unsparing critic of socialist doctrines who held Marx in deep respect. Young people of every ideological allegiance turned to him for political and intellectual guidance, but this he could not give. He was far too shaken by scruples and self-doubt.

Weber's untimely death in 1920 at the age of fifty-six robbed Germany of its leading social thinker. But his students and colleagues continued the study of sociology in the ideal-type framework that Weber had devised and in the close relationship to history that was congenial to the German tradition. In the process, inevitable alterations occurred. Among the older generations, Werner Sombart turned more and more to a semi-mystical interpretation of community spirit that eventually landed him in the Nazi camp. Among the juniors, Karl Mannheim tried to combine Weber's teaching with the analysis of the collective thinking of classes and social groups that the philosopher Max Scheler had baptized the "sociology of knowledge." The result was a shifting, many-layered type of sociological argument that pushed the relativist implications of Weber's thought to their logical conclusions. Mannheim's *Ideology and Utopia* (1929) constituted a summing up of two generations of political and intellectual debate in Germany on the eve of the National Socialist onslaught.

Italy had produced in the period before the war two great political sociologists—Vilfredo Pareto and Gaetano Mosca—but their influence was limited and perverted in the course of the 1920s. With the advent of Mussolini in 1922, there began an official direction of intellectual life that tried either to suppress social theory entirely or to steer it into support of the regime. Such "steering" proved to be relatively easy with Pareto's writings, which taught a hard, unsentimental doctrine of rule by elites in the tradition of Machiavelli; moreover, Pareto died in 1923 after having given fascism his qualified support. Mosca, in contrast, had expressed the same Machiavellian inheritance and the same emphasis on a "governing class" in terms of liberalism and constitutional government. His writings were clearly antifascist in tone, and from the floor of the Italian Senate—whose members were appointed for life—Mosca voiced his opposition in measured but uncompromising terms. So did another senator, Benedetto Croce, the dominant figure in Italian intellectual life. Yet Croce was hostile to the study of both psychology and sociology, and under his guidance, Italian social thought remained almost exclusively absorbed with history and philosophy. Not until the 1930s was Croce to expand the range of his historical thinking to embrace a full-scale repudiation of authoritarianism in all its forms (see Chapter 11, II).

One of the greatest strengths of the work of Émile Durkheim in France had been his combination of sociology and anthropology as a single academic pursuit. After Durkheim's death in 1917, this legacy remained, and the two subjects continued to be linked in the French curriculum. Indeed, of all the social sciences, anthropology made the greatest progress in the 1920s. This had been the last of these studies to be fully defined. In the nineteenth century it had still been largely in the hands of explorers, missionaries, and imaginative amateurs. After the First World War, it became more systematic, as the anthropologists of France, Britain, and the United States elaborated their techniques of field investigation. From France, the heirs of Durkheim applied in the field the lessons that their master had worked out at home; in England, a new generation of anthropologists put almost their whole emphasis on long residence in Africa or the Pacific, with only scant attention to the claims of theory.

Philosophy: Irrationalism and Logical Empiricism

In philosophy also, the irrational found enthusiastic exponents. Indeed it was here—at least on the more popular levels of philosophical expression—that the lessons of the previous generation were most seriously misunderstood in the postwar years. Men like Freud had emphasized the irrational only to understand it better, to master it, and to guide it into constructive channels. They were not irrationalists in the sense of being on the side of unreason. Yet in the postwar generation many writers did declare themselves frankly and enthusiastically for "thinking with the blood" and contributed to the advent of fascism in Italy and Germany by giving it a specious veneer of intellectual respectability.

The new and really revolutionary tendencies in philosophy, however, were embodied in what in most general terms can be called the analytic school. Analytic philosophy had its origin in the work of two Cambridge scholars, Bertrand Russell and Alfred North Whitehead, who in the years 1910–1913 published its founding charter, the *Principia Mathematica*. As its name implied, this treatise sought to recast philosophical prose in mathematical form. Disgusted by the vagueness of traditional idealism, Russell and Whitehead argued that only by using the unambiguous language of mathematics and symbolic logic could philosophy speak with the clarity and precision at which it had always aimed.

In the war and postwar years, these teachings made steady but unspectacular progress in the English universities. On the Continent, however, they impinged with explosive force. Here a number of young Germans and Austrians, inspired by Russell's example, formed the "Vienna Circle" in 1923. Their unofficial leader was Rudolf Carnap, but most people were to associate them with Ludwig Wittgenstein, whose *Tractatus Logico-Philosophicus*, published in 1921, became the most influential philosophical work of the entire half century. In this terse, intentionally provocative statement, Wittgenstein tried to reduce to nonsense nearly all the major concerns of traditional ethics and metaphysics. Nothing, he argued, that could not be talked about without ambiguity in the language of symbols or of ordinary speech deserved to be treated as philosophy at all. The rest was best left unspoken.

This new doctrine of logical positivism—or logical empiricism, as it was later called—never won much favor on the Continent. To Frenchmen and Germans, it seemed far too radically destructive. It took away too much of the traditional material of philosophical discourse by reducing it to a set of highly abstract propositions that only a few initiates could understand. Continental philosophers generally refused to make this sacrifice and continued in their loose and speculative ways, but in Britain and the United States, logical empiricism gradually became the new orthodoxy. And this receptiveness to the doctrines of the Vienna Circle was reinforced when in 1929 Wittgenstein emigrated to England—where he educated a whole generation of Cambridge philosophers to devote minute attention to the possibilities and pitfalls of ordinary language—and when, a few years later, Carnap went to the United States.

Analytic philosophy had originated in the Anglo-Saxon world, where empiricism and an antimetaphysical attitude had always been at home; its passage through Vienna seems in retrospect rather accidental. By the 1930s—when authoritarian government was stifling free inquiry in the German-speaking world and Austria had ceased to be a major center of thought—there was a complete philosophical cleavage between the Continent on the one hand and Britain and the United States on the other. Between German or French speculation on ethics and metaphysics, and Anglo-American analysis of the narrow problems that alone were compatible with the rigorous methods of logical empiricism, any sort of meaningful exchange had become almost impossible.

IV. IMAGINATIVE LITERATURE: EXPLORING THE INNER WORLD

The Postwar Mood: Expressionism, Dadaism, Surrealism

In imaginative literature—in poetry, drama, and the novel—the 1920s were the period in which the small groups of writers who before the war had constituted an experimental avant-garde suddenly found themselves in control of the field. Of course, realist writing of the late nineteenth-century type did not die out completely. In England, for example, Edwardian novelists like John Galsworthy and H. G. Wells continued to publish with great success. Throughout Europe most books remained in the realist vein. But such work was beginning to seem old-fashioned and conventional. The general public went on reading it, but those who considered themselves modern found it dull and turned toward more experimental writing.

The common denominator among these newer writers was a focus on the inner world of their characters—on the hidden depths of memory, aesthetic perception, and emotion—as opposed to the earlier emphasis on accuracy of external description and on dramatic plots. Virginia Woolf, for example, chided Edwardian writers for having "laid an enormous stress on the fabric of things" and insisted that they had thereby missed all that really mattered. In this, Woolf and other writers of the 1920s were continuing the attempts to find a more satisfactory alternative to realism that had inspired the French symbolist poets and the members of the English Bloomsbury Circle before the war. The postwar writers were interested in going still further toward delineating unexplored regions of the psyche: For them, reality was to be sought above all in the mind of the observer. They were also absorbed with the problem of language, preferring strikingly new uses of words and style in order to convey their insights. Independent of Freud and Jung, whose theories they later welcomed as confirmation of their own discoveries, they searched out the unconscious anxiety or passion that underlaid the apparent senselessness of human actions.

Common interests of this sort, far more than any specific and self-conscious movement, distinguished the postwar literary scene from what had gone before. There was no lack of regularly constituted movements, as experiments proceeded simultaneously in many directions, but they were more prominent during the war and immediate postwar years than in the major phase of the 1920s. In Germany there was expressionism, which tried to strip the mask from conventional behavior and to generate a vital intensity of feeling in fields as diverse as poetry, theater, painting, music, dance, and film. Jagged lines and twisted features, brutally juxtaposed images and shattered syntax—all proclaimed the primacy of the artist's emotional response to the world around him as the principal subject of art. In neutral Switzerland, the war years saw the birth of dadaism— an even more violent explosion of anger against "false values" of all sorts. In France its more mystical postwar successor, surrealism, sought a new reality, a "logic of nonsense," beyond the reality of commonplace experience. André Breton, the movement's founder and chief theoretician, proposed in 1924 that "automatic writing" be substituted for more self-conscious creativity, the better to liberate the deepest levels of the psyche. When he wrote of a "revolver with white hair," for example, Breton hoped to forge a new poetic vocabulary of arresting, subliminally suggestive images—poetry freed from staid logic.

Once the immediate postwar ferment was over, however, the rather pretentious manifestos of these movements began to sink into insignificance. What was truly exciting and creative in them was absorbed into the wider perceptions of major writers who gave their allegiance to no single school; the rest was forgotten. A similar experience characterized painting, which in these tumultuous years had been enrolled under the same banners as literature.

The Novel: Proust, Kafka, Mann, Woolf, Joyce

Two novelists to whom the new receptiveness of the postwar reading public granted a sudden and belated fame were Marcel Proust and Franz Kafka. Both died early: Proust lived just long enough to experience his own triumph, but Kafka died unappreciated, and with the bulk of his work still unpublished.

The first volume of Marcel Proust's vast novel *Remembrance of Things Past* had appeared just before the war under the title *Swann's Way*. In its elusive and infinitely elaborated analysis of the author's childhood and of the mysterious meaning behind apparently insignificant memories, it seemed tedious and incomprehensible to the general public. But when the second installment appeared in 1919, it enjoyed immediate success. Proust dissected the social pretensions of prewar French society with both humor and finesse; in this he proved himself the heir of the nineteenth-century tradition of social observation and critique embodied in Stendhal and Balzac. Yet Proust also showed himself fully a writer of the modern age in his parallel focus on the inner world of the mind and his fascination with how we perceive people and events around us through the distorting lenses of memory and anticipation. Sheltered by a devoted servant and her chauffeur husband, Proust spent his last years as an eccentric invalid recluse, writing in bed and going out only at night to gather new material. It was in this fashion that he worked on the revision of the final volumes of his great novel until he died in 1922 at the age of fifty-one.

Kafka was twelve years younger than Proust and far less sure of his own genius. Shy, tormented, and inordinately frightened of his father, he passed a difficult life working for a large insurance firm in the Czech-speaking city of Prague, where he felt doubly alienated from the people around him, first as a German writer and second as a Jew. When he died in 1924, still a young man, Kafka had published very little—notably the extraordinary short story *Metamorphosis*. It was his posthumous novels that were to bring him fame. *The Trial* (1925) tells of a hero accused of a crime he cannot remember, brought before a court whose workings he cannot understand; in *The Castle* (1926), the main character is hired as a surveyor by an employer he never meets, secluded in a castle whose grounds he cannot enter despite repeated attempts. Kafka's fiction offered the reader fantasies of a world of threatening, inexplicable necessity, which left the individual bewildered and helpless, and in which later readers were to discover intimations of the authoritarian practices of the next decade.

In Germany itself, the new temper was exemplified by Thomas Mann. Mann had already distinguished himself in the prewar period with the novel *Buddenbrooks* (1901), which recounted the decline of a patrician merchant family in Mann's native north German city of Lübeck, and a number of short stories on the themes of art and eroticism. His still more ambitious study of disease, death, and ideological debate in an Alpine tuberculosis sanitarium, *The Magic Mountain* (1924), ranked second only to the works of Proust and Joyce in subsequent literary influence. Mann was to achieve his greatest international fame two decades later, when he became a symbol of literary opposition to Nazi tyranny in American exile.

Across the Channel, Virginia Woolf was the one major novelist to come out of the cultural ferment of Bloomsbury, and she was also, second only to Joyce, the major innovator of this period in English fiction. Woolf converted the novel into a pattern of internal monologues, proceeding in an apparently random succession of images, thoughts, and emotions that attempted to re-create with the greatest possible accuracy the actual workings of the conscious mind. A book like *Mrs. Dalloway* (1925) thus distilled a wide range of human experience from the reflections and sensations of the heroine on a single decisive day of her life. There was very little overt action in Woolf's novels; instead she examined small events as seen from several "complementary" (in Bohr's sense) points of view.

With Virginia Woolf, the new stream-of-consciousness technique remained within the bounds of traditional literary language; with her Irish contemporary, James Joyce, the old conventions were broken almost completely. The author of *Ulysses* (1922) had spent a cloistered Catholic childhood in Dublin; self-exiled to the Continent, he stayed proudly aloof from the psychoanalytic movement. And in the novel that disturbed its generation more than any other—*Ulysses*, the account of a single day in the streets and pubs and middle-class houses of Dublin—he indulged his literary fancy to the full. Word plays and parodies, scraps of recollection, and fragments of foreign languages tumbled one on another in an apparently hopeless confusion whose careful articulations only

Virginia Woolf (1882–1941), whose novels pioneered the new stream-of-consciousness technique. *(Courtesy Corbis-Bettmann)*

close study would reveal. Its successor, *Finnegans Wake* (1939), was still more hermetic, and its appearance prompted critics to ask whether Joyce had not led the novel to its farthest limits, beyond which lay only dissolution or a return to more conservative techniques.

V. THE ARTS: THE TRIUMPH OF THE MODERN

Music: Schoenberg, Stravinsky, "The Six," Prokofiev

If "modernism" in literature meant attention to the inner landscape of the mind and to stylistic innovations with which to convey its mysterious contours, what did it mean in the arts? There the principal focus was on freeing the expressive elements of artistic language—color and form in painting, pitch and rhythm in music—from traditional uses so that they would stand on their own. No longer did a painting have to depict recognizable objects from the everyday world; its beauty could be expressed in pure color and shape—a yellow triangle or a red square. Similarly, a musical composition could be expressive in ways that departed from a nineteenth-century emphasis on melody and classical harmony. The search for new means of expression had begun before the war in both these fields, and grew logically out of experiments already commenced in the previous century.

Only in the 1920s, however, did the greatest stylistic revolution since the Renaissance attain its full potency.

In music, the two capitals of early twentieth-century artistic innovation were Paris and Vienna. Vienna—with an unbroken musical tradition stretching back beyond Mozart—now saw the birth of a "Vienna School" of composers, led by Arnold Schoenberg, who challenged that tradition in a radical way. Schoenberg's musical evolution spanned the lush, late romantic style of his *Verklärte Nacht* (1899) and the expressionist intensity of *Erwartung* (1909), a monodrama for soloist and orchestra, which abandoned traditional tonality altogether. His dissatisfaction with the anarchic formlessness of expressionism, however, led Schoenberg to conceive of a new, more systematic approach to musical composition. In 1923, after six years of silence, he revealed his twelve-tone, or "serial," method, exemplified in a series of five piano pieces, followed by a more polished Suite for Piano (op. 25) the following year.

The basic idea of the twelve-tone scale was relatively simple. It used all the notes of the scale—the black piano keys as well as the white—arranged into a pattern of the composer's own devising. Once selected, the sequence of notes could not be altered: This was Schoenberg's safeguard against the return of expressionism's chaotic randomness. It could, however, be modified by playing it backward (retrograde), upside down (inverted), or upside down and backward (inverted retrograde); it could also be transposed so that it began on a different pitch. In practice, this gave the composer a large margin of freedom, especially since several notes in the series could be played together as chords.

For the listener, however, twelve-tone music could be daunting. Since each new piece potentially used a different twelve-tone sequence, Schoenberg's musical language changed faster than audiences could assimilate it. The idea of finding beauty in dissonance seemed wrong-headed or perverse to many. Of all the stylistic innovations in twentieth-century art, twelve-tone music encountered the greatest public resistance.

Thus the twelve-tone scale made its way very slowly. But even before the war, Schoenberg—a hard-working, ultraserious teacher as well as composer—had found two Viennese pupils who were themselves to become influential composers: Anton Webern and Alban Berg. The latter is best known for his opera *Wozzeck* (1922), a grim and haunting story of an outcast soldier finally driven to murder and suicide by his wife's betrayal, based on a nineteenth-century play but given new topicality by the recent war. In *Wozzeck*, Berg used the twelve-tone technique with maximum dramatic effect and succeeded in creating an opera whose music, alternately harsh and warm, achieves a stunning emotional impact. In contrast with Berg's lingering romanticism, Webern chose to interpret the twelve-tone technique in a cooler, more controlled manner. A master of instrumentation, he composed little, but achieved in his limited output a conciseness of form and a wealth of musical effects that were to make him one of the most influential voices for the next generation of composers after the Second World War.

It would be wrong to imply, however, that atonality in any sense dominated German music in the interwar years. It remained an experimental style, and the vast majority of composers continued to work in a more traditional vein. In Germany and Austria, which had dominated nineteenth-century music, the memory of the old masters was close at hand—among them Gustav Mahler, who had died only three years before the war, and, of course, Wagner, whose lineal heir, Richard Strauss, was still Germany's best-known composer, however old-fashioned he might have seemed. (Berg included an out-of-tune Strauss waltz theme in the music for a tavern scene in *Wozzeck*—a joke at the expense of the "old music.")

Paris, with its reinforcement of Russian talent, was in the 1920s the liveliest and most versatile musical community in the world. There the experimentation in musical styles took forms both more varied and more accessible than in Vienna. The leading Paris musical figure was undoubtedly Igor Stravinsky, who had arrived from his native Russia in 1911 and proceeded to compose novel ballet scores for his compatriot and fellow exile, Diaghilev. The last and most famous of these, *The Rite of Spring* (1913)—frankly primitive in its powerful, throbbing rhythms—provoked a riot at its premiere. By the 1920s, Stravinsky had adopted a cooler, neoclassical style for many of the same reasons that had led Schoenberg to elaborate the twelve-tone method: It promised a means for imposing order on music recently freed from the constraints of inherited convention. His *Octet for Wind Instruments* (1923), published in the same year as Schoenberg's revolutionary *Five Pieces for Piano*, while not repudiating experimentation, brought it under tighter control.

A novelty of the immediate postwar period—the one closest to the world of entertainment and the ballet—was the emergence in Paris of a group of young composers who came to be called "The Six." Of these, three eventually achieved international recognition: the Swiss Arthur Honegger, a composer of powerful choral works, culminating in the episodic opera *King David*, originally produced in 1921; the Provençal Darius Milhaud, whose ballet score *The Creation of the World* (1924) made striking use of saxophones and ragtime rhythms, blending classical and jazz idioms with lyrical verve; and, finally, the Parisian Francis Poulenc, a versatile and elegant composer, slightly younger than his friends—who were in their mid-twenties at the war's end—and primarily known for his songs and his works for the piano.

The Russian exile Sergei Prokofiev shared with "The Six" a continuing faithfulness to tonality that made his works—though spiced with occasional dissonances—comprehensible to the average concert-goer. He also shared their humor—evidenced in his terse, deft *Classical Symphony* (1917), in his farcical opera *The Love of Three Oranges* (1921), and in his children's fairy tale *Peter and the Wolf* (1936). But Prokofiev was also a meticulous musical craftsman, whose clarity and simplicity served as a model to subsequent composers. When he returned to Russia in the early 1930s, his work became still simpler and closer to lyricism and folk themes; in this it reflected the reaction against modernism in the arts that was so marked a feature of the Stalinist era (see Chapter 10, V). Toward his country's new regime, Prokofiev took a different attitude from Stravinsky's. Stravinsky, who had already spent a large part of his youth in Western Europe, simply stayed on after the Bolshevik Revolution and subsequently emigrated to the United States; but Prokofiev—though apparently thoroughly "Westernized"—could not refuse the call of his homeland, where he became almost a composer laureate, alternately pampered and reproved by the guardians of official Soviet culture.

Painting: From the "Fauves" to the Abstract

In painting, as in music, a characteristically twentieth-century style began with a revolt against inherited tradition. Art ceased to be tied to a faithful representation of the visible world; instead, artists began to experiment with colors, shapes, and concepts that owed more to the artist's inner vision than to nature. No longer was it possible to judge a painting's excellence by the degree to which it resembled familiar objects. Artists now employed deliberate distortion in order to heighten the emotional power or shock effect of their canvases. "Nonrepresentational," or abstract, art—first produced on the eve of the First World War—was the culmination of the modern shift away from art conceived as a mirror of things seen.

The year 1905 is considered by most to mark the beginning of twentieth-century painting. In 1905 a group of young French painters joined together to exhibit their work in the Paris Autumn Salon. A visiting critic, struck by the boldness of their colors and brush work, called them *fauves*—wild beasts—and the name stuck. It suggested what these fledgling artists had in common: clarity of outline; strong contrasts that conveyed a sense of intense energy; and a brilliant palette characterized by clashing colors of red, green, and orange. Of the Fauves, the two who achieved the greatest subsequent reputation were Henri Matisse and Georges Rouault. However they later varied their styles and experimented with new techniques, they always remained true to their original Fauve inspiration. Matisse's *Woman with the Hat*, exhibited at the Autumn Salon of 1905, displays the essence of that inspiration—raw color used to convey emotions with arresting immediacy.

Two years after this first revolution, a second occurred. In 1907, another young Frenchman, Georges Braque, along with a recent arrival from Spain, Pablo Picasso, launched the movement that came to be called *cubism*. Deliberately banishing lyricism and bright color from their work, the cubists concentrated on form—on architectural reconstructions of fragmented objects, such as a wide glass or a violin, with disjointed and overlapping shapes. Cubism as a movement was at its height in the years 1910 to 1914, but its self-imposed austerity did not last long. Vibrant colors soon returned, and Picasso in particular went on to experiment with a range of new styles, which followed each other in bewildering succession for the next half century. Just before the war, both he and Braque tried the technique of *collage*, sticking actual objects, like colored paper or bits of fabric, on to their paintings. Picasso also became fascinated with work for the theater, including the inevitable designing of sets for the Diaghilev ballet.

The next major change in direction came from Germany. In 1910, a number of young expressionists in Berlin and Munich constituted themselves as *Der Blaue Reiter* (the "Blue Rider" group), dedicated to "pure form." The two who were to have the greatest influence—Paul Klee and the Russian-born Wassily Kandinsky—turned increasingly toward an abstract style that was to make them the progenitors of present-day nonrepresentational painting. Kandinsky justified his experiments in the treatise *Concerning the Spiritual in Art* (1911), which, along with Klee's *Pedagogical Sketchbook* of 1925, constitutes one of the founding documents of abstract art. Painting, Kandinsky wrote, must be "emancipated from the direct dependency on nature." His own steps toward that emancipation led him through a series of fantasy landscapes in fauve-like colors to the completely abstract "Constructions" series of 1912 and 1913. In the 1920s, Kandinsky began to use more geometrical figures in his paintings and shifted his palette toward black and the primary colors, giving his work an austere and formal aura not dissimilar from Stravinsky's neoclassicism. Klee, on the other hand, continued to paint in the poetic vein that had distinguished his work before the war—a private world of delicate colors and curious symbols, tinged with humor and owing a debt to children's art.

After cubism and the Blue Rider group there followed during the war and post-war years the manifestos of dadaism and surrealism. These were movements in literature as much as in art, but their influence on painting was, in the case of surrealism, deeper and more lasting than on poetry and the novel. Like the other artistic movements, surrealism was international in scope. While the Spaniard Salvador Dali created hallucinatory works in which extremely realistic objects were juxtaposed in bizarre assemblages (recalling the style of the late medieval mystic Hieronymus Bosch), the German Max Ernst and the Frenchman Yves Tanguy achieved a more radical transformation of reality. Tanguy's eerie landscapes looked as if they depicted another planet, empty and far from earth, while Ernst's early work showed how the collage technique could yield surrealistic results. Ernst also pioneered the technique of *frottage*—rubbing a piece of blank paper placed in wood with a soft pencil to pick up the pattern of the grain—another sign of how artists were continually trying to expand the means of expression at their disposal.

By 1930, the major innovators of the prewar years had become middle-aged men with established reputations, each cultivating his own style and his own subject matter with little regard for programmatic statements. Matisse had been producing still lifes and interior scenes of a highly decorative elegance; Rouault was specializing in clowns, old men, and prostitutes, whose powerful lines and dark colors reflected the artist's early training in stained glass; Picasso was turning from a classic and almost conventionally pictorial phase to the violent subjects he met with on his return to Spain in 1934—an evolution that was to culminate in *Guernica*, his personal reaction to the horror of bombardment during his country's civil war.

Since the influence of the established masters remained predominant, the years after 1925 saw far less innovation than had the two preceding decades. One tendency that was steadily gaining, however, was that of abstract art. Its ranks now included not only Kandinsky and Klee, but also the Spanish artist Joan Miró, the Englishman Ben Nicholson, and the Dutchman Piet Mondrian. Its greatest influence, however, was to come only after the experience of fascism and the Second World War had scattered and regrouped the world of art more thoroughly than any other catastrophe of modern times.

Architecture: The International Style of Gropius and Le Corbusier

In architecture, the 1920s witnessed the establishment of the "International Style," primarily through the work of Walter Gropius in Germany and Le Corbusier in France—the two founders, along with their predecessor and rival Frank Lloyd Wright in the United States, of contemporary construction and contemporary design.

The origins of modern architecture lay in the realization on the part of a few pioneers in the late nineteenth century that the new world of vast cities and of the machine demanded a wholly new conception of building. Not only had requirements changed—factories and offices, railroad stations and hospitals had been added to the previously standard demand for churches, town houses, and city halls—but it was also true that new materials had revolutionized construction possibilities. Steel, glass, reinforced concrete, and plastics gave a freedom from conventional limitations that only slowly sank into the minds of architects and of the public. Similarly, the technical complexity of these new types of buildings had changed the role of the architect himself. He could no longer be a mere academic designer of pleasing ground plans and façades; he must now understand something of engineering, sanitation, and electricity, and he must also be a town planner, moving old communities into the new framework that alone would fit the new society.

The most obvious feature of the modern idiom in architecture was its stress on the function of each building. The pioneers of the new style were impatient with the usual practice of copying parts of buildings from the past and adapting them more or less adequately to modern uses. They thought that the design of a railroad station should suggest the purpose it served, instead of imitating a Roman bath or a Renaissance palace. Similarly, they rejected the general tendency to use ornament in indiscriminate fashion. Form, they argued, should grow naturally from function.

Among the precursors of the International Style, the greatest continuing influence was that of Auguste Perret, who as early as 1903 had begun to design in Paris buildings of reinforced concrete that permitted great freedom in the arrangement of individual floor plans; the walls no longer carried the weight of the building; this was borne by a few concrete columns. In Germany also, early experiments with industrial design were proceeding in a similar direction. But the decisive break with the past came in 1911, when the twenty-eight-year-old Gropius was given the assignment of designing the Fagus Works at Alfeld-an-der-Leine for a client who was in complete sympathy with his views; the result was an elegant, light building, whose clean lines and walls of glass became the prototype of a style in industrial building that after the Second World War was to become almost standard both in Europe and in the United States.

In 1919, Gropius established the Bauhaus—a "school for creative art," aiming to bridge the gap between art and industry. At Weimar and subsequently at Dessau, the Bauhaus grouped a wide variety of talents including the painters Klee and Kandinsky, for Gropius believed in teamwork, in the union of art and techniques, and, unlike his contemporaries Wright and Le Corbusier, he was willing to keep his own personality in the background in order to achieve this result. He was primarily a teacher—the most influential of his whole era. Even when, in 1928, he returned to private practice, he produced buildings that again gave a clear direction to future planning. In the lofty, elongated slabs of the experimental housing schemes that he designed for suburban Berlin, subsequent architects found inspiration for some of the best work in city reconstruction in the years after 1945.

Under Gropius's influence, the Bauhaus also promoted a social vision. He and his colleagues at the school believed that high-quality housing and home furnishings could be mass produced in German factories at modest cost, thus for the first time making them available to all. Bauhaus designs for dinnerware, light fixtures, furniture, and rugs promised to create a total environment whose clean, harmonious lines would replace the jumble of contrasting styles and the shoddy workmanship of the prewar era. When the Weimar Republic embarked on a vast program of public housing in the late 1920s, many of the newly constructed neighborhoods and apartment projects bore the stamp of Gropius's ideas. Their new tenants, however, often clung to their accustomed possessions and defiantly softened the geometric contours of a Bauhaus interior with overstuffed armchairs and lace curtains.

The Bauhaus buildings in Dessau, Germany, designed by Walter Gropius and constructed in 1924–1925. Note the curtain of glass made possible by the use of a structural skeleton to support the weight. Such technological innovations underlay the daring new architectural style of the 1920s. (*Erik Bohr/AKG London Ltd*)

The Nazi regime forced Gropius into exile, first in Britain and then in the United States. During the same period, his Franco-Swiss counterpart, Le Corbusier, was finally coming into his own. Le Corbusier was as much of a visionary as Gropius, but he was more of an individualist. Throughout the 1920s he received no large commissions—his project of the Palace of the League of Nations was passed over in favor of a more conventional plan—and he was reduced to house design and to elaborating the principles of construction that he had originally learned in Perret's office. These included a flat roof; great freedom in planning interior space; horizontal ribbon windows, which sometimes even ran around corners; and a first floor lifted off the ground by columns, giving the building the effect of being suspended in air with a garden spreading under it. He also consoled himself with vast plans for rebuilding the center of Paris and for a "radiant city" of the future in which tall buildings would stand widely spaced among ample stretches of green.

In the 1930s, when Le Corbusier was at last able to turn from house design to public buildings, a reaction against the International Style was already setting in. Nazi Germany denounced it as "decadent," and France, whose building industry remained in the doldrums throughout the Great Depression decade, relapsed into a timid semiclassicism. Both Gropius and Le Corbusier left the Continent, the latter spreading to Brazil the message of the new architecture that Gropius was teaching in the United States. Thus it was in the smaller countries and outside Europe that the International Style continued to advance in the 1930s: Switzerland, the Netherlands, and Scandinavia became particularly hospitable. Here younger architects like the Finn Alvar Aalto turned away from the severe cubic designs of the pioneers to a warmer, more supple and curved style that was to reach full fruition only after the Second World War. When this conflict broke out, most new building in Europe, as in America, was still in one or another of the traditional styles, but the new idiom was now known everywhere. The triumph of the modern, in architecture as in so much else, was only a matter of time. The new generation that would come to take it for granted was already growing up.

READINGS

For the epoch-making changes in natural science, see the comprehensive, handsomely produced collaborative work, largely by French scholars, René Taton, ed., *Science in the Twentieth Century* (1966). For the revolution in physics, see Victor F. Weisskopf's *Physics in the Twentieth Century** (1972). Two excellent studies of Einstein's work in terms comprehensible to the layperson are Abraham Pais, *Subtle is the Lord: The Science and Life of Albert Einstein** (1982), and Jeremy Bernstein, *Einstein** (1973). Werner Heisenberg, in *Physics and Beyond: Encounters and Conversation** (1971), explores the philosophical implications of advances in physics during the 1920s from the point of view of a participant.

H. Stuart Hughes, in *Consciousness and Society: The Reorientation of European Social Thought, 1890–1930** (1958), gives a general interpretation of the work of the European social thinkers who dominated the 1920s; Peter Gay, *Freud: A Life for our Time* (1988) provides a detailed and balanced introduction to the most influential of them. Gay's biography can be usefully supplemented with Richard Wollheim's *Sigmund Freud** (1971). For sociological thought in particular, see Tom Bottomore and Robert Nisbet, eds., *A History of Sociological Analysis* (1978), and Raymond Aron, *Main Currents in Sociological Thought*, vol. 2: *Durckheim, Pareto, and Weber** (1970). In *Weimar Culture: The Outsider as Insider** (1968, 2001), Peter Gay analyzes with verve and discernment the precarious zenith of German cultural achievement, while John Willett, in *Art and Politics in the Weimar Republic: The New Sobriety, 1917–1930** (1980), places the work of the avant-garde in the illuminating context of contemporary politics. A comprehensive survey of high culture in Britain during this period is Boris Ford, ed., *The Cambridge Guide to the Arts in Britain*, vol. 8: *The Edwardian Age and the Inter-War Years* (1989).

The newer trends in literature are surveyed in Malcolm Bradbury and James MacFarlane, eds., *Modernism, 1890–1930** (1976), as well as in Edmund Wilson's older and insightful essay *Axel's Castle** (1931). A classic account of the stylistic innovations that enabled novelists to investigate the inner world can be found in the final chapter of

---

*Books marked with an asterisk are available in paperback.

Erich Auerbach's *Mimesis: The Representation of Reality in Western Literature** (1946). Joseph Machlis's *Introduction to Contemporary Music*, 2nd ed. (1979) surveys the music scene from the turn of the century onward in detailed fashion, while Eric Salzman's *Twentieth-Century Music: An Introduction,** 2nd ed. (1974) provides a succinct yet balanced overview. Charles Rosen's *Schoenberg** (1975) is an admirable, brief analysis of the work of one of the giants of modern music. Richard Taruskin's monumental study *Stravinsky and the Russian Tradition*, 2. vols. (1996) explores the native roots which inspired another great musical innovator of the early twentieth century. Igor Stravinsky, *An Autobiography** (1936) is the master's own account of his early career.

George Heard Hamilton, in *Painting and Sculpture in Europe, 1880–1940** (1967), gives a judicious overview of the subject, as does Herbert Read, in *A Concise History of Modern Painting** (1985). A now classic study of the one of the principal artistic innovators of the century is John Berger's *The Success and Failure of Picasso,** 2nd ed. (1989). Picasso's early career is treated in magisterial fashion by John Richardson in his *A Life of Picasso*, Vol. I: *1881–1906* (1991) and Vol. II: *1907–1917* (1996). The theories that guided another major artist to adopt non-representational painting on the eve of World War I are set forth in Wassily Kandinsky, *Concerning the Spiritual in Art** (1911). For the rise of the international style in architecture, see Nikolaus Pevsner, *Pioneers of Modern Design: From William Morris to Walter Gropius,** rev. ed. (1964), and Leonardo Benevolo, *History of Modern Architecture*, vol. 2: *The Modern Movement** (1960). Walter Gropius, *The New Architecture and the Bauhaus** (1925) is the programmatic statement of Bauhaus aims by the founder.

THE GREAT DEPRESSION, 1929–1935

Charity during the Great Depression: a "three-penny dinner" kitchen run by the Wesleyan Mission feeds the hungry unemployed in London's East End. *(Courtesy AP/Wide World Photos)*

I. ORIGINS AND CHARACTER

In the autumn of 1929 came the catastrophe that so few had anticipated but that in retrospect seems inevitable. Prices broke on the New York Stock Exchange, dragging down with them in their fall, at first, the economy of the United States itself, and subsequently that of Europe and the rest of the world. Financial losses of such magnitude had never before been known in the history of capitalist society, and the ensuing depression was also unprecedented in scope. There had always been business crises; economists had come to take them as normal and even to chart a certain regularity in their occurrence. But this one dwarfed all its predecessors. No previous depression had remotely approached it in length, in depth, and in the universality of impact. Small wonder that countless people were led to speculate whether the final collapse of capitalism itself, so long predicted by the Marxists, was not at last in sight.

Precisely because it was international in scope, the Great Depression assumed different shapes and guises in the different countries affected. Nor was its timetable uniform. As the United States began to emerge from the worst of the crash in the early 1930s, France had just begun its slide into crisis. Thus the Great Depression is best seen not as a single event, but instead as a multiplicity of national variations on the twin themes of economic weakness and confused political response. The initial events in the United States were both dramatic and unexpected; those that followed in Europe proved more damaging in the end.

On October 24, "Black Thursday" in the United States, more than 16 million shares of stock were sold in panic; in the next three weeks the general industrial index of the New York Stock Exchange fell by more than half. Nevertheless, it was by no means clear at first how severe the depression was going to be. Previous crises had originated in the United States—this was not the great novelty. What was unprecedented was the *extent* of the European economic dependence on America that the crash of 1929 revealed (see Chapter 6, III). This dependence varied greatly from country to country. Central Europe was involved first, as American financiers began to call in their short-term loans in Germany and Austria. These withdrawals of capital continued throughout 1930, until in May 1931 the Austrian Kreditanstalt suspended payments entirely. Thereafter, panic swept the Central European exchanges as bank after bank closed down and one industry after another began to reduce production and lay off workers.

Meanwhile the crisis had reached Great Britain. In September 1931, the country went off the gold standard, to be followed two years later by the United States and nearly all the other financial powers of the world. The great exception was France. With a balanced economy and relative self-sufficiency, the French held off the crisis longer than anyone else. Not until 1932 did its effects become severe. But late involvement did not help the country in the long run, for France was the slowest and the least successful of the major powers in pulling itself out of the Great Depression, which left a wound in French society that was far from healed when the Second World War broke out.

The fall in production and the fall in prices everywhere reached unprecedented depths. In Germany—which was hit worst of all—production had fallen by 39 percent, at the bottom of the Depression in 1932, and prices by only slightly less. In France, which was stubbornly holding to the gold standard, the price level in 1935 was just over half what it had been in 1930. Of all the manifestations of the Great Depression, however, unemployment was the most grievous and the one which most clearly left its mark on the whole era. In this respect, France was the least seriously affected; the number of those out of work never rose above 850,000. But here, as in Italy and in the agricultural nations in general, there was much semiemployment and concealed unemployment in the countryside. In Britain, the jobless numbered nearly three million—between a fifth and a quarter of the whole labor force. In Germany, unemployment mounted to the horrifying total of six million; trade-union executives estimated that more than two-fifths of their members were out of work entirely and another fifth employed only part time (see Figure 8.1). With roughly half the population in desperation and want, it was no wonder that the Germans turned to the extremist leadership that they had so narrowly avoided in the crisis of 1923.

Social unrest never reached such grave proportions elsewhere, but throughout Europe governments and peoples felt themselves on the edge of a precipice, as the turbulent and questioning mood of the immediate postwar years returned with redoubled intensity. What could be done to reverse this economic calamity? Economic experts proposed two contrasting and mutually exclusive solutions: one *deflationary*, the other *inflationary*. Those favoring deflation (generally on the political Right) argued that in a contracting economy, the government should live within its means by ruthlessly cutting expenditures. As incomes declined and tax revenues fell proportionally, governments should simply spend less. The danger of this strategy, however, was that the depression would become permanent. If government employees lost their jobs, if millions of other workers received nothing in unemployment compensation, then prices could fall without spurring an economic revival. The inflationary alternative required governments to borrow money. Only increased government spending, argued its advocates, could lift a country out of depression, since consumer purchasing power had effectively vanished. Here the danger was that increased money in circulation might cause prices to rise in turn, threatening the value of the currency.

Despite this danger, most European states opted in the end for inflation. Pressed by events, they reluctantly resorted to all sorts of measures of which the conservatives had initially disapproved. These measures came to follow a common pattern—most

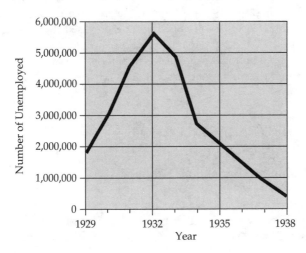

FIGURE 8.1   German unemployment statistics from the onset of the Great Depression to the eve of the Second World War. Note that the peak level began to fall *before* Hitler assumed power in 1933; the continued decline during the late 1930s was largely due to Hitler's rearmament policy.

countries turned inward, trying to save their own economies without reference to, or regard for, their neighbors, through raising tariffs. They sought to relieve the sufferings of the unemployed through extended subsistence payments, on the model of the British dole, and to provide new jobs through vast programs of public works and, eventually, through rearmament.

Most of these measures were mere palliatives, however, undertaken in skeptical and hesitant fashion, and only after years of delay had robbed them of maximum effect. The turn toward economic nationalism probably did as much harm as good, constricting the volume of world trade and still further reducing Europe's share in it. In Europe, as in the United States, the only policy that brought much lasting benefit was direct provision of new employment by the government. Even this was far less effective in its original form of public works than in its subsequent guise of war production. On both sides of the Atlantic, only rearmament proved a sufficiently powerful antidote to the Great Depression. It is sobering to note that the great power that was the most successful in pulling itself out of the slump—Nazi Germany—was also the one that plunged most wholeheartedly into preparation for war.

In effect, European governments were returning to the direct control of the economy they had exercised during the First World War. During the 1920s, most governments had attempted to shed their wartime economic responsibilities and return to the classical model of capitalist economy, where a "night watchman state" did little more than protect the uninhibited workings of the marketplace from outside interference. The postwar recession of 1919–1920 and the German inflation that followed had raised questions in the minds of some about whether the economy could really be trusted to heal itself unaided. But the years of stability from 1924 to 1929 made such fears seem excessive. Nostalgia for the "good old days," combined with the very real difficulties of forging a national economic consensus in peacetime, kept the role of the state a restricted one.

By the mid-1930s, however, the economic and social struggles of the decade had raised the question of the proper role of government in new and inescapable fashion. Could popularly elected governments in Britain and France simply watch as millions of citizens sank into the helpless poverty of unemployment? If not, what new model of the relations between government and the marketplace should replace that of capitalist laissez-faire? Fascist governments in Italy and Germany argued that their vision of a classless, corporatist society directed by an all-knowing state provided the only realistic response to economic crisis. Thus the Great Depression, in addition to the immense suffering it caused, also raised political issues about rival forms of government that were blending imperceptibly into the origins of the Second World War itself.

II. CENTRAL EUROPE: THE YEARS OF TURMOIL

Germany: From Brüning to Papen and Schleicher

The first European government to fall as a direct consequence of the Great Depression was the German ministry led by the Social Democrat Hermann Müller. The cause of its collapse was characteristic of a divergence on economic policy that was to split country after country in the ensuing years: The Left wanted increased unemployment relief; the Right argued for retrenchment and a balanced budget. In such a debate, the Conservatives initially held the stronger cards. They had on their side the weight of economic theory and the orthodox maxim that reduced spending was the proper way to move the business cycle out of depression. The Socialists were more hesitant. On problems such as these, Marxist theory was of little help, and they were obliged to fall back on arguments of humanitarianism and expediency. The new economics of John Maynard Keynes and the experience of the American New Deal had not yet taught them to see virtue in deficit financing.

Thus it was a conservative government that came to power in Germany in March 1930. It rested on that portion of the Reichstag Center and Right—still the larger part—which refused to follow Hugenberg and Hitler in their propaganda of unbridled nationalism. But the government had no majority in the Reichstag as a whole, nor did its chief inspire general devotion and loyalty. The new chancellor, Heinrich Brüning, was a man of rectitude and disciplined intelligence. As the first to reach political power of the generation that had actually seen front-line service during the war, he might have been expected to appeal to younger voters. But for this he was far too cold and rigid. Even in his own party, the Center, Brüning was not popular.

Yet he managed to stay in office for more than two years. Month after month, he doggedly stuck to his task, as the depression deepened, the army of the unemployed swelled to frightening dimensions, and both the Communists and the National Socialists made steady gains. In one sense, Brüning's might be called Germany's last democratic government of the interwar years; its leader did all in his power to resist the onslaught of nazism. In another sense, this ministry marked the beginning of the end for German democracy. Lacking a parliamentary majority, the Brüning government felt obliged to resort to the emergency decree powers that the constitution vested in the president, and beginning with the July budget of 1930, it enacted measure after measure by Hindenburg's fiat.

Meantime, the electoral returns gave mounting evidence of the Nazis' rise. In September 1930, they increased their seats in the Reichstag from 12 to 107—thus becoming the second largest party in the country and making the Reichstag itself still more unmanageable than before. Eighteen months later, when Hindenburg's term expired, the National Socialists decided on the bold maneuver of running their own man, Adolf Hitler, against Germany's undisputed father figure who, at eighty-five, was ready to do his soldier's duty by standing for reelection. Hindenburg won—but only because the Social Democrats felt driven to the paradoxical course of voting for a military hero to save what was left of German democracy.

At this point the former understanding between chancellor and president—which alone had permitted the Weimar system to continue working at all—broke down in unexpected fashion. Hindenburg, who was tied to the Prussian estate-owning class by origin and long association, refused to enact a land-reform decree that Brüning had laid before him. Brüning resigned. His successor was Franz von Papen, in name a member of the Center, but in fact a reactionary aristocrat and schemer who thought himself clever enough to give Germany a nationalist government without calling on Hitler for aid.

The advent of Papen in May 1932 began the eight-month agony of German democracy. The new "ministry of barons" did not pretend to have the confidence of the

Reichstag and relied solely on the support of President von Hindenburg. Its first acts clearly suggested its authoritarian sympathies. It lifted the ban on Nazi Storm Trooper activities, which had been imposed two months earlier by the Brüning government, and then, under the flimsy excuse that the constant street clashes between Communists and National Socialists made regular administration impossible, it went on to dissolve by police action the Social Democratic government of the key state of Prussia.

Now, if ever, was the time for Hitler's opponents to stand up and fight. From this point on it would be too late. But no one seemed prepared to take decisive action. The Democratic party had nearly vanished; the Center was paralyzed by its own internal divisions. The nationalist Right was increasingly conniving with the Nazis. Perhaps most surprisingly, the Communists, too, made common cause with the Nazi party against the Social Democrats, whom they dismissed as "social fascists," believing that a Hitler regime would pave the way for their own rise to power after the final collapse of capitalism. This split in the ranks of the Left made concerted opposition impossible. Even the Social Democrats, whose vigorous resistance had halted the Kapp *putsch* in 1920, found no similar fighting spirit with which to oppose von Papen in 1932. Electoral weakness, internecine struggles, opportunism, and weariness combined to reduce to mute impotence the German political forces that might have challenged Hitler's rise.

One consequence of the Great Depression was a rash of bank failures in Europe. Here, bank customers in Berlin wait to withdraw their savings in an atmosphere of tense expectation. (*Courtesy AP/Wide World Photos*)

In late July, another Reichstag election gave the Nazis more than 200 seats—thus ratifying their claim to being the strongest party in the nation. Unemployment stood at six million, and street battles between the private armies of the extremists had become almost a daily occurrence. Papen, like Brüning before him, found the ground slipping from under his feet. The Reichstag was completely unruly, and Hindenburg was losing confidence in the chancellor of his own choice. Bewildered and senile, the field marshal had only a few lucid hours a day, and in these was governed by those who were close at hand. Among them was General Kurt von Schleicher, still more of an intriguer than Papen and at least as confident of his ability to outwit Hitler. In early December, Schleicher became the German Republic's last chancellor.

Papen had behaved in office as a frank reactionary; his successor embarked on a more subtle policy. Schleicher decided to try demagogy, hoping to break the power of both the Communists and the Nazis through a pseudo-leftist appeal. And he felt that he had reason for optimism because Hitler, for the first time since the onset of the depression, had lost ground in the second Reichstag election of the year, and the economic situation was slightly improved. More particularly, Schleicher decided to investigate the illegal profits that some of the great landowners had made through the agrarian relief measures enacted by his predecessor. At this point conservatives took alarm—an alarm that put within Hitler's grasp the power that had very nearly eluded him (see Chapter 9, II).

Austria: Party Strife and the Accession of Dollfuss

To Austria, which had not wanted to be a separate state, the postwar years had brought less apparent turmoil than to Germany. After a battle with inflation almost as severe as that which the neighboring Reich was about to experience, Austria seemed to settle into relative stability. This impression of calm was reinforced by the fact that the Austrian political situation was far simpler than the German: Two great parties, the Socialist and the Christian Social, between them virtually monopolized the field.

This might suggest that Austria had found its way to the two-party system that students of parliamentary democracy—with the British experience in mind—usually regarded as the optimum. In reality, there was a thoroughgoing difference between Austrian and Anglo-Saxon politics. In Britain, the two parties agreed on fundamentals; and this remained true even after Labour had replaced the Liberals as the second party. In Austria, no such agreement was possible. The divergences between the parties split the national community wide open, reflecting not only the usual cleavage between Right and Left but also the two radically different types of society that the Treaty of Saint-Germain, in reducing Austria to its German-speaking provinces, had forced to live together.

On the one hand there was the city of Vienna, which had a quarter of the country's population—a vast metropolis shorn of its imperial function, cosmopolitan, industrial, and freethinking, with a large percentage of its inhabitants of Slavic or Jewish origin. Vienna regularly voted for socialism, which was rather more leftist and militant than its German counterpart. Joined to Vienna in unhappy union were the Danubian and Alpine provinces of the old empire—Tyrol, Salzburg, and the rest—overwhelmingly rural, conservative, Catholic, and inclining toward anti-Semitism and distrust of foreigners. These naturally voted Christian Social. This was a Catholic party not unlike the

German Center, with a tradition of paternalistic reform extending far back into the nineteenth century, but which, by the end of the 1920s, was increasingly tempted by authoritarian solutions.

A federal constitution alone enabled these two parties and the two types of society they represented to live together. For the better part of a decade they coexisted in a state of uneasy truce; the Christian Socials regularly dominated the federal government and the rural provinces, while the Socialists ran Vienna, which had been set up by itself as an urban province. Periodically the tension between the two broke out in vast street demonstrations in the capital—in 1926 and again in 1929, when the federal constitution was modified in a more authoritarian direction. The Christian Socials were scandalized at the fashion in which the Socialists ran Vienna—at high taxes and expensive public housing schemes. The latter contended that such measures were essential to relieve the economic distress of a ghost city that had lost its natural markets and was suffering grievously from the tariff policies of its neighbors. The Socialists had equal reason to distrust the Catholic party, for the Christian Socials were coming under increasingly heavy pressure from their fascist-minded direct-action groups, which by 1930 were beginning to receive secret help from Mussolini's Italy.

The coming of the Great Depression brought these latent tensions into the open. In 1931, the Austrian fascists made their first local bid for power; the next year the Christian Socials found the "strong man" they needed. With the accession of Engelbert Dollfuss to the chancellorship, a new era opened in Austrian history. The six years 1932–1938 were to be a period of growing authoritarianism, a semifascism, which steered a tortuous course between the democracy it had rejected and the ever-present menace of absorption into the Nazi state (see Chapter 9, III).

The International Aspect: The Abortive Customs Union and the End of Reparations

When the union of Austria with Germany finally came about in 1938, it was against the will of both major Austrian parties. Earlier, however, the idea of union, or *Anschluss*, had been very popular—indeed, it was almost the only thing on which Austrians were agreed. One of the failures that had undermined the authority both of Austrian democracy and of the Brüning government in Germany was the veto imposed by the French and their allies on the Austro-German plan for a customs union—an obvious first step toward *Anschluss*—which was broached in 1931. The matter finally went to the World Court, which declared against it in an eight to seven vote whose political motivation was only too apparent.

This marked the last time that the French were to take decisive action against their late enemies. From 1931 on, the trend toward revision of the Versailles settlement became irresistible. The British had always favored modification, and the Americans and Italians, for different reasons, agreed. The French found themselves isolated—particularly since they had chosen to exert their pressure for the dubious purpose of preserving Austria's freedom against the wishes of its own inhabitants.

Thus in international affairs, the years 1930–1932 can be regarded as a transition period between the Stresemann-Briand era of conciliation and the era of fascist aggression that was to follow. As the depression in Central Europe deepened and hit bottom in 1932, it became apparent that the vacuous optimism of the previous half-decade would no longer suffice. In international affairs, as at home, the battle against the Great Depression demanded something more substantial than high-sounding declarations of good will. The time of reckoning had come—the tangled knot of reparations and war debts now finally had to be unraveled. In the summer of 1931, on the initiative of President Hoover, the powers agreed to a moratorium on all intergovernmental debts. The following summer, at Lausanne, the powers in fact, if not in theory, canceled German reparations entirely. Simultaneously the payment of war debts came to an end. The problem of reparations and war debts had actually been swept away once and for all by the onrush of events.

This, far more than the long-awaited Disarmament Conference, which met at intervals for twenty months and achieved almost nothing, was the real accomplishment of 1932. The reparations nightmare had been lifted from Germany, and the Reich was well on its way to international equality. By now it was quite clear that the Germans were rearming, and that nobody was prepared to stop them. The "fetters of Versailles" were falling off one by one. Ironically, these very fetters were providing Hitler with his most reliable propaganda assets in his drive toward power. The German people failed to understand how much the last chancellors of the Republic—Brüning and Papen—had actually accomplished in strengthening Germany's international position. By the summer of 1932, these two—both nationalists to the core—had *already* set their country firmly on the course of patriotic revival that was later to be the Nazis' proudest boast.

III. WESTERN EUROPE: THE YEARS OF DRIFT

During the years of crisis when Germany and Austria were shaken by social unrest and moving inexorably toward authoritarian government, Britain and France drifted, safe from threat of revolution, but sure of nothing else. The illusory stability of the era of Baldwin and Poincaré had vanished. Government by businessmen had failed, but no clear alternative had emerged. Hence the rule of the Right continued, without talent and without imagination, until in the decisive year 1936 the people of Western Europe began awakening to the multiple threats, domestic as well as foreign, that were slowly undermining the societies in which they lived.

Britain: The Second Labour Government

In Britain, as in Germany, the Great Depression struck when a socialist government was in power. Here, as in the Reich, the Labour ministry proved incapable of coping with economic problems of such unprecedented dimensions.

The parliamentary elections of May 1929 returned Labour to power under conditions only slightly better than those that had confronted the party's first effort to govern in 1924. For the first time, Labour won more seats than the Conservatives. But it still lacked a majority; it was still dependent on Liberal tolerance; and it still had as its leader Ramsay MacDonald, whom age had made even vaguer and more hesitant than before.

The new government would be judged on how well it handled the crucial issue of unemployment, and here, almost immediately, it entered upon a desperate struggle with the financiers. Labour had been in power only four months when the Wall Street crash occurred. By the next spring, the effects of American withdrawals on the British economy were all too evident. Unemployment, which had stood at a million and a half at the beginning of 1930, reached two million by midsummer, and at the year's end was two and a half million. Obviously a Labour government could not let these people starve; it must support them somehow, and the only method available seemed to be giving the "dole" to larger and larger numbers of the unemployed.

This was a severe strain on the budget, already weakened by a fall in tax receipts. In the summer of 1931, the chancellor of the exchequer—whose financial principles were blamelessly orthodox—brought in the report of an expert committee on expenditure, which had concluded that the one way to meet the deficit was to reduce unemployment benefits. The somber picture it had drawn of Britain's financial position created a mood approaching panic. From mid-July to mid-August, banks of all sorts experienced heavy withdrawals; at the Bank of England the gold reserve was sinking to the vanishing point. With Parliament on vacation, MacDonald was left alone to deal with the crisis, and for such a position he was fit neither by his temperament nor by his minimal knowledge of economics and finance.

Recalled in haste from his holiday in Scotland, the prime minister summoned his cabinet on the weekend of August 22–23. He explained that the government and the country could find financial salvation only by accepting the recommendation to reduce unemployment payments. The alternative was bankruptcy. This was made quite clear by a group of New York financiers who refused to extend further loans to Britain unless its government carried out important economies. Half the cabinet refused. With the ministry deadlocked, MacDonald asked for and received the resignations of his colleagues. When the meeting adjourned, the ministers believed that a Conservative-Liberal coalition would replace them.

This was not MacDonald's plan, however. He had been to see the king, and the latter had talked to Baldwin. What emerged from these confabulations was a National Government, with MacDonald still prime minister and Baldwin as his deputy.

The National Government of 1931, like Lloyd George's Coalition from 1916 to 1922, was a mere façade for Tory rule. No more than three Labour ministers followed MacDonald into it, and there was only token Liberal representation. The prime minister, like Lloyd George before him, had become the prisoner of the Conservatives. He was beguiled into betraying his own party—by the pressure of financiers both British and American, by the patriotic pleas of the king, and by his own vanity, which could not resist the blandishments of the well born. It was a crushing blow for Labour. Although the party expelled MacDonald and the handful of members of Parliament who followed him, it needed a full decade to recover its strength. For the Liberals—who were entitled to expect a real share in power—it was one more step on the long downward path. For the country, it was a catastrophe parading as salvation; it meant nine years of fumble and muddle, with MacDonald and Baldwin, once political enemies, now pooling their talents for delay and obfuscation, at which they both so notably excelled.

Britain: The National Government: MacDonald, Baldwin, Chamberlain

Presumably, the National Government was formed to save the pound, but its first action was to go off the gold standard. This did not prove as catastrophic as the orthodox economists had feared. The pound fell from $4.86 to $3.40 on the international exchanges—and that was all. Parliament simultaneously swallowed the 10 percent cut in unemployment benefits at which the Labour ministers had balked.

Thus the financial crisis was surmounted with suspicious ease. Its sudden passing suggests that it had never been so grave as the financiers had pretended and that the Conservatives, as with the Zinoviev letter of 1924, once again were artificially creating fear in order to oust a Labour ministry. This suspicion was confirmed when the new government went to the country to ratify its mandate. The election of October 1931 was all too reminiscent of Lloyd George's "Khaki Election" of 1918. Under the guise of a coalition effort, the Conservatives preempted the greater part of the joint candidacies, and their electoral propaganda was unashamedly partisan. Consciously striving to create a mood of panic, the Tories threatened national disaster if Labour should win. Their tactics succeeded. The Conservatives emerged with the largest majority of the century—472 seats out of the 556 that went to candidates supporting the National Government. Labour, on the contrary, experienced the greatest debacle of its history—with only 46 members elected, it had lost five-sixths of its seats, including nearly all those held by former cabinet ministers.

The National Government, then, was in a position to rule almost without opposition. Once again, its first act was to ride roughshod over the principles of its Liberal supporters. It revived Baldwin's old program of tariff protection—now sponsored by the more forceful and convincing Neville Chamberlain—which it pushed through Parliament in early 1932. During the summer, it went on to make preferential trade agreements with the overseas dominions. Britain, which had always ranked as the citadel of free trade, was following the rest of Europe into economic nationalism. At this point, the Liberal ministers decided that they had had enough. They resigned from the ministry, leaving it an indisputably Tory preserve.

The party that MacDonald had betrayed meanwhile licked its wounds and made what show of opposition it could. Under younger and stronger leaders, Labour reorganized its cadres and slowly began to move away from its pacifist position in foreign affairs. By the autumn of 1935, the party was ready for the election suddenly announced as Parliament returned from summer recess. Labour's new confidence proved justified. When the votes were counted, the Conservatives had lost nearly seventy seats, while Labour had more than tripled its own. But the National Government still rested on an enormous Tory majority; Baldwin had put both opposition parties at a disadvantage by robbing them of their most appealing planks—internationalism and support of the League of Nations. No one yet knew that within a month the government was flagrantly to abandon these very principles, and that the House of Commons just chosen was to sit longer than any other Parliament of modern times. Its electoral origins long since forgotten, this same body was successively to endorse appeasement, war, and Winston Churchill, until in the moment of victory in 1945 it vanished unmourned (see Chapter 15, V).

In the intervening years, economic recovery had begun. After reaching its peak at the beginning of 1933, unemployment fell steadily, until it leveled off in 1936 at a little more than a million and a half. Production rallied in similar fashion. By 1937, it stood 20 percent above its 1929 level. Yet these figures were less encouraging than they seemed. Even before the Great Depression began, Britain had been in a state of semidepression, so that a return to "normal" did not mean what it did in other countries. The only reason the boat of the economy did not sink more, one contemporary observed, was that it was already half full of water. The plight of men on the dole was not eased, and resentment continued to smolder among the working classes in the depressed areas and in the country as a whole.

In undertaking state intervention, the National Government followed a line that was neither the hands-off attitude that Brüning or Hoover adopted in the early part of the Great Depression, nor the active policy later pursued by such sharply contrasting experiments as the American New Deal, the Nazi Third Reich, and the French Popular Front. Nothing done in Britain provided anything like their stimulus to morale, and its absence helps account for the apathy and discouragement that brooded over the country throughout the 1930s. In general, the National Government restricted itself to keeping interest rates low and sponsoring a substantial housing program. These were largely the work of the one decisive figure in the ministry, the chancellor of the exchequer, Neville Chamberlain.

Chamberlain was never popular, and his association with appeasement and the catastrophe of 1940 has injured his historical reputation. He was stubborn and unimaginative; his rasping voice, his dark clothes, and his perpetual umbrella symbolized all that was unlovable in the British business classes. But he was an excellent administrator who knew what he wanted and had complete confidence in his ability to carry it out. When Baldwin retired in 1937—having successfully surmounted the crisis of a royal abdication*—there appeared no alternative to making Chamberlain prime minister. He at least stood for *something*—the rest of the cabinet were little more than ciphers.

France: Tardieu, Herriot, and the Election of 1932

When Poincaré withdrew as French prime minister in the summer of 1929, no satisfactory successor appeared. Nobody combined as he did a basic conservatism with a thoroughly "republican" record calculated to reassure the part of the electorate that always suspected authoritarian tendencies on the Right. The men who followed Poincaré in office were too young to have such a record, and in the case of the three most important—Tardieu, Laval, and Flandin—subsequent dealings with fascism or approaches to fascism proved these suspicions amply justified.

---

*King Edward VIII, who had been on the throne for only eleven months, was forced to abdicate in December 1936 because of his insistence on marrying an American divorcée.

Poincaré's immediate heir, André Tardieu, was far too intelligent and far too undiplomatic to please most deputies. Originally a protégé of Clemenceau, he resembled the great war leader in his shortness of temper and impatience with opposition. In a time of grave national emergency, the Chamber of Deputies might endure leadership of this sort, but Tardieu could not convince his colleagues that the early 1930s were indeed such a period. The deputies continued in their customarily irresponsible attitude toward the national economy, and refused to listen to Tardieu's warnings that unless they consented to heavy investment in economic improvements, their country was bound sooner or later to be caught up in the worldwide depression. They preferred the leader who alternated in power with Tardieu—Pierre Laval—a sly and slippery fellow, converted from the Left to conservatism like so many successful deputies, who summed up in his own person all that was cynical and corrupt in French parliamentary politics.

By 1932, the Great Depression had in fact struck France, and in the election of that year the Left won easily. This put the Radicals under Herriot back in power for the first time in six years, with the Socialists providing support outside the government, as they had done in 1924. Once again—as had happened then—the Left ministry involved itself in insoluble financial difficulties. Herriot stayed in office half a year; of his four successors, only one remained for more than three months. The last of these—Edouard Daladier—had hardly begun his tenure when the storm broke that was to drown the Radicals in a torrent of well-orchestrated indignation.

France: The Riots of 1934: Doumergue and Laval

In December 1933, the police unearthed one of the widely ramifying scandals by which the French Republic was periodically shaken. The details of the Stavisky case are unimportant; indeed, they were never properly explained. They involved a provincial pawnshop, a fraudulent bond issue, and all sorts of unsavory minor details. The really sinister aspect of the case was its exploitation by the authoritarian wing of the French Right. French reactionaries spread reports that a number of leading political figures were involved in the scandal and that the government was concealing their guilt; thus democracy and the Republic itself were discredited in the minds of countless Frenchmen of conservative and patriotic views.

On February 6, 1934, the adherents of the leading rightist and patriotic organizations flocked into the streets of Paris to call for Daladier's overthrow. They failed in their attempt to storm the Chamber of Deputies: The police stopped them with gunfire, and eleven demonstrators lost their lives. But they did succeed in bringing down the government; Daladier had shed the blood of patriots, and Daladier had to go.

Not since the Commune of 1871 had France been so close to civil war. Although the riots of February 1934 were no more than an uncoordinated succession of street demonstrations, they were symptomatic of a deep-seated *malaise* that was gradually destroying whatever fragile consensus existed within French society. The government of the Left had failed. The Radicals had proved themselves unable to do anything coherent to meet the Great Depression, and they were hopelessly at odds with the Socialists in their notions of economic policy. The left-wing electorate was increasingly turning in disgust toward a new militancy and a near-revolutionary temper. On the Right a similar

Protesters pose with their makeshift weapons during a lull in the "Stavisky riots" of February, 1934. (*Courtesy UPI/Corbis-Bettmann*)

shift was occurring in still more threatening form. Weary of incompetent leadership, French conservatives were eyeing with growing admiration the fascist experiments beyond their borders.

And so—as had happened in 1926 and as was to happen once again in 1938—the French Left, after two years in power and with two years of its electoral mandate still to run, found itself bankrupt both financially and ideologically, and was thus obliged to hand over power to the conservatives. But the conservatives' attempt to repeat the financial "miracle" of 1926 did not succeed. The old ex-president whom they hoisted into office, Gaston Doumergue, was far from being a Poincaré, and his government failed to produce the anticipated national revival. Even the presence of the hero of Verdun, Marshal Pétain, as minister of defense, could not give it the proper patriotic flavor. Doumergue succeeded only in restoring a minimum of order in the national finances. When the old prime minister stepped down in November, to be succeeded by the dapper Pierre-Étienne Flandin, the country was well on its way back to politics as usual. When Laval replaced him the following June, all thought of national regeneration had long since vanished.

In the last half of 1935, under the rule of Pierre Laval, France touched its lowest point of the interwar period. In foreign affairs, Laval inaugurated an uninspiring policy of appeasement. In the economic sphere, the government had nothing better to offer than retrenchment, salary reductions, and a pedantic adherence to the gold standard. The other powers had abandoned gold and were beginning to move out of depression. France alone was holding firmly to a deflationary policy and sinking ever deeper into economic stagnation. Meanwhile, the paramilitary formations of the authoritarian Right were holding their parades with impunity. On the Left, a new unity was growing, as anger and frustration mounted at the impotence of French democracy and the spreading influence of fascism. The Socialists had joined with the Communists—while the Radicals limped more hesitantly behind—to forge the Popular Front that in the year following was to lead France into the most tumultuous and decisive period of its entire interwar history (see Chapter 9, V).

IV. SCANDINAVIA: THE MIDDLE WAY

The Role of the Smaller Democracies: The Belgian Language Question

From 1919 to 1939, the smaller democracies of Western Europe impinged only rarely on the wider sphere of international and ideological contention. Most of the time they followed their own course, secure in the conviction of unquestioning acceptance of the democratic way of life by the vast majority of their people. Of the large nations of Europe, Great Britain alone was as firmly settled in the electoral and parliamentary mold as were the Low Countries, Switzerland, and Scandinavia.

Since the mid-nineteenth century, Switzerland had lived almost without a history—that is, in the sense of wars, political reversals, and major divisive issues. Split as they were among four nationalities and two religions, the Swiss knew that their survival in unity depended on mutual forbearance. They realized that the only way to hold the nation together was through constant compromise and the maintenance of a delicate equilibrium among the interests of diverging languages and creeds. Politics and elections in Switzerland thus tended to become formalized; their main function was to ensure the national consensus by perpetuating the tacit compromises on which the federal system ultimately rested.

In the Netherlands also, inherent conservatism kept the country in the old political routines, but no similar national unity prevailed in neighboring Belgium. Like Switzerland, Belgium was linguistically divided. Roughly half its population spoke French; the other half spoke Flemish, a local variety of Dutch. Unlike the Swiss, however, the Belgians had never granted equality to the different national languages. French had ruled supreme as the language of the aristocracy and of business, of education, the law courts, and the administration. Only very slowly and after long parliamentary struggles was the Flemish-speaking population permitted to use its own language for all its public concerns.

Between 1922 and 1932, this battle was substantially won. But a minority of the Flemings still remained dissatisfied. Linked as they were by speech not only with the Dutch but with the Germans directly across their borders, they began to succumb to the blandishments of Nazi propaganda. Fascism never won real political power in Belgium—

but here, alone among the small democracies of Europe, it recruited a following that seriously weakened the nation when the Second World War struck.

The Socialist Record in Norway, Sweden, and Denmark

In the Scandinavian countries to the north, the interest of foreigners was chiefly aroused by the experience of Socialist government. Here, as opposed to the major countries of Western Europe, where interwar socialism produced little but disappointment and failure, democrats of Socialist sympathies could point to a record of administrative competence and substantial success in meeting economic difficulties.

In the 1920s, Socialist parties had attained power for the first time in all these countries and had become used to the responsibilities of office, but it was not until the Great Depression that they came to dominate political life. During these years they launched a series of experiments that gradually fused in the public mind with the wider image of a Scandinavian "way."

In the northern countries, socialism from the beginning had more to build on and was more congenial to local tradition than was true in the larger nations to the south. For Socialists everywhere, the crucial dilemma was reconciling collectivist economic philosophy with devotion to democracy and the rights of the individual. In France or Britain, Germany or Italy, these two goals frequently seemed opposed. In Scandinavia there was no such conflict of values. The individualism on which the Norwegians or the Swedes prided themselves had been accompanied by a strong emphasis on community action. A severe climate, a relatively sparse population, and a high degree of social homogeneity had encouraged an attitude that combined, in a fashion that was unique in Europe, a robust sense of personal freedom with a talent for working in common. The result had been the strongest movement of agricultural and consumers' cooperatives in the world—a movement that eventually came to include about half the population of Sweden and more than a quarter of the inhabitants of Norway and Denmark.

In addition, the Socialist parties of these countries—which resembled the British Labour party more than they conformed to any continental pattern—were notably undogmatic. They did not insist in doctrinaire fashion on the nationalization of basic enterprise; they preferred, where possible, to establish some mixed scheme for joint governmental and private regulation of the economy. The same was true of the trade unions. Far from confronting capital with uniform hostility and distrust, labor leaders were accustomed to settling their difficulties with employers through semiofficial procedures of arbitration and conciliation.

Thus, when the Great Depression struck, the Scandinavian nations were better prepared than were the nations to the south to deal in coherent fashion with the economic and social problems it raised. Working from the already existing tradition of common action, the Socialists substantially enlarged the sphere of government intervention in the economy. The Swedes, for example, concentrated from the beginning on maintaining purchasing power—a goal that the major nations of the Western world accepted only gradually, as the orthodox solutions of retrenchment and deflation revealed their inadequacy. The Swedish government was not afraid to borrow heavily in order to maintain jobs and prices; it used monetary policy systematically, as a weapon in economic planning. And throughout Scandinavia, social insurance schemes inherited from earlier years were extended and rationalized during the Great Depression to cover the hazards of sickness, invalidism, and old age for the entire population.

To observers from Britain, France, or the United States—oppressed by the fumbling of their own governments, by mounting class tension at home, and by the steady advance of fascism and communism abroad—Scandinavia in the early 1930s seemed to offer a haven of competence and good sense. Here governments ensured full employment and protected their people against want; capital and labor composed their differences across a conference table instead of fighting it out in bitter strikes; the economic and psychological barriers between classes were losing their rigidity as the welfare state imposed ruinous taxes on the rich and guaranteed a livelihood to the poor. Even the physical aspect of these countries seemed better. The cities were clean and trim and amply provided with parks and public housing. Indeed, the housing exhibition held at Stockholm in 1930 epitomized the whole trend; building after building reflected the influence of the new "International Style," which, like so many other twentieth-century innovations, had been accepted by the Scandinavians in common-sense fashion as the type of construction best suited to the requirements of contemporary life.

No wonder, then, that these observers hailed the Scandinavian course as the "middle way"—the way of pragmatic flexibility, steering between doctrinaire socialism on the one side and doctrinaire free enterprise on the other. It seemed to offer a new and heartening possibility for saving democratic government throughout the Western world. And such a fresh look at democracy was urgently needed. Nearly everywhere else in Europe, authoritarian government was confidently advancing, and democratic parliamentarism revealing its pitiable inadequacy.

V. THE CRISIS OF PARLIAMENTARY DEMOCRACY

By the mid-1930s, the Great Depression was beginning to lift. In all the major countries except France, the national economy had turned the corner: Production was mounting; unemployment was falling. But depression lifted only in the strictly economic sense. In political life and popular morale, the depression psychology persisted. The great democracies of Western Europe seemed sick—and none knew what remedy would cure them. In Italy and Germany, parliamentary democracy had disappeared. In Britain, it was functioning only lamely. In France, it seemed to be wallowing in political squalor. How long, people asked, could such a system maintain itself?

The parliaments of Europe had been caught unaware by problems of unprecedented scope and had failed to deal with them. Before 1914, it was possible for representative bodies to proceed in leisurely and amateurish fashion; the parliamentary practice of engulfing issues in floods of oratory had sufficed when the issues themselves were still of a political or ideological nature that demanded no special expert knowledge. But when the First World War, its liquidation, and the Great Depression raised their acutely complex economic and financial problems, the old political routines proved obsolete. Something else was needed to master a situation in which the role of government itself had increased so vastly. In this respect, as in so many others, postwar Europe never returned to "normal."

National leaders resorted to a variety of provisional expedients. None proved satisfactory; each raised as many problems as it settled. Among these expedients was government by coalition. A coalition of parties was, in itself, a proper and democratic way of setting up a government—that is, when it was honestly managed. In a multiparty state, the alternation in power of two great coalitions offered the only possible way of approximating a two-party system—as in France in 1919 with the Bloc National and in 1924 with the Cartel des Gauches. But this was true only if the coalitions stood for principles—if they were clearly of the Right or of the Left and had some vestige of a common program. When this was not true—as in Germany through most of the Weimar period—coalition government became a travesty; it distorted the verdict of the electorate without providing governmental stability in return.

A similar dishonesty characterized the "national" ministries to which Britain resorted in 1916 and 1931, and France in 1926 and 1934. Under the guise of rising above parties and expressing the unity of the nation, such governments proved themselves little more than a device for returning to power the conservatives who had lost the previous election. It was not surprising that the Left railed against these ministries—that the French Radicals, who had been tricked into such a combination in 1926, proved more wary in 1934, and that the British Labour party, which had seen the Liberals sold out during the war by their leader Lloyd George, reacted so violently to MacDonald's similar act of betrayal in 1931. Only by reviling him, expelling him from the party, and developing new leaders was Labour able to escape the fate by which the Liberal party had been overtaken.

If government by coalition might become mere fraud, the other favorite expedient—rule by decree—was even more doubtfully democratic. In the interwar years, Britain succeeded in avoiding this latter practice entirely, but in Germany and France, its general employment contributed heavily to discrediting democracy. When heads of government like Brüning and Doumergue insisted that the only way to cope with a recalcitrant parliament was to issue laws by executive order, it was quite obvious that democratic practices were breaking down. It was equally apparent that the locus of political power was shifting. The authority that was slipping from the hands of parliament was passing to the high civil servants—those anonymous but powerful persons who had always had more permanent positions and greater prestige in Europe than in the United States. They alone possessed the technical competence to deal with inflation and deflation, taxes and tariffs, monetary controls, and public works. The solutions they favored were generally conservative and paternalistic; for career public servants customarily came from the propertied classes. Indeed, in certain cases they carried into the postwar era the rule of the old aristocracy. Graduates of special schools and with a strong sense of caste, these "technocrats" scorned both public and parliament as mere ignoramuses; from this it was only a step to scorn democracy itself.

Here, too, the democratic Left felt betrayed. Winning elections did it no good: The "establishment" of the propertied and the well born always returned to power. Had the result been aristocratic rule in the true sense—that is, rule by the "best"—such defeat might have been less frustrating. But the expedients of the conservatives usually produced only government by pretentious mediocrities. This was what the fascist leaders pointed to when they vaunted their own "corporative" plan of drawing into the nation's service the best talent from business and the professions. And it was what Soviet spokesmen sneered at when they boasted of how they were raising a new and technically competent elite from the young men of promise among Russia's toiling millions. Both these authoritarian systems, in their widely contrasting fashions, seemed to have solved more adequately than had parliamentary democracy the problem of finding leadership that could give purpose and direction to the national life.

What, then, were these two systems which by their mere existence and example offered so perplexing a challenge to Western democracy in the depths of the Great Depression?

READINGS

For a general account of the European economy on the eve of the Great Depression, besides Landes (see readings for Chapter 5), there is D. N. Aldcroft, *From Versailles to Wall Street: The International Economy in the 1920s** (1977). John Kenneth Galbraith, in *The Great Crash, 1929,** 3rd ed. (1972), gives a spirited account of the beginnings of the Depression in the United States, while Charles P. Kindleberger, in *The World in Depression, 1929–39** (rev. ed., 1986), traces its spreading effects. Walter Laqueur and George Mosse, eds., *The Great Depression** (1970) contains a stimulating series of articles which first appeared as an issue of the *Journal of Contemporary History*.

Among books on individual countries that deal specifically with the political and social problems of the Depression, for Britain, besides Mowat and Stevenson (see readings for Chapter 5), see also Bentley B. Gilbert, *British Social Policy, 1914–1939* (1970), and Noreen Branson and Margot Heinemann, *Britain in the Nineteen Thirties* (1971). A classic documentary account of the Depression in one midlands town is George Orwell's *The Road to Wigan Pier** (1937), while Walter Greenwood, in *Love on the Dole** (1933), offers a contemporary novelist's view of the human costs of unemployment. For France, see Eugen Weber, *The Hollow Years: France in the 1930s** (1994), John T. Marcus, *French Socialism in the Crisis Years, 1933–1936* (1958), and Richard F. Kuisel, *Capitalism and the State in Modern France** (1981). For Germany, see Karl Hardach, *The Political Economy in the 20th Century** (1980), and Gustav Stolper et al., *The German Economy: 1870 to the Present* (1967). David Abraham, in his controversial but stimulating *The Collapse of the Weimar Republic: Political Economy and Crisis*, 2nd ed. (1986), points to the role played by economic rivalries in fatally weakening the Weimar regime. Hans Fallada's Depression-era novel, *Little Man, What Now?* (1933), conveys a sense of working-class life in Berlin at the height of the economic crisis.

The Scandinavian example during the Depression years is traced in sympathetic fashion in Franklin D. Scott, *Sweden: The Nation's History,** enlarged ed. (1988), and in Marquis W. Childs, *Sweden: The Middle Way*, new ed. (1947).

*Books marked with an asterisk are available in paperback.

THE FASCIST REGIMES

Surrounded by symbols of Nazi power and guarded by black-uniformed troops of the SS, Hitler is shown here addressing more than two million working men and women during a May Day celebration at the Tempelhof Airport in Berlin. (*Courtesy Getty Images, Inc./Liaison*)

Fascism was the great political surprise of the first half of the twentieth century. Communism, or something resembling it, had been threatening ever since the European revolutions of 1848; the novelty of communism after 1917 lay not in its ideology but in the eccentric twist given to it by its Russian abode. For the coming of a Socialist society in an authoritarian and intolerant form, the European mind was reasonably well prepared, and individual reactions to it followed a predictable course. Conservatives and liberals were hostile from the start; democratic Socialists, after an initial period of hesitation, usually swung around to determined opposition. It was not always easy to judge what Soviet Russia intended or was doing, but the main outlines of the system were clear to both friend and foe.

With fascism, it was quite different. In this case there had been no half century of preparation to warn Europeans of what was coming. To most of them, it appeared quite suddenly and unexpectedly with Mussolini's March on Rome in 1922. There had, of course, been a few premonitory signs before the First World War, including the brutalities of overseas imperialism, the "pan" movements, popular militarism, and the longing for war. These were but the bits and pieces of an ideology. The impact of the First World War was needed to precipitate a true mass movement, for fascism, far more than communism, was a product of war and postwar conditions—and of the sufferings of the Great Depression, which gave it the decisive chance.

Fascism seemed bewildering because it had no clear ideology. It spoke the language of socialism, but adopted an economic policy that buttressed the forces of large capital. It stressed its revolutionary origins, but carefully reassured the propertied and the tradition minded. Did fascism belong on the right or on the left, people wondered. Even the seating of its deputies in parliamentary bodies created a problem, although it was usually settled by putting the fascists alongside the ultraconservatives.

Fascism was—to cite the best simple definition that has ever been proposed—a "radicalism of the Right." Its ideals included an intense nationalism, a belief in the virtues of struggle and youth, and obedience to a charismatic leader; its sworn enemies included Marxism, liberalism, and racial minorities such as gypsies and Jews. When the old symbols of loyalty— "honor," "fatherland," and the rest—no longer seemed to bind society together, fascism reinvigorated them by an infusion of brutality and melodrama. It promised a united nation where economic conflict would give way to a "corporatist" inclusion of all productive groups in society within a single movement. It promised the isolated individual fulfillment in disciplined service to the nation as a whole.

So much for a tentative definition. For all their local variations, the fascist systems bore a considerable family resemblance. Both uniformities and contradictions are evident in the three main manifestations of the fascist phenomenon: Mussolini's Italy, Hitler's Germany, and the "clerical-corporative" regimes in Portugal, Austria, and Spain.

I. MUSSOLINI'S ACHIEVEMENT

Fascism advanced in three successive waves. First there was the period of postwar turmoil, in which it failed in Germany but brought Mussolini to power in Italy. Second there was the Great Depression, in which it triumphed in Central Europe. Finally there was the Second World War, in which German and Italian arms spread the system—or some facsimile of it—to the greater part of the European Continent.

Ideological Origins and the March to Power

Originally, Mussolini's success seemed an isolated occurrence, in sharp contrast to the ideology of democratic parliamentarism that predominated in Western and Central Europe in the 1920s. Mussolini indeed had acted in isolation. He had triumphed on his own without help from the outside. And his remained the original fascist regime—the only one called Fascist with a capital F—and the one that even after the advent of Hitler was more admired and imitated than the Nazi model. It is important to remember this when considering the later phases of Fascist history, in which Mussolini found himself overshadowed and humiliated by his German partner.

Benito Mussolini was a true proletarian. Born the son of a blacksmith in 1883, he was a Socialist by family inheritance and a revolutionary by temperament. After a youth of odd jobs, wide but spotty reading, and draft evasion in Switzerland, he early became the most dynamic figure within Italian socialism. When he was not yet thirty, he led the party's agitation against the Libyan War of 1911, and in the following year he succeeded in being chosen editor of the official Socialist newspaper and in expelling the "reformists" from the party's ranks.

Until 1914, Mussolini's career had followed a fairly usual course. His oratorical talents and his personal magnetism had brought him while still very young to a position of dominance not unlike Lenin's. And he seemed to belong with Lenin on the left or revolutionary wing of international socialism. But then the unexpected happened. A few months after the outbreak of the war, Mussolini changed his stand entirely—he declared for Italian intervention on the side of France and Britain, joining the motley ranks of those who followed the poet D'Annunzio in urging the government to go to war. At the time it seemed an act of political suicide: Mussolini was driven from his editorship and from the Socialist party itself. There was nothing left for him but to prove the reality of his conversion to nationalism by doing military service at the front.

Wounded and invalided out of the army, Mussolini languished in political obscurity. In 1919, when he formed his first "combat groups" (*fasci di combattimento*), from which his movement took its name, only very few answered his call. Not until D'Annunzio had been dislodged from his "regency" over the disputed port of Fiume did Mussolini, at the beginning of 1921, begin to enroll his first important body of recruits from the veterans of that tragicomic enterprise.

From then on, everything seemed to help the new movement. Italy was suffering from the usual dislocations and disillusionments of the immediate postwar period—rendered still more acute by the poverty of the country—and Mussolini was able to draw profit from nearly all of them. In addition, the nation had just embarked on the perilous experiment of political democracy. The new mass electorate of universal suffrage had swamped the Liberal and Radical parties, which before the war had dominated Italian politics. The Chamber of Deputies elected in 1919 had a far different composition from its predecessors. A majority of its members came from two great parties that appealed to the poorer classes—the newly organized Popular party, a Catholic formation not unlike the German Center, and, of course, Mussolini's former comrades, the Italian Socialists. Could these two have worked together, Italian democracy might perhaps have been saved. But that was never a real possibility. The Popular party leaders lacked experience, and as good Catholics, they distrusted the Marxist ideology of the Socialists. The Socialists were overflowing with revolutionary enthusiasm but had no coherent program. Their occupation of the factories in the autumn of 1920 had revealed the futility of the Maximalist attitude of simply waiting for the revolution to fall like bounty from the skies.

What helped Mussolini more than anything else, however, was the disappointment that Italian patriots had experienced at the Peace Conference of 1919. Their government, they felt, had betrayed them by failing to obtain the full price for Italy's entrance into the war. This sense of injury swelled to a chorus of indignation as a series of short-lived ministries proved unable to master the new political forces that the postwar turbulence had unleashed. Among these forces the Fascists soon eclipsed all their rivals in the vigor and brutality of their tactics. They beat up Socialists, trade unionists, and adherents of the Popular party; they burned and looted and administered almost lethal doses of castor oil. But to Italian conservatives they began to look more and more like avenging angels sent from heaven to ward off the perils of "bolshevism."

Actually, whatever "Bolshevist" threat there had been had disappeared by the end of 1920 with the failure of the occupation of the factories. It was the Fascists themselves who had replaced the revolutionary Socialists as the chief disturbers of law and order. By the spring of 1921, however, both the government and the propertied classes were winking at Mussolini's depredations and even occasionally treating the Fascist armed bands as auxiliaries of the regular police. In this attitude, Italian conservatives were encouraged by the fact that fascism from the start spoke a double language—it talked of revolution and of social leveling, but it also preached national revival and lauded the virtues of martial ardor, of hierarchy, and of discipline. As time went on, the latter themes gradually came to predominate. By the autumn of 1922, Mussolini sensed that it was time to give the conservatives still more specific assurances of good behavior. In early October, he formally renounced any intention of threatening the Italian monarchy.

In the next three weeks, Mussolini's black-shirted bands—which already controlled much of the northern countryside—prepared to seize power. In the end this proved unnecessary; the politicians in Rome lost their nerve and refused to fight. When the last prime minister of parliamentary Italy went to the king to ask for a proclamation of martial law, the monarch refused his signature. Instead he called on Mussolini to form a government. Thus the threatened "March on Rome" never occurred. This event—which was to figure in Fascist history as the foundation of the new regime—was no more than the token occupation of a citadel that had already fallen. As the Blackshirts began their anticlimactic entry into the capital, Mussolini was arriving by sleeping car from Milan to take over the reins of authority.

The Consolidation of the Dictatorship: The Murder of Matteotti and the Parliamentary Secession

The advent of Mussolini at the end of October 1922 was extraordinary in every respect. Technically it fell within the limits of constitutional procedure, but from the beginning Mussolini had no intention of governing as a parliamentary prime minister. For one

Benito Mussolini (1883–1945), flanked by other Fascist leaders at the time of the March on Rome, October 22, 1922. (*Courtesy Stock Montage, Inc./Historical Pictures Collection*)

thing, he did not have the requisite majority in the Chamber of Deputies. Only thirty-five Fascists had won seats in the last regular elections, held in the spring of 1921, and in order to make up his ministry Mussolini felt obliged to call on the Nationalists—whose program he had stolen and whose following he was about to absorb—and on the Popular party, which later regretted the grudging support it had given him. Besides all this, the new prime minister made no secret of his scorn for parliaments, elections, and democracy in general. "A gray and squalid hall" was what he called the meeting place of the Chamber of Deputies, and he taunted the parliamentarians with the boast that he might well have used it as a bivouac for his soldiers. To his constitutional functions he much preferred his party role of *Duce*, or chief, the title by which he was most often called in subsequent years.

Only gradually, however, did Mussolini impose full Fascist control over Italian life. For the first year and a half—still unsure of his tenure—he left a margin of liberty to the press, to the trade unions, and to the parties in parliament. In this period many Italians of liberal and democratic sympathies adopted a wait-and-see attitude toward the new regime or even gave it their qualified support. Since fascism was still so new, they did not know how far it would go. In its favor was the fact that it had brought order to the country, and moderate-minded people cherished the illusion that by participating in Mussolini's experiment they could influence it toward milder courses.

This honeymoon came to an abrupt end in the spring and summer of 1924. In April, Mussolini finally obtained a massive majority in the Chamber of Deputies through a rigged election in which violence and intimidation were freely employed. Two months later, the Socialist deputy Giacomo Matteotti disappeared. Matteotti had courageously spoken out against Fascist acts of terror. It was widely suspected and later proved that he had been murdered on official orders. In protest against this crime, some 150 deputies seceded from the chamber; they included nearly all the remaining representatives of Italian democracy, from the Socialist, the Popular, and the Liberal parties.

It initially seemed that the secession would bring Mussolini down. The *Duce*, badly shaken by the Matteotti murder, tried to brazen it out through disavowing his subordinates and imposing a strict press censorship. The secessionists failed to press their advantage, however. They delayed and argued and lost precious time. Still more important, they were unable to persuade the king to dismiss his prime minister. Hence, by the autumn of 1926, Mussolini felt sufficiently sure of himself to strike back. He accepted responsibility for all that had occurred, and he ordered the secessionists deprived of their seats in the chamber and their political parties dissolved. From this point on, the opponents of the regime had no choice but to keep quiet or to emigrate. The older and more eminent usually chose to leave. The younger stayed on to engage in clandestine activity; sooner or later, nearly all of them were arrested by Mussolini's political police and sent to prison or to forced detention on some barren island.

By the end of 1926 the Fascist dictatorship had consolidated its authority. The press and the chamber had been brought into line; the Fascist party had received a monopoly of political activity, with its Blackshirts acquiring official status as a militia of volunteers; the indoctrination of Italian youth was proceeding apace, as boys and girls of all ages were enrolled in semimilitary formations that taught fanatical loyalty to the regime.

The Corporate State

One reason why Mussolini felt safe in hitting back at his opponents was that he had finally reached a satisfactory understanding with the business leaders of the country. Most large industrialists had been skeptical of fascism at first; recruits for the new party had come rather from war veterans and the lower middle class, and what moneyed support it enjoyed was provided almost exclusively by the landowners of northern and central Italy. As time went on, however, and it became apparent that Mussolini would remain in power, some of the more farsighted leaders of Italian industry began to see that a mutually advantageous bargain could be struck with the new regime. Long negotiations followed, until finally, in the autumn of 1925, an agreement signed at the Palazzo Vidoni in Rome regularized the relations between fascism and Italian industry.

The Palazzo Vidoni agreement was little known outside Italy, and only a handful of foreign observers understood its importance. Essentially it gave organized Italian industry the privileged position of a state within a state in return for its implied promise to support the Fascist regime. The Federation of Italian Industrialists (*Confindustria*), which had negotiated with Mussolini, received semiofficial status as a self-governing body for the regulation of the economy. A similar official endorsement was subsequently granted to the organizations of larger employers in agriculture and commerce. Labor and the professions, on the other hand, enjoyed no such favors. *They* were compelled to enroll in Fascist-led formations, in which party representatives monopolized authority.

Together these various semigovernmental bodies made up what Mussolini called the *corporate state*. In official theory, they constituted the foundation of the regime, particularly after 1934, when they were reorganized on a much more elaborate basis, and 1938, when the Chamber of Deputies was transformed into a Chamber of Fasces and Corporations. It was similarly part of the theory of corporatism that bodies of this sort reconciled the conflict of classes by bringing capital and labor together under the benevolent auspices of the party-state. But the facts were rather different. In the corporative structure, capital alone enjoyed true self-government. Labor was shackled by the triple authority of the employers, the state, and the party, which usually managed to agree. Denied the right to strike and the right to leadership of their own choice, the workers of Italy might console themselves with a high-sounding "Charter of Labor" that was almost devoid of content.

Such was the reality of the corporate state. In the pretentious verbiage with which the regime enveloped it lurked a great deception. When the rhetoric was stripped away, Italian corporatism stood revealed as little more than an elaborate engine of class rule.

The Church, the Lateran Treaty, and Catholic Action

Mussolini was a forthright atheist. So were nearly all his chief party followers. As a realist, however, he fully appreciated the importance of Catholicism in Italian life. Among a people whose vast majority were of one faith, religion, if properly exploited, could serve as an invaluable reinforcement to national unity. Mussolini also saw that his predecessors, the parliamentary governments of Italy, had lost the support of millions of Italians by their anticlerical attitude and by the conflict with the Vatican that had lingered on for two generations, ever since the kingdom of Italy in 1870 deprived the Pope of his territorial dominion over Rome and the surrounding area.

Mussolini had good reason to conciliate Italian Catholicism. Among the other evidences of his turn to conservatism after 1922—paralleling his reassurances to monarchists and men of property—were a series of minor acts of favor to the church. Once sure of his own authority, Mussolini moved on to more important matters; he opened secret negotiations for the settlement of the "Roman Question" itself.

These negotiations—frequently difficult and at one point interrupted entirely—continued for nearly three years. Finally, however, they were completely successful. In February 1929, Pope Pius XI and the *Duce* announced that they had reached agreement on all the issues that had pitted church against state in Italy for nearly sixty years. By the Lateran Treaty and the Concordat that accompanied it, the Pope gained his minimum demands. He won territorial sovereignty over a few acres around the basilica of St. Peter's and the Vatican—thus securing that formal independence from the control of any temporal state on which the Papacy had always insisted; he also obtained a privileged position for the church in Italian public education and assurance that Italian marriage law would be brought into conformity with Catholic teaching.

The mood of harmony and of national jubilation created by the accords of 1929 did not last long. By 1931, church and state had returned to war. And the reason for the renewed conflict was symptomatic of the basic hostility between fascism and Christianity. Mussolini objected to the youth and university organizations run by the laymen's organization called Catholic Action; they competed, he complained, with his own Fascist formations. The Pope defended Catholic Action with all the polemical vigor at his command and denounced the "pagan intentions" of Mussolini's regime. After a summer of struggle, the two authorities reached a new compromise: The Catholic Action groups would continue to operate, but with a strictly limited program. After this, the old cordiality never returned; the relations between the Papacy and fascism remained strained until the outbreak of the Second World War.

Among the general public, however, the happy memory of the settlement of 1929 continued to predominate. This was certainly the most popular thing that Mussolini ever did, and it marked the zenith of his prestige and influence. As the 1930s opened, then, Italian fascism seemed forever established in the affections of the Italian people. Both at home and abroad, its authority was virtually unquestioned. At home, Mussolini had brought a new discipline and sense of purpose to Italian life. As the tourists put it, he had "made the trains run on time." Internal opposition had been crushed by the secret police, and the political exiles across the border were consumed with rage at their own powerlessness. Abroad, Mussolini enjoyed general respect as a strong ruler, essentially a moderate despite the regrettable strong-arm tactics of his subordinates. The *Duce* took care to encourage this impression of respectability by putting restraints on his own love of bluster and by cultivating the friendship of distinguished Englishmen. In return, such Tory worthies as Austen Chamberlain and Winston Churchill said complimentary things about him, implying that democracy might work for Anglo-Saxons but the more childish Italians required a stronger authority.

Only a bold prophet indeed in 1930 would have foretold that within thirteen years the Fascist *Duce*—his regime in full disintegration and his foreign ventures all come to naught—would succumb to the overwhelming hatred of his own people.

II. THE COMING OF HITLER

Mussolini made his way to power on the first wave of fascist agitation. His German counterpart, Adolf Hitler, had to wait another decade before reaching the same goal. This difference suggests the contrasting experience of German and Italian fascism and the divergent natures of their leaders and of the societies that they would strive to mold in their own image.

From Vienna to the Beer-Hall Putsch

Hitler was six years younger than Mussolini and of less proletarian social origins. His father had been a customs official on the Austro-German border and made pretensions to middle-class status that Mussolini's father would have scorned. This frontier situation, moreover, meant that Hitler could not take his nationality for granted as the future *Duce* did; it was something he had to fight and strive for. Technically an Austrian, Hitler longed for a wider fatherland.

It was natural, then, that when he went to Vienna to seek his fortune he should become a Pan-German, pledged to seek the unity of Austria and the German Reich. Nor was it surprising that Hitler, a bewildered and humiliated young man from the provinces, should learn to hate the Jews, who symbolized for him all that was cosmopolitan, sophisticated, and "decadent" in the Austrian capital. Hitler's own experience in Vienna was one of uniform failure—he was refused admission to the study of architecture, and he found himself reduced to menial tasks, to unemployment, and to living in dreary flophouses. His acquaintances of those days depict him as a moody, compulsive talker who was devoured by the sense of a mission both vague and vast. Here also there is a contrast to Mussolini. The future *Duce* made his way early in life; he had a clear, if rather cynical, mind and a robust emotional constitution; he knew what he wanted and was never the dupe of his own oratory. Hitler was a drifter and a dreamer; his mind bore the marks of the psychopath; he followed his political instinct, as he himself expressed it, "like a sleepwalker," and in his moments of oratorical exaltation he behaved as though in a trance.

The outbreak of the First World War found Hitler in Munich. Overwhelmed with joy at the news, he fell on his knees in thanksgiving. He enlisted in the German army, in which he served throughout the war, bravely and honorably but never rising above the rank of corporal. Army life suited him perfectly. Its comradeship gave him emotional security for the first time in his life, and its discipline supplied him with a sense of direction that he had never known before.

After the war Hitler joined the throng of jobless veterans, artistic bohemians, and political agitators who were making the Bavarian capital so lively a place in which to live. He specialized in rabble-rousing speeches that stressed nationalist and anti-Semitic themes. In 1919, he attached himself to a struggling group called the National Socialist German Workers' Party, which he raised from obscurity by infusing it with his own demonic force. Within a very short time he had become the Nazis' chief—the *Führer*, as he was to be known to history. Gradually he gathered around him the other leaders who were later to achieve fame—among them the corpulent, brutal Hermann Goering, who had been an ace flier in the war, and Josef Goebbels, a small, lame propagandist of burning intensity, who after 1926 ran the northern branch of National Socialism from his headquarters in Berlin. There were also sympathizers who were more loosely attached to the movement—notably old General Ludendorff, the dictator of the Reich in the First World War.

In Germany's years of torment between 1919 and 1923, conditions were at least as favorable for a fascist assumption of power as they were in Italy. Governmental authority wavered from month to month; street battles or assassinations became almost daily occurrences. Indeed, there was rather an excess than a lack of talent of an extreme nationalist and racist variety, whereas in Italy—after D'Annunzio's collapse at Fiume—

there was only one fascist movement and one undisputed chief. German fascism or semi-fascism thus remained dispersed and divided. Its main strength, rather than going toward politics, was thrown into the military activities of the Free Corps—irregular armed bodies of war veterans and young students, who served the government when it called on them in its moments of desperation, who fought Communists and Poles and murdered such democratic political leaders as Erzberger and Rathenau.

The Free Corps rose in the Kapp *Putsch*, the rightist insurrection which, in March 1920, forced the government to flee from Berlin and was beaten only by a general strike of the German trade unions. The next two years were quieter; democratic authority began to establish itself. But then came the terrible year 1923, with the French occupation of the Ruhr and the runaway inflation. The economic suffering and social dissolution of that year gave Hitler his chance. In November, the National Socialists made their own bid for power. It began with a tumultuous meeting in one of Munich's vast beer halls—hence the name "beer-hall *Putsch*" by which it is derisively known to history—and it ended with a street procession that was intended to turn into a general revolution. But Hitler had waited too long. Had he acted in the summer, he would have had greater chance of success. By autumn, however, Stresemann was in power and resolved on decisive action. The Nazi street demonstration was stopped by police fire. Old General Ludendorff, who was marching alongside Hitler, remained standing as he faced the bullets; the future *Führer* fell flat on the street, and two days later he was tracked down at the home of a friend and sent to prison.

From "Mein Kampf" to the Chancellorship

In the period of Germany's apparent stabilization, the Nazi party languished. Hitler was in jail, and nationalist extremism was everywhere on the wane. But these years were not wholly lost for the party. In his prison cell Hitler wrote *Mein Kampf (My Struggle)*, a vast, turgid autobiographical reflection that was to become the bible of the movement. And the lean years brought indirect benefits to the Nazis by ridding them of their rivals; as one after another of the extremist formations withered and died, National Socialism was left alone to incarnate the spirit of racial hatred and patriotic revenge.

At the end of 1924, when Hitler emerged from prison, he had revised his thinking about political agitation and concluded that better organization and discipline were required. He recast his movement as a regular political party, in which further putsches were discouraged and the "leadership principle," as he put it, was strictly enforced. By 1928, he was ready to make the alliance with Hugenberg's wing of the Nationalists that brought such rich returns in the form of joint agitation against the Young Plan and the chance to hound Stresemann to his death.

But the alliance with the Nationalists was only a temporary expedient and, with the coming of the Great Depression, Hitler felt strong enough to strike out on his own. The spread of unemployment finally gave the Nazis what they wanted—a rich field for the recruitment of desperate men. Tens of thousands of the jobless enrolled as Storm Troopers in the brown-shirted party army that corresponded to Mussolini's Blackshirts. Frequently their officers were former Free Corps men who knew how to kill and to inspire a rough loyalty among their followers. But their radicalism was in action rather than political ideology. The Free Corps had shown little interest in politics. And the National Socialists themselves were gradually forgetting the second term in their party label; their program was still sprinkled with socialist phrases, but these were vaguely expressed and it was doubtful how seriously the leadership took them. One straw in the wind was that in 1930 Hitler expelled from the party Otto Strasser, who had been attempting to steer the movement in a leftist direction.

The Nazis' electoral strength and their power in the streets grew steadily in the early years of the Great Depression. By the summer of 1932, they were riding high and sure of their ability to reach power within the very near future. But then an unexpected catastrophe occurred. In the second Reichstag election of the year, held in November, the Nazis lost votes. They were still the strongest party in the country, but they could no longer pose as an irresistible wave of the future rolling on from triumph to triumph. Indeed, they might already have missed their historic opportunity (see Figure 9.1). When the results of the voting came in, something like panic gripped the Nazi leadership. The series of elections following closely one on another had bankrupted the party treasury. There were literally no funds with which to pay the Storm Troopers—and this spelled disaster, for it was the promise of a square meal that had brought so many of these people to nazism in the first place, and the loss of their meal ticket would soon send them drifting away again.

At this point, Hitler held firm. Against the advice of his subordinates, he insisted that the Nazis should make no concessions and accept government posts only on their own terms. It was a risky gamble, but the decision to wait later proved to be fully justified. In the meantime, the party's shaky finances were propped up through a variety

FIGURE 9.1 The National Socialist vote in German national elections compared to the total percentage of eligible voters voting. Note the dip in the Nazi vote in November 1932. Even at its moment of greatest electoral triumph the following March, Hitler's party received less than half the votes cast.

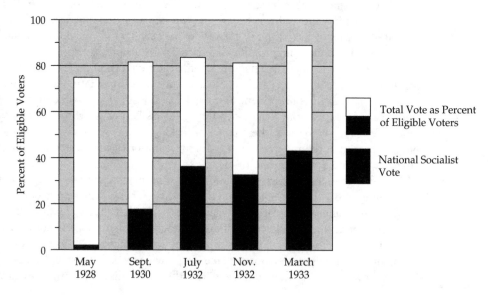

of expedients. The claim that Hitler received vital financial backing from Rhine-Ruhr industrialists in return for a promise to give German industry a free hand in the Third Reich is no longer accepted by most scholars; however, some individual businessmen did contribute to the party in its hour of need. Far more important for Hitler's future, however, was the refusal of industrial leaders, agrarian interests, and the army to back any government coalition that included the Left. Their fear of socialism proved far stronger than their distrust of a right-wing demagogue. When Chancellor Kurt von Schleicher attempted to bring trade unionists into his government in December of 1932, nervous German conservatives of all sorts began to bombard President von Hindenburg with advice to call Hitler to office. On January 30, 1933, the old field marshal bowed to what he had come to regard as the inevitable. He appointed Hitler chancellor with a coalition in which a majority of Nationalists and nonparty men (including former Chancellor von Papen) were intended to guarantee the preservation of conservative values.

Who must bear responsibility for Hitler's conquest of power? As in any major historical event, many actors contributed to the final outcome. The voters who backed the Nazis, the conservative politicians who believed they could manipulate them, the Communists who refused to oppose them, and the businessmen who were ready to deal with them all share some of the blame for having contributed to one of the greatest catastrophes of modern times. In the end, however, the chief responsibility lies with the conservatives. It was they who made the fatal judgment that a government led by Hitler was preferable to a government open to the Socialists and the trade unions. Intent on restoring the prewar, patriarchal Germany threatened by the Weimar regime, German conservatives insured instead that the old order—and much else of inestimable value in Germany—would perish within the next dozen years. When Hitler's supporters staged a gigantic torch-lit parade on the evening of January 30, they celebrated their victory and plunged Germany into the abyss.

The *Gleichschaltung*

Hitler accomplished in six months what had taken Mussolini four years. Within that time he had *gleichgeschaltet*—brought into line—nearly every phase of the national life.

First, he consolidated his political authority. A fire, which destroyed the Reichstag building—and which many thought had been set by his own henchmen—gave him an excuse to crack down on the Communists and to suspend constitutional guarantees of individual liberty. In the elections that followed, the Nazis used their position in the government to mount a propaganda campaign of unprecedented intensity and to give their Storm Troopers full license to terrorize the electorate. Still they failed to win a majority. The Social Democrats and the Center held firm.

When the new Reichstag assembled, however, Hitler made certain that it would not behave in the unruly fashion of its predecessors. He moved it out to the overawing atmosphere of the Garrison Church at Potsdam, where he staged an impressive ceremony suggesting his own solidarity with the conservative and imperial past. Behind the scenes, he neutralized the Center by a promise to respect the liberties of the Catholic church. Since the Communists were already nearly all in jail, this left the Social Democrats isolated in opposition. Alone they faced the storm of Hitler's abuse, and alone they voted against the Enabling Act that he had imperatively demanded.

The Enabling Act of March 23, 1933 was the cornerstone of the Nazi dictatorship. It gave the government power to rule by decree for four years—a power Hitler used to the full. Never again until the *Führer's* death was Germany to enjoy even the semblance of political freedom. With this act in his pocket, Hitler turned against the very people who had helped him to power. Papen and the Nationalists were left breathless; the chancellor whom they had intended to use for their own purposes began, on the contrary, to exploit them in ruthless fashion and had soon reduced them to the shabby function of window dressing for the regime. The Center fared no better. Its vote in favor of the Enabling Act was to no avail, and it disappeared along with Social Democracy when all political parties except the Nazis were dissolved the following spring and summer. The trade unions experienced a similar fate; one by one, virtually every independent body in every field of the national life was abolished or *gleichgeschaltet*. By the summer of 1933, Hitler's opponents were either in jail or in hiding, in exile or in concentration camps.

Even the Nazi party did not escape. In the following year came the turn of the dissidents within the movement itself. On the "Night of the Long Knives" of June 30, 1934, Hitler struck down those close to him who had deviated either to the right or to the left. Among the conservatives who perished in this night of terror was his predecessor as chancellor, Kurt von Schleicher. Among the "radicals" were some of the most prominent of the Storm Troopers and former Free Corps leaders, for the main purpose of the blood purge was to destroy the independent power of the Storm Troopers, which the army disliked and feared and whose unruly ways no longer befitted a party that was governing the state. Hitler's choice of executioners was again fateful for the future. He called on a newer and smaller body than the Storm Troopers, his own elite guard, or SS (*Schutzstaffel*). The SS wore black uniforms instead of brown, with death's head insignia, and functioned as an elite paramilitary force doing Hitler's bidding. They were specially selected for their "Nordic" qualities and physical fitness, and they were trained to an unhesitating, unquestioning obedience. "My honor," ran the SS motto, "means loyalty."

From the summer of 1934 on, the SS was to play an ever more important role in the Nazi state. As the power of the SA declined following the "Night of the Long Knives," the SS rose to prominence as the most ruthless of Hitler's armed supporters. It was to the SS that he would later give the cruel task of guarding Nazi concentration camps and executing their prisoners during the war. Parallel to them in importance as terror agents within and beyond Germany's borders were the feared secret police or Gestapo (*Geheime Staatspolizei*), which worked to destroy the domestic enemies of the Nazi regime, and the army, whose numbers grew as Hitler pursued rearmament in defiance of the Treaty of Versailles. But whereas the army clung to at least nominal independence, both the SS and Gestapo were directly subordinate to the new master of Germany, Adolf Hitler.

Five weeks after the blood purge, the eighty-seven-year-old Hindenburg conveniently died. With the passing of this sole remaining link to the past, Hitler was free to combine the offices of president and chancellor in his own person—a decision ratified by a plebiscite in which nearly nine-tenths of the German people voted yes. Thus Hitler early rid himself of the competing constitutional authority that in Italy, in the person of the king, was to plague Mussolini to the very end.

How much power did Hitler enjoy in the end? Historians are divided in their assessments. The school of "intentionalists" argues that Hitler encountered few checks to his own will. The Nazi party, the German government, and the military all served as willing tools to carry out the brutal racism and dreams of German expansion that he preached to the nation. The opposing school of "structuralists" counters that Hitler could not simply do as he pleased. They argue that no single command structure existed to carry out his orders; furthermore, those orders were frequently vague and imprecise. In their view, Hitler's obligation to delegate authority to others and his wish to keep German public opinion on his side by maintaining a high standard of living imposed real limits on what he could do alone.

As in most historical debates, there is something to be said for both views. Without Hitler's fanatical anti-Semitism or his determination to rearm Germany and attack its neighbors, Europe would most likely have been spared the Holocaust and the Second World War. Thus his intentions mattered a great deal. On the other hand, more recent research in the Nazi archives has yielded a picture of the Nazi state very different from the stereotype of compulsively efficient German organization. Despite the *Gleichschaltung*, the government that took power in Berlin in 1933 was prey to ongoing muddle and confusion within its own ranks. Competing and parallel organizations often tripped over one another, and their leaders fought protracted battles for bureaucratic supremacy. Hence the tendency to view the Nazi leader as a dictator who enjoyed total control over every aspect of German life should be balanced by a realistic appreciation of the many ways in which that control was limited by both economic and organizational constraints.

Racism and Anti-Semitism

As the *Gleichschaltung* proceeded, it became apparent that of all Germans, the Jews were faring worst. Anti-Semitism had been one of Hitler's favorite propaganda points in his drive to power, and it had behind it a long history in German popular legend and in sporadic outbursts of hatred and violence.

At Hitler's accession, the Jews of Germany numbered about half a million. In numbers and in social situation, the Jewish population of the Reich lay midway between the norm in Western Europe—where Jews were few and well assimilated into the national life—and that in Russia or Poland—where they numbered millions and suffered from periodic persecution and discrimination. In Western Germany, conditions similar to those in France prevailed; in Eastern Germany, assimilation had not gone so far. But in both areas, only in legend did the Jews dominate economic life. Actually, their participation in German industrial leadership was small; in retail trade and banking, on the other hand, they enjoyed some influence. Their real prominence lay in the professions, in intellectual life, and in the world of art and entertainment.

Nevertheless, throughout the latter half of the nineteenth century and the first part of the twentieth, German demagogues had regularly depicted the Jews as having a stranglehold on the business life of the country. Such agitators also described them as racially inferior and "impure," for along with anti-Semitic propaganda went an insistence on the racial superiority of the German people. The Germans, the racist propagandists claimed, were obviously superior, since they were tall and blond and had blue eyes. Even the most casual observer of the German scene might have noticed that this was true of only a minority of the country's population. It was in the Netherlands and Scandinavia, rather, that such "Nordic" or "Aryan" physical traits predominated. But Hitler and his followers apparently believed their own propaganda; they really thought that the "purity" of German "blood" was in danger from Jewish "contamination," and that it was their duty to the race to preserve it from further admixture.

The evidence is overwhelming that a very large part of the German people agreed with them. Little indignation was heard when Hitler began to take discriminatory measures against the country's Jewish population. Before attaining power, the Nazis had been forced to restrict themselves to attacking the Jews with slanderous and obscene language and to beating Jews and occasionally murdering them in the streets. From 1933 on, however, they were able to proceed in a more systematic fashion. The "Nuremberg Laws" of September 1935 forbade people of Jewish origin—defined as those with one Jewish grandparent—to marry or to have sexual relations with "Aryans." Two months later, Jews were expelled from the civil service, and a weeding-out process began that, by 1938, had virtually eliminated them from government, the professions, and cultural life. Then, in the summer of 1938, they were required to adopt first names that were easily identifiable as Jewish and to carry special identity papers. Finally, in November 1938 occurred the event that sent the anti-Semitic campaign into high gear: a Jewish boy, crazed by his people's sufferings, murdered a German diplomat called vom Rath. The vom Rath murder not only unleashed a storm of indiscriminate violence within the Reich; it also served as a pretext for new legislation forcing Jewish businessmen to liquidate their concerns at a loss and for starting a systematic roundup of the Jews who had not yet left the country.

After 1938, emigration was much more difficult; those who chose to leave now had to depart almost penniless. Many remained despite growing and ominous signs of danger, still attached to their homes, still hoping to survive in some fashion. They did not yet know that in 1941 Hitler was to decide on the "final solution" of the "Jewish Question," which would bring death to nearly all of them in the Holocaust of six million of their coreligionists that ranks as the greatest crime of modern times.

Economic Policy and Preparation for War

In the economic field, *Gleichschaltung* operated most unevenly. Labor was quickly curbed. As the Fascist regime had done in Italy, so in Germany the Nazis forced the German workers into a party-dominated Labor Front. As organized labor, workers had no real rights; instead, as individuals, they had the organization called "Strength through Joy," which provided free holidays and excursions into the country.

The majority of German workers probably accepted this sort of paternalistic treatment as good enough. They had a more important reason for being grateful to Hitler. Within five years, the regime all but eliminated unemployment through a massive program of rearmament and public works. This remained the bedrock of Hitler's popularity—as the Great Depression had brought him to power, so his solution to the problem of unemployment offered the most convincing reason for thinking he should stay here.

The rearmament of Germany was popular not only with the working classes, but also with industrial capitalists, to whom it guaranteed large orders and high profits. Hitler did not have to force German industry into line; it did not cost him very much to keep his implied promise not to tamper with ownership. Generally, the needs of the regime and the needs of heavy industry ran parallel—both had a vested interest in preparation for war. It was simpler for the government to deal with a few large concerns than with many small ones. Thus in practice the Nazis favored the economic concentration that had already been stimulated by the inflation of 1923. They were content to let the larger industrialists dominate the self-governing bodies that ran the various branches of the economy in corporative fashion. During the Second World War the government itself contributed to the process by "combing out" small and uneconomic enterprises. The leading industrialists were frequently rewarded with high party rank, and the Nazi chiefs for their part acquired large industrial holdings on their personal account—much of it through the plunder of Jewish property, which was euphemistically referred to as "aryanization." By the outbreak of the war nearly everyone had some reason to be content. Although wages remained low, jobs were plentiful, and the army was taking up what slack remained; industry was booming; and good Nazis enjoyed every opportunity to feather their own nests. Small wonder, then, that by 1939 Hitler's regime had attained extraordinary popularity within the Reich.

The Struggle with the Churches

Scarcely a promise of Hitler's was more flagrantly broken than the one by which he had undertaken to preserve the liberties of the Catholic church. Initially, however, everything seemed to be going well. The summer of 1933 saw the negotiation of a concordat with the Vatican that met nearly all the church's requirements. After a brief period of apparent harmony, however, the regime felt secure enough to attack. It then launched a vicious propaganda campaign against the members of religious orders, accusing both monks and nuns of smuggling, sexual immorality, and child abuse.

The reasons behind these wild charges did not take long to appear. The *Führer's* target was the Catholic schools and youth organizations, which threatened the monopoly of the "Hitler Youth," into which he was trying to enroll the young people of the Reich. By 1937, he had effectively destroyed the influence of church education. Nearly all Catholic schools were closed, and those that remained led a precarious and persecuted existence. There was nothing left but for German Catholics to bow their heads and for the Pope to protest in unmeasured terms. In one of his strongest encyclicals, *Mit brennender Sorge* (*With Burning Anxiety*), Pius XI condemned the Nazis' racial doctrine and their deification of the state. The papal castigation of fascism, which in Italy had been tempered by understanding, in Germany amounted almost to a declaration of war. Yet a complete break between church and state was avoided. During the Second World War, Pius XI's more diplomatic successor, Pius XII, refrained from speaking out against the horrors of the Nazi extermination camps in a fashion that might have shaken the national loyalties of Germany's Catholic citizens. His failure to condemn Hitler's policies as forthrightly as had the previous pontiff robbed anti-Nazi forces of a valuable ally and placed the Church in the morally ambiguous position of seeming to tolerate the destruction of the Jews.

In the early years of the Nazi regime, a few farsighted members of the German Catholic church hierarchy had already begun to warn their flock of the subtle poisons contained in Hitler's ideology. In his Advent sermons, Cardinal Faulhaber, the conservative archbishop of Munich, preached to overflow congregations on the theme of paganism in Nazi doctrine. To the north, Bishop von Galen of Münster spoke out in even sharper terms. The government left these ecclesiastics unharmed; they were the only people in Germany who enjoyed even a limited right of free speech.

Against dissident Protestants, however, Hitler proceeded with greater rigor. As the majority faith, German Protestantism offered opportunities for *Gleichschaltung* and enrollment in the national effort that were lacking in Catholicism, whose minority status and international affiliations limited its usefulness to the regime. Hitler initially tried to unify and to nazify the Protestants by forcing the church organizations of the individual states into a single Reich church under the rule of a "Reichsbishop." This the majority of Protestant pastors resisted. The Reichsbishop found his authority defied nearly everywhere and soon resigned in discouragement. But the nazified church organization remained. So did a number of "intact" churches in states whose bishops were sufficiently astute to avoid *Gleichschaltung*; these tried to keep their organizations out of the political struggle—as did the majority of the pastors of Germany. A strong minority, however, constituted themselves as the "Confessional" church, preaching root-and-branch opposition to racism, to the leadership principle, and to the association of Christianity with the Nazi state. The most eloquent spokesmen among the Confessional pastors were the former submarine commander Martin Niemöller, who in 1937, along with more than eight hundred of his fellows, was sent to concentration camp, and the inspiring theologian Dietrich Bonhoeffer, arrested in 1944 and executed by the Nazis soon thereafter.

Such was the extremely complex situation of German Christianity on the eve of the Second World War. The Nazis had failed in their effort to bring the churches into line. They had succeeded rather better with the Protestants than with the Catholics, but this was natural in view of the former's disunity, the greater pressure put upon them, and German Lutheranism's long record of nationalism and obedience to secular authority. At the same time, in the Confessional pastors, the Protestants had given the most courageous examples of defiance against the radically un-Christian practices of the Nazi state.

In general, then, the Christian churches were comparable only to organized business leadership in the limited autonomy they enjoyed within the confines of German fascism. Hitler would have been well advised to leave them entirely untroubled. For it was from the ranks of militant Christian laymen, Protestant and Catholic alike, that the future resistance to him was to recruit some of its most devoted adherents.

III.   THE CLERICAL-CORPORATIVE STATES

Nothing so clearly distinguished the milder fascist regimes from the German and Italian systems as the privileged position that the church enjoyed under them. These more moderate regimes have quite properly been called "clerical-corporative," for their two outstanding features were their clericalism and their corporative organization of economic life. They existed only in Catholic countries—in Portugal after 1930, in Austria after 1933, and in Spain (with some qualifications) after 1936 (see Chapter 12, III).

Portugal under Salazar

The assumption of power by Professor Salazar in Portugal brought order to a state that had been shaken by unrest ever since it deposed its ruling dynasty and became a republic in 1910. The Portuguese population was in economic terms the most backward, and in political terms the most uneducated, in all Western Europe. To rule it was comparatively simple. No elaborate ideology or pseudosocialist program was required; a strong hand alone sufficed.

Hence, although he was an admirer of Mussolini, Salazar restricted himself to the barest minimum of fascist practices. He did not organize a private army nor try to whip up the enthusiasm of the populace through frenetic appeals to national pride. He established a quiet dictatorship, in which the press was severely controlled and his own National Union enjoyed a monopoly of political activity. By the authoritarian constitution promulgated in 1933, Portugal was defined as a "new state" resting on the twin pillars of a corporative economic organization and the Catholic church.

Portuguese corporatism followed the Italian model in curbing the working classes while leaving the employers substantially at liberty to run their businesses as they pleased. Toward Catholicism, however, Salazar's policies diverged markedly from Mussolini's. He went far beyond merely granting the church a favored position in the state. An austere and devout Catholic himself, Salazar sincerely believed that he was carrying out Christian principles in ruling his country as he did, and that such should be the basis of any properly run society. Hence he gave the church a monopoly of education and tried to suffuse all aspects of Portuguese life with the spirit of a Catholicism that he interpreted in ultraconservative fashion as a doctrine endorsing quiescence and permanent stability in human affairs.

Austria under Dollfuss and Schuschnigg

In effervescent Austria, such an old-fashioned model of rule would not suffice. Engelbert Dollfuss, the authoritarian-minded chancellor of Christian Social origin who came to power in 1932, soon found it impossible to continue governing within the constitutional framework. With the advent of Hitler in January 1933, it became apparent that sympathy for nazism was spreading rapidly into Austria and that only a recourse to dictatorial methods could save the state from eventual subversion. The following March, Dollfuss suspended parliamentary government and a few months thereafter dissolved the opposition political parties. This latter measure was aimed primarily at the Austrian Nazis, but it also included the Socialists, who had been the Christian Socials' rivals for power in the years of constitutional rule.

Neither party accepted dissolution without protest. The Socialists were first to act. In February 1934, goaded to fury by a series of government raids, the Socialist paramilitary formations blockaded themselves in the great housing development called the Karl-Marx-Hof and prepared to resist by force of arms. Dollfuss's reply was to concentrate his army and police and to bombard the Socialists into surrender after three days of combat. Thus ended the threat from the Left; Austrian socialism was vanquished for a full decade. But the Nazis—backed as they were by the overwhelming strength of Austria's great neighbor—could not be dealt with thus easily. Five months after the Socialist uprising, a band of National Socialist conspirators forced their way into Dollfuss's office and killed him.

This first Nazi bid for power failed. Mussolini concentrated troops on the Brenner Pass and declared himself the protector of Austrian independence. Simultaneously Dollfuss's successor as chancellor, Kurt Schuschnigg, began to act with resolution and authority. A quiet, ascetic, scholarly figure somewhat like Salazar, Schuschnigg proceeded to apply the dictatorial constitution that had been voted into effect just three months before his predecessor's death. Under the new system, a single party, the Fatherland Front—which had absorbed most of the Christian Socials—received the usual fascist monopoly of political influence. Meanwhile the organization of corporative bodies proceeded slowly. It was in its clericalism, rather, that the Austrian regime showed where its primary ideological allegiance lay.

For nearly four years, Schuschnigg kept his country from the German and Nazi embrace. Within Austria, life remained deceptively calm; the dictatorship was relatively mild, and the average citizen had freedom to go about his ordinary concerns and to grumble against the government quite openly. Under the surface, however, the situation was far from placid. The Nazis were preparing in secret for the great day of annexation to the Reich, and the Socialists remained bitterly unreconciled. The government could not rely on *them* to help it when Hitler should decide to strike. Thus the regime drew support from a perilously narrow grouping: fragments of old-fashioned conservatism, nostalgia for aristocratic values, and, of course, clericalism. What ultimately kept it in power was the promise of Italian armed support. Should Mussolini falter, all would be lost. But in 1936, Italian Fascism began to align itself with its German counterpart (see Chapter 12, II). This spelled the end of Austria's freedom and of the moderate version of fascist rule that it had come to incarnate.

IV. THE NATURE OF THE FASCIST SYSTEM

As one follows the history of the major fascist regimes, certain similarities and uniformities emerge that may serve to define more precisely this new "radicalism of the Right." It is significant that the two societies in which fascism appeared full blown—the Italian and the German—had things in common that distinguished them from the societies of France and Britain on the one hand and those of Eastern Europe on the other. In the great Western democracies, middle-class values and the middle-class way of life predominated without question; despite the frequent bitterness of class feeling, there was a real homogeneity within the social structures of Britain and France that made them capable of withstanding the most severe political and ideological shocks. Similarly in Eastern Europe—before communism began its vast effort of economic transformation—there existed the more primitive homogeneity of a traditional agrarian society. Italy and Germany, in different ways, fell between these two norms; an old-fashioned rural or patriarchal society lived alongside and entangled with a modern industrial society. Lack of understanding and permanent tension were inevitable when two such different ways of life were condemned to an existence in common.

France and Britain, moreover, won the First World War; Germany lost it. To Italian patriots also—cheated as they felt themselves to be of the spoils of victory—the war seemed as good as lost. The origins of fascism in both countries thus lay in the disillusionment among returning veterans and in the thirst for action among boys just young enough to have missed the experience of combat. In more general terms, fascism arose out of the frustrations of the lower middle class from which so many of these former soldiers and dissatisfied students had come. Members of this class had particular reason to feel distressed and anxious in the postwar years. Threatened with proletarization—and unwilling to throw in their lot with the Marxists—these people were casting about for a new political movement that would give voice to their sense of profound injustice. Their bitterness appeared in its most desperate form in the great German inflation of 1923, when their grievances made them turn against their own government and blame a newly founded democracy both for their personal sufferings and for the humiliation of the nation, whose fate they identified with their own.

The original fascist leaders came from the ranks of the unreconstructed veterans. Down and out themselves, they appealed to others in similar straits. They prided themselves on their toughness; they disliked what was superior or distinguished or refined; more particularly, they disliked intellectuals—which was perhaps natural since a number of them were would-be intellectuals who had fallen short of their goals (as Hitler had failed in his ambition to be an architect). They were liars, they were bullies, and they were filled with resentments of all sorts. Indeed, the most curious feature of early fascism was its combination in the same individuals of the most ordinary petty-bourgeois grievances with absolutely limitless dreams of grandeur.

There was something seedy and even comic about the fascist parties in their early stages. Small wonder that so many people, reactionary and democratic alike, refused to take Mussolini and Hitler seriously. All their posturing and marching, this frantic eloquence, these solemn salutes with outstretched arms—all this seemed too ridiculous. Something more than that was needed to get fascism out of the back alleys of Milan or Munich and to make it a great national movement capable of seizing power.

This additional strength—and the sobering influence that went with it—came when men of property and conservative inclinations began to see in fascism a possible ally in their struggle with the political Left. In the immediate postwar years, when trade unionism and revolutionary socialism were at a high point—and again in the years of the Great Depression—conservatives were frankly frightened. The rising tide of Socialist or Communist agitation might carry to power a militant government of the Left that would deprive them of their property. Faced with this threat, the prosperous and propertied wondered whether their fathers and grandfathers had been right in espousing the cause of liberalism or democracy. If democracy led by inevitable progression to socialism, they reasoned, then perhaps democracy should be destroyed. Perhaps authoritarian rule offered the only solution. And this was exactly what fascism promised.

There was, of course, a great difference in temperament and background between the men of property, with their education and their refined manners, and the demagogues who led the fascist movements. This difference took a long time to bridge, and it was only hesitantly that businessmen and aristocrats began to extend the hand of

Uniformed Nazi party members summon citizens to contribute clothes to the Berlin Winter Aid campaign. As part of the policy of *Gleichschaltung,* Nazi propaganda stressed the need for Germans to come together as a nation and extend help to the victims of the Great Depression. *(Courtesy H. Armstrong Roberts)*

friendship to people whom they regarded as little better than gangsters. But they had urgent reason for doing so; in a time of crisis, they could not trouble about manners. Furthermore, they shared the fascists' hostility to Marxism in all its forms and agreed with the fascist emphasis on national honor and prestige. Those who made the first move or who remained most closely associated with fascism, moreover, were usually the less squeamish of their class—self-made men with new fortunes built on war and inflation, men with shady pasts who had good reason to worry about the legitimacy of their profits. To these a fascist government could give protection from embarrassing questions or parliamentary committees of investigation.

Men with older fortunes followed more slowly and accepted fascism more grudgingly. Some never accepted it at all. But most businessmen in both Italy and Germany eventually made their peace with the fascist system and prospered under it. From it, they won protection from social unrest and freedom from trade-union pressure; to it, they gave respectability and financial support. It was a profitable bargain for both sides.

This convergence between the fascist parties and the interests of the business class—more particularly the larger industrialists—was the central feature of the fascist regimes in practice. Their initial function was to solidify a tottering social and economic order and to bolster traditional elites by suppressing the working class that threatened Italian stability in 1922 and Germany in 1933. This they did with ruthless efficiency, reversing the gains that labor had made since its initial partnership with industry during the First World War. Here lay the crucial distinction between fascism and communism and the reason for not regarding the semi-Socialist or pseudo-Socialist statements in the fascist programs very seriously. The union between business interests and demagogy explains how fascism became that paradoxical phenomenon, a conservative regime in revolutionary clothing.

Yet it is incorrect to assert, as its Marxist critics did, that fascism was only a mask for rule by monopoly capitalism. In the crucial decisions, the party rather than the business interests had the last word. In both Italy and Germany, occasional spurts of radicalization as well as tough talk from the fascist chiefs showed who was the master. But this happened only infrequently—most of the time the interests of the regime coincided with the interests of the men of property.

Although Mussolini and Hitler governed police states and relied heavily on terror to enforce their will, they did not succeed in remolding Italian or German society in a truly totalitarian form. They did not smash an old organization of society and build up a new one as Lenin and Stalin did. They merely *superimposed* a fascist structure on the existing system, which they left largely intact. Even Nazi Germany—which went much further toward *Gleichschaltung* than did Fascist Italy—left extant some organizations that had existed before the regime came to power and that were to continue after its fall.

In both cases the authoritarian party did not absorb the functions of the state machinery, as it did in the Soviet Union. The traditional state—the civil service, the diplomatic corps, the armed services, and the judiciary—operated much as it had before. Its officials and officers were drawn from the same social groups as before 1933; despite claims from some historians that the Nazis inaugurated a "social revolution," evidence overwhelmingly points in the direction of continuity with the past. Two quite different elements in society enjoyed a situation of special privilege—large capital and the Christian churches. It is extremely significant that, for all his browbeating of the clergy, even Hitler never dared to mount a full-scale assault against the religious faith of the German people. This supports the "structuralist" argument that he held back.

There remains, however, a major distinction between fascism in its German form and fascism in its Italian form. In Hitler's Reich, the older centers of allegiance—the army, big business, and the church—existed only by the tolerance of the regime. Their situation was precarious, and their power limited. They could not effectively threaten the authority of the *Führer* or of the party he led. When Germany began to lose the Second World War—and when more traditional conservatives concomitantly lost confidence in Hitler—they could not get rid of him. They were reduced to secret conspiracy and to a desperate project to save their country by assassinating its leader. When this assassination attempt failed, they had no choice but to go along with Hitler to the bitter end.

In Italy, on the contrary, the old-line conservatives—including a number of dissidents within the Fascist party itself—threw Mussolini overboard in 1943 before it was too late. They were able to do this because the monarchy continued to exist, and the king provided an alternative symbol of loyalty around whom the discontented could rally. In broader terms, despite his longer period of rule, Mussolini's tenure had never been as secure as Hitler's. The Italian Fascists had always been more dependent than the Nazis on the conservative elements in society that had originally helped them to power.

Here also lay the crucial distinction between fascism in its fully developed form and the clerical-corporative regimes in Portugal and Austria. Perhaps these ought not to be labeled fascist at all; "authoritarian conservative" may be the description that fits them best. For they never moved much beyond the stage of "fundamentalist" reaction—a return to the old-fashioned values that liberalism, democracy, and socialism had undermined. Fascism always retained this reactionary spirit. It was apparent, for example, in the fascist attitude toward women, reasserting women's traditional inferiority by emphasizing their duties in the home and by restricting their educational opportunities. In Germany and Italy, however, policies of this sort played a minor part in the propaganda of the regime; in Portugal and Austria they were central.

Yet even these two latter countries did more than revert to old verities, for which the rule of a mere "strong man" would have sufficed. They tried—however lamely—to organize a single party and to proclaim a coherent ideology. And this, after all, was the core of fascist ideology—the effort to reinvigorate old values by giving them a new dynamism. A similar pattern characterized the fascist movements that arose in Eastern Europe during the interwar period, often in frank emulation of Italian and German models. The Arrow Cross in Hungary, the Iron Guard in Romania, and such shadowy organizations as the Iron Wolves in Lithuania all preached a defiant, antimodernist nationalism and anti-Semitism that appealed primarily to the young. In their glorification of the peasant—the symbol of premodern integrity and mystical union with the land— these Eastern fascist movements sought to revive national consciousness by force.

How far, then, did European varieties of fascism actually extend along the range of this dynamism? In Italy, it did not go very far. The Italian people were too skeptical by tradition to take Mussolini's propaganda at face value; most of them simply shrugged their shoulders and went their own way. The longer the Fascists stayed in power, the more obvious it became that their ranks were full of timeservers and profiteers. Nor did Mussolini for his part behave with the cruelty and thoroughness of Hitler and his henchmen. He organized no real concentration camps, and he embarked on an anti-Semitic policy only in 1938, when the pressure to follow German example had become overwhelming.

In the Nazi Reich, on the other hand, anti-Semitism and the concentration camps together created a demonic atmosphere of torture and frenzy that made Hitlerism unique in modern history. The persecution of the Jews was intensified after the outbreak of the Second World War (see Chapter 13, III). Similarly, the concentration camps frankly became places of extermination during the war. Before then, prisoners were merely worked to death, as undernourishment and privation gradually sapped their strength. No economic rationale lay behind the Nazi concentration camps: They served no productive function. They were simply abodes of torment through which perhaps half a million *Germans* passed, even before the war gave the Nazis the opportunity to round up millions more from the countries they had occupied. Over them presided the black-shirted SS and the secret police, the Gestapo—both headed by the pedantic, meticulous Heinrich Himmler, who looked more like a routine-minded German clerk than Hitler's chief executioner.

These demonic features, however, were not central to fascism. The tendency of historians to focus attention on such horrifying aspects of the system has frequently obscured the less spectacular side of its relationship to the society and the economy it dominated. Under fascism, the fundamentals of life for most of the population remained unchanged. Fascist rule did far more to shore up an old society than to build a new one. Thus the relatively temperate Mussolini, rather than the psychopathic Hitler, offers the more characteristic model for a fascist control of society. Not until the Second World War thrust Germany to the fore did the Italian image begin to wane. Only when the conditions of combat pushed fascism to its final extremities of cruelty did anti-Semitism and the concentration camp loom ever larger until, in the end, they blotted out everything else—leaving the fascist regimes nothing to show for two decades of exertion but mountains of ruins and millions of corpses.

The Popular Front Mentality

Long before fascism advanced to its final phase of systematic horror, European democrats had concluded that it was a force of cultural and ideological destruction that should be resisted at all costs. During the Great Depression, European democracy confronted a double threat—on the one side, fascism, and on the other side, Communist parties whose confidence was growing with the anticipated collapse of the capitalist system, and whose ranks, like those of the Nazis, were swelling month by month with the influx of the unemployed. In this two-front war, fascism presented the more immediate danger. Hitler's Germany was close at hand and was growing more aggressive every day. Stalin's Russia was far away and absorbed in the vast task of rebuilding its own society. In a military sense, it threatened nobody. In the 1930s, the Soviet attitude was almost purely defensive—the basic aim of Russian foreign policy in this period was to prevent an alliance of the Western capitalist countries that, with the new infusion of fascist energy, could overwhelm the Soviet experiment of "socialism in one country" before it was even properly launched.

In its vocabulary and in its aims, moreover, communism seemed far closer than did fascism to the aspirations of European democracy. It talked of human betterment, of the brotherhood of man, and of international concord, while Hitler and Mussolini preached hatred between races and nations. There were, of course, the terrorist and dictatorial aspects of Soviet rule—but in the 1930s European democrats of the Left were inclined to neglect these or to gloss them over as problems that could be dealt with in calmer times. What seemed of overriding present importance was that democracy and communism had a common enemy, before which they should sink their differences and present a united front. Thus the minds of left-wing democrats were prepared for common action against fascism when the Communist parties of the Western countries began to make advances to them in the summer of 1934.

The Origins of the Popular Front

What came to be called the *Popular Front* was originally Communist in inspiration. Indeed, better than anything else this showed that after a decade of sterility and bureaucratization, European communism was again on the march. It had been revived by the Great Depression in the sense of organization and numbers, but in the ideological sense the decisive event was the shock of Hitler's coming to power. Both the Third International and the German Communists had catastrophically underestimated Nazi strength and had never anticipated that Hitler would actually be able to accomplish his aims. Like Papen and the Nationalists, German communism had thought it could use the Nazis for its own purposes and subsequently order them to depart. In the Communist reckoning of the future, Hitler figured as the precursor of a Soviet Germany, the unconscious herald of the new society who would do the dirty work of clearing away the debris of bourgeois democracy and then succumb himself to the true revolution of the people. In line with this strategy, the German Communists in the last period of Hitler's march to power did little to oppose him and even sometimes cooperated with the Nazi Storm Troopers in their street battles with the Social Democrats. To their surprise, they found themselves after January 1933 treated no better—indeed worse—than Hitler's "bourgeois" and Social Democratic enemies, and they saw their party completely smashed within a few weeks.

The advent of Hitler precipitated great soul-searching and self-criticism among European Communists, particularly in France, which felt directly threatened by what had gone on in the Reich, and among Italian Communists in exile, who had already borne the iron hand of fascist tyranny. It was the French and Italian Communists who originally devised the idea of common action alongside Socialists and middle-class democrats. It was they who pressed the suggestion on the Comintern, which finally accepted it in 1935 as a major new departure in the International's policy. The Popular Front concept was that very rare thing in Communist history—a spontaneous initiative from a national party that was only later endorsed by Moscow. It offered the hope that a broad alliance of all the political groups opposed to fascism on the Left, whatever their past differences, could act together against their common enemy at last.

France: The Election of 1936
and the Blum Government

In France, a further event had added to the sense of urgency—the French had experienced the riots of February 6, 1934, which had apparently come close to overthrowing parliamentary democracy itself (see Chapter 8, III). Actually the peril was not as great as French Radicals and Socialists imagined. The rightist demonstrators of February had neither the intention nor the power to stage a fascist *Putsch*. Indeed, the "Leagues" of war veterans and patriots, which appeared to be the French counterparts to the Italian Blackshirts or the German Brownshirts, were not nearly so brutal or determined. Most of them were unarmed. Moreover, their leaders had only the vaguest ideas of how to recast the French state in more authoritarian form. They really never got beyond the stage of "fundamentalist" reaction. French society was still too secure—too solidly bourgeois—for fascism to have a mass appeal. Only the special conditions of defeat in war would give the French fascists their chance.

In 1934, however, French democrats of the Left could not be expected to reach so cool an assessment. They knew that in Germany people like themselves had underestimated the danger and they were determined not to make the same mistake. Hence when the Communists proposed a united front, the Socialists joined with alacrity at a special meeting of their national council held in mid-July. The Radicals also joined in the following year, and the three parties marked the national holiday, July 14, by staging an impressive demonstration of republican solidarity.

By this time, Laval was prime minister and inspiring no confidence at all in his ability to withstand fascist blandishments. He was followed in January by a stopgap cabinet improvised to tide over the interval until the spring elections—an interval of which Hitler took advantage to effect his decisive breach of the Versailles Treaty system. French prestige and French morale had never been so low as on that day in early May 1936 when the people went to the polls to cast their votes for a new Chamber of Deputies.

The result was an overwhelming victory of the Left—far more crushing than its previous triumphs of 1924 and 1932. This time the Popular Front added to the old alliance between Socialists and Radicals the new and untested strength of communism, and within the electoral coalition itself the shift toward the left was manifest nearly everywhere. The Socialists displaced the Radicals from their traditional position as the strongest party in the Chamber; still more, the Communists increased their seats from 10 to 73 to become for the first time a major force in French politics.

Thus the Socialists were the logical party to provide the new prime minister— again a departure from the established Socialist tradition of refusal to participate in government except in time of war. The designated leader was Léon Blum—Jewish, cultured, tolerant, humane—a perfect antithesis to Hitler. Yet for that very reason he aroused antipathies on the Right, which limited his ability to guide the country through a profound social crisis. Blum was a man of undoubted courage—as he showed when he rallied his shrunken party in 1920 after the secession of the Communists, and as he was to show again during the Second World War. But he was not sufficiently decisive to repulse two enemies at once: the open hostility of the French business community, which pursued him with a hatred to which anti-Semitism added a peculiarly bitter edge, and the covert hostility of the Communists, who ostensibly supported his ministry but who refused to participate in it and, in fact, made difficulties for it at every turn.

On the very day he assumed office, Blum faced an unprecedented situation. A million industrial workers of the Paris area, inspired by the Popular Front electoral victory but fearing that they would be defrauded of its fruits, as had so often happened in the past, were engaging in sit-down strikes in their shops and factories. The strikers were scrupulous about not damaging property, and there was scarcely any violence. But in these days of early June the propertied classes sensed revolution in the air; Paris was in a holiday mood that could readily pass over into civil war.

Blum's answer was to call the employers and the trade-union leaders together in his official residence, the Hôtel Matignon, and insist that they reach a settlement forthwith. Within two days these conferences produced the Matignon Agreements, which were to be the founding documents of the welfare state in France. The employers made nearly all the concessions—they granted labor the forty-hour week, a minimum-wage scale, paid vacations, and the right to collective bargaining.

The first month of Popular Front rule was its best. After June, nearly everything went wrong. Blum's government failed to maintain its reforming momentum. The new social reforms proved expensive, and productivity did not rise to keep pace with them. France had sunk into an economic morass from which only strong and coherent economic direction could lift it. The Popular Front offered goodwill and humanitarian sentiments, but these were not enough.

By the spring of 1937, Blum was being hounded by a host of enemies. The conservatives remained entirely unreconciled to the new relations he had established between capital and labor; as soon as they dared, employers started to evade and to sabotage the Matignon Agreements. The wealthy among them, fearing for the safety of their investments, began to smuggle large amounts of capital abroad. On Blum's left flank, the Communists continued to take advantage of their strategic situation—half in and half out of the governing coalition—to snipe at the ministry with impunity and to infiltrate Socialist-led trade unions. In June 1937, after a little more than a year of power, the Blum government succumbed to this combination of hostilities. Its resignation marked the end of the Popular Front era in France. The two ministries that succeeded it still gave lip service to the idea, but by April 1938, when Edouard Daladier returned as prime minister, the Popular Front concept had vanished without a trace.

Had the Popular Front, then, accomplished nothing? Had it failed in its double aim of pulling France out of the Great Depression and thus bringing to a halt the advance of fascism? True, despite the enthusiasm and devotion that had gone into it, the Popular Front's achievements were small indeed. The country's economic situation had improved only slightly. Blum's reforms had widened rather than bridged the chasm separating the owners from the laboring classes. He had failed to lead the workers from the marginal situation they occupied in French bourgeois society and to associate them more closely with the national consensus. Still worse, Blum's failure further embittered the workers and made them turn toward Communist leadership that was eventually to combat both the Socialist party and free trade unionism in France. As for stopping the advance of fascism, in some ways the Popular Front accomplished just the contrary, for French conservatives were so furious at what Blum had attempted to do that they became more than ever susceptible to authoritarian propaganda. To save the country from this Jewish schemer, they reasoned, the Republic itself might have to go—hence the slogan "Better Hitler than Blum" that was to do so much to sap French national morale in the years immediately preceding the Second World War.

Nevertheless, the legacy of the Popular Front was not wholly negative. The Matignon Agreements and the legislation that implemented them—despite continued violations—served as a model for succeeding governments. Like the American New Deal, these measures finally brought France abreast of the social legislation that for decades had prevailed in Germany, Britain, and Scandinavia. They provided the foundation on which the French postwar welfare state was to build. And when this welfare state emerged from the experience of its wartime resistance to Hitler and its collaboration with fascism, it was a patriotic movement that ranks as the proudest French memory in recent history. Indeed, the Resistance itself was to be a militant revival of the Popular Front—as Blum was to be one of its quiet heroes. In the achievements of the Resistance, the Popular Front, for all its weaknesses and failings, was to receive a retrospective rehabilitation as the *only* ideological movement in France in the whole interwar period that held any real promise for the future.

READINGS

Few subjects in twentieth-century European history have attracted more scholarly attention than the nature and history of fascism. For discriminating comparative analyses of fascist movements, see Stanley G. Payne, *A History of Fascism, 1914–1945** (1995), Renzo De Felice, *Interpretations of Fascism* (1977), F. L. Carsten, *The Rise of Fascism,** 2nd ed. (1980), Walter Laqueur, ed., *Fascism: A Reader's Guide** (1976), and Stuart J. Woolf, ed., *The Nature of Fascism** (1968). An outstanding collective attempt to situate Nazism within the broader framework of fascism is Neil Gregor, ed., *Nazism** (2000).

On the early phase of Mussolini's career, besides Wiskemann and Lyttleton (see readings for Chapter 6), Gaudens Megaro, in *Mussolini in the Making* (1933), traces in admirable detail his activities until 1914, while Angelo Rossi (Tasca), in *The Rise of Italian Fascism, 1918–1922* (1938), deals with his march to power. A biography synthesizing scholarship on the Italian Duce is Denis Mack Smith's *Mussolini* (1982). Philip V. Cannistraro and Brian R. Sullivan, *Il Duce's Other Woman* (1993) explores the role of the remarkable Margherita Sarfatti in helping Mussolini become Italy's youngest prime minister. Herman Finer's *Mussolini's Italy*, 2nd ed. (1935), and Gaetano Salvemini's *Under the Axe of Fascism** (1936; reprint ed., 1970) are still the best general studies, although they were written before the fall of the regime. Both are strongly antifascist. For economic history, Salvemini's account should be supplemented by more recent works such as Roland Sarti, *Fascism and the Industrial Leadership in Italy, 1919–1940* (1971).

For a modern view of the vexed church-state issue, see John F. Pollard's *The Vatican and Italian Fascism, 1929–1932* (1985). D. A. Binchy's *Church and State in Fascist Italy* (1941) is a dispassionate assessment by a liberal Catholic. Aspects of daily life under Mussolini are explored in Edward R. Tannenbaum's *The Fascist Experience: Italian Society and Culture, 1922–1945* (1972), and two works by Victoria De Grazia—*The Culture of Consent: Mass Organization of Leisure in Fascist Italy* (1981), and *How Fascism Ruled Women: Italy, 1922–1945* (1991). The fate of Italian jewry during the fascist years is recounted with empathy and insight in Alexander Stille, *Benevolence and Betrayal: Five Italian Jewish Families under Fascism** (1991).

The Nazi regime has received a comprehensive critical treatment in Karl-Dietrich Bracher, *The German Dictatorship** (1970), which still does not entirely supersede the older study by Franz Neumann, *Behemoth: The Structure and Practice of National Socialism*, 2nd ed. (1944). Jost Dülffer, *Nazi Germany, 1933–1945: Faith and Annihilation** (trans. 1996) offers a brief but insightful introduction which stresses the links between Nazi politics and the coming war. For Hitler's biography, Alan Bullock's *Hitler: A Study in Tyranny*, rev. ed. (1964) provides a balanced overview; it should, however, be supplemented

*Books marked with an asterisk are available in paperback.

by more recent studies such as Joachim Fest's detailed *Hitler** (1974) and Bullock's own *Hitler and Stalin: Parallel Lives** (1991), where the author explores revealing similarities between the two dictators. J. P. Stern's *Hitler: The Führer and the People** (1975) examines with great insight the popular expecations and the propaganda techniques that helped Hitler gain his following, while Martin Broszat's *The Hitler State: The Foundation and Development of the Third Reich** (1981) focuses more on the system than on its founder. The entire issue of *The Journal of Modern History* for March 1987 (Vol. 59, No. 1) is devoted to exploring aspects of National Socialism.

A classic account of the Nazis' political successes on the local level is William Sheridan Allen, the *Nazi Seizure of Power: The Experience of a Single German Town,** rev. ed. (1984). Dietrich Orlow's *The History of the Nazi Party*, 2 vols. (1969–1973) details the party's institutional growth during the Weimar period, while Martin Broszat's *Hitler and the Collapse of the Weimar Republic** (1987) explores the fateful relations between Germany's conservative elites and Hitler's mass movement. Henry A. Turner, *German Big Business and the Rise of Hitler* (1984) disputes the contention that German industrialists alone made that rise possible with their financial support. Two studies of the most powerful of Germany's industrial conglomerates under the Nazis are Joseph Borkin, *The Crime and Punishment of I. G. Farben* (1978) and Peter Hayes, *Industry and Ideology: IG Farben in the Nazi Era** (1987).

A topic of growing interest among researchers has been to identify the social origins of Nazi party members and voters. The emerging scholarly consensus that Hitler's support extended well beyond the lower middle class is forcefully argued in Richard F. Hamilton, *Who Voted For Hitler?** (1982) and Thomas Childers, *The Nazi Voter: The Social Foundations of Fascism in Germany, 1919–1933** (1984). A useful conspectus of other issues currently at the forefront of debate among historians of the Nazi period is Ian Kershaw, *The Nazi Dictatorship: Problems and Perspectives of Interpretation,** 2nd ed. (1989). Charles S. Maier explores one of the most acrimonious chapters in these recent debates—the argument over whether or not the Holocaust was unique—in *The Unmasterable Past: History, Holocaust, and German National Identity** (1988).

In the past two decades, a systematic attempt has been made by German and American scholars to extend our knowledge of daily life under the Hitler regime. The fruits of *Alltagsgeschichte* can be seen in Detlev Peukert, *Inside Nazi Germany: Conformity, Opposition, and Racism in Everyday Life** (1982) and Richard Bessel, ed., *Life in the Third Reich** (1987). Claudia Koonz, in *Mothers in the Fatherland: Women, the Family, and Nazi Politics* (1987), examines the implications of the widespread support for Hitler among German women. A remarkable collection of contemporary photographs by Otto Weber, showing small town life under the Nazis, was published in Germany in 1987 under the title *Tausand ganz normale Jahre* (*A Thousand Very Normal Years*), providing a rare window on everyday life under Hitler. Equally informative is the diary of Victor Klemperer, *I Will Bear Witness*, vol. I: 1933–1941** (paper ed., 1999).

George Mosse, ed., *Nazi Culture: Intellectual, Cultural, and Social Life in the Third Reich** (1969) offers a rich selection of documents illustrating the effects of *Gleichschaltung* in other domains. Berthold Hinz, *Art in the Third Reich** (1977) is an extensively illustrated guide to Nazi painting and visual propaganda, though Hinz's categories of Nazi art sometimes seem too inflexible. Nazi policies in architecture and Hitler's hostility to the Bauhaus are chronicled in Barbara Miller Lane's *Architecture and Politics in*

Germany,* rev. ed. (1985). Nazi policies toward organized religion in Germany are explored in Klaus Scholder's *The Churches and the Third Reich*, vol I: *1918–1934* (1988), John S. Conway's *The Nazi Persecution of the Churches* (1968), and Guenter Lewy's highly critical *The Catholic Church and Nazi Germany* (1964).

Eugen Kogon's *The Theory and Practice of Hell* (1950) remains the most impressive single volume in the extensive concentration camp literature; the author was both a sociologist and a survivor of Buchenwald. A moving, shorter eyewitness account is Primo Levi's *Survival in Auschwitz: The Nazi Assault on Humanity** (1958). A historical overview of the Holocaust is provided by Lucy Dawidowicz in *The War Against the Jews** (1976). Inga Clendinnen, *Reading the Holocaust** (1999) is a fascinating anthropological overview of how the Holocaust has been remembered and interpreted. A disturbing reminder of efforts to efface that memory is Deborah Lipstadt, *Denying the Holocaust: The Growing Assault on Truth and Memory* (1994).

Who was responsible for the Holocaust? Even today the issue continues to stir fresh debate, as scholars shift their focus from the Nazi state to its citizens. How even apolitical Germans could become mass murderers is a subject explored with chilling insight in Christopher R. Browning, *Ordinary Men: Reserve Police Battalion 101 and the Final Solution in Poland* (1992) and Daniel Jonah Goldhagen, *Hitler's Willing Executioners** (1996). The latter argues that an "eliminationist" strain of anti-Semitism in Germany predisposed its citizens to genocide. Eric A. Johnson, *Nazi Terror: The Gestapo, Jews, and Ordinary Germans* (1999) counters that indifference and submissiveness among the German population allowed a relatively weak Gestapo free reign.

For the clerical-corporative regimes, see Hugh Kay, *Salazar and Modern Portugal* (1970), an extended and scrupulous effort at fair-mindedness, and Francis L. Carsten, *Fascist Movements in Austria from Schönerer to Hitler* (1977). An older study that still merits attention is Charles A. Gulick, *Austria from Hapsburg to Hitler*, 2 vols. (1948). The phenomenon of British fascism is examined in Richard Thurlow, *Fascism in Britain: A History, 1918–1985* (1987) and Robert Skidelsky, *Oswald Mosely* (1975).

The French Popular Front is presented from the perspective of its chief architect in Joel Colton's *Léon Blum: Humanist in Politics,** rev. ed. (1987), while Eugen Weber charts the background of French fears of decline in *The Hollow Years: France in the 1930s** (1994). On Blum's social vision see also the relevant chapters in James Joll, *Intellectuals in Politics: Three Biographical Essays* (1960). Robert O. Paxton examines one right-wing response to the Depression in *French Peasant Fascism: Henry Dorgère's Greenshirts and the Crisis of French Agriculture, 1929* (1997). Alexander Werth's *The Twilight of France, 1933–1940* (1942) is an impressionistic but illuminating account of the last years of the Third Republic by an informed eye-witness observer.

THE STALINIST SYSTEM

One of Stalin's thorniest problems was the collectivization of Russia's peasants. Here, a line of tractors epitomizes the Soviet ideal of fully mechanized agriculture—an ideal that was seldom met. (*Courtesy Brown Brothers*)

I. THE CONSOLIDATION OF STALIN'S AUTHORITY

The Problem of the Succession to Lenin

When Lenin died in early 1924, no one knew who would succeed him as leader of both the Soviet Union and international communism. Nor had Lenin left any unambiguous instructions on the subject. This in turn was logical in view of the character of the authority that the founder of bolshevism had wielded. Lenin's dominance had always been extra-constitutional and informal. He had held no high office in the state machinery—indeed, this in itself was a sign of how completely the Communist party dominated the Soviet state. Not until the Second World War did the chief figure in the party, who for a decade and a half had been Stalin, consider it necessary to assume the office of prime minister, which Mussolini and Hitler had occupied from the start. In Lenin's day—and throughout the greater part of Stalin's period of rule—dictatorial authority derived solely from a leading position in the party. In Lenin's case, this position was almost entirely personal. He was simply the most persuasive and determined person in the five-man Politburo, which formulated the policy line for the communist party and through it guided the Soviet state.

In March 1919, at the same time that the Politburo had been set up, the congress of the Communist party had established two further bodies that were intended to handle the more routine questions of party organization and discipline. These were the Organizational Bureau, or Orgburo—again a committee of five members—and the permanent Secretariat. By the time Lenin died, Stalin had become the chief figure in both bodies. As secretary-general of the party, he controlled the complex network of local and regional party committees; as the leading member of the Orgburo, he was in a position to check any effort to review what he had done in the Secretariat. Finally, he was a member of the Politburo itself, and hence was authorized to know all the inner secrets of the party.

Stalin was not a Russian by birth but a Georgian, from the fertile and sunny regions south of the Caucasus Mountains. All his life, Stalin struggled to express himself in his second language, Russian, but never lost his heavy Georgian accent. In place of eloquence, he learned to use deception and guile. Those who knew him at close quarters, like his daughter Svetlana, have left us the portrait of a master of disguise, able to feign emotion while concealing his true thoughts. But his cruelty could not remain hidden. His wife, an independent-minded woman appalled at his actions, committed suicide. Thereafter Stalin had virtually no close personal friends. He had observed Lenin closely and learned how to crush the enemies of the Revolution without pity. He was now prepared to take the one step before which Lenin had hesitated and crush his rivals *within* the Communist party as well.

In the twenty months that Lenin lay incapacitated—from his first stroke in May 1922 to his death in January 1924—Stalin was able quietly to consolidate his own authority. At this time, he was far from being the most obvious heir apparent. He was a narrow party man, of limited education and almost no capacity to develop Marxist theory. At least three party leaders seemed to rank higher than he did—Trotsky, of course, and after him Gregory Zinoviev, who ran the Third International, and then the subtle theoretician Nikolai Bukharin. But all these men had serious counts against them. Trotsky was not an "Old Bolshevik." In the decisive years before 1917, when personal loyalties and associations were first forged, he had been the lone wolf of the Russian Left. Even after he had proved his organizing abilities both by launching the revolution itself and by beating the Red Army into shape, he remained isolated—too much of a visionary for the routine tasks of running a would-be socialist society, and too self-assured to share power easily with colleagues. Zinoviev, along with his inseparable companion Leo Kamenev, had hesitated in 1917. He had doubted the success of the Revolution and this had never been forgiven him. Finally, Bukharin—to Westerners the most appealing of the three—was too gradualist in his approach, too much of a "liberal" intellectual to survive in the jungle warfare that Stalin was about to inaugurate in his struggle for supremacy.

    In addition to the handicaps of their pasts, these three surprisingly lacked understanding of how political power actually operated—of what was needed first to acquire power and then to keep it. They apparently fancied that with Lenin's death, control over the party would revert to what it had always been in theory—the rule of a committee—and that in this collective leadership, Stalin would play a subordinate role. This was far from being Stalin's idea. His rivals made their supreme error in underestimating, because he was their intellectual inferior, a man who was to prove himself one of the craftiest and most ruthless rulers of modern times.

Leon Trotsky (1879–1940), photographed in his Kremlin office shortly before his break with Stalin. (*Courtesy Brown Brothers*)

The Struggle for Power

Though Stalin's method for reaching his goal was the old and simple one of "divide and rule," it fooled his adversaries, who never thought of combining against him until it was too late. First Stalin joined Zinoviev and Kamenev to form a *Troika* ("triumvirate") directed against Trotsky. Just a year after Lenin's death this tactic achieved complete success; faced with the implacable opposition of a majority within the Politburo, Trotsky resigned as commissar for war. This was potentially one of the strongest positions of power in the Soviet Union, controlling as it did the whole organization of the armed forces. Yet it apparently never occurred to Trotsky to rally the Red Army for his own defense. He was too much of a civilian and an ideologue. Also, he was far too loyal to the Communist party to resort to any such putschist tactics. In Trotsky's behavior are evident the beginnings of the attitude of deference and of self-doubt that was to handicap each successive group of Stalin's party opponents. They were so imbued with the notion of ideological solidarity that to oppose the party seemed to them the supreme, the unpardonable crime. They lost sight of the fact that the party was not a platonic ideal but rather was what flesh and blood human beings made of it—and that the man who after 1924 was restyling it to his own taste was their personal enemy and the enemy of nearly everything in which they believed.

With Trotsky's power broken, the *Troika* fell apart. Stalin now began to work with the right wing in the Politburo, the outstanding figure of which was Bukharin. At the same time, Stalin took care to protect his own interests by bringing into that body three new "center" members dependent on him alone; among them were Marshal Klementy Voroshilov, a military hero of the civil war, and V. M. Molotov, later to become famous in the West as "Old Iron Pants," the foreign minister who never conceded an inch. Zinoviev and Kamenev were thus isolated as the left wing of the party directorate. These two still controlled one citadel of power—the former capital of Petrograd, now renamed Leningrad, of which Zinoviev was party boss. Again nearly a year elapsed before Stalin struck. Finally, at the end of 1925, armed with a massive vote of confidence from the party congress—most of whose delegates were dependent for their positions on him alone—Stalin set out to break Zinoviev's power over the Leningrad machine with the well-tried and infallible appeal for party discipline.

Now, at last, Zinoviev and Kamenev thought of banding together with the discredited Trotsky. But when they acted, in the spring of 1926, it was too late. On November 7, 1927—the tenth anniversary of the Bolshevik Revolution—the opposition made its last public effort to stem the Stalinist tide. It held parades separate from those officially organized by the party. Retribution descended immediately; both Trotsky and Zinoviev were expelled from the party's ranks. Here their paths diverged. Zinoviev recanted his errors and was given a few years of grace. Trotsky, who bravely refused to bow, was exiled, originally to one of the Soviet Republics of Central Asia, and later abroad. Denied sanctuary by the governments of Western Europe, he lived first in Turkey and then in Mexico, where he served as an ideological rallying point for disillusioned Communists—the "Trotskyists" of the 1930s who attacked Stalin's politics and tried to return the party to its original "purity" of doctrine. And it was in Mexico in 1940 that Stalin's assassin sought him out in his fortresslike abode and slew him in cold blood.

All that now remained for Stalin was to deal with Bukharin and the "rightists," which he did in 1928 and 1929 in connection with his own swing toward the "leftist" economic policy. Like Zinoviev, Bukharin and his associates abjured their heresies. And like him, they were given a few more years to live before the great blood purge of the mid-1930s carried them off with nearly all the others.

"Socialism in One Country"

In one respect, Stalin's triumph was consistent with the basic situation in his country. After the final failure of communism in Germany in 1923, the Soviet regime had turned in upon itself. For a full decade it lived almost in isolation from the rest of Europe. The great nations of the West maintained only minimum relations with it, and the smaller countries that bordered on it served as what the diplomats called a *cordon sanitaire*—a zone of quarantine against contagion. Thus sealed off from Europe, the Soviet Union turned its back on the West and began to interest itself in Asia; Stalin's only foreign adventure in this period was an unsuccessful effort to exploit the revolutionary situation in China. Indeed, Russia as a whole seemed to be reverting to its half-Asian past, and Stalin's enemies saw a grim appropriateness in the fact that the country was being ruled by an "oriental despot" whose methods recalled those of Genghis Khan.

An important reason for the indecisiveness of the various opposition groups in the years after 1924 was their inability to adjust to this new situation. Most of Lenin's Bolshevik comrades believed it impossible for a socialist society to build itself in Russia unless the revolution spread to other and more developed countries. After the failure of 1923, the more sophisticated and internationally oriented of these leaders found themselves at a loss. Obviously they could not give up the struggle—they had to do *something*. Thus Trotsky and his allies continued to insist on keeping up pressure abroad and on pushing ahead with a socialist policy at home in order to maintain the momentum of the movement at all costs.

Stalin, with his simpler and harsher mind, found a clear answer. In the autumn of 1924, he launched the slogan of "socialism in one country." Russia, he proudly asserted, could create socialism alone, without help or support from the outside. Simplifying the issues and twisting them to his own purposes, Stalin depicted Trotsky and people like him as men of little faith and dangerous adventurers besides, who, with their doctrine of "permanent revolution," would lead the country into needless peril. The Soviet Union's vast resources were sufficient, Stalin argued, to overcome all its handicaps of backwardness and to win respect for a regime that already governed "one sixth of the world." This reassuring doctrine—with its undertone of smugness and its return to prerevolutionary patriotic themes—was well calculated to appeal to the new generation of organizers and managers whom Stalin had raised up in his party machine and who were far less concerned with abstract ideological speculation than was the generation of the Old Bolsheviks.

The Last Years of NEP and the "Scissors" Crisis

The only flaw in Stalin's reasoning was the virtual nonexistence of socialism in Russia. After the disappointing experience with war communism, Lenin had inaugurated the compromise with free enterprise called the *New Economic Policy* (NEP). NEP had given the country the minimum that the Soviet leaders had expected of it—a breathing space for consolidation. It had enabled the economy to start moving again after the civil war had brought it nearly to a stop. Once this basic goal had been achieved, though, NEP began to reveal serious shortcomings. For one, it was slow in raising industrial production. Not until 1926–1927 did industry as a whole reach the level of 1913; in per capita terms, it still remained below that level, since the population had increased by eight million. In addition, Russia's prewar industrialization had been far from adequate to satisfy the minimum demands of a European nineteenth-century society, let alone those a twentieth-century socialist one. In the countryside, where recovery had proceeded more rapidly than in the cities, NEP had accomplished no more than to return the agricultural population to the situation of 1913.

The gravest symptom of economic difficulty, however, was the "Scissors" Crisis, which first became apparent at the end of the summer of 1923. With agricultural production rising and industry lagging behind, a gap began to grow between the prices the peasants obtained for their crops and those they had to pay for the industrial goods they required. Two years of good harvest followed the famine year of 1921–1922, and with food plentiful at last, wholesale prices for agricultural products fell to just over half what they had been in 1913. Meanwhile, the corresponding prices for manufactured goods stood at nearly double their prewar level; industry could not possibly meet the demand. Caught between the blades of these closing "scissors," the peasants began to wonder whether it was worthwhile to deliver their produce to the cities at all. If they could get nothing they wanted in return—or if they had to pay exorbitant prices—they might do better to consume what they grew or to store it until the government agreed to a high price. From the mid-1920s on, the Soviet Union thus faced a chronic and growing crisis in feeding its urban population. The peasants, whom NEP had so notably strengthened, were proving themselves the strongest economic force in the nation, since they had in their power to starve the cities at will.

By 1927 it was apparent that the Soviet economy was caught, as it had been six years earlier, in a series of vicious circles. Ten years after the Bolshevik Revolution, Russia was scarcely closer to socialism than it had been at the start. The state-owned sector of the economy was still too weak to dominate the rest; the government organs of planning and control lacked the power to bring the countryside to terms. Quite simply, what was required was a strong and coherent policy that could cut through all the interlocking dilemmas at one blow: feed the cities, raise the level of industry, and provide new manpower for a new type of society.

II. THE GREAT TRANSFORMATION

Beginning in 1928, the Soviet Union underwent a "second Bolshevik revolution"—this time industrial rather than political—which transformed the country more profoundly than Lenin's original Bolshevik Revolution of 1917. For all its success in installing a new regime, the Revolution of 1917 had remained superficial in many respects. The new leaders had simply imposed a revolutionary government on a deeply traditional peasant society that accepted the new regime, once the civil war came to a close, without abandoning many of its ancient customs or beliefs.

The transformation begun under Stalin proved far more profound. It changed Russia economically and socially by destroying the peasant village and drastically accelerating the pace of industrialization. At the end of 1927, disillusioned by NEP, Stalin decided to adopt the policy of Trotsky that he had earlier attacked so fiercely. He now supported those who had argued that the Soviet Union must embark upon forced industrialization and the collectivization of agriculture if it was to survive. "We are fifty or a hundred years behind the advanced countries," he estimated later. "We must make up this distance in ten years. Either we do it or we go under."

Though Stalin saw the planned changes in agriculture and industry as linked, his chief concern was with industrial modernization—a program that could serve the needs of Soviet military defense. With equal measures of brutality and political skill, Stalin imposed this change of course, first on skeptical party colleagues, then on the country as a whole. He pursued his vision with astounding singleness of purpose—undeterred by mistakes, calamities, or the enormous human suffering it entailed. For more than a decade he whipped and drove his people into the greatest and most sustained economic effort made by a single nation in the history of modem Europe. In the end Stalin achieved his goal of making the Soviet Union a serious industrial power, but at appalling cost.

The Collectivization of Agriculture

By forcing peasants to merge their holdings in large collective farms, Stalin and his advisers hoped to produce a rural social structure that would be both more efficient and easier to control than the system of peasant landholding. Collectivization, they argued, merely followed the pattern of industry, where large units produced better goods and more cheaply than small ones. Thus transforming agriculture would be a test of the Soviet system. As Stalin decreed in the overblown rhetoric of the time: "Practical success in agriculture is the ultimate criterion of truth."

Beginning in 1928, teams of party agitators and industrial workers were dispatched to the countryside to urge the peasants to collectivize. At first the campaign seemed to sweep all before it. The official reports suggested that the peasants were rushing with enthusiasm to consolidate their holdings, and Stalin himself began to be carried away by the momentum of events. In mid-1929, he decided to speed the tempo of collectivization. Those who continued to refuse, he insisted, must be forced to comply.

The vast majority of peasants resisted. The government overcame their resistance by regular military operations in which recalcitrant villages were forced to capitulate at machine-gun point. In this fashion, two million peasant farmers, who with their families constituted a population of at least eight million, gradually succumbed. Some were killed; many more starved; the greater part were driven off to cultivate as well as they could the more remote regions of Siberia that needed to be exploited. Before they left—or before they submitted to joining a collective—the peasants did what they could to wreck the new experiment. They smashed their farm implements, burned their crops, and slaughtered their animals. In this way, more than half Russia's livestock perished. By

1933, by Stalin's official admission, the country had lost over half its horses, 45 percent of its cattle, and two-thirds of its sheep and goats.

Long before this, government and party had been obliged to call for a pause. In March 1930, Stalin indirectly conceded the extent of the calamity in the countryside in a statement bearing the curious title "Dizziness with Success." As in so many Communist pronouncements, the message that was actually conveyed was just the reverse of what it purported to be; it was an admission of failure rather than a hymn to success. In it, Stalin also resorted to the equally well-tried trick of shifting the blame to subordinates who had "misunderstood" his orders. In any case, the practical result was an easing of pressure on the peasants—collectivization proceeded more slowly for the next few months. But in 1932 and 1933 Stalin resumed his campaign, and this time the horrors of famine were joined to those of mass uprooting. The Ukraine—a fertile region producing a large part of the nation's wheat—was sealed off by cutting rail links with the rest of the country, and its harvest requisitioned at gunpoint. This policy, added to the disorganization of life in the countryside that collectivization had entailed, brought starvation to the Ukraine in 1932–1933 on a scale unknown for a full decade. Again, as in the case of the famine of 1922, it is impossible to say exactly how many perished. But demographers have estimated that the direct and indirect effects of the collectivization campaign together cost the country five million lives.

By the end of 1933, the government had won its battle against the peasantry. Meanwhile it had begun to reassure the country people that it was not going to make rural factory hands of them. By the basic statute of the collectives promulgated in 1935, these enterprises were granted their land in perpetuity, and the individual peasant members were permitted to keep a cow or a few goats and to cultivate as their own small garden plots not exceeding a couple of acres.

On this basis, the collectivization campaign continued into the latter part of the 1930s; by the outbreak of the Second World War, about 95 percent of the Soviet Union's farms had been collectivized. The basic type remained the regular collective, or *kolkhoz*, run by the peasants themselves (perhaps with a professional or party manager), varying in size from 1,000 to more than 7,000 acres, and consisting of from sixty to two hundred families. There were also a much smaller number of state farms, or *sovkhozes*, which served as models of management to the rest. Finally, there were the machine or tractor stations, holding a pool of expensive and scarce farm machinery that could be rotated among the collectives in a given area.

The foregoing, however, may give too tidy an impression. In actuality, even at the end of a decade of trial and error, the collective system on the land was still far from perfect. Not one of its goals was fully attained. After the terrible experiences of the period between 1928 and 1933, years were needed to rebuild agricultural production and livestock numbers to their earlier levels; and the collectives themselves frequently proved as reluctant as their independent peasant predecessors had been to make deliveries to the cities promptly and in the amounts specified. Millions of *kolkhozniki* were sullen and uncooperative, far from reconciled to the collective idea. Throughout the period of Russia's forced industrialization, agriculture was to present a most perplexing problem; along with transport—which was never adequate for the load put upon it—poor farm production continued to be the chief weakness of the entire Soviet economy.

Forced collectivization had been both brutal and senselessly wasteful of human resources. Russia's peasant population was in effect reduced once again to the status of serfs. When the system of internal passports was reintroduced into Russia in December 1932, these passports were denied to the peasants, who thus became tied to the land just as their forefathers had lived three-quarters of a century before under the tsars. Despite Stalin's claims of victory over the rebellious peasants, deported to labor camps or left to starve in their villages, they exacted a posthumous revenge. Soviet agriculture suffered enormous inefficiencies after forced collectivization. Significantly, no other Communist regime attempted to emulate the Soviet model of revolution in the countryside—for good reason.

The Five-Year Plans

A few months after the decision to collectivize the land, Soviet party leaders embarked on a second, related program that was at least as ambitious: the rapid industrialization of the Soviet Union through a systematic and coordinated plan. In so doing, Stalin and his colleagues resolutely repudiated the tolerance for private enterprise that had characterized the NEP period. They decided to utilize to the full the resources of state economic planning to make the Soviet Union a strong industrial country at last by building state-owned factories and electric power stations that would rival the greatest plants in the United States.

The First Five-Year Plan, to run from October 1928 to 1933, aimed to double overall Soviet production (see Figure 10.1). It placed chief emphasis on basic industry, which was scheduled to grow by 300 percent, and on electrification, which was to increase more than fivefold. At first, carried away by enthusiasm or anxious to curry favor with Stalin, the planners launched the slogan of completing the work in four years, as sector after sector apparently overfulfilled its quota. Then all sort of difficulties appeared. Fearing to fall behind in meeting their production norms, local officials often set about pilfering scarce supplies intended for neighboring factories. The railway system, which had not received high priority in the plan, remained in such a poor state of repair that goods could not be sent reliably from one factory site to the next, and often arrived late or not at all. Moreover, an unanticipated price rise and the continued resistance of the peasants to collectivization made all the original calculations of the Plan inaccurate. Yet in the end the overall output of Soviet industry was certainly more than doubled.

The Second Plan, running from 1933 to 1937, and the Third Plan, which was interrupted by the war, were originally intended to shift the earlier, almost exclusive emphasis on heavy industry and basic equipment to a more balanced development of the economy, in which the consumer would receive a share. Meanwhile, however, the international situation had begun to deteriorate. With the advent of Hitler, the threat of war, which had already influenced the original decision to industrialize, became acute and immediate. Hence heavy industry maintained its priority, and war preparation, particularly in the years after 1936, began to approach the level of Germany's. By the outbreak of the Second World War, then, Soviet economic development remained unbalanced and one sided—vast pockets of backwardness still existed alongside industrial complexes that ranked among the most modern in the world.

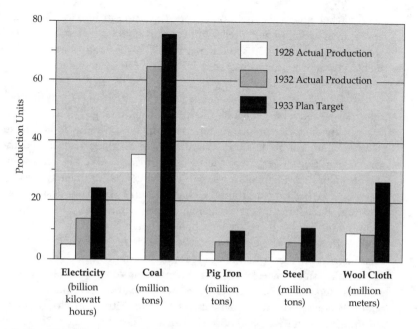

FIGURE 10.1   A comparison of the projected targets and the actual achievements of the first Five-Year Plan (1928–1933). In all cases, production fell short of the goals set, although heavy industry registered impressive gains. The amount of cloth produced, on the other hand—a barometer for consumer goods generally—actually fell from 1928 to 1933.

The Soviet production figures for 1937—the last prewar year in which halfway reliable statistics were published—bear eloquent testimony to the unevenness of economic growth under the first two Five-Year Plans. As compared to a decade earlier, the output of machinery and metal products had increased nearly fourteenfold, while that of coal and of pig iron had more than tripled and quadrupled, respectively. But the production of cotton cloth—a sensitive index of how consumer goods were faring—had risen by only a quarter. The percentages by which capital goods goals had been overfulfilled in the two plans balanced fairly evenly the extent of disappointment in the consumption sector. In the period of the First Plan, the Soviet factories turned out 127 percent of the capital goods expected; for consumer goods the figure was 81 percent. At the end of the Second Plan, the favored heavy industrial sector stood at 121 percent, while once again consumer products fell short by nearly 15 percent.

Nor were consumer goods the only area to suffer. In their efforts to increase production, Soviet planners and officials sacrificed concern for industrial safety and any thought for environmental protection. The new Soviet factory complexes rose quickly in part because their builders took every possible shortcut, creating assembly lines on which it was dangerous to work, in industrial areas polluted by smoke and chemical wastes. Worker housing was also shoddy and insufficient. The swollen population of the industrial cities lived huddled together, with several families sharing the same dreary, unsanitary quarters. Working hours were long and food supplies scarce, forcing tired workers to spend further time after their shifts ended, waiting in line for a few potatoes or a little sausage with which to feed their families. Nor should it be forgotten that how reliant Soviet industry remained on slave labor. By 1939, the Stalin's industrial enterprise fed on the blood and sweat of an estimated 2.9 million prisoners subjected to the most degrading work conditions imaginable.

Thanks in part to these expedients, by 1939 Russia had finally become a major industrial power. The very look of the land had changed. The vast dam spanning the Dnieper, the factories producing farm machinery at Stalingrad and Rostov-on-Don, the great metallurgical complex at Magnitogorsk—all these had altered the landscape beyond recognition. The last of these—Magnitogorsk—lay in Asia behind the Urals, for one of Stalin's subsidiary aims was to shift the centers of industry toward the east, where they would be less exposed than they had been in 1914 to war destruction and foreign occupation. Built largely by slave labor, the city stands as one of many monuments to Stalin's murderous will and to his people's collective suffering.

In terms of the Soviet Union's situation in 1928, the ten-year achievement had been impressive. World War II would reveal how much the Germans, for one, underrated its potential. True, Soviet slave labor and much outside help had been utilized; thousands of engineers and technicians were recruited abroad, particularly from Germany and the United States. These came as individuals, attracted by sympathy, curiosity, or the hope of gain. The governments of the West had not helped at all. There had been no official program of aid to an underdeveloped nation. Hence the capital for the colossal investment program that the Five-Year Plans entailed had to be squeezed from the Soviet peoples themselves.

By the end of the decade, then, the Soviet economy had been subjected to drastic changes. Planning had been heavily centralized, with an emphasis on those industrial sectors with military applications such as steel and machine tools, and a corresponding neglect of consumer goods. This emphasis—and the uneven pattern of development it created—was to be replicated in the Eastern European countries that fell under the Soviet sphere of influence following the Second World War (see Chapter 14, III). In the meantime, the power of the Soviet state to affect its citizens' lives for both good and ill had been enormously increased.

III. THE POLITICAL AND SOCIAL IMPLICATIONS

The Constitution of 1936

In 1936—as if to mark the fact that after two decades of Bolshevik rule the socialist society had at last become a reality—Stalin ordered the promulgation of a new constitution for the Soviet Union. On paper, it was—as sympathizers in the West liked to say—"the most democratic in the world." All the usual Western liberties received due attention, and the Soviet constitution makers added a few new ones. They abolished the limitations that earlier had deprived capitalists and aristocrats of the vote. And the roster of Soviet republics—which had already been increased in 1925—was raised to a total of eleven, thereby suggesting that the non-Russian peoples of the Transcaucasus and Central Asia were being given a larger share in the running of the Union. Finally, a change in terminology from "commissar" to "minister" created the impression that in the conduct of government the Soviet Union was going to behave as a parliamentary democratic state rather than as the party dictatorship it had been before.

Very little of this made any difference in practice. The Soviet Union remained a police state—indeed, from this standpoint there was deterioration rather than improvement. The real significance of the new constitution lay elsewhere. First, by ending the era of improvisations, it emphasized the fact that the Soviet regime had hardened into its final form; the abolition of the distinctions that had denied full rights to the former possessing classes most clearly epitomized the change by suggesting that the power of these classes had been broken and that they no longer represented a threat to the regime. Second, the new constitution provided excellent propaganda material for Western consumption. It seemed to mark the climax of three years of "liberal" policies that had put the Soviet Union into a light more favorable than any in which it was to appear during the whole interwar period.

After 1933—as if to underline the alternative he offered to the new threat of nazism—Stalin relaxed his pressure in the collectivization drive; he took his country into the League of Nations and made it a strong supporter of "collective security" at Geneva; by adopting the Popular Front idea, he seemed to endorse the notion of a "domesticated" communism that would be an acceptable ally to the Western democratic Left. There emerged the image of a strong and confident Russia that was setting out to build a socialist society at the very moment when the capitalist economies of the West lay crippled by the Great Depression. This picture stirred imaginations and led Western European democrats to slur over or conveniently forget the somber aspects of the Stalinist system that in ordinary times might have troubled them very deeply.

Most of these Western sympathizers did not know that at the very time the new constitution was being drafted Stalin had already entered on a phase of intensified terror that was to disillusion nearly all of them.

The Great Purges

In December 1934, a young assassin struck down the Communist party chief of Leningrad, Sergei Kirov. Stalin himself hurried to the scene of the crime and questioned the murderer. The official story that emerged from hours of interrogation was that an opposition existed within the apparently monolithic Soviet state, that the assassin had belonged to a group of young Communists who bitterly resented Stalin's oppressive rule and who regarded Zinoviev—with whom, apparently, they had no contact—as their ideological guide. Subsequent revelations, however, have brought to light a very different and far more sinister story. Kirov, it is now alleged, was put to death by the secret police on orders from Stalin himself, who both envied Kirov's popularity and wished to use his assassination to trap others.

Kirov's murder signaled the start of a wave of mass executions organized by Stalin, which in the space of four years would decimate the leadership of the Communist party and claim millions of other victims as well. Between 1935 and 1939, an estimated seven to eight million Soviet citizens were arrested. Of these, at least one million were executed outright; the remainder were sent to prison camps, where barely one-quarter survived. If the forced collectivization campaign had fallen most heavily on the peasants, the Great Purges, as they came to be called, hit hard at the Soviet elite.

In January 1935, Zinoviev and Kamenev were tried for treason and conspiracy and sentenced to long prison terms. They went on trial again a year and a half later, and this time they were executed. In early 1937, another group of high party leaders went on public trial—nearly all of them to receive death sentences—and in the spring and early summer, eight outstanding army leaders were convicted and executed in secret. Finally, in March 1938, came the turn of Bukharin and the old "Right," in the party. Thus, by the beginning of 1939, when Stalin officially announced the end of the purge, every possibility of opposition had been destroyed—two or three alternative governments had been eliminated. Only a handful of Old Bolsheviks—all of them loyal to Stalin—remained alive; the heavy hand of party orthodoxy had snuffed out every shred of independent initiative in the Soviet state.

Observers from the West, who were admitted to watch the more important trials, were puzzled by the abject fashion in which defendant after defendant entered the dock and declared himself guilty in the most circumstantial terms. Most of the stories they told seemed total fabrications; only in the case of the army leaders have subsequent historians admitted the probability of a true plot—and in their case one might argue that the Red Army's long years of clandestine military cooperation with Germany cast doubts on its high command's reliability in defending the country against the Nazi attack that now threatened. As far as the party men were concerned, however, there seems to be no evidence of any concerted opposition to Stalin. These Old Bolsheviks were already beaten and broken men; they had lost the political struggle at least a half decade earlier and they knew it. They did not like Stalin's methods, and they probably still grumbled against him in private, but they offered no real threat to his authority.

Thus they were easy game for the government interrogators and prosecutors who attacked them. Questioning often continued around the clock, often for days on end. Stalin's police made good use of the so-called conveyor method, where teams of interrogators relieved one another at regular intervals until the prisoner, broken and exhausted, confessed. Beatings, prolonged confinement in filthy freezing cells, threats against family and loved ones, and systematic torture were all used to extract confessions. Some prisoners were motivated by the hope of saving their lives and those of their families if they proved cooperative, though such hopes were seldom fulfilled. For Communist party members, yet another deciding factor was the weariness and resignation of defeat, coupled with the sense that the verdict of history had gone against them. This last, in terms of Marxist reasoning, was almost equivalent to an admission of guilt. If in the 1920s they had, in fact, opposed what proved to be the main course of history—that is, Stalin's rule—then in an "objective" sense, they were guilty of "antiparty" activities. From here, it was only a step to confessing whatever was charged against them.

So much for the defendants. There remains, however, the additional question of why Stalin behaved as he did. Why was it necessary for him to kill nearly all his old comrades-in-arms, who were no longer in a position to threaten him? Why did he further insist on imprisoning and murdering hundreds of thousands of teachers, doctors, artists, military officers, and members of the secret police itself, whose work was important for the state? We cannot know for sure. Some have suggested that Stalin was a madman. Yet someone completely beyond reason would not have been able to govern the Soviet

Union with Stalin's skill. Others argue that Stalin was less mad than cunning. Indeed, there was a perverse logic to the purges, since they swept away virtually all centers of independent thought and action within both the party and the Soviet government, and made the entire nation dependent on the whims of the "great leader" Comrade Stalin. He thereby achieved absolute power to a degree unparalleled in twentieth-century Europe.

Yet Stalin's success in liquidating his rivals, real or supposed, came at the price of perpetual suspicion. Like the Russian despots of old to whom he was compared both in praise and in condemnation—men like Boris Godunov and Ivan the Terrible—Stalin was possessed by the demon of universal doubt. As he aged and his crimes multiplied, he feared more and more for his own life and trusted fewer and fewer people—until in the end he was overcome by a paranoia that made his last years a nightmare for all those close to him.

The New Conformism

Beyond all this, men like Bukharin and Zinoviev recalled a past that Stalin wished to have hurled and forgotten. They recalled a time when revolutionary comradeship still existed and when, within the confines of the party at least, freedom of discussion and freedom of expression were permitted. Lenin, for all his preaching of Marxist ruthlessness, would have been more chary of murdering party colleagues.

By the 1930s, Russia was living in quite a different atmosphere—an atmosphere of "oriental" or "Byzantine" despotism. Party congresses had become mere rubber stamps;

Lenin and Stalin in 1923, a year before Lenin's death. The photograph was later used by Stalin to demonstrate the close bond between himself and the Revolution's founder. It was deliberately altered to make the two appear to be intimates. (*Courtesy The Granger Collection, New York*)

even the Politburo, which met in almost constant session, consisted solely of Stalin's creatures. The "great man" himself was virtually deified. He assumed the mantle of Marx and Lenin, arrogating to himself the role of high priest of theory and ideology, although he wrote in a flat, tasteless style and his thoughts were notably unoriginal. His chief claim as a theorist was his *Short Course on the History of the CPSU(b)*, a party history that magnified Stalin's role while vilifying that of his rivals Trotsky and Bukharin in a simplified narrative whose story of heroes and villains appealed to the popular mind. The Short Course became required reading at all levels. Stalin's most banal statements were welcomed by his sycophants as revelations from on high; indeed, authors who wished to find official favor were obliged to flatter him shamelessly and even to imitate the way he wrote. In all fields of culture a deadly conformism and sterility settled over Russian life, in stark contrast with the creativity of the 1920s (see Chapter 11, IV).

In the background, threatening at one time or another nearly everyone of any prominence in the country, lurked the dreaded secret police. As it had earlier changed its name from Cheka to GPU, so in 1934 it became the NKVD—the innocuous-sounding People's Commissariat of Internal Affairs. In fact it remained what it had always been: a machine for government by terror. With the great purges, its functions grew. It herded millions of political prisoners into what Alexander Solzhenitsyn later termed an "archipelago" of labor camps stretching across the Soviet Union from the outskirts of Moscow to the frozen wastes of Siberia. There the convicts were forced to work digging canals, mining gold and coal, logging, constructing factories—any task, in fact, that the central economic planners deemed essential. They, too, as we have seen, became toilers to fulfill the requirements of the Five-Year Plans.

The prisoner population and the death toll in these camps are impossible to determine with any accuracy, but both were high. Conservatively, the number of political prisoners laboring there in the late 1930s has been put at eight million, of which close to one million died of malnutrition and overwork each year. In many respects, the Soviet forced labor camps recalled the concentration camps run by the Nazis. They, too, were places of suffering and despair—of starvation, disease, and deliberate infliction of pain. It is perhaps pointless to ask which regime behaved more brutally toward its victims: the one that murdered millions with industrial precision, or the one that sent an even larger number to a lingering death brought on by starvation and exhaustion over months or years. In the end, the fact that should retain our attention is that both systems were created deliberately, with full knowledge of their effects, by governments that elected to employ terrorist institutions as a chosen instrument of rule.

The New Elite

Despite the terror, hardship, and turmoil of Stalin's economic revolution, a new Soviet generation was emerging that would form the country's leadership in the postwar decades. By the time the Constitution of 1936 was promulgated, fewer than half the people of Russia could remember the prerevolutionary era. This was a young population; unlike that of Western Europe, it was growing very fast. Far more than in the past, it was also a city population. Virtually the entire increase for the years 1926 to 1939 came in the cities alone; in this period, Moscow almost doubled in size, growing from just over two million to more than four million, and some of the smaller industrial cities quadrupled the number of their inhabitants. Of the entire urban population, two-fifths consisted of peasants who had lived in cities for fewer than twelve years.

The new generation took communism and the Soviet system for granted. The more gifted members found opportunities for advancement that they would never have known under the old regime—in part because of the rapid pace of economic expansion, in part because of the large number of posts vacated as older officials were imprisoned and executed in the Great Purge. Newly industrialized Russia was clamoring for technical talent, and could obtain it in sufficient quantity only by training the sons and daughters of illiterate peasants. During the NEP period, the regime had been obliged to rely on "specialists" from the prerevolutionary intelligentsia whom it had never fully trusted. During the First Five-Year Plan, it welcomed engineers from abroad. But what it really wanted was technicians of its own, and preferably of proletarian or peasant origin. Therefore, in the five years from 1933 to 1938, the Soviet Union sent a million young people into courses of higher education. From their ranks emerged a new intelligentsia of engineers and doctors, agronomists, teachers, research scientists, and factory managers. By Western standards, many of them were poorly and hastily trained, but they were enthusiastic, hardworking, and filled with pride in the new society that was theirs to create. It was on them that the regime very rightly rested its faith for the future.

A new elite emerged in the ranks of Communist party officials as well. Indeed, many of these began with a technical education as mechanical engineers or experts in metallurgy and were then drafted into party work. Whereas in the 1920s the party leaders such as Lenin, Trotsky, and Bukharin had been from a middle-class background, with university degrees in law or the humanities, party recruitment in the 1930s drew on those of peasant or working class stock, with education in the applied sciences. They were part of the so-called *nomenklatura*—individuals judged sufficiently reliable by Stalin and his aides for their names to appear on the list of those fit to occupy posts of responsibility within the party, the military, the government, and the economy. Here was further evidence of Stalin's emphasis on rank and hierarchy. The widening gap in income and standard of living between the mere worker or peasant and the highly paid party chief or factory manager suggested that the Soviet Union had left the revolution far behind and had found its own equilibrium of conservatism and stability.

For members of the *nomenklatura*, life in the Soviet system offered both great rewards and constant cause for anxiety. Fed, housed, and clothed by the state according to standards far above those allowed for ordinary citizens—allowed to shop in special stores and permitted chauffeured cars and country dachas—they enjoyed what even by Western criteria was a materially comfortable existence. At the same time, the powerful state that conferred these luxuries could also withdraw them at a moment's notice. Hence while the *nomenklatura* were rewarded for energy and ambition, the Soviet system also encouraged caution and political docility. If Soviet society was stable, that stability reflected the fear of doing anything that might put one's privileges at risk.

The System on the Eve of the War

What did the new elite actually think of the system of government under which it lived? How did it reconcile its optimism and Communist faith with the brutal realities of Stalinist rule? In the 1930s, these questions seemed unanswerable: Soviet Russia loomed up in the east as a vast paradox, in which devotion to the task of building a new society went alongside political behavior of a meanness and squalor rivaling that of the Fascists.

With the passage of time and the opening up of previously inaccessible Soviet archives, however, it has proved possible to gain some insight into the means whereby Stalinist society tried to reconcile these apparent irreconcilables. In practice, Soviet citizens seem to have adopted the habit of living on two levels at once: one public and conformist, the other private and more honest. Publicly the Soviet Constitution of 1936 might be acknowledged by everyone as "the most democratic in the world," yet all but the most idealistic or naive realized that any attempt by the average citizen to exercise the liberties enshrined in the constitution would result in arrest. Publicly the fact that millions were being sent to labor camps on trumped up charges in the late 1930s was not mentioned, yet almost everyone knew someone—a family member, neighbor, or coworker—who had "disappeared."

A similar willingness to tolerate a deep division between party line and reality was required in the realm of ideology. Lenin had, of course, argued that the Bolsheviks must be prepared to seize power ruthlessly and use that power to transform Russian society. But he had also at least partially realized the danger to liberty that would be entailed by the concentration of so much power in the hands of state and party. In his view, once the revolution was secure, the state would eventually shed its central, coercive role. Yet under Stalin, Lenin's self-professed disciple, just the opposite was occurring. The power of the state was increasing far beyond what the Old Bolsheviks had deemed desirable or even possible.

Stalin maintained the ideological link with the Leninist past while twisting Lenin's precepts to new uses. Lenin, for example, had relied on two devices to counteract the misuse of party power: "self-criticism," which would ruthlessly ferret out and correct past mistakes, and the system of "democratic centralism," by which each party echelon elected the one above it, thereby ensuring democracy at the base of the political pyramid. Under Stalin, these safeguards were thoroughly perverted. State and party elections became only a formal endorsement of a slate of candidates selected from above. "Democratic centralism" thus worked almost exactly in the reverse fashion from what had been originally intended. Similarly, "self-criticism" never touched the essentials of the system. Although there was constant discussion at all levels of the economic and party hierarchy—all the way from "town meetings" in each collective farm or factory right up to the deliberations of the Politburo itself—these discussions dealt solely with the technical details of policy; they did not go to the heart of the matter.

In essence, the safeguard of self-criticism was gradually altered to perform the opposite function from the one for which it had been devised. It served, not to correct the abuses of the dictatorship, but rather to strengthen the authority of the top party leaders through directed popular hostility toward the lower bureaucracy and toward specific technical mistakes. Thus criticism was "deflected away from policy itself to the execution of policy," while the central reality of the system was left untouched.* The result was a regularly recurring ritual of self-castigation. Certain abuses were in fact corrected in the process, but the main function of campaigns of this sort was psychological. They kept officials perpetually off balance, dependent on blindly following orders from above which

*Barrington Moore, Jr., *Soviet Politics: The Dilemma of Power* (Cambridge, Mass.: Harvard University Press, 1950), 403.

could change abruptly and without seeming cause. Above all, they ensured obedience—Stalin's major aim—by forcing his unfortunate subjects to jump through ideological hoops of his own devising.

By 1941, almost 20 million Soviet citizens had died as a result of Stalin's policies—ten million peasants in the mass starvation deliberately provoked in the years 1932–1933, eight million citizens of all descriptions executed on Stalin's orders during the Great Purge, and hundreds of thousands more who died a lingering death in labor camps or in frozen exile from their homes. On the other hand, the Soviet Union was for the first time a major industrial power, able to withstand the challenge of Hitler's Germany, the greatest industrial nation on the European continent. Was the cost justified? Could the same results have been obtained with less pain and suffering? These questions do not permit a definitive answer; we cannot replay Soviet history with, say, Bukharin replacing Stalin and compare the outcome. But historians are increasingly inclined to believe that Soviet industrialization could and should have been achieved at far lower human cost. Neither the deliberate starvation of the Ukrainian peasants nor Stalin's purges were necessary for this end. The purges were a moral abomination, visited on millions of innocent victims, causing death and misery on a scale which approached that of the Nazi Holocaust (see Chapter 13, III). They were also an act of political and economic folly. In the event, the purges weakened the Soviet Union at the very moment when it needed all its strength to counter the German threat.

The ordeal of the Second World War was to reveal in Soviet society a solidity that neither its friends nor its enemies had ever properly appreciated. But to see its heroic resistance to Nazi aggression as proof of the superiority of Stalin's policies or of Marxist ideology would be a mistake. In a very real sense, the Soviet Union succeeded in this undertaking thanks to a patriotic spirit and willingness to sacrifice that long predated the coming of the Bolsheviks, and succeeded *despite* Stalin. A half century after the war, Soviet citizens continued to debate, and to ponder, which calamity brought worse suffering to their country: Hitler or Stalin.

READINGS

A fine single-volume introduction to this and other aspects of Soviet history is Geoffrey Hosking, *The First Socialist Society: A History of the Soviet Union from Within** 2nd enlarged ed. (1992). See also Martin McCauley, *The Soviet Union, 1917–1991,** 2nd ed. (1993), which offers an excellent overview within a more traditional political framework of analysis, and Robert Service, *A History of Twentieth-Century Russia** (1997). The harvest of previously secret government records relating to the entire period of Soviet rule can be sampled in Dane Koenker and Ronald Bachman, eds., *Revelations from the Russian Archives: Documents in English Translation* (1997).

Several excellent works exist on Stalin and Stalinism, enriched by the revelations resulting from glasnost and opening up previously restricted archives. The most authoritative is Dmitri Volkogonov's *Stalin: Triumph and Tragedy** (trans. 1992). The best

*Books marked with an asterisk are available in paperback.

short treatment by a Western scholar is arguably Robert Conquests's *Stalin: Breaker of Nations** (1991). Robert C. Tucker, *Stalin as Revolutionary, 1879–1929* (1973) and *Stalin in Power: The Revolution from Above, 1928–1941* (1990), offer a more extended appraisal. Also noteworthy are Bullock (see readings for Chapter 9); Adam Ulam, *Stalin: The Man and His Era,** expanded ed. (1989); and two Soviet works: Roy Medvedev, *Let History Judge: The Origins and Consequences of Stalinism*, rev. ed. (1989) and Dimitri Volkogonov, *Stalin: Triumph and Tragedy** (1988, trans. 1992)—the former by a distinguished dissident, the latter by a former Soviet general given unparalleled access to the Communist party archives. For an account of life lived at the level of the common man, see Sheila Fitzpatrick, *Everyday Stalinism: Ordinary Life in Extraordinary Times** (1998).

The standard and detailed account of the early years of Stalin's rule is Edward Hallett Carr, *A History of Soviet Russia: The Interregnum, 1923–24* (1954), *Socialism in One Country*, 3 vols. (1958), and *Foundations of a Planned Economy*, 3 vols. (1969–1979), summarized in a one-volume synthesis, *The Russian Revolution from Lenin to Stalin* (1979). Carr's tendency to view Stalin's policies in a sympathetic light should be tempered by reference to the work of the more critical Hélène Carrère d'Encausse, *A History of the Soviet Union, 1917–1953,** 2 vols. (trans. 1982). Stephen F. Cohen's *Bukharin and the Bolshevik Revolution: A Political Biography, 1888–1938** (1973) examines the career of one of Stalin's principal victims against the background of the transformation of the Soviet Union into an industrial power. For Trotsky, in addition to Volkogonov and Deutscher (see readings for Chapter 3), there is Irving Howe, *Leon Trotsky* (1979).

For information on NEP, the collectivization of agriculture, and the Five-Year Plans, see Alec Nove's *An Economic History of the USSR: 1917–1991,** new and final ed. (1992). Collectivization is dealt with specifically in R. W. Davies, *The Socialist Offensive: The Collectivization of Soviet Agriculture, 1929–30* (1980), and Moshe Lewin, *Russian Peasants and Soviet Power: A Study of Collectivization* (1968, trans. 1975), while the centralizing forces behind Soviet industrialization are examined in Hiraoki Kuromiya, *Stalin's Industrial Revolution: Politics and Workers, 1928–1932* (1988). The effects of both campaigns on a single region have been documented on the basis of rich original sources in Merle Fainsod, *Smolensk Under Soviet Rule* (1958). Robert Conquest, *Harvest of Sorrow: Soviet Collectivization and the Terror Famine** (1986) links collectivization with purges of the 1930s.

The theory and practice of the purge are dealt with in Conquest's revision of his classic account, *The Great Terror: A Reassessment* (1990), and the same author's *Stalin and the Kirov Murder** (1989). Robert C. Tucker and Stephen F. Cohen, eds., *The Great Purge Trials* (1965) offers documents from the major show trials, especially Bukharin's. The most complete account of the labor camps, written by a former inmate, is Alexander Solzhenitsyn, *The Gulag Archipelago, 1918–1956,** 3 vols. (1974–1978). The effect on the victims is recounted in the memoirs of Eugenia Ginzburg, *Into the Whirlwind** (1967).

Russia on the eve of the Stalinist purges in the early 1930s forms the background of Anatoli Rybakov's novel *Children of the Arbat** (1988), where Stalin appears as one of the main characters; a fictional account of the purges that suggests the rationale that drove loyal Bolsheviks to confess to false charges is convincingly presented in Arthur Koestler's *Darkness at Noon** (1940). The harrowing details of a "good day" in a Soviet labor camp emerge in Alexander Solzhenitsyn's justly celebrated novella, *A Day in the Life of Ivan Denisovich** (1963).

11

EUROPEAN CIVILIZATION IN CRISIS

A scene from the 1931 movie version of Bertolt Brecht and Kurt Weill's satiric musical drama *The Three-Penny Opera*, showing Weill's wife, the singer Lotte Lenya, in the role of Jenny. *(Courtesy Brown Brothers)*

I. The Social Consequences of the Great Depression and Fascism

The Loss of Social Momentum

During the decade of the 1930s, when the Soviet Union was transforming itself from top to bottom, society and the economy languished in the West. Gripped by depression and the fear of war, countries like Britain and France made little technological progress. They lost the momentum of change that had characterized their history for more than a century; in many areas of national life, they could do no more than to maintain the equipment and procedures inherited from preceding generations. Still worse, much of this equipment lay idle or underutilized. The Great Depression years stand as a period of pause in the economic and technological modernization of Western Europe. And this decade was to be followed by a further half decade—that of the Second World War—in which innovation was almost entirely directed to military needs. Externally, the cities of the West that had been spared war damage did not look much different in 1945 from the way they looked in 1930. When economic progress was finally resumed in the late 1940s it came with explosive force.

The clearest indication of loss of social momentum was a further decline in the birthrate. In the 1930s, it sank to the lowest level known since regular records began to be kept in Western Europe. Faced with economic hardship and uncertainty, young people tended to postpone marriage and the arrival of children; birth control became so common a practice that governments began to worry about its effect on the strength of the nation. Among Northern and Western European democracies, in the Netherlands alone the figure for births remained significantly above that for deaths; elsewhere they were nearly in balance, with the population growing older. In the fascist countries, as might be expected, the regimes took vigorous counteraction. Both Italy and Germany encouraged large families through tax favors and special allowances; whether owing to these measures or to the natural tendencies of their people, both countries experienced a population rise that contrasted sharply with the situation among their neighbors.

Another sign of social stagnation was the near cessation of population movements in the early 1930s. When these did occur, they often reversed what had become normal in a highly industrialized society—as when city dwellers began to return to the farms, or when emigrants to the United States took ship for their old homelands. Nearly everywhere, governments tried to protect their own working population by keeping down the influx of foreigners seeking employment. This was a further manifestation of the turn to economic nationalism, reflected in the raising of tariffs and the official control of foreign trade. Even France, which had traditionally been hospitable to immigration, now began to limit the arrival of workers from abroad. In 1934, it admitted only one-third the number that had entered in 1930. Everywhere the national nightmare was the same—unemployment, the curse of the decade that put its stamp on nearly all aspects of social and cultural endeavor.

The Political Refugees

In one form, however, emigration continued and even increased, particularly in the latter part of the decade. This was the flight of almost 400,000 Germans from political and racial persecution. It was paralleled by a continued trickle of clandestine departures from Italy, which suddenly increased in 1938, when Mussolini imitated his Nazi ally by instituting discriminatory measures against the Jews. Finally, in 1939, with the end of the Spanish Civil War, nearly half a million Republican soldiers and refugees crossed over the border into France.

Only at the end of the decade did emigration of this sort begin to reach the proportions of a mass movement. In general, it was an emigration of elites rather than those of broad strata of the population, but for that very reason it had a social and cultural importance far beyond its numerical scale. The people who left Italy or Germany tended to be leaders in their fields—scholars and trade-union executives, members of parliament and financiers. Even the emigration of the Jews—although it involved every social class—had an elite character, since members of this faith were, on the average, both wealthier and better educated than the run of the population. Thus the flight from fascist persecution in a very real sense impoverished the countries that drove these people out and enriched those that received them. When Germany lost through emigration its most original composer, Arnold Schoenberg (who was Jewish), and its most influential novelist, Thomas Mann (who was not), the national culture experienced an irrevocable loss; indeed, as the departure of intellectuals from Germany continued, it became apparent that the country was suffering a drain of talent which a whole generation could not make good. As cultural levels in Italy and Germany declined, they rose in the countries that opened their doors to the refugees—at first primarily France, where the Italians in particular felt most at home, and later the United States, where, after the war, so many émigrés moved to find a second home.

If for the mass of the population the fundamentals of life did not change under fascist rule, this was true only of the torpid and conformist majority. For the minority of the free-spirited, the creative, and the "racially" alien, life changed catastrophically. The persecution of the Jews and the denial of free thought under fascism came to rank as the second nightmare of the decade—adding a further note of grimness to the earlier specter of unemployment. The jobless worker and the refugee from fascist oppression—whether Jew or intellectual or perhaps both—became the twin symbols of the 1930s. Together these symbols suggest why in cultural terms the period was one of "engagement"—of protest against injustice and of enrollment under the banners of social reform.

II. The Literature of "Engagement"

To writers who found themselves face to face with the two great evils of the time—the Great Depression and fascism—it seemed impossible to maintain any longer the attitude of a detached aesthete. Sooner or later nearly all of them were swept up in the drive for social justice. Seeing intolerable conditions around them, even those who had earlier shown no interest at all in the condition of their fellow men began to ask themselves why all this suffering had to exist, and whether humankind could not find a new organization of society that would make life freer and happier. They revived the utopian strain that had figured so prominently in the thought and action of the nineteenth century and put new life into the old ideologies of progress. From this standpoint, the 1930s appear as an Indian summer of the previous century—the decade of despair was also a decade of hope.

Obviously, European intellectuals did not discover ideology overnight with the coming of the Great Depression. The previous generation had boasted many writers whose work either directly or by implication furthered political causes. But most of these were isolated individuals who prided themselves on their freedom from humanitarian prejudices. Like D'Annunzio in Italy, they combined sensualism with a glorification of war and killing. When they did show interest in political action, it was usually in the service of fascist or near-fascist movements. It was against writers of this sort that the French philosopher Julien Benda warned in 1927, when he published his influential polemic *The Betrayal of the Intellectuals*.

In the 1930s, as fascism in practice revealed both its brutality and its intellectual shoddiness, writers who had earlier welcomed it as a movement of protest began to desert it. They turned instead toward restoring human fellowship and rational behavior. Some embattled writers of the 1930s were Marxists and some were "bourgeois" democrats; but they had a common vision of a better society that would end forever the blundering incompetence that had produced the Great Depression and the disappointment of human hope that had led to fascism and the menace of war. This vision of the future was often extremely eclectic. It combined elements both of traditional Marxism and of traditional liberalism; it tried to reconcile them or to go beyond them to a type of society whose outlines were vague but would express the new realities of the twentieth century more adequately than either of them. Among writers, as among politicians, there grew a Popular Front mentality.

One further quality these writers shared was a new simplicity and directness. They were profoundly concerned with being *understood*—as had been true neither of the literary forebears of fascism, who had affected a "rich," mannered style and scorned the common herd, nor of the frankly experimental novelists and poets of the 1920s. From this standpoint, the decade of struggle against the Great Depression and fascism marked a pause in literary innovation or even a step backward; writers seemed to be telling themselves that the times had become too grave for mere technical experiments. What counted now was to transmit their message to a broad public as sharply and as decisively as possible.

Neo-Marxism: Communist and Social Democratic

The Great Depression and the Popular Front gave Marxism a crucial importance among European ideologies. Indeed, these events put Marxists in the strongest position they had enjoyed since the early 1920s—when the split between Communists and Socialists weakened both wings of the movement, and the consolidation of parliamentary government under the leadership of conservatives cut the ground from under them. After 1933, this situation was reversed. Capitalism was now on the defensive for having allowed the Great Depression to occur and for having encouraged, or at least tolerated, the coming of fascism; Communists and Socialists were militant and self-confident and were beginning to sink their differences in common action against a common foe.

In both cases, however, Marxist doctrine required renovation. Under Stalinist orthodoxy, communism had transformed Marxism into little more than a stereotyped set of principles that could be twisted to justify anything the Soviet Union might choose to do. In the case of democratic socialism, conduct no longer jibed with theory: Parties that for a generation had been parliamentary and legalist still mouthed the language of violent class struggle. In the 1930s, each tried to bring theory up to date and both failed.

After Lenin and Bukharin, European communism produced only one important thinker who combined party leadership with theoretical writing—the Italian Antonio Gramsci. Gramsci, however, was arrested by Mussolini's police before he had had time to measure his strength and influence against Stalin's. As the newly chosen chief of the Italian Communist party, he was imprisoned in 1926 and not released until just before his death in 1937. Gramsci's thought and example were expressed, not in his party's councils or in those of the Third International, but in fragmentary prison writings, which were published only after the Second World War. In these, Gramsci placed new stress on the subjective and noneconomic elements in Marxism. "Every revolution," he wrote, "has been preceded by an intense critical effort of cultural penetration." He therefore dealt with popular culture and with its relation to the old literary culture of the educated classes and to the new society dominated by the machine; he struggled with the problem of how a Marxist social consensus could be achieved after a successful seizure of power, but he never reconciled his own longing for spiritual freedom with his unquestioning acceptance of the necessity for single-party dictatorship.

Similarly, the other great theoretician of neocommunism, the Hungarian-born and German-educated Georg Lukács, always ultimately bowed to party discipline. Again and again he fell afoul of the official leadership. His own theory, which, like Gramsci's, was primarily cultural and subjective, was based on the idea of a "class consciousness" existing independently of political and economic conditions. It opened the way to an individual judgment of events—which in terms of Communist orthodoxy was the supreme danger. Lukács more than once had to repudiate what he had written, but he stubbornly returned to his favorite themes. As an old man he was to find at last in the Hungarian revolution of 1956 a brief satisfaction for his constantly repressed rebelliousness (see Chapter 19, IV).

Although neither Gramsci nor Lukács had much direct influence outside a narrow circle of the Communist elite, similar ideas gradually filtered down to the party rank and file. This was particularly true during the wartime Resistance period, when thousands of Communists, left to their own devices and thrown into close association with former class enemies, worked out for themselves a more liberal interpretation of Marxist principles, and again, after Stalin's death in 1953, when individual national versions of communism began to gain ground. In the 1930s, however, tendencies of this sort had little chance. One after another they were smothered by the dead weight of Stalinist orthodoxy.

By the 1930s, a number of Socialist leaders had decided that the old and crude slogans of class warfare no longer sufficed. Among them was the French Popular Front chief, Léon Blum, who tried to change Marxism into an inclusive doctrine of humanism and humanitarianism in which all men of good will could recognize their own aspirations. But Blum's formulation of this goal remained vague, and in his day-to-day activities as a political leader he was chained to the traditional routines of his party. On the other hand, Socialist leaders who did succeed in making a clean break with the class warfare dogmas of the past fell into worse difficulties. A significant number finally compromised with fascism by consenting to work with the Nazi authorities in the period of wartime occupation.

Thus European socialism failed to renew itself. It found no fresh vocabulary to explain how and why it had become the nondogmatic catchall for European democrats who longed for a more just and efficient organization of society. Nor did it develop a new economic doctrine to replace the Marxist theory in which it only half believed, and the orthodox principles of capitalist finance that it applied most of the time when in office, since it knew no other. The task of devising a fresh theoretical approach fell to an English economist—a non-Socialist and even an enemy of socialism—John Maynard Keynes, the most influential economic thinker of the whole half century.

The New Economics of Keynes

Keynes was a man of lively and versatile mind who had had a number of careers before the 1930s, when he formulated his principles of economics. He was far from being simply an economist. An associate of Bertrand Russell and Ludwig Wittgenstein at Cambridge, he had written a treatise on probability, which was an early contribution of the new analytic philosophy; he was a member of the Bloomsbury Circle of aesthetes, sharing its characteristic enthusiasm for French painting, psychoanalysis, and the Russian ballet. He had been a high-ranking civil servant, an influential figure at the Paris Peace Conference, from which he returned disillusioned and angry, to write *The Economic Consequences of the Peace*, a little book that did much to create the bad conscience of the British about the Treaty of Versailles in general and German reparations in particular.

As Keynes observed the stagnation of the British economy in the late 1920s and its crisis in the half decade following, he began to reconsider the orthodox principles of economics that he had been teaching. Preoccupied, like most of his compatriots, with the nightmare of unemployment, he came to question nearly all the dogmas of "sound" financing, deflation in time of crisis, and free enterprise at all costs. The result of these reevaluations, *The General Theory of Employment, Interest and Money*, appeared in that extraordinary year 1936 when so much else in Europe was astir.

Keynes undertook to prove that government could manipulate the economy—through such devices as altering the interest rate, monetary expansion, public investment, and public works—without resorting to socialism. Scornful of the orthodoxies of laissez-faire, he judged economic policy on the strictly practical criteria of the total output of goods and the volume of employment that it succeeded in creating. Moreover, he added to the classical principles of economics a novel psychological element. These principles, he explained, might be correct in the abstract, but they did not work out in practice, since real human beings often refused to think like the proverbial economist—trade unionists, for example, stubbornly denied the logic of taking a wage cut in a time of depression and falling prices. In line with this practical turn of thought, Keynes stressed "macroeconomics"—the analysis of interconnections within the economy as a whole, as opposed to the conventional method of isolating individual problems for detailed study.

John Maynard Keynes (1883–1946), the century's most influential economist, at the time of the publication of his *General Theory*. (*Courtesy Brown Brothers*)

It was also characteristic of him to emphasize short-run considerations, in contrast to the comforting conviction of the orthodox that in the long run all difficulties would resolve themselves. In a crisis like the Great Depression, Keynes argued, there simply was not time to wait for the ineffable logic of the economy to set things right. "In the long run," he observed, "we are all dead."

Keynes scorned socialism nearly as much as he did laissez-faire. He called it "a dusty survival of a plan to meet the problems of fifty years ago, based on a misunderstanding of what someone said a hundred years ago." The "important thing for government," he further explained, was "not to do things which individuals are doing already . . . but to do those things which at present are not done at all."* Not government ownership, but government intervention at the key points in the economy, was the substance of Keynes's message. Yet despite his hostility to the Socialists, he was to become their teacher; he taught them where they had made their mistakes and what they were really seeking— after they had found Marxian economics inapplicable, class warfare distasteful, and nationalization of basic industry a panacea that was far from sufficient. Had Blum and the leaders of the Popular Front in France known of Keynes's work, they would have had a

*"The End of Laissez-Faire" (1926), in *Essays in Persuasion*, new ed. (London: Rupert Hart-Davis, 1951), 316–317.

clear substitute to offer for the deflationary policy of their predecessors, which they knew to be disastrous but whose economic premises they never succeeded in escaping. British Labour was in a more fortunate situation. It came to power only in 1945, when it had absorbed Keynes's teaching and was able to apply large parts of it in the postwar reconstruction of the British economy.

In general, it was in the United States rather than in Europe that Keynes first exerted practical influence. In America, his writings were used to justify theoretically what the New Dealers had been doing by a process of trial and error. Indeed, in its simplest form, this was the historical significance of Keynes's work: It provided a sanction of theory for the unorthodox practices that necessity had forced upon governments during the Great Depression—deficit financing, for example, and the effort to maintain full employment by state action. Along with this sanction went the heartening assertion that it was not necessary to make an all-or-nothing choice between doctrinaire socialism and laissez-faire capitalism. Both were at fault; both had failed to see how much that was new could be done within the old framework of a private-enterprise economy. Like the Scandinavian governments whose practice had anticipated and paralleled his own theory, Keynes offered the possibility of a "middle way."

Literature and the Primacy of Politics

In imaginative literature, the tendency of the 1930s toward ideological "engagement" and a new directness of expression appeared both in the work of younger writers who first achieved recognition in this period and in that of established authors who found themselves turning to new themes.

Among the elders, Thomas Mann offered the outstanding example. Even before the Nazis came to power, Mann had begun a series of novels dealing with the Old Testament story of Joseph and his brothers, and it was with the manuscript of the second of these novels that he went into exile, first in Switzerland and later in the United States. Mann's *Joseph* books—which were to be published in succession between 1933 and 1943—set their biblical theme in a contemporary ideological context. In the character of Joseph, Mann conveyed his own image of the bourgeois humanist, wise, tolerant, and efficient—with a flavor of the welfare-state administrator. Through this mythical figure presented in modern dimensions, Mann was evidently seeking to restore to honor the humane values that the Nazis had trampled on and to express his personal solidarity with the Jewish people in their years of persecution.

Among the younger writers, it was the French and the British, rather than the Germans, who continued and broadened in the 1930s the postwar tradition of the ideological novel. Many of these writers were Marxists or "fellow travelers" on the Left—fascinated by the dynamism and revolutionary hopes of the Communists, but unwilling to subordinate their independence to the demands of Communist party discipline. Notable among the French writers who explored political themes in their fiction during this decade was André Malraux, an eloquent adventurer who had spent part of his youth in Southeast Asia and had imbibed its exoticism and spirit of revolutionary ferment. Returning to France in the late 1920s, he began a series of novels marked by graphic depictions of action and courage in times of crisis, interspersed with meditations on the

Thomas Mann (1875–1955), awarded the Nobel Prize for Literature in 1929, shown here at his writing desk. *(Courtesy Brown Brothers)*

meaning of commitment. In *Man's Fate* (1933), he portrayed the warmth of comradeship and the self-knowledge gained during a failed attempt at revolution in the Chinese city of Shanghai; in *Man's Hope* (1938), he wrote from first-hand experience of the heroism of the Republican forces in the Spanish Civil War. Though Malraux's political sympathies clearly lay with the revolutionaries and Spanish Republicans, his chief concern was less to provide a primer for activism than to explore the way in which ideals determined the choices of men and women and united them with others in the great ideological struggles of their era.

The Civil War in Spain, more than any other series of events, marked the high point of ideological commitment in the 1930s. For European intellectuals, it began on a note of hope. They regarded it as a crusade for social justice and human rights—and, like the decade, it ended in profound disillusion. This disillusion sprang from two sources—the Communist perversion of the Republican cause in Spain, and the dictator Francisco Franco's eventual victory over the Communists and their allies (see Chapter 12, III). It was a foretaste of the defeat that their ideals would suffer at the hands of the Nazis in turn, soon after Franco made good his claim to power.

Yet some refused to abandon the belief that idealism could survive the political chill now creeping across Europe. In his *Homage to Catalonia* (1938), the British writer George Orwell offered what was to become the classic account of life among the troops striving to defend Republican Spain against the forces of Franco. Orwell did not hide his disgust at the Communists or his growing war-weariness; yet at the end of his account he still maintained that what he had learned from the struggle was worthwhile. "Curiously enough," he wrote, "the whole experience has left me with not less but more belief in the decency of human beings."* Orwell's vivid rendering of his reactions to the Spanish conflict demonstrated how the writer could serve as the conscience, as well as what he termed the "unofficial historian," of Europe in a time of crisis.

III. THE RELIGIOUS REVIVAL

Quadragesimo Anno and Its Sequels

In May 1931, just as the church's struggle with Mussolini over Catholic Action was beginning, Pope Pius XI issued the encyclical *Quadragesimo Anno*. This pronouncement marked the fortieth anniversary of *Rerum Novarum*, the basic papal statement on the nature of modern industrial society, whose central principles it intended to reaffirm and bring up to date. The coming of the Great Depression had given this anniversary a burning topical interest.

Quadragesimo Anno, like its predecessor, severely criticized the capitalist order for its heartlessness and its exploitation of the working classes; it endorsed the intervention of the state to correct intolerable abuses and the association of workingmen in unions for their mutual protection and improvement. In ideological terms, it steered carefully between individualism and collectivism, between traditional liberalism—which "had already shown its utter impotence"—and socialism—which it called "a remedy much more disastrous than the evil it is designed to cure." As a substitute for both of these, it advocated harmony between classes. It was more precise about how to achieve this understanding than *Rerum Novarum* had been; among the devices it recommended were profit sharing and the establishment of "vocational groups" within each branch of the economy.

The Pope couched these recommendations in such broad terms that Catholics in diametrically opposed ideological camps could find in his words an endorsement of what they were already doing. Economic conservatives interpreted his statement about "vocational groups" to mean self-governing bodies of the corporative type associated with fascist or quasi-fascist states. Indeed, clerical-corporative rulers like Salazar and Schuschnigg argued that they were building their regimes on the very principles set forth in *Quadragesimo Anno*. On the other hand, Christian Democrats of leftist and strongly antifascist orientation found in the same encyclical support for their own advocacy of militant social action in favor of the laboring classes.

Thus *Quadragesimo Anno* faced in two directions. It served both as an endorsement for the milder forms of fascist rule and as a summons to almost revolutionary activity. At the time, the former interpretation appeared the more justified. By its attacks on liberalism and socialism, the encyclical seemed to add still another powerful voice to the chorus of condemnation of European democracy, which had been so closely associated with both of those ideologies. As the years passed, however, and the shams and deceptions of fascism and corporatism were gradually exposed, the Christian Democratic inter-

*Homage to Catalonia, new ed. (London: Secker & Warburg, 1967), 247.

Pope Pius XI (pontificate 1922–1939), who signed the Lateran Treaty with Mussolini in 1929 and two years later issued the stirring encyclical *Quadragesimo Anno*. (*Courtesy Brown Brothers*)

pretation came to predominate. Then Catholics began to stress the quiet criticism the encyclical had made of corporatism in practice—of its denial of freedom and its domination by the state. During the war years the principles of *Quadragesimo Anno*, interpreted in this fashion, inspired the Christian Democrats of France, Italy, and Germany, who played a militant role in Resistance movements. In the immediate postwar period, these same principles stimulated widespread Catholic support of the welfare state.

Such activity always stopped short of socialist measures, however, for on one point the encyclical had been categorical. Even though it distinguished European socialism from communism as far less dangerous to the proper organization of society, it had still condemned it as a "mitigated" evil. This injunction was to have important effects in the postwar period. Cooperation between Christian Democrats and Socialists—the main support on which European democracy rested in the critical years from 1944 to 1948—was always to be grudging and limited. Papal condemnation of the Socialists confirmed their suspicions of Christian Democratic "clericalism." The wall of mutual distrust was never breached—with highly damaging results for European democracy.

The Theological Aspect: French Catholicism and Protestant Neoorthodoxy

The important place that a papal pronouncement must be given in an account of social and cultural currents in the 1930s suggests the new significance that Europeans in this period began to attach to religious concerns. The ideologies of progress had usually neglected religious values; they either were hostile to religion or regarded it as of little importance to the direction of society and government. After 1930, however, as these ideologies were forced on the defensive nearly everywhere, their adherents were obliged to reconsider their attitude toward religion—or at least to take it seriously into account as a social force they had underestimated. Was it not possible, they wondered, that people were now rushing with religious fervor to embrace fascism or communism for the very reason that this emotion had earlier been thwarted and denied? Were not these militant ideologies themselves a perverted answer to a religious need? The nineteenth-century ideologies of progress had allowed men's souls to atrophy, and in the fourth decade of the twentieth century they began to pay for it.

The religious, both Catholic and Protestant, found their consciences aroused by the human suffering that the Great Depression and fascism had brought about. They realized more sharply than they had before how closely people had come to associate the Christian churches with the propertied and the well born and how, as a consequence, the urban working class had fallen away from organized religion. If the unemployed were turning by the thousands to fascism or to communism, it was partly because they felt abandoned by the churches; there were not enough priests or pastors who cared about their fate. The more socially conscious of Europe's religious leaders began to urge a great effort of re-Christianization. They preached the need of missionary activity within Europe itself to fill the spiritual void among the masses and to bring congregations back to the empty churches.

It was characteristic of the temper of the 1930s for a revival of religion to go hand in hand with a strong social conscience. The drive for social reform and the drive to restore theology to honor were often exemplified by the same individuals. This was particularly the case in France, where de-Christianization had gone furthest and where the revival of religious thinking attained the highest level. The separation of church from state in 1905 had been a harsh and vindictive measure but, in impoverishing Catholicism and driving it back on its own resources, both economic and spiritual, it had prepared the way for its rejuvenation. As opposed to the situation in Italy or Ireland, Poland or Portugal, where the church enjoyed official favor and did not need to change, in France both clergy and laity were obliged to reconsider their earlier certainties. In this respect, twentieth-century French Catholicism offered a stirring example of what the historian Arnold Toynbee called the "virtues of adversity."

Among the French religious thinkers whose influence extended far beyond the confines of their own country, three were outstanding: Gabriel Marcel, an eloquent opponent of the inhuman practices of industrial civilization; Emmanuel Mounier, founder of the left-wing Catholic review *Esprit*, in which he expressed his "personalist" solution for the crisis in European values through reasserting the central importance of human personality; and finally, Jacques Maritain, a "theologian of culture," who applied the old categories of Catholic thinking to the new problems of European politics and society. Maritain shared with Marcel an exemplary position as a convert to the Catholic faith; he shared with Mounier the fact that he had become a democrat and a leftist in his social views. These new allegiances suggest the key position of French Catholics on the eve of the Second World War as leaders both in re-Christianization and in reinterpreting the church's message in less conservative terms.

In the theological revival within the Protestant world, Germany and Switzerland took the lead. Here the most influential figure was the Swiss, Karl Barth. Just after the First World War, Barth had startled theologians with his epoch-making commentary on St. Paul's Epistle to the Romans. In 1921, he went to teach in Germany, where he remained for more than a decade until the advent of Hitler drove him back to Switzerland.

Barth's goal was to restore the fundamentals of Protestant doctrine as they had been enunciated in the sixteenth century. He was impatient with the "liberal" interpretation of dogma that more recently had come to dominance in the Calvinist and Lutheran churches. This, he argued, was merely a feeble compromise with Christian truth. It was because the clergy offered such thin fare that their congregations had deserted them. Barth's neoorthodoxy was a trumpet call for a return to first principles. It was also an appeal for the active practice of Christian charity through social endeavor among the de-Christianized working classes. Finally, it preached uncompromising opposition to all forms of tyranny. It was indicative of the moral conviction behind neoorthodoxy that the pastors of the Confessional church who resisted Hitler most actively came from among those influenced by Barth rather than from among the "liberal" theologians.

While in the West both Catholicism and Protestantism were renewing themselves, in the Soviet Union the Orthodox church was slowly succumbing to Communist pressure. From the start, the Bolsheviks had set out to destroy Christianity. Militant atheists themselves, they saw nothing but evil in the "opiate" of religion, which tried to console the poor rather than arouse them to revolutionary protest against their lot. The new rulers of Russia persecuted the church; they shut its places of worship, even sometimes turning them into antireligious museums. They taught atheism in the schools and through the Communist party. After a decade and a half, such methods brought substantial results; the Orthodox church itself, whose clergy was frequently corrupt and uneducated and whose close association with the old order had damaged its prestige, failed to arouse among the people the spontaneous response of solidarity that supported Western Catholicism or Protestantism in their periods of persecution. By the mid-1930s, the new Soviet intelligentsia had grown to maturity without religion; the regime was so sure that atheism had come to stay that it even granted the church a grudging tolerance. Orthodox Christianity in Russia had become what it was to remain for many years thereafter—the barely tolerated faith of a minority of women and old people.

IV. THE PEOPLE AND THE ARTS

The Cultural Reaction: Germany, Italy, the Soviet Union

Along with its other retrograde tendencies, nazism spelled reaction in the sphere of culture. Hitler and his henchmen rejected abstract art and experimental music, the modern style in architecture, and such novel practices as psychoanalysis. They drove the Freudians into exile—including, finally, Sigmund Freud himself who, one year before his death, was forced to leave Austria in 1938 on its annexation to the Reich. Hitler derided and hounded abroad Germany's leading artists. He imposed on the country a barren neoclassicism in painting, sculpture, and architecture. This effort was expressed in monumental form when he opened in Munich in 1937 a colossal House of German Art to contain the painting and sculpture of which he approved. Across the street, in cramped and squalid quarters, he ordered displayed as horrible examples the "decadent" art of the 1920s that he had banned. The art-loving citizens of Munich, however, jammed the "decadent" show day after day and left all but empty the echoing marble corridors of the official museum.

In Italy there reigned a similar "fascist" style. Cold, formal buildings, intended to suggest the country's imperial mission, aped the symmetry of the classical without its grace of proportion and decoration or its honesty of workmanship. Sham classicism as a cultural manifestation of fascist rule did not surprise Europeans very much—it seemed of a piece with the rest of the system. They were more surprised to see the Soviet Union turning in a similar direction. Here again, architecture took the lead. In 1931, the competition for the new Palace of the Soviets was won by a totally unimaginative and tasteless design for a neoclassic skyscraper looking rather like a wedding cake.

This turn to artistic conventionality in Russia was one aspect of the general imposition of Stalinist orthodoxy. Stalin, like Hitler, hated what was experimental or demanded an effort of understanding, so he laid down the law that architecture must follow traditional styles. Painting must be pictorial and "realistic," music must be tuneful, and writing must deal with optimistic themes calculated to inspire confidence in the workers' state. The guiding principle was "socialist realism"—a formal notion of reality that would further socialist goals, a far cry from the tolerance or even welcoming of artistic experiment that had characterized the Bolsheviks in their first years of rule. It seemed almost miraculous that works of any merit at all succeeded in emerging from such a setting. Most of them were aesthetically worthless—propagandist novels and plays; pompous oil paintings of revolutionary incidents; clumsy, overdecorated buildings. Not until after the Second World War would Soviet art and literature begin to recover from the damage suffered under the suffocating dictates of Stalinist conformity.

The Popular Arts and the Classic Age of Film

The 1930s were an era of mass entertainment on a scale that Europe had not experienced before. Radio and motion pictures, first widely disseminated during the previous decade, now attracted a mass audience of millions. Some saw in these new developments the threat of a single, commercialized culture, crushing regional variations in speech and taste beneath the weight of bland conformity. Some interpreted the growth of the mass media as an opportunity to raise the cultural standards of the nation by making fine music and theater available to all. Still others saw in radio and film a potent propaganda weapon that would weld a fragmented people into a disciplined body guided by a single will. In fact, the mass media served all these ends over the course of the decade.

Hitler and Mussolini had been quick to grasp the propaganda potential of the media and made effective use of radio speeches to mold popular support for their regimes. The Weimar movie industry soon saw its studios and actors *gleichgeschaltet* to serve the

Reich. In addition to commissioning films with patriotic or anti-Semitic themes, Hitler also entrusted the young woman director Leni Riefenstahl with the task of making documentaries of the 1934 Nazi party rally in Nuremberg and the 1936 Olympic Games in Berlin. The result was visually compelling propaganda whose aesthetic beauty masked its manipulative intent. Riefenstahl and her film crew captured the disciplined, ominous power of the Nazi ranks marching through the city of Nuremberg and the delirious welcome accorded the *Führer* in *The Triumph of the Will* (1934). Stalin, too, used motion pictures as a propaganda tool, following in this the example set by the Bolsheviks in the 1920s. From Soviet studios in 1938 came Sergei Eisenstein's brilliant epic *Alexander Nevsky*, a historical film whose action prophetically depicted the clash between Germans and Russians in war, with a musical score composed by Prokofiev.

The advent of sound endowed the films of the 1930s with greater power to move audiences than in the silent 1920s. Silent movies had been an appropriate medium for conveying the surrealists' dream fantasies, and for entertaining the public with the comic pantomimes of Charlie Chaplin; sound added the missing element needed to broaden their expressive range.

Just before the Nazis commandeered the German film industry, the director Josef von Sternberg had created *The Blue Angel* (1930), one of the first successful German sound films, starring Marlene Dietrich as a husky-voiced temptress and Emil Jannings as the aging teacher who succumbs to her charms. The film's music included cabaret songs memorably sung by Dietrich, and a background score that highlighted the dramatic closing scene. It was in France, however, that the cinema of the 1930s produced its greatest triumphs in the films of Jean Renoir, the gifted son of the impressionist painter. Renoir's principal theme was French society and its class antagonisms. In *The Grand Illusion*, class differences are overcome when both officers and enlisted men join to help the planned escape succeed. Three years later, however, in *The Rules of the Game* (1939), Renoir showed the French social order on the brink of collapse. A hunting weekend at a French chateau became the occasion for romantic rivalries and violence resulting from the characters' failure to respect the rules of the film's title. Like Eisenstein's *Alexander Nevsky*, *The Rules of the Game* conveyed a premonition of a grim future that was soon to be confirmed. In films such as these, and in the directors who conceived them, Europeans were to discover in retrospect a classic age of film.

In addition to film, the popular arts in the 1930s embraced jazz (imported from America) and cabaret theater. Jazz rhythms and sonorities inspired the German composer Kurt Weill, who turned from austere classical music to a jaunty, acerbic idiom when collaborating with the playwright Bertolt Brecht on *The Three-Penny Opera* (1928). Brecht's words and Weill's music transformed the plot of the English eighteenth-century *Beggars' Opera* into a spectacle adapted to the contemporary milieu of postwar Germany—it was bright, it was cynical, it was full of bitter social satire. It was also a huge success. Brecht and Weill repeated their partnership in the opera *Mahagonny* (1930), but in Germany's changed political climate, their satire against bourgeois values now drew bitter attacks. With Hitler's rise to power, theater was no longer permitted to traffic in left-wing politics, and both Brecht and Weill were soon forced to take the road of exile.

The success of *The Three-Penny Opera*—which not only was a popular triumph in its stage and film versions but also won "highbrow" acclaim—suggests the new attitude toward art and entertainment that was to gather strength during the 1930s. Since the end of the war, artists had sought a broader audience and had aspired to transform society through their art. The Bauhaus was only the most visible attempt to place the products of high culture within reach of a mass public. But Weill's music and Renoir's films incorporated influences from "lowbrow" spheres as well. The balance was not always a comfortable one, and many artists at length despaired of meeting the demands of mass taste while still remaining true to their own standards. Yet both the socially conscious temper of the 1930s and the search for new sources of artistic inspiration combined to ensure a commitment to increased communication between the artist and a widening public.

READINGS

For an analysis of French social thought in this period, see H. Stuart Hughes, *The Obstructed Path* (1968). Laura Fermi, in *Illustrious Immigrants: The Intellectual Migration from Europe, 1930–41* (1968), traces the experience of the anti-fascist emigration. Lescek Kolakowski, in *Main Currents of Marxism*, vol. 3: *The Breakdown* (1978), duscusses the development of neo-Marxist theory over the past half century, while James Joll's *Gramsci** (1977) is a succinct, balanced appraisal of one of its most creative exponents. For a sympathetic introduction to the work of the leading economist of the period, see Robert Skidelsky's magisterial *John Maynard Keynes*, Vol. I: *Hopes Betrayed, 1883–1920* (1986); *John Maynard Keynes*, Vol. II: *The Economist as Savior, 1920–1937* (1992); and *John Maynard Keynes*, Vol. III: *Fighting for Freedom, 1937–1946* (2002). An overview of his life, work, and subsequent influence is Robert Lekachman's *The Age of Keynes** (1966).

In the field of imaginative literature, Henry C. Hatfield, *Modern German Literature** (1966), traces the careers of the most influential German writers, and Henri Peyre, *The Contemporary French Novel** (1955), deals with parallel developments in France. Herbert R. Lottman, *The Left Bank* (1982), discusses in its early chapters the Parisian cultural milieu at the time of the Popular Front, while André Malraux's contribution to the literature of engagement is analyzed in David O. Wilkinson's *Malraux: An Essay in Political Criticism* (1967). Bernard Crick's *George Orwell: A Life** (1980) presents the best detailed introduction to the writer's work; Raymond Williams's *George Orwell** (1971) is brief but insightful. The theological revival is covered in a selection of texts with brief introductions by Will Herberg, ed., *Four Existentialist Theologians* (1958).

For Hitler's impact on officially sanctioned art and architecture in Germany, besides Mosse, Hinz, and Lane (see readings for Chapter 9), there is Robert R. Taylor, *The Word in Stone: The Role of Architecture in the National Socialist Ideology* (1974). For Soviet cultural policy and the effects of "socialist realism" on the arts, see the relevant chapters in Orlando Figes, *Natasha's Dance: A Cultural History of Russia* (2002); Sheila Kirkpatrick, ed., *Cultural Revolution in Russia, 1928–31** (1978); and Edward J. Brown, *Russian Literature Since the Revolution,** rev. ed. (1969). Andrei Sinyavsky, *Soviet Civilization: A Cultural History* (1988, trans. 1990) offers a penetrating view of Soviet ideals and their effects on culture by a noted dissident writer.

*Books marked with an asterisk are available in paperback.

For a penetrating survey of the most important of the new popular arts, see Gerald Mast, *A Short History of the Movies*, 4th ed. (1986). More specialized works include Siegfried Kracauer's classic *From Calagari to Hitler: A Psychological History of the German Film** (1947); David S. Hall, *Film in the Third Reich* (1969); and the fine study by Alexander Sesonke, *Jean Renoir: The French Films, 1924–1939** (1980). The medium viewed by a pioneer is presented in the essays of Sergei Eisenstein, *Film Form** (1949), ed. Jay Leyda.

12

THE ROAD
TO CATASTROPHE,
1935–1939

A bomb explodes in a Madrid street in 1937 during the Spanish Civil War—a conflict that was to prove the prelude to an even greater struggle two years later. (*Courtesy AP/Wide World Photos*)

Contrary to the First World War, whose origins were extremely complex and responsibility for which was spread among a number of nations, the Second World War was the work of one man, Adolf Hitler. Of Europe's national leaders, Hitler alone brought about the conflict. The only serious controversy among historians has occurred over the question of whether or not he wanted to accomplish his purposes by war and precipitated it at a moment of his own choosing. Certainly Hitler had no clear timetable. The documents alleged to present such a schedule are contradictory both with each other and with the actual course of events, and it seems plausible that (like most statesmen) he would have preferred to get his way without resort to arms. He embarked on his earlier adventures uncertain as to exactly how far he would go and prepared to withdraw if international opposition became too intense. In addition, a gradual abdication of responsibility by the French and a peculiarly inept alternation between conciliation and resistance on the part of the British played directly into his hands.

When all this has been said, however, the fact remains that Hitler's goals at the very least involved the subjugation of three European nations—Austria, Czechoslovakia, and Poland—and that by the time he had gotten to the third of these, the French and British had no idea where he would stop. The *Führer* made no secret of the fact that restless expansion and eventual hegemony over Europe were essential to the Nazi dynamic. And after his initial gambles had succeeded, he was quite frank about stating (both in public and in private) that he would not shrink from war in the future. No other national leader was anywhere near as determined a bully as he. All the others whose aggressiveness or ineptitude encouraged the drift toward war—even Mussolini—were only auxiliaries in the process.

The war was the climax of five years of blundering and bluff, of the irresolute diplomacy of the Western powers pitted against Hitler's demonic force and unswerving dedication to his goal. Its main origins lay in the successive stages of Nazi expansion. Yet the most important single series of episodes was the Spanish Civil War—that tragic prelude to the major international conflict—in which Hitler played only a secondary part and in which the chief actors and sufferers were the Spanish themselves.

I.   REARMAMENT AND THE RHINELAND

The first major act of aggression breaking the false calm of the post-Locarno years came in 1931, not from Germany, but from Japan, with the conquest of Manchuria (in northeastern China). Six years later, this conquest was to expand into an undeclared war against China and eventually to merge into the Pacific phase of the Second World War itself.

The failure of the League of Nations to stop the Japanese advance, though little noted by Europeans at the time, was an ominous sign of the inability of international bodies to halt a determined aggressor. A League mission undertaken by the British Lord Lytton in 1932 attempted an even-handed approach by condemning the Japanese invasion, while at the same time recommending a compromise which granted limited autonomy to Manchuria in exchange for guarantees of Japanese economic rights in the region. Yet when the League Assembly adopted the terms of Lytton's report in February, 1933, the Japanese delegation stalked out—a rebuff to which the League proved powerless to respond.

The Vogue of "Collective Security": Barthou and Litvinov

In the early 1930s, the League's weakness was not nearly so obvious as it was to appear in retrospect. Indeed, the three years between Hitler's appointment as German chancellor in early 1933 and the last decisive action in the League's history at the end of 1935 were a period of intense interest in maintaining peace through the collective action of the European powers.

This vogue of what came to be called "collective security" was partly based on illusion. Millions of peace-minded people in the democracies of the West hoped that it would be possible to restrain the Nazis through moral pressure alone. It was also based on the fact that Hitler's coming to power required three years to produce its logical results; the new international alignment had not yet crystallized. In 1933 and 1934, the two fascist powers still stood far apart, and the pattern of Nazi expansion was as yet unrevealed. The other European powers did not know how seriously to take Hitler's frantic rhetoric. They still did not realize that he meant quite literally the program for German domination of Europe that he had outlined in *Mein Kampf*.

At the start, moreover, Hitler tried to reassure the statesmen of Europe. However he might bluster at home, his diplomats spoke more suavely abroad, leaving their listeners with the impression that the new German regime would be modest in its demands. True, Hitler's predecessors, Brüning and Papen, had already succeeded in removing the worst of the burdens that the Treaty of Versailles had laid on the German people: Six months before the Nazis came to power, reparations had disappeared. When Mussolini proposed that the French and British join with him in a Four-Power Pact with Hitler to maintain the peace, there seemed to be no good reason for refusing. In July 1933, such a pact was in fact solemnly signed. In retrospect its clauses sound strangely irrelevant. The final text of the treaty merely reaffirmed the spirit of the 1920s by engaging each power to continue to respect its undertakings under the Covenant of the League and the Locarno Treaty.

Two months later the Germans cast off the mask. In October, Hitler announced that he was withdrawing both from the Disarmament Conference—whose nearly two years of labor had failed to produce a satisfactory formula for German military equality—and from the League of Nations. These two actions produced a preliminary awakening on the part of Europe's statesmen—the first of a series of brusque shocks that were to punctuate the history of the next six years. In France, Hitler's moves occasioned only passing activity; in the Soviet Union, they produced a major policy change.

In Paris—as a side effect of the riots of February 1934 and of the formation of Doumergue's government of national union—for the first time since Briand's retirement there came to power a foreign minister with a clear notion of his goals. Louis Barthou was an elder statesman and a solid republican of conservative views. His foreign policy was simple: to build a wall against Nazi expansion by strengthening France's alliances in East Central Europe. By associating the Poles and the members of the Little Entente still more closely with France's policy, he hoped to convince Hitler that aggression would not pay. Barthou had barely begun this reconstruction of his country's alliance system when he was killed in October 1934. His death seriously weakened the policy he had personified; under Premiers Flandin and Laval, the French foreign ministry showed less determination to resist Hitler's international aims.

To the Soviet Union, on the contrary, German withdrawal from the League came as a heaven-sent opportunity to gain international respectability and a measure of security against German expansionist aims in Eastern Europe. Germany had not been a year absent from that body when, in September 1934, partly owing to Barthou's persuasions, Russia joined the organization that in the previous decade had kept it in quarantine. The moral seemed clear: With Germany out and Russia in, who could doubt which country was the more devoted to peace? The Soviet representative at Geneva, Maxim Litvinov, underlined the lesson by preaching more strenuously than anyone else the doctrine of collective security. Litvinov was an Old Bolshevik of the international type; with an English wife and strong ties to the West, he was ideally equipped to present Soviet policy in a new and attractive guise. This change helps explain the appeal of the Popular Front and the prestige that Russia enjoyed among European democrats in the years 1934–1936.

The First Breaches of the Versailles and Locarno Treaties

In March 1935, Hitler formally announced that he would no longer abide by the disarmament clauses of the Treaty of Versailles. He restored the system of peacetime conscription that Germany had employed up to 1918 and that characterized such important continental powers as France, Italy, and the Soviet Union. There was a certain consistency in Hitler's contention that he was merely trying to raise Germany to a position of equality with other European nations. By their failure to disarm, he implied, they had themselves made German rearmament inevitable.

Partly for this reason, the reaction to Germany's unilateral action was relatively mild. Clandestine German rearmament had been going on for years before Hitler came to power; the only novelty in the 1935 declaration was the reintroduction of conscription. The League of Nations, of course, condemned the action. A week before the League meeting, representatives of France, Britain, and Italy, in a conference at the Italian lakeside resort of Stresa, had agreed on common action against the German menace, but this "Stresa Front" proved as transitory as the other Italian initiative in international affairs, Mussolini's Four-Power Pact.

In the meantime, Italy had continued preparations for the conquest of Ethiopia. With the powers divided and their attention riveted on Africa, Hitler was in an excellent position to take decisive action once more. On March 7, 1936—scarcely a year after his denunciation of the disarmament clauses in the Versailles Treaty—he sent German troops into the Rhineland cities that the same treaty had demilitarized. They were greeted by delirious crowds: At last Germany seemed to have attained full international equality. Hitler waited, nervously wondering whether his gamble would succeed.

But the French army did not move. Although it was still stronger than the German, its strategy had become exclusively defensive, and it was quite unprepared to march into the Reich. The government, moreover, was weak and hesitant, merely trying to muddle through the remaining few weeks until the May elections that would bring the Popular Front to power. The Italians were alienated; the British were unimpressed; in the end the French and the League of Nations itself were reduced to ineffective protests against this breach not only of the Treaty of Versailles, which Germany had accepted under duress, but of the Locarno Pact, to which the Reich had freely consented.

Hitler's troops stayed in the Rhineland. The first—and the best—opportunity for nipping Nazi aggression in the bud had been lost. After the crucial year 1936, it would be too late.

II. THE ETHIOPIAN WAR

Meanwhile, the other fascist dictator, Benito Mussolini, had finally given free rein to the vocation for conquest, which he had been talking about for a decade and a half, but until now had prudently held in check. No doubt the example of Hitler helped to spur him on. The effect of Mussolini's actions in 1935 and 1936 was certainly to bring about the alignment of his country with Nazi Germany, an alignment the British and French had earlier been fortunate enough to avoid.

Italy's Imperial Disappointments

In the scramble for Africa at the end of the nineteenth century, Italy had gained the least. Repulsed by the forces of the emperor of Ethiopia in 1896, the Italians had been obliged to content themselves with two barren strips of coastline in East Africa and the equally barren shore of Libya, which they had added in 1911. This was a meager "empire." Along with Italy's disappointments at the Paris Peace Conference, the memory of colonial repulses had rankled all through the 1920s in the minds of Italian nationalists.

The continued independence of Ethiopia seemed to stand as a permanent taunt to Italy's martial valor and abilities as a colonial power. The great defeat of 1896—one of the worst that Europeans had ever suffered at the hands of "natives"—clamored for vengeance. Since the French acquisition of Morocco in 1912, Ethiopia had ranked as the only important area in Africa which had never submitted to colonial conquest. What could be more natural, then, than for Mussolini to set out to occupy nearly forty years later the great mountain empire that Italians had so long regarded as rightfully theirs?

The European attitude toward colonial wars, however, had changed. The better part of a generation had passed without further acquisition of colonies. Indeed, the tide had turned. With native nationalist movements springing up in so many parts of Asia and Africa, the problem for Europeans was now to hold what they already had rather than to acquire new territories. Along with increased difficulty in ruling the colonies had come a new guilt about doing so at all; the Socialist parties in particular were turning to a militant anticolonialism. Mussolini was much mistaken when he thought that other Europeans would regard an Italian war of conquest in the 1930s as casually as they would have in the 1890s. Colonial war no longer was what everybody else was doing.

The Consequences: The End of the League and the Rome-Berlin Axis

On October 3, Italy had launched its invasion of Ethiopia. Within little more than a week, the Council of the League had declared Italy an aggressor, and its Assembly had voted economic sanctions in the form of embargoes under the terms of Article 16 of the Covenant. On November 18—four days after the British election—sanctions actually went into effect. In Europe, opinion seemed united against Italy and behind the League, and in Ethiopia the emperor's forces were putting up a stout resistance.

But this was not the end of the story. Despite the League's decision, Britain and France still refused to impose the one form of sanctions that would really hurt, an embargo on oil. Britain seemed bellicose—at one point its Mediterranean fleet was even put on the alert—yet it did nothing decisive. France was even less militant, the French Right arguing quite sensibly that with German power growing, it was folly to antagonize Italy. The sanctions that the League had voted in the autumn proved ineffective, or perhaps even worse than ineffective, since they infuriated Mussolini by denying him much-needed goods, but failed to cripple his war effort. By the spring of 1936, the Italians had

The strength and determination of the Axis powers in 1937 is triumphantly displayed as Hitler and Mussolini review a German labor corps. (*Courtesy Brown Brothers*)

broken Ethiopian resistance. On May 5, they marched into the capital, Addis Ababa, and a few days later Mussolini bestowed on his king the new title of emperor.

Such was the first real war that Europe had known since the sequels to the First World War had come to an end in 1922. The Ethiopian conflict introduced four years of alarms following closely one on another until at last the major European powers themselves went to war. More important, it ended one international institution and inaugurated another. It killed the League. The failure of sanctions against Italy was too flagrant to be explained away by the pious phrases of internationalism; after 1936, it was impossible to consider the League seriously as an instrumentality for keeping the peace. Simultaneously with the disappearance of Geneva as a center of influence in foreign affairs, there emerged a new alignment between Fascist Italy and Nazi Germany. Almost overnight, what came to be called the Rome-Berlin Axis took its place as the strongest force in Europe. Their experience of French and British hostility—of being considered one after the other the bad boys of Europe—finally drove the two fascist leaders together. The Rome-Berlin Axis did not come into effect officially until the following October, but by the summer of 1936 it already existed in fact—as the next great international crisis, the outbreak of the Spanish Civil War, was so amply to prove.

III.   THE SPANISH CIVIL WAR

The Origins: Alfonso XIII and the Dictatorship of Primo de Rivera

Spain's twentieth-century time of troubles began with its defeat by the United States in the war of 1898. The Spanish-American War destroyed the last lingering illusions about the country's traditional greatness. It not only stripped Spain of nearly all its colonies and ended what remained of its great-power status; it also revealed how many aspects of the national life were corrupt or decayed or functioning badly.

The war exposed in all its nakedness the selfishness and inefficiency of the small minority of wealthy or aristocratic people who, behind the façade of a constitutional monarchy, actually ruled the nation. The war also became the starting point for mounting revolutionary agitation in three distinct forms. There was first the working-class movement, which came later to Spain than to France or Italy, since Spanish industrialization was less far advanced. Then there was the growing demand for autonomy in areas whose speech and tradition differed from the dominant Castilian, more particularly in the two regions bordering on France, the Basque provinces to the west and Catalonia to the east. Finally, there was a marked resurgence of anticlericalism, which directed its attacks against the vast wealth that the Catholic Church had acquired in the last quarter of the nineteenth century.

These three currents of discontent converged in the city of Barcelona, the Catalan capital. Enterprising, modern, oriented toward France—with its speech in fact very close to the ancient language of the southern French—Barcelona epitomized the new or centrifugal energies that were threatening to tear apart the traditional Spanish state. In

1909, the city was shaken by five days of wild rioting and convent burning. Thus a quarter of a century before the Civil War the pattern was already established that would make Barcelona the focal point of autonomist, anticlerical, working-class protest during Spain's years of fratricidal struggle.

Spain avoided involvement in the First World War. But isolation from the rest of Europe during the great conflict intensified its existing difficulties by creating a boom in certain sectors of its economy and a depression in others. Meanwhile the military had seized control. They were encouraged by the reigning sovereign, Alfonso XIII, who had been a king literally since the day of his birth and who cherished anachronistic ideas of the possibilities of monarchy in the twentieth century. Alfonso hoped that if the parliamentary constitution were destroyed, he would become the real power in the country. Hence he did nothing to oppose the military coup d'état that brought General Miguel Primo de Rivera to power in September 1923.

Primo de Rivera was not prepared to merely serve the king, however—he wanted to rule Spain himself. Unfortunately, he had no clear notion of what he intended to accomplish once in power. Aside from aligning the country diplomatically with Fascist Italy, he allowed it to drift; under the surface of a military dictatorship, Spanish life remained as anarchic and invertebrate as before. Finally, the king himself grew tired of his "strong man." In January 1930 he dismissed him, and the majority of Spaniards rejoiced. But when two months later Primo de Rivera died in Paris, the full consequences of his dismissal descended on Alfonso's head. With the dictator gone and buried, the Spanish had lost the target of their hatred, and they turned on the king instead. In response, Alfonso announced the restoration of the constitution and, as an initial token of the return of liberty, scheduled the election of municipal councillors for mid-April 1931.

The election campaign quickly mounted into a full-scale national consultation. The leaders of the various republican parties—whose strength had grown steadily in the last half decade—concerted their efforts and converted the municipal elections into an informal plebiscite on the monarchy. When polling day came, they had already won over the cities. While urban areas voted almost solidly for republican candidates, the countryside remained generally monarchist. Yet the vote of Madrid and Barcelona and the other major centers made the greatest impression. Shaken by what appeared to be a tidal wave of opposition, the king left the country without abdicating. On April 14, 1931, the Spanish Republic was proclaimed.

The Republic: Azaña, Gil Robles, and the Election of 1936

It was easier to proclaim a republic than to make it a reality. The Constituent Assembly, or Cortes, which assembled in July, was divided at least four ways in its interpretation of what the new regime meant. To the left were those who wanted social revolution; to the left of center was the party of Republican Action, liberal moderates who followed the one true statesman whom the revolution produced, Manuel Azaña; then came the scheming and corrupt party of the Radicals; finally on the right were the clericals, who accepted the Republic in their public professions but despised it in their hearts.

For the first two years of the Republic's history, under Azaña's leadership, the new regime seemed to be making some progress in developing a coherent program out of these contrasting tendencies. Azaña's government acted constructively. It curbed the army, granted autonomy to Catalonia and to the Basque provinces, and stimulated popular education. But it failed to take the dramatic action toward breaking up the great estates of the south and the southwest that would have stirred the popular imagination; during 1932 and 1933, land reform proceeded at a very slow pace. And by their army reforms, Azaña's ministers brought down upon themselves and upon the Republic the implacable opposition of the military. A revolt of high-ranking army officers in August 1932—which the government suppressed without difficulty—gave a foretaste of the far graver threat that was to come four years later.

At the end of 1933, with the dissolution of the Constituent Assembly, the first elections for a regular Cortes returned a conservative majority. There followed the *bienio negro*—the "black" two years of clerical reaction. As the government and the Cortes began to reveal their true colors—as they undid one by one the reforms of the Azaña era—it became apparent that the most powerful man in the country was now the clerical leader, José Maria Gil Robles. Under Robles's skillful prodding Spain was moving toward the quasi-fascism that already existed in Portugal and that in these very years was being established in Austria.

To stop this threat, the parties of the Left and Left-Center banded together for the elections of February 1936. As their counterparts in France were simultaneously doing, they formed a Popular Front that embraced groups ranging from the Azaña type to revolutionary Socialists and Anarcho-Syndicalists. This coalition won a narrow victory, and Azaña's friends now returned to power. For a moment it seemed as though Spain was merely returning to the situation that had existed before the reaction set in at the end of 1933.

But to believe that was to mistake the dynamics of the Popular Front. The electoral campaign had released a great wave of revolutionary enthusiasm, which was not to be stopped by prudent counsels of moderation. The extreme left parties in the victorious coalition had not formed its majority—but they had provided its fighting force. And this was driving toward social revolution. Brushing aside the temperate policies of Azaña and his like, the Left took matters into its own hands and resorted to direct action. In the spring of 1936, land seizures, revolutionary strikes, and even murder became everyday occurrences; outrages against churches and the clergy grew more and more frequent. In reaction, army leaders and the conservatives raised the standard of counterrevolution and began that summer to converge on Madrid.

The Civil War: The Military Aspect

The Spanish Civil War can be regarded from at least three different standpoints. It can be treated as a civil war in the narrower sense—a desperate, bloody struggle, which lasted nearly three years and periodically bogged down in a trench stalemate not unlike that which the First World War produced. It can be viewed as an international conflict—a dress rehearsal for the Second World War. Finally, it can be seen as a battle of ideologies—a social revolution aborted not only by the forces of military and clerical reaction but also, in paradoxical fashion, by a party that itself professed revolutionary aims, the Spanish Communists and their Soviet chiefs. The Spanish Civil War was each and all of these.

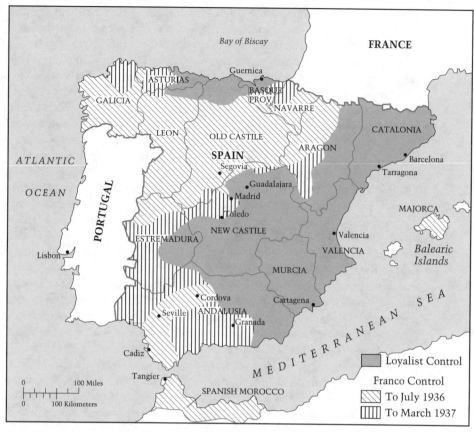

MAP 12.1 The Spanish Civil War.

From the military standpoint, the Civil War began on July 17 with the revolt of an important garrison in Spanish Morocco and the arrival of General Francisco Franco from the Canary Islands to take command. The next day, a number of mainland generals took up arms. The insurgent forces rapidly dominated the south and west—the more backward half of the country—and this remained throughout the war the headquarters of their strength. But it was in Burgos, to the north, that at the end of July they set up their Junta of National Defense, which ten weeks later named General Franco chief (*Caudillo*) of the Spanish state.

Franco himself was a wily man, small, heavy-set, and imperturbable in manner. His leadership of the Nationalist cause had come about somewhat accidentally; the more prominent general who was scheduled to direct the movement had been killed in an airplane accident just at its start. But once installed in power, Franco proved well equipped to bind together the heterogeneous coalition that was assaulting the Republic. With no clear ideology of his own, except hatred for the Republic and respect for tradition and discipline, Franco was sufficiently skeptical of all ideologies to take his own followers no more seriously than they deserved, particularly the Spanish fascist party, the Falange, which provided much of the drive and enthusiasm behind the Nationalist cause but certainly did not account for the bulk of its strength. The majority of Franco's followers came, rather, from the various monarchist factions, and more generally, from landowners and propertied people and those loyal to the Catholic church.

By November, the Nationalists—who began the war with the great advantage of having most of the regular army on their side—had reduced the defenders of the Republic to approximately the positions they were to occupy for the next two years. The Republicans were holding at bay the forces besieging Madrid, from which the government had fled to the east coast city of Valencia. Farther north along the coast, Barcelona ranked as the third major center of Republican loyalty. A fourth area of strength, but isolated from the others, was the Basque provinces, conservative by tradition, but which had thrown in their lot with the Republic in an effort to preserve their newly won autonomy. The Republican forces were thus on the defensive nearly everywhere (see Map 12.1).

The Republican coalition was as ill assorted as the one which Franco led. Once the war began—more particularly, once the government decided to arm the workers for its defense—control slipped from the hands of the moderate democrats. In early September, the appointment as prime minister of the leftwing Socialist Francisco Largo Caballero marked the triumph within the Republican camp of the forces pressing for social revolution. But even the revolutionary Left was much divided: Besides the Socialists, there were the Communists, the Trotskyite POUM,* and the Anarcho-Syndicalists. The last of these represented the strongest single power among the Spanish people—a force characterized by spontaneous revolutionary enthusiasm and a wild cult of liberty. In Catalonia in particular, the Anarcho-Syndicalist drive reinforced the Catalan autonomist spirit to make the city of Barcelona the focus of revolutionary sentiment on the Republican side.

In this fashion—after the original momentum of Franco's forces had been stopped—the war settled into something approaching a stalemate, in which intervention from outside, and with it the pressure of foreign ideology on both camps, was gradually to change the character of the Civil War almost beyond recognition.

The Civil War: Foreign Intervention

It was obvious from the beginning that the two fascist powers, Italy and Germany, sympathized with the Nationalist insurgents. It was equally obvious that Léon Blum's new government in France sympathized with the sister Popular Front that was defending itself across the Pyrenees. Although Hitler and Mussolini actively aided Franco's cause, the French Popular Front restricted itself to semiclandestine encouragement of the shipment of war materials to Madrid and Barcelona. In this difference of policy lay the crucial difficulty that eventually was to spell ruin for the Spanish Republic.

Italy and Germany scarcely made a secret of what they were doing. Under the guise of "volunteers," Mussolini even sent regular ground troops to swell Franco's forces; Hitler limited himself to providing aviation and tank units and other specialist personnel—using Spain as a proving ground for testing his new military equipment. On his orders, the Condor Legion of the German airforce destroyed the defenseless Basque town of Guernica with saturation bombing in April, 1937, killing hundreds of innocent civilians.

*Partido Obrero de Unificación Marxista (Workers' Party of Marxist Unity).

A stolid General Francisco Franco gives the fascist salute to parading troops during the Spanish Civil War. *(Courtesy Corbis-Bettmann)*

(This brutal act inspired Pablo Picasso to paint one of the century's most powerful pictures, entitled simply "Guernica," in protest at the carnage.)

Against all this the British protested vigorously. With a conservative government in power and the people profoundly divided over Spain, Britain's leaders tried to steer a strictly neutral course. One reason, in turn, that the French government found it impossible to aid the Spanish Republic was Britain's neutral stand. The French hesitated to take more active measures without British support. In addition, France itself was grievously divided. Indeed, the Spanish Civil War was paralleled by a "cold civil war" among the French people. Partisans and enemies of the Popular Front lined up in similar fashion in their attitude toward Spain and found in its armed conflict a projection of their own domestic struggle. Faced with this bitterness and division of feeling among the French people, Blum could take no decisive action. After his fall in June 1937, his successors were even less concerned than he had been for the fate of the Spanish Republic.

With the default of France, the role of protector of the Spanish Republic devolved on the Soviet Union. The Russians were slower than the Italians or the Germans to intervene in the Spanish Civil War; they did not act until October 1936. But when they did, it was as massively as geographical remoteness and limitations of transport permitted. Like Hitler, Stalin sent no ground troops, but he provided war materials of all sorts, plus technical advisers, pilots, drivers—and political commissars. The last of these, who came from among the leaders of both Soviet and Western European communism, had as their task not only to advise and guide the Spanish Republic but also to indoctrinate the International Brigades, which first went into action in November 1936 in the defense of Madrid.

The International Brigades consisted of volunteers in the true rather than in the Italian sense. Those who enrolled in them were mostly young idealists of democratic or leftist convictions—antifascist émigrés from Italy or Germany and also Englishmen and Americans. Just over half were Communists when they enlisted, but since Communists served as the political commissars of the Brigades, a larger number fell under Communist ideological influence during their Spanish service. The historical importance of the International Brigades extended far beyond their strictly military role. Their chief significance was in swelling the legend of the Civil War as a struggle for democracy and in sustaining the sympathy for the Spanish Republic among Western European intellectuals that so strongly marked the literary atmosphere of the late 1930s. For Italian antifascists there was also the stirring memory of the defeat they helped inflict on Mussolini's "volunteers" at Guadalajara in the spring of 1937. In the minds of Italians, still more than in those of the French, the Spanish Civil War provided a welcome arena for fighting out domestic quarrels on foreign soil.

On both sides, foreign intervention changed the character of the opposing coalitions. Mussolini's and Hitler's help brought Franco closer to fascism; Stalin's aid to the Republic gave its defense a Communist tone that had been almost wholly absent at the beginning. Influence from abroad operated most unevenly in the two camps. In Franco's case, it was not decisive. Despite his dependence on Italy and Germany, the *Caudillo* kept the Nationalist movement firmly in hand, and its essentially Spanish character remained intact. With the Republic, it was quite different: President Azaña and Prime Minister Largo Caballero found it impossible to resist Soviet pressure. They had no recourse; no other champion had come forward. As they became ever more dependent on Russian and Communist aid, they found their cause perverted and at the last almost completely deprived of its spontaneous Spanish character.

The Civil War: The Ideological Transformation

Soviet intervention in the Spanish Civil War had the opposite effect from what might have been anticipated. It did not strengthen the forces of social revolution; rather, it stopped the revolution in its tracks by sacrificing everything else to the goals of military efficiency and international respectability.

At the beginning of the war, the workers in a number of areas had taken matters into their own hands by seizing control of factories, landed estates, and even commercial enterprises. The arrival of Soviet "advisers" halted all this, for Stalin had decreed a policy of no socialism in Spain in an effort to reassure the Spanish middle class and Western "capitalist" opinion. Abroad, this pragmatic and even cynical policy failed. The "modernization" that the Soviet Union imposed in Spain was so obviously calculated that it carried little conviction to Western conservatives. It merely disillusioned a number of Republican sympathizers like George Orwell, who returned home bitterly disappointed with the treatment that the Spanish revolutionaries had received. Within Spain, it stimulated the growth of a peculiar sort of communism. At the beginning of the war, the Spanish Communists had been insignificant. Now, with the possibilities of protection that Soviet aid afforded, large numbers enrolled in the Communist party. It became an ideological catchall and a refuge for the timorous and the opportunistic.

Meanwhile within the government, some middle-class political leaders began to cooperate with the Spanish Communists against Prime Minister Largo Caballero. For this strange alliance there were compelling practical arguments. The Soviet and Communist organizers were the only people in Spain who could provide the bureaucratic competence and the military discipline that the Republic required if it was ever to survive against its better trained enemies; moreover, as the indispensable source of funds and supplies, Stalin's deputies had an unanswerable argument for getting the last word.

In the early months of 1937, Communist influence spread relentlessly throughout Republican Spain. On the fighting fronts, units of the Communist-trained People's Army began to replace the less disciplined workers' militia. The showdown between the two came in the streets of Barcelona at the beginning of May. After three days of sporadic fighting, the revolutionary formations of the POUM and the Anarcho-Syndicalists were overwhelmed. The POUM was dissolved and its leaders imprisoned or killed, while the representatives of the Anarcho-Syndicalists were dropped from the government. Thereafter, until the end of the war, the Soviet Union and the Communists were firmly in control. With bourgeois politicians cooperating with them, they used their dominance of the army, the police, and the propaganda department to mold according to their own desires the whole Republican cause.

Franco's Victory and the Balance Sheet of Terror

In mid-1938, the Soviet Union decided to abandon the Spanish Republic. The policy of moderation, Stalin realized, was not working; it had not persuaded the great Western democracies to come to the help of Spain. Hence he determined to cut his losses and to abandon the struggle. Although few realized it at the time, this decision appears as the first sign of Soviet disillusionment with the four-year-old policy of Western orientation, of "collective security" and Popular Fronts, that would lead eventually to a cynical settlement with the Nazis in August 1939.

With the end of Soviet aid to the Republic, Franco's armies broke the stalemate and began to roll once more toward victory. In December 1938 they mounted their great offensive against Catalonia. The following January, Barcelona fell; Madrid and Valencia,

A Loyalist soldier carries a comrade wounded during the Spanish Civil War. (*Courtesy Robert Capa/Magnum Photos, Inc.*)

whose position was now hopeless, fought on until the end of March. With their fall, the Civil War ended. Hundreds of thousands of Republican soldiers and refugees poured over the Pyrenees to a miserable life of internment in France.

Franco had won, and the quasi-fascist government he had established was recognized by the Western democracies. Although France and Britain and the United States bowed to the accomplished fact, within those countries debate over the Civil War continued to rage. Those who had favored Franco spoke of his followers as "Christian crusaders" against "bolshevism." The far more numerous apologists for the Republic depicted the latter's struggle as a fight for democracy, for a legal and popularly chosen regime pitted against the forces of reaction and military tyranny.

Both of these views were gross simplifications. Neither reflected the realities of the Spanish situation, in which the usual categories of Western ideological debate simply did not apply. The legal argument was largely meaningless. The election of 1936 had been very close, and following it the left parties in the Popular Front had made no secret of their intention to break all legal norms by launching a social revolution. Nor, on the other hand, was it realistic to depict as virtuous warriors of the church the soldiers of General Franco who murdered wherever they went. Indeed, the atrocities on both sides were sickening. The war was without pity for prisoners or civilians. On the Republican side, the killing of priests and nuns at the start of the war and Communist terror against leftist dissidents at war's end added the horrors of sacrilege to the miserable spectacle of a revolution devouring its own children. But the Nationalists slaughtered more than the Republicans. To the 600,000 victims who perished during the war itself, Franco added an additional 50,000 summarily executed as Communist sympathizers and a million more thrown into prison or concentration camp at its close.

The Spanish Civil War can be described most succinctly as a class struggle in which the rich defeated the poor. The majority of the Spanish people doubtless were only helpless bystanders. Yet it was quite apparent that the Republic had more popular support than did Franco. As evidence one need only point to the fact that despite the aid of the regular army, and the massive help they received from Mussolini and Hitler, the Nationalists needed nearly three years to win. Moreover, although the Civil War was not a struggle *for* Western democracy, Franco's victory represented a major defeat for democratic values throughout Europe. While the democratic powers had shown themselves weak and vacillating in their attitude toward Spain, the fascist states had stood strong and united. This was to be further demonstrated in the next great international crisis—the German annexation of Austria—which erupted when the Civil War in Spain had run but a little more than half its course.

IV. THE FALL OF AUSTRIA AND CZECHOSLOVAKIA

The Anschluss of 1938

After two years of deceptive quiet and a steady increase of armed strength at home, in March 1938 Hitler struck again. He sent his tanks rolling into Austria, which succumbed without a fight. The next day the country was formally annexed to the German Reich.

The *Anschluss* had been preceded by a month of intense pressure on the Austrian government. On February 12, Hitler had summoned Chancellor Schuschnigg to his Bavarian mountain retreat at Berchtesgaden and, after long hours of table-pounding and invective, bullied him into submission. Schuschnigg agreed to an amnesty for imprisoned Austrian Nazis and to appoint a Nazi as his minister of the interior. In short, he was bludgeoned by Hitler's "Trojan Horse" tactics into opening the way to slow absorption of his country by its powerful neighbor.

On his return to Vienna, however, Schuschnigg's attitude stiffened. He reaffirmed his intention of maintaining Austria's independence and began to mobilize public sentiment behind him. The Austrian Nazis replied with uprisings all over the country. With civil war threatening, Schuschnigg saw no recourse but to call for a plebiscite to ratify his policy. This drove Hitler to fury. He sent an ultimatum demanding postponement of the plebiscite, and when this was refused, he began to concentrate troops on the frontier. Schuschnigg finally resigned, leaving the government to a Nazi minister who invited the Germans into the country.

Two problems are crucial in judging the origins and the consequences of the *Anschluss*. First, what was the attitude of the Austrians themselves? This is an extraordinarily difficult question, and historians will doubtless still be debating it for years to come. One might approach it by calling attention to the 99.75 percent of the electorate that ratified the annexation in a plebiscite held in April. But this in fact meant very little. As in all Hitler's plebiscites, there was no real alternative, and pressure and terror were freely employed to obtain the desired results. Undeniably, Nazi and pro-German sentiment had been steadily growing in Austria in the years immediately preceding the *Anschluss*. Before Hitler's advent in 1933, the Austrians had been almost unanimous in desiring union with their great neighbor, whose speech and tradition were almost indistinguishable from their own. Then, in the half decade from 1933 to 1938, Chancellors Dollfuss and Schuschnigg had tried to stir to life an Austrian national consciousness, on a basis of religious and traditional values. But this was only partially successful; the whole Austrian Left, for one thing, had remained alienated. Most of the country's citizenry had sunk into apathy and had fallen away from political concerns. When the *Anschluss* came, a large minority were enthusiastic, and the majority accepted it with resignation.

The second question concerns the attitude of the other European powers. Why did none of them come forward to protect the independence of Austria? The answer is that none of them simultaneously wanted and was able to do so. Fascist Italy, which had mobilized troops on the Brenner Pass at the time of the first Nazi threat in 1934, no longer stood as the guarantor of Austrian independence. Since the establishment of the Rome-Berlin Axis in the autumn of 1936, Mussolini had aligned himself with Hitler instead. The *Duce* resented not being informed of what his German friend was planning in Austria, but when the annexation had been accomplished, he swallowed his humiliation and sent the *Führer* his congratulations.

What about Britain and France? In London, Foreign Secretary Anthony Eden, the chief champion of resistance to fascist aggression, had been dropped from Chamberlain's cabinet less than a month before the *Anschluss*, and under the prime minister's own leadership the British government was moving toward the policy of conciliation with Mussolini and Hitler that came to be known as "appeasement." Long before the Germans struck, Chamberlain and his chief colleagues had already accepted the absorption of Austria into the Reich. In Paris, the situation recalled what it had been two years before at the time of Hitler's remilitarization of the Rhineland. Once more the French had a weak government—indeed, this time they were between ministries and had no government at all.

Blum was about to make his last despairing effort to revive the Popular Front. He was to be followed, after less than a month in office, by a prime minister who promised a sterner policy. Edouard Daladier, the last prewar premier of France, had been burned twice in the past—once when he had ordered the police to fire against the rightist rioters of February 6, 1934, and again two years later when he had led the faction within the Radical party that had endorsed the Popular Front. As a result, Daladier was well liked neither in the country nor in his own party, to which the memory of participation in Blum's government had grown highly distasteful. But he had a reputation for tenacity and force of character. In April 1938, Daladier put together (under technically Radical auspices) a government that in fact was both conservative and nationalistic. By serving simultaneously as minister of defense, he gave notice that he put the highest priority on France's preparation for war. The next great crisis was to test whether Daladier meant what he said—whether he would really stand against Hitler when the showdown came.

The Problem of the Sudetenland

Hitler had scarcely finished with Austria when he began political operations against his other small neighbor to the southeast, Czechoslovakia. Czechoslovakia was a far stronger state than Austria. It was almost twice as populous; its industries were busy and up to date; and among the small nations of East Central Europe, it alone had maintained its post-1919 democratic institutions (see Chapter 14, II). This relative success reflected the high level of education and efficiency among the Czechoslovak people; it also reflected the wisdom of its statesmen, more particularly the founder-president, Thomas G. Masaryk, and his faithful coadjutor, Eduard Beneš, who had succeeded to the presidency on Masaryk's retirement in 1935.

But Czechoslovakia had one grievous problem. The Paris Peace Conference, in one of its less happy decisions, had awarded to the Czechs the Sudetenland, a mountain rim of territory around the Bohemian and Moravian borders that was inhabited by three million German-speaking people. Masaryk and Beneš had maintained most convincingly that this was the only logical solution; the new Czechoslovak state, they argued, needed a natural mountain frontier for its defense, and Bohemia and Moravia formed a historical and economic unit that should not be broken up. It would have been impossible, moreover, to draw a boundary along clear linguistic lines, since in many areas Czechs and Germans lived mingled together. Masaryk and Beneš won their case, for in this instance, as in so many others, the conference in the end decided against the vanquished.

In the first decade and a half of Czechoslovakia's history, the Sudeten Germans created little trouble. They received far better treatment than did most national minorities in East Central Europe, and in comparison with what occurred in other countries, their grievances were distinctly minor. But after Hitler came to power, these grievances suddenly flamed into life. As had happened in Austria, local Nazi agents went busily to work, and they had soon won over most of the German-speaking population. For here, as opposed to Austria, there was no competing national loyalty to restrain the inhabitants of the Sudetenland from ardently seeking annexation to the Reich.

Once Austria was safely annexed, Hitler felt free to espouse the Sudeten grievances. In concert with the local Nazi leadership, he took up the demand for Sudeten autonomy within the Czechoslovak state. Autonomy was all that he openly sought; but the way in which he phrased his claim left no doubt that annexation was his real objective. President Beneš and his colleagues knew it; hence they resolved to resist German pressure even to the point of war.

The Meetings at Berchtesgaden, Bad Godesberg, and Munich

The Sudeten issue first flared up in late March, scarcely more than a week after the annexation of Austria. There followed consultations between the French and British governments that set the pattern for everything that was to follow. The French were prepared in theory to honor their treaty obligations by going to Czechoslovakia's defense, but in practice they were far from ready to do so. In this attitude they were greatly influenced by the advice of their military chiefs, who warned them that the French army was in no condition to fight a war beyond its own borders, since it had put all its trust and most of its resources into the row of fortifications called the Maginot Line along the country's northeastern frontier.

The British, who, unlike the French, were not bound to Czechoslovakia by treaty, had no desire to fight at all. In their discussions with Daladier and his colleagues they found allies in the members of the French cabinet who were already in favor of appeasement. Thus the tacit result of the meetings between the two governments was an agreement that they could go no further together than the British would consent to move alone. In fact, this meant an abdication of French responsibility. In the spring of 1938, the relationship was established that was to persist until the outbreak of the Second World War. The power less involved in continental affairs took the lead, while France—whose concern for what went on in Central Europe was far more direct—meekly followed in Britain's wake.

The events of the summer and early autumn of 1938 showed how far this process had already gone. As tension and disorder mounted in the Sudetenland and Hitler's tone grew more violent, Prime Minister Chamberlain increasingly took diplomacy into his own hands. First he sent to Czechoslovakia a special mediator, whose pro-German sentiments soon became obvious. Next he began to reveal the way his own thought was tending by insisting that the Czechoslovak government make concessions. Finally, when in mid-September it became apparent that Hitler was preparing an armed attack and that Beneš and his colleagues were resolved to resist, Chamberlain suddenly decided to go and see the *Führer* himself.

The spectacle of an elderly and peace-loving man, armed only with his inevitable umbrella, getting into a small plane to make the first flight of his life, stirred the imaginations and the sympathies of democratic-minded Europeans. It was quite evident that Chamberlain was prepared to grant Hitler anything within reason in order to preserve the peace. And this he apparently accomplished; he returned from Berchtesgaden with a formula of "self-determination" for the Sudeten Germans that he forced first on his own cabinet, then on the French, and lastly on the Czechs themselves. By September 21, when Beneš had finally bowed to British and French pressure and consented to the amputation of thousands of square miles from his country, the crisis seemed to have passed.

But the next day, when Chamberlain went once more to see Hitler, this time at Bad Godesberg on the Rhine, everything had changed. The *Führer*, dumbfounded at the acquiescence of the French and British to his demands, felt defrauded of his triumph. For the past two weeks he had been stirring his people to a fever of patriotic excitement; his troops were massed for action on the Czech frontier; and now he was being asked to forgo the military occupation of the Sudetenland. This he refused to do. He insisted that his soldiers must march into the German-speaking districts of Czechoslovakia at once.

Here, at last, the long-suffering Chamberlain called a halt. Even he would not submit to this sort of bullying. Deeply discouraged, the British prime minister returned home to report failure to his colleagues and to the French. For the first time the two great democracies began seriously to face the possibility of war. The French started to mobilize—the British to dig protective trenches against air raids and to distribute gas masks to the civilian population. But on neither side of the Channel was there a real conviction that war was coming. To nations who had lived for twenty years at peace, the prospect of armed conflict was still unthinkable.

Both cabinet ministers and ordinary people were ready to grasp any last straw of salvation from whatever source. The savior was Mussolini—suitably prompted by the German government. In this moment of almost total despair, the Italian *Duce* stepped forward with a renewal of his old four-power proposal. He stood ready, he told his German partner, to meet with Hitler, Daladier, and Chamberlain to settle the Sudeten issue. All three quickly accepted. Their deliberations were equally brief. On September 30, 1938, in the city of Munich—where the Nazi movement had begun—the four leaders agreed to Hitler's maximum program. The only modifications of the *Führer's* Bad Godesberg demands were face-saving clauses providing for the occupation of the Sudetenland in stages and for the final delimitation of the frontier by an international commission. Hitler had won, but the peace had been saved for another year.

V. THE LAST YEAR

The Aftermath of Munich

The Munich settlement is notorious in history—it has become synonymous with capitulation, appeasement, and treachery to small allies. But this verdict is a judgment of hindsight. At the time, the vast majority of the British and French welcomed the agreement with relief and jubilation. When Chamberlain returned to London, bearing with him the document promising "peace in our time," he was received with intense enthusiasm by a vast crowd waiting at the airport. For the first time in his life he was really popular. The same was true of Daladier. The French prime minister, who had fewer illusions than Chamberlain and knew very well that he had signed away his country's whole alliance system in the East, expected to be all but lynched at his return. Instead he was greeted as a savior. Only a minority of leaders in either country, such as Winston Churchill, bitterly criticized the Munich settlement and foresaw its consequences.

In defense of Munich, it can be said that it gave people in the Western democracies another year in which to prepare their minds for war. In September 1938, they were completely unready for the horrors of conflict; a year later, although they still loathed the idea of war, they finally knew what they confronted and, in the case of the British at least, were prepared to face the facts. They had been pushed to this sober estimate of international realities by months of mounting evidence that Hitler's word meant nothing and that he and Mussolini were bent on further and apparently unlimited conquest.

The basic premise of the Munich agreement had been that Hitler would now be satisfied and would consent to live at peace with his neighbors. That hope defined the policy of "appeasement." But the very implementation of the settlement proved that this was not so. On the international commission delimiting the German-Czech boundary, the Nazi representatives were stubborn and overbearing, and the frontier as finally established was far more unfavorable to the Czechs than had originally been contemplated. Meanwhile, Mussolini had begun to threaten France. At the end of November, he mounted a great propaganda offensive for the annexation of the French territories of

Nice, Corsica, and Tunisia. As a feeble gesture in reply, Daladier's appeasement-minded foreign minister in early December signed a mutual guarantee of France's frontier with Germany. The proof that German agreements were worthless came the following March—Hitler's favorite month for action—with the destruction of what remained of Czech independence.

This Second Czechoslovak Crisis and Its Consequences

The annexation of the Czech parts of Bohemia and Moravia was carried out in characteristic Nazi fashion. Hitler summoned to Berlin the elderly, ineffective figure who had succeeded Beneš as president,* and with the protracted tongue-lashing he had given Schuschnigg just a year earlier, bullied him into submission. Thus, in March 1939, the rump Czechoslovak state that had remained after Munich ceased to exist; with their mountain defenses gone, the Czechs had no capacity to resist. The Czech lands became a "protectorate" of the Reich; Slovakia achieved independence under a clerical and authoritarian government; and the Hungarians added a further slice of the country to the territory they (and the Poles besides) had acquired in the wake of the Munich settlement.

This second Czechoslovak crisis differed in two important respects from the earlier crises Hitler had precipitated. First, it showed that the Nazi annexationist drive was now extending to non-German peoples. Until then, Hitler had claimed that he sought only to incorporate *German* territories into the Reich, and this argument seemed unanswerable to people who, like most of the British, had always had their doubts about Germany's Versailles boundaries. Now Hitler threw off the mask; after the annexation of the Czech lands it was apparent that he wanted far more than mere reunion with the Germans who lived outside the Reich.

In addition, Hitler was caught in a flagrant breach of his word. He had broken the Munich agreement less than six months after its signature. This rankled in Chamberlain's mind. The British prime minister believed in doing things in businesslike fashion. To him the pledged word was the foundation of commercial intercourse, and hence, of civilized society. He was deeply and sincerely (if perhaps naively) shocked that the statesman whose promise he had trusted should have betrayed him.

In the weeks after the demise of Czechoslovakia, Chamberlain—with Daladier in his wake—swung around sharply to a policy of resistance to Hitler. Thus the British and French prime ministers were not at all willing to compromise when the *Führer* began his next annexationist move, this time seeking to incorporate the last major group of Germans outside the Reich, the inhabitants of the Free City of Danzig and the Polish Corridor. Indeed, Chamberlain and Daladier did the contrary. They pledged military aid to Poland and later to Rumania and Greece, and they notably speeded rearmament. In April, for the first time in their history, the British instituted a program of peacetime conscription.

*Beneš, whose personal position had been destroyed at Munich, had retired and left the country the previous autumn.

Danzig, the Polish Corridor, and the Nazi-Soviet Pact

Meanwhile the Spanish Civil War had ended in triumph for the fascist powers. Ten days later, on April 7, Good Friday, Mussolini annexed the small Balkan country of Albania, which had long been a veiled Italian dependency. Throughout Southern Europe the forces of militant fascism seemed to be sweeping everything before them. These, however, were only sideshows. The real point of danger lay on Germany's eastern frontier, and during the next four months the crucial and agonizing problem for the British and French was to provide aid to Poland in a form that the Poles themselves would accept.

For Britain and France to make their stand for Poland rather than for Czechoslovakia was logical from neither the military nor the ideological standpoint. Poland merely happened to be the next issue that arose after Chamberlain's and Daladier's patience were exhausted. Without natural protection for its frontiers, Poland was far more vulnerable than Czechoslovakia; its army was less modern, and its armaments industry less important. Furthermore, it had long since ceased to be a democracy, even in theory. Ever since Marshal Pilsudski seized power in 1926—and after his death in 1935—Poland had lived under an oligarchic dictatorship, with real power in the hands of a narrow military and political clique. In its quasi-feudal pattern of landholding and social relations, Poland ranked with the most reactionary countries in Europe: Spain and Portugal and Hungary.

The presence of German-speaking minorities within this area gave Hitler a pretext for invasion which he would prove only too happy to invoke by posing as their protector. France and Britain, for their parts, could not defend Poland without Russian help. The Poles, however, were sworn enemies of the Russians. How could the British and French persuade the Poles to accept the Russians as allies against the Nazi threat of imminent invasion?

Chamberlain and Daladier carried out this assignment in the half-hearted and dilatory manner to be expected of men whose own minds were divided. As a good conservative, Chamberlain detested the idea of casting in his lot with bolshevism, and Daladier was scarcely enthusiastic about implementing his country's alliance with the Soviet Union, which had been allowed to languish ever since it had been signed four years before. So they quite literally sent low-ranking officers on a slow boat to negotiate a military agreement with the Russians.

Meanwhile, Stalin had grown suspicious. He saw no advantage in siding with the British and French against Germany. In a speech to the Politburo on March 19, 1939, he warned that Hitler's war with the Western democracies would be long and bloody; better to wait until the two sides were exhausted and then enter the conflict in support of a communist revolution in Germany, which England would be too weak to oppose. An alliance with Hitler, on the other hand, could yield a position of dominance or control in Finland, the Baltic states, and eastern Poland "up to the gates of Warsaw." In early May he accordingly dismissed his foreign minister, the Western-oriented Litvinov, and replaced him with the tougher and more provincial Molotov.

Meanwhile, Hitler had determined to seek an understanding with the Soviet Union, as Stalin's mind also began to turn toward a dramatic reversal of alliances. In mid-August, he informed the *Führer* that he was ready to start political conversations. Once the German foreign minister, Joachim von Ribbentrop, arrived in Moscow, events went

A cartoon by David Low, which appeared in the *London Evening Standard* on September 20, 1939, satirizing the Hitler-Stalin Pact. (*Courtesy The London Evening Standard*)

at a rapid pace. He and Molotov talked as one realist to another, and it was not hard for them to agree to carve the spoils of Poland between their two countries. Secret clauses in the ensuing treaty awarded the Soviet Union the Baltic States of Estonia and Latvia, as well as the southern territory of Bessarabia in return for Soviet pledges to give Hitler a free hand elsewhere in Eastern Europe.

On August 23, the greatest diplomatic bombshell of the century exploded over a stunned Europe. The Nazis and the Soviets announced that they had reconciled all their differences. The impossible had happened—the two ideological systems sworn to eternal enmity had signed a nonaggression pact and agreed to live at peace with one another. Most fascists throughout Europe accepted the Nazi-Soviet pact in cynical fashion as a clever bargain. To Communists it came as a shattering blow; from this moment on, true believers in Western Europe began to desert the party in droves.

Now that he was protected from the Russian menace, Hitler felt free to strike. The Nazi-Soviet pact made war inevitable. The next day, the local Nazis took over control of Danzig. In the Corridor also, the Germans redoubled their agitation. Meanwhile, Britain and France began to mobilize. On the last day of August, the Germans presented their final demands to Poland. These were merely for the record: Hitler did not even wait for an answer. In the small hours of September 1, the German planes launched the attack, and the armored columns began their advance. On the morning of September 3, Britain declared war. In the afternoon, France followed, after the appeasers within Daladier's cabinet lost their last-ditch campaign for conciliation. For the moment, Mussolini stayed neutral. The Second World War had begun.

READINGS

The general diplomacy of the period is covered in Keylor (see readings for Chapter 1), Craig and Gilbert (see readings for Chapter 6), and in Winston S. Churchill, *The Second World War*, Vol. I: *The Gathering Storm** (1948). The alignment between Hitler and Mussolini is traced in Gerhard L. Weinberg's magisterial *The Foreign Policy of Hitler's Germany,** 2 vols. (1970–1980), while the diplomacy preceding the Ethiopian War is narrated in sprited fashion by George W. Baer in *The Coming of the Italian-Ethiopian War* (1967) and in *Test Case: Italy, Ethiopia, and the League of Nations* (1976). Anthony Adamthwaite, *France and the Coming of the Second World War, 1936–1939* (1977), explores the hesitations of French leaders confronting a resurgent Germany, on the basis of extensive work in the French diplomatic archives.

The fateful approach of the conflict in the months between the Munich Agreement and German attack on Poland is chronicled by Donald Cameron Watt in *How War Came: The Immediate Origins of the Second World War, 1938–1939* (1989). Watt's contention that Hitler deliberately sought to provoke hostilities is a powerful rebuttal of the "revisionist" argument advanced almost half a century ago in A. J. P. Taylor's *The Origins of the Second World War,** 2nd ed. (1966), which asserted that the conflict could be flamed in great part on Anglo-French blundering and that Hitler had no conscious intention of going to war. Gerhard L. Weinberg defends conclusions similar to Watt's in *Germany, Hitler, & World War II** (1996). For a survey of both Taylor and his critics, see Gordon Martel, ed., *The Origins of the Second World War Reconsidered** (1986). Hitler's foreign policy objectives are surveyed in Klaus Hildebrand's *The Foreign Policy of the Third Reich** (1973) and in Norman Rich's *Hitler's War Aims,** 2 vols. (1973–1974). The case for accepting *Mein Kampf* as a coherent blueprint for the invasion of Russia and the destruction of the Jews is convincingly made in Eberhard Jäckel, *Hitler's World View** (1981).

For the Spanish Civil War, Gabriel Jackson's *The Spanish Republic and the Civil War, 1931–1939** (1965) and Gerald Brenan's *The Spanish Labyrinth*, 2nd ed. (1960) present the background and the struggle itself from a scholarly and liberal standpoint. Hugh Thomas, *The Spanish Civil War*, (rev. ed. 1977, reissued 1987), is a full-scale history that tries to be fair to all parties. Anthony Beevor, *The Spanish Civil War** (1982) is especially good at detailing the military side of the conflict. Both David T. Cattell's *Communism and the Spanish Civil War* (1955) and Burnett Bolloten's *The Spanish Revolution: The Left and the Struggle for Power During the Civil War** (1979) offer a detailed analysis of Communist influence on the Republican side. In *The Anarchists of Casas Viejas* (1982), Jerome R. Mintz pains a revealing portrait of an indigenous Spanish social movement whose presence was strongly felt during the civil war years.

The Spanish Civil War aroused a striking degree of foreign interest and attracted many combat volunteers as well as observers from abroad. George Orwell's *Homage to Catalonia** (1938) recounts in memorable fashion both the enthusiasm and the subsequent disillusionment of one such volunteer in the POUM militia; Franz Borkenau's *The Spanish Cockpit** (1937, reprint ed. 1963) combines the immediacy of eye-

*Books marked by an asterisk are available in paperback.

witness description with the analytic detachment of a trained sociologist. Ronald Radosh, Mary R. Habeck, and Grigory Sevostianov, eds., *Spain Betrayed: The Soviet Union in the Spanish Civil War* (2000) presents a collection of hitherto unpublished Soviet documents that paint a dark picture of Comintern duplicity during the civil war, as the Soviet Union first supported and then betrayed the Republican cause. The difficulties of reporting the war and the challenges it posed to accepted ideologies on both Left and Right are explored in James Wilkinson, "Truth and Delusion: European Intellectuals in Search of the Spanish Civil War," *Salmagundi*, No. 76–77 (Fall 1987–Winter 1988). A strikingly original account of the role of popular religion during the years of the Republic is William A. Christian, Jr., *Visionaries: The Spanish Republic and the Reign of Christ* (1996).

Among the many novels written by participants, Ernest Hemingway's *For Whom the Bell Tolls** offers an emotionally charged account of an American's sacrifice for the Republican cause, while André Malraux's *Man's Hope* (1937) presents a panorama of the first two years of the Civil War, interspersed with philosophical meditations on its meaning. Peter Stanksy and William Abrahams, *Journey to the Frontier: Two Roads to the Spanish Civil War** (1966) traces the itinerary of two young English poets from indifference to political commitment in Spain, and in so doing suggests why the Spanish struggle assumed such importance as a European moral crusade. Ronald Fraser's *Blood of Spain: An Oral History of the Spanish Civil War* (1979) weaves several eye-witness accounts of survivors into a rich and moving narrative.

For the annexation of Austria, see Gordon Brooke-Shepard, *Anschluss: The Rape of Austria* (1963), and the personal account by Kurt Schuschnigg, *Austrian Requiem* (1946). Telford Taylor, *Munich: The Price of Peace** (1980), and J. W. Wheeler-Bennett, *Munich: Prologue to Tragedy** (1948) are two standard works on the crisis of 1938 and the fruits of "appeasement." For an explanation of the Western democracies' willingness to seek accommodation with Hitler, see A. L. Rowse, *Appeasement: A Study in Political Decline* (1961); William R. Rock, *British Appeasement in the 1930s** (1977); and Wolfgang Mommsen and Lothar Kettenacker, eds., *The Fascist Challenge and the Policy of Appeasement* (1983).

13

THE SECOND WORLD WAR

A German motorized column rolls through a Polish town heavily damaged by German bombing in September 1939. *(Courtesy Corbis-Bettmann)*

I. ILLUSION AND BLITZKRIEG

For the democracies of the West, the Second World War opened on a paradoxically sour note. From the moral standpoint, their cause was blameless. Britain and France had gone to war to defend a threatened ally and to stop the spread of fascism; they sought nothing for themselves, and the sympathies of the neutrals were overwhelmingly on their side. From the beginning, the Second World War was what the first war had become only after Wilson had redefined it: a war for democracy.

Yet most of the French and British felt otherwise. They went into the conflict without conviction, quietly, even sullenly. From one point of view, their lack of enthusiasm was a sign of maturity. The days of bands and flag waving were over, and people faced soberly and without illusion the suffering that lay ahead; even the Germans showed no real eagerness for the conflict until they had experienced the intoxication of Hitler's first victories. But this absence of martial ardor also revealed a deep-seated malaise among the French and British people. They were going into the war under leaders tainted by past appeasement, whose present public statements gave no evidence of profound belief in their own cause. The disillusionments of the Spanish Civil War and the betrayal of Czechoslovakia brooded over them. Why, people asked themselves, were they fighting to defend reactionary Poland rather than the democracy of Spain or Czechoslovakia? Beyond this there was a sense of danger and disappointment because France and Britain were fighting alone; the other Western democracies of Scandinavia, the Low Countries, and the United States were not with them. Finally there was the sickening suspicion that the West had declared a war that it could neither properly fight nor fully win—an unreal struggle that seemed to have no logical end. This became evident as the Germans disposed of Poland in less than a month and the war in the west settled into a weary winter of waiting.

The Conquest of Poland

Against Poland, the Germans for the first time tested their tactics of *Blitzkrieg*, or "lightning war," which they were to use again and again in the next two years. For this sort of fighting, Poland offered almost ideal terrain. The country was one vast plain—from northern Germany to the swamps and forests on the Russian border there was scarcely a natural obstacle to stop the advance of an invading army. The new German strategy aimed at taking the enemy everywhere by surprise. While massed aircraft raided his cities, ammunition dumps, and communications centers, columns of tanks raced ahead of the infantry, cutting supply lines and spreading confusion and terror in his rear.

The *Blitzkrieg* tactics worked with speed and efficiency as a German army of a million and three-quarters overwhelmed Polish forces only a third as large. By mid-September the Germans had advanced so far into the country that the Russians took alarm. On September 17, Stalin ordered the invasion of Poland by the Red Army, which moved forward almost without opposition until it met the Germans two days later. After a further week of fighting, Polish resistance ended with the capture of the capital city of Warsaw. The government fled—eventually to take refuge in London, where it became the first of the continental governments-in-exile that existed throughout the war under British protection.

With Poland completely crushed, Hitler and Stalin proceeded to divide the spoils. However, Hitler took a larger share than foreseen in the nonaggression pact that Germany and the Soviet Union had signed five weeks earlier. Thanks to the success of his *Blitzkrieg* offensive, the *Führer* now controlled most of the country. Accordingly, he annexed outright the former Free City of Danzig, the Corridor, and a number of additional districts in the west. The central part of the country he set up as a German protectorate—as he had done with the rump of Bohemia-Moravia—to be called the Government-General. For his part, Stalin annexed eastern Poland up to (and slightly beyond) the frontier that Lord Curzon had originally proposed in 1919. This area, which had a majority of Ukrainians and White Russians rather than Poles, the Soviet leaders had always regarded as rightfully their own, and they claimed that they were only rectifying a twenty-year-old injustice when they joined it to the Ukrainian and White Russian Soviet Republics. In "compensation" for accepting reduced Polish territory, the Soviets also annexed the Baltic state of Lithuania.

The "Phony" War

The French and British stood helpless as the Poles reeled under the German attack and Poland then disappeared from the map. They had gone to war to save Poland's independence, but now they found themselves half unable, half unwilling, to go to its aid. It was impossible for them to send ground troops overland; their navies could not enter the Baltic, which the Germans had effectively closed; their air power lacked the means to traverse the entire Reich. Their inability to help the Poles made the French and British feel guilty from the outset and gave them a first taste of how the war was to prove entirely different from what they had imagined.

After a few tentative advances to secure better defensive positions, the Allied commander-in-chief, General Maurice Gamelin of France, decided upon a stationary war. Obsessed with memories of the First World War, too much convinced of that war's lesson of the superiority of the defense over the attack, he decided to sit it out in his Maginot Line fortifications. Similarly, the French and British chose to husband their aircraft rather than to bomb the Reich. At the beginning of the war, they had expected massive Nazi bombardments and even gas attacks: People had left the cities by the thousands, and children had been systematically shipped to safety. But when the bombs did not fall, life returned to normal; those who had fled the cities came back, and gas masks were discarded. A tacit and informal truce reigned on the Western Front.

But this truce was profoundly demoralizing. As the French soldiers—who accounted for the bulk of the Allied ground troops—waited through the late autumn and winter in the Maginot Line, they began to wonder why they were at war. The Germans, facing them in equal inaction on the Siegfried Line, knew that sooner or later their *Führer* would give the order to advance. The French had no such consolation. This *drôle de guerre*, this *Sitzkrieg*, this "phony" war, as it came to be called, seemed less and less war than a long succession of wet, dreary days of meaningless boredom. Under these circumstances, it was not surprising that the soldiers lost confidence in national leaders who themselves appeared to have so little idea of how they proposed to win. Meanwhile the French Communist party, under orders from Stalin's Comintern, further undermined morale by protesting against a war that benefitted only the "capitalists."

Hitler's Spring Offensive

With the coming of spring, Hitler struck at last. In three months from April through June 1940, Nazi forces overran Norway, Denmark, the Netherlands, Belgium, and the greatest prize of all: France.

Surprise, superior strategy, and the meticulous preparation of the German troops combined to overwhelm their foes. Of the countries which Hitler conquered in the spring of 1940, however, France alone possessed armed forces large or well equipped enough to match the German *Wehrmacht*. The French army was reputed to be the finest in the world. It had prevailed over Germany's armed forces in the First World War; many expected it to do so again. But in fact the opposite occurred. Despite the lessons of Poland's fall, the French general staff failed to grasp the nature of the German *Blitzkrieg* until it was too late. Obsessed with memories of the previous war, they thought in terms of defense and fixed lines of combat, whereas the Germans prized offense and rapid movement. This strategic failure decided the outcome.

The German high command found a way past French defenses in the hilly, wooded country of the Ardennes, which the French had dismissed as impassable for a modern army. Again, as in 1914, the invaders avoided the French fortifications in the northeast by swinging around on the right flank. Bringing their main force of tanks and troops through the supposedly impenetrable Ardennes forests, Hitler's generals were able to take the French defenders completely be surprise, then fan out behind French lines to create panic and destruction in the rear.

By the third week in May there was no stopping the Nazi armies as they drove relentlessly south. Their fighter planes strafed at will, scattering the retreating French columns and the millions of refugees, French and Belgian, who clogged the roads with cars and carts piled high with their possessions, and who obstructed French attempts to mount a counterattack. Meanwhile, further east, the Maginot Line remained intact but irrelevant; in a few more days it would be seized by the *Wehrmacht* in an attack from the rear.

The *Führer*'s goal was Paris. He was determined to avoid the mistake that Moltke had made in 1914 by letting up too soon, and instead sought to maintain momentum in a drive on the French capital. Hence he failed to capitalize fully on the parallel successes that his armies had scored in driving west to the Channel. The *Führer*'s inattention allowed one Allied success amidst a string of humiliating defeats. An improvised, amphibious retreat at the end of May ferried some 335,000 British and French troops from the beaches at Dunkirk across the channel to safety in England in the greatest rescue operation of all time. Though their equipment remained behind, they had escaped death or imprisonment to fight again.

With the end of the Dunkirk evacuation on June 4, the agony of France began. The prime minister, Paul Reynaud (who had succeeded Daladier in late March), succumbed to the faction among his cabinet that favored peace at any price. Since the beginning of June they had acquired a distinguished spokesman in Marshal Pétain, whom Reynaud accepted as vice-premier. The hero of Verdun, now eighty-four, was the sole survivor of France's great leaders in the First World War—the symbol of patriotism, rectitude, and solid traditional values to much of the nation. With his white hair, piercing blue eyes, and military bearing, Pétain looked and acted like the father figure many French men and women instinctively sought at a time of crisis. They little thought that the man they trusted was about to create a four-year dictatorship. When Pétain advised abandoning the fight, it was difficult for mere civilians in the government to resist his immense moral authority. On June 17, the marshal sued for an armistice "with a heavy heart." Five days later the Germans, who already occupied more than half of France, imposed their will on the vanquished in the very same railroad car at Compiègne in which Marshal Foch had handed his armistice terms to the Germans in November 1918.

The fall of France came as the greatest shock that Western democracy had ever sustained. In Britain, the United States, and among the smaller neutrals, the news was greeted with incredulity and anger. How could France have fallen, and in so short a time? Much of the responsibility, as we have seen, lay with an incompetent and self-deluded French military command. But their failure of intellect was paralleled by a general failure of nerve. In the end, many French resignedly accepted defeat and occupation. When Hitler received the news of the capture of Paris, the photographers caught him in an improvised dance of triumph: He exulted vulgarly and shamelessly at the end of more than twenty years of German "dishonor." Now that France was gone, he calculated, surely Britain would see reason and come to terms as well. But Hitler had failed to reckon with the British people—and with their leader, Winston Churchill.

II. "THEIR FINEST HOUR"

Churchill's Leadership

On May 7 and 8—just before the Nazi storm broke—British Prime Minister Neville Chamberlain had sustained a furious attack in the House of Commons. Like Daladier, Chamberlain had not known how to put his country on a war footing. Profoundly and stubbornly a man of peace, he had neither mobilized the energies of his people nor given them a clear vision of the task before them.

His successor was Winston Churchill, a fighter and a maverick by nature. Born to an American mother and a British father of impeccably aristocratic lineage, he was raised as a Conservative, but entered Parliament as a Liberal in 1900 and served Lloyd George as First Lord of the Admiralty during the First World War. After the war he reverted to his Conservative roots, serving as chancellor of the exchequer under Baldwin, but was obliged to withdraw from the Conservative leadership for his criticism of the policy of conciliation with India in 1931.

Thus deprived of influence by his exclusion from the cabinet, Churchill became the most redoubtable foe of the Baldwin and Chamberlain governments. With only a handful of followers, he tirelessly denounced the policy of appeasement and demanded more energetic preparation for war. Many members of Parliament thought him a warmonger—self-aggrandizing and prone to exaggeration. Yet events proved him right. In May 1940, four decades after he had first entered the House of Commons, Churchill at last received the prize he had coveted his entire political life: the post of prime minister. Conservatives and Labour alike reluctantly agreed that he was the logical person to assume leadership at this moment of crisis. Members of both parties accepted posts in the new government. Thus from the beginning, Churchill's war ministry was what Lloyd George's had never been—a true coalition and a true expression of national unity. Chamberlain himself came to trust Churchill, and in heated War Cabinet debates now supported his refusal to surrender to Hitler during that bleak month of May.

Churchill proved to be an incomparable war leader. It is true (as his enemies so often alleged) that he was vain, domineering, and insensitive to the feelings of others. But he was also self-confident, energetic, and tenacious—qualities very much needed in wartime. Like the British bulldog, whose features resembled his own, once he sank his teeth into an opponent he would not let go. Above all, Churchill was an eloquent and inspiring speaker, one of the great orators of the twentieth century and in fact of any age. At a time when Britain lacked the resources to prosecute the war alone, his words became potent weapons. His rich prose and the measured cadences of his speeches gave the British a sense of the majesty of their history and of the great task that had devolved on them, now that they stood alone. But he also knew how to bring his rhetoric down to earth. When Churchill told his countrymen bluntly that he could offer them nothing but "blood and toil and sweat and tears," most accepted the prospect with stoic resolve. Now at last all illusion had been stripped away and Britain knew what lay ahead.

The Battle of Britain

The mood of England in the summer of 1940 was epitomized by the remarks attributed to an apocryphal cockney on a London bus: " 'Ere, wot ye grousin' about? We're in the finals, ain't we? We're playin' at 'ome, ain't we?"

Indeed, the British seemed almost happy to be alone. They had never had much regard for their French ally, and now that this vexation was eliminated, the war had become blessedly simple. It had been reduced to a question of national survival. Realistically, it appeared impossible for the British to hold out. Only the intervention of the United States or the Soviet Union could give them hope of victory. Meanwhile they went about the business of defending their country with brisk self-confidence. They were quite prepared, as Churchill had warned them, to fight on their beaches, in their cities, and eventually—if their whole island should be lost—in the dominions overseas. These had been with them from the start, and if the British government should be forced to fall back on Canada, it seemed almost certain that the United States would enter the war.

Hitler himself was far less sure of his next step. The rapid fall of France caught him by surprise: It put him ahead of schedule, and he had no plans ready for his next move. Thus his military chiefs were obliged to improvise a plan for invasion on short notice. Operation "Sea Lion"—surely the most transparent code name ever devised—called for an initial assault in September by 90,000 men, who were to be transported by a flotilla of more than 1,000 craft. Hitler ordered Reichsmarshall Hermann Goering, his right-hand man and the commander of the German air force (*Luftwaffe*), to soften up the

"VERY WELL, ALONE"

This cartoon by David Low of June 1940 captures the British mood of grim defiance against the threat of Nazi invasion. (*Courtesy The London Evening Standard*)

British defenses. Goering was full of confidence. Indeed, he was certain that he could subdue Britain by air attack alone without resort to the hazardous expedient of invasion.

But Goering did not know the high level of combat efficiency that the Royal Air Force (RAF) had attained in the past year. The British had used to good advantage the year's respite they had gained at Munich. By 1939, they were producing more than six hundred aircraft a month—almost equalling the German rate of output. More important, their fighter planes were superior in design. The British had gone into mass production a couple of years later than the Germans, and their new models, the Spitfires and Hurricanes, were more advanced than the Luftwaffe's planes. Finally, the British possessed decided advantages in their ability to detect the movements and discover the plans of their enemy. They had invented radar shortly before the war, and at the beginning of October 1940, activated their first radar warning system. They had also acquired an exact model of the German code encryption device, named Enigma, through which military orders passed from Hitler and the German High Command to units in the field in the form of complex mathematical ciphers. With this machine in their possession, the British soon broke the German military code and listened in on Goering's orders to his pilots, thus gaining precious advance warning of where the next attack was to come. In a final intelligence coup, they also penetrated the code of the German secret service (*Abwehr*) and identified Nazi spies working undercover in Britain. When arrested and threatened with imprisonment, they agreed to cooperate with the British, and fed their Nazi superiors misinformation throughout the war right up until the eve of the Allied invasion of Normandy in 1944.

The cumulative weight of British aircraft and intelligence superiority was to prove of increasing value as the war progressed. Still, in the summer of 1940 the German air force outnumbered the British by almost two to one. If it had concentrated its attacks on the airfields and fighter forces, it might have broken Britain's power in the air. Instead, the *Luftwaffe* made the strategic error of continually shifting its target. In late August, it struck at British ports and shipping; then it attacked airfields; finally (in early September), it launched its great Blitz against London, Coventry, and other industrial centers. Night after night, it struck at the British capital; each day, it seemed as though government and inhabitants could not hold out much longer in the burning and heavily damaged city. But the Londoners reacted with grim fortitude. Most of them filed patiently into cellars and subways to get what sleep they could, while those who had jobs to do—antiaircraft crews, fire fighters, and air-raid wardens—manned their posts with quiet efficiency.

Meanwhile, the weather itself was helping the British. During the six decisive weeks from mid-August until late September, there was an abnormal amount of fog and rain. Goering never got the fortnight of clear weather that he needed to mobilize his force with maximum effectiveness. As September wore on, his losses of aircraft grew more and more alarming. By the end of the month, it was obvious that bombing alone would never force the British to their knees. On October 12, "Sea Lion" was postponed until the following spring. In fact, although no one dared tell Hitler so, the project of an invasion of Britain had been abandoned. A few thousand intrepid pilots of the RAF had saved their country. They had won the Battle of Britain. As Churchill was to express it with his customary felicity: "Never in human history have so many owed so much to so few."

Hitler's Diplomatic Offensive: Mussolini, Pétain, Franco

In the autumn of 1940, then, Hitler was left without a war to fight. The conquest of Britain had eluded him, and Churchill continued to reject his feelers for peace. He could try to cripple British trade with his submarines—and here he was scoring a notable success—but this was not enough to bring final victory within his grasp.

Frustrated in the west, Hitler turned south toward the Mediterranean. Here he had to deal with three Latin powers, all, in one form or another, allied or subjugated to him. If he could weld these together into an effective military bloc, then at least he might be able to strike at Britain overseas, at the powerful bases of Gibraltar and Malta and at Egypt—formally independent but now occupied by the British army—which held the key to the Near East and India.

Unfortunately for the Führer, the three dictators of Italy, France, and Spain were proud men and strong nationalists who had no intention of subordinating their countries' aims to Hitler's military needs. In Italy, Mussolini felt angry and humiliated by his own role in the war: His army's record in its single week of fighting against France had been mediocre, and his navy and air force in the Meditarranean were being battered by far smaller detachments of the British, who were also holding off his attempts to advance from Libya into Egypt. Hitler, therefore, saw no reason to give his tardy ally any substantial reward. He merely permitted the Italians to remain in the small area of southeastern France they had occupied in June, while postponing indefinitely the award Mussolini really wanted—Nice, Corsica, and Tunisia.

The *Führer's* cavalier treatment of Mussolini reflected his concern for what was going on in France. Here Marshal Pétain—or rather his vice-premier, Pierre Laval—less than three weeks after the armistice had bullied the French Chamber into voting him full powers to govern and to alter the constitution as he saw fit. Armed with this grant of power, Pétain and Laval had replaced the democratic French Republic with an authoritarian and quasi-fascist "French State." It was referred to as the Vichy government, from the resort city in central France where it established its headquarters. This change of capital had been necessitated by the armistice terms. Pending the conclusion of a final peace, the Germans were to remain in control of an Occupied Zone, which included Paris, the north, and the whole Atlantic coast; although, in form, Pétain was the ruler of this part of France too, his effective power was limited to the Unoccupied Zone in the center and the southeast.

When Hitler finally met the marshal at Montoire on October 24, Pétain proved evasive. No substantial promise of collaboration was forthcoming. The same had been true of Hitler's conversation with Franco the day before at the frontier city of Hendaye. The *Caudillo* had been polite, even courtly. He had listened for nine long hours to the *Führer's* urgings that he enter the war, but in the end he refused, summoning all sorts of objections: The Spanish economy had been shattered by the Civil War; its Catholic people detested the German pact with the Soviet Union; he himself had no desire to play host to a foreign army. Hitler had at last met his match. The mild-mannered *Caudillo* had talked even the eloquent *Führer* into exhaustion. "Rather than go through that again," Hitler lamented, "I would prefer to have three or four teeth taken out."

So Hitler failed in his efforts to construct a Latin fascist bloc and to seal off the Mediterranean. In retrospect, this failure was to appear one of the major mistakes in his whole conduct of the war, for it left French North Africa at liberty and vulnerable to the maneuvers of his enemies.

The Conquest of Yugoslavia and Greece

With the fall of France, the small states of East Central Europe that had looked west for protection found themselves at the mercy of their great neighbors. Once more Germany and the Soviet Union took parallel action. Stalin continued his program of restoring the Russian frontiers of 1914 by seizing Bessarabia from Romania and annexing the remaining Baltic states of Latvia and Estonia. Hitler added no more territory to the Reich, but he brought three more countries under his control as dependent nations. First he undertook to protect Romania against Russia; in return he ordered the Romanians to give up additional territory to their neighbors—half of Transylvania to Hungary and a smaller area south of the Danube to Bulgaria. Hitler held them in his power through the hope of further gain and the fear of further loss. Earlier, by buying up their agricultural surpluses in the Great Depression years, the Nazi Reich had put these countries in a state of economic dependence. Now it had them in a state of political dependence as well.

Hitler found Yugoslavia's leadership weak and divided when, in the spring of 1941, he put the same sort of pressure upon them that he had earlier exerted on the Romanians and Hungarians. On March 25, the regent, Prince Paul, adhered to the German-Italian alliance, which since the previous September had included the Japanese as well. Yugoslavia seemed to be safely in the Nazi orbit. The next day, though, Belgrade began to stir: A conspiracy of high-ranking army officers overthrew the regent and his prime minister and established the boy king, Peter II, in his place. The new government repudiated the German alliance and, sustained by a great wave of patriotic enthusiasm, prepared to resist the invasion that was sure to come.

Hitler's retribution descended swiftly and brutally. On April 6, the German attack began, both from the north and from Bulgaria to the east. Once more, *Blitzkrieg* tactics worked with precision. In eleven days, all was over with Yugoslavia. Meanwhile, Greece, too, had been invaded. Hitler had come to the aid of his Italian allies by attacking their Greek adversaries from the rear. A week after the capitulation of Yugoslavia, Greece signed an armistice. The Germans had now won complete domination over the Balkan peninsula.

The End of the Nazi-Soviet Pact

Despite the pact signed with Stalin in 1939, Hitler had never really buried his hostility to Bolshevism. He had merely concealed it for strategic reasons in order to protect his eastern flank while he dealt with France and Britain. Eventually—as he had announced in *Mein Kampf*—he was resolved to eliminate the power of Russia once and for all, transforming its vast lands into an outpost for German settlers to colonize and arm as a new addition to the Reich. But he intended to do this only when he had forced the West to make peace. At all costs, he wished to avoid what he considered the supreme mistake made by his imperial German predecessors in 1914—a war on two fronts. His timing, however, was disturbed by two unexpected developments: Britain's failure to admit that it was beaten and the Soviet Union's refusal to accede to the Nazis' ideas on the division of the world.

On November 12, 1940, Foreign Minister Molotov arrived in Berlin for political consultations. There Hitler proposed a gigantic apportionment of spheres of influence. To the Russians he offered a chance to expand south "in the direction of the Indian Ocean." This proposal impressed Molotov not at all. The Soviet foreign minister made it quite clear that he was not interested in hypothetical gains from a still undefeated British Empire with which his country was not even at war. A British air raid on the German capital interrupted the negotiations, underscoring Molotov's doubts. When his Nazi hosts insisted that England would soon capitulate, Molotov is reported to have asked: "If that is so, then why are we in this shelter, and whose are those bombs which are falling?" Only a delimitation of spheres of influence within Europe itself would satisfy the Soviet Union, Molotov informed his German hosts, including the domination of Bulgaria and the Bosporus Straight, thus guaranteeing the Soviet Black Sea fleet access to the Mediterranean.

That much Hitler conceded. Once Germany had won the war, Berlin was prepared to cede control over Romania as well additional territory in the eastern Balkans.

But behind this façade of conciliation, Hitler was preparing to deal his rival to the east a death blow. Shortly after the meeting with Molotov, the Führer determined that "the final struggle against Bolshevism" must begin the following spring with a massive attack on the Soviet Union. Stalin received reports of this decision from his own ambassadors and secret agents, but stubbornly ignored them. All his actions in the first half of 1941 suggested that he believed time was still on his side. By avoiding all provocation of its fearsome adversary, the Soviet Union could prolong Germany's war with England and thus avoid attack. As late as June 13, when the German troop concentrations on the Soviet frontier had been almost completed, an official press communiqué vigorously denied any deterioration in relations between the two countries.

Incredible as it may sound, Stalin and his colleagues deceived themselves as to the imminence and nature of Hitler's attack. There would be no German *Blitzkrieg* tactics used against them, they believed, despite their enormous success in Poland; the attack itself would come exclusively from the southwest, rather than along a broad front. Prey to calamitous wishful thinking, they did not even listen to the friendly warning that the German ambassador gave them on the eve of the onslaught. And when, on June 22, the greatest invasion of all time began to roll, they were disastrously unprepared.

Now at last the war had entered on its major phase. Hitler had fallen into the trap he had sworn to avoid—a war on two fronts. And the British were no longer alone. They had survived their year of supreme peril—"their finest hour," as Churchill called it. The Russians were with them—and in less than six months, the Americans would be fighting too.

III. THE WAR IN THE BALANCE

The German Invasion of Russia

For his reckoning with the Soviet Union, Hitler had massed a total of nearly four million German troops comprising 180 divisions, and with them more than 3,000 tanks, 7,000 pieces of artillery, and 2,000 airplanes. Once more overruling the advice of his military chiefs, he had decided to advance all along the line, rather than to concentrate his forces for a single decisive blow. Three army troops were to invade the Soviet Union on a front that would eventually extend for 2,000 miles. Their commanders were the same aristocratic generals, now field marshals, who had won the victory in France: Leeb in the north, with Leningrad as his objective; Bock in the center, headed toward Moscow; Rundstedt in the south, with the endless wheat fields of the Ukraine stretching before him. They were accompanied by satellite forces from Hungary, Romania, Slovakia, and Italy.

At first it appeared as though the Germans would sweep everything before them. The wide encircling operations they had planned proceeded with deadly accuracy against the Russian troops massed close within their country's frontiers. Parallel columns of tanks drove forward through open country, meeting little resistance, and then, when they were far in the enemy's rear, wheeled toward each other to close the jaws of a vast trap. Again and again, the Nazi armored divisions ambushed the Russians in this fashion.

The latter seemed paralyzed with fear or astonishment; encircled and bewildered, they surrendered by the hundreds of thousands.

Even Stalin was privately forced to admit that the Germans had achieved a series of tremendous victories that placed the Soviet Union in mortal danger. After three months of war, Hitler had succeeded in inflicting massive losses on the Red Army—2.5 million men killed, wounded, or taken prisoner (out of a total of 4.5 under arms); a force of 15,000 tanks reduced to a pitiful remnant of 700. Now the folly of purging the top ranks of the Red Army in 1937–1938 came back to haunt the Soviet dictator at his hour of greatest need. Who would replace the over 300 marshals, generals, and division commanders whom he had ordered shot? It was fortunate for Stalin that his territorial annexations of 1939 provided some buffer through which his armies could fall back while he sought to reorganize the general staff.

The invasion thus reached its autumn climax. As the Ukrainian capital of Kiev fell, Hitler ordered his tank divisions north to the central front, intent on seizing Moscow before winter arrived. The drive for Moscow began on the last day of September and at first seemed unstoppable, as units of the German army swiftly advanced to within fifty miles of the city's outskirts. For three days in mid-October, panic seized the Soviet capital. As government offices were evacuated to the east and a flood of refugees left the city, riots erupted in the streets and the Soviet regime seemed about to topple. Stalin himself disappeared, leaving some to speculate that he had fled before the German invaders. But on October 19, Stalin reappeared in the Kremlin. He recalled his ablest surviving general, Zhukov, whom he had earlier sent to organize the defenses of Leningrad, back to the capital and declared a state of siege. Tens of thousands of Muscovites now dug tank traps and a defensive perimeter on the city's outskirts, while Stalin ordered fresh reserves of troops transferred from the Far East.

For six weeks the fate of Moscow hung in the balance. The Germans, halted by heavy rain and snow in late October, returned to the attack in mid-November as soon as the ground had frozen solid. But in the end Zhukov's stubborn defense prevailed. On the day of testing, December 2, the Soviet lines held firm. They had won the battle of Moscow—the first major Russian victory in the war. The supreme danger was over.

By this time, full winter had arrived. The German soldiers were huddling miserable and half frozen in their advanced positions, vainly attempting to ward off the cold. Hitler had issued no winter clothing to his troops, assuming that the war against Russia would be won by autumn. But on December 8, even he was obliged to bow to realities and announce a suspension of operations on the Eastern Front. Two days earlier, Stalin had ordered a counteroffensive. And on the seventh of the same month, the Japanese attack on Pearl Harbor had brought the United States into the war.

The Great Coalition

With the American intervention, the Second World War attained its final form. It became a coalition struggle of the two greatest democracies of the West in declared or tacit alliance with the homeland of communism. These ill-sorted bedfellows had been thrown together by a series of historical accidents. Britain and the United States shared with the Soviet Union a common enemy in fascist terror and aggression, but there was little else to hold together two such radically different types of society, whose history during the previous quarter-century had been marked far more often by hostility than by friendship. On both sides, at the end of 1941, a massive legacy of distrust barred the way to harmonious cooperation.

Already that August—four months before America entered the war—Winston Churchill had ventured across the dangerous waters of the North Atlantic to meet with his future partner and ally, Franklin Roosevelt, off the coast of Newfoundland. From on board Churchill's battleship came a joint proclamation later called the Atlantic Charter, where the two leaders pledged "to respect the right of all peoples to choose the form of government under which they will live." The Soviet Union (along with emissaries of seven German-occupied European countries) signed the same Charter a month later in London. Though the decisions later made at the Yalta and Potsdam Conferences appeared to violate the principle of self-determination, Churchill was certainly right to insist that the Allies must declare the fundamental principles that inspired their resistance to Hitler. Unlike World War I, where patriotic self-interest dominated attempts to justify the war until the final year of the war, World War II was fought for much higher stakes.

At the outset, the British served as the connecting link between the Russians and the Americans. For one thing, the British owed more to the Russians—with the German invasion in June, the *Luftwaffe*'s attacks on British cities had come to an abrupt end. Hence Churchill voiced the sentiment of the overwhelming majority of his fellow citizens when, on the morrow of the Nazi attack on the Soviet Union, he pledged Stalin all the aid he could spare. Roosevelt, however, was unwilling to go that far. He well knew that an influential segment of the American people would never countenance an alliance with a Communist state. The Japanese attack on Pearl Harbor rescued Roosevelt by forcing his hand; now the country had no alternative. The president was also spared the dangers of a congressional debate over whether to declare war on Germany and Italy as well as Japan. The two fascist states themselves took the initiative by inaugurating hostilities with the United States in conformity with their Tripartite Pact with Tokyo.

Japan had been at war with China since 1937—a conflict which in hindsight appears as the opening salvo of World War II. With the fall of France in 1940, the Japanese seized North Vietnam, hitherto a French colony, and soon overran South Vietnam as well. Thus by the time of their attack at Pearl Harbor, Japanese armies controlled much of the East Asian mainland and were poised to seize still more. Japanese military leaders calculated that their position was now too strong for a serious challenge by the Allies, whose resources were already stretched to the limit by the war in Europe.

In a few months in early 1942, Japanese forces overran the rest of Southeast Asia with the same ease with which the Germans had conquered Europe. As Hong Kong, the Philippines, and Singapore fell one after another, the weakness of the Western colonial powers was revealed for all to see. Grimly, the Americans and their allies prepared to do battle on two fronts—in Europe and in the Pacific. Eventually, their superior naval and air power would prevail against Japan's far-flung empire, inaugurating a process of liberation which would bring much of Southeast Asia independence from colonial rule of any kind. But victory, and the ensuring wave of decolonization, lay far in the future.

For the moment, American leaders were only too aware of their country's inability to fight and win both a Pacific and a European war simultaneously. Therefore, Roosevelt and his military advisers were forced to reach a crucial decision within a month after Pearl Harbor: They determined to give the defeat of Germany priority over dealing with Japan. Although this meant that some sort of coordination with the Russians was essential, the U.S. government was resolved to limit such coordination to the military sphere. But some sort of aid was imperative. When the Red Army finally halted the German invasion in December 1941, the situation of the Soviet Union seemed all but hopeless. It had lost its richest lands and more than half its industrial resources; overall industrial production had fallen by more than half, and famine in the cities was beginning to take a dreadful toll.

Yet in this moment of deepest crisis, the Soviets launched a winter counteroffensive. From December to May, the Red Army pushed forward, disengaging an ample protective zone before Moscow and dislodging the Germans from their advanced positions in the Ukraine. Their campaign showed how much the Red Army had learned from their earlier reverses. This resiliency of the Russians—their ability to fight back after the terrible defeats of the summer and autumn—amazed and delighted their well-wishers in occupied Europe and in the West. It seemed to betoken some peculiar strength in the So-

The Big Three at Yalta, February 1945. From left to right: Winston Churchill, Franklin Roosevelt, and Josef Stalin. Roosevelt's poor health is evident in this photograph; he died two months following the conference. (*Courtesy Brown Brothers*)

viet peoples or in the system of government under which they lived. Thus the winter of 1941–1942 marked the beginning of a new wave of pro-Soviet and pro-Communist feeling in Europe. Stalin's peace with Hitler in 1939 had completely deflated his country's reputation. Now the rupture of that pact and Soviet resistance to the Nazi invasion brought a sharp and steady rise in Russia's standing. The years between 1941 and 1944 saw Soviet prestige higher than ever before.

The War in Eastern Europe and the Anglo-American Contribution

For nearly three years, the war in the East dwarfed the struggle in the West. The Nazi-Soviet conflict was without precedent in history. In the extent of territory it covered, in the forces engaged, in the ruthlessness displayed on both sides, certainly no modern war was comparable to it.

Against the over four million men that the Germans and their satellites had sent to Russia, the Red Army had mobilized a roughly equal equal force. Their equipment was also of equal quality, especially the new T-34 tank (built on an American design). But as the war continued, and as Russia's population advantage began to tell, the weight of numbers fell ever more heavily on Stalin's side, despite the frightful losses that the Soviet peoples suffered. These again were without precedent. At the end of the war, total Soviet deaths—civilian and military—were estimated at 20 million. Millions had died in combat; millions more had starved or frozen to death. The Germans had slaughtered countless others among the civilian population behind the lines or worked them to death as prisoners of war. The Soviet Union was not a signatory of the Geneva Convention, and the Nazis saw no purpose in conforming to its provisions in dealing with enemies whom they regarded as subhuman. On neither side, then, had a prisoner much chance of humane treatment. In most cases, imprisonment meant brutality, hardship, and a lingering death.

With the Soviet Union bearing the brunt of the fighting, there was mounting pressure on the British and the Americans to come to the aid of the Russians by opening a second front on the European continent. Stalin pleaded for it in terms that alternated between polite suggestion and peremptory demand. Public opinion in Britain and the United States clamored for it. Neither the Russians nor the Anglo-American public understood that the Western Allies were *already* contributing mightily to the common war effort, but that this contribution was more dispersed and harder to grasp than the Russian, reflecting the complex and wide-ranging commitments of a truly global struggle. American forces were engaged against the Japanese in Asia and the Pacific; the British (and by 1943 the Americans as well) were fighting in the Mediterranean. Moreover, the Americans on all fronts, and the British on most of theirs, were operating at the end of supply lines that were thousands of miles in length, which meant that many Anglo-Americans in uniform remained absorbed in transport and resupply.

Finally, the critics of British and American strategy forgot that all the prospective operations in the West involved an amphibious assault against a heavily defended coastline. The great democracies had almost to invent the technique of amphibious warfare. The Germans had not dared to launch "Sea Lion" against England; the Russians had no need for, or experience in, major landing operations. These were to become the Anglo-American specialty—their great contribution to the art of modern warfare. But the Western Allies could make their supreme attempt—a major cross-Channel invasion of France—only after gaining experience in the Mediterranean and the Pacific. The true second front was not to materialize until the very last year of the war.

The Nazi "New Order": Racism and Collaboration

By the end of 1941, Hitler had conquered the most extensive empire that European history had ever known (see Map 13.1). Directly or indirectly, he ruled over all the former democracies of Western Europe, save for neutral Sweden and Switzerland; he held the whole of the Balkans and East Central Europe, the Ukraine, and a vast zone in European Russia. Italy was closely allied to him; Spain, more loosely. Except for minor bits and pieces, all the Continent lay in his grasp.

In the weary and disillusioned Europe of 1940 and 1941, an influential minority of both the leaders and the led was willing to accept German hegemony. The Germans were the most numerous and the most industrially advanced of the major peoples of Western and Central Europe, and after the collapse of France, leadership seemed to devolve on them almost by right. Hitler offered the Europeans a "New Order." He promised them a stern justice under which each nation would be assigned its fitting role. But the reality of the New Order bore little resemblance to the promised ideal. By the end of 1942, at the very latest, the majority of the populations of occupied Europe had turned against Hitler and the nation he led. In 1943, the Italians, too, were to become his enemies, and with them a small but resolute minority among his own people. By the war's end, nazism was universally hated as the most dreadful tyranny that Europe had known since the Dark Ages.

What had changed people's minds? First was the fact that the Nazi "New Order" subordinated Europe's captive nations to the needs of Hitler's war machine. With methodical and ruthless purpose, the rulers in Berlin fashioned a system of economic exploitation where countries occupied by German troops not only had to bear the costs of the occupation, but were also obliged to ship food, raw materials, and manpower to the Reich in ever-increasing quantities.

The German need for labor proved especially difficult to satisfy. With the invasion of the Soviet Union in 1941, Hitler began to face a stringent manpower shortage. The Russians alone outnumbered the Germans—and the *Führer* could not send all his troops to the east, since he also needed to garrison France, Norway, and the Balkans. Under these circumstances, his sole recourse was to withdraw every able-bodied German male out of agriculture and industry and send him to the front. Nazi ideology forbade women any role outside the home, and few were allowed to replace men in the fields and factories. The only remaining manpower reserve lay in the occupied territories. Thus the Nazis began to resort to labor drafts abroad. By the last year of the war, millions of foreigners working in Germany had been degraded to an army of slave laborers. Young men fleeing from forced labor in the Reich had become the chief source of recruitment for the resistance organizations that were springing up everywhere.

Still worse was Nazi racial policy. In *Mein Kampf*, Hitler paraded his ideas of German superiority and his contempt for most of the peoples of Europe. Any effort to re-

MAP 13.1 Nazi-occupied Europe in 1941.

organize the Continent under German leadership immediately collided with the flagrant contradiction of Nazi racial doctrine. What incentive was there for Europeans to collaborate with their new masters when most were relegated in advance to the category of "inferior peoples" in the Nazi racial hierarchy?

The Nazis displayed grudging respect for fellow "Nordics"—the Dutch, the Norwegians, and the Danes—who were invited to join the Germans as "master races" in the New Order. Next came the French and the Belgians, "mixed" peoples who were rather perplexing to racial theorists. One stage lower ranked the Slavs—the Russians, the Poles, the Yugoslavians, and the Czechs—of whom the Czechs alone, who were peacefully inclined and vital to German war production, escaped the worst of Nazi brutalities. Finally, of course, in the lowest order, came those whom the Nazis regarded as pariahs—the Jews and the Gypsies, as well as the mentally handicapped and homosexuals from all racial groups. These people were to be exterminated. In early 1942, Hitler and his inner circle ratified a "final solution" of the "Jewish question," and in the next three years his faithful SS detachments destroyed six million Jews in the gas chambers and crematories of Auschwitz and other concentration camps. Thus perished during the Second World War about three-quarters of European Jewry—two-fifths of all the Jews in the world.

The Holocaust

In January 1939, more than half a year before the war began, Hitler had prophesied the "annihilation of the Jewish race in Europe." He came perilously close to accomplishing his aim. It may be, as some historians have argued, that the Nazi campaign evolved over time from sporadic toward ever more systematic destruction. Certainly it was not until they had subjugated much of Eastern Europe in 1942 that the Nazis found themselves in a position to carry out genocide on a mass scale. The majority of Europe's Jews lived in Poland and the Ukraine, which now fell under Hitler's control. In the months after the invasion of the Soviet Union, Nazi officials experimented with various methods of mass murder before undertaking a full-scale campaign of genocide. Shooting the victims with special execution squads (the so-called *Einsatzgruppen*) proved more difficult than asphyxiating them in gas chambers; thus the death camps were born.

The architects of the "final solution," Heinrich Himmler and SS General Reinhard Heydrich and their staffs, planned it with the ruthlessness of mass murderers and the technical efficiency of industrial engineers. Four huge extermination centers were constructed in Poland at Belzec, Maidanek, Sobibor, and Treblinka; a fifth center, Auschwitz, was converted from an existing concentration camp within Germany, which had formerly housed Polish political prisoners. All were designed as factories of death. Trains delivered their human cargo to these camps, where they were gassed and incinerated with the methodical precision of the assembly line. At the peak of its activity, Auschwitz attained the murderous rate of 12,000 victims a day. As the war dragged on, Germany's desperate need for working hands meant that some of the intended victims were spared at the last minute for hard labor—selected at the camp gates by SS doctors such as the infamous Josef Mengele, the "angel of death" at Auschwitz.

After the war, many Germans protested that they had known nothing of the Holocaust. This claim is extremely difficult to disprove, but even more difficult to believe. While the Nazi authorities did take measures to hide the full dimensions of the "final solution" from the German public (there were no press reports on the number of Jews killed, for instance, and no visitors allowed in the death camps), at the same time the disappearance of so many from cities such as Frankfurt, Hamburg, and Berlin could not fail to attract notice. Soldiers on the Eastern Front were even more likely to witness killings and deportations of Jews, and would have told some of what they saw when on leave to those at home. In the final months of the war, huge convoys of prisoners tra-

Frightened Jewish families forced from their homes by German troops begin the long journey to extermination camps after the Warsaw Ghetto uprising in April 1943. (*Courtesy Corbis-Bettmann*)

versed parts of Germany on foot. Thus most Germans doubtless knew something. Yet if they did not actively persecute these prisoners, they chose to turn a blind eye to what was happening—some because they felt powerless to intervene, others because they were truly indifferent to the sufferings of the Jews. That indifference had lethal consequences. As the anti-Nazi Protestant pastor Martin Niemöller is reported to have said after the war:

> First they came for the socialists, and I did not speak out—because I was not a socialist. Then they came for the trade-unionists, and I did not speak out—because I was not a trade-unionist. Then they came for the Jews, and I did not speak out—because I was not a Jew. Then they came for me—and there was no one left to speak for me.*

The Resistance: Tito and de Gaulle

Just as Nazi occupation policy—and the racial theory of which it was an outgrowth— were unprecedented in European history, so were the choices with which it confronted individuals among the conquered peoples. It had earlier been assumed that populations who temporarily fell under enemy control in wartime would obey the orders of the in-

*Quoted in Michael Berenbaum, *The World Must Know: The History of the Holocaust as Told in the United States Holocaust Memorial Museum* (Boston: Little, Brown & Co., 1993), 41.

vader; relations between the two might not be friendly, but they were supposed to be "correct." In the Second World War, circumstances were quite different. At first, a great many local officials tried to conform to the older pattern, and some of them—who sacrificed their good names to what they regarded as their duty—rank among the unsung heroes of the conflict. But as Nazi occupation policy hardened, it became ever more difficult to reconcile German orders with the voice of the local officials' own consciences, and when they were asked to help herd Jews or forced laborers, some of them refused.

Under these circumstances, only a handful remained with the Germans until the end. The prototype of such true "collaborationists" was Vidkun Quisling of Norway, whose name was given to the whole species. But Quisling had few followers in Norway, and elsewhere in the west Hitler found no suitable leading figure to govern in his name. He organized Belgium and Holland as military commands—as Poland had been. In France there was Marshal Pétain, but he was no Quisling. On the contrary, the marshal was a perplexing borderline case, whose presence at the head of the Vichy government confused and divided the French through most of the war. Another—and more sinister—borderline figure was Ante Pavelich, the ruler of Croatia, which Hitler had separated from the Serbian lands of Yugoslavia in conformity with his characteristic tactics of divide and rule.

These special cases can be understood only in the light of that other phenomenon—counterpoise and deadly enemy of collaboration—the Resistance movements. Resistance meant sabotage and guerrilla warfare against the Nazi occupiers. It meant the establishment of shadow governments and shadow political parties to prepare the ground for the day of liberation. It also meant liaison with governments-in-exile, where such existed.

Throughout Europe, the conditions that stimulated such activity were much the same. Resistance grew in rural areas, where mountains or forests offered cover, and also in cities, where workers felt threatened by the labor draft. It sprang up where there were idealistic or desperate men whose hatred of the invader impelled them to leave their ordinary jobs to go underground or take to the hills. The Resistance tended toward the left. Its recruits most frequently came from the working classes or from young intellectuals with a social conscience; it was strong at the extreme ends of the social scale—among the poor and among the upper classes, whose sense of adventure and martial tradition brought the Resistance a precious reinforcement of military talent. The great middle class and the richer peasantry generally stood aside. People of this sort, cautious by tradition and wedded to routine, hesitated to take the risks that Resistance activity entailed.

The Second World War on the continent of Europe has sometimes been called an international civil war. It was such a conflict in a double sense. First, it was a desperate struggle between resisters and collaborationists—between patriots who were trying to drive the invaders out of their country and the smaller number of traitors who put themselves at the service of Nazi Germany. This was a war without mercy; a Resistance fighter well knew that if he fell into the hands of the black-shirted SS, only torture and death awaited him. Alongside this avowed conflict raged another and quieter civil war, yet one which was scarcely less cruel—the war of Communists against non-Communists within the Resistance itself. The examples of Poland, Yugoslavia, and France may suggest how this latter struggle developed in three widely different settings.

The Poles very early organized a strong and united Resistance movement. Here collaborationists were virtually nonexistent; the cruelty of German occupation policy saw to that. The Poles were proud that they never produced a Quisling, but they were not exposed to the temptations that assailed the Scandinavians or the Dutch; Poland was never invited to collaborate in the Nazi New Order, and its people were immediately treated as inferiors. Nor was there a problem of Communist influence. In Poland, traditional hatred of Russia and of communism had only been intensified by Stalin's connivance with Hitler in the partition of the country. The Polish Resistance was both conservative in tone and supported by the overwhelming majority of the people. It carried on a regular underground government, with law courts, bond issues, even a rudimentary educational system, and, through a remarkable organization of clandestine couriers, it maintained contact with the Polish government-in-exile in London.

Stalin had no regard either for the government in London or for the underground regime in Poland itself. When the Red Army crossed the Polish boundary on its triumphal advance west, he chose to ignore both of them. Instead he set up his own puppet regime of Communists who had been indoctrinated in Moscow, and he let the authentic Polish Resistance fighters be destroyed by the Germans while making only the most perfunctory moves to save them.

Yugoslavia, in contrast, produced both a non-Communist and a Communist-led Resistance movement of major dimensions. Indeed, the Yugoslavs never really demobilized after their defeat in the spring of 1941. A number of Serbian army officers, under the command of Colonel Draja Mihailovich, fled with their weapons and continued the struggle in the country's mountain fastnesses, where they organized bands of guerrilla fighters called *Chetniks*. Mihailovich's exploits soon aroused widespread sympathy in the West. The Yugoslav government-in-exile appointed him minister of war and relied increasingly on him to assure its return home at the end of the conflict.

Meanwhile, however, Churchill and Roosevelt had begun to have grave doubts as to whether Mihailovich was mobilizing Yugoslav Resistance to the full. The Chetnik leader made no secret of his intention of enforcing Serbian supremacy on the country's liberation, and he neither tried nor desired to appeal to the Croats, Slovenes, and other minority peoples within Yugoslavia. This role fell to another resistance leader, Josip Broz, better known by his revolutionary nickname, Tito.

Tito's movement began later than Mihailovich's but soon outdistanced it. For Tito was a Croat; and although he had long since cast off the ancestral Catholicism that characterized Croatia, he had no love for Serb supremacy, and he preached reconciliation and unity among the Yugoslav peoples. He condemned both the Serbian collaborationists and the Croat leader Pavelich, who was taking his revenge for the humiliations his people had suffered at the hands of the Serbians by slaughtering tens of thousands of them with Hitler's and Mussolini's blessing. Tito was a Communist, and his bands of Partisans—as they were called to distinguish them from Mihailovich's *Chetniks*—were systematically indoctrinated by Communist political commissars. During the war, however, Tito kept his own communism in the background; rather, he followed the Popular Front formula when he organized a Yugoslav underground government in November 1942.

Tito fought the Germans and fought them hard. By 1943, he was keeping at bay at least ten enemy divisions. Mihailovich, in contrast, remained quiescent, holding his

Opponents of Nazism risked imprisonment in concentration camps such as this one at Sachsenhausen near Berlin. In this photograph from February 1941, shivering prisoners stand at attention in 10°F weather. A hanged prisoner can also be seen on a gallows behind the massed inmates. (*Courtesy H. Armstrong Roberts*)

forces in reserve. This was the evidence the Allies needed to make their choice. In 1943, first Churchill, and later Roosevelt, withdrew support from Mihailovich and gave their help to Tito instead.

In France, as in Yugoslavia—and as was to occur later in northern Italy—Communists played a very prominent part in the Resistance. But France found in Charles de Gaulle a military and nationalist leader who was far more successful than Mihailovich in counteracting their influence. An expert in tank welfare from whose books the Germans learned the *Blitzkrieg* tactics they were to apply so devastatingly against the French, de Gaulle had been a prophet without honor in his own country. Called by Premier Reynaud in France's hour of supreme peril to serve as undersecretary of war, he had come to office too late to stay his army's collapse. Yet he was able to use his official position to maintain the link with Britain after France's defeat. Refusing to accept Pétain's armistice, he flew to London, where on June 18, 1940, he broadcast a message calling for French citizens to continue the fight. Reminding his listeners that their nation was engaged in a world war where "France is not alone," he promised them that "the flame of French resistance must and will not die."

In Britain, de Gaulle established a Free French National Committee to serve as an embryo government-in-exile. Recruits arrived in a slow trickle. Most of the French took a "wait-and-see" attitude—which was only natural since Pétain's government in Vichy still seemed to speak with the voice of legitimacy. Nowhere else in Western Europe were people's allegiances so cruelly divided. Churchill gave de Gaulle his support—although he found the general extremely difficult to deal with and complained that the Cross of Lorraine (de Gaulle's emblem) was the heaviest cross he had to bear. Roosevelt, on the contrary, distrusted the Free French leader as an authoritarian and refused to grant recognition to his National Committee.

This distrust proved mistaken, but it was understandable in view of de Gaulle's excessive pride and his tendency to regard his country's destiny as incarnate in his own person. An imposing figure at six feet three inches tall, unbending in his insistence on protocol befitting a head of state, the general made up for his lack of military and financial resources through sheer stubbornness and force of personality. Though he held a weak hand at first in his British exile, he played his political cards with the cool deliberation of someone determined to bluff the other players into submission up to the very end.

By 1942, however, de Gaulle began to make definite progress in his own quest for legitimacy. A sizable segment of the French overseas empire—including equatorial Africa, the Pacific islands, Madagascar, and Syria—had come under his control. Pétain's regime was steadily losing prestige as its impotence to shield France against the German occupation grew more evident. The vast majority of the Resistance organizations within France recognized the general as their chief. A number of their leaders joined him in London, including several prominent Socialists, whose arrival gave the Free French movement a more representative and democratic flavor. By the autumn of 1942—when the British and Americans were preparing for a landing in French North Africa—it was apparent to all except those irremediably prejudiced against de Gaulle that the active and militant element within France had deserted Vichy and had transferred its sympathies to the Free French movement.

IV. THE TURNING OF THE TIDE

In the autumn of 1942, the tide turned. For more than three years, events had moved in Hitler's favor. The war had been a long succession of German victories—the greatest the world had ever seen. The best his enemies had been able to do was to stop his advance in the air Battle of Britain and before Moscow and to defeat his Italian ally in the Mediterranean. At the end of 1942, the trend was reversed: the Russians held firm at Stalingrad, the British broke out of Egypt, the Americans landed in French North Africa. In two widely separated theaters of combat, the Allies were preparing vast encircling operations that would bring the Nazis their first major defeats. From this point on, the victory of Britain and America and the Soviet Union was never in doubt. The only question was how long it would take—and the answer to that question depended on the great strategic decisions which the Allied leaders were to make in their efforts to fight a coalition war of unprecedented scope and intensity (see Map 13.2, p. 336).

The Battle of Stalingrad

Hitler changed his military command after the failure before Moscow. His old field marshals, disappointed by the *Führer's* interference with their strategy, retired and were replaced by younger men, who were more pliable and closer to the Nazi party. And Hitler himself assumed the post of commander-in-chief for the first time.

Although the military amateur was now in charge, the plan for the campaign of 1942 showed a more coherent strategy than that pursued in 1941. The attack was to be on one front alone; the whole weight of German arms was to be concentrated in the south, where Hitler hoped to achieve the decisive results that had eluded him the previous year. He planned to drive from the Ukraine to Stalingrad on the Volga, and to the Caspian Sea, thereby literally cutting the Soviet Union in two. By seizing the Caucasus, he hoped both to deny the Red Army its major source of oil and to solve his own most urgent supply problem.

At first, the German tanks rolled forward as relentlessly as they had the previous summer. In early July, they took Sevastopol in the Crimea; at the end of the month, they were in Rostov and preparing to cross the Don. Once across the great river, they raced ahead almost without interruption. By late summer, they were just short of the oil center of Grozny in the north Caucasus, and their advanced patrols had reached the Caspian Sea.

Meanwhile, on August 22, the Battle of Stalingrad had begun. Stalingrad was a key city in every sense. It was dear to Stalin's heart; under its original name of Tsaritsin it was the place where he had first made a military reputation during the civil war. It was also a major industrial center—one of the new manufacturing complexes that had been built up safely remote from the Soviet frontiers during the Five-Year Plans. Finally, it was a strategic position of first importance: Situated on the Volga just where the Don bends closest to its sister river, it stood farthest east of the great cities of southern Russia. Beyond Stalingrad lay little but open steppe. Should it fall into enemy hands, communication between the south and the center of the country would be effectively severed.

Stalin gave the order to hold at all costs. With their backs to Asia, the city's defenders stood their ground. But the Germans, though suffering enormous losses, still inched steadily forward. By mid-September they were in the city itself; defenders and besiegers fought desperately at close quarters in streets and factories. For a few days the position of the defenders seemed hopeless.

Once again Stalin kept his nerve. While the defense of Stalingrad hung in the balance, Zhukov and his military staff were completing their plan for a great pincers movement that would catch the Germans in a trap. On November 19, the first Soviet attack began. Isolated at the end of a dangerously stretched communications line, and poorly supported by the Romanian and Italian troops dug in beside them, the besiegers of Stalingrad now had to turn to face a new threat to the rear. By November 23, after four days of fierce fighting, the Russian pincers began to close. If the Germans were to escape, it had to be before winter set in. But Hitler refused to give the order for evacuation. "We are not budging from the Volga," he declared, and ordered a relief army under General Manstein east to the rescue. On Christmas eve, within sound of the guns of Stalingrad, a defeated Manstein turned back—the rest was one long German martyrdom. Hunger, frost, and typhus took a mounting toll. By the new year, the Germans were reduced to a ragged rabble of sick and half-crazed men. On February 2, 1943, when the final surrender came, only 80,000 remained alive to be led off to captivity.

So ended the greatest battle of human history.

The War in North Africa

For two years, the desert war in North Africa had seesawed back and forth with no decisive victory for either side. The Italians had first invaded Egypt from their own colony of Libya. Then, in December 1940, the British launched a surprise counterattack, driving the Italians back 500 miles and capturing 130,000 of them, with casualties on their own side totaling fewer than 2,000. At this point, Hitler saw the necessity of bolstering his groggy ally. He sent to Libya one of his ablest tank leaders, General Erwin Rommel, with reinforcements of German armored troops and instructions to supplant the Italians in command. By the spring of 1941, Rommel had pushed his enemy back to the Egyptian frontier.

For the ensuing year, the two opposing forces lay deadlocked as Rommel's advance stalled. Then a new British general, Sir Bernard Montgomery, arrived in Egypt and quietly began painstaking preparations for a counteroffensive to rob Rommel of the prize he seemed close to taking. In late October of 1942 the British artillery opened fire on Rommel's forces at El Alamein, only seventy miles from Alexandria, with the heaviest barrage that the African continent had ever known. After ten days of intense tank and infantry combat, Rommel's lines finally broke, and he was forced to retreat. Relentlessly, methodically, Montgomery pursued him along the Egyptian and Libyan shore. On January 24, 1943, the British at last captured Tripoli, and the road to Tunisia lay open.

The advance from El Alamein formed one claw of another great pincers movement—a campaign that the British and Americans devised to liquidate once and for all the Axis position in North Africa. The second was a series of landings in French-controlled Morocco and Algeria that Churchill and Roosevelt had decided was to be their major effort for the year 1942. When, on November 8, the great Allied invasion armada approached the African coast and the untried American troops scrambled ashore, the French army and navy stationed to defend this part of the French Empire followed Pétain's orders and resisted. Ironically, it seemed at first that France might block the campaign to free North Africa. Then a local Vichy official ordered surrender in return for Allied backing as the region's governor; he had barely assumed power when he was assassinated. Into the power vacuum now moved General de Gaulle with energy and consummate skill. By the autumn of 1943, de Gaulle was heading what was in reality (if not yet in name) a new provisional government of the French Empire. The Vichy government had become a mere shadow, since the Germans had used the North African landings as a pretext for occupying the whole of France. As the moment of liberation approached, all eyes turned toward de Gaulle.

The Conquest of Sicily, the Fall of Mussolini, and the Invasion of Italy

Meanwhile, the Allied pincers had closed on Tunisia. Its reduction had taken longer than the British and Americans had expected, but the delay brought additional Axis reinforcements and thus a larger number of prisoners when Axis resistance finally ended in May 1943. The next step was Sicily. Once more Churchill and Roosevelt had decided to give priority to clearing the Mediterranean. Meeting at the Moroccan port of Casablanca in January, they had determined to occupy the great Italian island that nearly divided the Mediterranean in two.

The attack on Sicily began on July 10. It was the largest landing that the British and Americans had yet undertaken: 160,000 men participated. After sharp fighting on the beaches, the conquest of the island proceeded rapidly. The Germans fought hard, but the Italians, who constituted the bulk of the island's defenders, offered little more than token resistance. They were already sick of the war—disgusted by constant defeats, by the domineering of their German allies, and by the way Mussolini had lied to them about their nation's strength and its readiness for war.

For the *Duce* himself, the play had almost ended. On July 25, just after the fall of the Sicilian capital of Palermo, he was toppled from power. A combination of monarchist conservatives and Fascist dissidents persuaded the old king to dismiss him and make him prisoner. Mussolini's successor was Marshal Pietro Badoglio—the conqueror of Ethiopia and a very recent convert to antifascism, to say the least. Badoglio hoped to take Italy out of the war unscathed, and in this he faithfully expressed the longings of his people. In the month and a half that followed Mussolini's fall, the country lived in a strange euphoria; free political activity revived as though by magic, and the Italians cherished the illusion that they were entering on a new era of peace, liberty, and national harmony.

Actually, their troubles had only begun. For Italy, the second phase of the war was to be still more cruel than the first. Badoglio was forced to make an unconditional surrender to the Allies as their troops landed south of Naples; meanwhile, Hitler, well aware of Badoglio's plans, began pouring men and supplies over the Brenner Pass to hold in check his faithless ally. For the next year and a half, Italy was to remain cut in two. In the north, Mussolini, whom the Germans had dramatically freed from imprisonment, wielded nominal authority as a pathetic and powerless Quisling. The king and Badoglio, whom the Allies were supporting in the south, were scarcely less feeble and unrepresentative of the Italian people. Between the two hovered the uncertain mass of Italians—half starved, half frozen, and miserable in the damp Mediterranean winter.

Teheran and the Great Strategic Decisions

After its victory at Stalingrad, the Red Army swept on to further winter triumphs. It drove back the German besiegers before Leningrad,* cleared an additional zone west of Moscow, retook Rostov and began the liberation of the Ukraine. In the spring of 1943,

---

*The seige was finally lifted a year later.

however, as had happened the year before, the Germans struck back. In March, they recaptured the recently liberated city of Kharkov, and in early July they attacked with a massive tank offensive 100 miles farther north in the region of Kursk and Orel. But this was their last effort; never again were the Germans to regain the initiative on the Eastern Front. Having blunted the German advance, in mid-July the Soviet summer counteroffensive began to roll. It was the beginning of a campaign that continued for almost two years and reached its end in the smoking ruins of Berlin.

With the British and Americans at last ashore on the European continent and with the Russians advancing relentlessly toward their own borders, a new coordination had become urgent. As long as the campaigns in the east remained widely separated from those in the west, it had been possible to treat them as two separate wars. Now it was essential to knit them together. This was the purpose of the first of the two meetings that brought Churchill and Roosevelt into personal contact with Stalin—the meeting held in November and December of 1943 at the Persian capital of Teheran.

For nearly two years Stalin had been pleading for a major second front—preferably in France—that would relieve German pressure on his own forces. The great achievement of the Teheran Conference was an agreement that a major landing by the Western Allies would be made in France in May of 1944. The commander of the operation was to be General Eisenhower. Stalin, much gratified, promised to open a simultaneous offensive on the Eastern Front. The strategy had been established that would bring total victory in the last year and a half of the war.

V. THE FINAL ASSAULT

The Liberation of Rome and Northern Italy

The Teheran decisions had put the Italian campaign in a paradoxical position. It was to be both an active front and a secondary front. It was the only place on the Continent where the British and Americans were actually fighting, but its needs were constantly subordinated to the task of building up strength in England for the cross-Channel operation in the spring. Hence it was always short of manpower; again and again, a planned offensive dwindled and failed because of a lack of reserve troops.

These handicaps were already apparent in the first efforts to break the winter stalemate south of Rome. In January 1944, the Allies made a landing at Anzio, only 30 miles from the Italian capital, and a simultaneous assault on the Germans defending the mountain abbey of Cassino. They hoped to catch Hitler's forces off guard by attacking them at two points at once and then by advancing quickly to the liberation of Rome. Both expectations were cruelly disappointed. It was not until late May that the British and Americans at last broke out of the Anzio beachhead. Once the mountains had been breached, the way to Rome lay open. The Germans did not try to defend the Italian capital; throughout the campaign it was treated by both sides as an open city. On June 4, the Allies entered Rome in triumph, to the wild rejoicing of its inhabitants.

Rome was the first of the continental capitals to be freed from the Nazi grasp, and its liberation inaugurated a new era in European political history. It marked the beginning of postfascist politics—of the reconstruction of democracy on the ruins of authoritarian regimes. Six weeks before Rome fell, Badoglio had been persuaded to reconstruct his ministry to include the leaders of the chief antifascist political parties. In early June, the Italian king relinquished his functions. Badoglio also had to go. The democratic political leaders insisted that they would serve under him no longer and that the new chief of government should be Ivanoe Bonomi—the next to the last prefascist prime minister of Italy—who had been chairman of the clandestine Committee of Liberation during the German occupation of Rome.

Thus, after its entry into the capital, the government of southern Italy presented a much more democratic face to its own people and to the outside world. In this it reflected the desire of antifascist Italians to get back into the war—to "work their passage home," as Churchill put it. The Italian capital had produced a real Resistance movement, and north of Rome the Resistance was strong and militant. When the Allies reached Florence in early August, they found that its citizens had already taken up arms for their own liberation. By the time the campaign had again frozen into a winter stalemate in the mountain chain running between Florence and Bologna, the military achievements of the Italian Resistance had been universally recognized. A new Italian army was being trained to take its place beside the British and the Americans and the French in the final push to liberate the northern cities. In the last six months of the war, the Italians had been all but accepted as full Allies in the common cause.

The Landings in Normandy and Southern France

The liberation of Rome was overshadowed by a greater event—the most dramatic of the whole war—which occurred only a day and a half later: the Allied landings in Normandy.

The great build-up of forces in southern England had mounted throughout the winter and spring until, as the soldiers put it, the island seemed about to sink under the weight of men and materiel it was carrying. The target date for the invasion, like the advance on Rome, had been subject to repeated and frustrating delays. At last Eisenhower decided to press ahead despite unfavorable weather, and was rewarded for his resolve when, on the dawn of D-day, the seas unexpectedly began to calm.

The landings began in the early morning of June 6 on a 60-mile arc along the broad indentation of the Normandy coast between Cherbourg and Le Havre—close enough to the English coast to permit continuous air cover with fighter planes. It was not the *Luftwaffe* that the invaders now had to fear; it was the Germans' artillery, their barbed wire, their underwater obstacles and mines—all the heavy defenses that they had been preparing for three years against just such an attack. Casualties were heavy on D-day, and for long hours the outcome hung in the balance. Yet the invaders were able to profit by German indecision. In far-off Berlin, Hitler and his Chief of Staff, Friedrich Jodl, remained calamitously deceived about their intentions. Believing that the Normandy landings were only a feint, and that the main invasion would come in the Calais area, where the Channel was narrowest, the *Führer* ignored pleas from local commanders to counterattack and kept his armored forces in reserve until it was too late. When they finally began to move, the harassing attacks of the French Resistance held them to a slow crawl.

Throughout June and most of July, Eisenhower's forces consolidated their beachhead and steadily increased their strength. Within a week of D-day, more than 300,000 British and Americans were ashore, and, through artificial harbors built off the beaches, a steady stream of supplies began to flow in. On July 25, the American forces began a breakthrough at Saint-Lô. From there they went on to the cathedral town of Coutances, cutting off the enemy's retreat from the Cherbourg peninsula. By early August, the dashing tank commander, General George Patton, was out in open country at last, heading off on a great race across northern France.

At this point de Gaulle went into action. His prize armored division, under General Leclerc de Hauteclocque—which had been held in reserve for just such an eventuality—was given the order to advance on Paris. Here the Resistance had already risen; for ten days it fought bitter street battles with the occupying forces. Finally, Leclerc's tanks settled the issue. By August 26, the city was free. The day before, General de Gaulle—now universally recognized as the liberator and leader of the French—had arrived to assume authority. On a glorious summer afternoon he walked in triumph from the Etoile down the Champs Elysées to the Place de la Concorde, and then drove by car to Notre Dame, where the Te Deum of thanksgiving was interrupted by the desperate rifle shots of unyielding collaborationists.

Allied troops move from their landing craft onto the beach of Normandy on the morning of D Day, June 6, 1944. (*Courtesy H. Armstrong Roberts*)

The German Resistance and the Attempt on Hitler's Life

The Germans knew that they were beaten. For four years, death had been raining down on them from the skies, and as the Anglo-American air offensive mounted in intensity, the German cities and communications system were steadily crumbling. The Allies had won unquestioned mastery of the air; the *Luftwaffe* had failed completely. With the collapse of his promise of victory through air power, Reichsmarshal Goering had retired into obscurity. By the last year of the war, he no longer ranked among the top Nazis. The real directors of the German war effort were now three: an ambitious young architect, Albert Speer, who was reorganizing the economic front to make the most efficient use of the nation's resources; the SS chief, Heinrich Himmler, whose machinery of terror kept the population in line at home and whose black-shirted private army was trained to a ruthlessness and fanaticism that won for it an increasingly prominent role on the fighting fronts; finally Josef Goebbels, book burner and rabble rouser, whose task was now to mobilize the energies of the German people for a last-ditch stand—the utterly faithful Goebbels, who never wavered in his loyalty to his chief and who alone among the Nazi leaders chose to share Hitler's fate at the end.

The official propagandists had told the Germans that an Allied landing in France could never succeed—that it would be thrown back into the Channel with a staggering loss of life. By July, when it was obvious to all that the Normandy invasion had in fact succeeded, Hitler's subjects were left to draw their own conclusions. A courageous minority decided that the only recourse was assassination. They could see no other way to save their country from further destruction. On July 20, they planted a bomb in the temporary shelter on the Eastern Front where Hitler was holding a staff conference. The Führer escaped as if by a miracle; although a number of those standing around him were killed, and although he himself received injuries from which he never fully recovered, he lived to continue the war and to take frightful revenge on his enemies.

These enemies included a large group of late converts to the opposition—military men, like Rommel, who turned against Hitler only when they realized that the war was lost. But the core of the conspiracy consisted of dedicated and high-minded men—a few generals, diplomats, and civil servants, Protestant and Catholic clergymen, Social Democrats, and trade-union executives. Most of them were anti-Nazis of long standing. They were revolted by Hitler's tyranny, and they phrased their opposition in moral, and frequently in religious, terms. In embryo they presented the small, conservative, but extremely distinguished German counterpart to the Resistance movements that had sprung up in the occupied countries.

The failure of the July 20 bomb plot meant that the war was to continue until the total defeat of Hitler's Reich. It meant that the Germans would have no such escape from their bondage to a half-mad war lord as the Italians had found the year before with the overthrow of Mussolini. It also marked the last act in the gradual subjugation of the German army to Hitler's control; so many of his outstanding generals had been involved directly or indirectly in the plot that henceforth the military leadership was under a cloud. Finally, and most important, the failure of the assassination attempt brought the destruction of the flower of German antinazism. In the savage repression that followed it, at least 300 oppositionists lost their lives—a political elite that was to be sorely missed when the Germans began the difficult task of building up a new democracy.

The Soviet Breakthrough: Poland and Romania

A month before the fateful bomb exploded, the Red Army had opened its promised summer offensive. In the spring it had completed the liberation of the Crimea and the Ukraine. Now it began advancing along an 800-mile front against enemies reckoned at two million—as compared to the one million facing the Allies in the west. It drove the Finns to sue for peace; it reached German soil at the border of East Prussia; it crossed both the old and the new boundary of Poland and seemed on the verge of delivering the capital city of Warsaw.

At this point, the Polish Resistance rose in arms. On August 1, it began to fight the Germans in the streets of Warsaw. The Red Army was just across the Vistula River, but now refused to move. Despite anguished pleas from Churchill and Roosevelt—despite their efforts to send supplies to the fighters in Warsaw over an impossibly long air route—Stalin remained adamant; only at the very end would he offer even token help to the Polish insurgents, who could not maintain the unequal fight. After two months of hopeless struggle, they succumbed to German arms; thus ended the authentic and independent Polish Resistance.

The official reason for Stalin's inaction was that the Poles had risen irresponsibly and prematurely—before his army was ready to go to their aid. Most Western historians have found this argument unconvincing. They suspect that Stalin had ulterior motives in allowing the Poles to perish—that he was pleased to see eliminated a Resistance movement which would have proved extremely troublesome to him. From the merely military point of view, however, Stalin's strategic argument made sense, for it was true that the Red Army had no immediate need to push on to Warsaw: Poland could wait—it was already all but in Soviet hands. To the south, a greater prize glittered. In the late summer of 1944, the collapse of the whole German position in the Balkans began to loom on the horizon.

Thereafter—as had happened the week before in France—the Germans had no recourse but to evacuate the peninsula as fast as possible. Following Romania, Bulgaria sued for peace and reentered the war alongside the Soviet Union. In early October, as the Germans began their retreat from Greece, the British arrived from Egypt almost unopposed and took up the thorny task of trying to persuade the Greek Resistance to accept the return of the government-in-exile. In Yugoslavia, Tito redoubled his attacks on the retreating Germans; slowly his Partisans advanced from the mountains into the Serbian plain until, in late October, they entered Belgrade in triumph. Tito had swept away the Serbian Quislings; he had driven out the Croat terrorist Pavelich; Mihailovich he had captured and held prisoner. Only the Yugoslav government-in-exile stood between him and the undisputed power he craved—but to the exiled king and his government Tito was resolved to pay as little heed as possible.

As opposed to the Communist leaders in Poland, who were completely dependent on Stalin and the Red Army, Tito had done the job himself. He had received help from the Red Army only at the very end, when it marched through his country from Romania on its way to attack the Germans in Hungary. This was to be the secret of Tito's stubbornness and strength in his subsequent conflicts with the Soviet Union. In Hungary, the Red Army at last encountered a firm German stand. Here it was to be stalemated for most of the winter. Once more it shifted the focus of its efforts—this time back to the plains of Poland. The Red Army had already achieved the essentials of Stalin's purpose: Virtually the whole of East Central Europe now lay under Soviet domination.

The Churchill-Stalin Agreement on Spheres of Influence

It was this harsh reality that prompted Winston Churchill to pay a call on Stalin in early October. He was acting alone, and he was fully aware of the risks he was taking, but he was convinced that there was not a moment to lose and that he should try to save what could be saved before it was too late. He could not wait for Roosevelt to accompany him: The American president was fully occupied with his own campaign for reelection, and at least another month had to pass before he would be free to exert his influence in the great political and territorial decisions that the vertiginous course of the war had raised.

Churchill himself has given the classic account of what passed between him and Stalin:

> The moment was apt for business, so I said, "Let us settle about our affairs in the Balkans. Your armies are in Rumania and Bulgaria. We have interests, missions, and agents there. Don't let us get at cross-purposes in small ways. So far as Britain and Russia are concerned, how would it do for you to have ninety percent predominance in Rumania, for us to have ninety percent of the say in Greece, and go fifty-fifty about Yugoslavia?" While this was being translated I wrote out on a half-sheet of paper:
>
> | | |
> |---|---|
> | Rumania | |
> | Russia | 90% |
> | The others | 10% |
> | Greece | |
> | Great Britain (in accord with U.S.A.) | 90% |
> | Russia | 10% |
> | Yugoslavia | 50–50% |
> | Hungary | 50–50% |
> | Bulgaria | |
> | Russia | 75% |
> | The others | 25% |
>
> I pushed this across to Stalin, who had by then heard the translation. There was a slight pause. Then he took his blue pencil and made a large tick upon it, and passed it back to us. It was all settled in no more time than it takes to set down.*

In this simple fashion, Stalin and Churchill marked out their spheres of influence in the Balkans. On just such an issue had the Soviet understanding with Nazi Germany broken

*The Second World War, VI: Triumph and Tragedy (Boston: Houghton Mifflin Company, 1953), 227.

down four years earlier. Now Stalin had obtained from Churchill what Hitler had refused to grant him—a position of preponderance in the eastern part of the Balkan Peninsula.

It is easy to criticize the spheres of influence agreement of October 9, 1944. Indeed, the U.S. government—true to its consistent refusal to make deals while the war was in progress—never accepted it. True, it was a calculated, realistic bargain in the old tradition of power politics. True, the minor percentages of influence were impossible to enforce; Churchill might better have written 100 percent for Romania and Bulgaria on Stalin's side, and for Greece on his own, rather than 90 percent or 75 percent. Still worse, the 50–50 agreement for Hungary eventually broke down completely, as did the similar understanding about Yugoslavia. Finally, the whole arrangement had the fatal weakness of omitting Poland—the country where the war began and which during all its stages was the source of bitterest contention between East and West.

Nevertheless, it is only fair to add that Churchill was playing from a desperately weak hand. He probably got the best agreement that could have been obtained in the existing circumstances—certainly one more favorable to the West than the situation that was to emerge at the end of the war. And—paradoxically enough—the 50–50 arrangement for Yugoslavia eventually proved to be far less a lost cause than it seemed in the first months of 1945. After Tito's break with Stalin three years later, this was about where Yugoslavia stood, precariously poised between East and West.

But the most telling argument in favor of the spheres-of-influence agreement was its effect in Greece. Here, two months after the meeting between Churchill and Stalin, the Communist-led Resistance (the EAM-ELAS) rose in revolt against the newly returned government-in-exile. Fighting flared in the streets of Athens, and the situation grew so serious that the British prime minister himself felt obliged to fly to Greece to calm the storm. He curbed the Communists by military force, and he mitigated the country's internal differences by arranging for a regency under the archbishop of Athens. His task was immensely simplified, moreover, because the Soviet Union gave no support to the Communist insurgents. In this one instance at least, Stalin stood strictly by his word: Greece was treated as a British sphere of influence.

The Battle of the Bulge

On the Western Front, meanwhile, the advance toward Germany was continuing at a slow pace, as Eisenhower's forces gathered themselves for a final assault on the Reich (see Map 13.2). Then, in mid-December, the unexpected happened: The Germans struck back, powerfully and with stunning effect. For this, his last offensive effort, Hitler called on his ablest and most experienced commander, old Field Marshal von Rundstedt. Rundstedt's plan was bold and well conceived; he tried to cut through the Allied armies at their weakest point and, by capturing the great supply base of Antwerp, to demoralize them and disorganize their rear. The place he chose to strike was the same rugged and woody Ardennes where the Germans had breached the French defenses four and a half years before.

Rundstedt's plan came uncomfortably close to success. Favored by a spell of cloudy weather that prevented Allied planes from reconnoitering his troop concentrations, he caught the Americans thoroughly off guard. Soon a whole sector of the Allied

Allied Advances
⊞ January 1944 - January 1945
▬ February 1945
(Time of Yalta Conference)

0   250   500 Miles
0   250   500 Kilometers

NORTH
SEA

NORWAY

SWEDEN

FINLAND

Leningrad

BALTIC SEA

Riga

Smolensk

IRELAND

GREAT
BRITAIN

London

DENMARK

NETHERLANDS

BELGIUM

Paris

LUX.

FRANCE

SWITZ.

SPAIN

Marseilles

CORSICA

SARDINIA

GERMANY

Berlin

Munich

AUSTRIA

ITALY

Rome

POLAND

Warsaw

Prague

CZECHOSLOVAKIA

Vienna

Budapest

HUNGARY

YUGOSLAVIA

Belgrade

ADRIATIC SEA

MEDITERRANEAN SEA

SICILY

U.S.S.R.

Kiev

RUMANIA

Bucharest

BULGARIA

Sofia

BLACK
SEA

ALBANIA

GREECE

TURKEY

MAP 13.2   The Second World War: The Eastern and Western fronts in the last year of the war.

line in Belgium and Luxemburg was staggering back: A great "bulge" opened that had to be closed at all costs. It was a gloomy Christmas in Paris and Brussels—the victory that had seemed so close had once more been thrown into doubt. By the third week of January, Eisenhower's forces had stopped the German offensive and pushed the attackers back out of the bulge. But the Battle of the Bulge, as it came to be called, had shaken the Allies and disorganized the timetable of their advance into the Reich.

Once again the Western war effort seemed far less impressive than the Russian, for while the Americans and British were recovering from the shock they had received in the Ardennes, the Red Army was setting out on another spectacular winter offensive. Resuming the attack in Poland where they had broken it off five months earlier, the Russians captured Warsaw in mid-January 1945 and then swept on 300 miles to penetrate deep into Germany itself. East Prussia and Upper Silesia were in their grasp; before them literally millions of Germans were fleeing in the bitter cold. The Red Army did not pause until it reached the Oder River, only forty miles from Berlin.

This was the situation when the Big Three of the wartime alliance met on February 4 for the second (and last) time at the Crimean resort of Yalta. Their talks were overshadowed by the enormous Soviet successes and the partial Western reverse on the battlefield; to most prognosticators it seemed that the Russians would be in Berlin long before the British and Americans had advanced very far into the Reich. The Red Army's cannon could already be heard in Hitler's capital, while the Western Allies were still on the German frontiers more than 300 miles away. What Churchill and Roosevelt did not know was that the Ardennes offensive had exhausted the *Führer*'s last reserves—that in fact it had hastened rather than delayed the hour of victory in the West.

The Yalta Conference

The Yalta Conference has aroused more controversy than any other event of the whole war. In the United States it has been attacked in the bitterest terms: Roosevelt, his enemies have claimed, was "duped" by Stalin into "selling out" Eastern Europe and Manchuria to communism.

More than a year had passed since the meeting at Teheran. In this climactic fourteen months, the character of the war had changed entirely. Eight nations had been freed from the Nazi grasp, and final victory was now in sight. A multitude of problems stood in urgent need of immediate solution—problems to which the spheres of influence agreement of the previous October had offered only a partial and unsatisfactory answer. The procedure for reaching *strategic* decisions that had worked comparatively well at Teheran began to break down in dealing with the essentially political decisions that were the chief subject of discussion at Yalta. There was simply not enough time to argue them out to a clear conclusion. Hence the Big Three had recourse to loosely drafted formulas that gave a fallacious sense of an agreement that did not really exist. As soon as the conference adjourned, the deep antagonisms between East and West revealed themselves; each side had a conflicting interpretation of what it had agreed to do.

This was particularly true of the Declaration on Liberated Europe, which the Big Three issued. Based on the Atlantic Charter, it promised to assist the nations newly freed from Nazi tyranny, to help them solve their problems through democratic means and by free elections. But in the outstanding case in point—Poland—certain other decisions of the conference implicitly violated these high-sounding phrases. For in substance, Churchill and Roosevelt agreed to what Stalin wanted to do with the Poles. The Western leaders consented to the frontier that he had been demanding all along—roughly corresponding to the Curzon Line—and to his proposal for compensating Poland by extensive annexations to the West at Germany's expense. Stalin also secured Western consent to forcibly repatriate Soviet POWs and slave laborers even from areas of liberated Germany under American or British control. This ill-considered concession ensured the death or Siberian imprisonment of tens of thousands of Soviet citizens after the war's end.

In the other decisions regarding Germany, however, the West fared rather better. For one thing, the more punitive proposals for the postwar treatment of the enemy were nearly all abandoned. Although the conference decided in theory to break up the Reich into several separate states, it did nothing concrete about it, and in the succeeding weeks the idea was quietly buried. In a more positive vein, the Big Three agreed to admit France to equal partnership in the future control of Germany, including a zone of occupation of its own.

In all these matters, it was Churchill who fought the battle both for France and for Germany—for the preservation of both as future bulwarks of the West against Soviet power. Roosevelt, on the other hand, seemed hesitant and unsure, siding now with Churchill and now with Stalin. He distrusted communism—but he also distrusted British imperialist aims (which was a perfectly valid suspicion, as long as Churchill was in power). Hence he failed to coordinate adequately with his British friend, and he was prepared to make large concessions in the interests of Allied unity. Furthermore, he was less vigorous in expressing his opinions than he had been at Teheran. Churchill thought him very frail just after the adjournment at Yalta: In two months he was dead.

In short—however the harsh reality might be covered by soothing phrases—Roosevelt conceded to Stalin the domination of East Central Europe that the latter had won by his pact with Hitler in 1939 and more recently by his spheres of influence agreement with Churchill. The American president gambled that the Soviet leader would respond positively to this kind of generosity—more particularly in the planned organization of the United Nations, which was also discussed at Yalta. The alternative was to refuse to recognize the fait accompli of Soviet conquest, as the United States was subsequently to do in the case of Communist China. This course President Roosevelt rejected. He was convinced that public opinion in his own country and in Western Europe would be grievously disappointed if the war leaders at Yalta failed to reach an agreement, and in this conviction he was probably right. It would have come as a stunning blow to the veterans of the Resistance in particular to learn that the unity of the great alliance had been broken before the war had even been won. That was how things looked at the time. Posterity has judged otherwise.

The Last Campaigns: Vienna, Berlin, Prague

Within three months of the adjournment of the Yalta Conference, the war in Europe was over. Roosevelt was dead. And the Red Army held all three of the major capitals of Central Europe as the result of an extraordinary sequence of events.

In early March, Eisenhower's armies began a general advance toward the Rhine. When the forward units in the center reached the river, they discovered to their astonishment that the retreating Germans had failed to blow up one of the bridges—the railroad bridge at Remagen south of Bonn. This stroke of fortune changed the whole military outlook. Rather than having to wage a desperate and bloody struggle to cross the Rhine, the Americans were over the river at one bound. Bradley rolled up the German resistance in the Ruhr, trapping more than a quarter-million of Hitler's last troops. And when this battle came to an end, the Americans set off to the east to cut the Reich in two. On April 11 they reached the Elbe River, only sixty miles from Berlin.

Three days earlier, the final offensive in northern Italy had begun. In little more than a week of intensive fighting, the Allies broke the Germans' mountain defenses and

The bombed-out ruins of the city of Cologne, Germany, in 1945. To the right of the Gothic Cathedral—one of the very few buildings left standing—note the railroad bridge lying half submerged in the Rhine River. (*Courtesy National Archives and Records Administration*)

poured down into the north Italian plain. The Resistance fighters rose to meet them, as one city after another accomplished its own liberation before the Allies arrived. By the end of April, all Italy was free: The Germans laid down their arms. Mussolini, deserted by his protectors, tried to escape to the Swiss frontier, where he was discovered by a local Resistance detachment and summarily shot.

In the east, the Red Army had once again, as in the previous summer, shifted its main blow to the south. While Stalin was at Yalta, his commander in Hungary, Marshal Rodion Malinovski, was finally winning the long struggle for Budapest. In mid-February, German resistance ceased in the Hungarian capital. The road to Vienna lay open. And in eight weeks more the Austrian capital was also in Soviet hands. The race for control of Central Europe was already going in Stalin's favor.

Before Berlin, however, the greatest of the Soviet commanders, Marshal Grigori Zhukov, had paused for two months, preparing his forces for the final assault. In front of him lay Hitler's last hope—the most desperate and fanatical of his soldiers, whom he had ordered to stand their ground and die in defense of the Nazi capital. Berlin was now a mass of ruins. Indeed in the last winter of the war the Allied air forces had roamed at will over the Reich; virtually every city had been blasted again and again. With legitimate strategic targets exhausted, the British and American aviators struck almost at random, ruthlessly obliterating the architectural monuments of Germany's past and rendering millions homeless. The fire bombing of Dresden in February 1945, in which tens of thousands lost their lives, ranks among the most terrible events of the entire war.

Still Hitler refused to recognize the inevitable. He decreed that the German people should go down with their leader in a macabre Götterdämmerung, and he immured himself in the air-raid bunker below the Reich Chancellery as the battle for Berlin began to rage above him. On April 16, Zhukov opened his offensive. Nine days later he had the city surrounded. As the Russian tanks smashed into the capital, Hitler knew that the end had come. On the last day of April he shot himself, and his body was burned in the Chancellery courtyard. A week later the German High Command, in a surrender ceremony at Eisenhower's headquarters at Reims, finally brought the Second World War in Europe to a close.

But the war in the Pacific continued. The Allied decision to give priority to operations against Hitler had slowed the war effort against Japan. Now, with the German surrender, the American army prepared to re-deploy troops to the Far East. During the next three months, preparations intensified for an assault on the Japanese itself, which military experts predicted would cost a million Allied casualties and at least that many Japanese deaths. Then on August 6, 1945, the United States dropped an atomic bomb on Hiroshima, an industrial city of 200,000 in Western Japan, obliterating the city and killing 78,000. The Soviet Union, which had promised at Yalta to enter the war in the Far East on the side of the Americans, declared war on Japan two days later and invaded Manchuria. On August 9, a more destructive atomic bomb destroyed the city of Nagasaki, and the Japanese at last sued for peace. At last, on September 2, 1945—almost six years to the day since Hitler had invaded Poland and begun the Second World War—the bloodiest conflict in modern history was at an end.

READINGS

Once again, the most wide-ranging and spirited account by a participant is by Winston S. Churchill, *The Second World War,** 6 vols. (1948–1954). Among one-volume studies, the finest overall is Gerhard L. Weinberg's magisterial *A World at Arms: A Global History of World War II** (1994). The best single-volume treatment of military events is John Keegan's *The Second World War** (1990). Other sources include Peter Calvocoressi and Guy Wint, *Total War: The Story of World War II,** rev. ed. (1979), a massive 900-page survey; and Gordon Wright, *The Ordeal of Total War, 1939–1945** (1968), which deals far more with social, economic, and psychological questions than with the military campaigns. See also Charles de Gaulle, *The Complete War Memoirs* (1964), which rival Churchill's in literary quality, though not in scope.

Herbert Feis, in *Churchill, Roosevelt, Stalin: The War They Waged and the Peace They Sought,** 2nd ed. (1967), and in *Between War and Peace: The Potsdam Conference* (1960), analyzes the diplomacy of the Allied coalition in balanced and understanding fashion. Gordon A. Craig and Francis L. Loewenheim, eds., *The Diplomats, 1939–1979* (1994) provides a fine introduction to wartime and postwar diplomacy alike in the spirit of Craig and Gilbert's earlier volume on interwar diplomacy (see readings for Chapter 6). Robert Beitzell, in *The Uneasy Alliance: America, Britain, and Russia, 1941–1943* (1973), examines the difficult beginnings of the Allies' military partnership, while Robin Edmonds, in *The Big Three: Churchill, Roosevelt, & Stalin in Peace and War** (1991) charts its course through the end of the World War II. Lloyd C. Gardner's *Spheres of Influence: The Great Powers Partition Europe, from Munich to Yalta* (1993) argues that a divided Europe was preferable to an unstable or warring Europe after 1945.

Marc Bloch's *Strange Defeat* (1949; reprint ed., 1981) offers a highly suggestive interpretation of the fall of France by an eyewitness and master historian. Guy Chapman's *Why France Fell* (1968) and the relevant chapters in Stanley Hoffmann's *Decline or Renewal? France Since the 1930s* (1974) provide additional analysis of the end of the Third Republic. Two excellent biographies of Winston Churchill emphasize different aspects of his career: Roy Jenkins, *Churchill, A Biography** (2001) analyzes his political career from the perspective of a seasoned politician, while John Keegan's briefer study, *Winston Churchill* (2002), is best on military affairs. John Lukacs, *Five Days in London: May 1940** (1999), argues that Churchill made Allied victory possible by refusing to concede defeat at the moment of Hitler's triumph in France, despite heavy pressures from his own cabinet. Richard Overy, *The Battle of Britain: The Myth and the Reality** (2000) offers an excellent account of the Battle of Britain; Richard Hillary's *The Last Enemy** (1942), the somber memoirs of an RAF pilot, reveals the human costs of England's "finest hour." The triumphs of British espionage and code-breaking during the war are recounted in detail in F. H. Hinsley's *British Intelligence in the Second World War,* 2 vols. (1979–1981), while J. C. Masterman, *The Double-Cross System in the War of 1939 to 1945* (1972) and F. W. Winterbotham, *The Ultra Secret* (1974) provide fascinating specifics about two of the most telling espisodes in the undercover war.

*Books marked with an asterisk are available in paperback.

Angus Calder, in *The People's War: Britain, 1939–1945* (1969), gives a vivid picture of life on the home front, as does Tom Harrisson, *Living Through the Blitz** (1976). Paul Addison, in *The Road to 1945: British Politics and the Second World War** (1994), argues that government war planning paved the way for the postwar Welfare State in Britain. For the war in the Soviet Union, besides the excellent treatment in Geoffrey Hosking (see readings for Chapter 10) there is Richard Overy, *Russia's War: Blood Upon the Snow* (1997), written to accompany a joint British-Russian television documentary using previously classified material. Alexander Werth's *Russia at War, 1941–1945* (1964) presents a panorama of the conflict on the Eastern Front by an eyewitness. For a more recent assessment of the forces which shaped domestic Soviet history during the war, see John Barber and Mark Harrison, *The Soviet Home Front: A Social and Economic History of the USSR in World War II** (1991). The difficulties of the early months of the war are vividly recounted in the first volume of Nikita Khrushchev, *Khrushchev Remembers,** 2 vols. (1977). Norman Kogan's *Italy and the Allies* (1954) deals with Italy's change of alliance and subsequent activity as a cobelligerent of Britain and the United States. A comprehensive portrait of the Nazi regime and the German home front during the war appears in the second and concluding volume of Ian Kershaw's monumental biography, *Hitler: 1936–1945, Nemesis* (2000).

For Hitler's "New Order," see Alexander Dallin's *German Rule in Russia, 1941–1945*, 2nd ed. (1981), Louis de Jong, *The Netherlands and Nazi Germany* (1990), and Vojtech Mastny, *The Czechs Under Nazi Rule* (1971). France's somber experience under both Vichy and Nazi control is detailed in Robert O. Paxton's astringent *Vichy France: Old Guard and New Order** (1972), Philippe Burrin's masterly *France under the Germans: Collaboration and Compromise** (1993, trans. 1996), and *The Sorrow and the Pity: A Film by Marcel Ophuls* (1972), the text of an outstanding documentary. The alternatives of resistance and collaboration may be followed in M. R. D. Foot, *Resistance: European Resistance to Nazism, 1940–1945* (1976); Stephen Hawes and Ralph White, eds., *Resistance in Europe, 1939–45* (1975); and Henri Michel, *The Shadow War* (1972). Women participants in the Resistance have also attracted the attention of scholars; an excellent example is Margaret Collins Weitz, *Sisters in the Resistance: How Women Fought to Free France, 1940–1945* (1995). Sheila Isenberg, *A Hero of Our Own: The Story of Varian Fry* (2001) tells the unlikely story of a lone American who orchestrated the escape of hundreds of artists and scholars from wartime France. Opposition to Hitler within Germany is analyzed in Peter Hoffmann's penetrating study *The German Resistance to Hitler, 1933–1945** 3rd. ed. (1996), which can be usefully supplemented by Joachim Fest, *Plotting Hitler's Death: The Story of the German Resistance* (1996). Ian Kershaw, *Popular Opinion and Political Dissent in the Third Reich, Bavaria 1933–1945* (1983) and Inge Scholl, *The White Rose: Munich 1942–43** (1952) both deal with the motives and limits of German Catholic opposition.

The collaboration of neutral countries with the Nazis, especially that of Switzerland, has become a topic of recent interest due to the compensation claims of Jewish survivors. See Isabel Vincent, *Hitler's Silent Partners: Swiss Banks, Nazi Gold, and the Pursuit of Justice** (1997) and Jean Ziegler, *The Swiss, the Gold, and the Dead: How Swiss Bankers Helped Finance the Nazi War Machine* (1997). A detailed account of the Nazi confiscation of art treasures and the scarcely less predatory behavior of Swiss art collectors and Soviet and American troops at war's end can be found in Lynn H. Nicholas, *The Rape of Europa: The Fate of Europe's Treasures in the Third Reich and the Second World War* (1994).

On the Nazi treatment of the Jews, besides Levi and Dawidowicz (see readings for Chapter 9), there are Michael R. Marrus, *The Holocaust in History** (1987), Raoul Hilberg, *The Destruction of the European Jews,** 2nd rev. ed. (1985), and Sarah Gordon's study of German attitudes in *Hitler, Germans, and the "Jewish Question"** (1984). Walter Laqueur, ed., *The Holocaust Encyclopedia* (2001), the result of a massive collaborative effort, presents the prehistory, unfolding, and sequels of the Holocaust in penetrating detail, with excellent photographs. The memories of Jewish survivors and Polish neighbors of Auschwitz are juxtaposed with telling effect in another documentary film transcript, Claude Lanzmann's *Shoah: An Oral History of the Holocaust** (1985). A classic investigation of the motivations and mentality of those who carried out the "final solution" is Hannah Arendt's *Eichmann in Jerusalem: A Report on the Banality of Evil,** rev. ed. (1976). Nor were Germans and Jews the only players in this tragedy. Jan T. Gross, *Neighbors: The Destruction of the Jewish Community in Jedwabne, Poland** (2002) demonstrates how native Polish anti-Semitism was unleashed by the Nazi conquest of 1939, with murderous effects, while Jonathan Steinberg, in *All or Nothing: The Axis and the Holocaust, 1941–43* (1990) examines how Italian officials unexpectedly protected Jews in the areas of Yugoslavia under their control.

Anthony Beevor, *Stalingrad: The Fateful Siege, 1942–1943** (1998) recounts the harrowing struggle that proved to be the turning point of the war in the East. His descriptions of the suffering of soldiers on both sides makes for grim reading. John Keegan, in *Six Armies in Normandy** (1982), offers a detailed analysis of the crucial battle on the Western Front, while Hans Speidel's *Invasion 1944* (1950), gives a professional military account of the Normandy landings from the German standpoint. For an analysis of the most important of the inter-Allied conferences, see Diane Shaver Clemens, *Yalta** (1970). Lloyd C. Garner, *Spheres of Influence: The Great Powers Partition Europe, from Munich to Yalta* (1993) argues that the decision to divide Europe among the victors spared Europe a more serious conflict after 1945. H. R. Trevor-Roper, *The Last Days of Hitler** (1947), chronicles the macabre end of the Nazi Reich. His classic account can usefully be supplemented with another graphic account by Anthony Beevor, *The Fall of Berlin 1945* (2002), much of it based on archival material unavailable to Trevor-Roper.

Literary accounts of World War II, the occupation, and the Resistance by participants are as important a supplementary source for understanding this conflict as they are for World War I. Among the best are Jean-Paul Sartre's portrait of France in its hour of defeat, *Iron in the Soul** (1949); Simone de Beauvoir's study of resistance and its moral dilemmas, *The Blood of Others** (1945); Italo Calvino's irreverent but moving account of Italian Resistance in the North, *The Path to the Nest of Spiders* (1947); Alfred Andersch's *Winterspelt* (1974), which explores a German officer's failed attempt to surrender his unit to the Americans before the Battle of the Bulge; Konstantin Simonov's patriotically inspired *The Living and the Dead* (1960); and Vasily Grossman's harsh, epic portrait of Soviet Russia at the time of the Battle of Stalingrad, *Life and Fate* (1980). The American novelist Alan Furst, though not, like the previous authors, an eyewitness, has nevertheless recaptured the trials and ambiguities of Europe's descent into World War II, most especially *The Blood of Victory* (2002). Among the many films dealing with the war, Daryl Zanuck's *The Longest Day* (1966), depicting the D-Day Normandy invasion of 1944, remains one of the most accurate and impressive.

14

EASTERN EUROPE: THE YEARS OF REVOLUTION, 1945–1949

Josip Broz Tito, while leader of the Yugoslav Communist partisans fighting the Nazis, arrives on the Dalmatian island of Vis to meet Dr. Ivan Šubašić, representative of King Peter's government. (*Courtesy Brown Brothers*)

I. THE WAR'S END

The Second World War was never formally terminated. No peace treaty ratified the defeat of Germany, as in 1919. With the lesser belligerents—Italy, Hungary, Romania, Bulgaria, and Finland—treaties were finally concluded, after several adjournments and protracted wrangles between the Soviet Union and the Western powers. These treaties embodied hard-won compromises on the questions on which technical agreement could be reached, such as boundaries, reparations, and the limitation of armed forces. They did not touch the wider dispute as to the character of the regimes under which the states in question should live. In dealing with Germany, disagreement between East and West on these larger issues was so great that it proved impossible to draft a formal treaty even for more technical matters. Instead, the postwar settlement merely developed gradually, as one practical decision led to another in the efforts of hard-pressed administrators to make postwar Germany a viable community.

To a lesser degree this was true of Europe as a whole. No great conclave of powers, such as had met in Paris in 1919, drew up a blueprint for the reconstruction of the Continent. Rather, it was a series of imprecise agreements concluded while the war was still in progress, such as the Churchill-Stalin understanding on spheres of influence or the Yalta Conference, that set the stage for the postwar settlement which eventually emerged during the half decade 1945–1949. The results were notably different in Western Europe from what occurred in the areas occupied by the Red Army in the East. In the West there was a substantial return to the prewar or prefascist situation—a conservative solution, which the Americans did their utmost to encourage. In the East there occurred a major revolution imposed by the occupying power.

Neither in the East nor in the West did the years immediately following the war see the sort of spontaneous revolutionary outbreaks that had flared up in Central and Eastern Europe after 1917. Instead, the political climate was largely influenced by the two nations whose dominance over the Continent emerged as one of the major new developments of the immediate postwar period: the Soviet Union and the United States. In the earlier postwar settlement of 1919, both victors and vanquished belonged within the European camp; England and France had imposed their will upon Germany and decreed an end to the Austro-Hungarian Empire. Now Europe lay prostrate, exhausted by a second war that had lasted longer and exacted a greater toll by far in lives and destruction than the first. The forces that would shape the new postwar era were thus largely beyond European control.

Population Displacements

More than the First World War, the Second World War had been a "total war." To a far greater extent than in the years 1914–1918, civilian populations felt the direct effects of combat. Constant bombardment from the air and the wide sweep of operations on the ground had brought the realities of war directly into the homes of tens of millions of Europeans who had been spared by the first conflict; the uprooting of people through flight, forced labor, or political persecution had occurred on a scale that dwarfed anything Europe had experienced before.

In the first three and a half years of the war alone, 30 million Europeans had fled or had been driven from their original homes. These included a million and a half people deported from the Polish areas annexed by Germany into the "Government General," which became one vast dumping ground; it also included 100,000 Alsace-Lorrainers resettled in unoccupied France, and 400,000 Germans, long resident in Eastern Europe, whom Stalin insisted that Hitler move to the west as a token of fidelity to the Nazi-Soviet pact. A large percentage of these people subsequently went east again—as the *Führer* tried to set up German colonies in the occupied parts of Russia and the Ukraine—only to flee headlong back to the Reich in the great retreat of 1944.

Meantime, some 12 million Russians had left their homes for the interior of the country. In the Balkans and Hungary, as a result of Hitler's boundary changes, several hundred thousand more people had found themselves uprooted. And by 1944, eight million foreign workers were toiling in the Reich. These formed the bulk of the more than 12 million "displaced persons" whom the Allied armies and international relief agencies gradually returned home at the close of hostilities. Added to these in 1945 were an estimated 3 million Germans expelled from the Czech Sudetenland and Hungary by the new Czech and Hungarian governments, and a further 3.5 million driven from the former German provinces of East Prussia, Pomerania, and Silesia by the Poles. The result of this great reshuffling of peoples—and of the hunger and cold and sickness that had gone with it—was death, disease, and a massive war-weariness that was without precedent.

Military Occupation

In 1945 and 1946, most Europeans were simply too tired to do other than acquiesce to the fact that the government which succeeded Hitler's was not of their own making. Military occupation on a novel scale was the rule in both East and West. After the First World War, the occupying armies of the victorious Allies had been stationed only in the Rhineland and in a few scattered areas of Central and Eastern Europe; elsewhere there had been little organized armed force to oppose the activities of local revolutionists. In 1945, on the contrary, military power was everywhere. In the West, the British and Americans had millions of men stationed in France, Italy, and Germany; in the East, the Red Army had six nations in its shadow. In both areas, the military authority, either directly or implicitly, frowned on any sort of spontaneous revolutionary gesture. In the West, this was obvious. In the East, it was less apparent, because the Soviet Union was fostering the activities of local Communist parties—but in its own way and at its own pace. It was *imposing* a revolution, a strange and novel revolution—guided and bureaucratic—that was directed both against conservatives and against indigenous revolutionary stirrings. The central paradox of the great change imposed by Stalin on East Central Europe in the years 1945–1949 was that it stifled in embryo the genuine and popular revolution for which all the elements were present when the Red Army arrived.

II. THE PRECONDITIONS

The six nations of East Central Europe that, in the course of the military operations of 1944 and 1945, came under Soviet influence or occupation had already passed through much common experience in the interwar years. To a superficial observer, these states appeared extremely heterogeneous. Two, Hungary and Bulgaria, had been among the vanquished in the First World War; two more, Romania and Yugoslavia, had been with the victors and had been vastly enlarged as a result; two others, Poland and Czechoslovakia, had been revived in 1919, as new births of old nations that had disappeared long ago. In political structure, too, these states were very different. The three Balkan countries were kingdoms, the two new nations were republics, and Hungary was a kingdom with a vacant throne. Poland, Czechoslovakia, and Hungary were Catholic; Yugoslavia was divided in faith; whereas Romania and Bulgaria were Eastern Orthodox. From the standpoint of language and cultural tradition, all were Slavic except Hungary and Romania.

Underlying this tangled catalogue of differences, however, the six nations had in common their peasant character and the problems that character entailed. But this their rulers refused to recognize. With rare exceptions, the governments of East Central Europe in the period from 1919 to 1939 tried to behave as though they were ruling great powers in miniature—they concentrated their attention on question of national prestige and neglected the more practical tasks of alleviating the poverty of their fellow citizens.

Nationalities, Minorities, and Politics

The chief public concern was the question of minorities and national frontiers. The treaty makers of 1919—by their own admission—had assigned a fifth of the population of the area to nations to which the people affected did not wish to belong (see Map 14.1). Approximately 22 million of the 110 million human beings in East Central Europe were officially considered as belonging to minorities and, at least in theory, were protected by special minority clauses in the peace treaties. But these were violated with depressing regularity and did not even apply to another category of people who also felt themselves aggrieved—members or offshoots of official "majority" nationalities who thought that their distinctive cultural traditions were not adequately respected. In Hungary, which had suffered more than any other country at the hands of the treaty makers of 1919, the question of minorities and frontiers became the national obsession. Elsewhere, public absorption with the same problem was almost as intense. Nearly everywhere, concern for national rights served to deflect interest from economic and social issues and from the possibility of attempting to solve them by work in common.

The same lack of realism characterized the political parties. These called themselves "liberal" or "radical" as the case might be, but for the most part, the parties actually consisted of cliques of city lawyers who had acquired the manners of the West and knew little of the countryside and its problems. Nor were their broader political principles very solidly anchored. Most of them passed over quite easily to the service of the dictatorships into which the parliamentary regimes of these countries had evolved by the 1930s. The

MAP 14.1   Territorial changes in Central Europe following the Second World War.

great exception, of course, was Czechoslovakia, where the political parties maintained their democratic allegiance until the disaster at Munich. Czechoslovakia—or rather its Czech lands of Bohemia and Moravia—was the exception in other respects also. In its level of education and industrialization, it seemed closer to the West than it did to the peasant societies of East Central Europe.

There were also Marxist parties, but these were not of first importance. In the countries that had a significant number of urban workers—Poland, Czechoslovakia, and Hungary—there existed Socialist parties on the Western model. In the Balkan peninsula, on the other hand, communism had begun to establish itself on a small scale, for in a predominantly agrarian society, where there were almost no trade unions to canalize the aspirations of the poor, Communist agitators found a free field. In such a society, intellectuals were in an ideological vacuum in which political extremism could flourish unchecked. This was particularly the case in Yugoslavia, where, in the 1930s, the University of Belgrade became a seedbed of Communist influence. It was from idealistic students of the Left—disgusted with the corrupt dictatorship under which they lived—that Tito recruited the young intellectuals who in the war years were to lead his Partisans to victory.

Generally, the leaders of "peasant" or "agrarian" parties were no exception to the usual Eastern European politicians. Like "liberals" or "radicals," they, too, tended to be economically unrealistic and ideologically illiterate. Most of them were of urban origin, and their notion of rural life was bucolic and sentimental; they idealized the peasants without making adequate distinctions between the problems of those who were desperately poor and those who were self-sufficient, and they failed to see the importance of industrialization in alleviating rural misery. Among the "peasant" politicians, however, there were a few leaders who had a wider vision. The left wings of these parties produced persons of stature, with a real grasp of peasant needs. Men such as these proved themselves the most impressive national leaders in the immediate postwar years—Stanislaw Mikolajczyk in Poland, Ferenc Nagy in Hungary, Iuliu Maniu in Romania, and G. M. Dimitrov and Nikola Petkov in Bulgaria.

The Agrarian Dilemma

The more imaginative agrarian leaders at least dimly understood the problem of rural overpopulation. Here outsiders often misjudged the true situation—they thought in terms of the old stereotype of aristocratic dominance and the need for breaking up the great estates. In most parts of East Central Europe the concentration of landed property in the hands of the nobility was not a currently serious problem. Only in Poland and Hungary had quasi-feudal conditions persisted similar to those that prevailed in southern Italy and Spain. Elsewhere, small peasants holdings were the rule. In Bulgaria and in much of Yugoslavia, this had been true even under Turkish suzerainty. In Romania and Czechoslovakia, post-1919 reform measures had redistributed the land on an extensive scale.

The real problem, rather, was the misery and low level of productivity among the peasant masses, however independent in theory a great part of them might be. Almost everywhere, the peasants were the majority of the population. Only in Bohemia and

Moravia were they less than half, and in Bulgaria—the most rural and "primitive" of the six nations—they accounted for more than three-quarters of the inhabitants. But the peasants had little influence on the conduct of affairs. Lacking the education or debating experience that would have equipped them to participate in politics and parliamentary life, they were ordinarily represented by city dwellers who had an inadequate understanding of their needs. These needs were those of any underdeveloped and depressed agrarian society—Russia, much of Asia, Latin America, and the Iberian Peninsula offered comparable examples—that is, better farming methods and the economic stimulation of an expanding industry.

In absolute terms, East Central Europe may not have been overpopulated; it had far fewer people per square mile than England or Belgium. But these were highly industrialized nations which had a very small percentage of their people on the land and whose population was remaining relatively stationary. In the peasant countries to the east, on the contrary, population was increasing, and the increase was pressing against the available productive resources. The land was becoming overfragmented; between two-thirds and three-quarters of the landholding peasants cultivated plots that were too small for their own needs. In addition, there were millions of landless peasants working as farm hands—a reserve of unskilled labor that kept agrarian wages permanently depressed. Since so much cheap labor was available, there was little incentive to improve farming methods. "On a given unit of land" in one Balkan country, "four times as many people produced three times less wheat than in Denmark."*

As a result, poverty was increasing and the peasants found few chances to break out of the vicious circle of misery in which they were caught. Educational opportunities were meager, as indeed were nearly all other possibilities of self-improvement. The organization of cooperatives offered one vista of hope, but governments were not interested in encouraging them. Industrialization offered another, but here both ingrained prejudice and lack of capital stood in the way. Realistically considered, industry alone could break up the old routines in the countryside and drain off the excess agricultural population to find new and productive work in the cities and thus to raise living standards for all. This had been the experience of Western Europe in the nineteenth century, as it was to be that of Russia in the 1930s. But East Central Europe lacked the coercive leadership that Stalin provided when he transformed his country from top to bottom. This, then, was the problem that the interwar years left to the future: How could the peasant nations of the East learn from Soviet experience while avoiding the barbarity and human suffering that the great transformation of Russia had entailed?

The Legacy of Nazi Occupation

These problems were themselves sufficient to produce a revolutionary situation. Beyond them, the demand for change was intensified by the experience through which East Central Europe passed during the war years.

---

*Hugh Seton-Watson, *Eastern Europe Between the Wars, 1918–1941* (Cambridge: Cambridge University Press, 1945), 98.

From 1941 to 1944, the whole area was in the Nazis' grasp. This was also true of Western Europe, of course, but German behavior in the East differed markedly from German conduct in the West. In the West, the occupying power was dealing with peoples whom it regarded as relatively superior; these peoples were assured of decent treatment most of the time provided they did not try to resist German orders. In the East, it was quite different. Here the Nazis dealt with nations they considered inferior both "racially" and culturally, and their concern with the conquered peoples was limited to making them serve the German war effort.

Hence in East Central Europe it was much harder to stand aside and wait for the war to end, as so many people succeeded in doing in the West. Of the occupied countries, only the Czech lands received even moderately good treatment, and of the peoples allied with the Germans, the Hungarians alone were dealt with in any sense as equals. Elsewhere the alternative was clear—one could either suffer as a nation, like the Poles, or accept the humiliating relationship of an "alliance" that actually meant subjugation. The latter policy was the most common. Willingly or coerced, the rulers of Hungary, Romania, and Bulgaria—joined by the new puppet states of Croatia, Serbia, and Slovakia—became minor auxiliaries in the German war effort.

Most people of property or standing in the community collaborated with the Germans. Worse still, on the extremist fringe of profascist activity in Eastern Europe, violent outbreaks of anti-Semitism punctuated the war years. In Romania, the Iron Guard, a

The destruction in Eastern Europe left by World War II is clearly evident in this 1946 photo of a street in Warsaw, Poland. (*Courtesy Corbis-Bettmann*)

native fascist movement launched by Corneliu Codreanu in the mid-1930s, was itself responsible for the murder of many Romanian Jews before the Nazis finally crushed it as a potential rival in January 1941. In short, the East produced far more homegrown fascism than did Scandinavia or the Low Countries or even France. Anti-Nazi leaders in the East clearly understood that the departure of the Germans alone would not cleanse their countries of the fascist contagion. Much remained to be done in ridding their land of its own fascist sons and daughters. Here also lay an impetus to revolution.

III. THE TWO REVOLUTIONS

At the very least, one might foresee that the end of the Nazi tyranny over East Central Europe would produce three revolutionary changes: land reform in the areas where great estates still existed, industrialization, and a thorough purge of fascists and collaborationists. These were the elements of the spontaneous and indigenous revolution that began to appear almost everywhere once the Germans had left and the Red Army had taken their place.

The natural leaders of this revolutionary change were the respected figures within the peasant parties and those who had fought the Germans during the war as Resistance chiefs. Their natural adversaries were the Moscow-trained Communists who had, quite literally, arrived in the baggage train of the Red Army. The first phase of liberation from the Nazis was to be marked by a continually frustrated effort on the part of the indigenous leaders to realize their ideal of a spontaneous and democratic revolution as against the Stalinist concept of an orthodox Communist revolution imposed from outside.

"People's Democracy"

At first, the peasant leaders' cause did not seem utterly hopeless. In the early stages of Soviet occupation, the democratic parties in most countries of East Central Europe enjoyed some margin of liberty. Already, however, there were two great exceptions. In Yugoslavia, Tito's grass-roots Communists had the local situation firmly in hand, and in Poland—which in international and strategic terms was the most important country of all—the Soviet puppets, who had first established themselves in Lublin and then moved into the ruins of Warsaw, were desperately trying to maintain their power. The Polish Communists knew very well that they had almost no backing in the country and that if free elections ever should be held Mikolajczyk's Peasant party would sweep the field. Hence they effectively quarantined the Peasant party leader and the three colleagues he brought with him under the terms of the post-Yalta agreement for enlarging the Polish government. Mikolajczyk himself, after two years of political frustration, first within the government and then in open opposition to it, finally fled the country in despair.

These were two special cases at the two poles of Communist influence. In Yugoslavia, the Communists were so strong that they did not need to share authority with other political groups. In Poland, they were so weak that they did not dare permit anyone else to exert influence, and they relied unashamedly on the Red Army to keep them in power. Elsewhere, coalition government was the rule. In Bulgaria and Romania, the phase of true coalition lasted only a few months; in Czechoslovakia, it lasted nearly three years. There and in Hungary, relatively free elections were held.

The formula of government was everywhere the same—what came to be called "People's Democracy." To the Communists and their Soviet sponsors it suggested a transition regime—something more proletarian than the "bourgeois" democracies of the West, reflecting a situation that was not yet ripe for true communism, since the old social structure and ways of doing things still persisted. To non-Communists, on the other hand, "People's Democracy" meant a Popular Front, distinctly leftist in tone, but with communism accepting the limited role of revolutionary vanguard. Obviously, these two concepts would not long be compatible. Yet for the short term, the disparate coalitions of Communists, Socialists, Agrarians, and miscellaneous democrats that governed the various People's Democracies were held together by an emergency program on which all could agree: the purge of fascists, land reform, and other acts of social equalization that the postwar situation urgently required.

In this unstable relationship, the degree of liberty permitted to the individual varied greatly from region to region and from one department to another of the national life. In most places there was considerable tolerance of free speech and free meetings, but at the same time people found it inadvisable to say anything openly derogatory about the Soviet Union and its representatives. What freedom they enjoyed was extremely precarious, and the power of communism behind the scenes was far greater than it appeared to be on the surface. Everywhere the Communists held control of three vital levers of power—the ministry of propaganda, the ministry of the interior (which directed the police and local administration), and the army general staff.

Was People's Democracy, then, a mere fraud from the outset? Or was it a form of government and society in its own right that might have lasted longer had historical circumstances been different? In operation, it showed itself both fraudulent and short lived. But when People's Democracy was first introduced, a number of leaders of unimpeachable democratic conviction—men like Eduard Beneš of Czechoslovakia and Ferenc Nagy of Hungary—believed in it and were willing to try it. If Stalin had died earlier, or if the onset of the Cold War had been delayed, People's Democracy might have had a better opportunity to evolve in a tolerably free direction. Perhaps two of the six nations in question might have remained close to the Western definition of democracy.

The Return to Soviet Orthodoxy

Within the Soviet Union, however, changes were already in process that spelled disaster for the democratic leadership of East Central Europe. During the war, Stalin had somewhat relaxed the iron hold of Communist ideology and discipline in his own country. This respite was partly owing to necessity. The dislocations of wartime, the German occupation of the Ukraine and of the western part of Russia itself, and the mobilization for military service of trusted local Communists made it impossible to keep the people in the tight check characteristic of the previous decade. Moreover, the slogan of national unity

The imposition of Soviet orthodoxy in Eastern Europe is seen in these massed marchers, celebrating May Day in Hungary in the early 1950s. Note the twin portraits of Lenin and Stalin carried in the procession. (*Courtesy H. Armstrong Roberts*)

in the war effort was applied at home as well as abroad, and this dictated the same moderation that was being imposed on the foreign Communist parties. In the desperate struggle he was waging to halt the German invaders and drive them out of the country, Stalin was willing to accept help from any quarter, no matter how alien to Communist principles. He not only appealed to the patriotic memories of the Great Russian past, he also mobilized the force of religion by granting small favors to the Orthodox clergy and encouraging them to make statements in support of his regime.

In the days of victory, the tide of patriotic emotion was at its height. The heroes of the hour were the military chiefs—first among them Marshal Zhukov, the defender of Moscow and conqueror of Berlin, who remained in Germany as commander of the Soviet occupation forces. Stalin was jealous of his generals. Although during the war he had put on a marshal's uniform and directed the course of military operations himself, he had not actually participated in the fighting. He never witnessed a battle, as Churchill so often did; he stayed, rather, within the Kremlin, as mysterious and shut off from his own people as he had been during the prewar years.

For many Russians, faced with the daunting task of rebuilding their country, the postwar period nevertheless seemed to promise a continuing liberalization of Communist party rule. The colossal losses suffered by the Soviets—some 20 million dead (civilian and military), 1,700 cities and towns heavily damaged, 31,000 factories destroyed, 25 million people homeless—had set the country's economic progress back by at least a decade. Faced with a similar economic catastrophe at the end of the civil war, Lenin had elected to loosen party controls and launch the New Economic Policy. Stalin's willingness to tolerate some degree of private farming and marketing during the war in order to boost scarce food supplies suggested that he might also follow Lenin's example at the war's end.

But in this the Russians were mistaken. Now that the moment of crisis was past, Stalin insisted on retracting the economic and ideological concessions he had been forced to make during the war years. The first sign that the regime was returning to its prewar policy of rigor was the recall of Zhukov from Berlin, in March 1946, and his reassignment to an obscure command in the Russian provinces. A purge of the armed forces was already in full swing. Officers and soldiers, including former prisoners of war, who had become ideologically "contaminated" by contact with the West were systematically rounded up. The forced labor camps in Siberia received these by the hundreds of thousands, along with the minority peoples of the Crimea and the Caucasus, such as the Chechens whom Stalin accused of having collaborated with the Germans.

A similar reimposition of Stalinist orthodoxy occurred in the economic sphere. The fourth Five-Year Plan, launched in 1946, again reflected the priorities of the 1930s. Heavy industry received the most attention, with housing and consumer goods far down the scale of priorities. Having only barely survived the war, Stalin believed, the Soviet Union was in no position to allow itself the luxury of diverting its resources into rewarding its long-suffering population with increased food supplies or more consumer goods. The years of economic progress lost in the struggle against Hitler had to be recouped, even at the cost of further privation.

These policies were bound to be unpopular. Thus the Stalinist leadership simultaneously took pains to stifle what little freedom of expression had been enjoyed during the war. The change was especially evident in the arts. On music, on literature, and even on science—upon all cultural life—the pall of Communist orthodoxy descended once again. The leader in this reimposition of ideological control was a young favorite of Stalin's, Andrei Zhdanov. It was Zhdanov who, on the occasion of the twenty-ninth anniversary of the Bolshevik Revolution, in the autumn of 1946, called for internal indoctrination and discipline in the Cold War that was opening with the West. It was Zhdanov whom Stalin entrusted with the task of bringing to heel the writers who had permitted their fancy to wander during the war years.

Zhdanov was quite obviously a candidate for succession to the aging Stalin. His rival was a man of the same generation—a leader of the new type who had never known anything but the Stalinist atmosphere of intrigue and terror—Georgi Malenkov. In Zhdanov, something of the spirit of Old Bolshevism survived; in ideological terms, he was a doctrinaire, and he believed in a policy of revolutionary militancy for the foreign Communist parties, both in the East and in the West. Malenkov, on the other hand, was the pure bureaucrat—an administrator with a natural bias toward caution. In the early phases of Soviet postwar initiatives in East Central Europe, Zhdanov's militancy predominated. The later phases were to be marked by the less imaginative and more routine imposition of Communist control through Soviet agents who bore the Malenkov stamp.

The Communist Crackdown

In Bulgaria and Romania, assertion of Communist control began during the war itself, when the Soviet Union had not yet turned toward ideological rigor at home. As with Yugoslavia and Poland, where Communist domination had existed from the outset, the contrasting cases of the two eastern Balkan monarchies reflected the comparative strength of pro-Soviet elements in one nation and their total dependence on the Red Army in the other.

Bulgaria probably had more genuine pro-Russian sentiment among its population than any other country of East Central Europe. It alone among the Axis satellites had refused to contribute troops for the invasion of the Soviet Union. And in the coalition government, called the Fatherland Front, which was formed in the autumn of 1944 after Bulgaria changed sides in the war, the Communists very early began to take the initiative. By the following January, they already felt strong enough to start attacking the other parties. Striking at the one political group that could really threaten their power, they deprived the Agrarian League of its talented chief, G. M. Dimitrov, by forcing his resignation and driving him out of the country. Thereafter, Communist pressure was unrelenting. In September 1946, the monarchy disappeared; the next month a manipulated election gave the Communists a majority in the Grand National Assembly, and by the end of the year the opposition parties had been reduced to utter impotence.

The Soviet representatives remained behind the scenes during the process of consolidating Communist control over Bulgaria. In Romania, on the other hand, they played a leading role from the beginning. Six weeks after the Communist onslaught had opened in Bulgaria, in February 1945, the Soviet deputy foreign minister, Andrei Vishinsky, arrived unexpectedly in the Romanian capital of Bucharest to give Stalin's orders on the spot. Here the coalition government had been working very poorly from the Soviet standpoint—it had neither proceeded with sufficient rigor against the old ruling classes nor contributed adequately to the prosecution of the war. Hence Vishinsky forced King Michael II to dismiss his prime minister and to appoint instead a pro-Communist figurehead, Petru Groza. The British and Americans protested, to no avail. Indeed, the issue of the Romanian government was one of the nagging conflicts with the Soviet Union that clouded Roosevelt's last weeks. With Soviet help, Groza and the Communists had come to stay. By the time the king himself was forced out at the end of 1947, all power was in Communist hands.

The experience of Hungary and Czechoslovakia was quite different. There, the formula of People's Democracy was something more than a mask for Communist control, and democratic political leaders were able to exert real influence for two or three years. In Hungary, the Soviet occupation authorities actually permitted free elections. In November 1945, the peasant Small-Holders party led by Ferenc Nagy won a clear parliamentary majority, and Nagy himself became prime minister. In Czechoslovakia, where former President Beneš had returned to the leadership of his country with Stalin's blessing, a similar experiment yielded rather different results. The Czechoslovak parliamentary elections of May 1946 showed no party the clear victor, and the Communists emerged as the single strongest group. It was natural, then, that Beneš should appoint their leader, Klement Gottwald, to head the government.

For the better part of the next two years, the Communists of Czechoslovakia behaved with comparative moderation, and the country continued on the democratic course to which it had become accustomed in the prewar years. In Hungary, however, a storm was already building. The extent of the Small-Holders' victory had taken the Hungarian Communists and their Soviet sponsors by surprise, and the latter were resolved that this sort of thing should never happen again. They began to pressure the majority party, seizing its secretary-general and finally putting him to death. Meanwhile, Prime Minister Nagy, harassed from all sides, was steadily losing control of the situation. In May 1947, the Communists took advantage of his absence on vacation in Switzerland to force him to resign his office. The demoralization of the Small-Holders party followed, and with it the gradual imposition of Communist rule.

Nine months later, Czechoslovak democracy succumbed. In a bloodless coup d'état in February 1948, the Communists seized power in Prague and the last glimmer of democracy flickered out in East Central Europe. In one country after another, the process had been the same. First, the authentic leaders of the democratic parties had been forced out. Then these parties, under new and more pliant leadership, were reduced to the role of mere façades, or—in the case of the Socialists—were obliged to fuse with the Communists. Finally the monolithic control of a single party was imposed on the country, together with the distinguishing marks of Communist rule—a campaign to collectivize agriculture, a speeding of the tempo of industrialization, and an end to what vestiges of personal liberty still remained.

IV. THE SUPPRESSION OF OPPOSITION

The Communist suppression of organized opposition proceeded in three stages. First, the democratic political leaders were attacked. Then came a series of trials of prominent churchmen. Finally, the Communists began to purge their own ranks, as a deadly duel opened between the "Muscovites" loyal to Stalin and the homegrown leaders accused of "nationalist" deviations.

The Democratic Leaders and the Churchmen

During 1947, the democratic leadership of East Central Europe all but disappeared. Mikolajczyk of Poland and Nagy of Hungary both escaped abroad; Iuliu Maniu, the veteran Peasant party leader in Romania, was condemned to life imprisonment; Nikola Petkov, who had succeeded G. M. Dimitrov as the chief figure in the Bulgarian Agrarian Union, was tried on false charges and summarily hanged.

With these people eliminated—and with the older conservative leadership either extinct or discredited—the Christian churches alone remained as possible centers of opposition. Communist rule was by very definition anti-Christian, but the rigor it displayed toward the church varied greatly from country to country. These local differences reflected both the strength of religious sentiment in the particular country and the degree to which church organizations themselves were equipped to offer resistance to Communist control.

Within the nations of Orthodox faith, the influence both of religious sentiment and of church organization was comparatively weak. In the three Orthodox areas of the Balkans—Bulgaria, Romania, and the Serbian parts of Yugoslavia—the religious pattern resembled that of Russia before 1917; that is, the level of education among the clergy was low, and the people had little religious militancy. Nor was there any central leadership abroad, such as the Papacy offered in the Catholic world, to which the Orthodox faithful could look for encouragement in time of persecution. On the contrary, each nation had its separate church organization, linked to the others solely by spiritual ties, and with a tradition that emphasized national solidarity and obedience to the authority of the secular state. Hence it was not too difficult for the Communist rulers of Bulgaria, Romania, and Yugoslavia to make their Orthodox clergy conform. Some priests and bishops merely bowed their heads and did what was expected of them; others gave active support to the new regimes; but in neither case did they present a serious problem to those in authority.

In the Catholic countries, it was quite different. Here—except possibly in the Czech lands—religious faith was strong, and respect for the priests was nearly universal. The Catholics of East Central Europe, moreover, enjoyed active support from outside: Not only the Vatican but millions of Catholics in Western Europe and the United States gave them constant encouragement in their struggle to preserve their faith.

The Communists were wise enough not to proceed directly against religion itself. They chose rather to limit the church's role in education and to frighten the clergy into submission by striking at the chief figure, or primate, within each country. In Yugoslavia, Tito brought to trial the spiritual leader of the Croats, Archbishop Alois Stepinac, who was condemned in 1946 to a long prison term. A similar fate befell the primate of Hungary, Cardinal Joseph Mindszenty—whose trial in 1949 recalled the Soviet purges in the defendant's public admission of the most unlikely charges—and Archbishop Beran of Prague, who was deported from his see in 1951. All these proceedings bore a melancholy resemblance to one another, but the character and policy of the defendants were by no means uniform. Beran was a true democrat. Mindszenty was a popular figure and a personality of heroic stature; the son of peasants, he was a conservative of the old stamp who had opposed land reform because it would entail financial loss for church education. Stepinac presented a still more doubtful case from the standpoint of East European democracy. As primate of Croatia, he had countenanced the fascist regime of Ante Pavelich during the war years and hence, at least indirectly, shared responsibility for the mass murder of Serbs under this most sinister of Axis puppets.

However much the moral justification of these trials might vary, the result they achieved was the same. By the early 1950s, the Catholic church in Croatia, Czechoslovakia, and Hungary had been terrified into submission. But the Polish experience was different. Among the Poles—who ranked with the Irish as the most profoundly Catholic people of Europe—it was impossible to take the same stern line that had succeeded among the Catholic peoples to the south. In Poland, solidarity between clergy and people was too strong, and religious feeling was too intense to yield to merely political pressure. Hence the Polish Communists moved warily—they did nothing to interfere with the succession to church leadership of Archbishop Wyszynski in 1948, and they allowed church-state relations to drift along with no clear victory for either side. This was one of the chief reasons why the Communist regime in Poland was to follow after 1956 a course that markedly diverged from that of its ideological partners in East Central Europe (see Chapter 19, IV, and Chapter 22, III).

Tito's Heresy and the "Nationalist" Deviation

One other country had diverged still earlier from the model that the Soviet Union laid down: Tito's Yugoslavia, which in June 1948 was expelled from the Stalinist camp and subsequently undertook to establish its own definition of Communist goals.

That Yugoslavia should be the first Communist nation to leave the common fold presented a most striking paradox, for in the early postwar years, Tito's regime ranked as the most advanced of all—the country where Communist control had proceeded the furthest and where People's Democracy came closest to Soviet standards. For this very reason, however, the Yugoslav Communists fell under suspicion in Moscow from the start. They had been *too* successful; they had achieved power by their own efforts—aided rather by Britain and the United States than by the Soviet Union. Stalin never forgave Tito his wartime traffickings with the West, and as the Soviet leader grew older and more suspicious he came to detest the resilient self-confidence of the Yugoslavs and the feeling of national self-sufficiency that went along with it.

Tito, for his part, strenuously objected to Russian domineering and to the tendency of the Soviet secret police to treat his country as its own preserve. The issue between him and Stalin, then, was chiefly one of national independence. This was already evident five months before the break, in January 1948, when the Communist official organ in Moscow rebuked Tito for the plan of a South Slav federation that he had been discussing with the Bulgarian Communist leaders. It was quite clear that Stalin wanted no competition from any secondary affiliations within the Communist camp. Hence it should not have come as a complete surprise when in the following June the newly founded association of Communist parties, or Cominform (see Chapter 17, I), expelled the Yugoslav Communists on the patently false charge that they had faltered in the campaign to collectivize agriculture.

At first Tito seemed shaken by his expulsion. He kept insisting that he remained a loyal Communist, and he was slow to reply to the insults that the press and radio of the other East European countries poured upon him. Indeed, during the first year of Yugoslav isolation, it appeared that Tito's regime might not withstand the united onslaught of its neighbors. Gradually, however, Tito's peculiar assets for such a struggle made themselves evident. His Resistance record had given him a position as a national as well as a Communist hero—and his break with Stalin immensely increased his popularity by putting the emphasis on this patriotic aspect of his past. The Russians failed in their efforts to turn the Yugoslav Communists against him; the army, the party cadres, the secret police remained loyal. As he gathered confidence, the Yugoslav leader himself began to grope his way toward a definition of his new position. He stressed the Leninist purity of his doctrine, as opposed to Stalin's perversions of it, and he took the first steps toward reopening his contacts with the West and toward the liberalization of his regime at home.

The real influence of Tito's new form of Communism was to become apparent only in the 1950s (see Chapter 19, IV). Meanwhile, Tito's success hastened the final round in the suppression of opposition to communism in East Central Europe. Zhdanov died in the summer of 1948, his policy of revolutionary militancy discredited by the failure of the Cominform to bring Tito to terms. After Zhdanov's death, his followers within the Soviet Union were systematically purged. At the same time, the Soviet leadership adopted a tactic of keeping a tight rein on the East European Communists. The Russian leaders urged them to follow Soviet example and purge their own ranks, in an effort to eliminate all those who might fall under suspicion of a "nationalist" or Titoist deviation.

In this purge, which extended from the spring of 1949 to Stalin's death four years later, several of the most responsible of the East European Communist leaders lost their lives. Of those accused, only Wladislaw Gomulka of Poland, who was merely imprisoned without trial, lived to play a prominent part in the post-Stalinist era. In many respects, this new purge resembled what Russia had experienced in the 1930s, but with an important difference. In the Soviet Union, from 1936 to 1938, Stalin's new men had purged the "Old Bolsheviks." Now it was the older men, the "Muscovites" trained to iron discipline, who were slaughtering the newer type of leadership that the war and postwar years had pushed to the fore and that thought at least partially in national rather than in Stalinist terms. In both cases, however, the results were the same—the stifling of talent and independent initiative and the imposition of a gray bureaucratic uniformity on the whole party.

The Balance Sheet

By the end of 1949, the five states of East Central Europe that still remained within the Soviet camp had brought their two revolutions to an end. In each, the power of the old ruling classes had been destroyed; the churches had been deprived of their influence everywhere but in Poland and had been all but forced out of the field of education, which they had earlier dominated. By the same process, political democracy had also perished.

The postwar revolutions in East Central Europe bore a striking resemblance to the "second revolution" unleashed by Stalin in the Soviet Union two decades before, in 1928. The resemblance was far from fortuitous; buoyed by his earlier success, Stalin now saw little need to alter abroad the methods he had tried at home. In both instances, revolution had come from above, administered by a centralized Communist party with the help of its secret police. In both, basic industry was stressed and the economy governed by five-year plans on the Soviet model. The plans had some positive results. By 1953 these economic measures were to result in doubling the area's steel production and in a three-year increase of almost 100 percent in overall industrial output in both Poland and Czechoslovakia. The collectivization of agriculture was proceeding apace—although at a less rapid rate than had been true of the Soviet Union in the 1930s, since it was even more stubbornly resisted by the peasantry.

With these industrial gains came some of the now familiar ills of the Soviet system—glaring inefficiencies in distribution, too few consumer goods, environmental degradation, broad possibilities for graft and corruption, and the stifling conformism that party patronage brought to cultural life. For those who had suffered through the Nazi occupation, "liberation" by the Red Army merely meant subjugation to a new and different occupying force.

Even in the realm of economic progress, however, the people of Eastern Europe derived little advantage from their efforts. The Russians diverted a considerable amount of the new production for their own internal needs, eventually appropriating some 20 billion dollars worth of goods. The work week was long and factory discipline severe; in a few sectors of the economy, forced labor was being used. With the industrial labor force increased by about a third, overcrowding in the cities was becoming a grave problem. The breathless pace at which industrialization occurred brought massive pollution, as factories were erected with no thought of how to reduce damage by smoke or chemical waste. As the 1940s ended, East Central Europe might be said to have begun to face up to its basic economic problems. Yet its exploitation by the Soviet Union slowed that economic progress considerably, leaving the region far behind its Western neighbors in the race to industrialize.

READINGS

For the interwar background of social and political problems, besides Crampton, Jelavich, and Wolff (see readings for Chapter 1), there are Hugh Seton-Watson, *Eastern Europe Between the Wars, 1918–1941* (1946), and David E. Kaiser, *Economic Diplomacy and the Origins of the Second World War* (1980). Kaiser argues that the small Eastern European states were economically subservient to Germany well before the war. Seton-Watson, in *The East European Revolution,* 3rd ed. (1956), gives a general history of events from the collapse of Nazi power to 1949. On the expulsion of Germans from Czechoslovakia and Poland immediately after the war, see the relevant chapters in Norman M. Naimark, *Fires of Hatred: Ethnic Cleansing in Twentieth-Century Europe** (2001).

For the subsequent course of Communist rule in East Central Europe, see François Fejtö,* *History of the People's Democracies,** 2nd ed. (1974); Teresa Rakowska-Harmstone, ed., *Communism in Eastern Europe,** 2nd ed. (1984); and Zbigniew K. Brzezinski, *The Soviet Bloc: Unity and Conflict,* rev. ed. (1967), which traces both the consolidation of the bloc and its internal strains after Stalin's death. A comprehensive view of the aims and contradictions of state-planned economies in Eastern Europe is presented in János Kornai, *The Socialist System: The Political Economy of Communism** (1992).

On individual countries, see R. J. Crampton, *A Short History of Modern Bulgaria** (1987) and Joseph Rothschild, *The Communist Party of Bulgaria* (1959); Stephen Fischer-Galati, *The New Rumania: From People's Democracy to Socialist Republic* (1967); Hans-Georg Heinrich, *Hungary: Politics, Economy, and Society** (1986) and Bennett Kovrig, *The Hungarian People's Republic;* Hans Renner, *A History of Czechoslovakia since 1945** (1989); Josef Korbel, *Twentieth-Century Czechoslovakia* (1977); and Morton Kaplan, *The Communist Coup in Czechoslovakia* (1960). A vivid memoir detailing the author's struggle to survive first the Nazi camps and then Stalinist repression in postwar Czechoslovakia is

*Books marked with an asterisk are available in paperback.

Heda Margolius Kovály, *Under a Cruel Star: A Life in Prague, 1941–1968** (1986). The difficulties of economic reconstruction under Soviet tutelage are detailed in A Zaubermann's *Industrial Progress in Poland, Czechoslovakia, and East Germany, 1937–62* (1964).

Yugoslavia under Tito and the dramatic break with Moscow have given rise to a voluminous literature. See Wayne S. Vucinich, ed., *At the Brink of War and Peace: The Tito-Stalin Split in a Historic Perspective* (1982); Dennison Rusinow, *The Yugoslav Experiment, 1948–1974* (1977); and Jozo Tomasevich et al. (Wayne S. Vucinich, ed.), *Contemporary Yugoslavia: Twenty Years of Socialist Experiment* (1969). The historical background to the recreation of a Yugoslav state under Tito is meticulously and fairly detailed in Aleksa Djilas, *The Contested Country: Yugoslav Unity and Communist Revolution, 1919–1953* (1991). Two memoirs of absorbing interest are Vladimir Dedijer, *The Battle Stalin Lost: Memoirs of Yugoslavia, 1948–53* (1971), and Milovan Djilas (father of Aleksa), *Rise and Fall** (1983). The elder Djilas, in *Conversations with Stalin** (1962), offers a rare glimpse of the dictator during the final decade of his rule by an observant Kremlin visitor.

15

WESTERN EUROPE:
THE YEARS OF
RECOVERY, 1945–1949

The end of sweets rationing in postwar Britain brings a rush of eager young customers to a candy store in a northwest London suburb. *(Courtesy of Getty Images, Inc./Hulton Archive Photos)*

In Western Europe, the postwar settlement—both social and political—emerged from a long struggle between two opposed movements. The first was the ideology of the war-time Resistance, an active force of renovation and change. The second was the entrenched power of old institutions and attitudes, which might seem no more than a force of passivity and inertia, but which in fact had behind it the bulk of inarticulate public sentiment. This was the basic contrast between the two. Those pressing for change were both articulate and devoted to the public welfare—but they were only a minority. Those who wanted to return to the old ways were for the most part silent and absorbed in their private concerns—but they were the more numerous. In the final amalgam, there was to be far more of conservatism than of innovation in the postwar West.

The quiet, largely undeclared struggle between these forces dominated the half decade 1945–1949. By the end of the 1940s the issue was decided; the main lines of social and political settlement that were to persist through the whole subsequent decade had been firmly established.

I. THE MOMENT OF LIBERATION

The end of the war in Europe was greeted everywhere with an enormous sigh of relief. True, the war in the Pacific was far from over—and the general assumption was that it would continue longer than it actually did—but most Europeans were not much interested in the Far Eastern struggle. It had been from the beginning the Americans' war, and it was only the professional military men of Europe and people with a special concern for the colonies who had their eyes fixed on Asia in the late spring and summer of 1945. To the rest of the population, these imperial questions seemed remote and of little importance. Indeed, people already appeared to sense the outcome, that the former colonies would be reoccupied only temporarily and that they would very soon break away from the mother country. But this problem still lay in the future (see Chapter 18). Both Britain and France were busily redeploying their forces for service in the Far East when the explosion of the atomic bomb at Hiroshima in August 1945 brought the war against Japan to an unexpectedly early close.

In actuality, the end of the war, like the postwar settlement, came about piece-meal. Each captive community in Western Europe experienced the supreme moment of liberation in turn. Each felt a nightmare lifting and a brief thrill of fraternity and human renewal. At this moment, the forces of the Resistance occupied the center of the stage.

The Ideology of the Resistance

The European Resistance movements tended toward the left. They included both Socialists and Communists, and also Catholics of advanced social views, who usually called themselves Christian Democrats. A minority of Resistance leaders distrusted the Communists from the outset and tried to exclude them from positions that might entitle them to postwar influence, but, for the majority of the Resistance fighters, particularly the rank

Charles de Gaulle, leader of the Free French Resistance, acknowledging the cheers of the crowds lining the Champs-Elysées on August 26, 1944—four years after Hitler's troops had celebrated their victory parade along the very same route. *(Courtesy Corbis-Bettmann)*

and file, the Communists were comrades-in-arms like any others. Non-Communists gave them their friendship and hoped that in return the Communists would prove cooperative in the rebuilding of postwar democracy.

This was the vision of the Resistance—a vision both vague and generous. It resembled the ideal of the Popular Front, but it went beyond the prewar concept of a merely temporary expedient or a minimum program to embody a whole new view of European society. To the Popular Front's goal of social justice it added the Christian Democratic ideal of class reconciliation. It sought to bridge the gap between Communists and democrats—and also the chasm that had so long separated Catholics from anticlericals—by creating a new and nonsectarian socialism. By the same token it strove to supplant the old political parties with a new movement that would bring to national leadership men who were both more public-spirited and more technically competent than the usual parliamentary politicians of the old stamp.

This vision—like the corresponding image of People's Democracy in Eastern Europe—was not wholly unrealistic. At the beginning, it corresponded to a yearning for political and social renewal that was widespread on the European Continent. In 1944 and 1945, most of the more thoughtful people in France and Italy and Germany considered it impossible to return to the former routines of parliamentary democracy; they were convinced that something more active and vital and efficient was required. Even in their view of communism the optimists of the Resistance were not wholly mistaken: Western European communism *had* changed during the war years. The Resistance experience had brought to the fore new and younger men who tended to think first of their own country's needs, rather than of Moscow's orders, and who preferred a political system in which the essentials of personal liberty were preserved. But men of this sort seldom held posts of top command; the great question in the months immediately following liberation was how much practical influence they would be able to exert on the postwar activity of their parties.

In the end, that influence proved slight indeed. As tensions between the Soviet Union and the United States and its European allies escalated into what came to be known as the "Cold War" (see Chapter 17), Stalin brought the Western Communist parties to heel and reimposed the old discipline upon them through "Muscovite" leaders on whom he could rely. At the same time, the non-Communist Resistance chiefs, with a few notable exceptions, were finding it impossible to dominate the reviving parliamentary life of their respective countries. With the first postwar elections, the older—and presumably discredited—parliamentary leaders began to return in large numbers to positions of influence. In the unfamiliar conditions of peacetime, the Resistance chiefs were showing themselves no match for the seasoned politicians. Faced with the tricky infighting of the parliamentary arena, the veterans of the Resistance behaved like inexperienced amateurs. The only Resistance leaders who were able to make a permanent mark on the postwar scene were those who had very early joined some regularly constituted political movement.

The Purge of Fascists and Collaborationists

This failure to recast in a new form the party framework of continental democracy was the first great defeat for the Resistance. The second was the failure of the purge of fascists and collaborationists. At best it would have been an enormously difficult task to punish the guilty and to redress the grievances inherited from years of tyranny. In the atmosphere of 1945 and 1946, which was heavy with both weariness and political passion, it proved impossible for the new political authorities to find a judicial formula that could convince the average citizen that justice was being done.

In the moment of liberation itself, the Resistance fighters dealt out their own retribution. Mussolini perished at the hands of Italian partisans after the barest semblance of a trial. In all the countries that had suffered under Nazi oppression, the more extreme Resistance leaders took advantage of the interregnum between the departure of the Germans and the arrival of regular Allied authority to settle old scores and to shoot down their enemies as they chose. This was particularly true of Communists and of criminal elements that had attached themselves to the Resistance late and for their own personal advantage.

Under these circumstances, it is not surprising that crimes were committed under the cover of patriotism. The number of suspected fascists and collaborationists shot out of hand is extremely hard to determine. In France, between 8,000 and 9,000 were summarily killed during the liberation. Nearly 1,500 more were executed after regular trials of one sort or another. For those guilty of lesser offenses, de Gaulle's government devised a series of penalties which ranged from discharge from public service to prison terms and temporary loss of citizenship rights.

In Italy, in the Low Countries, and in Scandinavia, the new democratic governments followed similar procedures. Throughout liberated Europe, both public administrators and the judiciary tried to carry out the purge in conscientious fashion, but nearly everywhere the results were disappointing. It proved impossible to establish exact gradations of collaboration; it was even difficult to determine with any precision who had been responsible for another man's death. As a result, the public soon lost interest; worse, the average citizen concluded that it was all a matter of politics and that one set of politicians was simply taking revenge on its adversaries. Thus, the postliberation purge almost entirely failed to accomplish the moral purpose that the Resistance leaders had intended. Far from "purifying" the atmosphere of politics, as the Resistance had hoped, it poisoned it further through a massive injection of hatred and personal rancor.

Germany offered the crucial test. Here, where the anti-Nazi forces were weak and would have had great difficulty accomplishing the purge on their own, the Allied occupation authorities assumed the task of "denazification" themselves. But to "denazify" Germany was a far harder task than to rid France, for example, of fascists and active collaborationists. In the latter country, only a small minority was involved; in Germany, the great majority of the adult population had been associated with the Nazi party in one form or another. Denazification thus proved to be an enormous and unmanageable operation. It bogged down in masses of paper, as millions of Germans filled out elaborate questionnaires; it foundered in quiet sabotage and a conspiracy of silence among the population at large. It frequently proved simpler to try the lesser offenders first, since their cases were easier to untangle. This resulted in an unanticipated injustice: As denazification degenerated into an unsavory comedy, the only feasible course seemed the granting of amnesties on an ever wider scale—and these, naturally, were of greatest benefit to those whose cases had not yet come to trial. Thus many insignificant people who had been tried earlier received heavy penalties, while some important offenders whose cases had been postponed escaped scot-free. Finally, the simplest solution was to call a complete halt. Denazification never officially came to an end; it just dwindled away.

The mass of the German people followed the denazification procedures with complete skepticism. To the German public, denazification conveyed no clear impression of justice being done or wrongs being righted. This was particularly true of the Allies' greatest effort to teach the Germans a lesson: the trial of the major war criminals held at Nuremberg from November 1945 to September 1946.

The Allies spared no pains to make the Nuremberg trial an impressive example. A Lord Justice of Great Britain presided over the eight judges sitting on the bench, and a Justice of the United States Supreme Court served as chief prosecutor. The case was meticulously prepared. The crime of waging aggressive war and the "crimes against humanity" for which the defendants were being tried were carefully defined and supported in great detail. The accused included all the leading Nazis except for Hitler and

Goebbels, who had taken their lives in the Chancellery bunker in Berlin, and Himmler, who had committed suicide just after his capture by the British army.

But to the Germans as a whole, the trial carried no moral message. The defendants' compatriots saw it as an act of revenge inflicted by the victors on the vanquished, and whatever signs of impartiality the court displayed were canceled out in the German mind by the fact that Soviet judges were participating along with the British, the Americans, and the French. The final verdict was received with apathy as a foregone conclusion. The only surprise, perhaps, was that three of the defendants, including former Chancellor von Papen, were acquitted. Seven received prison sentences, among them Albert Speer, Hitler's architect and productivity expert in the last year of the war. The remaining twelve were all condemned to be hanged, but Goering at the last moment escaped the noose by taking poison in his cell.

Elsewhere the major auxiliaries of the Nazis had been tried by their own people. In Norway, Vidkun Quisling was condemned to death and executed; in France, the same fate befell Pierre Laval. But Marshal Pétain, who had likewise received the death penalty, was granted clemency by de Gaulle and his sentence commuted to life imprisonment on an island off the Breton coast. The trials of Laval and Pétain had been far from edifying; they had been carelessly prepared and marked by outbursts of political invective. Here, as in Germany, the conclusion was the same. The punishment could not be made to fit the crime—the retribution exacted was inadequate for what had gone before. The wrongs committed in the Nazi era had been so vast and so diffused that no proper punishment could be devised. What the Resistance leaders had intended as a great moral lesson had degenerated into a series of spiteful attacks against a few thousand broken and bewildered human beings.

II. The Economic Problem

The Extent of War Damage and War Losses

When the war came to an end, vast stretches of Western and Central Europe lay in ruins. Although no one region was so terribly devastated as northeastern France had been in the First World War, the total damage done in the second war was far greater and spread over a far wider area. Nearly everywhere transport had been completely disorganized. Bridges and railway stations had ranked as high-priority targets for Allied aviators and had been systematically bombed in preparation for the final advances. Port installations had suffered almost as much. Thousands of square miles of farmland lay devastated. In Germany, nearly all the great cities were in ruins, and even in France, which had escaped with less damage, the Cotentin Peninsula and such seaports as Brest, Le Havre, Saint-Nazaire, and Toulon were more than half destroyed.

In Britain, war damage was concentrated in the ports and industrial cities; in Italy, it lay chiefly in the two swathes of countryside where the Allies' advance had successively come to a halt in the two last winters of the war—the area between Naples and

Rome, and that between Florence and Bologna. The Italian seaports were also grievously damaged, as were such industrial centers as Milan and Turin. In contrast, the northern countries fared rather better. Denmark had escaped almost without destruction; neither here nor in Norway had there been any regular fighting at the end of the war, which found the Germans still in occupation. Similarly, Belgium's rapid liberation had helped preserve its cities: Antwerp and the region of the Ardennes were the places most heavily damaged. But in the Netherlands, where the Germans had remained almost until their final defeat, devastation and human suffering had been very severe; at the end, the urban poor were close to starvation, and the Allies were obliged to send emergency supplies by parachute.

In France, half a million buildings had been completely destroyed, and another million and a half seriously damaged. Half the country's cattle had disappeared, along with more than three-quarters of its railroad engines. Only one-tenth of its trucks and automobiles were fit for service. Industrial production at the beginning of 1945 stood at less than half what it had been in 1938. But in Germany things looked far worse. In a city such as Frankfurt, its beautiful medieval quarter laid waste by Allied incendiary bombs, less than a quarter of the houses were still standing. As late as 1946, the output of German industry had risen to only one-third of its volume of ten years before.

In Germany, however, appearances were deceptive. Under the surface of unprecedented destruction, a major share of the nation's assets remained intact. Large parts of the German countryside had been spared, along with most of its smaller towns and villages. Moreover, at least three-quarters of its industrial plant was still usable. The melancholy fact was that British and American aviators had been far more successful in destroying artistic monuments and workers' housing than they had been in crippling German industry. This was one of the chief reasons for the German "miracle" of economic recovery in the years after 1949.

Experts viewing the devastation of France and Germany estimated that it would take twenty years to rebuild. Actually, the larger part of the task was completed in a single decade. But this covered only the material losses. As far as human losses were concerned, it was harder to make an estimate, for here there had been intangible drains that only time would fully reveal.

Of the major belligerents in the West, Germany alone lost more men in the second war than it had in the first. More than a million and a half Germans had been killed in action, an additional two million were missing, and another million and a half were prisoners. Elsewhere—in Britain, in France, and in Italy—the numbers of those who perished in combat fell far below what they had been in the earlier war. But civilian losses were much higher. Two and a half million French men and women had been held in captivity in Germany as prisoners of war, forced laborers, or concentration camp inmates. Of these, more than 200,000 had been executed or had died of hardship and starvation. Countless others returned home crippled in body and in spirit. The six-year torment of the war eroded Europe's population both physically and psychologically. Once the first flush of joy at the coming of peace was over, it became apparent how much in fact the war had cost—how tired and depressed people were, and how few were fully capable of making the strenuous effort required to restore Europe's economy to a state of vigorous health.

Reconstruction, the Black Market, and American Aid

The initial pace of reconstruction was very slow. For the first few months, governments and people concentrated on the immediate tasks of restoring communications and essential services and reopening the coal mines, on which everything else depended, but they did not pursue these goals with any consistent policy. They wavered between an attitude of laissez-faire and an effort to keep wages and prices strictly in line. Only in the Low Countries and in Scandinavia—particularly in Belgium and in Norway—were governments strong enough to take stern action to limit currency circulation and thereby to hold inflation and the black market in check.

In France and Italy, on the other hand, inflation and black marketeering completely escaped control. Price regulation proved almost wholly ineffective. Soon the black market became the real market, since goods were unobtainable at the official prices. Meanwhile, the value of money fell steadily. The French franc, which had been officially established at the rate of 50 to the dollar at the time of the Normandy invasion, stood at about 300 when it reached a temporary plateau in early 1948. The following year, the Italian lira, which Allied Military Government had valued at 100 to the dollar, was finally stabilized at 625. Yet these results had been achieved only at the cost of abandoning controls entirely and of letting prices outstrip the wage level. In Italy, the postwar lira had fallen to one-fiftieth of its prewar purchasing power; in France, the fall had been at least half as great. This inflation was not as ruinous as that experienced by Germany in 1923, but it was enough to destroy once again the class of small investors and to wipe out nearly all private savings.

Even this modest economic stabilization, moreover, occurred only with American aid. Such help had reached Western Europe in successive waves. First there had been the emergency aid in the form of food and essential supplies that the Military Government had brought to Italy and the corresponding Civil Affairs officers had handled for France. By the end of 1945, however, the American army in France and Italy had finished its work and gone home. The new funnels for aid were the United Nations Relief and Rehabilitation Administration (UNRRA) and a number of direct grants from the United States to individual countries. These expedients in turn proved entirely inadequate. Not until the American government—in the context of the Cold War of 1947—inaugurated the Marshall Plan did Western Europe at last find its way out of the economic morass which had almost engulfed it (see Chapter 17, I).

III. THE OCCUPATION OF GERMANY

In Italy, the Military Government had been only a temporary expedient. In France, the Allied armies had restricted themselves to supply and civil liaison functions. In Germany, on the other hand, the Military Government ruled the country for four full years. There seemed to be no alternative, for here the unprecedented had happened: The German central government had disappeared. All that was left were local officials—and in the East even these were often lacking, since mayors and district administrators had departed along with the population fleeing before the advance of the Red Army. In his last statement, Hitler had delegated his powers to his naval chief, Admiral Karl Doenitz, and for a few days the admiral tried to run a semblance of government from his headquarters in Flensburg. But the Allies soon brought this to an end. By mid-May of 1945, the slate had been wiped clean. The four occupying powers were left alone with their problems and with each other; they must both rule their separate zones of Germany and devise a common policy for the government of the country as a whole.

The Potsdam Decisions: The Oder-Neisse Line

The Western Allies had wavered back and forth between moderation and rigor in their planning for postwar Germany. In September 1944, eight months before the end of the war, Roosevelt and Churchill had temporarily agreed on the extremely harsh scheme proposed by the American secretary of the treasury, Henry Morgenthau, Jr. The "Morgenthau Plan," as it was called, was based on the notion of a "pastoral" Germany; the Reich was to be stripped of its industrial potential. Its inhabitants, by returning to the bucolic conditions under which they had lived in the days of Kant and Goethe, were presumably to lose their taste—along with their capacities—for waging aggressive war.

The Morgenthau Plan was economic madness. None of the secretary's advisers who had drafted it ever explained how it would be possible for Germany to support its swollen twentieth-century population with an eighteenth-century economy. As this simple truth dawned on the British and Americans, they quietly shelved the Morgenthau proposals. By the time of the Yalta Conference, Churchill was pleading for humane treatment for Germany, while Roosevelt seemed irresolute and hesitant. Something of the Morgenthau Plan attitude still lingered. In the final directive issued to Anglo-American Military Government, the key formula specified a level of economic activity just sufficient to prevent "disease and unrest." This ambiguous wording was capable of two different interpretations. At first it was treated as a strict maximum that the Germans were not to exceed, but its interpretation was subsequently modified to allow them to raise their standard of living as far as their own resources permitted.

Stalin and his advisers were clearer about what they wanted from Germany. They were interested in a social revolution that would transform their zone—or preferably the whole nation—into a People's Democracy, and in receiving substantial reparations as compensation for the destruction their own country had suffered. Beyond that they wanted a boundary for Poland sufficiently generous to help the Poles forget what they had ceded to the Soviet Union and to tie them firmly to Russia's policy. These concessions Stalin had failed to obtain at Yalta. The final conference of the Big Three, held in Potsdam, just outside Berlin, the following July, gave him an opportunity to return to the attack.

Much of the criticism that Yalta generated should more properly have focused on Potsdam, for it was here that the British and Americans finally consented to the Oder-Neisse boundary for Poland and the sum of ten billion dollars in reparations for the Soviet Union, which Churchill had succeeded at Yalta in having postponed for later decision. But Churchill was able to participate only in the first part of the Potsdam Conference; toward its end he was obliged to give up his seat to Clement Attlee, whose party had just defeated Churchill's Conservatives in the British parliamentary elections. Likewise,

President Truman had taken Roosevelt's place. Of the original trio of war-time comrades-in-arms, only Stalin remained. It was certainly not without influence on the Potsdam decisions that the Soviet leader was facing two inexperienced Western negotiators.

The Oder-Neisse boundary—which put under Polish rule an area inhabited by nine million Germans—was never formally conceded by the British and Americans; they simply agreed to the de facto administration of the area by Poland, pending final decision by a regular peace conference. This proviso really meant very little. It did not prevent the expulsion by the Poles of the vast majority of the Germans within their new borders, to whom the Czechs added nearly three million more by driving out the Germans of the Sudetenland. The problem of absorbing 12 million expellees and refugees became the most agonizing difficulty that German administrators faced in the immediate postwar years. But on one matter at least Truman and Attlee held firm. They did not grant Stalin's third demand—an interallied control of the Ruhr that would have associated the Soviet Union in the administration of Germany's most important industrial area and so given it an opportunity to spread Soviet ideological influence into the very heart of the country. The Western leaders thereby made certain that experiments in People's Democracy would be restricted to Russia's Eastern Zone.

The Partition of the Country

Just before the Potsdam Conference met, the four Allied powers moved into the occupation zones that had been formally assigned the previous spring. Earlier they had been administering on a temporary basis the areas that their troops had occupied during the course of hostilities. Now they redeployed their forces behind the definitive zonal demarcation lines—the Russians in the east, the British in the northwest, the Americans in the south, and the French in a smaller zone to the southwest bordering on their own country. In substance, this meant American withdrawal from such central German regions as Thuringia and Saxony and their reassignment to Soviet control.

At the same time, the occupation powers arranged for a similar four-way division of the city of Berlin—which was entirely surrounded by the Soviet Zone. This was an awkward arrangement, and it was to cause repeated international crises in succeeding years, but the Allies hoped to mitigate the Berlin problem and to give a minimum of unity to the country by establishing in the former capital a number of central German agencies. These would have the task of ensuring uniformity in carrying out the less controversial of the Potsdam decisions—which included the level to which German industry would be limited, a pledge to treat the country as a single economic unit, and provisions for the demilitarization and democratization of German society.

Quite obviously, however—as Eastern European experience was demonstrating—the Russians interpreted the term *democratization* differently from the British and Americans. By it, they meant the unquestioned leadership of Communist and pro-Soviet elements.

In the spring of 1945, as Marshal Zhukov's armies reached the outskirts of Berlin, a group of German Communists led by Walter Ulbricht arrived from Moscow to prepare for the postwar German government in the Soviet Zone. Ulbricht—like Klement Gottwald in Czechoslovakia and Wladislaw Gomulka in Poland—was a "Muscovite" who had spent the war in the Soviet Union. During the Weimar years, he had risen through the ranks of the German Communist party (KPD) thanks to his organizational skills and astute sense of political opportunism, in the end serving as a Communist deputy in the Reichstag before being ordered into exile in 1933.

Upon returning to Berlin in 1945, Ulbricht and his associates at first tried to fos-ter the illusion of political pluralism. They revived the German Communist party, banned by Hitler in 1933, and three other parties as well: Social Democrats, Liberal Dem-ocrats, and Christian Democrats. Then in the spring of 1946, they forced the East Ger-man Social Democrats to merge with the Communists in the new Socialist Unity party (SED)—a process in which the former party (originally much the stronger) entirely lost its identity. By the end of the year, the Soviet occupation authorities—acting through Ulbricht and the SED—had firmly set their zone of Germany on the same course that the satellite states of East Central Europe were simultaneously following.

Similarly, in economic policy, the Russians made sure that East Germany served their interests. They exacted reparations not only by dismantling factories and shipping them to the Soviet Union—which was permitted by the Potsdam Agreement—but also by tapping current German production—which had been expressly forbidden. By operat-ing their zone as a self-contained economic entity, they violated the provision that Ger-many was to be treated as a unit for purposes of foreign trade. This behavior evoked retaliation from the West. In late 1946 and 1947, the British and Americans moved to-ward a separate economic policy of their own. They ceased dismantling factories, they raised the permitted level of German industry; in short, they began to shift from treating the Germans as enemies to preparing them for a role as future allies.

In December 1946, the Americans and British agreed to fuse the economic ad-ministration of their two zones into what came to be called the *Bizone*—the nucleus of the future state of Western Germany. Meanwhile, a series of conferences between the Western and the Soviet foreign ministers had ended in total deadlock. In the same fash-ion, the Allied Control Council, which consisted of the four zonal commanders, had also broken down. It held its last meeting in March 1948, when the Soviet representative walked out in protest against the invitation the British and Americans had extended to the French to join the Bizone. Three months earlier, the foreign ministers had adjourned their final conference without agreement. The rupture was complete. By the spring of 1948, the partition of Germany between East and West was an established fact (see Map 15.1).

The Establishment of State Governments, Political Parties, and the Bonn Parliamentary Council

In the winter of 1945–1946, Germany was at its nadir. Industry was languishing, millions were living in cold and squalor in cellars and temporary barracks; the old and infirm were dying of hardship, and the expellees from the East were receiving a chilly welcome as unwanted guests. Social dissolution seemed imminent, as parents lost control over their children, and prostitution and black marketeering flourished on the fringes of the occupation armies.

Yet at this very moment, Western Germany was taking its first steps toward political and moral revival. Toward the end of 1945, the British and American occupation authorities began the reconstruction of German administration above the local level. They established state governments within their zones—four in the British Zone and four in the American. These states did not exactly correspond to the former divisions of Germany. A few, like Bavaria, which was the largest in territorial extent, were genuine revivals of the old middle-sized states of the Reich. Others, like North Rhine–Westphalia, the most populous, were formed from provinces of Prussia, which at last disappeared from the map. In general, however, this redrawing of administrative boundaries benefited the country; it tended to equalize the states in size and to group together areas with common interests.

With the organization of the Bizone, the state governments began to acquire a new political significance. Indeed, the bizonal Council of Ministers-President of the individual states became a West German government in embryo. These ministers-president—or prime ministers—had received their appointments from the Military Government as trusted anti-Nazis. Some had been imprisoned under Hitler; some had lived in exile; some had remained at liberty within the Reich but had succeeded in avoiding involvement with the Nazi tyranny.

The ministers-president and their ministerial colleagues gave tangible evidence of the revival of German democracy. Most of them were older men who had acquired political experience under the Weimar Republic, and the parties they represented were similarly reincarnations of Weimar models. Two parties dominated the field from the outset. Neither the right-wing parties nor the Communists were able to win much support. The former were discredited by their collusion with the Nazis; the latter, by their association with the Russians, who were too close for comfort. The Social Democrats and the Christian Democrats, rather, found the postwar atmosphere congenial and emerged almost equal in strength from the first elections to state diets, or parliaments.

The Social Democrats—who had kept alive their organization in exile—had never broken their ties with the Weimar years. They had found a new kind of leader, however, in Kurt Schumacher. Schumacher offered a striking contrast to the older type of bureaucratic, routinized Social Democratic leadership. A veteran of twelve years in concentration camp, he had emerged shattered in health, with both an arm and a leg missing, but with a passionate faith in the future of his party; by his intense, frenetic drive and his burning oratory, he steered the Social Democrats toward a more nationalist course and away from their former exclusive dependence on the trade unions.

German Christian Democracy was also for the most part a revival of an earlier party—the old Catholic Center. The new name suggested a broadening of its base to include a substantial Protestant wing. Its leader, however, was a Catholic and a prominent centrist from the Weimar years: Konrad Adenauer—whose personality and influence were to dominate a decade and a half of post-Nazi German history—had already ranked as an important figure in the 1920s and early 1930s. But he had largely restricted himself to local affairs, serving as lord mayor of the Rhineland city of Cologne. Under the Nazis

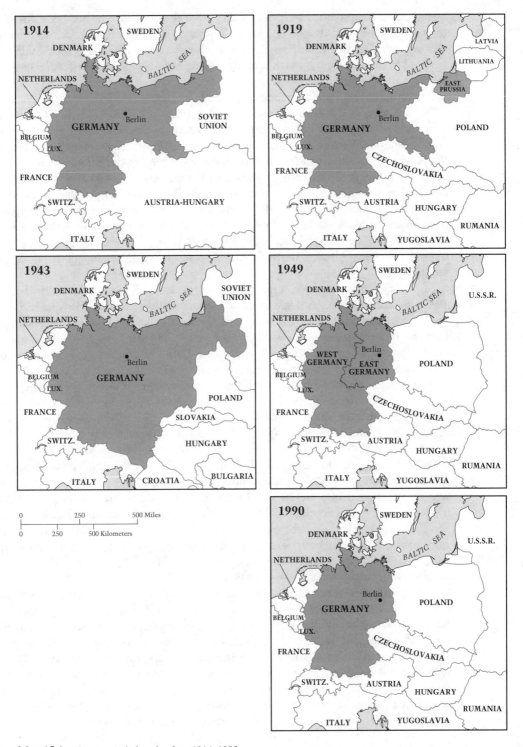

MAP 15.1 Germany's shifting borders, 1914–1990.

he had never compromised with the regime, yet at the same time he had been careful not to engage in the more dangerous kind of Resistance activities. Except for two brief periods in prison, he had simply waited out the twelve years of Hitler's rule. In 1945 he emerged from retirement—tough minded, astute, astonishingly robust for his sixty-nine years—to become his country's guide and savior as it groped its way toward its second experiment in republican and democratic government.

It was largely under Adenauer's influence that the Rhineland university town of Bonn was selected as the place where a "Parliamentary Council" was to meet to draft a constitution for Western Germany. In September 1948, after the French had accepted the Anglo-American invitation to join their smaller zone to the Bizone, representatives of the West German state diets convened in Bonn to establish at last a federal government. Three months earlier, the Western occupation powers had proclaimed a currency reform. By a conversion of old marks into new at a rate of ten to one, they cut the ground from under the black market and prepared the way for rapid economic revival. The Soviet Union, meanwhile, had precipitated the first great crisis over Berlin, in an effort to force the Western Allies to desist from their plan of establishing a federal government (see Chapter 17, I).

The Parliamentary Council proceeded, undaunted, with its labors. In February 1949, the constitution, or "basic law," was substantially completed. Two more months were needed to alter it to suit the occupying powers. By summer, however, everything was ready for its ratification by the West German people and for the election of the first federal parliament. In these elections, the Christian Democrats scored a narrow victory over their Social Democratic rivals; Konrad Adenauer became the first chancellor of the new German Federal Republic, which was formally inaugurated at Bonn in September.

The following month the Soviet Union, not to be outdone, proclaimed its own puppet German Democratic Republic in the Eastern Zone. The new republic was formally led by Wilhelm Pieck, an aging and amiable figurehead, but real control remained in the hands of Walter Ulbricht, who assumed the title of General Secretary of the Socialist Unity party the next year. With the founding of a separate East German state, Ulbricht's campaign of Stalinist conformity picked up its pace. Stalin's own *Short Course* was now translated into German and made required reading in schools and factories. Those suspected of harboring doubts about the wisdom of maintaining close ties with Moscow were ruthlessly purged from the party, while youth groups and other organizations sponsored by the Communist regime dispensed the political party line. At the same time, a large Russian garrison remained quartered within East Germany to ensure the country's ultimate loyalty to the Soviet bloc.

While Soviet occupation remained a reality in the East, in the West the occupation was now over in essentials, if not yet in theory. Although the Western powers reserved certain rights to themselves under an "Occupation Statute" and although their troops also remained in the country, West Germany had in fact become a sovereign nation once again. The new Federal Republic contained the bulk of the country's industrial resources and two-thirds of its population—which gradually grew to three-quarters, as hundreds of thousands of refugees from political oppression crossed the demarcation line from East to West. Within a year after its foundation, the German Federal Republic was being courted as an ally by the military coalition the United States was building.

The Austrian Parallel

Post-Nazi Austria resembled a Germany in miniature. The Danubian republic, whose independence the wartime allies had decided to restore, also found itself partitioned into four occupation zones, with its capital surrounded by the Soviet Zone and divided four ways. But there was one important difference. From the beginning, the Austrians possessed a central government at Vienna. Although this government had originally been established under Soviet auspices, it soon received full recognition from the Western powers. The Communists, who had played only a minor part in its formation, eventually dropped out entirely. The federal government continued as a semipermanent coalition of the People's Party and the Socialists, who roughly corresponded to the two leading German parties. Thus Austria was in an excellent position to take full advantage of the possibilities for military evacuation and neutrality which were to appear in rather surprising form ten years after the war's end (see Chapter 19, II).

IV. FRANCE AND ITALY: THE ERA OF "TRIPARTISM"

Communism, Socialism, Christian Democracy

In the first general elections of the postwar era, held in France in October 1945, and in Italy the following June, three parties clearly dominated the field. Two of them were the old parties of the Left—the Communists and the Socialists. The other was Christian Democracy. In Italy this group was the heir of the Popular Party of the period of 1919–1922, but in France it was almost a new creation. Together the trio of parties polled nearly three-quarters of the vote, reducing their adversaries to mere splinters or pathetic reminders of former greatness. In France, the three emerged nearly equal; in Italy, the Christian Democrats outstripped their rivals to the left.

Flushed with its victories in the combats of the Resistance, communism emerged for the first time as a major force in Western European politics. This Resistance prestige was one reason for its new importance; another was its control of organized labor, which it had wrested from the more moderate, Socialist-oriented trade-union leaders during the war years. Finally, the economic hardships of the years 1943–1946—particularly among the urban poor—encouraged the spread of Communist influence; economic desperation pushed whole classes of the population toward the extreme left. But poverty was never the chief reason for the appeal of communism. Its hold depended rather on what the French called its *mystique*—its power to inspire devotion and sacrifice among its adherents. This was especially true of intellectuals and of young people—the two groups of converts in whom Communist organizers took most pride and who generally knew communism only in the moderate and patriotic guise it had assumed during the war years.

In contrast, socialism seemed tired and stuffy. It was true that old Léon Blum had declared, after his release from prison in Germany: "Socialism is the master of the

hour." It was also true that the ideology of the Resistance movements was broadly socialist. But this was only in the sense of general goals; most Resistance veterans had little regard for the Socialist *party* as a regular political organization. The inability of the
Resistance to effect a regrouping of Western European political forces was also a defeat
for socialism. After its failure to become the nucleus of a wider and less doctrinaire type
of movement—which was what Blum had in mind—the Socialists were thrown back on
their old organizational base. With a cadre of aging leaders, they resumed the attitude
they had maintained before the war. In the intervening years, however, circumstances
had changed drastically. Socialism's new position as the middle group among the three
mass ideologies was not as favorable as it initially seemed, for it cast the Socialists in a
difficult role as mediators under pressure from both sides and made them appear far more
"center" than "left." This was particularly true in their relations with communism: Whatever the Socialists did proved wrong. Where they resolutely kept their independence
from the Communists, as in France, they were accused of having a merely negative policy
and of splitting the working-class and the labor movement; where they cooperated
closely with the Communists, as in Italy, they found themselves reduced to the position
of helpless "fellow travelers."

Christian Democracy was actually a more conservative ideology than socialism,
but it had a fresher look—as a movement based on Catholic principles, it alone could
challenge communism on the grounds of faith and personal devotion and compete with
it for the allegiance of the young. Like communism, it was closely associated with the Resistance tradition. In France, the new Christian Democratic party—called the Popular
Republican Movement (MRP)—was founded in November 1944, by former Resistance
leaders, chief among them de Gaulle's foreign minister, Georges Bidault, who had served
as chairman of the clandestine Resistance directorate. The MRP also let it be understood
that it had the general's secret blessing. This de Gaulle never confirmed, but the image of
the French Christian Democrats as the "party of fidelity" to the national leader certainly
helped them in the first postwar elections.

They were also helped by the fact that in France, as in Italy, millions of conservatives whose own parties had disappeared in the wave of revulsion against fascism voted
for them as the least objectionable of the three mass formations. This influx of grudging
support swelled the ranks of the Christian Democrats far beyond their leaders' most optimistic hopes. For the short term, it was a source of strength, but in the long run, it created difficulties by deepening the cleavage between conservatives and reformers
characteristic of political parties whose common denominator was religion rather than a
coherent social philosophy.

In the period 1945–1947, however, this problem still seemed remote. The most
urgent questions for the reviving democracies of Western Europe were economic rather
than political and, in solving them, a "tripartite" formula of government was far from
ideal. Of necessity, the immediate postwar ministries in France and Italy were based on a
nearly equal sharing of power by the three mass parties. Yet agreement on such a basis
was almost impossible; the differences among the parties were too great. The split over
economic policy found the Communists and Socialists, as Marxists and proponents of
state action, allied against the Christian Democrats, who preferred free enterprise. On
questions of personal liberty, on the other hand, the Socialists stood together with the
Christian Democrats against the authoritarian Communists. Thus the tripartite govern-

ments were riven not by one cleavage but by two—with the Socialists in the uncomfortable middle position in both cases. Both conflicts needed to be resolved before postwar democracy in France and Italy could face its problems with any strength or coherence.

France: De Gaulle and the Politicians; the Welfare State

During the fourteen months after France's liberation, Charles de Gaulle governed his country as a benevolent dictator. Aided only by the advice of the Consultative Assembly—which had been enlarged with new members from the Resistance and the political parties following its move from Algiers to Paris—the general and his ministers directed the French war effort and took a number of long-range decisions on economic policy. De Gaulle sought to restore his country's great-power status by making a maximum contribution to the winning of the war; the first great success he scored was the decision of the Big Three to admit France to equal partnership in the occupation of Germany. He also inaugurated a welfare-state policy in order to associate the working classes in a new spirit of national unity and to deprive the Communists of their most telling propaganda points.

With the end of the war, however, and with the election of a Constituent Assembly the following autumn, de Gaulle began to feel more and more uncomfortable. An authoritarian by temperament, he had worked only reluctantly with the Socialists and the other political leaders who rallied to his movement in the war years. He never had liked politicians nor accustomed himself to their methods. The parliamentary leaders, for their part, had deferred to him during the war emergency only because they saw no alternative. With the coming of peace and the restoration of a popularly elected Assembly, a rupture was unavoidable. De Gaulle believed in a strong executive; the politicians wanted an executive of the old parliamentary type who would be strictly dependent on the legislature. For three months the general tried to adjust to the new situation. In November, he reorganized his ministry to take account of the proved electoral strength of the three mass parties, but almost immediately he began to quarrel with the Socialists, who refused to approve a military budget of the size he demanded. De Gaulle saw no alternative but resignation. Accordingly, he abandoned his office in January 1946 and retired to his home in the country.

With de Gaulle's resignation, the real era of "tripartism" began. It continued for a year and a half, under alternating Socialist and MRP leadership. With this succession of tripartite ministries, the regime of "politics as usual" returned to the Assembly. The governments lacked coherent direction; they postponed dealing with urgent problems or concealed their evasions of responsibility under meaningless compromise formulas. Almost overnight the Third Republic atmosphere of intrigue and behind-the-scenes maneuvering resumed its previous sway.

Yet for all its faults, the era of tripartism constructed one lasting monument, for on one thing, at least, the three governing parties agreed: the welfare state. Resuming where the Popular Front had left off nearly a decade earlier—and building on what de Gaulle had already accomplished in the same direction—the tripartite ministries vastly enlarged the role of the state in French economic and social life. In the first six months of 1946, they laid the foundations of a welfare-state system that all subsequent governments accepted as an accomplished fact.

Among these reforms was the nationalization of the coal mines, gas and electricity, and major banking and insurance enterprises, as well as a system of additional pay for workers and employees with children, based on the principle of family allowances, which was almost the only positive legacy left from the unhappy Vichy period. The latter measure formed part of a comprehensive body of social security legislation, which eventually covered more than half the population and absorbed about 16 percent of France's total national income. The social security system was bitterly criticized as a "monster" strangling French economic life. No doubt it was excessively bureaucratic in its administration, and employers did tend to pass on its costs to the consumer in the form of higher prices, but, in providing protection against the worst forms of want, it acted as a powerful brake to social unrest during France's years of inflation and economic hardship.

Finally, in establishing a national planning office under Jean Monnet, the French government provided itself with a framework for future economic expansion that Italy and Germany completely lacked. The Monnet Plan was to be of immense benefit in canalizing the country's resources when production at last began to soar in the boom years of the next decade.

Italy: Parri, De Gasperi, and the Socialist Split

Originally, Italy seemed less fortunate than France in not having an unquestioned national chief like de Gaulle, but it finally acquired a leader whose tenure in office was to be far longer than that of the French general. The great paradox in the situation of France and Italy—whose courses during the immediate postwar years ran so closely parallel—was that France lost its national leader at the very time that Italy was at last finding its own.

In June 1945, the triumphant Resistance leadership of the newly liberated North forced a change of prime minister. They pushed the old and ineffective Bonomi out of office and substituted their own man, Ferruccio Parri. Parri had been one of the three main chiefs of the northern Resistance. An engineer by training and an antifascist of more than twenty years' standing, he had served a period of detention on one of Mussolini's penal islands in the late 1920s. He had subsequently helped establish a clandestine political formation, the Party of Action, which was dedicated to that nonsectarian form of socialism to which so many of the Resistance fighters aspired.

Parri was a man of towering moral stature, but as an administrator he was no more effective than his predecessor. His party soon proved to be one of leaders without followers. Although it had played a Resistance role second only to that of the Communists, and although it included a large part of Italy's foremost intellectuals, it failed to win support among the wider public. The pressure of the three mass parties proved overwhelming. Far from attracting the Italian Socialists into its own orbit, moreover, the Party of Action was forced to stand helplessly by while the Socialist leader, Pietro Nenni, moved toward an alliance with the Communists, which was to cripple his own party for more than a decade.

By the autumn, this disastrous alliance was leaving Parri isolated in his own ministry. Yet it was the Right rather than the Left that finally torpedoed the experiment in government by militant anti-Fascists. In late November, a loose coalition of conserva-

Italy's Christian Democratic leader, Alcide De Gasperi, speaks to a dense throng in the center of of Milan shortly after the war. (*Courtesy of Getty Images, Inc./Hulton Archive Photos*)

tives—who had been steadily regaining confidence during the past few months—brought Parri down. His successor was the Christian Democratic leader, Alcide De Gasperi.

As foreign minister under the two preceding governments, De Gasperi had gradually been strengthening his position and preparing for his advent to power. A supple parliamentarian and a man of quiet tenacity, he had already figured among the younger leaders of the Popular Party in its brief pre-Fascist history. After serving a prison term in 1927 and 1928, he had waited out the last decade and a half of Mussolini's rule as a librarian in the Vatican. During 1943, however, he had cautiously begun to reconstitute his former party and to add to it newer Christian Democratic elements from among the clandestine opposition to fascism. Two years later, he had done his work so well that he was leading the single strongest force in Italian public life.

De Gasperi's policy combined antifascism and moderate reform with a basic conservatism. Hence although his own record under Mussolini had been impeccable, he was sufficiently indulgent toward the holdovers from the Fascist past to reassure the politically apathetic or those with a slightly tarnished ideological background. Furthermore, he won the men of property over to his side by reasserting the authority of the state. De Gasperi's deeply ingrained sense of state power was exactly what was needed to bring order out of the chaotic conditions into which Italy was falling in the winter of 1945–1946.

In the course of the year 1946, the Italians realized that a firm hand was finally in control. Early the following year, this hand was strengthened by the secession of a minority of democratically minded Socialists from Nenni's pro-Communist leadership. With the Socialists split, the stage was set for a dramatic showdown between De Gasperi and the Italian Communists.

The Dropping of the Communist Ministers and the End of Tripartism

In early May 1947, the Communist ministers were forced out of the French government. They were actually not too sorry to go. They were confident that they could prove the impossibility of ruling the country without them, and that the Socialists and the MRP would soon be obliged to consent to their recall. In fact, nothing of the sort happened; the departure of the Communists from the French government proved to be permanent. Later in the month, the same thing occurred in Italy, where De Gasperi now felt strong enough to dispense with his Communist aides entirely.

The Italian prime minister, like his French counterpart, had had his resolution stiffened by assurances of support from the United States. In the opening phase of postwar rivalry with the Soviet Union, the Truman administration was anxious to see the governments of its allies safely in anti-Communist hands. The dropping of the Communist ministers ranked as one of the opening acts in the inauguration of the Cold War. It also settled the two issues that had plagued the postwar governments of Western Europe from the beginning. In the realm of economic policy, it meant a victory for free enterprise and conservative solutions; on the question of personal liberty, it meant that the traditional Western freedoms would be preserved and no compromises made with the more slippery definitions of People's Democracy. In the new political phase that was opening, the Socialists found themselves more and more pushed to the side; for the next half decade the Christian Democrats, in Italy and France as in Germany, were destined to take the lead (see Chapter 17, II).

V. THE BRITISH LABOUR GOVERNMENT

In July 1945, midway between the end of the war in Europe and the armistice in the Far East, the British held the first of the European postwar elections. The result was a resounding defeat for Winston Churchill and his Conservative party. For the first time in its history, Labour emerged with a clear-cut majority. With 393 seats in the House of Commons to 198 for the Conservatives, it received an ample mandate to carry out its Socialist program. Indeed, the Labour victory of 1945 was also the first time in history that a Socialist party had ever won a parliamentary majority in a major European country.

American observers, stunned by the news, interpreted it as an act of base ingratitude toward the peerless leader who had won the war. This was far too sentimental a reading of what had occurred. In fact the Labour victory was the logical outcome of the way the British war effort had been managed; it flowed almost inevitably from the economic and social legacies of the war itself.

The Postwar Economic "Imperatives"

Of all the major Western belligerents, the British had most thoroughly mobilized their people and their economy for war. Far more efficiently than the Germans, they had allocated manpower and womanpower and rationed the necessities of life for the whole population. The result had been a "semisiege economy," based on the principle of "fair shares" for all. In Britain, the black market had been almost nonexistent; rich and poor had fared alike. A nation profoundly united against the Nazi menace had expressed its solidarity in the first experiment in economic equality that a great Western democracy had ever made.

During the years of wartime austerity, the poor people of Britain had actually seen their standard of living rise. Both money wages and the workers' share of the total national product increased; infant mortality dropped to the lowest level ever known; milk for every child in Britain became the most striking symbol of wartime equality. Obviously, this current could not be reversed once the war had ended. Whichever party was to govern, it must continue the egalitarian policy, for there had come into being during the war an "implied contract between government and people"—in return for doing everything the government demanded for the winning of the great conflict, the British people were assured that their rulers would pursue an advanced social policy at the war's end. Three major "imperatives" for the future faced any postwar government:

> First, it would have to take steps to divert an increased share of the country's current output of goods to the export market so that the balance of payments could be restored; second, it would have to find means of directing into investment a larger proportion of the national income in order to satisfy the necessity for greater and more efficient production; third, it would have to provide for a tremendous new outlay on the social services and, consequently, maintain taxation at a high level.*

In short, Britain was faced with the necessity of pulling itself up by its own bootstraps. It had consumed all its economic fat and liquidated all its overseas investments during the war. Totally dependent on imports for its survival, it had to find a way to pay for these imports and at the same time provide for the social needs of its own population. This could be done only by increasing the export of finished products—and that in turn required heavy outlays for the modernization of Britain's antiquated industries in order to make them fully competitive. The British themselves, meanwhile, must do without woolens and Scotch whisky and the other luxury exports that could buy precious dollars. And they must pay extremely high taxes.

On this policy of continued austerity combined with an extension of social services the two major parties were in agreement. Indeed, the Conservatives in Churchill's National Government had already concurred in postwar plans for vastly increasing public

*Keith Hutchinson, *The Decline and Fall of British Capitalism* (London: Jonathan Cape, 1951), 283, 285.

educational facilities and for establishing a National Health Service (which in the United States would be called "socialized medicine"). But such a policy was uncongenial to the Tories. To Labour, on the contrary, it was the natural fulfillment of what the party had been advocating for decades. The voters of Britain seemed aware of this, and they cast their ballots for the party better suited to carry out the policy that was coming in any case; a massive defection of the middle class from the Conservatives to Labour suggested that millions among the electorate had understood the imperatives of the hour.

Finally, in explaining Labour's victory, it should be noted that the British Socialists were in a far better campaigning position than their adversaries. They knew it very well: It was they who broke up the wartime coalition and insisted on an early election, refusing to listen to Churchill's pleas that they wait until the war against Japan had been won. This favorable position again grew out of the role Labour had played during the war. In the allotment of ministries in the National Government, the Labour men had received the assignment of supervising the home front. Their leader, Clement Attlee, became deputy prime minister—in practice, the man who provided governmental continuity during Churchill's long absence overseas. Attlee's strongest associate, Ernest Bevin, applied his wide experience in trade-union leadership to directing the ministry of labor, which handled workforce allocations. The Conservatives, on the other hand, headed the foreign ministry and most of the military service ministries. The Tory assignment was to run the war on the fighting fronts, for which the Conservatives were fitted by tradition and temperament, just as Labour was fitted to manage the domestic economy. A large number of Conservative MPs served as officers in the armed forces, whereas the Labour people more frequently remained at home. Thus—as the Conservatives bitterly lamented—by going off to fight the war they had lost touch with their home constituencies. Labour had stayed behind, free to rebuild its political fences and to prepare its program for the postwar era.

The Labour Program: Nationalization and Its Consequences

The record of Labour in power during the six years 1945–1951 was very nearly unique in still a further respect. Prime Minister Attlee and his colleagues did what political leaders almost never do—they carried out to the letter the program on which they had been elected.

Some of these measures were contributions to the new welfare state and showed the influence of Keynesian economics: the National Health Service, the extension of educational facilities, and an integrated program for new housing and for the rehabilitation of depressed areas. Such measures aroused little controversy. It was against Labour's more strictly Socialist proposals that the Tories directed their fire. The controversial center of the Labour program was the series of nationalization acts that sought to bring the "commanding heights" of the economy into public ownership. Even here, however, opponents made distinctions. It was difficult to fight with much conviction against the nationalization of the coal mines, which had been a sick industry ever since the 1920s and which the government alone could provide with the capital needed for the urgent task of modernization. It was on steel, rather, that the Conservatives chose to make their stand. For in Britain, as in any modern industrial country, the production of steel was the key to the whole economy.

The parliamentary struggle over the nationalization of steel was intense and bitter. In order to force the measure through before their mandate expired, Attlee and his colleagues felt obliged to alter the constitution itself. They used their crushing majority in the House of Commons to modify the Parliament Act of 1911 by reducing the power of the House of Lords once again; in the future, the Lords would be able to delay legislation for no more than a single session. By the time this hurdle had been surmounted, however, and the nationalization of steel had become law, Labour had only one year of power left. In 1951, the Conservatives returned to office, with the denationalization of steel as the first item on their agenda.

Nearly all the other nationalizations survived. The Conservatives did not try to reverse these any more than they sought to undo the Attlee government's welfare-state measures. In this sense, Labour accomplished a permanent, irreversible revolution in British life that would not be threatened until Margaret Thatcher became prime minister in 1979. But Labour's very success also presented it with an insoluble dilemma. By the end of four and a half years in office, it had almost completely accomplished its program. What was it to do now?

The great change that Socialists had dreamed of for a century had come at last, but life continued much as before. The most glaring economic inequalities had been eliminated, class hatred had been enormously reduced, but still the intangible barriers of speech, education, and manners separated class from class. Nor did the workers themselves experience the qualitative change in the whole atmosphere of life that socialism had promised. The man in the coal mines or in the nationalized railroads did not feel that he now *owned* his place of work in his capacity as a citizen. This was partly because of faults in the nationalization acts, which had organized state enterprise in too centralized and bureaucratic a fashion and had made almost no provision for worker consultation. Nationalization, people now saw, was not the final end and aim of economic policy; it was only one of a number of weapons at the disposal of the welfare state, partial and fallible like any other. The failure of nationalization in Britain to accomplish what had been hoped for was a major cause of the crisis of confidence that was to shake European socialism as a whole in the decade of the 1950s (see Chapter 20, III).

VI. The Parliamentary Restoration

Parliamentary democracy was restored throughout Western Europe at the end of the war. It was a restoration in a very real sense, for the norms of parliamentary life had been overthrown or suspended everywhere, except in neutral Sweden and Switzerland. Even in Britain the system had not functioned fully, since no general election was held for ten years—the Parliament elected in 1935 sat longer than any such body of modern times—and by-elections were not contested between the parties.

In the smaller countries, the governments-in-exile returned and picked up the threads of political life where they had dropped them in 1940. Norway, Denmark, and the Netherlands resumed their parliamentary systems unchanged; the only marked alteration was a shift in political influence toward the left which, as in Britain, reflected the austerity and the economic imperatives inherited from wartime. In Belgium alone real difficulties arose. King Leopold III, who, unlike the sovereigns of Norway and the Netherlands, had remained in his own country throughout the war, labored under a double suspicion—he was accused of having capitulated prematurely in May 1940 and of subsequent acts of collaboration with the Germans. The "royal question" threatened to tear the country apart. The Flemings in general supported the king, whereas the French-speaking Walloons demanded his withdrawal. Not until 1950, when Leopold abdicated in favor of his son, did Belgium return to civil peace.

In Scandinavia and the Low Countries, the restoration of parliamentary democracy in its old form came as no surprise. More worthy of comment was the return of the major states of Western and Central Europe to their former constitutional patterns. In France, this was perhaps only natural, since the Third Republic from 1870 to 1940 had proved the most enduring of the recent political systems under which the country had lived, and the Vichy regime ranked as scarcely more than an interlude. But in the nations that had passed under fascist dictatorship—in the one instance for twelve years, in the other, for more than twenty—the restoration of parliamentary institutions in the old style was certainly not a foregone conclusion.

The Constitutions of France, Italy, and Western Germany

The surprising thing about the postwar constitutions with which France, Italy, and Western Germany provided themselves was that they showed so little trace of the criticism to which their earlier institutions had been subjected—even by democrats—during the years of dictatorial rule.

In France, both among the Resistance and among the more immediate followers of General de Gaulle, the conviction had been almost universal that the constitution of the Third Republic would not do. Similarly, the popular referendum held in October 1945 had shown an overwhelming majority for giving the country a new institutional framework. But, as the Constituent Assembly (which had been elected at the same time) labored through the following winter, it became apparent that the new proposals which were taking shape only intensified the eccentric features of the Third Republic. The left bloc which dominated the Assembly—and whose historical memories went back to the Jacobin tradition of 1793—imposed its view that a single parliamentary body should concentrate nearly all power in its own hands. De Gaulle and the Christian Democrat MRP were opposed and, by taking their case to the conservative mass of the French people, ensured the rejection of the new constitution by a narrow margin of the electorate in a second referendum held in May 1946.

Thus it became necessary to elect another Constituent Assembly and to draft another constitution. In the new Assembly—although the "tripartite" character remained—the MRP increased its representation, and the two parties of the Left lacked the slight majority they had held in the earlier body. The second draft constitution was more conservative than the first. Indeed, when in the autumn it received the people's endorsement and the "Fourth Republic" was formally inaugurated with the first regular parliamentary elections, the representative bodies looked much as they had before 1940. The Chamber of Deputies was renamed the National Assembly, and the second Chamber, now called the Council of the Republic, did not enjoy the full powers of the old Senate; but both of them met in their traditional halls and conformed to their old procedures, and soon the councillors of the Republic were referring to themselves as senators and claiming nearly all the prerogatives of the former body. Meanwhile, the only other major constitutional innovation—a new procedure for designating the prime minister—was operating in just the opposite way from what had been intended. It was supposed to make the appointment of the prime minister more straightforward and his tenure more secure. In practice it made his appointment harder, and his stay in office proved more precarious, as ministries under the Fourth Republic lasted even a shorter time on the average than they had under the Third. No wonder that the citizenry soon grew skeptical about a constitution which had actually been accepted by only a third of them; the massive abstentions in the second constitutional referendum—more than 30 percent of the eligible voters—already showed how little the French were satisfied with their new institutions.

In Italy, the old constitution was even more obviously in need of renovation than was the French. It had not only been in suspension for more than two decades; it was also nearly a century old and reflected an earlier age in its provisions for a monarch with more than nominal powers and for a Senate appointed by the king. In June 1946, the monarchy disappeared in a popular referendum that was held simultaneously with the election of a Constituent Assembly. This Assembly labored for nine months. The new republican constitution it produced was a massive document specifying all sorts of novel human rights—most of which in practice proved inoperable. Except for making the Senate elective and substituting a president for the king as the titular chief of state, the Italian constitution that came into effect in January 1948 reproduced with astounding fidelity the main features of its antiquated predecessor.

One change, however, was so little discussed that it passed almost unnoticed: women's suffrage. In Italy, as in France, women won the vote without a struggle. What had seemed scarcely within the realm of possibility in 1939 was accepted by nearly everyone at the war's end as the natural consequence of the changed role of women in economic and social life.

In Western Germany, the Parliamentary Council at Bonn labored under a handicap that did not affect the French and Italians. The Germans had to pay heed to the wishes of the occupying powers, which had reserved the right to request modifications in the completed document. More particularly, this meant an insistence on decentralization—which the Americans characteristically associated with the concept of democracy. The German constitution makers of 1949 simply bowed to foreign pressure when they gave more powers to the states than these had enjoyed under the Weimar system. For the same reason, they renamed the Reichstag the *Bundestag* ("Federal Assembly"). In other respects, the Bonn constitution followed the Weimar model fairly closely. There were, however, two significant changes in the federal executive. The emergency powers of the president, which had opened the doors to the Nazi tyranny, disappeared from the 1949 constitutional document, and the German president became no more than a ceremonial figure in the normal Western European pattern. In his place, the chancellor was assured of a more stable tenure through an ingenious device that permitted a vote of no confidence only when the opposition had already agreed on a candidate for the succession.

The Problem for the Future: Legitimacy against Apathy

In postwar Europe, parliamentary democracy proved that it had become the normal and "legitimate" form of government. Its restoration was accepted by the vast majority of the population as a return to natural and well-tried forms of rule. Indeed, in some respects it appeared to have profited by its period of suspension. The party structure had become simpler, now that three major parties—as in France and Italy—or two—as in Britain and Western Germany—dominated the field. On the Continent, the old multiparty system seemed likely to disappear; in Britain, a two-party alternation in power was functioning properly for the first time in a generation.

Yet this simplification of the party structure meant that discipline within the individual parties was becoming tighter, and the resulting "tyranny of party machines" made average citizens think that politics was a professional game with which they had no concern. Such was the more threatening aspect of the ease with which parliamentary government had been restored: The other face of general acceptance was public apathy. One reason why people concurred in the return of the old practices was that they did not know what to put in their place. They were not particularly enthusiastic about parliamentarism, but they could think of no alternative. The paradoxical result of the effortless parliamentary restoration was a massive falling away from political interests.

With it went a parallel loss of concern for ideology. The Resistance experience had been the last great explosion of the ideological fervor that had characterized European political life for more than a century and a half. The failure of the Resistance to recast the Continent's politics in its own image was also a failure of the whole ideological approach to human society. As Europe returned to "normal" at the end of the 1940s, it became apparent that the old ideologies that had provided the guiding thread for so much of its history no longer really counted. To young people in particular, they seemed stale and irrelevant. What counted now was the split between East and West—the gulf between the Communist way of looking at things and all the other points of view, whose differences one from another were coming to seem less and less important, since they shared the same enemy. The Communist–anti-Communist cleavage immensely simplified the European ideological landscape. Indeed, for a while it seemed to have obliterated it entirely. It was only in the middle and late 1950s, with the reduction in the intensity of the Cold War following Stalin's death, that true ideological debate returned to European politics—but in a greatly altered form, with new problems and a new vocabulary (see Chapters 19 and 20).

READINGS

The rebuilding of democracy in the three major countries of the Western European continent is dealt with in the following works. Jonathan Story, ed., *The New Europe: Politics, Government, and Economy since 1945** (1993) is ambitious and detailed but assumes some prior knowledge of the topic. For postwar Germany, see the comprehensive treatment by Dennis L. Bark and David R. Gress, *A History of West Germany*, 2 vols. (1989). Other studies include Alfred Grosser, *Germany in Our Time: A Political History of the Post-War Years* (1971); Peter H. Merkl, *The Origin of the West German Republic** (1963); Gabriel A. Almond, ed., *The Struggle for Democracy in Germany* (1949); and the memoirs of General Lucius V. Clay, *Decision in Germany* (1950). The Potsdam Conference is described with abundant detail in Charles L. Mee, Jr., *Meeting at Potsdam* (1975). Telford Taylor, *The Anatomy of the Nuremberg Trials: A Personal Memoir* (1992) chronicles the most famous of Europe's postwar trials from the viewpoint of one of the chief American prosecutors.

On the creation of the regime in East Germany, see Norman M. Naimark, *The Russians in Germany: A History of the Soviet Zone of Occupation, 1945–49** (1995). Wolfgang Leonhard, *Child of the Revolution* (1958), is a vivid memoir by one of the original members of the "Ulbricht Group," while Carola Stern, *Ulbricht: A Political Biography* (1965), offers a balanced assessment of the country's unloved leader. An excellent and accessible introduction to the history of the German Democratic Republic is Anne McElvoy, *The Saddled Cow: East Germany's Life and Legacy* (1992). Henry Ashby Turner, Jr., *The Two Germanies Since 1945** (1987) provides an introduction to the twin paths taken by East and West Germany after the war.

For France, see Gordon Wright, *The Reshaping of French Democracy* (1948; reprint ed., 1970); Jean-Pierre Rioux, *The Fourth Republic** (1983; reprint ed. 1989); Philip Williams, *Crisis and Compromise: Politics in the Fourth Republic* (1966); and Bruce D. Graham, *The French Socialists and Tripartism, 1944–1947* (1965). For Italy, the finest single work on the postwar period as a whole is Paul Ginsborg, *A History of Contemporary Italy: Society and Politics, 1943–1988** (1990). See also Stuart J. Woolf, ed., *The Rebirth of Italy, 1943–1950* (1972); H. Stuart Hughes, *The United States and Italy,** 3rd ed. (1979); and Giuseppe Mammarella, *Italy After Fascism: A Political History, 1943–1965* (1966). Alan Sked and Chris Cook, *Postwar Britain: A Political History,** 2nd ed. (1984) and David Childs, *Britain Since 1945,** 2nd ed. (1986) both provide excellent overviews of British politics since 1945, while Michael Sissons and Philip French, eds., *The Age of Austerity** (1986) offers a series of penetrating vignettes of Britain in the lage 1940s. A highly sympathetic account of the British Labor government is given by Keith Hutchison in *The Decline and Fall of British Capitalism* (1951), while Kenneth Harris's *Attlee* (1984) details the life and policies of the Labor head of government. Charles S. Maier draws a balance sheet of the political reconstruction following both world wars in "The Two Postwar Eras and Conditions for Stability in Twentieth-Century Western Europe," *American Historical Review*, 86, no. 2 (April 1981).

*Books marked with an asterisk are available in paperback.

On economic problems, besides Aldcroft and Landes (see readings for Chapter 5), there are the general survey of Frank B. Tipton and Robert Aldrich, *An Economic and Social History of Europe From 1939 to the Present*** (1987) as well as the perceptive analyses by M.M. Postan, *An Economic History of Western Europe, 1945–1964* (1967), and Andrew Schonfield, *Modern Capitalism: The Changing Balance of Public and Private Power,** corrected ed. (1969). On the origins of the Marshall Plan, see Michael J. Hogan, *The Marshall Plan: America, Britain, and the Reconstruction of Western Europe, 1947–1952** (1987, reprint ed. 1989). More recent scholarship tends to downplay the importance of the Marshall Plan as the primary engine for Europe's recovery and stresses instead the resources and domestic policies of the countries concerned. For an excellent statement of this revisionist view, see Alan S. Milward, *The Reconstruction of Western Europe, 1945–1951** (1984). The social origins of the welfare state in Britain and Scandinavia are charted in Peter Baldwin, *The Politics of Social Solidarity: Class Bases of the European Welfare State, 1875–1975** (1990).

16

CULTURAL
RECONSTRUCTION,
1945–1965

Pope John XXIII (pontificate 1958–1963) is carried in the procession toward St.
Peter's Basilica for the formal opening of the Second Vatican Council in the autumn
of 1962. *(Courtesy Corbis-Bettmann)*

I. THE HERITAGE OF THE RESISTANCE

The Demand for Ethical Renewal:
From Silone to Camus

Postwar cultural life in Europe began with the Resistance to fascism. It began while the war was still in progress when, from their hiding places, from exile, or from concentration camps, the opponents of Hitler and Mussolini took up the task of defining the new cultural values. Even in the blackest hours of the war, this Resistance literature was a literature of hope. It was just as "committed" in the ideological battle as the writing of the 1930s had been, but it directed its struggle with tyranny less toward specific political goals than toward the renewal of Europe's humanist and humanitarian tradition, defined in the broadest possible terms. Christians and atheists, Marxists and liberals, could all find a place in the ethical vision of the Resistance years.

The values that emerged from the Resistance fight against fascism, not surprisingly, tended to reject or negate those imposed on Europe by Hitler's "New Order." Against the power of the state, the Resistance defended the rights and worth of the individual. Against hierarchy and blind obedience, it espoused equality and critical thought. And instead of a brutal amorality in political affairs, it urged a return to firm standards of ethical conduct. Such values, Resistance writers felt, should not merely be piously invoked, but must also guide the actual practice of leaders and citizens in the postwar world. Only thus could the sacrifices and suffering of the antifascist forces in wartime be redeemed.

The sudden and vigorous renaissance of a free press in newly liberated Europe gave these writers a forum in which to convey their vision of ethical renewal to a broad public. In newspapers and magazines, journals and pamphlets, as well as in books, poetry, and plays, they attempted to define and encourage the adoption of their ideals. Like the writing of the 1930s, the literature of the succeeding decade aimed at simplicity and directness. Here again, fascism provided a compelling negative example of what to avoid. The swollen oratory of Mussolini and the sinister euphemisms of Nazi rule—where the term *final solution* meant the murder of millions—bred a desire for plain words that expressed the truth. Ethical integrity and stylistic clarity appeared to many writers to be equivalent necessities in the Europe now taking shape.

A literature that sought to inspire moral reflection and to attain a sturdy simplicity of form had already been created during the Resistance years, though censorship prevented it from attaining the wide circulation it enjoyed following the Liberation. An example could be found in the work of Italy's leading antifascist writer, Ignazio Silone, who had published in Swiss exile his novels *Fontamara* (1930) and *Bread and Wine* (1937), which chronicled the struggles of the southern Italian peasantry to preserve their land and their lives from political and economic exploitation. Silone, who appears to have led a double life as a Fascist informer in his youth, was at pains in his maturity to portray an ethic of compassion that could be applied in the real world. "Morality can live and flourish only in practical life," asserts the main character in *Bread and Wine*. "We are responsible for others as well."* This outlook was also reflected in the work of Silone's

---

*Ignazio Silone, *Vino e pane*, rev. ed. (Milan: Arnaldo Mondadori, 1955), 360.

countryman, Carlo Levi, whose *Christ Stopped at Eboli* (1947) similarly dealt with the poverty of southern Italy and the necessity of change. Levi had been exiled by Mussolini's police to a remote village in the south. Here, in his years of forced retirement, the author had discovered an Italy unknown to cultivated northerners like himself—and whose existence as revealed in his book helped to stimulate a widespread demand for social and economic reform in the postwar years.

In Germany, the most forceful protests against oppression took the form of explicit and harrowing memories of life in the concentration camps. Such were Ernst Wiechert's *The Forest of the Dead* (written in 1938–1939 but first published in 1945) and the more detailed analysis by the left-wing Catholic publicist Eugen Kogon, *Der SS-Staat* (1947), translated under the title *The Theory and Practice of Hell*. From these accounts there emerged an ambiguous and troubling view of human nature under appalling stress. On the one hand, writers who had lived through the concentration camp experience gave countless examples of self-sacrifice and human solidarity; yet they also told without shame of the stratagems and compromises with the camp authorities essential to survival and how, in the last stages of hunger and suffering, human feeling could disappear almost completely. Many readers were shocked to discover the extent to which the camps had been run by the prisoners themselves, who had beaten and extorted food from their fellow inmates under the sadistic supervision of the SS guards. Still, the final message of these accounts was hopeful rather than dispiriting; not all had succumbed to the pressures, and those who resisted to the end displayed a resiliency and courage as inspiring as it was rare.

The most influential book to emerge from France's wartime Resistance was the brief novel by "Vercors" (Jean Bruller), *The Silence of the Sea*, published clandestinely in 1942. Vercors sought to portray an officer of the German occupation in sympathetic guise while indicating that his human qualities were powerless to alter the criminal occupation policies of Hitler's Reich. Although the heroine of the story falls in love with the officer, she refuses to break her vow to remain proudly silent in the presence of the German invaders. In the end, the officer himself is forced to admit that he had been an unwitting agent of the Nazi "New Order" and sadly abandons his dream of Franco-German understanding in time of war.

Albert Camus, however, remains the most representative of the French writers marked by the Resistance. Camus was Algerian French by birth, accustomed since childhood to life in a culturally mixed community where allegiances were unclear and ethical principles undefined. This Algerian background had suffused his first novel, *The Stranger* (1942), the portrait of a murderer indifferent to his crime and dissociated from the world around him. But Camus's subsequent experience as editor of the clandestine Resistance newspaper *Combat* gave him a more sympathetic understanding of humanity and a greater belief in the political responsibilities of the writer. His masterpiece, *The Plague* (1947), embodied the insights he had gained during his years in the French underground. As an allegory of the human struggle against disease and death, it carried echoes of the author's own wartime stand against the resurgence of a barbarism that civilized peoples were supposed to have outgrown centuries ago.

The Plague also demonstrated the abiding qualities of Camus's work—its direct, classic style, its ethical scrupulousness, and its concern for the human condition in its broadest sense. Camus was anything but a moral preacher; he detested merely rhetorical

Albert Camus (1913–1960), French novelist and moral thinker who, with Jean-Paul Sartre, dominated the immediate postwar French cultural scene. *(Courtesy AP/Wide World Photos)*

positions and believed that individuals could do little more than "bear witness" against the evil they saw around them. But he felt at the same time—as he declared on receiving the Nobel Prize for literature in 1957—that he was serving as a representative of the new generation of Europeans born during the First World War, whose whole youth had been passed in political and social chaos and who were now seeking to recreate the values of purposeful activity and human solidarity.

The Vogue of Existentialism: Heidegger, Sartre, Beauvoir

Just after the war, a new philosophical movement gained rapidly in appeal and notoriety, first in France, then throughout Western Europe. Existentialism in fact traced its origins back to the nineteenth century, more particularly to Kierkegaard and Nietzsche. But it was never a systematic philosophical school; instead, it represented an outlook best described as one that took the experience of daily existence as the philosopher's chief focus and asked how men and women confronted the meaning of their own lives. Existentialism received a powerfully invigorating contribution from the work of the German philosopher Martin Heidegger during the 1920s. Heidegger's chief work, *Being and Time* (1927), sought to create a new mode of discourse for encompassing the questions of dread, despair, and death, which he felt to be central to human existence, and to explore the notion of "authenticity," which defined the individual's personal responses to the challenge of being itself.

It was the French writer and philosopher Jean-Paul Sartre, however, who in the mid-1940s transformed a body of thought little known outside of German academic circles into a philosophy with wide appeal. Sartre's own major philosophical treatise, *Being and Nothingness* (1943), contained brilliant insights but proved difficult for all but the most philosophically literate. Sartre followed this work, however, with a rapid succession of plays, novels, and essays that formed the basis of his reputation during the immediate postwar years and gave to his theoretical views a concrete meaning couched in the language of his time.

Existentialism, as Sartre redefined it, focused its attention on the very human problems that war, collaboration, and resistance had forced into the consciousness of nearly everyone. It emphasized extreme situations and moral dilemmas—the freedom and the responsibility of every human being to reach a choice in ambiguous contexts in which right and wrong were far from clear. Again and again, Sartre returned to the fact that men and women are defined by choices which they cannot evade, yet which they are constantly tempted to pass off as the work of fate or as imposed by others. Failure to accept responsibility for one's own actions Sartre condemned as "bad faith." His characters in plays such as *The Flies* (1943) or novels such as *The Age of Reason* (1945) were shown confronting the temptations of "bad faith" as they wrestled with the difficult decisions laid before them. In the monthly journal that he founded in the fall of 1945, *Les Temps Modernes*, Sartre emphasized the special responsibility of the writer himself to keep such issues of ethics and self-knowledge before the public.

A major contributor to what she later termed the "existentialist offensive" of the 1940s was Sartre's companion and fellow writer, Simone de Beauvoir. Although she would subsequently achieve greater fame for her pioneering study of the condition of women entitled *The Second Sex* (1949), Beauvoir attempted in *The Ethics of Ambiguity* (1947) to define a coherent statement of existentialist morality. She rejected the accusation that existentialism was actually a creed of despair, pointing instead to its faith in men's and women's ability to make positive choices for themselves and for others. But what, then, qualified as a "positive choice"? The answer was the humanism espoused by the Resistance. "We can take as our starting point," Beauvoir wrote, "that the welfare of an individual or of a group of individuals deserves to be considered the absolute goal of our action."*

Yet just as the special situation of the war and the postwar period had given these ideas their relevance, so in the new ideological atmosphere of the 1950s they began to lose their cogency. With Europe returning to something resembling "normal," the vogue of existentialism passed, and more traditional and academic philosophy resumed

---

*Simone de Beauvoir, *Pour une morale de l'ambiguité* (Paris: Gallimard, 1947), 198.

its sway. Both Sartre and Beauvoir attempted to find new ways to reconcile humanist goals and practical politics, turning to Marxism and to revolutions in the Third World as possible answers once the promise of a moral transformation in Europe finally waned.

II. THE NEW TALENTS IN LITERATURE AND THE ARTS

The Losses in the War

In the First World War, the European aristocracy suffered the heaviest losses as a single class; in the second war, it was the intellectuals who paid most severely with their lives and talents. A disproportionately high number of them were killed in the Resistance or perished in concentration camps. This was to be expected, since so many intellectuals were dedicated to the antifascist cause, and since Hitler—and Stalin, too—made a systematic effort to "decapitate" subject peoples by depriving them of their intellectual leaders.

This "decapitation" operated in several different ways. First there were the concentration camps themselves, which deadened the intellect even when they did not kill (although in a few favored cases, political prisoners were able to make good use of their years of detention to write books of a notable sweep and moral elevation). Then there was the near destruction of the Jews, who had supplied so high a proportion of the century's intellectual leaders. Finally there was emigration. Of the thousands of European scholars and writers who fled to the New World during the 1930s or the war years, at least half remained in their new homes and were permanently lost to the European intellectual community.

In the initial flush of liberation, people did not quite appreciate how serious these losses had been, for the first effect of the war's end was to unleash a torrent of creativity. All the thoughts that had been dammed up for years suddenly began to pour forth. As wartime censorship ceased, as paper and printing facilities gradually became available, writers took out of their desk drawers the work they had labored on in secret during the era of tyranny. Now at last they could speak the truth; now at last they could relieve their minds of all the pent-up thoughts and emotions they had been obliged to hold back for so long. The result was a sense of new power, of variety, of a deeper truth. Men and women were jubilant at the possibility of writing about human experience as it actually had been, free of the doubts and constraints that fascist domination had laid upon them.

Once this first outpouring was over, however, it became apparent that less was really new than had at first appeared. Once writers had had their say about war and tyranny—once artists had grown accustomed to their postwar freedom of expression—they began to feel other limitations and to find other reasons for doubt. They saw how thin were the ranks of those with major talent; as the younger men held back in hesitation, the older intellectual and artistic leaders resumed their sway. Thus there was no dramatic assumption of leadership by the avant-garde, as had happened following the First

World War. There was hesitation, rather, and groping for new forms of expression and, with it, a great uncertainty about the new intellectual and aesthetic direction. The United States was frequently the answer; one byproduct of the Second World War was a shift of the center of gravity in a number of cultural fields to the other side of the Atlantic. Of the European countries, Germany, of course, had suffered the most irreplaceable loss of talent. But everywhere in Europe, to a greater or lesser degree, the younger writers and artists needed time to find their way and to become conscious of their own claims as a new aesthetic generation.

Imaginative Literature: Neorealism and Its Sequels

In the novel, the "old masters" were André Gide in France and Thomas Mann in Germany. At the war's end, Gide assumed a position of unquestioned preeminence as France's first man of letters, which he held until his death in 1951. With Mann, it was different. Long years of exile had separated him from the life of his native country, and when he finally returned to Europe from his California home, he chose to settle in Switzerland rather than in Germany. Before leaving America, however, he had published his final masterpiece—*Doctor Faustus* (1948), an allegory of his own country's fate and that of its greatest creative artists, as expressed in the life of a composer who had in him something of Nietzsche and something also of Schoenberg.

It was Italy that first produced a new school of fiction as a group of younger men began to write in what they called the "neorealist" vein. They came from all parts of Italy, and they were only loosely linked to one another. Perhaps the best known abroad were Elio Vittorini, who was Sicilian; Vasco Pratolini, a Florentine; and the north Italian Cesare Pavese. Despite their marked differences, they had in common a definition of goals that went beyond the merely photographic aim of nineteenth-century realism, with its pretense of absolute objectivity, toward a new art which would be more popular, more poetic, and more politically "engaged." The neorealists combined a concern for the sufferings of the poor with an optimistic faith in the future. They wanted to distill from the squalor of poverty an aesthetic beauty that would prefigure the better life to come. Most of them, at the outset at least, were convinced Communists.

Post-Nazi Germany produced little that was comparable to Italian neorealism. Its first literary efforts after the great defeat tended to be memoirs of war and privation—a "literature of the ruins." But here also there was an effort to tell the truth as people had actually experienced it. The most successful literary studies of the postwar German scene were those of Heinrich Böll, especially his collection of short stories entitled *Children Are Civilians Too* (1947) and his brief novel *Adam, Where Art Thou?* (1951). Böll's fiction—focusing on the victims of war and their quiet but tenacious struggle to survive—offered the reader both a sober reckoning of the human costs of war and a moral critique of a nation still unwilling to admit its complicity in the Third Reich.

In England the counterpart to neorealism could be found in a loosely associated group of authors known as the "angry young men." The majority of the group were writers of lower-middle-class origin who had benefited by the postwar democratization of British life, but who at the same time were depressed by what they felt to be the drabness of the welfare state and incensed at the invisible social barriers that still persisted. The novel which seemed most representative of the whole school was Kingsley Amis's *Lucky Jim* (1954)—a half-hilarious, half-pathetic story of the mishaps of a young instructor at a provincial British university. The hypocrisy and stuffy intolerance of the academic establishment were held up to ridicule as the hero, Jim Dixon, found himself unable to conform to the games required by his superiors. A career of a different sort was chronicled in John Brain's *Room at the Top* (1957), whose hero brazened his way to a success far less honorable than Jim Dixon's university failure.

By the mid-1950s, at the time when such realistic novels of social criticism appeared in England, new literary currents were beginning to make themselves felt on the Continent. The French "new novelists" returned to an internal meditation on individual experience, expressed directly and without the familiar paraphernalia of "realism" or of psychological explanation. But since their works made heavy demands on the reader, their appeal remained confined to a restricted audience. In Italy, too, younger writers of fiction, like Italo Calvino, began to turn away from neorealism and toward more fanciful themes. Calvino's tales mixed fantasy and satire in an arresting, personal blend of literary invention. A similar reaction was also evident in Germany, where Böll was now joined by younger and more flamboyant writers—chief among them Günter Grass, the author of *The Tin Drum* (1959). Surrealist in manner, corrosive in his treatment of moral clichés, and with a virtuoso range in his use of the German language, Grass's work heralded a German literary renaissance that was to continue through the succeeding decade.

Drama: Older Masters and the Theater of the Absurd

The evolution of the postwar drama roughly paralleled that of the novel. Here, too, there were older masters, whose works enjoyed general esteem even when they were not popular successes. In the East, Bertolt Brecht returned from exile to become the chief literary luminary of the Communist world and Europe's most influential dramatist. Although Brecht theorized about the need for the theater to banish illusion and awaken its audiences' critical faculties through "distancing devices" (*Verfremdungseffekte*), the power of his later plays remained overwhelmingly emotional rather than dryly political. Both *Mother Courage* (1941) and *The Caucasian Chalk Circle* (1949) moved the public with their human drama rather than amused them with the wit and satiric verve so apparent in the *Three-Penny Opera*, as Brecht's social protest now yielded to a richer and more potent blend of criticism and compassion.

In France, theater in the 1950s was dominated by two foreigners long resident in that country who had become thoroughly assimilated to French culture—the Romanian Eugène Ionesco, the author of a series of short, "experimental" plays in a surrealist vein, and the Irish expatriate Samuel Beckett, whose *Waiting for Godot* (1952) achieved a stunning effect with its spare, understated dialogues onstage. Both Ionesco and Beckett shared preoccupations that led critics to baptize their work the "theater of the absurd." Both insisted on confronting the audience with characters enmeshed in situations that defied logical analysis and whose seeming meaninglessness suggested the frustrations and moral ambiguities of modern life. Just as the French novelists of the 1950s had turned away from realism as their chosen literacy vehicle, so Beckett and Ionesco discovered in the "theater of the absurd" an expressive potential lacking in more conventional drama. *Waiting for Godot* showed two tramps on a bare stage, awaiting the arrival of a mysterious

M. Godot, who had still not appeared by the play's end just as, Beckett suggested, men and women of his time wasted their lives while expecting better days. Ionesco, though less complex an artist, produced in his *Rhinoceros* (1960) a memorable condemnation of the social pressures leading to conformity. Its hero watches helplessly as those around him are transformed into the lumbering animals of the play's took its title and finally blames himself for not resembling them.

Film: From Italy to the French "New Wave"

By 1945, the aesthetically conservative no longer questioned that the cinema had become an art form at least the equal of the "legitimate" theater and even perhaps superior to it. In the first twenty years after the war, a greater share of original talent went into the producing of films than into the writing of plays for the stage. Indeed, the number of superior motion pictures was so great and their character so varied that it was extremely difficult to find the main trends among this embarrassment of riches. Along with a continued high level of excellence in France and Britain, films from Italy and Sweden, two countries that had made scarcely any contribution to the cinema arts during the prewar years, now moved into the front rank.

Death confronts a mailed knight playing chess for his soul in this scene from Ingmar Bergman's allegorical film *The Seventh Seal* (1957). *(Courtesy of the Lester Glassner/Neal Peters Archive/Neal Peters Collection)*

In Italy, neorealism in the novel had an exact parallel in the films, and the relationship between the two was very close. The war had not yet ended before a new generation of producers was trying to put on film the misery of the conflict and its sequels as the Italian people were still experiencing them. The results were the classics of the Italian postwar cinema—among them Roberto Rossellini's *Open City* (1944) and Vittorio De Sica's *Bicycle Thief* (1948). Like the neorealists of the novel, Rossellini and De Sica sought to show the reality of poverty and at the same time to tinge it with poetry and hope. Far more than was true of the novel, the character of these motion pictures derived from the physical limitations of the postwar years. Wanting simply to film what they had seen, and lacking both studios and money, the Italian directors worked outdoors, using real streets and amateur actors and frequently improvising rather than following a formal script.

By the 1950s, the dominance of Italian neorealist cinema had ended. Yet just as Italian literature had sought new avenues of creativity in Calvino's prose fantasies, so Italian film now took on a more subjective tone in the works of younger directors destined to reshape the Italian cinema during the next decade and a half. Most prominent among them was Federico Fellini, whose first critical success, *I vitelloni* (1953), still displayed traces of neorealist inspiration in its portrait of the aimless existence of a group of young friends in an Italian city modeled after his native Rimini. *La dolce vita* (1960), which brought Fellini international acclaim, investigated aspects of modern Italian culture from a satiric viewpoint not unlike Calvino's.

Meanwhile in Sweden there appeared another new director of major talent, Ingmar Bergman. His two principal films of the 1950s—*The Seventh Seal* and *Wild Strawberries*, both released in 1957—probed the dark side of human emotions in a powerfully personal blend of allegory and realism, reminiscent in its visual boldness of early German expressionist cinema. *The Seventh Seal*, set in medieval Sweden at the time of the plague, depicted the struggle of a disillusioned knight seeking to defeat Death in a chess match, which he purposely forfeits in the end to spare the lives of a young couple. Thus, despite its moments of gloom, the film closed with an affirmation of human solidarity.

At the decade's end, the advent of a "New Wave" in French film returned France to the forefront of European cinema. In 1959 there appeared François Truffaut's autobiographical film about a young rebel living at the margin of society, *The 400 Blows*, followed two years later by his masterpiece, *Jules and Jim*, the story of an amorous triangle and its dramatic dissolution, alternately lyrical and tragic in tone. The year 1959 also saw Jean-Luc Godard release his first feature film, *Breathless*, which, despite its indebtedness to American gangster movies, was primarily a poetic evocation of freedom threatened by society's rules and constraints. Godard's subsequent films of the early 1960s made less use of plot and became increasingly experimental, to the point where they abandoned any pretense to precise meaning and instead explored the suggestive power of abruptly dissociated story fragments. Different as the styles of Truffaut and Godard were, however, what bound their work together in a recognizable school was their insistence that the director be allowed to shape his own material (the so-called *auteur* theory of film making). Common to both was also their interest in the oblique, the ambiguous, the surprising, and the problematical sides of life, which allowed them to present a less tidy but more "realistic" vision of the world than had the documentary films of the late 1940s.

Fine Arts: The Reconciliation
of the Abstract and the Figurative

Although Paris still retained its traditional preeminence in European painting, it was more and more challenged by other centers. The reputation of France in the arts was in great part due to the continued activity of major painters surviving from the first quarter of the century—Picasso, Braque, and Matisse. Of these, only Matisse, with his novel *papier découpé*, or cut-paper compositions, struck out on a bold new path in old age which was to influence younger artists with its simplicity and stark colors. Most of the younger generation, however, now looked as much to American abstract art in New York and to the figurative tradition of German expressionism for guidance as to Paris. The result was a great variety of styles, with nonrepresentational art in the ascendant, but little pronounced change in direction.

As in the novel and in films, so in painting Italy made the most dramatic leap from obscurity to the front rank, and for the same reasons. The end of fascism and the lifting of its atmosphere of cultural mediocrity and formalism released new talent in the plastic arts. In comparison with the work of French painters, that of the postwar Italians tended to be warmer and more serene. It was also more figurative—in strong contrast to the dominance of abstract art in France and Germany. The Italians tried to reconcile the new awareness of design, color, and balance, which nonrepresentational art had brought to the fore, with the more traditional values—such as emotional evocation and a feeling for subject matter and recognizable shapes and forms—which linked them to the great art of the past. Typical of this approach was the art of Renato Guttuso, whose strong, simplified rendering of working men and women conveyed both the dignity and the enduring resilience of Italy's peasants in a manner that recalled Silone's literary descriptions of the peasant world.

A similar desire to bridge the gulf between abstract and figurative art could be seen in sculpture, which underwent a revival during the immediate postwar years. Here the two major talents were a Swiss and an Englishman: Alberto Giacometti and Henry Moore. Giacometti's emaciated figures, frozen in midstride and condemned to solitude, seemed to capture the same sense of human isolation that Beckett explored in his spare, absurdist dramas. Henry Moore, on the other hand, created more comfortable "biomorphic" wood and metal sculptures that took their inspiration from the reclining human figure, yet at the same time so radically simplified and recast its contours that the resulting forms achieved a monumental, abstract quality of harmonious repose.

Architecture: Postwar Reconstruction
and the Engineering Influence

In painting, Americans in the years after 1945 won real respect from the Europeans for the first time. But it was in architecture and music that the American effect on the Old World was most pronounced. In these fields—whose artistic idiom had always been highly international—the United States had begun to move into a position of leadership as early as the war years. This was partly because influential architects who had emigrated from Germany—such as Walter Gropius and Mies van der Rohe—chose to remain in their new home. It also reflected the character of postwar architecture, which made heavy demands on engineering, at which the Americans excelled. During the war years, moreover, when very little building was done in Europe, the modern style had been steadily advancing in the United States.

By 1945 the triumph of the modern on both sides of the Atlantic was assured, and the vast job of reconstructing the cities that had been devastated during the war offered a unique opportunity for bold new design. But in general the results were disappointing. Although most of the rebuilding was in some variety of modern style—except where respect for traditional artistic monuments absolutely dictated the contrary—the individual buildings usually lacked imagination, and they tended to be erected in haphazard fashion. In most cases it proved too expensive and legally complicated to draw up a uniform plan for a city and to devise a whole new street layout. The pressure was for rebuilding as fast as possible, with only secondary regard for aesthetic considerations and the harmony of the whole. Where reconstruction was somewhat delayed, however, the results were more satisfactory. This was true in Coventry, in parts of West Berlin, and in the French seaport of Le Havre, where the patriarch of modern French architecture, Auguste Perret, designed what was virtually a new city with broad avenues and parks, heavy and conventional in detail, perhaps, but admirable in its overall effect.

The Italians once again showed themselves the boldest postwar innovators. And it was also in Italy that the engineering influence proved strongest. The Italians became particularly interested in industrial design and in the virtuoso use of reinforced concrete, whose master was Pier Luigi Nervi. In his employment of slabs and beams and shell domes, Nervi developed a whole new series of architectural possibilities. The results were buildings of an astonishing lightness that seemed to stand almost without support, such as the exhibition hall at Turin, dating from 1948–1949, and the stadium constructed for the Olympic Games in Rome in 1960.

Music: Shostakovich, Hindemith, and the Heirs of Schoenberg

After 1945, as had been true ever since the pall of Stalinist orthodoxy descended, Soviet artists and writers lived under such tight restrictions that they could contribute very little of importance to European cultural life as a whole. It was only with the death of Stalin in 1953 that even the most cautious sort of innovation became possible once again (see Chapter 20, II).

In music, however, despite the way in which Andrei Zhdanov brought the Soviet composers to heel—along with everyone else who had strayed from the narrow ideological path during the war—Russian work continued to command respectful attention abroad. The war itself had seen the emergence of Dmitri Shostakovich as the Soviet Union's most influential composer. Less witty and original than Prokofiev, Shostakovich specialized in the grander and more obvious musical effects, as displayed to maximum advantage in his Seventh Symphony, written during the siege of Leningrad. Chastened by having twice fallen into official disfavor, Shostakovich eventually learned to curb his more experimental tendencies.

In Western Europe, however, just the contrary occurred. Under the influence of younger American composers and of major European composers who continued to live in the United States, the continental leaders of the musical world turned toward bold experiment. Of the great Germans who had remained in America, the most important remained Arnold Schoenberg, the prophet of atonal music. Schoenberg's greatest influence came only after the Second World War, as the new generation began to adopt his twelve-tone form of composition. Among the elders, Schoenberg's contemporary and fellow Californian by adoption, Igor Stravinsky, also turned to experimenting with similar techniques. When Schoenberg died in 1951, he had finally won recognition as the most important musical innovator of the century. At the Festival of Contemporary Music held at Cologne in 1960, Americans joined with Europeans to celebrate the triumph of the modern, which in music, as in painting and architecture, had finally been ensured.

III. Reforms in Education

The Influence of American Science

In science, even more than in the arts, postwar Europe was profoundly influenced by the United States. The wartime development of nuclear physics had been a joint Anglo-American effort, but in the public mind the Americans won most of the credit. A fairer judgment would also have emphasized the fact that a very large number of the leading nuclear physicists who had aided the United States—like the Italian Enrico Fermi—were refugees from fascist oppression.

The postwar prestige of American science did not derive solely from its wartime achievements. It derived also from the very realistic consideration that the United States alone—particularly in the years of hardship in Europe immediately following the war—had the money and the resources to build the great laboratories that the new demands of experimental science required. This material weakness faced European scientists with a severe crisis of self-confidence. They began to send their students in large numbers to the United States for advanced training; they argued strenuously for the introduction of laboratory exercises in the secondary school curriculum, which had always been a weak point of European education. At the same time, they tried to emphasize the theoretical aspects of scientific research for which they did not suffer under the same sort of material handicaps.

In social science also, American scholars overwhelmed the Europeans with their larger numbers and the more elaborate research facilities at their disposal. Here again the contrast was partly one of empiricism as against theory. In the United States, economists, sociologists, and anthropologists emphasized teamwork and quantitative method; in Europe there was a tendency to continue using the older literary and discursive approaches. In any event, the decade and a half following the war saw no major innovations in European social science. The British and the Swedes maintained their ascendancy in economics; the French continued to combine anthropology with sociology in the tradition of Durkheim; the Germans, in this as in so many other fields, were fully absorbed in recovering the ground they had lost during the twelve years of Nazi tyranny.

The one significant exception to this pattern was the return to Germany in 1950 of the "Frankfurt School" of sociologically oriented philosophers—chief among them Theodor W. Adorno and Max Horkheimer—after a decade and a half of exile in the United States. Their arrival not only signaled the fact that one eminent segment of the Weimar Republic's intellectual Left had survived the Nazi era; it also suggested that it was possible to combine a subtle, nuanced version of Marxism with psychoanalysis, and even with American-style empirical method. In the same year that Adorno and Horkheimer reestablished residence in Frankfurt, the book that was the chief fruit of their collaboration with American sociologists, *The Authoritarian Personality*, was published and immediately acclaimed as a classic study of prejudice. Using typically American research tools, such as clinical interviews and Thematic Apperception Tests administered to over 2,000 respondents, its researchers had amassed an impressive set of empirical data that was then interpreted in a typically European, theoretical manner to yield broadly suggestive general conclusions. The Frankfurt School thus demonstrated to its younger German followers the possibility of a marriage between Continental and American traditions in social science.

School Reform and the Church Question

In teaching, as in advanced research, the postwar years found the Europeans undergoing a major crisis of self-criticism. The experience of war and tyranny—which nearly everywhere had lowered educational levels and even for brief periods closed down the schools and universities entirely—intensified and brought out into the open a number of long-range problems of European education that the previous generation of teachers had either minimized or denied (see Figure 16.1).

First there was the problem of numbers. This came about through the combination of three separate developments that reinforced each other: a postwar population spurt; the educational interruptions of wartime, which frequently meant that two differ-

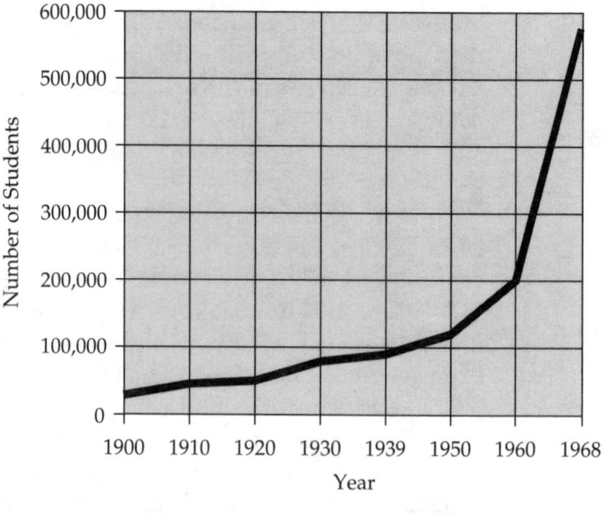

FIGURE 16.1 French university enrollment from 1900 to 1968, showing the precipitous climb in the student numbers after 1950. The overcrowding that resulted was to play an important role in igniting the student protest movement of the late 1960s.

ent age groups were crowding the schools and the universities at the same time; and the democratization of life, which prompted poor and lower-middle-class parents to seek educational advantages for their children that they would never have expected for themselves and which in turn induced governments to raise steadily the age at which adolescents could legally leave school. In Britain, the Labour government first set fifteen as the prescribed age, then raised it to sixteen. In France, in the late 1950s, the school-leaving age jumped from fourteen to sixteen.

The outcome of all these changes together was an unprecedented rise in the number of students. In Germany, the number of those attending universities was more than double what it had been before the war. In France, by the 1950s, one out of five adolescents was attending the elite high schools or *lycées*, whereas the prewar figure had been one in fifteen. This swelling of numbers usually meant overcrowded classrooms and a shortage of teachers, whose pay often failed to keep pace with the rising cost of living. In a poor country like Italy, the schools and universities were overwhelmed, and the level of instruction fell correspondingly. Britain just barely kept abreast of the new demands, and France, which had always taken particular pride in its public educational system, found itself lagging behind.

With the vast increase of numbers—and with a different type of student now flooding the high schools—the question of the curriculum itself suddenly became urgent. European education, far more than American, had traditionally been literary and classical. It had put primary stress on the humanistic training of a comparatively small and privileged element within the population. In the postwar world, much of this teaching seemed antiquated and irrelevant, and it had little meaning for boys and girls from the poorer classes, who had but remotely shared in the cultural heritage of the aristocracy and the upper bourgeoisie.

This situation produced a series of reforms in school curricula directed toward strengthening natural science and contemporary subjects. There were also efforts to build "bridges" between classical and vocational schools, so that gifted pupils from the second group could move into the first and become eligible for admission to a university. Able and ambitious students from families with modest means were similarly aided by a vast increase in public scholarship funds. This process went further in Britain than in any other major country. By the 1950s, the extension of higher education to members of the British working class had drastically changed the student composition of the universities and was already beginning to transform the whole character of the national elite (see Chapter 20, III).

IV. THE CHURCHES AND SOCIETY

In the immediate postwar period, the Christian churches wielded extraordinary influence. The part that individual ecclesiastics and the militant lay public had played in the Resistance gave them a new type of prestige, and in places where civil government had broken down, the clergy frequently became the sole rallying point of the forces of order. In East Central Europe, the Nazi yoke had scarcely been lifted when the Catholic church was plunged into a bitter struggle with communism; here once again the opponents of tyranny closed ranks behind the clergy.

The Jewish Survivors and the Attraction of Israel

In Central and Eastern Europe, and to a lesser extent in the West also, a dreadful memory weighed on the consciences of all convinced Christians: the destruction of six million Jews. Hitler's mass slaughter had permanently altered the religious map of Europe. In the West, the change was relatively slight. Most of the French and Italian Jews had survived, and a large number of them owed their lives to the protection of the Catholic clergy; these small and well-assimilated Jewish minorities resumed their positions in society after the war almost as if nothing had happened. In countries like Germany and Poland, however, the change was catastrophic. Vast communities of Jews had been reduced to mere fragments—in Germany only 30,000 out of 600,000 remained—and the few who had survived Hitler's extermination camps frequently found it impossible to take up their former lives. Too many ties had been broken, and too many terrible memories lay between Jew and Christian. Although both the Communist governments in East Germany and Poland and the Christian Democratic government in Bonn officially condemned anti-Semitism—and although the West German regime agreed in 1952 to pay three and a half billion marks in restitution for what the Jews had suffered—anti-Semitism lingered among the people. Consequently, the surviving Jews felt that they could never trust their fellow citizens again; while the older ones returned to their former homes, the younger and more active decided to emigrate abroad.

Thus the Jewish emigration of the 1930s—which had mostly been from Germany and Austria to the New World—was followed in the postwar years by another wave of departures, this time primarily from Poland and Romania. The goal was Palestine, which in 1948 became the independent state of Israel. The Soviet government generally refused to let its nationals emigrate; the Communist-dominated governments of East Central Europe pursued a more uncertain policy, sometimes permitting, but more usually forbidding, their Jewish citizens to leave. There was, however, much clandestine emigration. In all, perhaps half a million Jews were able to make their way from Eastern Europe to Israel in the decade 1945–1955.

Social Catholicism and the Worker-Priests

At the end of the war in Europe, the prestige of the Catholic church stood higher than it had for nearly a century. Pope Pius XII—who had come to the papal throne just a few months before the outbreak of the conflict—had failed to condemn either the Nazis or the Holocaust in more than the most cautious terms. Yet his aloofness did not prevent the emergence of Christian Democratic parties into positions of leadership in the mid-1940s. Some Catholic politicians, emphasizing the plight of the working classes, were interpreting the basic social documents of the contemporary church, *Rerum Novarum* and *Quadragesimo Anno*, in a sense of uncompromising protest against the exploitation of one class by another. This it seemed that Catholic social values might at last find able defenders at the very highest levels of government.

Within a decade, however, more conservative views prevailed. The Christian Democrats in power proved rather different from what they had been in the Resistance years, and social Catholicism gradually became reduced to the position of a barely tolerated left wing on the fringe of the official parties. This was particularly apparent in the case of the most imaginative experiment the church had ever made to win back the de-Christianized workers of the great industrial centers—the worker-priest movement in France.

The idea animating the worker-priests was that the only way to reconvert the hostile and the apathetic among the laboring classes was to offer dramatic proof that the clergy was not so separated from, and uninterested in, the life of the factories as its enemies had asserted. If the workers refused to go to church, then the church itself must come to them. Beginning in 1946, a few specially trained French priests began working—in ordinary laborers' clothes—in the factories of the Parisian industrial area. They were only gradually to reveal their identity and to begin their active mission, as little by little they won the confidence of those who worked alongside them.

By 1951, ninety worker-priests were in the factories, and the idea had received the enthusiastic endorsement of the French episcopate. But then the difficulties began. In Communist-led rioting in Paris, two or three of the priests fell into the hands of the police, and it was discovered that they had become infected by Marxist doctrine. The Vatican took alarm. Pope Pius XII forbade the further recruitment of worker-priests and severely limited the scope of those already active. For seven more years the dispute within the church dragged on—with the French cardinals constantly pleading for the continuation of the experiment. In 1959, shortly after the installation of a new Pope, John XXIII, the Vatican rendered its final verdict: Work in factories, it decreed, was "incompatible with the life and obligations of the priesthood."

Pope John XXIII, the Vatican Council, and His Successors

The decision concerning the worker-priests did not give an accurate guide to Pope John's own attitude. It was characteristic, rather, of his first two years on the papal throne, when he was proceeding with caution and following the advice of the elderly Italian cardinals who dominated the Curia, or central administration of the church. Although an old man himself, the new Pope was youthful in spirit and a bold reformer. Of peasant origin, with a simple, profoundly human approach, his whole style was in strong contrast to that of the chilly and autocratic Pius XII. Pope John's unfailing affability and warm humor brought the Papacy close to the mass of Catholics—and to Protestants, Jews, and unbelievers, who came to love him almost as much as did those of his own faith. In his brief four and a half years of office, he made a greater change in the Catholic church than any Pope of the twentieth century.

The keynote of Pope John's policy was *aggiornamento*—bringing the church up to date by squarely confronting the problems of the contemporary world. Such ideas were embodied in his two great encyclicals—*Mater et Magistra* of 1961, and *Pacem in Terris*, published shortly before his death in the spring of 1963. The first, as its date implied, continued the series of social pronouncements begun in 1891 with *Rerum Novarum*. Pope John's *Mater et Magistra* drew attention to the poverty of the underdeveloped world and the responsibility of Europeans and Americans to share their wealth with those less fortunate. *Pacem in Terris*, for its part, contained a stirring appeal for peace, coupled with a condemnation of thermonuclear war. It both reflected and reinforced the progress toward international understanding that had marked the preceding decade of European history.

Yet the most extraordinary of Pope John's innovations was the calling of a church council—the first since the Vatican Council of 1870 and the most important since that of Trent, in the late sixteenth century, which had met the challenge of Protestantism by laying the basis for a Catholic reformation. The council of the 1960s—Vatican II as it came to be called—brought together more than 2,500 cardinals and bishops from the entire Catholic world. Its agenda was enormous—so great, in fact, that observers frequently questioned whether it would ever be possible for so large and unwieldy a body to deal with more than a fraction of what it had undertaken to debate. Several times its machinery seemed to be grinding to a halt. Yet in four successive autumn sessions, lasting about three months each, it managed to inaugurate the most extensive reforms the church had experienced in the modern era.

The first session, in the autumn of 1962, already showed where the council's center of gravity lay. In organizing their proceedings, the church fathers (with the Pope's evident support) gave preference to "progressives"—characteristically those from France, Germany, the Low Countries, North America, and the underdeveloped world—as against the conservatives who dominated the Curia and the Italian and Spanish hierarchies. There was an exhilarating sense of renewal as the assembled fathers cast off the control of the Curia and engaged in a free debate that astounded non-Catholics accustomed to regarding the Church as a monolith. However, it was agreed that final decisions on the most controversial issues must be postponed to a further session. Then, in the ensuing period of adjournment, Pope John died, and the whole idea of the council seemed in danger. But the College of Cardinals elected as his successor the figure closest to the deceased pontiff among the Italian hierarchy—Giovanni Battista Montini, archbishop of Milan, who chose to be called Paul VI. Although in manner and in training Pope Paul recalled Pius XII, with whom he had worked for many years, in policy he tended to follow the line that John XXIII had marked out.

Yet the new Pope's guidance was less sure than that of his predecessor. When the council reassembled in September 1963, hesitations appeared. Not until the third session, the autumn following, did the delegates discuss such sensitive subjects as disarmament and birth control with realism and frankness. The fathers voted that in the future the bishops should participate alongside the Pope in the government of the church; they completed the constitution on ecumenicism and pushed forward the one on the relation of Catholicism to the modern world. But on two of the most hotly debated drafts the reformers, though in the majority, were unable to have their viewpoint officially promulgated—a declaration absolving the Jews of responsibility for the death of Jesus (which had served so often in the past as a pretext for anti-Semitism), and a statement on religious liberty intended to inaugurate a new era of understanding with non-Catholics. Only when the council reconvened for the fourth—and final—time in September 1965 did it finally approve the substance of the declarations on religious liberty and on the Church's relations with Judaism.

Quite apparently in the last session of the council, Pope Paul was trying to act as a mediator between the conservatives and the reformers. But this task proved almost insuperably difficult; the pontificate of John had released a flood of new tendencies within the church that subsequently traveled under their own momentum. In some of them John's successor shared to the full. He broke with papal precedent by making dramatic journeys to Israel and to India, to South America and to Africa; he remodeled the Curia in Rome, retiring from its direction the more reactionary cardinals. He drew the line, however, at the notion of fully sharing his authority with the bishops, and he expressed his frank alarm at the widespread questioning of religious tradition and the malaise among the younger members of the clergy that led them to want to marry or even to leave the priesthood entirely. The clearest sign of the Pope's evolution to the right was the encyclical *Humanae Vitae*, issued in the summer of 1968, which reaffirmed the intransigent Catholic stand on birth control.

On the death of Paul VI in 1978, the conclave of cardinals had initially chosen another Italian, who took the name John Paul I. He, however, had in turn died after only five weeks in office. When the cardinals met again, they broke precedent by looking beyond the Alps and for the first time in four and a half centuries electing a non-Italian. Their choice, Karol Wojtyla, who took the name of John Paul II, as Archbishop of Cracow in Poland had behind him a record of successfully resisting Communist infringements on the rights of Catholics. A man of strength and good humor, an athlete and a scholar, he radiated vigor and confidence. On a number of the crucial issues that were shaking the church, he ranked as a conservative; he insisted on theological precision, a disciplined clergy, and the inadmissibility of contraception. Yet at the same time his down-to-earth approach suggested a Pope attuned to the modern world and one with a lively concern for human freedom and dignity, in his own continent and in the non-European world alike. In John Paul II, Catholicism found a spiritual leader richly equipped to consolidate the *magisterium*—the teaching authority—of an institution nearly 2,000 years old.

READINGS

James Wilkinson, in *The Intellectual Resistance in Europe** (1981), explores the cultural impact of the Second World War and the heritage of the Resistance during the 1940s in France, Germany, and Italy. George Steiner, *Martin Heidegger** (1979) is a skillful introduction to a centrally important yet elusive philosopher. For postwar French thought, besides Hughes (see readings for Chapter 11), there are Mary Warnock's *Existentialism* (1970) and Mark Poster's *Existential Marxism in Postwar France* (1975). Patrick McCarthy's *Camus* (1982) and Annie Cohen-Solal's *Sartre: A Life** (1989) offer guides to the life and thought of two dominant figures on the postwar French cultural scene. The political creeds and choices of the French existentialists are explored in Roy Pierce, *Contemporary French Political Thought** (1966), and Michel-Antoine Burnier, *Choice of Action* (1969).

*Books available in paperback are marked with an asterisk.

The French intellectuals' ambiguous relationship with left-wing politics is detailed with verve and insight in Tony Judt's *Past Imperfect: French Intellectuals, 1944–1956* (1992).

Postwar Italian literature is surveyed in John Gatt-Rutter, *Writers and Politics in Modern Italy* (1979). Silone's personal vision of politics and morality is assessed in R. W. B. Lewis, *The Picaresque Saint* (1959). For literary developments in Germany, see Peter Demetz, *Postwar German Literature* (1970) and *After the Fires: Recent Writing in the Germanies, Austria, and Switzerland* (1986). A compendious survey of the English literary landscape since the war is Boris Ford, ed., *The New Pelican Guide to English Literature*, vol. 8: *The Present** (1983). Martin Esslin, *Brecht: A Choice of Evils,** 4th ed. (1984), traces the German playwright's evolution from Weimar to postwar theater; the same author's *The Theatre of the Absurd*, 3rd ed. (1973) provides an excellent introduction to both Beckett and Ionesco. For more on Beckett, see A. Alvarez, *Samuel Beckett** (1973). For the French "new novel," see John Sturrock, *The French New Novel: Claude Simon, Michel Butor, and Alain Robbe-Grillet* (1969).

For postwar European film, besides Mast (see readings for Chapter 11), there are the excellent studies by Mira Liehm, *Passion and Defiance: Film in Italy from 1942 to the Present** (1984); Pierre Leprohon, *The Italian Cinema* (1972); and James Monaco, *The New Wave* (1976). Leo Braudy and Morris Dickstein, eds., *Great Film Directors: A Critical Anthology** (1978), contains first-rate studies of Fellini, Bergman, Godard, and others. Ingmar Bergman surveys his own career in *The Magic Lantern: An Autobiography** (1988), while Don Allen's *Finally Truffaut** (1985) is a well-illustrated chronological study of Truffaut's entire oeuvre.

A reliable introduction to postwar art on both sides of the Atlantic is Edward Lucie-Smith, *Movements in Art Since 1945,** new rev. ed. (1984). Werner Haftmann, *Painting in the 20th Century*, new ed. (1965), is especially good on the art of the 1950s. For developments since the 1970s, see Brandon Taylor, *Avant-Garde and After: Rethinking Art Now** (1995). On sculpture, see Udo Kultermann, *The New Sculpture* (1968). Developments in architecture are traced in Benevolo (see readings for Chapter 7) and in G. E. Kidder Smith, *The New Architecture of Europe** (1962). For postwar music, besides Machlis and Salzman (see readings for Chapter 7), there are the studies by Geoffrey Skelton, *Paul Hindemith: The Man Behind the Music* (1975), and Norman Kay, *Shostakovich** (1971).

The standard treatment of the Frankfurt School is Martin Jay's *The Dialectical Imagination: A History of the Frankfurt School and the Institute of Social Research, 1923–1950** (1973). On changes in education, see Fritz K. Ringer, *Education and Society in Modern Europe* (1979), which deals chiefly with the situation in France and Germany, and Lawrence Stone, ed., *Schooling and Society* (1976).

Jewish emigration and the founding of the state of Israel are discussed in Howard M. Sachar's detailed study, *A History of Israel** (1979), and in Tom Segev's *1949: The First Israelis* (1986). On the Catholic Church's troubled response to the Nazi threat, see Guenter Lewy, The Catholic Church and Nazi Germany,* 2nd ed. (2000). John Cornwell, *Hitler's Pope: The Secret History of Pius XII** (1999) contains a sharp indictment of the wartime pontiff, based on extensive archival research. Peter Hebblethwaite's *Pope John XXIII: Shepherd of the Modern World* (1985) and Thomas Cahill, *Pope John XXIII* (2002) both offer admiring introductions to Pius XII's reforming successor. For Vatican II and its effects, see Langdon Gilkey, *Catholicism Confronts Modernity* (1975); J. Derek Holmes, *The Papacy in the Modern World, 1914–1978* (1981); and E. E. Y. Hales, *Pope John and His Revolution* (1965).

THE COLD WAR,

1947–1953

A view through barbed wire and across the wall at the Brandenburg Gate between East and West Berlin—symbol of the Cold War division of Europe. (*Courtesy Photo Researchers, Inc.*)

I. The Split between East and West

America's Postwar Role: Preconception and Realities

President Roosevelt had based his wartime policies on a few general ideas about what his country's position was in the world and what the postwar international scene would be like. Convinced that Woodrow Wilson had gone astray through lack of "realism," he wanted to avoid his predecessor's mistakes by making full allowance for the brute facts of power politics. His vision, like Wilson's, was "idealistic"—but its idealism was tempered by a recognition of the limits imposed on constructive statesmanship.

In retrospect, Roosevelt frequently appears to have been overcautious about these limits. He was sure, for example, that his compatriots would tolerate the stationing of American troops in Europe for only a very brief period, and it was partly for this reason—in order to get a settlement that would not need American policing—that he was accommodating with Stalin at Yalta. In his view of the future, each European power had its anticipated role. The Soviet Union would dominate Eastern Europe and would aid in controlling Germany; Britain would take the lead in the Mediterranean, and France on the western European Continent—and the united power of the wartime partners would then serve to keep Germany firmly in check.

One by one, as the postwar years went by, these preconceptions proved unfounded. First came the disputes with the Soviet Union over the government of postwar Germany. Then Britain confessed its inability to guard the Mediterranean. France meanwhile—deeply involved in colonial warfare and in domestic struggles both economic and ideological—was recovering its strength more slowly than had been anticipated. Soon Germany was to be split, with each of its two halves taken into rival alliance systems by its occupiers. By 1947 at the very latest, the preconceptions on which the American government had based its European policy had all proved erroneous. The central international drama of the next two years was the forging of an anti-Soviet alliance by the United States to cope with these new circumstances and the corresponding consolidation of the Communist world under the authority of the aging Stalin.

The United Nations: Unforeseen Weaknesses and Unanticipated Strengths

The United Nations, like its predecessor the League, grew out of the victorious wartime coalition. Indeed, it was founded while the war was still in progress. The initial drafts for its organization were worked out by the four "sponsoring powers"—the United States, the Soviet Union, Britain, and China—at Dumbarton Oaks, in Washington, in the autumn of 1944, and its final Charter was signed by the representatives of fifty nations at the conclusion of the conference held in San Francisco from April to June of the following year.

At first sight, the Charter of the United Nations looked much like the old Covenant of the League. Like its predecessor, the new international organization aimed at nearly universal world membership. During the decade and a half after its foundation, it admitted about fifty additional members—some from among wartime enemies or neutrals, but the majority from the former colonial areas of Asia and Africa. Like the League, the United Nations had a General Assembly in which all its members participated with an equal vote; a Council, renamed the Security Council, on which the five Great Powers (including France) occupied permanent seats, with the smaller powers electing six from their own ranks on a two-year rotation basis; specialized agencies for economic and cultural affairs, whose functions had now been vastly enlarged; and a system for guiding toward nationhood the former colonies of defeated enemies—which previously had been called *mandates* and were now renamed *trusteeships*.

These changes in terminology, however, meant more than merely revising an old institution—just as the shift in the organization's headquarters from Geneva to New York symbolized a real change in its center of gravity. It was no longer a predominantly European enterprise; the membership of the United States and the Soviet Union made its claims to world jurisdiction far more real than had been true of the League. Moreover, this non-European character grew steadily, particularly after 1955–1956, when twenty new members were added, many of them from Asia and Africa, and after 1960, when there came a further influx of sixteen African states. Finally, both of the United Nations' deliberative bodies were slightly different in character from what their counterparts in the League had been, and these differences were to become decisive in the first decade and a half of the new organization's existence.

Churchill and Stalin had agreed with Roosevelt that the United Nations should more frankly recognize the predominant role of the Great Powers in international affairs than the League had done. Hence they had strengthened the authority of the Security Council by conferring on it "primary responsibility for the maintenance of international peace and security," under the terms of Article 24 of the Charter. At the same time, in Article 27, they had ensured that no Great Power could be put in a minority; a unanimous vote of the Big Five was required on all major decisions. Stalin had insisted on this at Yalta, and Churchill and Roosevelt concurred—on the thoroughly realistic basis that if the Great Powers were in disagreement, the Security Council would not be an effective agency for enforcing the peace. But the events of the immediate postwar years once again changed these preconceptions. In 1949 the whole Chinese mainland passed under the control of the Communists, who were denied a seat on the United Nations Security Council. The remaining four powers, as the cleavage between East and West widened, began to vote regularly three to one, with the Soviet Union casting its veto not merely in exceptional cases, as the Charter had anticipated, but almost as a matter of routine.

With the Security Council paralyzed, attention shifted to the General Assembly. Here the founders of the United Nations had again changed the former machinery of the League by substituting a two-thirds majority for the earlier rule of unanimity. Thus when the Security Council was unable to act, the Assembly could frequently muster the requisite majority. From 1950 on, this became the increasingly regular pattern of United Nations activity. There developed with this pattern a new importance for the non-European nations, the neutrals between the two Great Power blocs, and the middle-rank states, whose voices grew ever more influential in the General Assembly.

For the settlement of *European* concerns, however, the United Nations proved almost powerless. Nearly all its major early decisions—on the independence of Israel in 1947–1948, on the Korean War in 1950, on the Suez crisis in 1956, on the Congo in 1960—lay outside the confines of Europe. On the Continent itself, the gap between the

Communist and the non-Communist world was too wide to be bridged by any international organization. Here the two power blocs went their separate ways, organizing their rival security systems independently and sometimes in defiance of the United Nations that they themselves had taken the lead in founding.

The Peace Treaties with the Axis Satellites

After their adjournment at Potsdam, the Big Three turned over to their foreign ministers the task of making the peace. Pursuant to this decision, the U.S. secretary of state, James F. Byrnes, Britain's new foreign minister, Ernest Bevin, and the Soviet Union's Vyacheslav Molotov constituted themselves a Council of Foreign Ministers. They met first in London in September 1945, then in Paris the following summer, where they were joined by the French foreign minister, and finally in New York at the end of the year, to work out the final details of settlement.

The outcome of more than a year of discussion was a series of peace treaties with Italy and with the four minor German satellites: Bulgaria, Hungary, Romania, and Finland. Essentially, these treaties were the work of the Big Four alone, although the advice of the lesser allies was sought, and they signed the final documents. The treaties followed a common pattern: They imposed reparations, limited the armed forces of the defeated countries, and made few territorial changes. Except for the enormous alteration in the frontiers of Poland and the disappearance of the Baltic States—both matters that lay outside the sphere of the peace treaties—the boundaries of Europe returned substantially to those established at Paris in 1919. Once again, however, as at Yalta, the Soviet Union insisted on retaining the territorial gains it had made during the war. The peace treaties ratified its annexation of Bessarabia from Romania and of the Karelian Isthmus and the Arctic seaport Petsamo from Finland. Without the sanction of a formal treaty, the Soviet Union also annexed Estonia, Latvia, Lithuania, and East Prussia, including the ancient German city of Königsberg (renamed Kaliningrad) on its western borders.

The Big Four attempted to reduce Italy's new frontiers to conform more closely to ethnic lines. The question of where its eastern border should now lie was the most serious the peacemakers faced, for it brought the new anti-Fascist Italian regime into conflict with another product of the wartime Resistance—Tito's Communist government in Yugoslavia. The new Yugoslav government claimed not only Venezia Giulia, most of which the Western powers were quite ready to concede, since the bulk of its people were Yugoslavs; they also demanded the seaport of Trieste, whose population was overwhelmingly Italian. In the end, the Big Four adopted a solution that satisfied neither side by declaring Trieste a *free territory*, much as Danzig had been between the wars. In 1954, this attempt at compromise ended when the city of Trieste was annexed by Italy, while the rural part of the free territory went to Yugoslavia.

In the case of the former Italian colonies, the Big Four also failed to supply a definitive solution. After disagreeing among themselves, they referred the question to the United Nations, which at length decided to grant independence to Libya, federation with Ethiopia to Eritrea, and an Italian trusteeship (preparatory to independence) to the Somali coast. Quite against their expressed intent, the Western powers had been driven to accept a plan that inevitably hastened the drive for freedom throughout the African continent (see Chapter 18, III).

Within less than three years, the fundamental assumption on which the peace treaties were based—that of a wartime coalition imposing its will on the vanquished—had vanished. By the end of 1947, it was apparent to everyone that a Cold War between the Soviet Union and the West had replaced the process of international consultation. Italy had won full acceptance as a military ally of the West, while Bulgaria, Hungary, and Romania were functioning as obedient satellites of the Soviet Union. Finland alone remained outside both of the Great Power blocs.

The Truman Doctrine and the Marshall Plan

This change of circumstances had already become amply apparent when the foreign ministers turned their attention to making a settlement with Germany. Twice during 1947—in March and April in Moscow, and in November and December in London—they tried to reach some minimum accord. Their efforts failed completely; the standpoints of East and West were much too far apart.

Discord first erupted into actual violence in the eastern Mediterranean. The Greek Communists—in whose suppression Churchill had played an active role at the end of 1944—took up arms once again in September 1946. This time they were aided by the fact that Greece's northern neighbors, Albania, Yugoslavia, and Bulgaria, were all under Communist regimes and were able to send them clandestine help across the border. They were also encouraged by the widespread popular dissatisfaction with the postwar Greek regime, in theory a parliamentary monarchy but in fact a corrupt right-wing oligarchy, almost entirely dependent on British armed support. When the British announced in early 1947 that they could no longer afford to provide that support, President Truman rose to the challenge. In March, he announced to the American Congress that in the future the United States would "support free peoples who are resisting attempted subjugation by armed minorities or by outside pressure." Shortly thereafter, American military missions traveled to Turkey and Greece, where they promised aid to Greece's right-wing government.

The Truman Doctrine became the cornerstone of a new interventionist policy of the United States in European affairs, replacing the inconsistencies and hesitations that had characterized the first year and a half of peace. Its counterpart in the economic sphere was the plan for European recovery first enunciated by Secretary of State George C. Marshall at a Harvard Commencement address the following year. Truman, Marshall, and their advisors feared that without massive U.S. economic assistance, Europe would be unable to rebuild and would instead remain sunk in a permanent depression which might breed political extremism, just as the Great Depression had fed both fascism and communism. In its original formulation, however, the Marshall Plan was not, strictly speaking, a Cold War maneuver. It offered aid to *all* European countries, irrespective of ideology, provided they would coordinate their economic proposals to use U.S. assistance to maximum effect.

Perhaps the clearest sign of how the cleavage between East and West was making impossible any overall European cooperation was the manner in which the Marshall Plan gradually became transformed into an instrument of the Cold War. This process of perversion occurred on both sides of the great ideological divide. In the East, the outcome was at first uncertain. Most of the Soviet satellites held back, distrustful of Secretary Marshall's invitation, since it required prospective aid recipients to decide in concert how that aid would be apportioned among former foes and allies alike. The Poles and the Czechs were nonetheless willing to accept until they were sharply called to task by their Russian masters. By midsummer of 1947, it had become quite clear that the Soviet Union would permit no Communist participation in the Marshall Plan. The U.S. president and his advisors were now free to continue the distortion of the original proposal by presenting it to Congress as the economic complement to the military program of the Truman Doctrine. When the Marshall Plan—or, to use its official name, the European Recovery Program—went into effect in early 1948, it had become exclusively a Western European enterprise. Moscow's response appeared the following year, when the COMECON (Council for Mutual Economic Aid) was founded in an attempt to shape the economic recovery of Eastern Europe to Soviet advantage (see Chapter 20, II).

The Cominform and the Communist
Bid for Power in France and Italy

The forced refusal on the part of the Czechs and the Poles in July 1947 to participate in the Marshall Plan inaugurated the decisive eighteen months in the split between the two ideological camps. Until the end of 1948, one event followed closely on another in tragic sequence.

In September 1947, the Communist parties of the Soviet Union and its satellites, together with the two Western European Communist parties of major importance—those of France and Italy—revived the Third International under a new name. The reestablished Comintern was called "Cominform," to suggest that it was no more than a vehicle for the exchange of information. In fact, during the next five and a half years of intense Cold War, the Cominform allowed the Soviet Union to coordinate the ideologies and economic plans of the East European Communist states, to reinforce their solidarity against the West, and to spur the militancy of the French and Italian parties. But it never achieved the prestige or importance of the Third International, in part because of its restricted membership (only two Western Communist parties were included, and Yugoslavia was soon expelled), in part because Soviet strategists found other, more direct ways to dominate Eastern Europe. In April 1956, having outlived its usefulness, the Cominform officially disbanded.

The new stance of toughness toward the West adopted by the Cominform first became evident in the actions of the French Communist party in the fall of 1947. On November 12, the Communist leaders who dominated the General Trade-Union Federation (CGT) issued a "manifesto to the French working class" calling for an insurrectionary general strike in the factories, railways, and coal mines to protest poor pay and working conditions. For a month, the very existence of the regime seemed to hang in the balance as violence and sabotage spread. But little by little, decisive government action brought a reversal of momentum. The Socialist minister of the interior, Jules Moch, did not hesitate to call out special police forces and even used the army against the strikers—who finally lost heart when they discovered that they were threatened with the loss of their social security benefits. A month after it began, the crisis was over, and the French production index began to climb as the value of the franc held steady.

In April 1948, the Italian electorate went to the polls to choose the first parliament under the new constitution. The voting was preceded by the most frenetic electoral campaign of postwar European history. The Communists and their Socialist allies had formed an electoral alliance called the People's Bloc. Prime Minister De Gasperi's Christian Democrats had made a similar alliance with three smaller democratic parties and profited as well by the backing of the Vatican and the U.S. government, which for the first time in history tried to influence the outcome of a European election. When the votes were tallied, De Gasperi and his allies had swept the field. Together they won more than 60 percent of the seats in the Chamber of Deputies. The Communists and their allies had been held to half that total—a level of popular support that was to remain almost unchanged for the next decade.

Thus the Italian Communists' bid for power had failed. They recovered their militancy briefly in July, when their leader, Palmiro Togliatti, was wounded in an assassination attempt, and they staged a dramatic general strike in protest. But the mere threat of military force was enough to bring about the movement's collapse.

By the end of 1948, the economic and ideological offensive of the Western European Communists had been broken and the Soviet bloc had experienced a further defeat in its failure to bring Tito to terms. After being expelled from the Cominform the previous June, the Yugoslav Communists were now groping their way toward establishing a position of neutrality between the two power blocs. In the meantime, the architect of the Soviet policy of revolutionary militancy, Andrei Zhdanov, had died with his work in ruins. Had he won a free hand earlier, the Italian and French Communists might have come closer to success. As it was, the movement had started too late. With the United States now once again fully involved in European affairs, it was doomed from the start.

The Berlin Airlift

The last and most protracted crisis in this year and a half of constant alarms was the first great international conflict over Berlin. In June 1948, having failed to dissuade the British and Americans from their plan of organizing a West German government, the Russians decided to put pressure on the weakest and most exposed point in the Anglo-American defensive position: They cut off railway and road access to the three Western sectors of Berlin and simultaneously tried to force the city government into line. But the Western powers would not be bullied. They supported the democratic majority on the Berlin city council—whose resistance forced the Soviet authorities to set up a separate administration for the eastern part of the city—and they mobilized every available transport plane to supply Berlin by air. All through the summer and autumn, the great airlift went on. Then winter brought a new problem. Surely, the Russians thought, the Western aircraft could not bring in enough coal to supply the needs of the two million people in their sectors. But the Americans and British simply increased the number of their planes and added coal to the food and essentials they were already carrying. By spring the success of the Berlin airlift was evident to all. In May, the Russians called off the blockade. The Western position in Berlin was safe for the future.

In Greece also, the West was winning the Cold War. With Tito's defection from the Soviet camp, the Greek guerrillas lost their most important supply base. Hard pressed

Inhabitants of West Berlin greet a plane bringing them supplies during the Berlin Blockade of 1948–1949. *(Courtesy H. Armstrong Roberts)*

by their assailants, they retired into an ever-smaller sector of the northern mountains. In the autumn of 1949, the last Communist guerrillas laid down their arms.

II. THE NORTH ATLANTIC ALLIANCE AND THE GOVERNMENTS OF THE CENTER

In the spring of 1949, the Western powers formally established the ideological and military alliance toward which they had been moving during the past two years. The Atlantic Pact (not to be confused with the earlier Atlantic Charter), signed in April in Washington, brought together ten European nations, the United States, and Canada. It included France and Britain, the Low Countries, Italy, and the two Scandinavian na-

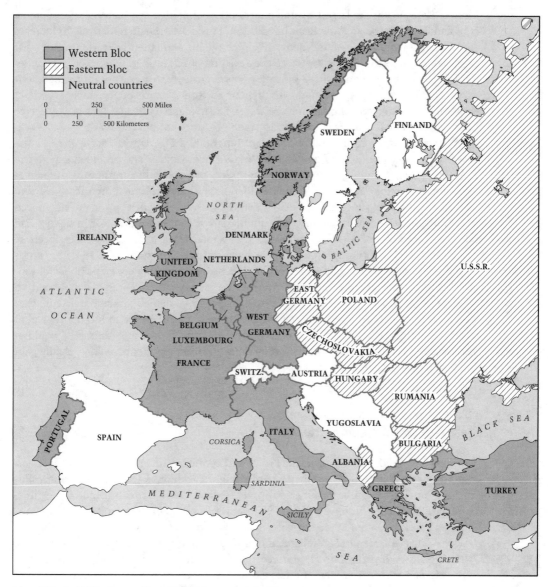

MAP 17.1 Cold War Europe: The NATO Alliance and the Warsaw Pact.

tions, Denmark and Norway, which had fought in the war on the Allied side. Portugal and Iceland also joined, and subsequently Greece, Turkey, and Western Germany (see Map 17.1).

The North Atlantic Treaty Organization (NATO) was, strictly speaking, no more than a military arrangement for mutual protection. Each member nation undertook to provide ground, air, or naval contingents in proportion to its means, with France supplying the largest number of ground troops and the commander of the central sector. The

United States made the largest overall contribution of money and material; the supreme commander was to be an American. In addition, President Truman undertook to increase the American military commitment in Germany by permanently stationing combat troops along the Rhine. This was to be the keystone of Atlantic military policy—the defense of Western Germany, with a force that was eventually to consist of fifty Allied divisions. Such an army was obviously insufficient to stop a major Soviet advance, but it could fight a costly delaying action, and the Atlantic planners trusted that it would give Stalin sober thoughts about launching any probing attack toward the West.

In addition to its primary military function, the Atlantic Pact expressed the growing ideological solidarity among the Western democracies and provided experience in working out common policies that was subsequently to find expression in the movement for European unity. The Marshall Plan was already pushing in that direction; throughout the late 1940s and early 1950s, the U.S. government constantly encouraged European initiatives for economic and administrative cooperation. Never in history had relations between the United States and the Western European democracies been so close and cordial. During the four years of his second administration, 1949–1953, President Truman and his secretary of state, Dean Acheson, pursued a coherent policy of supporting and strengthening governments of the democratic Center. They hoped to stimulate the growth of a "Third Force" in Europe—a moderate parliamentary rule that would prove equally resistant to Communist subversion on the Left and to the revival of authoritarian doctrines among conservatives. This Third Force, they surmised, would at last provide a plateau of stability on which democratic government would gradually gain the confidence of the disaffected masses.

Government by Christian Democrats: De Gasperi, Adenauer, Schuman

From 1948 to 1950, this policy seemed to be succeeding. With the threat from the Communists checked and the inflationary spiral brought to a halt, democracy in Western Europe was finally beginning to function in an approximately normal fashion. The three chief nations of the Western continent, moreover, had leaders who understood one another and spoke a common ideological language. In Italy, after his sweeping electoral victory of April 1948, De Gasperi remained in uninterrupted power for more than five years. Although his own party followers formed the core of his ministry, the Christian Democratic premier preferred to give it a less clerical character by associating with, whenever possible, the leaders of the three minor democratic parties who had fought the electoral battle at his side. Chief among these was Count Carlo Sforza, a veteran diplomat and a "good European" who, as foreign minister in the period 1920–1921, had tried to pursue a policy of international conciliation and who from 1947 to 1951, under far more favorable circumstances, returned to the same office with hopes undimmed.

In Germany, another Christian Democrat, Konrad Adenauer, began in September 1949 the hitherto longest chancellorship in German history—indeed, the longest single tenure of power that any democratic statesman had held in the entire modern history of Europe. The duration of Adenauer's stay was all the more remarkable given that fact that he assumed office as chancellor at the ripe age of seventy-five. For the next fourteen years *"der Alte"* ("the old man"), as he was known, steered West Germany in the direction of reconciliation with France and toward a close working relationship with the United States. Adenauer combined the patience of a diplomat with the pragmatism of a political realist. His long and bitter experience of the costs of German nationalism had convinced him that his homeland could recover its sovereignty and some measure of independence within Europe only by adopting the modest role of partner within an international framework. Like Gustav Stresemann in the 1920s, Adenauer sought to reassure former enemies that Germany was now committed to a policy of diplomatic "fulfillment" as a member of the broader community of Europe.

Adenauer's authority throughout his postwar political career remained still more unshakable than De Gasperi's. France, in contrast, with de Gaulle in the shadows, found no single unquestioned national leader. Nevertheless, the element of continuity was provided by Christian Democrats—the MRP leaders Bidault and Robert Schuman—who between them almost uninterruptedly held the foreign ministry during the first postwar decade. Of the two, Schuman was both the more responsible and the more imaginative. A Lorrainer who had been a German citizen before 1918 and had even served in the German army during the First World War, Schuman spoke French and German with equal fluency and was admirably equipped by education and temperament to act as mediator between the cultures of his two homelands.

Adenauer had the reputation of being pro-French. As a fledgling politician in the early 1920s, he had been accused of sympathy with French annexationist schemes for the Rhineland. The third member of the trio—De Gasperi—had a similarly varied political past. Before 1914, as a young "irredentist" from the South Tyrol, he had been elected to the Austrian Parliament, and he spoke German fluently. Indeed, he is said to have expressed surprise and pleasure at discovering that he and Schuman had a second language in common. And this, in fact, was true in both the literal and the figurative sense: De Gasperi, Adenauer, and Schuman spoke a common language. They were "good Europeans" who saw the urgent necessity of united action to preserve their Christian heritage.

In Italy and Germany, the tempered conservatism of Christian Democratic rule found expression in measures of social equalization. Although these were in no sense Socialist, they significantly altered the internal balance of economic forces in favor of the laboring classes. In Italy, the most pressing problem was agrarian poverty, for which De Gasperi had promised remedial action during the election campaign of 1948. Another year was needed, however, for the government to submit specific legislation to parliament, and still another eighteen months to carry an initial measure for the redistribution to poor peasants of a million and a half acres of land held in great estates. This reform measure fell far short of De Gasperi's original proposal; it provided for the needs of only a small part of Italy's landless peasantry, whose standard of living remained depressed. But it started the long-overdue process of breaking the economic power and social prestige of the large landowners and lifting the economy of the backward southern part of the country to bring it closer to that of the industrial north.

In Germany, the most dramatic reform undertaken by the Adenauer government was the law voted in 1951 for "codetermination" in the factories. Although the idea of giving workers a share in management had originated among Catholic trade-union leaders and the left wing of the Christian Democrats themselves, Adenauer and his ministerial colleagues were reluctant to make so radical an innovation in the face of vehement opposition by employers. Only the pressure of the Social Democrats and the threat of a strike by the powerful metal workers' union finally ensured the passage of a law providing for worker representation on supervisory boards in the iron, steel, and coal industry. The following year, however, when it was proposed to extend codetermination to the rest of German industry, the conservative opposition was more successful. A second law, passed in 1952, significantly reduced the power of the workers' representatives on the boards.

The Schuman Plan

By the spring of 1950, the economic aid that had been arriving from the United States under the Marshall Plan (see Figure 17.1) during the past two years was beginning to show substantial results. In France and Italy, production levels stood well above those of 1938. This was only a modest achievement, and the economic gains were partially canceled out by a 10 percent increase in population, but it at least showed that Western Europe had emerged from its economic stagnation and made up the ground lost during the war years. Meanwhile, the "miracle" of German industrial expansion had begun. At the beginning of 1949, less than a year after the Anglo-American currency reform had at last set the German economy moving, the production index stood at 85 percent of the 1936 figure.

During the first two of the four years that the Marshall Plan was scheduled to run, American aid averaging four billion dollars a year had resulted in a 30-billion-dollar expansion of annual output. Overall production of goods and services had gone up by 25 percent—an increase of 15 percent over the prewar figure. Industrial output as a whole had risen by nearly a third—with steel setting the pace with an increase of more than half. Thus, despite the slow start of postwar economic reconstruction—and despite the

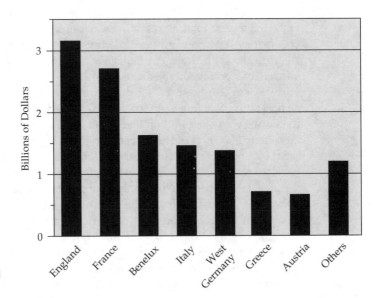

FIGURE 17.1 Graph showing Marshall Plan aid to individual European countries. Note the large shares of England and France compared to those of the other recipients.

far greater extent of devastation in 1945 than in 1918—recovery had proceeded more rapidly and more evenly following the Second World War than it had after the First. In addition, Western Europe had gained precious experience in cooperative economic endeavor.

It was in this context that Robert Schuman, in May 1950, came forward with the most imaginative proposal that postwar Europe had yet heard and the one from which all subsequent progress toward European integration stemmed: the project for a European Coal and Steel Community, which came to be called the Schuman Plan. The French foreign minister suggested a pooling of heavy industrial resources and an elimination of tariffs in the "core" nations of Western Europe—France, Italy, Western Germany, and the Low Countries. The idea caught on quickly. By the following April, representatives of the six nations were ready to sign the treaty establishing the Community. They guarded themselves by providing that it was to come into effect only gradually during the five years following its ratification; a half decade of grace was granted for all the threatened vested interests to adjust themselves to the new competitive situation.

Meanwhile, the international outlook had changed drastically. The European atmosphere in which the Coal and Steel Community treaty was signed was radically different from the one in which it had been proposed.

III. THE KOREAN WAR AND THE GOVERNMENTS OF THE RIGHT

In June 1950, the army of Communist North Korea crossed the thirty-eighth parallel to attack the American-endorsed government of South Korea. The United States responded quickly: President Truman decided to send military aid to the South Koreans. Subsequently the United Nations voted to support the U.S. intervention, and a number of Western European countries agreed to supply troop contingents for an international army under U.S. command.

This distant Asian war had immediate and profound repercussions in Europe. The quiet and undeclared conflict between the Communist and the Western camps that had been going on for the past three years had suddenly flared into open violence, and no one knew if and when the struggle would spread to Europe itself. Many recalled how a local war in Spain fourteen years earlier had set the stage for a major international conflict. Most Western Europeans were relieved that the Americans had gone to the aid of South Korea; the prompt American response suggested that the United States was faithful to its allies and that the year-old Atlantic Pact would stand the test of war. But once the crisis was past, and the North Koreans had been driven back, Europeans began to have second thoughts. When the American army in its turn crossed the thirty-eighth parallel and invaded the territory of the enemy—thereby provoking the intervention of the Communist Chinese—the Europeans feared that the war was being pursued beyond its minimum objective of saving the South Korean government and that it might become a global conflict. Thus the Europeans' original gratification that the United States had gone to the aid of a small ally was gradually transformed into anxiety lest they themselves be drawn into a struggle for power in Asia, with which they had only a very limited concern.

The Economic and Military Effects: The EDC

From the economic standpoint, the immediate result of the fighting in Korea was an increase in raw-material prices throughout the world, which, in turn, set off a new cycle of inflation. For the statesmen of Europe, this was heartbreaking. They had scarcely finished establishing their countries on what seemed at last to be a secure economic plateau, when the whole weary spiral of price rises, social unrest, and wage adjustments began once again. Nor was U.S. aid this time as unstinting and as free from conditions as it had been in the previous two years. With the outbreak of the Korean War, the emphasis in Washington changed. In the later phases of the Marshall Plan and its sequels, "military support" replaced economic aid as the basis of U.S. appropriations for Europe. The Cold War perversion of Secretary Marshall's original vision was thus pushed one step further.

From the purely military standpoint, the Korean War induced a mood approaching panic. With the threatened spread of the conflict to Europe, the U.S. government expressed the fear that the existing strength of NATO would prove inadequate to withstand a Soviet attack on Germany. The United States began to insist that the West Germans be armed for their own defense. Without a German military contribution, the Americans argued, the protection of the West against a Communist assault would be perilously fragile.

For the Europeans in the North Atlantic Alliance—and for the French in particular—this American demand raised a cruel dilemma. Most West European statesmen disliked rearming Germany only five years after Hitler's defeat; they recalled that the demilitarization of the country had been one of the few aims on which all the occupying powers had agreed. At the same time, the European nations were entirely dependent on the United States for military and economic support, and they could not afford to dispute the wishes of their great ally. In this major international quandary, the French proposed a dramatic compromise solution: The Germans would be rearmed—but only as the soldiers of a European army. The sting would be taken out of a revived German militarism by making certain that the country had no national army, but only contingents in a special force under international command.

This was the central idea behind the European Defense Community (EDC), whose founding treaty was signed at Paris in May 1952 by representatives of the six countries of "Little Europe," which were already bound together by the Schuman Plan. From the standpoint of European integration, the proposals seemed to be another step forward along the path that the French foreign minister had already marked out. In actual fact, the new Defense Community was rather different from the Coal and Steel Community that had preceded it. First, it was not a pact between equals. Under its terms, West Germany alone was to have no national army; France, Italy, and the Low Countries, on the other hand, were to retain separate forces of their own in addition to those they contributed to the European command. Still more important, the EDC leaped over a succession of stages that "good Europeans" thought should logically have preceded it. The Schuman Plan had been intended as only the first of a series of "communities" that were gradually to link the economies of the six member states. Subsequently, as through the years "Little Europe" grew accustomed to work in common, a joint political authority would naturally and inevitably follow. The direct leap to a military community—logically the very last stage in the succession—meant the short-circuiting of this whole process.

The final paradox of the EDC was that its initial sponsors, the French, eventually proved to be the prospective members who were least enthusiastic about it. They had originally put it forward as a neat contrivance for avoiding a threatening obstacle. When the contrivance finally became reality, they began to have grave doubts. While the other national parliaments one by one ratified the EDC accord, the French Assembly held back. For two full years, the question of the EDC hung suspended over France's parliament, poisoning the political life of the country and contributing significantly to the slow but already painfully apparent decline of the Fourth Republic.

Gaullism and the Conservative Revival

In the political sphere, the Korean War encouraged a trend toward conservative government that had already been apparent in the two years between mid-1948 and mid-1950, when economic stability seemed to have been attained at last. With the return of something approaching "normal," social protest and the demand for change had begun to lose their edge. The outbreak of war in Asia greatly accelerated the conservative revival; the remilitarization of Europe naturally played into the hands of parties that had always stressed nationalism and the tradition of fighting "natives" overseas. By 1950, the Communists' power had been broken. They could still embitter the political atmosphere but could no longer hope to influence national policy.

A series of national elections extending through the years 1951 and 1953 most dramatically showed the new balance of forces. First France went to the polls, in conformity with the new constitution of the Fourth Republic, which had set the term of the National Assembly at five years. In the French election of June 1951, the "tripartite" arrangement of 1946 was replaced by a "hexagon" of six parties roughly equal in strength; in the redistribution of political forces, the two parties of the Center—the MRP and the Socialists—were the chief losers, whereas great gains were made on the Right. At the end of the year, the British electorate also gave its verdict. In the elections held in October 1951, the Conservatives bested Labour by a narrow margin, and Winston Churchill returned to power for the last time.

In 1953, the Italian Chamber of Deputies and the West German Bundestag both came up for reelection. On the surface, the results of these two elections seemed to be in complete contrast. In Italy, Prime Minister De Gasperi's Christian Democrats lost ground to the Right; in Germany Chancellor Adenauer's followers gained. But the actual effects on national life were much the same. In both countries, Christian Democracy in power had become a far more conservative force than it had been at the outset. The major reform acts of previous years—land redistribution in Italy, codetermination in Germany—had gradually been confined in scope by the pressure of the propertied classes. In Germany, however, the conservative revival expressed itself *within* the Christian Democratic leadership, whereas in Italy it spoke through revived parties of the Right, which were openly backed by the larger businessmen and landowners.

The gradual triumph of conservatism was accompanied by a corresponding change in Europe's political leadership. In Italy, Count Sforza was forced out of the foreign ministry in the summer of 1951, while his French counterpart, Robert Schuman, was dropped from the same office at the beginning of 1953. Half a year later, De Gasperi also departed after more than seven years in office. He died in 1954, pleading until the last for the ratification of the treaty establishing the EDC.

One by one the "good Europeans" were being moved off the scene. In an effort to salvage something of their former position, they were reduced to electoral strategems that brought them only further discredit. For the election of 1951, the French government modified the proportional system that had been instituted in 1945. The new electoral law provided that a party (or coalition) that won a majority of the vote in any constituency was to be assigned *all* the seats for that area. In Italy, which also operated under a proportional system, De Gasperi and his colleagues devised a still more transparent maneuver; here a coalition that had gained a narrow majority in the *whole country* was to be rewarded with a bonus of two-thirds of the seats in the Chamber.

In both cases, these electoral tricks disappointed the expectations of their contrivers. In Italy, the unpopularity of the "*legge truffa*" or "swindle law," as its enemies called it, contributed to the decline of the democratic parties; when the votes were counted, it was discovered that their coalition had just missed its majority and that hence the proportional system would operate as before. In France, the electoral law of 1951 actually did reduce the power of the political extremes on Right and Left, but it failed to provide the reinforcement of Center rule that its sponsors had anticipated.

France most clearly showed what were to be the new tendencies of the early 1950s. At first it seemed that the 1951 election had brought to the fore a revived authoritarianism of the Right. In the new Assembly, the strongest single party—which had narrowly ousted the Communists from first place—was the Rally of the French People (RPF) led by Charles de Gaulle. In the spring of 1947, the general, disgusted by the weaknesses of the restored parliamentary regime, had emerged from retirement to found his own political movement. It rapidly won support. Conservatives and authoritarians of all sorts flocked to de Gaulle's banners. But it reached its high point too early; in the first autumn of its existence it polled 40 percent of the vote in municipal elections throughout the country. Then de Gaulle faced his usual dilemma. Lacking a popular majority and with no general election scheduled for nearly four years, the Gaullists of the RPF could maintain only a sterile opposition, which in fact benefited the Communists.

Hence the RPF electoral success of 1951—in the teeth of the special law that had been devised to thwart it—came too late. Those who really profited from the new parliamentary situation were the old Radicals, now transmuted into frankly conservative representatives of small business, and the so-called Independents, who spoke for the larger propertied interests. Together these two parties replaced the Socialists and the MRP as the dominant influences in French political life.

In the spring of 1953, de Gaulle realized that his party had failed; he gave his followers their "liberty of action" and retired once more to his country home southeast of Paris. In Italy and Germany, too, authoritarian appeals were failing to win favor. In the elections of 1953 in both countries, neo-Fascist and neo-Nazi forces made a poor showing. By 1953, old-fashioned conservatism, rather, with a strong tinge of traditional nationalism, had emerged as the dominant political force in Western Europe.

IV. EASTERN EUROPE: THE CLIMAX OF THE TERROR

At the end of his life, Stalin sank into a state approaching paranoia. Life became a nightmare for those around him. The aging despot suspected everyone, and one favorite replaced another with a capriciousness that defied explanation. Rumors circulated that Zhdanov's death in 1948 had not been accidental; the press announced a mysterious "doctors' plot" to poison the leaders of the Soviet state. A number of the doctors' names were Jewish; one of the most sinister features of Stalin's last years was an appeal to the latent anti-Semitism among the populations of Eastern Europe.

In short, a new purge, comparable to the great terror of 1936–1938, seemed to be threatening. This atmosphere of universal danger was intensified by the grim international outlook. Just as the West was concerned lest the Soviet Union extend the scope of the Korean War to Europe, so Stalin was equally afraid lest the United States pass over to the attack. If the "American imperialists," he reasoned, had gone to war for so little a thing as Korea, what was to prevent them from assaulting the Communist camp in Eastern Europe itself?

Sequels in Eastern Europe

For the satellite nations of East Central Europe, this threat of war meant the intensification of Soviet pressure to step up heavy industrial production and to postpone still further the adequate provision of consumer goods. It also meant the decline of the Cominform, already under suspicion by Stalin since the defection of Yugoslavia. A process of anticipating Stalin's orders on the part of his satellite lieutenants or of receiving indirect instructions through the Soviet ambassadors and "advisers" in the Eastern capitals replaced the formal consultations that this body had been intended to provide. Finally, it meant that the purge of leaders suspected of "national" deviations took a new and still more sinister turn.

This second wave of the purge appeared in its most intense form in Czechoslovakia. Between 1950 and 1952, the Czechoslovak Communist party was shaken by the most severe internal crisis that East Central Europe had yet seen. One reputation after another toppled, as accusers followed accused into the defendant's box. When the trials ended—in December 1952—eleven top leaders were hanged, several of whom were Jews, for the new element in the Czechoslovak purge trials was a scarcely concealed anti-Semitism. Under the transparent euphemism of "cosmopolitan" tendencies, the Jewish Communist leaders of Eastern Europe were systematically accused of sympathy with Israel and with the West. In Hungary, too, old-line Communist leaders, such as Laszlo Rajk, and Jewish party members, such as Anna Pauker, were singled out for attack.

The Cold War reached its climax at the end of 1952. Just as nationalist and conservative tendencies were gaining in the West, so in the Soviet sphere the narrowest and most isolationist definitions of communism were in the ascendant. At the very moment that "good Europeans" were losing ground in France and Italy, in the East the mere suspicion of "cosmopolitanism" was becoming sufficient to bring imprisonment and even death. With each month that passed, the two armed camps of divided Europe appeared to be drifting farther and farther apart. When 1953 opened, it seemed that only a miracle could save the old Continent from a new and still more deadly world war.

READINGS

Since the end of the Cold War, the literature on its origins and course has grown at a rapid pace. Martin Walker, *The Cold War: A History* (1993), presents a balanced overview by a respected British journalist. John Lewis Gaddis, *We Now Know: Rethinking Cold War History** (1997) offers a number of provocative conclusions based on recently available archival material, including his return to the old thesis that Stalin made the Cold War inevitable. Jeremy Isaacs and Taylor Downing, *Cold War: An Illustrated History, 1945–1991* (1998), based on the CNN TV series, offers a wealth of visual materials to supplement the above accounts. Vladislav Zubok and Constantine Pleshakov, *Inside the Kremlin's Cold Cold War: From Stalin to Khrushchev** (1996) makes a persuasive case for considering Stalin's foreign policy decisions in light of internal Soviet politics. Europe's role—too often neglected in the shadow of superpower relations—is explored in A. W. DePorte, *Europe Between the Superpowers*, 2nd ed. (1986), and in Charles S. Maier, ed., *The Cold War in Europe: Era of a Divided Continent** (1991). A balanced summary of the transition from the Second World War to the Cold War may be found in William R. Keylor's *The Twentieth-Century World: An International History,** 4th ed. (2001). William Stueck, *Rethinking the Korean War: A New Diplomatic and Strategic History* (2002) shows how errors on both sides helped to precipitate one of the early chapters in this global conflict.

For the individual Western European countries, besides the books by Grosser, Williams, and Ginsborg (see readings for Chapter 15), one may consult Francis Boyd, *British Politics in Transition, 1945–63* (1964); Raymond Aron, *France: Steadfast and Changing* (1960); Richard Hiscocks, *The Adenauer Era* (1966); and Norman Kogan, *A Political History of Post-War Italy*, 2 vols. (1966–1981). Walter Laqueur, *Europe in Our Time: A History, 1945–1992** (1992), lacks an overall thesis but offers a wealth of informative detail. The series of essays edited by Francis O. Wilcox and H. Field Haviland, Jr., *The Atlantic Community: Progress and Prospects* (1963), traces the growth of the Atlantic idea, while F. Roy Willis, *France, Germany, and the New Europe, 1945–1967*, rev. ed. (1968), details the often difficult first steps toward reconciliation between the two dominant powers of Western Europe.

On Eastern Europe, besides Fejtö (see readings for Chapter 14), there are Jacques Rupnik, *The Other Europe: The Rise and Fall of Communism in East Central Europe* (1989); Chris Harman, *Bureaucracy and Revolution in Eastern Europe* (1974); J. F. Brown, *The New Eastern Europe* (1966); and the thorough, scholarly essays on Yugoslavia, Poland, and Hungary in the first volume of a collaborative study edited by William E. Griffith, *Communism in Europe: Continuity, Change, and the Sino-Soviet Dispute* (1964).

*Books available in paperback are marked with an asterisk.

THE LOSS OF
COLONIAL EMPIRE

French President Vincent Auriol signs a treaty with Laos at the Elysée Palace in 1949, while the king of Laos looks on. (*Courtesy Corbis-Bettmann*)

In the fifteen years from 1945 to 1960, the European powers almost completely liquidated their colonial empires. Most of these colonies had been acquired in a mere decade and a half at the end of the nineteenth century, and the decisive acts in their liberation came in an equally brief time span. By 1960, nearly all the more important of the former colonial areas of Asia and Africa were fully independent, and most of the rest had formal independence scheduled for a very early date. A decade later, colonial rule of the old type lingered on in only a few territories, the greater part of them in sub-Saharan Africa, though informal ties with their former colonies allowed European powers to continue to exercise influence throughout much of the Third World.

The reaction against colonization had already begun during the interwar period (see Chapter 6, III). The local nationalist movements coincided with deepening doubts about the justification for empire with Europe itself. Both France and Britain had made efforts to train native elites, who now quite understandably began to desire a say in administering their own countries. At the same time, some Europeans themselves began to feel uneasy at the apparent conflict between Wilsonian calls for self-determination at the end of the First World War and the continued imposition of colonial rule. Both the push for independence and unease at refusing to grant it intensified after the Second World War. But so, too, did European fears of falling into second-class status without the resources of empire. Especially in the case of France, a weakened international position after 1945 made the prospect of decolonization seem distasteful, though perhaps inevitable.

In some instances, the process of colonial liberation occurred peacefully. In others, the European powers agreed to retire only after long and bloody wars. But almost everywhere, the departure of the Europeans was forced in one form or other. Only through the steady growth of local nationalist movements were the colonial powers led to realize that their days were numbered and that it was wiser to grant independence with good grace than to continue a hopeless delaying action.

I. THE SETTING

Asia and Africa in the War Years: The Loosening of Colonial Ties

In the Middle East, in Africa, and in Southeast Asia, the Second World War had been fought by the Europeans and Japanese with scant regard for the local populations. The major belligerents decided the "natives'" fate as the necessities of war dictated and rarely troubled to seek out the views of the leaders on the spot. Thus the British brought India into the war without consulting the spokesmen of the Congress party, Gandhi and Nehru. They agreed with the Russians to a joint occupation of the formally independent nation of Iran and, in Egypt, which was also supposed to be independent, they took advantage of their special treaty rights to set up at Cairo and Alexandria their main military bases for the Mediterranean. The French were no more considerate of local feelings. The allegiance of one colony or another to Vichy or to de Gaulle depended almost entirely on the decision of individual French governors or military commanders; in Algeria or Morocco the French were as little concerned with what the local Moslem population thought about the war as the British were in Egypt.

Thus the Asians and Africans of the European colonies lived through the great conflict as passive spectators—except, of course, for those who were recruited into the Indian army, which fought for the British in the Near East, or the French colonial forces, which made so splendid a record in Italy and in the liberation of southern France. But though colonial peoples remained necessarily on the sidelines, they could not fail to see what was happening. In particular, local nationalist leaders realized how the war itself had undermined the foundations of colonial rule. The German defeat of France in 1940, and the Japanese defeat of the British and the Dutch in Southeast Asia in 1942, severely damaged the prestige of the European powers. This was particularly true in areas like Burma, Indochina, and Indonesia, where the Japanese were still the occupying power when the war in the Pacific came to an end. It was also apparent in more remote regions, where the presence of foreign armies—particularly the anticolonialist Americans—shook the local populations out of their accustomed attitudes. Almost everywhere a similar lesson applied: After the shocks that the war had administered, colonial authority could never be the same again.

Even before the war ended, the British and French had reached this conclusion about the Arab countries of the Near East. The European conflict hastened the liberation of the territories France and Britain had received as Class A mandates from the spoils of the Turkish Empire in 1919. Iraq had already achieved its independence from Britain in 1937. The French—after protracted squabbles with the British, whom they feared as postwar rivals in the Levant—in 1945 honored their prewar promise to free Syria and Lebanon. In 1946, the British, not to be outdone, gave independence to the small kingdom of Transjordan, which was enlarged two years later (and renamed Jordan), when it conquered the central part of Palestine that remained outside the new state of Israel. In 1954, with the British agreement to evacuate the Suez Canal Zone within twenty months—and thus to end the indirect control over Egypt that had been crucial during the war years—there disappeared the last traces of European suzerainty over the Arab nations of the Eastern Mediterranean.

The Attitude of the Remaining Colonial Powers: Assimilation, Commonwealth, and Intransigence

The victors in the First World War had ended the colonial rule of one power, Germany. The victors in the second war similarly reduced the number of their rivals overseas by eliminating Italy. By 1945 there were only five significant colonial powers left. Besides the two major nations, Britain and France, three small European countries—Belgium, the Netherlands, and Portugal—retained important holdings in Southeast Asia and Africa.

These five powers varied greatly in their attitude toward colonial rule. In general, the British faced the end of imperialism with the greatest realism and equanimity. Through their formula of a Commonwealth of self-governing dominions, they had developed a framework both for preparing colonial areas for nationhood and for retaining economic and cultural ties with them after their liberation. Nevertheless, the British had reasons for doubt and hesitation. It was not clear whether the Commonwealth formula—which previously had been applied only to areas of European settlement such as Canada and Australia—would work equally well for nations with Asian and African populations and governments. The British were divided, moreover, on the issue of the pace at which liberation should proceed. The Conservatives still had a strong imperialist wing, with which Winston Churchill himself was in sympathy. Indeed, the great war leader had declared quite bluntly that he had no intention of liquidating "His Majesty's Empire." Labour, on the contrary, stood united in its resolution to give independence to the colonies as rapidly as individual circumstances would permit. It was fortunate for the cause of colonial liberation that the British Labour party was governing the country during the decisive postwar years. When the Conservatives returned to power in 1951, their imperialist wing had been much weakened, and it was too late in any case to reverse a process that had by now become irresistible.

France's counterformula for colonial evolution—the assimilation of native elites to French culture—was far less flexible than that of the Commonwealth, for it depended on the actual desire of Asians and Africans to become French, and it was incapable of rapid extension to whole populations. Should the majority of natives gain the vote, it would break down completely. This was what in fact happened after 1945. During the war, de Gaulle had promised the colonies that rallied to his Free French movement a democratic suffrage and the reorganization of France's Empire as a "French Union." In subsequent years, the Union proved generally to be a disappointment. Although the new French constitution of 1946 provided for consultative institutions for the empire, they never acquired real power, and the individual territories under French control continued to be governed from Paris, much as they had been in the past. Yet the extension of the vote—despite official delays and chicanery—gradually became a reality. Both the Constituent Assemblies of 1945 and 1946 and the regular parliaments that followed them had about eighty overseas deputies, who vigorously defended their constituents' interests and who eventually came to regard themselves as the spokesmen and founders of future nations.

The smaller colonial powers were far less "enlightened" than Britain or France. All three proposed to keep their colonies while making an absolute minimum of concessions. In the case of Portugal, such a policy was practicable. Its two vast but undeveloped colonies in Africa—Angola and Mozambique—showed few signs of restiveness in the postwar years. It initially appeared that Belgium had the same advantage. The great Belgian colony of the Congo enjoyed an unexampled prosperity during the war and its aftermath—partly due to the newly discovered importance of its uranium deposits—and its rulers carefully restricted the education of the natives to the essentials of technical training. Not until the very end of the 1950s did the liberation of the Congo suddenly become urgent.

The Dutch, in the Indonesian archipelago, had one great colony that accounted for much of the wealth and prestige of the home country, but their postwar situation was more tenuous than that of the Belgians. Although they had pursued an equally stern policy of resistance to advances by the native people, they faced circumstances that were much more unfavorable to continued colonial rule. Indonesia was six times as populous as the Congo and infinitely more developed culturally. Furthermore, whereas the Belgian government-in-exile had held possession of the Congo throughout the war, the Dutch had lost Indonesia to the Japanese under humiliating circumstances. At the war's end, it proved impossible for the Netherlands to reestablish its control. The independence of Indonesia was to rank as one of the two key events of the late 1940s that decisively set the colonial world on its new course.

II. THE LIBERATION OF SOUTHERN ASIA

The British Withdrawal: India, Pakistan, Burma, Ceylon, Malaya

The most important single act in the end of empire was Britain's liberation of India. With its population of 400 million, India alone had as many people as all the rest of the colonial world together. It was the keystone of British overseas rule—the epitome and symbol of imperial authority.

India, moreover, was better prepared for independence than any other major colony. For half a century the British had been systematically training its aspiring young men to staff the civil service and the judiciary, and in the Congress party it possessed a reservoir of talented political leaders. Although India had taken long strides toward self-government in the interwar years, this process had not been rapid enough for the nationalist spokesmen; they rejected the offer of quasi-independence which Britain made in 1942 and, during the latter part of the war, Nehru and his colleagues were in jail. When the conflict ended, it was obvious that the Congress party would be satisfied with nothing less than complete independence.

This the Labour government was resolved to grant. The only obstacle was the attitude of the Moslem League—the rival of Congress—which insisted on the establishment of a separate state for India's Moslem minority. The British were reluctant to do this, since there was no natural way to divide the country and in many areas Moslems and Hindus lived closely intermingled. Partition eventually became unavoidable, however. This crude and unpalatable solution—which had already been applied to Ireland, which was occurring de facto in Germany and Korea and which was soon to be extended to Palestine and Indochina—proved to be the only one possible. In the summer of 1947, India and the Moslem territories, which took the name of Pakistan, became independent nations within the Commonwealth. The definition of the Commonwealth was stretched one step further to permit the two Asian nations to participate as republics in an institution that necessarily honored a monarch as its symbolic head.

The island of Ceylon, on achieving independence, likewise chose to remain within the Commonwealth, but Burma, whose conquest by the Japanese during the war had decisively broken the tie to Britain, determined to cut the last link. Burma became a neutralist nation, torn by internal strife during the first years following its independence and precariously poised between India and Communist China. Indeed, throughout Southeast Asia the victory of the Chinese Communists in 1949 brought the threat of insurrections led by influential Chinese minorities. This happened in Malaya—another dependency of Britain, which had fallen to Japan in 1942; here the British felt obliged to fight a long and cruel jungle war against Communist guerrillas before they considered it safe to offer self-government to the peninsula. Yet the struggle with local Communist movements could delay, but not halt, the process of liberation. In 1957, a pacified Malaya became the fourth independent Asian nation within the Commonwealth.

The Struggle for Indonesia and Indochina

The French and Dutch did not give up their Southeast Asian possessions so easily (see Map 18.1). Both Indonesia and Indochina had to fight for their independence against the dogged resistance of stubborn imperialists.

MAP 18.1 Former European colonies in Asia; the date after the name of each country refers to the year when it became independent.

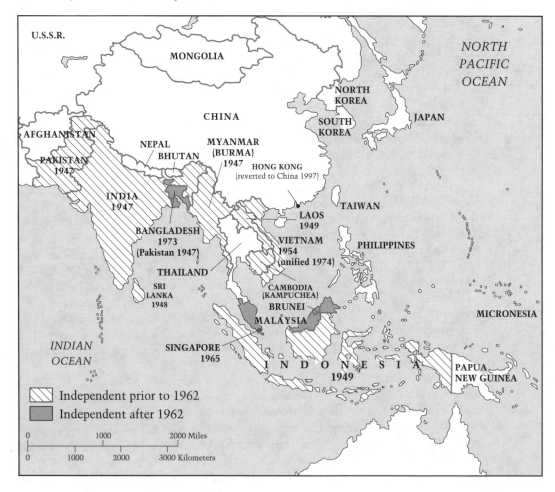

When the Dutch returned to Indonesia after the war, the local nationalists—who had developed their clandestine organizations during the years of Japanese rule—were already in substantial control. The only recourse was to negotiate with them for self-government short of independence. But the negotiations soon broke down, and the former colonial power shifted to an attempt at coercing the nationalists by force. For four years the fighting continued in desultory fashion. Finally, however, the Dutch realized that they lacked the military means to bring the Indonesians to terms. In 1949, Indonesia became an independent nation.

In Indochina the story was much the same, but here the fighting continued longer and the solution was less clear-cut. From the beginning, the situation of Indochina was extremely complex. Of the major French colonial territories, it alone had remained loyal throughout the war to the Vichy regime and hence neutral in the world conflict. For this reason, it was not until the very end of the war that the Japanese took formal control of Vietnam. By that time, the clandestine struggle for power had become at least five-sided. Besides the Vichy French and the Japanese, there were agents sent out by de Gaulle who were trying to establish their influence in preparation for the hour of victory; there were Chinese infiltrating in the north; and there was the Communist-trained nationalist leader Ho Chi Minh, who was organizing the native cadres for a republic of Vietnam in the eastern part of the country. The two western Indochinese protectorates, Cambodia and Laos, remained outside the power struggle.

When the war ended and the Gaullist agents were able to operate freely, their first inclination was to negotiate with Ho Chi Minh, who appeared to be at least partially independent from Moscow's control and who was leading a nationalist movement with a broad popular base. This was also the view of the French ministry at home, which invited the Vietnamese leader to Paris for consultations on self-government for Indochina. But while Ho Chi Minh was away in France, a catastrophe occurred—a subordinate French commander precipitated fighting on his own authority. The government in Paris was too weak to resist; by the end of 1946 it had allowed itself to be pushed into war. Thus there was set the dangerous precedent of local French representatives literally blackmailing the more liberal ministries at home into support of their own uncompromising colonial policies.

The war in Indochina dragged on for more than seven years. It became a steadily increasing drain on France's military forces, its economy, and its national morale. In its worst years, it killed more young officers than the French national military academy could produce, for this was a war fought by professional soldiers; it was so unpopular among the French people that the government dared not send conscripts to Asia, as the United States was to do in Korea. It was a war that seemed without end and without possibility of a favorable outcome. As the French were obliged to make more and more concessions to those Indochinese who opposed the authority of Ho Chi Minh, the army gradually found itself in the paradoxical position of the British in Malaya—fighting a Communist-led national movement in the name of non-Communist native nationalists who also laid claim to independence.

The victory of the Communists in China in 1949 intensified the Vietnamese struggle by providing Ho Chi Minh's forces with a northern supply base similar to that which the Balkan Communist states had offered the Greek insurgents two years earlier. By the same token, it put Ho's movement itself under firmer Communist control. The next year the Korean War broke out—followed in a few months by the intervention of the Chinese. The Chinese intervention at first seemed to improve the outlook for the French struggle in Indochina. It made that conflict a part of the Cold War, as it became apparent that the Communist Chinese were now supporting two parallel threats to Western influence, one on their northern border and one on their southern border. The result was a drastic alteration in U.S. policy toward Indochina. The United States government, which had formerly condemned the French for adhering to a discredited colonialism, now shifted to support of the Indochinese war as a contribution to the joint Western attempt to hold the line against communism.

The change came too late to save the French. Although the U.S. government poured money and supplies into Indochina, the French military position continued to deteriorate. When the Korean War came to an end in 1953, the Communist Chinese were free to increase their pressure toward the south. The Americans, on the contrary, sick of war in Asia, decided not to intervene in Indochina. At this point, the French command committed an act of supreme folly. It threw nearly all its remaining resources into the strong point of Dien Bien Phu near the Chinese border. The Vietnamese and Chinese Communists—fully aware of the fortress's symbolic importance—assaulted it unsparingly. In May 1954, Dien Bien Phu was overwhelmed, and with it the last hopes of the French in Indochina.

The fall of Dien Bien Phu was the first of the great shocks that were eventually to destroy the Fourth French Republic. It swept into power Pierre Mendès-France, the most talented and courageous of France's political leaders in the early 1950s, who had consistently declared that his country must cut its losses and make peace in Indochina (see Chapter 19, II). In July, a conference of foreign ministers at Geneva settled the matter by partitioning Vietnam, as Korea had been, along the seventeenth parallel of latitude. To the north, Ho Chi Minh's Communists were to rule. South of the parallel, an independent Vietnam joined the states of Cambodia and Laos, which earlier had been granted their freedom, and these in turn found themselves linked to Burma and Indonesia in a perilous neutrality between East and West. French rule in Asia had come to an end. The renewed war on the part of the United States to preserve the pro-Western regime in South Vietnam still lay in the future.

III. THE AFRICAN AWAKENING

In Africa, the postwar change was even more dramatic than in southern Asia (see Map 18.2). The independence of the latter area, which had an ancient and advanced culture and strong nationalist movements, could not be denied after 1945; qualified experts had been almost unanimous in predicting what would happen if the Europeans tried to stand against the tide. In Africa, it was quite different. Here the process of liberation surprised the specialists themselves by its swiftness and irreversibility. Most of Africa was far less developed than Asia, and its nationalist movements were infinitely weaker. Once started, however, the drive toward liberation gathered its own momentum; colonial authority began to crumble in places where a decade earlier it had scarcely been questioned. Indeed, the Europeans sometimes seemed to be urging the African spokesmen themselves toward independence when both sides knew that they were not ready. In this process, as in Asia, the British took the lead, while the French followed more reluctantly.

In 1945, the map of Africa was not much different from what it had been in 1914. Except for the transfer of the former German colonies to British and French tutelage, and the largely theoretical independence of Egypt, almost nothing had changed. The pockets of freedom were the same as they had been in the past—Ethiopia, Liberia, and the white-dominated Union of South Africa. Less than a tenth of the continent was even formally independent. As the 1950s opened, the map was still unaltered, but in the preceding five years pressure had been building behind the torrent that was to come. The independence of Libya in 1951 set the course for a decade of furious movement. By 1960, the colors on the map had been reversed; now only scattered pockets of Africa were neither already free nor well on their way to independence.

The British Example: The Independence of Ghana and Nigeria

The British Labour government had instituted an Africa-wide program of colonial preparation for independence by establishing plans for economic development and systematically turning over authority to native officials, but it was the Conservative ministries of the 1950s that actually presided over the course of liberation. The process began in 1954 with the termination of British treaty rights in Egypt. The logical sequel occurred at the beginning of 1956, with the liberation of the Sudan, which had been under joint British and Egyptian authority. The really decisive event, however—at least for Africa south of the Sahara—was the independence gained by the Gold Coast, which in 1957, under the new name of Ghana, became the first purely African nation within the Commonwealth.

The Gold Coast was a natural place to begin: It was prosperous, it was economically developed, and it had almost no European population. Indeed, the fact that West Africa had never been an area of European settlement greatly simplified the problem of its liberation, for the French as well as for the British. It was logical that the next British colony after Ghana to become independent should be the west coast territory of Nigeria—the continent's most populous country—which from the moment of its liberation in 1960 moved into the front rank of African power.

Britain's other West African territories, which were smaller and poorer than Nigeria and Ghana, progressed more slowly toward independence, but their future was no longer in doubt. They soon became African countries ruled by their own black leaders. British East Africa, however, presented a different picture. Here, small but influential minorities of European settlers feared the government of native Africans and insisted on retaining their privileges. They had a model of stubbornness in the Union of South Africa, which pursued an unyielding policy of white dominance and strict separation of the races.

From 1952 to 1956, the East African colony of Kenya was torn by bitter racial strife. In protest against the whites' monopoly of the best highland farming country, the secret society of the Mau Mau swore to drive them out by a campaign of systematic terror. Here, as in Malaya, the British could see no alternative to a stern campaign of repression. Once the Mau Mau were beaten, however, the British turned almost immediately to

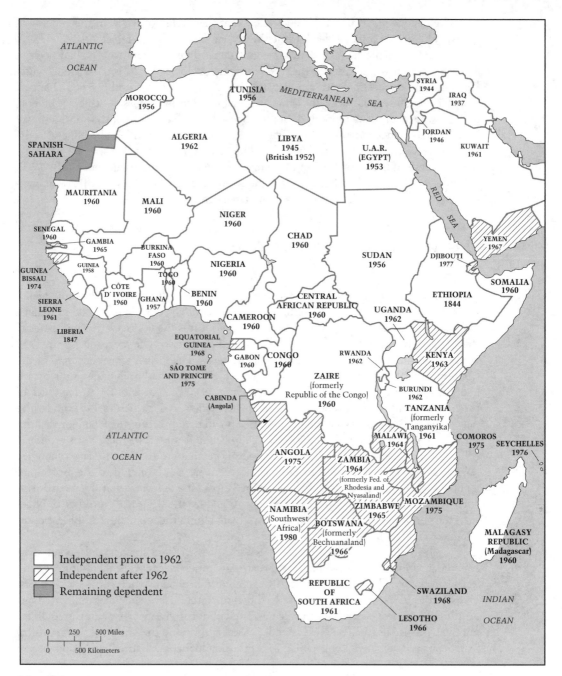

MAP 18.2 Former European colonies in Africa; the date after the name of each country refers to the year when it became independent.

conciliation. The liberation of British East Africa came a few years later than that of the west coast colonies, but the result was much the same. By the mid-1960s, not only had Kenya become independent but also its neighbor Uganda and the former territories of Tanganyika, Nyasaland, and Northern Rhodesia, which took the new names of Tanzania, Malawi, and Zambia. In the early stages of this process there had been talk of multiracial government—as opposed to the rule of the whites in South Africa, on the one hand, and on the other, to the West African formula of an all-black nation. This proved impracticable. Those Europeans who chose to remain in the new East African states did so at their own risk and as merely tolerated partners in an economic development geared to the needs of the black majority.

The one exception was Rhodesia (formerly Southern Rhodesia), where the whites were numerous and resolved to maintain their racial supremacy. In 1965, after having rejected a settlement worked out in London that would have extended representation to the blacks by gradual stages, Rhodesia declared its independence, staving off a series of half-hearted British efforts to bring it to heel, until a domestic black resistance movement finally compelled whites to share power in the nation—newly renamed Zimbabwe—in 1980.

French North Africa and the Algerian War

French postwar policy in Africa made a bad beginning, with the repression of two native revolts—a local one in Algeria in 1945 and a far more widespread and serious insurrection on the island of Madagascar two years later. In both cases, the revolts were put down with a brutality that effectively discouraged any further such attempts for another decade. In Algeria, as in Madagascar, the French were extraordinarily successful in keeping news of their operations from the Western press.

France's real difficulties began with the independence of the former Italian colony of Libya in 1951. For the freeing of Libya—the most backward of the five Arab countries on the southern shore of the Mediterranean—not only drew attention to the vestiges of British control in Egypt; it also, and rather more seriously, underlined the dependent position of France's three North African territories—Tunisia, Algeria, and Morocco.

These were the only areas of the continent comparable to South Africa in the extent of their European settlement. There were about 200,000 Europeans in Tunisia, 300,000 in Morocco, and one million—of whom roughly half were of French origin—in Algeria. Of these, the settlers in Tunisia and Morocco created the less serious problem. Besides being fewer in number than the Europeans of Algeria, they had been established on the land for a shorter period, and they were living in a society that even the French recognized as predominantly Moslem in character. Tunisia and Morocco were formally not colonies at all; they were protectorates, still in theory subject to their traditional native rulers, and both had well-organized nationalist movements under leaders who were moderate in temper and oriented toward the West—in Tunisia, the forceful orator Habib Bourguiba, and in Morocco, Sultan Mohammed ben Youssef. On March 2, 1956, Morocco severed its ties with France. Tunisia logically had to follow; later the same month it too achieved nationhood.

The French were ready for a rapid settlement with Tunisia and Morocco, partly because a major insurrection had recently broken out in Algeria, the territory that lay between them. Algeria was far more precious and important to France than were its neighbors. It was the chief area of French settlement overseas; indeed, in theory it was not a colony but an integral part of France. It had operated on a double standard of citizenship, however; both in its economy and in its administration, the European settlers were all-powerful, and these, like the whites of South Africa, regarded themselves as having at least as much right to the country as the native population. Many of them had lived there for three or four generations and considered Algeria rather than France to be their homeland.

When revolt broke out in the autumn of 1954—less than four months after the end of the war in Indochina—the French were in no mood to negotiate with the rebels. Their humiliation at Dien Bien Phu rendered them determined not to yield again. They decided for military repression, and this remained their basic policy for the rest of the decade. The last governments of the Fourth Republic tacked and veered in their attitude toward Algeria; a move toward negotiation was invariably followed by a renewed resort to military action. Whatever the hesitations of the ministries at home, the French in Algeria never wavered—the army and the settlers agreed that the only possible policy was resistance to the last. In one sense, they were right. The negotiation of a solution for Algeria was like trying to square the circle. The rebels in the hills insisted on independence; the local French knew that this would result in a Moslem-ruled country and the end of their privileges. It was not clear how much of the Moslem population actually backed the rebels—the latter did not hesitate to murder and terrorize natives who refused to accept their leadership—but it was quite evident that between the French position and that of the Algerian nationalists there was no middle ground.

Under these circumstances, it soon became apparent that the war in Algeria would be still costlier and more cruel than the struggle for Indochina. Indeed it lasted longer, absorbed far more manpower, and undermined even more disastrously the nation's strength and self-confidence. By 1956, the French had 400,000 troops in Algeria, including the young conscripts who had never gone to Indochina; almost all the divisions assigned to NATO were eventually drained off to service in North Africa. The war these soldiers were called on to fight was a merciless struggle in which the French replied to the cruelty of their adversaries by the use of physical torture in the interrogation of prisoners. Countless young Frenchmen were revolted by what they were forced to witness or participate in; at home the consciences of the intellectuals and the clergy were deeply troubled. The government found no better way to deal with its critics than by resorting to arbitrary arrests and sporadic censorship of the press.

After nearly four years of inconclusive warfare, the long-awaited explosion came. The impasse in Algeria precipitated the fall of the Fourth French Republic and the establishment in its place of a new and more authoritarian regime under General de Gaulle. But even the prestigious general was unable to reach a quick solution. In view of the profound divisions in French opinion at home, it took him nearly four more years to come to an Algerian settlement. The war had dragged on for the better part of a decade when it was finally brought to an end—and on the Moslem rebels' maximum terms. In mid-1962, Algeria became an independent Moslem nation. After a desperate last-ditch uprising against the inevitable in the cities of Algiers and Oran, about three-quarters of the European population of Algeria chose to "return" to France—if such a term could properly be applied to the migration of hundreds of thousands of people who had never before in their lives seen Europe (see Chapters 19, II and 20, III).

The French "Community" in Black Africa

South of the Sahara, as if to balance their stubbornness in Algeria, the French pursued a far more conciliatory policy. Indeed, for a year or two they seemed almost to be outstripping the British in their concessions to the black populations of West Africa. First came the enactment of a "framework law" in 1956—which ranked as the only substantial achievement of the Fourth Republic's last phase—granting representative institutions to the twelve West African territories under French rule and to the island of Madagascar. Two years later France made the greatest leap in its history of imperial policy. In the referendum on the new Gaullist constitution, the colonies were given the option of voting either for independence or for the status of an autonomous republic in the "Community" that was to replace the French Empire. Only one—the small territory of Guinea—chose independence. The rest were satisfied with autonomy in the framework of the Community.

Within two years, however, the Community itself was proving to be only a transition phase. By the end of 1960, all the new African republics had successfully negotiated their independence from France, and all but one had become members of the United Nations. Of the seventeen states admitted in that year, eleven were former French African colonies. Earlier, a number of the local leaders had discussed West African federation into larger units, but in the end the planned federations either broke down or failed to gain significant powers. As a result, several of the new nations found themselves too weak and sparsely populated to function successfully as independent entities.

Thus the French Community experienced a paradoxical fate. From a juridical standpoint, its former constituent parts had less cohesion and less recognition as an international entity than the nations of the Commonwealth. In practical terms, however, most of the former French colonies remained more dependent on the old mother country than did the territories liberated by the British. Their weakness made continuing European aid a necessity of life, and the French were more generous than the British in supplying civil servants free of charge and in extending economic assistance. Indeed, in the 1960s, France ranked second only to the United States in the aid it gave to the underdeveloped world. Moreover, the continued use of the French language in the administration and the educational systems of the new nations contributed more prestige to the home country than did the prevalence of English elsewhere in Africa; for French was the preserve of France alone, whereas English was rapidly becoming an international language not necessarily associated with the British tradition. Thus the African nations "of French expression," as they termed their cultural affiliation, looked more frequently to France for guidance than their English-speaking counterparts did to Great Britain. Most of them voted with France in the United Nations and lined up on the conservative side in the informal division of African states between the moderates and those oriented to the left.

However favorable such a situation might be for the maintenance of French influence, the proliferation of new sovereign states—the "Balkanization" of the African

Jubilant marchers celebrate Algeria's official independence from French rule on July 3, 1962, in the streets of Algiers. *(Courtesy AP/Wide World Photos)*

continent—was of questionable benefit to the Africans themselves. In these unprecedented circumstances, the term *nation* lost its old meaning. Boundaries followed the lines of European conquest rather than of tribal divisions, and what national consciousness existed was largely confined to the narrow circles of the educated elite that monopolized political life. Indeed, a few of the states seemed to depend on little more than the personality of a single political leader to whom they offered a political base. At the same time, old tribal hatreds were constantly threatening to erupt into murderous violence. Friendly observers agreed that Africa needed larger and more logical national groupings, but no one knew how to go about redrawing the map of the continent.

The Independence of the Congo;
The Portuguese Possessions

In the climactic year 1960, the former German colonies and French trust territories of Cameroon and Togo also became independent, as did the former Italian colony of Somalia. But the most dramatic and unexpected event of the year was the sudden decision of the Belgian government to liberate the Congo. By none of the usual criteria of nationhood was the Congo ready for independence. Its educated elite was very small, its nationalist movement of recent origin, and it was still riven by tribal antagonisms that threatened to tear the new state apart even before its foundation. But the example of the neighboring French colonies had suddenly galvanized into life its latent hostility to European rule. After the Congo capital had been shaken by nationalist riots in early 1959, the Belgians decided that a gradual approach was no longer possible. They decreed the election of a parliament and the proclamation of independence for June of the next year.

The result was chaos. As the Belgians began to depart, the native Congolese army mutinied and the new government proved unable to enforce its authority. At one point there were three different Congolese leaders competing for authority—and autonomist regimes in two of the Congo states. It took the rest of the decade for a relatively stable government to come into being.

Beyond the perennial danger of an explosion in the heart of Africa loomed the whole question of the southern third of the continent, rich in minerals, where European influence was still far from being a spent force. Here Rhodesia and the Union of South Africa remained as bastions of white domination. And here the Portuguese colonies of Angola and Mozambique continued as relics of an earlier era. These were special cases in a number of respects. They were ruled by an authoritarian nation rather than by a democracy; hence, the gap between the practice of government in the colonies and at home did not loom as large as in a state with free institutions. The almost total absence of racial discrimination among the Portuguese, coupled with the unusually strong influence of the Catholic church, had accustomed the natives to a sleepy paternalism. Finally, the Union of South Africa, which favored the status quo in Angola and Mozambique as a buffer against the spread of African nationalism, encouraged Portugal in its retrograde course. But even here the independence of the neighboring Congo had an unsettling effect. In 1961, a revolt broke out in Angola that eventually spread to Mozambique, obliging the Portuguese government to promise local reform and to maintain 80,000 troops in its African dominions. Old-fashioned colonial rule in the Portuguese territories was to persist thirteen years longer until independence was achieved in 1974, but its twilight had already begun.

IV. THE EFFECTS IN EUROPE

By the 1960s, the Europeans faced the prospect of retiring within the old frontiers from which they had set forth so bravely 500 years before. It was a vast change for the nations of Western Europe, and one to which many people, particularly of the older generation, found it extremely difficult to adjust. For commercial companies and the national economy as a whole, it frequently meant the loss of precious overseas investments. For individuals and corporate groups, such as colonial administrators, financial middlemen, and army officers, it entailed a severe diminution of prestige and income. In addition, there were the settlers and planters who found themselves no longer welcome in the new nations and who returned by the tens of thousands to their unfamiliar home countries. Before 1960, these settlers came mostly from the Netherlands Indies and the former French protectorates of Tunisia and Morocco; they returned embittered by their losses, filling the ears of their fellow citizens with the tale of their grievances. Those Europeans unwillingly repatriated from the colonies swelled the ranks of the remaining imperialists at home, urging them on to make a final, stubborn stand against the tide of Asian and African nationalism.

The Last Stand of Imperialism: The Suez Expedition

Thus the loss of the colonies brought a temporary reinforcement to the nationalist Right. In France, the two hopeless imperial struggles that between them spanned virtually the entire postwar era—the Indochinese war and the Algerian insurrection—reduced the army to a state of intense frustration. It felt betrayed by the politicians at home, who had given it inadequate support, and it again resolved to accept no more defeats.

In Britain, the imperialists were concentrated in the Conservative party and had considerable influence on the new prime minister, Anthony Eden, who in the spring of 1955 took over from the eighty-year-old Churchill. The Conservatives faithfully carried out their pledge of the year before to evacuate the Suez Canal, but they were outraged when the Egyptian nationalist leader, Gamal Abdel Nasser, seized possession of the canal itself from its European stockholders. They resolved to punish Nasser and to check the spread of extremist nationalism throughout the Arab world. The French were glad to co-operate in a joint venture. They knew that Egypt was giving both moral and material help to the Algerian insurrection, and they hoped that by cutting off the insurgents' source of supplies, they could begin to reduce them to terms.

On November 5, 1956, a British and French parachute attack swooped down on the Suez Canal. The expeditionary force suffered minimal casualties, and it seemed that nothing could stop its march on Cairo. But in the meantime, worldwide indignation was gathering. The British and French had allowed the best occasion for intervention slip by. They had failed to act in September, when irritation against Nasser's move had been nearly universal, but had waited until midautumn, when the canal was functioning normally again, and Western European ships were passing freely. What had triggered the British and French action had been secret information that the Israeli government was planning its own attack on the Sinai Peninsula.

Even then, however, Eden and his associates across the Channel let precious days pass. On October 29, the Israeli invasion began. Two days later the Anglo-French air force went into action against the canal. Nearly a week more passed before the parachute landings came. The date of the attack itself—one day before the presidential election in the United States—seemed a little too cleverly calculated to take advantage of a temporary paralysis in American policy. Meanwhile, the Soviet Union had sent an ultimatum calling on France, Britain, and Israel to desist from the attack.

Faced by complete lack of support from the United States and by the condemnation of a crushing majority in the United Nations, Eden and his French partners were

Large areas of Port Said, Egypt, were destroyed by the air and sea bombardment that accompanied the Anglo-French invasion of November 14, 1956. (*Courtesy Corbis-Bettmann*)

obliged to retreat. A special United Nations police force replaced the Anglo-French expeditionary command in the canal zone. By the end of December, the final contingents of the invasion army had sailed for home.

The Suez Expedition was the last stand of old-fashioned imperialism. It surprised its own sponsors by the vehement reaction it provoked, creating overnight a solid front of opposition among the Asian and African nations. Suez showed that never again could Europeans coerce "natives" in the old manner. But the Suez incident was an episode, rather than a genuine reversal, in the process of freeing the colonies. Once its lesson had been digested, the course of liberation was resumed, and at a still swifter tempo.

The Economic Consequences: Oil and Prosperity

Even from Asia, however, the Europeans had not completely withdrawn their influence. The chief remaining area of imperial control was the Persian Gulf, where Britain still "protected" a number of sheikdoms with fabulously rich sources of oil. By the 1960s, oil represented the last great overseas investment of the Europeans, but even here conditions were slowly changing. Italy, which had been despoiled of its colonies, was successfully undercutting the established oil-exploiting nations by offering Middle Eastern governments far more favorable terms. The time was not far off when native rulers would be masters in their own lands again, and in control of oil resources.

Most Europeans believed that the continued exploitation of oil in the Middle East was essential to their prosperity. But economists were beginning to doubt this and advanced the persuasive argument that the enormous profits of European oil companies in Asia did not really benefit the economies at home, since they merely represented a higher price charged to the consumer. This, in broader terms, was true of colonial exploitation as a whole. *Under contemporary conditions*, it enriched the small group of Europeans with investments or well-paid positions overseas while scarcely affecting at all the majority of the home population. In fact, it was beginning to be apparent that colonies no longer even paid for themselves; they were a drain on the European nations rather than a source of profit. The most telling case in point was the contrast between France and Germany: France, which had tried to retain its colonies, had lagged behind in economic progress; Germany, which had lost its colonies a generation earlier, had experienced a great industrial boom. By 1953, when Europe as a whole entered on a period of general prosperity, it was becoming obvious that the end of empire was a source of benefit rather than of loss to the economic expansion and social welfare of the old Continent.

READINGS

The most useful general introduction to the subject of colonial liberation remains Rudolf von Albertini, *Decolonization: The Administration and Future of the Colonies, 1919–1960** (1971, reprint ed. 1982). Franz Ansprenger's *The Dissolution of the Colonial Empires** (1989) is comprehensive but uneven. On Britain's lengthy process of disengagement from its imperial role, see John Darwin, *Britain and Decolonisation: The Retreat from Empire in the Postwar World** (1988), and Wm. Roger Lewis, "The Dissolution of the British Empire," in Judith M. Brown and Wm. Roger Louis, eds., *The Oxford History of the British Empire*, vol. 2: *The Twentieth Century** (1999). Raymond F. Betts, *Uncertain Dimension: Western Overseas Empires in the Twentieth Century** (1985), offers important background on the developments preceding decolonization. See also A. J. Stockwell, "Southeast Asia in War and Peace: The End of European Colonial Empires," in Nicholas Tarling, ed., *The Cambridge History of Southeast Asia*, vol. 2 (1992). For a critique of the colonialist mentality, see Edward Said, *Culture and Imperialism* (1993), as well as D. Mannoni, *Prospero and Caliban: The Psychology of Colonization** (1956). Said's thesis that racism fueled colonialist policies is challenged in David Cannadine, *Ornamentalism: How the British Saw Their Empire* (2001), which argues that class prejudice united British imperialists with the elites of the lands they colonized. Thomas R. Metcalf, *Ideologies of the Raj** (1995) ex-

*Books available in paperback are marked with an asterisk.

plores the shifting concepts of identity and difference through which the British attempted to justify their presence in India and defend colonialism.

On Britain's subsequent retreat from India and the Indian drive for independence see John Gallagher, *The Decline, Revival, and Fall of the British Empire* (1982); A. Seal, *The Emergence of Indian Nationalism* (1968); and Erik Erikson, *Gandhi's Truth: On the Origins of Militant Nonviolence** (1969). Also of interest is Mahatma Gandhi's *Autobiography: The Story of My Experiments with Truth* (1948).

The French experience in Indochina is chronicled in John T. McAlister's *Viet Nam: The Origins of Revolution* (1969), and Bernard Fall's *Street Without Joy: Indochina at War, 1946–1954*, 4th ed. (1964). Fall narrates the course of the climactic battle in the Indochina conflict in *Hell Is a Very Small Place: The Siege of Dien Bien Phu* (1967). For the Algerian War, see Alistair Horne's *A Savage War of Peace: Algeria, 1954–1962** (1977), and John Talbott's *The War Without a Name: France in Algeria, 1954–1962* (1980). On the important question of how politicians and the public reacted at home to these events, see Miles Kahler's *Decolonization in Britain and France: The Domestic Consequences of International Relations* (1984).

On the emerging nations of Black Africa, an overview of changing colonial relations may be found in Prosser Gifford and William Woger Louis, eds., *The Transfer of Power in Africa* (1982). Basil Davidson, *The Black Man's Burden: Africa and the Curse of the Nation-State** (1992), argues that African nationalists sought to secure liberation from colonial rule by creating nation-states on the European model, with disastrous results. Edward Mortimer's *France and the Africans, 1944–1960* (1969), and Richard Adloff's *West Africa: The French-Speaking Nations, Yesterday and Today* (1965), address the issue of France's continuing role in the region. Crawford Young, in *Politics in the Congo: Decolonization and Independence* (1965), discusses the shortcomings of Belgium's colonial policies; while John D. Hargreaves, in *The End of Colonial Rule in West Africa: Essays in Contemporary History* (1979), analyzes the more successful British attempts to cooperate with native elites. The British role in East Africa is examined in Crawford Pratt's *The Critical Phase in Tanzania, 1945–1968: Nyerere and the Emergence of a Socialist Strategy* (1976).

For a spirited, scholarly, and highly critical account of the Suez expedition, see Hugh Thomas, *The Suez Affair* (1966). Another excellent—and equally critical—treatment of the topic is Anthony Nutting, *No End of a Lesson: The Story of Suez* (1967).

A New Equilibrium,

1953–1960

Hungarian rebels defend a border post during the doomed uprising of October 1956. (*Courtesy Corbis-Bettmann*)

I. THE CHANGE IN THE INTERNATIONAL CLIMATE

The Relaxation of the Cold War

In the first eight months of the year 1953 there occurred four events whose joint effect was to reduce the international tensions that in the previous half decade had seemed to be mounting inexorably. Eisenhower replaced Truman in the U.S. presidency; Stalin died; the Korean War came to an end; and the Soviet Union announced that it had perfected a hydrogen bomb. Once more Europe reached a turning point such as it had experienced in 1947 with the beginning of the Cold War, and in 1950 with the outbreak of the conflict in Korea. The events of 1953 did not end the international struggle between East and West, but they notably changed its character, adding to the previous exclusive concentration on preparing for war an alternative vista of "peaceful coexistence." This was what the neutralist states, the dissident Communist regimes in Eastern Europe, and the Socialist opposition parties in the West all wanted—and with them the vast mass of inarticulate public sentiment on both sides of the ideological divide.

The advent of the Republicans to power in the United States meant the rule of a party that was more detached from European concerns than the Democrats had been. President Eisenhower and Secretary of State John Foster Dulles were less understanding and sympathetic with the Europeans than were Truman and Acheson—indeed, Dulles aroused hostility nearly everywhere—but the result was the beginning of a "salutary neglect" of Europe by the United States and a new feeling of independence on the part of the Europeans. With the departure of a U.S. administration that they had liked and trusted, European statesmen became more inclined to go their own way. They no longer deferred so readily, as in the past, to the wishes of their great ally across the Atlantic. By the late 1950s, it appeared that the postwar subordination of the old Continent to America was making way for greater European independence.

Moreover, Eisenhower and Dulles were able to accomplish what the Democrats could have managed only with the greatest difficulty—to make a compromise peace in Korea. The end of the Korean War in July eliminated the most serious single threat to the delicate international balance. It also meant that the U.S. master demagogue, Senator Joseph McCarthy of Wisconsin, no longer enjoyed the vast unofficial power as self-appointed prosecutor of "traitors" that he had wielded during the years of the Korean conflict. With the coming of peace and the lifting of the national atmosphere of tension and frustration that had favored his rise, McCarthy began to lose influence; within another year his power had been completely broken. This also was reassuring to the Europeans, who had feared that McCarthy might be leading America to a new home-grown fascism.

Stalin's death brought to power in the Soviet Union younger leaders who were aiming at a "thaw" both in the international climate and in the dictatorship at home. In the succeeding years, this thaw progressed most unevenly. It was subject to sharp checks and reversals of course, particularly in the years 1956 and 1960. For Europe as a whole, however, the effects of the Soviet thaw were cumulative; by and large, the danger of war receded as the decade wore on. And—paradoxically enough—such also was the effect of the Soviet Union's announcement, in the very month following the Korean peace, that it possessed the secret of the hydrogen bomb. This did not make Europeans more nervous, as Russia's explosion of its first atomic bomb four years earlier had done. Rather it made them realize that the "balance of terror" was now complete—the United States no longer held a decisive lead in weapons, and the preservation of the peace had become more urgent than ever.

The Failure of EDC and the "Summit" Meeting of 1955

It was in this atmosphere of relaxed tension that in August 1954 the French National Assembly, after more than two years' delay, finally voted on the treaty establishing the six-nation European Defense Community. Nearly everything had changed since the treaty was signed; the wartime urgency that had originally stimulated it had now passed. The Korean War was over, and only the month before, Prime Minister Mendès-France had brought to an end the eight-year struggle in Indochina. The cause of EDC had become hopeless: Mendès-France simply laid it before the Assembly and without expressing his own opinion allowed the treaty to go down to defeat.

Next autumn the Western European powers contrived a substitute. Exhuming an almost forgotten five-nation treaty that had been signed in Brussels in 1948, they added Italy as well as Germany to the signatories—thereby reassuring the French, who felt they needed reinforcement against German influence in an international military force. The new treaty of 1954 did not organize an international army on the model of the EDC; it merely established within the framework of NATO—which Western Germany had joined in 1952—an inner circle to serve as a holding company for the German military contribution. Indeed, German rearmament materialized after the great pressure for it had already passed. Germany entered NATO just at the time the organization itself was beginning a long process of reexamining its basic assumptions. With the nuclear arsenal of both superpowers still growing, the old concept of a defense of the West by conventional ground divisions seemed obsolete, but the strategic substitute for it was far from clear.

The summer following the defeat of EDC saw the decade's most dramatic display of the new international atmosphere—the meeting at Geneva of the "Big Four." This "summit" meeting reached no tangible decisions, but it was the first time since the Potsdam Conference of ten years before that the leaders of the United States and the Soviet Union had come together. To Europeans, the mere fact that President Eisenhower and the new master of Russia, Nikita Khrushchev, had actually spoken with each other in an amicable fashion seemed to give a tenuous guarantee of peace. It was widely believed that the two leaders of the supernations had exchanged tacit pledges that as long as they were in power, the Cold War would not be pushed to a final decision.

Hence in the mid-1950s Europe began to turn in on itself and to occupy itself with its own concerns. In 1953 and 1954, the economic boom, which previously had been restricted to Germany, spread to Britain, France, and Italy. This in itself was a powerful incentive for concentrating energies at home. Another was the loss of colonial empire. Except for France and Britain's desperate gamble at Suez and the running sore of the conflict in Algeria, the main trend of the decade was toward liquidating overseas commitments. The thaw in the East, moreover, was at last making possible a limited amount of cultural exchange between the Communist and the Western democratic world. This also strengthened the notion of Europe for Europeans—raising the hope that the sorely tried Continent, which had been torn by two fratricidal wars and a postwar ideological split that was very nearly as bitter, might finally recover its old cultural unity and with it its old self-confidence.

II. CONSERVATIVE DEMOCRACY IN THE WEST

In Western Europe, the years from 1953 to 1960 saw a reinforcement of the previous trend toward conservative government. By the end of the decade, the Socialist opposition parties were weaker than they had been for nearly a generation, and they were beginning to wonder whether they would ever again win a major election. Hence the dominance of the conservatives was far from being an unqualified benefit to Western European democracy. It suggested stability, it was true, and it expressed the satisfaction of material prosperity, but this satisfaction also meant complacency and absorption with private concerns. It carried one step further the public apathy and the drift away from political interests that had already begun to characterize the late 1940s. At the end of the 1950s, both Germany and France were living under "father figures" who lulled the electorate into a sense of security by keeping controversial issues from public discussion—in Germany, Konrad Adenauer, whose more than ten years of rule had profoundly altered the original intentions of the constitution makers at Bonn; in France, Charles de Gaulle, whose return to power had ended one French republic and installed another.

Britain: The Churchill, Eden, and Macmillan Governments

The return of the British Conservatives to power at the end of 1951 did not mean abandonment of Labour's postwar reforms. On the contrary, the Tories were emphatic in their claim to being a conservative party that was fully abreast of the times, and their chief spokesman for domestic affairs, R. A. Butler, proudly asserted: "The Welfare State is as much our creation as it is that of the Socialists." Gone were the days of a narrow businessman's party led by men like Baldwin and Chamberlain. In returning British Conservatism to the leadership of aristocrats, Churchill had broadened rather than narrowed its base, restoring its feeling for the interests of all classes of the population.

As prime minister from 1951 to 1955, Churchill limited himself to ending Labour's nationalization of steel and of inland transport and to reducing the expenses of the National Health Service by instituting a few relatively minor fees. In short, he and his colleagues behaved like responsible conservatives, rather than reactionaries, in accepting the great change that had gone before, while lopping off its more extreme features and improving its administration. They won back the confidence of the middle-class citizens who had deserted them in 1945 by ending the "austerity" and the war-born controls over economic life that Labour had prolonged beyond their period of maximum usefulness.

This return of the middle-class electorate to the Conservatives became amply apparent in the sudden and unexpected parliamentary election held in May 1955. The Conservatives returned 345 members of parliament to 277 for Labour, thereby securing a comfortable majority for the next half decade. Within less than eighteen months, however, they involved themselves in a major crisis. The Suez Expedition of November 1956 brought down upon Eden not only the condemnation of a majority within the United Nations but also the vehement opposition of the British Labour party. As the storm broke over his head, Eden's health collapsed; his failure at Suez ended his prime ministership, and he was obliged to give way to another protégé of Churchill, Harold Macmillan.

Macmillan, who was not an aristocrat like Churchill and Eden but the heir of a Scottish publishing family with strong American ties, was exactly the leader the Tories' embarrassing situation demanded. Astute, tactful, calm in crisis—"unflappable," as his admirers called him—and possessing the confidence of all wings of the Conservative party, he was able to soothe the feelings of the die-hard imperialists, who were outraged by the withdrawal of the expeditionary force from Suez, while at the same time assuring the outside world and the moderate majority among his followers that he would embark on no more such adventures. In short, Macmillan healed the wounds of Suez in an astonishingly brief time and restored the Conservatives' unity and self-confidence for the political battles that lay ahead.

Within three years they were ready once more to risk an early election. This time they succeeded even more brilliantly than in 1955. In the election of October 1959, Labour was totally overwhelmed; the Conservatives increased their majority once again, scoring their greatest popular triumph since their landslide victory of 1935. For the Labour party, the electoral results came as a shattering blow. It was the third successive election in which they had been beaten, and the fourth in which they had lost seats—a situation almost without precedent in British parliamentary history.

Labour's 1959 defeat precipitated a major battle within the party. It called into question the moderate attitude of Hugh Gaitskell—who had replaced Clement Attlee as party leader after the 1955 election—which had reduced the traditional emphasis on nationalization and other socialist measures and differed only in detail from the Conservative foreign policy of reliance on the United States and nuclear deterrence. Labour's left wing was weakened by the death of its leader, Aneurin Bevan. Bevan's followers, however, were growing increasingly militant. In the course of the year 1960, there began to gather a ground swell of protest against Gaitskell's "me-too" political strategy, coupled with vociferous demands for Britain's renunciation of nuclear weapons.

Germany: The Adenauer System

In Western Germany also, the party in power reinforced its control in the late 1950s. Chancellor Adenauer's Christian Democrats—whose basic conservatism was by now quite apparent—in the election of 1957 once more increased their vote, receiving for the first time a clear popular majority. Like the Tories in Britain, German Christian Democracy had won three successive elections, each time raising its percentage of the national total.

Defeated in 1949 and 1953, and now once again in 1957, the Social Democratic opposition in Germany confronted the same necessity of reexamining its position as faced the British Labour party. The internal criticism within German Socialism concentrated on the routine leadership of Erich Ollenhauer, who had succeeded Schumacher on the latter's death in 1952, and on the party's tendency to continue its mechanical repetition of outworn Marxist slogans. In its new program voted in November 1959, the party all but discarded its Marxist inheritance, reducing its emphasis on nationalization, accepting the remilitarization of the country, and renouncing the notion of class warfare as the basis of Social Democratic policy. The following year, the dynamic young mayor of West Berlin, Willy Brandt, replaced Ollenhauer as the party's official candidate for the chancellorship.

The Christian Democratic victories of 1953 and 1957 were endorsements of the laissez-faire economic policy of the minister of economics, Ludwig Erhard, whose corpulent joviality expressed to perfection the joys of material prosperity. Their electoral triumphs also amounted to personal plebiscites on the rule of the old chancellor. On passing his eightieth birthday, Adenauer did not retire, as Churchill had done. He continued to govern and to tower over his ministerial colleagues by his long experience, his indomitable will, and his vast prestige both at home and abroad. Not since Bismarck had a single individual so completely dominated a free German society.

Adenauer's long rule began to alter profoundly the workings of the Bonn constitution. In place of a true parliamentary or cabinet system, it substituted the government of one outstanding personality who reduced the ministers to clerks and the opposition to impotent frustration. In this situation, the Bundestag became less and less important; the realities of power in Germany were increasingly concentrated in the hands of a bureaucracy responsible in the final reckoning to the chancellor alone.

Meanwhile, Germany continued to be divided between East and West. As long as this was true, foreign policy necessarily dominated public discussion. In the diplomatic realm, Chancellor Adenauer—reinforced by the success of his party's policy at home— operated virtually as he chose. Like almost all other Germans, Adenauer refused to accept the partition of his country, but his attitude toward the Communist regime in Eastern Germany was so uncompromising that in effect it prolonged the East-West split. By insisting on free elections throughout the country—a position that the East German government and its Soviet sponsors could not possibly accept—the West German chancellor blocked any negotiated solution.

Italy: Christian Democracy in Flux

In Italy, as in Germany, the Christian Democrats maintained themselves in power throughout the 1950s and, as with the German party, their basic conservatism generally increased. But the Italian situation lacked the stability of the German. There was no unquestioned national leader. After De Gasperi's retirement in 1953, no single dominating figure emerged from the Christian Democrats' ranks. Furthermore, Christian Democracy was unable to regain the majority position in the Chamber of Deputies that it had temporarily won in the dramatic electoral battle of 1948. Ten years later, it reconquered some of the ground lost in 1953, but the election of 1958 still left the party obliged to find parliamentary allies to ensure its tenure of power.

The leader of West Germany during the first two postwar decades—Konrad Adenauer (1876–1967). (*Courtesy AP/Wide World Photos*)

Thus Italy was in the paradoxical position of having a single party that was far stronger than all its rivals and alone able to supply a prime minister, but that at the same time was too weak to govern by itself and was profoundly divided by internal factionalism. In the seven years following De Gasperi's retirement, six prime ministers followed each other in office at approximately yearly intervals. They came from the left, the right, and the center of Christian Democracy's ranks. Sometimes they tried to govern in alliance with the smaller democratic parties, as De Gasperi had usually done; more often they acted alone as a single-party ministry dependent on the benevolence of a Chamber of Deputies in which they lacked a majority but which could not unite to elect an alternative government that excluded the Christian Democrats. They experimented with all possible formulas of government and succeeded with none; no ministry lasted as long as two years.

The result was a situation of permanent flux underlying the apparent stability provided by the continued rule of the same party. As the 1950s wore on, Italian political life became increasingly concentrated within the confines of Christian Democracy itself. The real decisions in Italian politics were made, not in the public competition among the parties, but in the private factional squabbles of the governing group. These factions were legion. Two attitudes, however, dominated the rest, and Christian Democracy would eventually be forced to make a choice between them. The most dynamic figure within the party, Amintore Fanfani, argued for an "opening to the Left" and a reinvigoration of social and economic reform. This viewpoint took on added cogency in the autumn of 1956, when—as a result of vast disturbances in Eastern Europe—Pietro Nenni led his Socialist party away from its alliance with communism.

Christian Democracy's powerful backers, both in economic life and in the church, effectively vetoed Fanfani's idea of an "opening to the Left." Instead they favored the other major tendency within the party, that of the Christian Democratic right wing. In the late 1950s, the winds of change were already blowing strongly through Italian political life, but the ruling party was still standing firmly against them. It was becoming ever more clerical and obscurantist, and it had almost forgotten its original goal of combining Christian values with moderate reform and a sturdy insistence on its independence from external direction of all sorts.

France: The Decay of the Fourth Republic; Mendès-France and Mollet

While parliamentary conservatism was consolidating its position in Britain, West Germany, and Italy, in France the parliamentary system itself was going into a steady decline. The four years of the decay of the Fourth Republic, from mid-1945 to mid-1958, opened with one great crisis of confidence and closed with another. Between lay two abortive efforts at revival.

The fall of Dien Bien Phu and the collapse of the French position in Indochina in 1954 inaugurated France's time of troubles. But it also brought to power Pierre Mendès-France, a statesman who had the courage to face at last the major international and colonial issues whose constant postponement had been poisoning the country's political life. The new prime minister liquidated the war in Asia and the EDC, and he began the process of conciliation with the North African protectorates; yet his real concern was not for foreign affairs at all, but for France's domestic welfare. His great goal was to modernize the French economy, to lift its retrograde sectors in agriculture and small industry to the level attained by the more advanced of the country's enterprises in the postwar years. The irony of Mendès-France's prime ministry was that during six of his seven months in office he was compelled to concentrate on diplomatic and imperial concerns that he believed to be secondary; he had scarcely turned his attention to his plans for economic modernization, when a motley coalition of his enemies—who hated him as a reformer, a Jew, and the "gravedigger" of the Empire and the EDC—brought him down.

With the fall of Mendès-France in February 1955, French politics returned to the old game of compromise and delay, as the Moslem revolt in Algeria widened its scope. Parliamentary elections were due the following year, however, and these provided an opportunity for a second attempt to revive the country's energies. The joint campaign conducted by Mendès-France and the Socialist leader, Guy Mollet, had something in it of the old Resistance spirit of social and moral reinvigoration on the democratic Left; it promised both reform at home and peace in Algeria.

In the election of January 1956, this left-center coalition made the greatest gains. Hence it was logical that it be asked to form the government and that Guy Mollet, as the leader of the largest group within it, should become prime minister, with Mendès-France as his deputy. But the Mollet ministry proved itself unable either to revive the democratic Left or to carry out the program on which its supporters had campaigned. It had scarcely been installed in office when it was overwhelmed by reactionary pressure. On the one hand, a new party of authoritarian rowdies—a protest party of small tradesmen and peasants led by the demagogue Pierre Poujade, which had surprised everyone by electing more than fifty deputies—kept the Assembly in an uproar by its incessant tumult and obstruction. At the same time, the Algerian French resolved to block all plans for conciliation with the rebels. When the new prime minister visited Algiers in February, he was greeted by catcalls and rotten fruit from an angry mob; appalled by his experience, Mollet quickly abandoned the notion of a new departure in Algerian policy.

For the next fifteen months, then, France witnessed the extraordinary spectacle of a Socialist prime minister conducting a colonial war of repression. The Right was satisfied to have Mollet stay in office; it was far more convenient to allow the democratic Left to bear the onus of a reactionary policy rather than to apply that policy themselves. But in the spring of 1957, when the government finally took up the task of revising the tax system in favor of the less prosperous classes, the conservatives decided that the time had come. They overthrew Mollet—and with him the last ministry of the Fourth Republic worthy of the name.

The last year of the regime was merely a long death agony. Mollet's two successors were young men of promise but little stature, who were chosen because neither had yet had time to offend anyone and because the more experienced statesmen were reluctant to accept the post. After eight months of walking a tightrope at home and trying to combine military action with half-hearted efforts at reform in Algeria, the government finally blundered into a major crisis. In February 1958, a local commander, acting (in the now familiar pattern) on his own authority, bombed the Tunisian frontier town of Sakhiet, which was serving as a protected base for the Algerian insurgents. Once again, as at the time of the Suez incident, the Asians and Africans within the United Nations set up a great cry of indignation. The United States and Britain, in order to save something from the debacle, tried to serve as mediators between the French and the outraged Tunisians, but the Anglo-American "good offices" wounded the susceptibilities of the French Right.

On May 13, a loose coalition of semifascist groups, acting in understanding with the local French army command, seized control of the Algerian administration. Two years before, when Mollet had bowed to mob pressure, the Fourth Republic had suffered a shock from which it never recovered. The far more serious demonstration of May 1958 finally killed it.

France: De Gaulle and the Fifth Republic

The insurrection of May 13 installed in power in Algiers a new and revolutionary authority in competition with the legal government in Paris. The North African "Committee of Public Safety" consisted of resolute and desperate men, both soldiers and civilians, who were determined to impose their own views on the home country. They wanted an authoritarian regime that would call a halt to the steady retreat from overseas dominion.

With the bulk of the French army in North Africa, the Algiers committee had the weight of military strength on its side. It also had many sympathizers in France, among conservatives and nationalists in general and the followers of de Gaulle and Poujade in particular. In contrast, the government in Paris felt its power slowly slipping away as the month of May wore on, and this steady retreat turned into a rout when it became known that General de Gaulle himself stood ready to form an alternative government.

De Gaulle's candidacy was not what the insurrectionists in Algiers had originally intended; they had hoped for somebody more fascist and less conciliatory toward colonial aspirations for freedom, but they had no particular champion in mind. The Gaullists, on the other hand, knew exactly what they wanted. Once de Gaulle's name was launched by the small group of faithful followers who had remained loyal to him, the idea quickly won favor. Indeed, it soon became apparent that a government headed by the general was the only possible solution. De Gaulle—the liberator of his country—was still the "first citizen of France." His military background and his authoritarian preferences were congenial to the nationalist Right; his Resistance record and his known distaste for the tactics of a coup d'état made him acceptable to most of the democratic Left. On June 1, the French National Assembly bowed to the inevitable and invested de Gaulle as prime minister.

The general's return to power after his twelve years of retirement was, in form, a completely constitutional procedure—but, in fact, it was a revolutionary change imposed by a determined minority on a divided and irresolute majority, and it was so interpreted by both the French people and their elected representatives. As a sign of the gravity of the change, the latter, before disbanding forever, voted full power to de Gaulle's government to rule France as it chose for a period of six months, and to draw up a new constitution for the "Fifth Republic."

By September, the constitution was ready. In a popular referendum, it was accepted by 80 percent of the French people with only the Communists and a tiny minority of doctrinaire democrats voting against it. Two months later, in elections for a National Assembly, the rightist parties won an overwhelming victory. A new and hastily formed Gaullist party, the Union for the New Republic, placed first; the old Independents of Pinay stood second; together these two secured almost three-quarters of the seats, while all the other parties were reduced to mere splinters. The Communists, handicapped by a new electoral system, fell to ten seats; the Poujadists simply disappeared.

The final act of establishing the new regime was the election of de Gaulle in December as president of the Republic by a specially chosen list of local "notables." The general's move from the prime ministry to what had formerly been a largely ceremonial office betokened the great change in the locus of power that the new constitution had effected. The Fifth Republic was not to be a strictly "presidential" regime like that of the United States. Its constitution provided for a hybrid organization—part presidential and part parliamentary—and it retained a prime minister, who was to be responsible to the Assembly, for the conduct of day-to-day business and for parliamentary liaison. But this Assembly had had its sessions shortened and its powers notably curbed. The weight of influence—which under the Third and Fourth Republics had fallen overwhelmingly toward the legislature—had been shifted to the executive branch and, within the executive, the final power of decision lay with the president rather than with the prime minister. Thus the Fifth Republic gradually established its character as the rule of a bureaucracy presided over by a prestigious figure into whose hands a much-tried and much-divided people had delivered its fate.

Rather than being recognizable as either a democracy or a dictatorship, the new regime in France began to assume an old-fashioned monarchical character. De Gaulle governed his country as a monarch—remote and benevolent at the same time—refusing to involve himself in the sordid details of politics and administration, but ready to intervene at any time to arbitrate differences among its citizens. It was in this role of national "arbiter" that de Gaulle preferred to regard his own office. He conceived it in such a way because he was interested above all in the "unity" of the people, and he insisted on the unity of the French because he believed that they had always been destined for "greatness"—which was the third of his trinity of central ideas. In pursuit of greatness for his country, de Gaulle sought a more independent French policy within the Western coalition. He protested against the favored position of Britain as the chief ally of the United States; he aligned himself with Chancellor Adenauer, whose position as a national leader in so many ways resembled de Gaulle's own; and early in the year 1960, he exploded an atomic bomb in the Sahara desert, thereby making France the fourth world power to have a nuclear capacity of its own.

Thus de Gaulle's regime presented a puzzling face to the outside world. On the one hand, it had efficiency and the modernization of the country for its objective, taking up the task of national renewal where Mendès-France had been forced to halt a half decade earlier. On the other hand, the regime looked back to the past—with its notion of "greatness" that recalled an age when the national state was unquestioned and when the French still had the population and resources to play a major role in world affairs. In the 1960s, such a view of the position of any one European nation had become something of an anachronism.

The Neutralist Fringe: Finland and Austria

Of the twelve democracies of Western Europe, all except Sweden and Switzerland were members of NATO and formed part of the loosely knit ideological coalition of the West. The latter two carried over into the period after 1945 the traditional neutrality they had preserved so successfully during both World Wars. Their cultural and ideological ties were completely Western, and in a more intangible sense than membership in NATO, they also could be counted with the Atlantic Pact nations. Two other democracies, however, which directly bordered on the Soviet sphere, were confined by necessity to a stricter form of neutrality.

The first was Finland. Despite the fact that they had twice been at war with the Soviet Union in the years from 1939 to 1944, the Finns succeeded in keeping free of Russian domination and even in maintaining reasonably cordial relations with their great neighbor in the postwar period. At the same time, they preserved their democratic institutions at home, gradually ousting the Communists from the positions of influence in the government and the economy that they had won at the war's end. To outsiders—viewing the fate of the other states of East Central Europe that had passed under the shadow of the Red Army—Finland's continued independence seemed a miracle. In fact, its explanation was comparatively simple. In their dealings with the Russians, the Finns proved themselves both tenacious of their liberty and punctilious in the fulfillment of their reparations and other obligations to the Soviet Union. For their part, the Russians were not sorry to have in the East a "show window" like Finland to display how tolerant they could be when they wished.

Austria was the second special case. In May 1955, after ten years of four-power occupation, the Austrians won their independence from foreign control. Under the terms of the "State Treaty" signed by representatives of Britain, France, the United States, and the Soviet Union, Austria became, as its neighbor Switzerland had been for generations, a nation whose neutrality was guaranteed by the Great Powers. Within the country, political life proceeded much as before. The government continued to be a coalition of the two major parties—the Catholic People's Party and the Socialists—with the former, which was slightly stronger than its rival, regularly providing the chancellor. The Austrian economy, moreover, which had been so unstable following the First World War, also began to prosper, for with the development of light industry, the country finally found a secure financial base.

III. THE IBERIAN DICTATORSHIPS

On the Iberian peninsula, authoritarian conservative regimes continued to exist after the defeat of fascism in the Second World War. Spain and Portugal were obviously not democracies, but in the rhetoric of the Cold War, Western propagandists counted them with the "free world." Portugal ranked as a member of NATO; Spain did not, for anti-Franco sentiment continued sufficiently strong in Britain and Scandinavia to keep the Spaniards from formal membership. But since Franco received military aid from the United States and permitted the establishment of American bases on his country's soil, Spain necessarily became a de facto partner in the Western coalition. Both here and in Portugal, an uncompromising hostility to communism was one of the major ideological supports on which the regime rested.

Salazar's Portugal

By the 1960s, Prime Minister Salazar had become the senior ruler of Europe. He had been in power for more than a generation, longer than any other such dictator in the Continent's history. Yet he remained very little discussed. Quiet, ascetic, scholarly, Salazar hated publicity, and he effectively kept his country out of major ideological controversy during the crucial decade after the war's end.

While maintaining the essentials of his authoritarian control, the Portuguese dictator tried to modify its appearance so as not to offend the sensibilities of his democratic allies. In speaking of their economic institutions, the Portuguese dropped the term *corporate state*—which had a fascist ring—and referred to their *new state* instead. At intervals, moreover, Salazar lifted the censorship of the press and authorized something that resembled a free election. In 1953, the opposition was able to contest municipal elections in the three largest cities, polling 20 percent of the vote, and again five years later there was a temporary relaxation of control for a presidential election campaign. But these sporadic acts of leniency scarcely changed the nature of the dictatorship. No real political life existed in Portugal. The regime had been in power so long that the political education of the people had never developed—its level was by far the lowest in Western Europe—and the opposition leaders had become elderly, cautious, and out of touch with their prospective constituents. Many were veterans of long jail terms, and occasionally one of them was sent back to prison after an unsuccessful electoral campaign. Still worse, in the spring of 1965 an opposition candidate for the Portuguese presidency was found murdered just across the Spanish frontier. Only the military—who in the early 1960s attempted three armed coups against the regime—could even remotely threaten Salazar's authority.

Portugal's greatest difficulties, however, were economic. Despite the stimulus of indirect state control over the economy through Salazar's corporative institutions, Portuguese industry and agriculture failed to keep pace with the country's needs. The rate of investment remained low—economic expansion was far from adequate to cope with the needs of the nation's population, whose growth was one of the most rapid in Western Europe. As the 1950s passed, poverty and undernourishment became appalling. Salazar was careful to keep the center of Lisbon neat and clean to impress tourists, but elsewhere conditions were so bad that the Catholic hierarchy itself sounded an alarm. In 1954, the archbishop of Beja issued a pastoral letter in which he denounced the growing poverty and the regime's callousness to the misery of its people.

Salazar finally decided that remedial steps were necessary. In 1955, he launched a five-year development plan. The initial results gave modest reason for encouragement. Portugal equipped itself with a steel industry, and the rate of economic growth began to average 5 percent a year—which, however, was still far from adequate for a country with about two-fifths of its working population underemployed. Then, just after a second five-year plan had been inaugurated, revolt broke out in the African territory of Angola. Military expenses quadrupled, cutting deeply into funds for economic growth. By the mid-1960s it had become apparent that Portugal's problems were all of a piece. Economic sluggishness, authoritarian rule at home, and repression overseas reinforced each other in the dubious legacy of nearly four decades of Salazar's paternalism.

Franco's Spain

In Spain, too, poverty was the central national problem, but Franco was less successful than his neighbor Salazar in keeping such matters from public discussion. Unlike Portugal, Spain was not a backwater protected from the main currents of European life. Its Civil War had made it of crucial interest both to Europeans and to Americans, and in the generation following the war's end, Spain was never long absent from news and discussion abroad.

In 1945, many people assumed that the Franco regime would simply disappear, caught up by the same worldwide indignation that had swept away Hitler and Mussolini. Yet Franco did not depart from the scene. He maintained his power and, temporarily at least, even consolidated it. This paradox, which puzzled many Europeans at the time, was the logical result of the Spanish dictator's extremely clever wartime policy.

At the beginning of the war, Franco's "nonbelligerence" was distinctly favorable to the fascist rulers of Italy and Germany who had helped him to power. But by the autumn of 1940, he had already become sufficiently skeptical of Hitler's victory to refuse to join him in an attack on Gibraltar. Two years later he took another step away from the Axis by adopting an aloof attitude toward the Anglo-American landings in French North Africa. By the end of the war, his neutrality had turned to favor Britain and the United States. Yet this pro-Allied stand was never complete. Franco always made a distinction between the Western powers and their Soviet cobelligerent. He treated the war on the Eastern Front and that in the West as two separate conflicts, and to the German invasion of Russia he even contributed a Spanish "volunteer" division. This uncompromising anti-Soviet attitude at first caused difficulties for Franco with the Western democracies, but once the Cold War began, the Spanish dictator seemed vindicated. Now he needed only to point to his record as an anti-Communist crusader before the rest of the Western world had awakened to its peril.

During the first half of the 1950s, Franco's authority was unquestioned. In reality, however, the character of this authority had changed greatly in the years that had passed since the end of the Civil War. The Spanish fascist party, the Falange, which had originally served as the spearhead of the Nationalist coalition, had lost most of its influence; Franco was less and less inclined to play the role of its *Caudillo*. The old-fashioned conservative forces gained ascendancy, and it gradually became apparent that the Spanish dictator was at least as much their prisoner as he was their leader. Chief among these forces were the interlocking interests represented by the army, the landowners, the monarchists, and the church.

The army, of course, had produced General Franco himself and, like the dictator who had sprung from its midst, the army officers corps had no clear ideology. Except for a generalized respect for strong authority, it was interested chiefly in its own privileges. Most of the great landowners were similarly nonpolitical and concerned only with keeping control of their estates. Insofar as they did have a political viewpoint, it tended to be monarchist. Some form of monarchism was the usual ideal of Spanish conservatives and, as the decade of the 1950s wore on, the monarchists became increasingly strong and self-confident. There emerged something resembling a two-party system within the authoritarian framework, as those loyal to the exiled pretender to the throne began to challenge the former political monopoly of the Falange. Even Franco seemed to be moving in that direction. In 1947, he issued an Act of Succession promising in vague terms that on his death or retirement the country would be ruled by a king once more. Seven years later he allowed the monarchists to contest the Madrid municipal elections and, in 1955, the pretender's son, Prince Juan Carlos, was permitted to return to Spain to study.

As far as the church was concerned, although the Civil War had largely been fought to preserve it from harm, its leaders were far from being uniformly satisfied with Franco's course. The Spanish hierarchy had traditionally been ultraconservative, and perhaps the majority of the bishops and archbishops remained in the reactionary mold. Ecclesiastics of this sort inspired the ascetic, semisecret laymen's organization called *Opus Dei*, which was able to install a number of its members in high office when Franco reorganized his ministry in 1957. But a growing minority of bishops and priests took quite a different stand, preaching social reform and trying to dissociate themselves from the policies of the regime. The clergy of the Basque provinces were particularly militant; some even went so far as to side with the workers in the illegal labor demonstrations that marked the decade's end.

Yet popular discontent stayed under control. The reasons for this stability were mostly negative. Spain's losses in the Civil War had been so frightful that almost nobody wanted to renew the struggle. Thus throughout the decade 1945–1955 the country was outwardly calm; opposition was restricted to grumbling (which the regime permitted), and although the vast majority of the people were dissatisfied, they remained inert and apathetic. Then, at the end of 1955, a militant opposition suddenly flared up. There were strikes in Barcelona and the Basque provinces—the old centers of autonomist sentiment—and the university students staged an impressive demonstration in Madrid in honor of the recently deceased Ortega y Gasset, Spain's most influential thinker and an avowed opponent of the Franco regime. One of the student leaders was the nephew of García Lorca, the great poet who had been slain by the Nationalists during the Civil War.

Both among workers and among students, the new generation had abruptly and unexpectedly come into its own. The twenty-year-olds, too young to remember the horrors of the Civil War, had revived Spain's languishing political awareness. The police and the law courts bore down on the strikers and students and effectively curbed their unrest. Yet the lesson was already apparent: The trial of the student leaders, who received light sentences, became a courageous condemnation of the whole regime. Franco remained in power, but after 1955 he could never feel entirely secure (see Chapter 21, III).

IV. EASTERN EUROPE AFTER STALIN

The death of Stalin in March 1953 set in motion a whole series of interlocking changes in Eastern Europe. With the passing of the old tyrant, it was quite evident that the system of rule that had been so completely associated with his name and personality could not continue unchanged, either in the Soviet Union itself or in the satellite nations. Stalinism as such was no longer practicable, but the new formula that would replace it remained undefined. It required a full five years for the post-Stalinist system to establish itself. Only after the Soviet leadership had passed through successive phases of adjustment to the realities of the mid-1950s did it reach something approaching a new equilibrium.

The Malenkov Era

No single individual could replace Stalin. Obviously the succession would have to be divided among his heirs, and some form of collective rule was the only one possible. In the first post-Stalinist phase, an informal five-man directory governed the Soviet Union. Its members represented the main centers of power in politics and society—Georgi Malenkov for the bureaucracy, Vyacheslav Molotov (minister of foreign affairs) for the old-line Stalinists, Marshal Bulganin (minister of defense) for the military, Lavrenti Beria for the secret police, and a more obscure figure, Nikita Khrushchev, for the party apparatus. Malenkov seemed to be the dominating figure. Since the death of Zhdanov five years before, this pudgy, impassive manipulator had ranked as the closest approximation of an heir apparent to Stalin, and his assumption of the prime ministry suggested that he would take command over his four colleagues.

Within three months, the five-man directory had been reduced by one. In June, the others combined against secret police chief Beria, stripped him of his authority, and executed him the following December. Beria was the most feared and hated man in the Soviet Union. His fall meant that the secret police was no longer to wield the almost unlimited powers that had made it the nightmare of the Russian people during the last years of Stalin's life. It certainly did not disappear from the Soviet scene—but it resorted less often to arbitrary arrest, and the average Russian citizen became less conscious of its existence. As far as the Soviet directory itself was concerned, moreover, the execution of Beria marked the last time in the decade that a disgraced leader paid for his mistakes with his life. The following years were marked by frequent purges and reorganizations in the Soviet political command, but the purge no longer meant physical extinction—it merely brought demotion and exile to a remote post.

With Beria's downfall, there occurred a number of small but significant changes in the Soviet machinery of control. Anti-Semitism was curbed, as the "doctors' plot," which had epitomized the climax of the terror at the end of Stalin's life, was revealed to have been a fabrication of the secret police itself; writers and artists were granted more freedom of expression; and conditions in the forced labor camps were slightly improved. Stalin's victims, meanwhile, had decided to test the extent of his successors' lenience.

In June there was an uprising in East Berlin and other cities of the German Democratic Republic—the first open revolt against Soviet and Communist authority in the satellite world. Angered by the imposition of new production quotas that effectively lowered wages, and frustrated by continuing shortages of staples ranging from potatoes to coal, workers spilled into the streets to demand that their old work norms be restored. Emboldened by their initial success, they soon voiced political demands as well, including calls for party chief Ulbricht's resignation and for free elections. When Ulbricht publicly voiced indignation at the workers' lack of gratitude to the state, the playwright Bertolt Brecht, then living in East Berlin, commented dryly that if the East German government was dissatisfied with the populace, they should elect a new one. The workers' revolt against the self-proclaimed "Workers' and Farmers' State" was finally quelled only with the help of Soviet tanks and troops.

Soviet military intervention was also required to crush uprisings within Russia itself. In July, prisoners in the forced labor camp of Vorkuta, a place of desolation north of the Arctic Circle, overwhelmed their guards and temporarily gained control of the camps; a similar rising had already occurred at the Norilsk camp (northern Siberia) in May. In both cases the prisoners barricaded themselves in the camp compounds and refused to resume work until their demands for better food, shorter work hours, and a reexamination of their sentences were met. Their brave acts of defiance at first stunned the camp administration into negotiations, but at length Moscow called a halt and again sent in tanks and soldiers to bring this challenge to a bloody end.

Once these threats were dealt with, Malenkov and his colleagues continued on their course of cautious retreat from Stalinist practices. What moved them to act was the realization that repression alone would not prevent future camp revolts, and that it was more effective to ensure public order by the use of carrots as well as the Stalinist stick.

The growing unrest in Soviet satellites erupted into open rebellion after Stalin's death. Here armored tanks move in on street fighters in East Berlin in the wake of calls for free elections during the summer of 1953. (*Courtesy Getty Images, Inc./Liaison*)

Conditions in the labor camps gradually improved. More broadly, Malenkov sought to reduce the previous stress on heavy industrial production and preparation for war. Abroad, he relaxed the pressure of Soviet economic exploitation on the satellite states—agreeing among other things to lower the work norms that had so incensed East German workers. At home, he planned to provide consumers with the goods they had been denied for so long. The new Five-Year Plan he devised for the period 1956–1960 sought to double Soviet consumption levels, to provide housing for the 17 million new people who had been added to the population of the Soviet cities during the last half decade, and to cope with the permanent agricultural crisis by propitiating the peasant masses.

As the program unfolded in the course of the year 1954, the orthodox Stalinists found it too much to swallow and the military were even more recalcitrant. In February 1955, after the greatest intraparty debate that the Soviet Union had seen for a quarter of a century, Malenkov resigned—alleging, in traditional Communist fashion, his own inability to cope with the problems his partial abandonment of Stalinism had called forth.

The Military Interlude and the Warsaw Pact

In the new directory that followed Malenkov's fall, the military naturally played a prominent role. Marshal Bulganin became prime minister, and Marshal Zhukov, the conqueror of Berlin, emerged from retirement as minister of defense. The influence of the military brought a new shift in economic plans and a return to an emphasis on armaments and heavy industrial equipment.

The major achievements of this change of direction were in relations with the Communist states of East Central Europe. In mid-May 1955, the satellite nations for the first time were bound together in a formal military alliance with the Soviet Union. The Warsaw Pact, as the alliance was called, was the Eastern response to NATO and to the Western plans for rearming Germany, which had joined NATO the previous year. Its creation also followed the withdrawal of Soviet troops from Austria, which became independent and neutral in 1954. Austrian independence removed the legal justification for stationing Soviet troops in Czechoslovakia, Hungary, and Romania, where they had ostensibly been guarding supply lines for Soviet troops stationed to the west in Austria. Now a new legal justification was needed—one supplied by the fiction of a defensive military pact among equals.

Thus like the North Atlantic Alliance, the Warsaw Pact was theoretically created for the mutual protection of its signatories, which included Bulgaria, Czechoslovakia, East Germany, Hungary, Poland, Romania, and, of course, the Soviet Union. The military command of the Warsaw Pact forces was unified under Russian control—the supreme command was permanently retained by the Soviet Union—and its strategy in the event of a NATO attack was to be an armored *Blitzkrieg* counteroffensive that would sweep up to the English Channel. In reality, apart from joint annual maneuvers similar to those held by NATO, the sole collective action undertaken by the Warsaw Pact since its founding was to be the invasion of Czechoslovakia (without the participation of the Czechs and Romanians) in the fall of 1968 (see Chapter 21, I).

Soviet leaders also tried to improve their relations with Tito's Yugoslavia. Yugoslavia did not join the Warsaw Pact; it maintained the neutrality between the two Great Power blocs into which it had at last settled after breaking with Moscow in the early 1950s. But two weeks after the signature of the pact, Nikita Khrushchev, whose star was now definitely in the ascendant, journeyed to Belgrade to seek to end the seven-year-old quarrel with Tito. The talks were extremely amicable, and the final communiqué, which spoke of "mutual respect for . . . different forms of Socialist [that is, Communist] development," suggested that Tito had been right all along.

Indeed, it appeared that under cover of a temporary alliance with the military, Khrushchev was advancing his own power and was returning to a view of Soviet policy that was not too different from Malenkov's. As first secretary of the Communist Party's Central Committee, Khrushchev occupied the position that had been Stalin's before the latter's rise to dictatorial authority. It was curious that the parallel did not occur to the other Soviet leaders and put them on their guard. Once more, as had happened a generation earlier, control of the party machinery proved to be the most direct avenue to dominance over the Soviet state. But Khrushchev's advance to power was more humane than Stalin's. He simply pushed his rivals out instead of crushing them completely. In October 1955, the last of the Old Bolsheviks, Molotov, who had differed with Khrushchev over the reconciliation with Tito, confessed his errors—a sure sign of his impending resignation as foreign minister, which duly followed in summer 1956.

The demotion of Molotov and the gradual revelation that Bulganin was no more than an imposing figurehead signaled the emergence of Khrushchev as the most important leader in the Soviet Union. This became clear when the new master of the Russians dropped a bombshell that rocked the whole Communist world.

"De-Stalinization"

On February 25, 1956, Khrushchev mounted the rostrum to address the Twentieth Congress of the Communist party of the USSR in Moscow. With his customary ebullience and self-confidence, the first secretary launched into what gradually unfolded as the most important Communist statement thus far in the postwar period. One by one and with mounting intensity, Khrushchev detailed the "crimes of the Stalin era." His audience followed him with breathless attention, alternately aghast and delighted. No doubt the speaker was carried away by his own eloquence and said rather more than he intended. But there was also calculation in his apparently extemporaneous outburst; all the pent-up hatred and fear of the deceased despot was crying out for expression, and there was no better way for the first secretary to consolidate his authority than by giving voice to it at last. By exposing some of Stalin's crimes, he could hope to avoid criticism for complicity in others. Moreover, Khrushchev evidently hoped to win favor in the West by serving notice that he had definitely departed from the Stalinist path. The central thesis of his long, rambling utterance was that there were several possible ways to reach "socialism" besides that of Communist orthodoxy.

Khrushchev's address was supposed to be kept within party circles, but its text soon leaked out, both to the Communist and to the anti-Communist press. Nearly everywhere, its effects were immediate and thoroughgoing. Within the Soviet Union, it started a new ideological "thaw," of which the comparative leniency of the Malenkov era had given only a foretaste (see Chapter 20, II). Hope sprang up once more in the forced labor camps, writers and artists were again held in looser rein, and Khrushchev launched a program of cultural exchange with the West which included a number of official visits of his own. In the ranks of the foreign Communist parties, the "de-Stalinization" policy produced a minor earthquake. The hardened and experienced leaders whom the late dictator had promoted to power felt the ground trembling beneath them. The more patriotic and "liberal" Communists who had come to the fore during the wartime Resistance period raised their heads once more. Both in the Communist parties of the West and in those of the satellite states, the most intoxicating perspectives seemed to be opening. Freedom from Soviet dominance was one aspiration, liberalization of the Stalinist ideological discipline another. All through the spring and summer of 1956, a vast soul-searching and examination of conscience within the Communist world mounted in intensity. Then in the autumn the explosion came.

The Polish "October" and the Hungarian Revolution

This post-Stalinist ferment reached the highest pitch in Poland and Hungary. Along with Czechoslovakia, these were the most industrialized and Western-oriented of the Soviet satellites. Czechoslovakia differed from its two immediate neighbors in having a pro-Russian tradition and a Communist party that had purged itself of deviationists more thoroughly than any other during Stalin's last years. Poland and Hungary, on the contrary, cherished bitter memories of hostility to Russia, and their Communist parties harbored leaders who stood ready to guide them toward a new course.

In Poland there was Wladislaw Gomulka, the only major "national" Communist to survive Stalin's final purge. In Hungary there was Imre Nagy,* a comparative liberal and humanist in communism's ranks, who had served as prime minister in the Malenkov era and had left good memories behind him. In both countries, hope for a change from rigid Stalinist direction centered on a single individual, who soon became a symbol of the most varied aspirations for a freer life. These aspirations found their chief vehicle of expression in literary discussion groups that sprang up in the wake of Khrushchev's February speech and that soon entered into contact with the more articulate urban workers. In the spring and summer of 1956, Hungary's and Poland's courses ran parallel. Not until the autumn did they diverge, the one to end in tragedy, the other in a cautious advance toward more liberal goals.

The signs of change first became evident in Poland. At the end of 1954, Gomulka had quietly been released from prison, and his ideas soon began to spread among the intermediate echelons of the Communist party. Then, in June 1956, a workers' uprising at Poznan (the former German city of Posen) showed that the grip of the Polish Stalinists was weakening, and that a relaxation of discipline over both factory and intellectual life was becoming imperative. As the summer wore on, and as the talk in the discussion groups waxed bolder, the Stalinist leaders were forced out one by one. In early October, the last important one resigned; less than a week later, Gomulka, for the first time since his disgrace, attended a meeting of the Politburo, which he clearly intended to dominate. Faced with the prospect of a Gomulkaist Poland, the Russians took alarm. On October 19, a delegation of the major Soviet leaders, headed by Khrushchev, flew unexpectedly into Warsaw. Their arrival was accompanied by menacing Red Army troop movements toward the Polish capital. But though Khrushchev bullied and blustered, Gomulka and his colleagues held firm. The Poles insisted on proceeding with the election of the "national" Communist leader as first secretary of the party, which duly occurred on October 21. After the Soviet delegation returned to Moscow, Khrushchev canceled the troop movements and accepted Gomulka as director of Poland's future course.

The decision had evidently been difficult and bitterly fought. As far as outsiders could tell, it was based on three major considerations. First, the Soviet leaders were convinced—and correctly so—that Gomulka was a good Communist who for all his apparent heterodoxy still intended to keep the party firmly in control. Second, the Poles agreed to stay within the Soviet orbit by maintaining their membership in the Warsaw Pact. Finally, the eruption of far more serious difficulties in Hungary counseled caution on both sides. To the Russians, it suggested the inadvisability of becoming involved in active intervention in two places at once; to the new Polish leadership, it gave an occasion to preach calm to their people lest they suffer the fate of their Hungarian friends.

In Hungary, as contrasted with Poland, there occurred no gradual shift of influence to Communist leaders who were more acceptable than the old Stalinists to the

*Not to be confused with Ferenc Nagy, the Small-Holder party's prime minister in the period 1945–1947.

The Hungarian revolution: Lenin's
works burn in the streets of
Budapest in late October, 1956.
(*Courtesy Magnum Photos, Inc.*)

people at large. The diehards at Budapest clung to power until the last and, when they
did go, it was not through an intraparty change of authority, but through an explosion of
popular anger. On October 23, a vast crowd of demonstrators—inspired by the events in
Poland—was calling for the resignation of the government when the secret police
opened fire. This event transformed into open revolution what had earlier been only a
massive movement of protest. It swept Imre Nagy into the premiership, but it soon overwhelmed Nagy himself, driving him far beyond his Communist affiliations into a pledge
of free elections and withdrawal from the Warsaw Pact. As the ten days of Hungary's experiment in national communism proceeded, it became apparent that the party was no

longer in control and that the revolutionists would not halt at the liberalization of the Communist system but were aiming rather at democracy of the Western type or even at a restoration of the old regime.

After grave debates in the Kremlin, the Soviet leaders took a decision contrary to the one they had made in the case of Poland. They decided to intervene, sending back into Budapest the troops which they had withdrawn from the Hungarian capital, on Nagy's request, at the end of October. On November 4, the Soviet tanks brutally bore down on the revolutionists. The outside world stood aghast, but the Russians had chosen their time well. No one lifted a finger to save the Hungarians; to intervene militarily would have meant that the West was willing to cross the fragile boundary separating cold war from hot belligerency, with the danger of nuclear exchanges that would have rendered Europe a wasteland. As it would five years later at the time of the Berlin Wall, America and its NATO allies chose reluctant inaction to potentially deadly confrontation. Cardinal Mindszenty took refuge in the American Embassy; Nagy, in that of Yugoslavia. The Soviet Union returned the old Stalinists to power, as tens of thousands of Hungarians fled across the Austrian border, and the mass of the people submitted sullenly to their fate.

The "Refreeze" and the New Equilibrium in Yugoslavia and Poland

The suppression of the Hungarian revolution came as a shattering blow to Western Communists. Like no other postwar event to date, it revealed the ideological bankruptcy of their movement. During Stalin's last years, they had suffered under the deadening effects of orthodoxy imposed from the outside, and the life and the enthusiasm had gradually been drained out of them. Then the post-Stalinist "thaw" gave them a new hope and a new appeal. This brief revival of spontaneity made the succeeding disappointment all the more bitter—the shock of Hungary was the greater because of the illusions that had gone before. It bore particularly hard on intellectuals, who had followed the developments in Hungary with interest and sympathy and who had learned that such figures as George Lukács, the respected Marxist theoretician and literary critic, had thrown in their lot with the revolutionists. After the Soviet military action, both party members and "fellow travelers" began to desert communism in droves. Perhaps half the writers and artists who had ranked as the great ornament of the French and Italian parties abandoned the ideological allegiance to which they had clung for so long. After the autumn of 1956, communism still represented a major block of sullen discontent standing against the prevailing conservative temper on the Western European continent, but it had lost much of its idealism and self-confidence.

In Yugoslavia, too, the suppression of the Hungarian revolution meant a loss of ideological prestige. After a brief period of hesitation, Tito decided to endorse the Soviet intervention. Subsequently, he released his guest, Imre Nagy, whose execution in June 1958 served as a grim warning to Communist leaders who might be tempted to stray beyond the borders of permissible deviation. These actions dimmed Tito's aura as the leader and model of national communism. At the same time, they only confirmed the course the Yugoslav regime had taken since its early years of unorthodox experiment. By 1954, Tito's initial period of innovation had come to an end. In the economic realm, he had decentralized his country's industrial direction and called a halt to agrarian collectivization and the compulsory delivery of crops. From the standpoint of individual liberty, he had strengthened the rights of the citizen before the courts and the secret police, granted a limited freedom of speech, reopened cultural channels to the West, and released Archbishop Stepinac (without restoring him to authority). Then Tito suddenly stopped the process of change. He reacted with a sharp negative when his former trusted subordinate, Milovan Djilas, proposed to establish in competition with Tito's special brand of communism a liberal socialist movement that would, in effect, have converted Yugoslavia into a two-party state. After repeated rebukes, Djilas was condemned to a long term in jail. The Communist monopoly of power remained unbroken. It is significant that the great intellectual ferment of 1956, which stirred Poland and Hungary so deeply, found few echoes among the Yugoslavs.

In Poland, the wave of popular protest that had swept Gomulka into power at first threatened to travel as far as the Hungarians had gone. In late October and early November there were anti-Soviet demonstrations throughout the country and a massive undercurrent of sympathy for Hungary. But Gomulka—who was a far more decisive figure and a more hard-bitten Communist than Nagy—succeeded in keeping his people under control. He was aided by the Catholic primate, Cardinal Wyszynski, who saw that Gomulka's rule was the best that Poland could hope for under the circumstances and who counseled his flock to vote for Gomulka-backed candidates in the elections to the Sejm (parliament) scheduled for January 1957.

This tacit alliance with the church turned the elections into a personal triumph for Gomulka. According to Western standards, these were far from free, but they did result in the return of a minority of non-Communist deputies and the beginning of real debates in a body that earlier had been no more than a rubber stamp for the regime. Throughout the following winter and spring, the process of liberalization went on unchecked. The forced collectivization of agriculture came to an end; the workers' councils, which had sprung up before and during the great demonstrations of the previous October, received official endorsement and the right to champion the grievances of the men in the factories and workshops; the activity of the secret police was curbed; and political prisoners were released. The intellectual ferment continued. The tone of the press became openly non-Communist or even anti-Communist, as the censorship collapsed, and the Resistance fighters of 1944, whom the Red Army had allowed to go down to defeat, were granted a posthumous rehabilitation.

Then Gomulka called a halt. Striking out both against the remaining Stalinists within the ranks of Polish communism, and against the far more influential "revisionists" who were trying to push him into something resembling Western social democracy, he consolidated his authority over his party and his state. The danger signal that a reimposition of official control was on the way was the closing down of a militant Communist youth journal just under a year after the October effervescence had started. Thereafter one action inexorably followed another. Intellectuals and writers were restrained, the powers of the workers' councils were reduced, the secret police began its spying once again, the old war of pinpricks against the church was resumed, and Gomulka lashed out ever more bitterly against his critics both on the right and on the left.

Still, something had changed. As Poland in the course of the year 1958 settled into the Gomulkaist mold, it became apparent that the results were not notably different from the point that Titoist Yugoslavia had reached four years earlier. In both cases, the process of liberalization had disappointed the original expectations. Yet in Poland, as in Yugoslavia, there remained a residue of significant change which marked these nations off from their orthodox Communist neighbors. In both countries, the peasants were largely left to their own devices, and the urban workers enjoyed more individual and collective rights than they did elsewhere; in both countries, speech was freer, and the possibilities of contacts with the West more numerous and satisfactory. One nation had been forced to stay within the Soviet orbit; the other continued outside, but with a neutrality which, after 1955, leaned rather toward Russia than toward the West. In Yugoslavia there was more national independence; in Poland, more intellectual and literary vitality. In both, the Communist party, as symbolized in the personality of one towering leader, refused to relinquish its monopoly of power. Together, however, they offered an alternative to the Soviet model of Communist rule, which served as a tenuous bridge between East and West and had a growing appeal for the newly liberated nations of Asia and Africa.

Khrushchev Consolidates Power

Once he had swallowed the bitter pill of Hungary, Khrushchev continued to consolidate his control over the Soviet Union. In the summer of 1957, Malenkov and Molotov (who actually had very little in common and represented the two extremes of the Soviet leadership) were denounced as members of an "antiparty" group and exiled to obscure posts. The following autumn, Marshal Zhukov, whose popularity obviously competed with Khrushchev's own, was dropped from the defense ministry and in the spring Khrushchev finally took the premiership from Bulganin. After 1958 the new master of the Soviet Union stood unchallenged. With the power of the secret police broken by the fall of Beria and that of the bureaucracy and the army curbed, the Communist party once more concentrated in its own hands all the major levers of authority.

Jaunty, full of earthy quips, and supremely self-assured, Khrushchev maintained an uneasy balance between ideological rigor and grudging tolerance. To the West he directed two years of soft speech, trying to repair the damage to his country's prestige that its intervention in Hungary had caused. But in the autumn of 1958, he shifted to a more provocative manner. Once again the Soviet Union put pressure on the Western position in Berlin, inaugurating a period of renewed tension in international affairs that culminated in the complete failure of a "summit" meeting with President Eisenhower in Paris in May 1960. At home the great "thaw" was over, but although sterner controls were again imposed, they fell far short of what had been common practice in the Stalinist era. Too much had changed in Soviet society to permit a return to the situation of 1953. As contacts with the West continued and standards of living slowly but cumulatively rose, it became apparent that Russia had entered on a new phase of Communist rule whose outlines were still unclear but whose push toward a relaxation of tension and terror was unmistakable.

READINGS

Gaullist France is analyzed by Philip M. Williams and Martin Harrison in *Politics and Society in de Gaulle's Republic* (1971), and by Stanley Hoffmann et al., in *In Search of France* (1963); the former book is more critical, the latter more sympathetic in tone. The leader himself is portrayed by Brian Crozier, *De Gaulle: The Statesman* (1973), and by Jean Lacouture in his excellent two-volume biography, *De Gaulle: The Rebel, 1890–1945** (trans. 1990) and *De Gaulle: The Ruler, 1945–1970** (trans. 1991). De Gaulle's own account of his dramatic return to power, *Memoirs of Hope: Renewal and Endeavor* (1971), is inevitably biased but valuable nonetheless.

The years of Conservative rule in Britain after 1951 are chronicled in the early chapters of Sked and Cook (see readings for Chapter 17) and Vernon Bogdanor and Robert Skidelsky, eds., *The Age of Affluence, 1951–1964* (1970). The course of the other Western European states, where the break with the earlier postwar era was less sharp, may be followed in Grosser, Hughes, and Hiscocks (see readings for Chapters 15 and 17); in M. P. Fogarty, *Christian Democracy in Western Europe* (1957); and in Kurt Sontheimer, *The Government and Politics of West Germany* (1973).

On Eastern Europe, in addition to Hoskings, Fejtö, Brzezinski, and Griffith (see readings for Chapters 10, 14, and 17), there is Merle Fainsod, *How Russia Is Ruled*, new version by Jerry F. Hough under the title *How the Soviet Union Is Governed* (1979), which traces the changes in institutions and economic practice after the death of Stalin. Seweryn Bialer's *Stalin's Successors** (1980) details the rivalries and power shifts within the Kremlin in the late 1950s. Two notable studies of the man who next assumed leadership in the Soviet Union are William Taubman, *Khrushchev: The man and His Era* (2003) and Roy Medvedev's *Khrushchev** (1983). Of interest are also Khrushchev's rambling but revealing memoirs, *Khrushchev Remembers,** 2 vols. (1970–1974). On the soviet labor camps and the impact of de-Stalinization, see Anne Applebaum, *Gulag: A History* (2003).

György Litvan, *The Hungarian Revolution of 1956: Reform, Revolt, and Repression, 1953–1963* (1996) offers a detailed view of the revolution from its origins to its aftermath. François Fejtö, *Behind the Rape of Hungary* (1957), explains the great explosion of 1956. Nicholas Bethell, *Gomulka: His Poland, His Communism* (1969), explores events surrounding the Polish "October," while Stephen Fischer-Galati, ed., *Eastern Europe in the Sixties* (1963), offers a series of essays by individual specialists on topics cutting across national frontiers.

On Iberian developments after the Spanish Civil War, besides Kay on Portugal (see readings for Chapter 9), there is Stanley G. Payne's compact and admirably balanced *Franco's Spain* (1967) and Max Gallo's *Spain Under Franco* (1976).

*Books available in paperback are marked with an asterisk.

ACHIEVING
PROSPERITY, 1960–1968

Growing European affluence during the 1960s led to an upsurge in the purchase of consumer goods. Here, a French salesperson advises a young family on the verge of buying an automatic washing machine. (*Courtesy Henri Cartier-Bresson/Magnum Photos, Inc.*)

As the 1960s opened, Europe was crossing the threshold of the new and more prosperous society that forty years before had been promised but not achieved. In the 1920s, there had been visible on the horizon an economy and a way of life that strongly resembled those of the United States—a mobile, mechanized society in which consumption levels were high and class lines were fluid. This great change had failed to occur: Europe's momentum had been lost, with the narrowing of economic vistas in the 1920s, the Great Depression of the 1930s, and the war and the period of slow recovery in the 1940s. The first twentieth-century effort of reinvigoration had failed.

A generation later, however, Europe was ready to start again. A half decade after the end of the Second World War, the prerequisites existed once more, as they had in the mid-1920s, for an era of rapid economic expansion. This time, the promise did not fail. The five years after 1950, unlike those after 1924, brought more than disappointments and half-fulfilled hopes. Instead they marked the start of an unprecedented boom, which was to continue for over two decades.

In the interval between 1930 and 1960, something had been learned. The new generation of leaders in government, business, and the trade unions had widened their vision and their tolerance for experiment. They now knew better both how to control the economy and how to project its development into the future. The steady economic expansion that had begun in the early 1950s was a new phenomenon in twentieth-century Europe in both its length and breadth; the two uninterrupted decades of growth touched nearly all sectors of society. Although inequalities of income still existed, the gap between rich and poor in Western Europe narrowed appreciably during these years. Economic security was still further enhanced by the willingness of governments to provide health and retirement benefits for their citizens—the system of guaranteed support that was now nearly universally termed the "welfare state."

Taken together, the factors influencing Europe's economy in the 1960s provided a powerful push toward consumption. Advances in technology, such as consumer electronics and household appliances, found a ready market, which in turn prompted further innovation. Already in 1957, British Prime Minister Harold Macmillan proclaimed that his countrymen "had never had it so good." A decade later, looking back at twenty-two years of peace (another record for the century) and continuing signs of affluence, most Europeans would have had to agree.

I. THE EUROPEAN POPULATION

The Postwar Population Spurt

In the period after the First World War, the slowing down of population growth—and its complete cessation in some places—had acted as a powerfully depressing force. The reverse happened after the Second World War. Europe entered on an era of rapid rise in population, and this growth was spread more evenly throughout the Continent than such spurts had been in the past. Thus, Italy, which until about 1950 had had one of the highest rates of increase in Europe, after midcentury began to see its number of births slackening off. Conversely, Britain, whose prewar population had been almost stationary, experienced a slow but steady natural increase of about 0.5 percent a year. Another highly urban country, the Netherlands, jumped to first place in population growth among the nations of Western Europe.

Yet the greatest postwar surprise occurred in France. The people who had ranked as the epitome of an old, stable, and even stagnant society suddenly began to multiply. In 1945, for the first time in a decade, France registered an excess of births over deaths. The year 1949 had the highest number of births that the country had seen for half a century. The nine years ending in 1954—a census year—showed a net population increase of 300,000 annually, and a total population gain of more than three million.

The result of such gains, however, was not to increase European pressure for emigration abroad. That pressure had existed only in the first postwar years, when the economy of Europe had not yet recovered sufficiently to absorb the new age groups looking for work. After the midcentury, there was less need to leave. The European economy itself was absorbing the population excess; of the industrial nations of the Continent, Italy alone had a continuing unemployment problem.

A Culture of Cities

As opposed to the population growth of the interwar period, which was concentrated in the rural societies of Southern and Eastern Europe and served merely to increase agrarian misery and discontent, the post-1945 spurt was confined almost entirely to the cities. Although the countryside still maintained a higher birth rate than the urban areas, it no longer kept its excess people on the land. Young men and women left the farms for the cities, where industrial and clerical jobs awaited them. In the 1950s the cities of Europe thus grew rapidly, while the population of the countryside remained stationary or even fell. This was just as true in the East as in the West. In the satellite states of East Central Europe, the forced industrialization program produced a massive influx of workers into the cities; in the Soviet Union, just under half the population of 1959 consisted of town dwellers. In nation after nation, the decade following the midcentury saw a loss of population from the country to the city, both in relative and in absolute terms.

For many peasants and rural dwellers, particularly of the older generation, the depopulation of the countryside was a source of grief and anxiety. The sense that a traditional way of life was departing prompted the rise of reactionary political movements, such as monarchism in southern Italy and Poujadism in southwestern France. Yet these political protests were only temporary. Their period of importance was confined to the mid-1950s, when the loss of influence on the part of the countryside first became apparent. In the longer view, the rural depopulation was a source of benefit rather than harm to the agricultural areas. It meant abandonment of marginal land and more intensive cultivation of what remained. It encouraged the consolidation of scattered plots and the elimination of "dwarf" holdings and, by reducing the excess of agricultural manpower, it tended to raise wages and to stimulate the introduction of tractors, reapers, and other types of mechanical equipment.

The new society was dominated by the cities. As in the past, the cities set the styles and the consumption patterns for the people as a whole, but no longer were there vast backcountry areas which lay beyond the influence of urban attitudes. By 1960, almost all of European society had been permeated by the culture of the cities.

The New Affluence and Popular Culture

This urban culture was coming increasingly to resemble that of the United States, especially in its strong orientation toward consumption. As the general prosperity of the 1950s gained momentum, the demands of European consumers became ever more pervasive and imperative. As more women entered the work force, the need for products and appliances to reduce the burden of household chores began to be widely felt. Supermarkets now made it possible to do all food shopping under one roof, thereby saving precious time; frozen foods made food preparation easier once the shopper returned home. The sale of so-called consumer durables—items such as electric refrigerators, washing machines, and vacuum cleaners—reached remarkably high levels as economies of scale allowed them to be produced at steadily lower prices. Whereas only 8 percent of British homes could boast a refrigerator in 1956 (the others used iceboxes), by 1962 the rate had reached 33 percent, and by 1971 had increased to 69 percent—a more than eightfold jump in a mere fifteen years.

Private and individual transport was another need that was finally met in the postwar boom. The number of automobiles in Europe more than doubled in the 1950s, and millions of motor scooters were circulating. This sudden multiplication of private transport effected what amounted to a class revolution. Before the war, only the well-to-do had been able to afford motorcars and distant vacations; the mass of the population went to work by streetcar or bicycle and traveled very little. By the 1950s, all this had changed. Even people of modest means had begun to buy automobiles, and a whole new class had been inserted between the bicyclists and the car owners—the intermediate stratum of those (mostly young) who traveled by motor scooter.

This new mobility was not an unmitigated blessing, however. The European Continent was simply too small for such traffic pressure. Lacking the open spaces and broad highways of the United States, it began to suffer under the strain. Crooked, narrow city streets that dated from the Middle Ages were hopelessly clogged with traffic; quiet vacation resorts had their peace shattered by massive arrivals from the cities. People fleeing noise and congestion moved out to the suburbs, as they were simultaneously doing in America, but adequate housing was in short supply nearly everywhere. This was the one important area in which, by 1960, the losses of the war had not been fully made up. Wartime destruction had merely aggravated a problem of obsolescence in housing that had already been apparent at the end of the 1930s. During the Great Depression far too few dwellings had been built; then had come the bombardments of the war; and finally, to cap all this, the post-1945 growth of population and the general rise in standards of living had enormously increased demand.

The postwar boom also made itself felt in the field of entertainment. Scarcely had the thirst for motion pictures and radio been satisfied when television and cassette tape recorders began to spread. Cultural conservatives lamenting such changes usually blamed them on American influence—much as they had during the "jazz age" of the 1920s. True, American music, American styles, and American motion pictures held and even increased their popularity in the postwar period; but these were only the superficial manifestations of a deeper tendency. Europe was actually not so much being influenced by the United States as traveling of its own will the same path that America had pursued a generation before. Consumption levels were rising and life was becoming democratized. The rest followed almost automatically.

Professional sports, which had already come to play a prominent role in European popular culture after World War I (see Chapter 5, III), assumed still more important dimensions during the boom years of the 1960s. Soccer was the undisputed king, with mass followings in all the major cities and many smaller ones, and with each team sporting distinctive colors and cheers. But cycling and rugby also drew large crowds. The Tour de France bicycle race and indoor events such as the *Sechstagerennen* (six-day bicycle races) in Germany reached a new audience through television; so did rugby's Tournament of Five Nations, which pitted the official teams of France, Britain, Scotland, Wales, and Ireland against one another in prime time. In a Europe where many younger people were moving to new cities in search of work, professional sports teams provided a common link and social bridge. Strangers could unite in supporting the home team in the stadium or in an office betting pool. Despite periodic outbreaks of fan violence and periodic accusations of corruption, such matches offered a precious opportunity to feel part of a larger community.

Not all leisure activities were spectator sports. Tourism reached new levels with the advent of inexpensive package tours, which allowed working-class families from the British midlands to taste the pleasures of a week on Spain's Mediterranean coast. Other tourists bundled their family and a family-sized tent into the family car and set off on a journey tailored to meet their personal tastes and pocketbook. For the more affluent, jet travel promised rapid connections with more exotic lands. Brazil became a favorite destination of French tourists, while the sun of Turkey and North Africa attracted Germans and Scandinavians. The result was a broadening of horizons, a "deprovincialization" of Western and Central Europe, where, though most still preferred to spend their vacations at home, a growing number sought adventure and relaxation abroad.

European popular culture in the 1960s was designed to appeal primarily to the young—students and working singles who had money to spend and the leisure time to enjoy what it brought. What this meant in practice was clothes, films, and music which formed the basis for an international style that was casual, cut across class lines, and mocked a more conservative elder generation by not taking itself too seriously. The ubiquitous 1960s uniform for the young included blue jeans, brightly colored T-shirts, and (for women) the option of the mini-skirt, which had originated in Britain in the fall of 1965 and then scandalized the French when young British tourists appeared in Paris on Easter holiday in 1966. Favorite films included American westerns and comedies (John Wayne and the Marx Brothers had many devoted European fans). But what typified popular youth culture above all in the 1960s was its music—folk, blues, and American and British rock and roll. When the Beatles sang about "Strawberry Fields" and the Rolling Stones extolled "Jumping Jack Flash," the lyrics eluded those Europeans who spoke no English, but the dreamy escapism of the first and the energetic iconoclasm of the second were universally appreciated among the new rock audience.

Not all Europe shared in this revolution of consumption and of class attitudes. It was most marked in the industrialized and otherwise "advanced" areas of Western and

Central Europe—Britain, Scandinavia, the Low Countries, France, Western Germany, Switzerland, Austria, and Northern Italy. As in the past, the Mediterranean world lagged behind. But the greatest postwar change was in Eastern Europe. Although Soviet consumption standards still remained far below what they were in the West, the difference was narrowing. Blue jeans and Beatles tapes were eagerly sought items in Prague, Warsaw, and Leningrad. The colossal effort at industrialization in the 1930s and the frantic pace of reconstruction in the 1940s were at last beginning to show results.

II. EASTERN EUROPE: THE NEW MIDDLE CLASS

The Later Five-Year Plans and the New Pattern of Soviet Population

In the postwar period, as had been true in the 1930s, the Soviet Union maintained the most rapid rate of industrial expansion in the whole of Europe. It continued its former practice of setting its economic goals in terms of five-year plans, which became both more realistic and more flexible as the planners gained experience. Yet many of the old faults persisted. This was particularly true in agriculture which, by Khrushchev's own admission, was still lagging behind its targets in the late 1950s.

The Soviets' Fourth Five-Year Plan (1946–1950) not only aimed to reconstruct war damage and to restore Soviet production to its prewar level; it also continued the earlier stress on heavy industry and on the economic growth of the eastern parts of the country. The Fifth Plan (1951–1955) marked a more decisive change in Soviet society. Previously, Russia had been an underdeveloped country in the sense that shortages of raw materials and equipment had limited industrial growth, although labor had never been lacking. After 1955, this ceased to be true; the countryside was no longer able to furnish manpower wholesale. The Soviet labor reserve had fallen—as it had earlier in the advanced economies of the West—and thus the life and productivity of the individual worker had become more precious.

This change reinforced the demand for consumer goods and a better standard of living that mounted to a clamor after Stalin's death in 1953. The Sixth Plan—which was scheduled to run from 1956 to 1960—precipitated a great debate on economic policy. Its first two years proved to be a period of experiment such as Russia had not known since the 1930s. The most important innovations decreed by Khrushchev and his colleagues provided, on the one hand, for decentralizing the execution of the plan, and on the other, for further concentration in agricultural management. In 1957 the Soviet leaders decided to delegate to regional economic councils the administration of the details of the plan. The following year they agreed on the gradual transformation of the rural Machine Tractor Stations into Repair Technical Stations. The latter change was the logical sequel to a gradual consolidation of collectives and state farms into larger units that possessed their own mechanical equipment.

Then, in November 1958, the unprecedented happened. Khrushchev announced the decision to shelve the Sixth Five-Year Plan and to replace it by a Seven-

Year Plan to run until 1965. This new plan, which aimed to increase overall industrial production by nearly 80 percent, was the first in which the Soviet leaders openly declared their intention of overtaking the Americans in per capita output. Moreover, the Seven-Year Plan at last struck a balance between the continued growth of heavy industry and the satisfaction of consumer demand, more particularly in the provision of housing, where 15 million new apartments were called for.

One of the reasons for superseding the old plan was to take advantage of the information gathered in the general census of 1959. This census, besides documenting the massive growth of Soviet cities since the war, also revealed a number of significant changes in the general pattern of the country's population. Once more, as in the 1930s, the greatest industrial development had occurred to the east, in the Asian areas behind the Urals, and it was here that new cities had mushroomed from nothing. But this change, which was only beginning in the prewar years, had decisively altered the distribution of the Soviet peoples by 1959. It had scattered the Great Russians throughout the Soviet Union, as skilled workers and administrators took employment in the newly developing parts of the country. In the census of 1959, 114.6 million of the Union's 208.8 million inhabitants declared themselves to be Russians (see Figure 20.1). Only 97.8 million lived in the Russian Soviet Federated Socialist Republic (RSFSR); the remaining 17 million had migrated elsewhere, drastically changing the population pattern of some of the Asian republics. In Kazakhstan in Central Asia—the center of a boom in cotton growing—the Russians had become the largest single element (43 percent) in the population. In the neighboring Uzbek Republic, they numbered more than a million.

With Russians filling most of the responsible positions and setting the social tone in the Asian republics, it was small wonder that these were threatened by russification. Although the official policy continued to provide for local autonomy and the fostering of indigenous culture, its practical application was becoming restricted to the realm of art and entertainment. The local literatures steadily lost in importance, as more and more people adopted Russian as their everyday language. This spread of Russian influence, however, was less a national change than a further example of the Europe-wide triumph of the city over the countryside and of advanced technology over the more primitive. Moreover, the resistance to it paralleled the tenacity of ethnic identity that

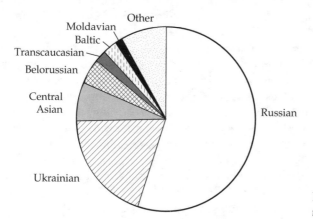

FIGURE 20.1   Distribution of ethnic groups in the Soviet Union, 1959.

was simultaneously becoming apparent in the West (see Chapter 21, II) and reflected the fact that birthrates among Asian Moslems were far higher than among the Russians.

The other great change revealed in the census was the comparatively small size of Soviet families. The average number of children recorded was just over two—a figure that seemed incompatible with the annual natural increase of population of 1.75 percent. The explanation, apparently, was a high marriage rate and great progress in cutting down childhood mortality. Broadly speaking, the small size of families reflected the fact that a very high proportion of Soviet women went out to work during the day and that the people as a whole were raising their expectations and hence restricting the number of their children, as parents had done in Western and Central Europe a generation or two before.

The Drive for Improved Living Standards

This rise in expectations was the most strongly marked feature of Soviet society in the 1950s. After more than a generation of denial and hardship, Russian consumers, like their counterparts in the West, were clamoring for the good things of life. For almost forty years, they had suffered one calamity after another; time after time they had been urged on by their rulers to exertion and sacrifice in the Communist cause. First had come the World War of 1914–1918, then the still greater horrors of the civil war, and after that—following the brief breathing space of the New Economic Policy—the rigors of collectivization, the Five-Year Plans, and the Great Purge. Scarcely had these ended when the Soviet peoples had been plunged into the Second World War, with its frightful devastation and human losses, which seemed for a time to have canceled out all the gains of the preceding decade.

By 1953, however, when Stalin died, this ground had been recovered. Reconstruction was substantially complete, and the country was moving on to new levels of industrial achievement. The pressure of the Cold War was also lessening. For the first time since the Bolsheviks had come to power, there seemed to be no urgent reason for exertion, and the Soviet leadership began to give heed to consumers at last. As Khrushchev eventually realized, the deepest longings of his people were for a more comfortable life and an end to the fear of war. These two aspirations went together. The sentiment for peace was intense among a people whose every family had lost some member in World War II and whose leaders for decades had justified their dictatorial rule by pointing to the danger of capitalist attack.

In the 1950s, such arguments were wearing thin. The Soviet population no longer consisted of an inert and inarticulate mass manipulated by its rulers at will, plus remnants of the old regime who were too frightened to protest. The new generation educated and trained in the 1930s had now come to positions of authority in the party and in the economy. The census of 1959 revealed that illiteracy—which as late as the mid-1920s had afflicted nearly half the population—had been nearly eliminated, and that almost four million people had received a university education. By the end of the 1950s, the party, led by Khrushchev, was again in unchallenged control of Soviet society, but it was no longer the militant party of the prewar years driving a reluctant people toward the goal of a collectivized economy. By 1960, this goal had been achieved; the days of heroic exertion were over. The new aspirations for peace and personal comfort had affected the lower and intermediate ranks of the party itself, and the old separation between party and people was ending.

In brief, what had emerged in the Soviet Union was a new middle class, which was not notably different from its counterparts in the "capitalist" West. Like Americans and Western Europeans, the new stratum of Russian managers and professional people desired material well-being, private security, and a relaxation of tension. With the reduction of the power of the secret police, they were also beginning to long for freedom of expression and inquiry, both in ideological discussion and in the arts.

The Cultural "Thaw" and Its Sequels

In 1954, Ilya Ehrenburg, who earlier had ranked as a pillar of Communist orthodoxy, published a novel entitled *The Thaw*. Two years later, at the height of the excitement over Poland and Hungary, a less-known writer, Vladimir Dudintsev, in his novel *Not By Bread Alone*, went still further in expressing the view that Russian writers should be free of ideological constraint in attacking bureaucracy in state and party.

These two books suggest the sudden loosening of intellectual supervision that followed the death of Stalin. The earlier phrases of the post-Stalinist era were marked by a revolt against the tyranny of "socialist realism" and a widespread search for a freedom that Russia had almost forgotten. Subsequently, this "thaw" was followed by a "refreeze." The limitations that were reimposed on Soviet writers and artists emerged most clearly in the case of Boris Pasternak's *Doctor Zhivago*.

Pasternak was an influential and respected poet of the prerevolutionary school who, after years of occupying himself mostly with translations, had finally written a novel, which he sent abroad to be published. It first appeared in Italy, but it was the publication of the English-language edition in 1958 that brought its author international fame. The novel became a best seller in the Western world—a success that was bound to displease the Soviet authorities, since the spirit of *Doctor Zhivago* was meditative and individualistic and sharply critical of the Bolshevik regime. This displeasure became open anger when Pasternak was awarded the Nobel Prize for literature. The author of *Doctor Zhivago* was not forbidden to go to Stockholm to receive the prize, but it was clear that such a trip would mean his permanent exile. After some hesitation, Pasternak declined the award, explaining in a letter to Khrushchev that he was "tied to Russia" by his "birth, life, and work" and that for him "to leave and go into exile abroad was unthinkable."

Thus Pasternak bowed to official pressure and continued to live quietly in the country house the Soviet state provided for him. In early 1960 he died, surrounded by the admiration of the more independent figures in the Russian literary world, and with hundreds of copies of his novel circulating clandestinely in Moscow and Leningrad. Pasternak's had been a voice from the past; that was one reason why his revolt had failed. But his lesson was not lost on the younger generation. Although the Soviet Writers' Congress of 1959 took a rigid position on the ideological commitment of literature, the signs of intellectual ferment continued. A number of younger authors began to experiment with new techniques and new themes, some of them (especially those who portrayed life in the Russian countryside) deriving their inspiration from Italian "neorealism." In the realm of painting, a revolt against the old formalism and conventionality was in full swing; an exposition of Polish experimental art in the spring of 1959 gave occasion for re-peated demands for shaking off "the yoke of slavish imitation."

The same oscillation from thaw to refreeze—and then back to a precarious bal-ance between the two—was apparent in the field of science. In his last years Stalin had officially enforced the teachings of the biologist Trofim Lysenko, who had denied the Mendelian theory of genetics by reviving the early nineteenth-century notion of the in-heritance of acquired characteristics. Such a position was obviously congenial to Marx-ists, who insisted on the ability of humans to change the evolution of nature. In 1948, at the climax of the postwar reimposition of ideological control, Lysenko's scientific oppo-nents were reduced to silence. For eight years the official theory held sway, as Soviet sci-ence separated itself almost completely from the mainstream of research in genetics. Then, in 1956, the Russian scientists, like the writers and artists, declared their indepen-dence from ideological control. Their concerted opposition forced Lysenko's resignation as president of the Lenin Academy of Agricultural Sciences. By 1959, however, he was back again in official favor—only to fall once more when after Khrushchev's own depar-ture he lost his key role as director of the Institute of Genetics in the Soviet Academy of Sciences.

On balance, the post-1956 control over Soviet culture was far looser than Stalin's had been. Most scientists were now at liberty to speculate as they chose, and the writers enjoyed more freedom than they had known since the 1920s. They could now write of Soviet society in terms of distinctions and shadings—as opposed to the black-and-white stereotypes on which Stalin had insisted—and they could depict communism as a faith that was changing and developing away from the monolithic orthodoxy of a former day. By the early 1960s the younger and more experimental writers were con-stantly getting into trouble—but they continued to publish nonetheless. Alexander Solzhenitsyn wrote of the forced labor camps in his *One Day in the Life of Ivan Denisovich* (1962); Victor Nekrasov published an honest and objective diary of his travels in Amer-ica; and Yevgeny Yevtushenko captivated audiences both at home and abroad with read-ings from his own poems, one of which, "Baby Yar," castigated the anti-Semitism that remained so ugly a feature of Soviet society.

The younger writers and artists and scientists did not, like Pasternak, question Communist society as such. They accepted it as a fact of life—after all, they had never known anything else. But at the same time they were striving for a more liberal type of rule, one in which individual talent would enjoy the freedom it required for its full devel-opment. And this, in a wider sense, was the aspiration of the whole new middle class that the Soviet regime had raised to influence and authority.

The Satellites' Push for Economic Independence

Similar pressures for a fuller and a freer life also appeared in the satellite states of East Central Europe—more particularly in Hungary, Romania, and Czechoslovakia, which had remained securely tied to the Soviet Union after the cataclysmic events of the au-tumn of 1956. Within half a decade of the suppression of the Budapest rising, the Hun-garian government began to loosen the reins of police control; by the mid-1960s, personal conversation and cultural exchange with the West had become almost as uninhibited in Hungary as in Poland and Yugoslavia. Romania soon embarked on a similar course of liberalization, but at a slower pace. Paradoxically enough, it was Czechoslovakia, the most "Western" and the most industrial of the Eastern European states, which adhered most closely to the old despotic model. The Czech Communist leadership remained more Stalinist than did other regimes; it lacked the imagination to see the benefits it might derive from appealing for cooperation to non-Communist technicians and intellectuals, as the Hungarians were doing.

Economic policy was the chief area in which the new drive for independence manifested itself. By the end of the 1950s, all the East European economies faced a knot of nearly insoluble dilemmas. The most serious was in agriculture. Here the Yugoslavs and Poles, who had brought collectivization to a halt, could point to the superiority of their productive record. The former announced an increase in farm output of 50 percent in the three years 1956–1959, and the latter claimed a 10 percent rise in the year 1961 alone. Elsewhere, with agriculture almost completely collectivized, stagnation threatened. The overall population of the area was increasing at a rate of one million a year, while farm production was failing to keep pace. Meanwhile the governments did almost nothing to conciliate the sullen opposition of the peasant masses. Still more, their agrarian policies were self-contradictory. Although the state planners stressed the importance of raising farm output, they starved agriculture of development funds and diverted its workforce to the needs of industry. By the mid-1960s, the old nightmare of rural overpopulation was a thing of the past; the new problem was one of an aging labor force—the average farmer was between forty and fifty years old—cultivating huge stretches of land with inadequate and outmoded equipment.

The needs of agriculture, then, were almost everywhere being sacrificed to industrial expansion. Yet even the industrial sector experienced vexing difficulties. In East Central Europe, as in the Soviet Union, the later 1950s brought the realization that an adequate provision of consumer goods could not be delayed forever and that to give the public some satisfaction in this respect was the surest way to reduce popular opposition to Communist rule. Beyond that, the economic planners began to recognize—as was simultaneously happening in the West—that further coordination within the bloc was necessary if Eastern Europe was to maximize its potential as an economic market.

That much could readily be agreed on. But the exact means of accomplishing it aroused heated debate among the Communist governments. In 1958, Khrushchev decided to breathe new life into the COMECON (Council for Mutual Economic Aid), which had been founded nine years earlier as the economic forerunner of the Warsaw Pact (see Chapter 17, I). At its meeting in Bucharest in June, the COMECON announced its intention to bring into harmony the major national economic targets up to the year 1975. Consensus on such an abstract goal was not hard to reach; already most of the national plans were trying to remedy past deficiencies by utilizing capital and labor resources more efficiently and by keeping investment going up at a steadier pace.

But when, in the autumn of 1962, Khrushchev became more specific in his proposals for creating a "unified planning organ" to coordinate the national investment plans, his smaller allies began to balk. Those with less-developed economies protested that their interests were being sacrificed in the name of a division of labor among the member nations of the bloc. The Romanians in particular pointed out that it was unjust and illogical to build a "Socialist" world on the basis of a division between "industrial and agrarian, developed and undeveloped" economies. In brief, Romania served notice that it was not prepared to remain a grain and oil reservoir for the rest of the COMECON nations and that it was going to industrialize, as Czechoslovakia, Poland, and Hungary had already done; nor was there any way that Khrushchev could prevent it. By the summer of 1963, Romania had won its case; construction was progressing rapidly on a great new steel plant on the Danube. The Soviet leader had failed in his effort to bring the East European economies into line.

The Sino-Soviet Rift and the Fall of Khrushchev

In the spring of 1960, a series of officially inspired articles in the Chinese press began to attack the whole basis of Khrushchev's foreign policy. The Soviet leader's efforts at international conciliation, the Chinese claimed, were totally mistaken. Not only were they failing to bring results, but they also weakened the revolutionary militancy of Asians and Africans who looked to the Communist world for help and guidance and whose struggle for political and economic independence must be given first priority. Khrushchev's doctrine of coexistence with the capitalist world and his warnings on the dangers of thermonuclear war seemed nothing less than a betrayal of Communist first principles. In Chinese eyes, the Soviet Union and its European allies had joined the camp of the "haves" against the "have-nots." The same tendencies toward moderation that had been greeted in the West with relief and gratitude were now being condemned in China as ideological treason.

Khrushchev answered the Chinese polemics, at first cautiously, later with increasing asperity. And as the ideological duel continued throughout the next four years, all the East European countries except one supported the Soviet Union. Only Albania—

Nikita Khrushchev (1894–1971), shown here protesting with his foreign minister, Andrei Gromyko, at the United Nations in 1958. (*Courtesy H. Armstrong Roberts*)

weak, backward, and geographically isolated from the rest—aligned itself with China. After vainly attempting to force a change in Albanian leadership, Khrushchev broke off further relations. The result was to leave the small country on the Adriatic in a state of hostility with all its neighbors—with Western-oriented Greece and Italy, with neutralist Yugoslavia, and with Bulgaria and Romania, which were still within the Soviet orbit. But if the vast majority of the European Communist leadership sided with Khrushchev, they were far from happy about the way he was conducting the exchange with the Chinese. A number of the East European parties thought that China should be dealt with more gently and privately—that it was dangerous and unbecoming for Communist countries to debate before the whole capitalist world—a point of view that was echoed by the powerful Italian Communist party.

Moreover, there was some truth in the Chinese contention that Khrushchev's foreign policy was not accomplishing its purpose. If it had been wholly conciliatory, it might have succeeded better. But the Soviet leader alternated soft approaches with truculent challenges. In August 1961 he authorized the East German regime to cut off the flow of escapees to the West by building a wall between the two parts of politically divided Berlin. A year later he secretly installed medium-range missiles in Castro's Cuba. The first of these gambles succeeded; the Western powers were caught unprepared with no concerted response in mind. But in the Cuban case, the outcome was a Soviet defeat. After a tense week of Soviet-American confrontation, Khrushchev was obliged to withdraw his missiles.

In retrospect, the building of the Berlin Wall and the Cuban Missile Crisis together proved a major turning point in the Cold War. Now the lines of demarcation between East and West were finally drawn for all to see. The United States would not challenge Soviet control of East Berlin, nor would the Soviets attempt to expand into Cuba. Instead each side tacitly accepted the status quo—and thus the legitimacy of the other's sphere of influence. Kennedy's imposition of a naval "quarantine" around Cuba (a word chosen to sound less hostile than "blockade") might have triggered Soviet defiance or even a missile attack. As it was, American promises not to invade Cuba and to dismantle missiles in Turkey aimed at the Soviet Union allowed Khrushchev to accept Kennedy's demand that no Soviet missiles remain on Cuban soil. But nations around the globe held their breath while the two superpowers engaged in nuclear brinksmanship. Never, before or since, has the world been closer to atomic destruction.

Meanwhile, Khrushchev was encountering difficulties on the domestic front. Although he radiated optimism and energy, his interventions within the Soviet economic bureaucracy had an improvised quality that dismayed his subordinates. He kept tinkering with the planning machinery; he shook up factory management, first emphasizing local initiative, later returning to control from the center. Most questionable of all, he tried to solve the perennial farm problem by shock tactics, ordering the ploughing up of vast stretches of "virgin lands" in such barren areas as the Central Asian steppe. The result was an ecological catastrophe. The harvest of 1963 proved disastrous, obliging the Soviet government to buy wheat from abroad, notably from the United States. No more than had his predecessors, Khrushchev failed to heal the ills plaguing Soviet agriculture, leaving the economy weaker than before.

Beyond all this, there was the question of Khrushchev's "style." Although he had attacked the Stalinist cult of personality, his own rule had gradually become a one-man show. And there was much in this performance that offended the new "middle class" generation of Soviet managers and political leaders. Khrushchev's manners were boorish, he talked too much, he favored his own family, and he acted impulsively and sometimes irresponsibly. Still more, he was a living reminder of the unhappy past. Khrushchev, after all, had been raised to a position of influence by Stalin himself. Though he had repudiated the dead despot's legacy, he was tied to it by his own earlier career. A transition figure, Khrushchev might lead his people out of the era of unbridled tyranny, but he was neither by training nor by temperament the sort of man who could adequately represent the new forces at work in Russian society.

So, as Khrushchev's difficulties mounted, both wings of Soviet communism found reason to question his leadership—the old Stalinists because he had disgraced and humiliated them, the "liberals" and technicians because of his blunderbuss tactics. The final straw was Khrushchev's proposed draft of a new Party Program, whose "term limit" provisions threatened the Stalinists (himself excepted) with enforced retirement. Driven to action, a temporary coalition among his enemies finally removed Khruschchev from power. In the autumn of 1964, the Executive Committee of the Soviet Communist Party seized the opportunity of his absence from Moscow on vacation to strip him of his state and party offices. In this thoroughly bureaucratic palace revolution of October 1964, Khrushchev's nine years of undisputed power abruptly came to an end.

His successors were men of the new stamp—party-machine products, moderate in speech and colorless in personality—Aleksei Kosygin as prime minister and Leonid Brezhnev in the ordinarily more influential role of party first secretary. Aside from eliminating Khrushchev's flamboyance and cultivating a suaver style, the new leaders seemed to differ little from him in their concrete decisions. Indeed, the post-Khrushchev era began quietly enough with what looked like a further move in the direction of "liberalization." Without questioning the basic Communist premise of collectivized industry, Prime Minister Kosygin encouraged individual plants to shift to a system that would emphasize profits and stimulate the initiative of managers. These reforms reflected the exchange of ideas between Soviet and Western economists that had taken place quite openly during the previous decade. It was not until the latter part of the 1960s—and with Brezhnev in the ascendant over Kosygin—that Soviet policy took a more sinister turn that once more gave rise to alarm in the West.

III. WESTERN EUROPE: LESSENING NATIONAL AND IDEOLOGICAL DIFFERENCES

When, in May of 1965, Europeans paused to reflect that their continent had been at peace for twenty years, they could find reason for solid satisfaction in the road they had already traversed and in the prospects before them. More particularly, a comparison between the Europe of 1938 and that of 1965 was all in favor of the latter. Two decades after the end of the First World War, the situation had been bleak in the extreme. A society barely emerging from the Great Depression and riven by a three-cornered ideological struggle had just seen the peace saved at Munich—but with each passing week it was becoming more apparent that only a postponement had been gained and that a further great conflict was all but inevitable. In contrast, the twentieth anniversary of Hitler's defeat found Europe prosperous, confident, and no longer obsessed by the fear of war. The world was still full of alarms—but the danger spots lay beyond Europe's borders, in Asia, in Africa, or in the Middle East. An increasing number of Europeans were beginning to believe that should war erupt in one of these places, it would be possible for them to avoid involvement in it. This hope was reinforced by the informal détente—the tacit understanding to refrain from nuclear threats—which had characterized Soviet-American relations since the confrontation over Cuba in the autumn of 1962.

Almost no one argued that Europe's boundaries—as they had existed, virtually unaltered, since 1945—were entirely satisfactory. Yet at least they had acquired the sanction of habit and resigned acceptance through the passage of time. The disappearance of the Baltic States was the most obvious violation of national sentiment, but there seemed not the remotest chance that this injustice would be rectified. Similarly, many Germans refused to be reconciled to their amputated eastern frontier, but it was hard to imagine Germany dragging its allies into a war to recover the lost provinces from the Poles. In East Central Europe, as before 1939, half a dozen national minorities were dissatisfied with their lot—but they voiced their complaints less bitterly than in the interwar years. Their grievances were further attenuated by the fact that all the countries in question were living under Communist regimes in which the pressure of economic and social adjustment dwarfed older and more sentimental issues. Indeed, the great remaining problem of Europe was its ideological division down the center; on both sides of the divide, people longed for the restoration of a continent-wide economy and culture. Even here, however, East and West alike saw reason for hope. As opposed to the steady exacerbation of ideological hostility in the 1930s, in the 1960s such hatreds and misunderstandings were diminishing, and the barrier that Winston Churchill two decades earlier had baptized the "iron curtain" had been punctured so often that in most places the term was no longer appropriate to the new realities.

Yet in one crucial area the iron curtain was still the dominant fact of life. A line of barbed wire and watchtowers still separated West from East Germany. This was the outstanding anomaly in a Europe that had settled into its midcentury equilibrium. Within the division of Germany, the wall across Berlin visibly symbolized the fact that, here at least, the Cold War persisted. The bizarre situation of the former German capital—the isolation of one-half of it as a beleaguered outpost of the West—was the last unresolved legacy of the Second World War. Khrushchev had been well aware of its importance. Nearly his whole tenure of power had been occupied by an endemic Berlin crisis, as he kept urging the need for a permanent settlement. Yet though he multiplied his threats and exhortations, he constantly postponed his deadlines and never pushed matters to a final showdown.

An agreement between the Western powers and the Soviet Union on Berlin seemed next to impossible. The former insisted on ironclad guarantees for their rights of access and freedom for the West Berliners to organize their government as they chose; the latter sought a way of reinforcing the East German regime, whose popularity was almost nil and which was transparently the weakest and most dependent within the Communist bloc. Between a West unyielding in its defense of the status quo and a Soviet leadership intent on tidying up a standing challenge to its prestige, the city of Berlin remained suspended in limbo.

Germany: The Succession to Adenauer

Such at least was the state of affairs as long as Chancellor Adenauer stayed in power. But in October 1963, his fourteen-year tenure of office came to an end. In the election of September 1961, Adenauer's Christian Democratic Union had emerged victorious for the fourth time, but with a reduced percentage of the vote. These electoral losses suggested that the German public was growing weary of Adenauer's authoritarian leadership, and the succeeding year and a half was occupied by bitter party infighting, with the octogenarian chancellor trying to block the path of Ludwig Erhard, whose popularity as the architect of Germany's "economic miracle" (see Figure 20.2) made him the logical candidate for the succession. Eventually Erhard won. No other party leader had remotely as good a claim as he. In April 1963, the Christian Democrats named him their candidate for chancellor, specifying that the change should take place in six months' time.

Erhard's style of government was very different from Adenauer's. Affable, frequently irresolute, and unschooled in party intrigue, the new chancellor granted both the Bundestag and his ministerial colleagues a freedom to which they had long grown unaccustomed. Adenauer had treated his subordinates like schoolboys; Erhard gave them the sense of being his collaborators and equals. The result was a shift from one-man government to a more traditional cabinet system. Such a change had already been implicit in the outcome of the "*Spiegel* incident" the previous year. Franz-Josef Strauss, the minister of defense, had arbitrarily ordered the arrest of the editors of Germany's leading news weekly on the charge that they had published secret military information. After a vast

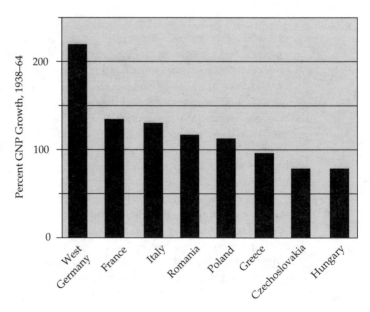

FIGURE 20.2   The growth in the gross national product of several European countries between 1938 and 1964. Note the strength of West Germany's economy compared with those of France and Italy, and the relatively poor performance of Eastern bloc countries.

outcry in the press and the universities, Strauss had been obliged to resign—a result that was generally interpreted as salutary in giving greater content and reality to German democracy.

A similar reinforcement of democracy was evident in the new self-confidence of the Social Democratic opposition. Under the buoyant guidance of the young mayor of West Berlin, Willy Brandt, the Social Democrats emerged greatly strengthened from the election of 1961; their vote had gone up by nearly 5 percentage points, which was almost exactly what the Christian Democrats had lost. Brandt was a man attuned to the 1960s, sturdily optimistic and pragmatic, with a notion of socialism that had little of Marx left in it and that was closer to British or Scandinavian practice. Under his leadership, the Social Democrats strengthened their hold over West Berlin in the municipal election of 1963; they similarly controlled four of the nine West German state governments. But after having made such gains in local influence, they were disappointed that the parliamentary election of September 1965 pushed their vote up by only three additional percentage points, still leaving the Christian Democrats in control.

The moderation of the German Social Democrats reflected public satisfaction with the continuing prosperity of the country. At the same time, the steady growth in the party's strength underlined the fact that a decade and a half of Christian Democratic rule had left many areas in Germany's economy and society woefully neglected. For one thing, there was the problem of absorbing nearly a million foreign workers, who after the Berlin wall went up in 1961 began to take the place of escapees from East Germany as recruits for the labor force. Still more important was a great backlog of unfilled public needs. Germany's highways were proving far from adequate for the new traffic, its European lead in technology was slipping, and the construction of schools and hospitals was failing to keep up with the country's requirements. It was apparent by the mid-1960s that in Germany, as in the United States, expenditures for public welfare had been sacrificed to private affluence and that the Social Democrats had a mounting sentiment behind them when they blamed such deficiencies on Christian Democracy's unbroken tenure of power.

In foreign affairs, the difference between the parties was less noticeable. By the election of 1961, the Social Democrats had abandoned any thought of a neutralist stand and had aligned themselves on a position of loyalty to the United States and to NATO that was scarcely different from that of Adenauer. At the same time, they criticized him for having done too little about reunification. There was some justice in this reproach. By his rigid and uncompromising attitude toward the East German regime, the old chancellor had in fact ruled out any realistic progress toward reuniting the country.

At the beginning of 1963, nine months before his retirement, Adenauer—piqued by what he regarded as a cooling in relations between Washington and Bonn since President Kennedy had taken over from Eisenhower—had signed a treaty of friendship with France. This document might mean everything or nothing. Its chief purpose was to codify for the future something of the cordiality and esteem that had grown up between Adenauer and General de Gaulle. But so personal a relationship could not be inherited by Adenauer's successor. And it was soon apparent that between him and de Gaulle relations were more distant than they had been under his predecessor. For Erhard was at the very least reluctant to support the drive for leadership in Europe and a world role overseas that the general had inaugurated after putting in order his own domestic difficulties.

France: De Gaulle's Claim to European Leadership

In the course of the year 1962, Charles de Gaulle achieved two successes that marked a decisive turning point in his tenure of power: He brought the Algerian War to an end, and he reinforced his own office in a way that gave a new sense of permanency to the regime he had created.

The struggle in Algeria, of course, was closely linked with de Gaulle's return to national leadership. The fear of the Algerian French that the politicians in Paris were about to "sell them out" to the Moslem rebels had precipitated the complex chain of events that eventually hoisted the general into power. Once in office, however, he disappointed the conservatives and nationalists who had hoped that he would pursue a policy of colonial repression. Equally dismayed were those of the Center-Left who had voted for him in the expectation that he would try to meet the Moslems' demands. De Gaulle did neither of these, following instead a zigzag course that alternated military action with vague conciliatory gestures and ended by confusing both his friends and his enemies. It was impossible to tell whether he was feeling his way without having a clear goal in mind or whether he knew all along what the outcome would be and was simply giving his people time to accustom themselves to the idea of letting Algeria go.

General Charles de Gaulle (1890–1970), French head of state in the years from 1944 to 1946 and again from 1958 to 1969, here shown beside German Chancellor Konrad Adenauer (1876–1967) at a rally supporting European integration in a small German town in 1962. (*AKG London Ltd*)

In any case, in the nearly four years that he took to bring the war to an end, de Gaulle gradually eliminated all intermediate solutions. First he dropped as impracticable the idea of "assimilating" Algeria to France—that is, of making a reality of the Moslem Algerians' theoretical status as full French citizens. Next he tacitly ruled out the notion of an "association" of Algeria with France that would fall short of complete independence. Finally, in the spring of 1961, he began negotiations that ten months later were to bring about a solution earlier thought acceptable by only a handful of French intellectuals and leftists—the unconditional liberation of Algeria.

In the meantime, however, the long delay and the ambiguity of the general's statements had exasperated public opinion at home. By the autumn of 1960, scarcely any articulate French citizen seemed any longer to be a convinced Gaullist. The regime was apparently resting on an ever narrower base of support as it turned now this way, now that, to face a double and contradictory opposition. On the Right, the nationalist irreconcilables resorted to direct action. In April 1961, the military leaders in Algiers staged the fourth insurrectionary demonstration to shake that effervescent city since 1956. This time, as he had done the previous year, de Gaulle sternly repressed the challenge to his authority; in France itself the army stuck by him, but it was quite obviously astir with discontent. No longer in a position to count on the military, the rightist opposition at home turned to conspiracy and terrorism with a succession of plastic-bomb explosions in Paris itself. These criminal acts, which were directed against prominent Frenchmen known to favor conciliation with the Algerian Moslems, actually claimed few victims; their main effect was to discredit the cause they were intended to serve by gradually convincing the mass of apolitical Frenchmen that the nationalist diehards were both ruthless and irresponsible.

The democratic and leftist opposition, in contrast, stuck strictly to nonviolent protest. The furthest it went was a manifesto signed by 121 intellectuals—among them Jean-Paul Sartre—calling for civil disobedience in what they regarded as an unjust war. Most of those who objected to the prolongation of the Algerian conflict took a more moderate stand. The main target of their attacks was the barbarous behavior into which a war without mercy had led the special French units charged with the work of repression. First the Protestant clergy, later the chiefs of the Catholic hierarchy denounced the practices of torture, reprisals, and summary executions. Those who opposed the Algerian War could not understand the government's balancing tactics and the way it gave equal treatment to two oppositions so different in character. The police seemed at least as zealous in breaking up student or trade-union demonstrations against the war as in pursuing the authors of bomb outrages. In February 1962—just one month before the negotiations with the rebels were successfully concluded—a Socialist-led protest against police brutality turned a million and a half people into the streets of Paris, the largest public demonstration that the French capital had seen since the Second World War.

Once the Algerian conflict ended, however, the nationalist opposition melted away. This was apparent in the results of the special election of November 1962, by which de Gaulle sought to reinforce his authority.

The previous August he had barely escaped assassination by rightist fanatics. This—the closest shave he had yet had in several attempts that had already been made against his life—convinced the general and his advisers that something should be done about the succession to the presidency. The provision in the constitution of 1958 that the head of state should be chosen by a list of local "notables," rather than by the people directly, had ensured de Gaulle's own election, but it was far from certain that in the event of his sudden death that it would produce a president of similar views. With the Algerian War over—with the crisis that had originally brought him to power successfully surmounted—there was a real possibility that France would return to politics as usual. Most of the local officials who ranked as presidential electors were adherents of one of the old parties of the Third and Fourth Republics. What guarantee was there that they would not choose a politician of the same stamp who would be totally out of sympathy with the institutions and practices of the Fifth?

To meet this danger, de Gaulle instructed the new prime minister whom he had just installed in office, Georges Pompidou, to propose a constitutional amendment providing for the popular election of the president. The proposal in itself was enough to alarm the parliamentarians of the National Assembly; the form in which it was presented drove them to fury. Pompidou bypassed the amending procedure specified in the constitution by announcing that the change would be submitted to a popular referendum for ratification. Faced with this violation of a constitutional document that had been purposely tailored to de Gaulle's own requirements, a large majority of the deputies closed ranks and girded for battle. They overthrew the Pompidou ministry—to which the general replied by dissolving the Assembly and calling for new elections.

The election of 1962 was the great watershed in the internal history of de Gaulle's rule. It brought a new type of man into the Assembly; nearly half of those elected had never served as deputies before, and most of these were political pragmatists, impatient with the guidance of the old party war horses. More broadly, the election was a repudiation of the traditional parliamentary leadership. The voters, particularly the young, had shown that they were dissatisfied with old-fashioned politics—or, at the very least, bored by it. All this suggested that the Fifth Republic could no longer be regarded as the temporary expedient that its critics had called it.

The most telling issue against de Gaulle was the independent nuclear deterrent that the general was developing. Indeed, this was just about the only remaining question on which the opposition in the Assembly could mount a first-class debate and rouse the French public from its post-Algeria lethargy. The nuclear striking force cost a great deal of money; its critics could easily point to the way it diverted funds from such urgent purposes as education and housing. But de Gaulle refused to compromise his military program: The independent deterrent was central to his conception of his own role and that of the nation he led.

To American policy makers, the general's defiant stand frequently seemed mere cantankerousness; in his own mind it formed part of a logical and coherent view of the future. The United States, de Gaulle argued, could neither unite Europe nor be counted on to use its nuclear deterrent for the defense of the Continent. A master of *Realpolitik* and an unabashed exponent of national egoism, the general was skeptical of apparently generous or altruistic gestures in international relations. The Europeans, he contended, must rely on themselves. Of course, they must draw closer together; but they should maintain their separate national identities and defer to the leadership of the one power that by geography and tradition was equipped for the role—Gaullist France. This line of thinking further implied an indissoluble Franco-German understanding and a concerted effort to lure the states of East Central Europe away from their Soviet ties.

De Gaulle's foreign policy bewildered both Frenchmen and other Europeans. The enthusiasts for European unity tended to distrust him; they disliked his nationalist language and regretted the passing of the Christian Democratic leaders whose vision of the future had been international and federalist. On the other hand, they recognized that a federal Europe could not be built without France, and that until that happy solution was reached, there was no alternative to playing along with France's ruler. One people, however, was almost uniformly hostile to de Gaulle's policy: British of all political persuasions saw it as a threat to their own position, for the general's notion of his country's European and world role challenged Britain almost as much as it did the United States. Whatever party was in power in London, distrust between de Gaulle and the British remained a constant in the international politics of the 1960s.

Britain: Labour's Half Decade of Power

The Conservatives had already governed Britain for more than a decade when articulate public sentiment finally began to turn against them. Elsewhere—in Eastern Europe, in Germany, in France—politics and the national economy seemed to be on the move as the 1950s came to an end. The British alone remained in the doldrums, apparently hypnotized by Prime Minister Macmillan's soothing rhetoric.

Yet under the surface of prosperity there was much to criticize in the Tory conduct of affairs. In comparison with the record of its neighbors across the Channel, Britain's economy was stagnating. Inflationary pressures were not being absorbed by industrial expansion; investment was going into high-profit concerns rather than into those that could best aid the economy as a whole; and the excess labor force was unable or unwilling to move to the places where new jobs were available. Moreover, the years of Conservative rule saw a slow erosion of the welfare-state practices that the Labour government had installed and that the Tories had initially accepted. The National Health Service reinstituted charges for such medical help as prescriptions, eyeglasses, and dentistry, and the government freed certain categories of buildings from rent control; the latter measure encouraged a private construction boom at the expense of public housing.

Meanwhile, British nationalists who had been incensed at Prime Minister Eden's knuckling under to the United States during the Suez crisis were further outraged when Macmillan apparently did likewise in the matter of nuclear arms. At the end of 1962, at a meeting with President Kennedy at Nassau in the Bahamas, he accepted a new arrangement that subordinated the small British nuclear force to American supply and production schedules. Indeed, the change was so drastic as to make people question whether Britain any longer ranked—although far behind the United States and the Soviet Union—as the world's third nuclear power. The contrast with the thoroughly independent fashion in which the fourth such power—de Gaulle's France—was readying its striking force was only too apparent.

It was neither economic nor nuclear policy, however, that at length discredited the Macmillan government. It was a series of internal difficulties within the Conservative party itself. First came a sensational sex scandal, complete with national security implications; then the following autumn, Macmillan learned that he would have to undergo an operation and resigned. He was succeeded by Sir Alec Douglas-Home—a former earl who had renounced his title in order to assume the post of prime minister. In less than a year, the general election of 1964 pitted Sir Alec and his party against another newcomer, the new Labour leader, Harold Wilson.

Projecting an essentially "classless" image to the British electorate, Wilson was by nature a peacemaker. He tried to bridge the gap between Labour's right and left—and at the same time to modernize the party—by calling on the new class of technicians and managers to cooperate in the great work of building a planned society. He stressed the need to expand educational opportunities, systematically outbidding the Tories, who had already endorsed a proposal for more than doubling university enrollments in the next generation. This was the great novelty of the election campaign—an appeal to the new middle class that went beyond the conflict between private enterprise and nationalized industry by offering a coherent program of industrial investment, realignment of private incomes, and the use of scientific knowledge under state direction.

In the end, Labour won the election by the extremely narrow margin of five seats. Once installed as prime minister, however, Wilson chose to behave as though he had received an unqualified mandate for change. He announced that his government would proceed to reinvigorate public housing construction; it would "intervene selectively" in the economy by establishing public industries in depressed areas and in "growth" regions of technological advance; it would enlarge social security coverage and restore a full system of medical care without charge; it would redistribute incomes by simultaneously raising pensions and taxes on large earnings. It was clear that Wilson intended to make good on the early postwar promises of the "welfare state" philosophy, whose stated goal was to relieve the individual from the burdens of having to bear the cost of housing, health care, and retirement alone. Wilson was returning to the spirit of the Labour government of 1945 by insisting that Britons had economic as well as political rights that the government must honor.

Paradoxically enough, Labour's greatest strides in carrying out this program came in its initial period of rule, when its parliamentary majority hung on a handful of votes. In his first year and a half in office, Wilson did in fact succeed in doing some of the things he had promised. Social services grew markedly; public housing and slum clearance increased sharply. In short, Labour made good on its pledge to shift resources from the private sector to the public—and eventually even exceeded its announced goal in this front. Yet after winning a resounding reelection triumph in 1966, Wilson encountered mounting problems. Social reforms cost money, and that money could be found only if the government produced a high rate of economic growth. Such growth, however, was dependent on a favorable trade position, and Labour had inherited from the Conservatives a balance-of-payments deficit and an overvalued currency.

After a year of hesitation, Wilson finally moved to devalue the pound sterling in November, 1967, in order to boost British sales abroad. But the move, while economically sound, was a blow to British pride. The pound was a major international currency—second only to the dollar in its worldwide influence. To devalue the pound, then, meant to take another step in Britain's slow, dignified abdication as a great power. To this, too, Wilson and his colleagues saw no alternative. They announced that their country would give up its military responsibilities east of Suez; for the first time in the postwar period, they set the budget for education higher than that for defense. Thirteen years of Tory rule had masked the extent to which Britain had already relinquished its overseas commitments. The return of Labour put the final seal on the long, drawn-out end of empire.

Italy: The Failure of the "Opening to the Left"

In Italy, too, the Socialists returned to power in the early 1960s. But here they were far from being strong enough to govern alone: They commanded less than 15 percent of the vote, as opposed to the Christian Democrats' 40 percent and the Communists' 25. Moreover, they were burdened by the memory of two decades of close cooperation with the Italian followers of Stalin. Not until the events of 1956 had shaken them loose from this alliance were they in a position to offer a reinforcement to Italian democracy—to participate in that "opening to the Left" which Prime Minister Amintore Fanfani had so long advocated.

In the spring of 1962, the restless Fanfani was at last able to carry out his design. The hesitations of his own Christian Democratic party were resolved when it became apparent that the Vatican no longer opposed an understanding with Italian socialism; Pope John's policy of coming to terms with the modern world was already having its effect. For their part, the Socialist leaders agreed with Fanfani on the urgency of reform and a planned economy. They realized, as he did, that the economic boom was affecting Italian society most unevenly, and that only vigorous government action could redirect public and private investment into those sectors that were currently being neglected. Many of the more old-fashioned or ideologically militant Socialists were reluctant to go along with an economic program that owed far more to Keynes than to Marx. But even these could appreciate the benefits that might accrue to Italian workers by having some of their spokesmen in on the planning process.

The original opening to the Left meant simply that the Socialists would support a revamped Fanfani government without supplying any ministers themselves. By 1963, however, when parliamentary elections gave a 60 percent majority to the parties that had endorsed the new course, a closer alliance seemed preferable. At this, an influential minority among both the Christian Democrats and the Socialists began to balk. It took a summer and autumn of complex party jockeying—and a colorless caretaker government—to convince the two parties that there was no alternative. Not until the very end of the year was it possible to put together a new ministry in which the Socialists were full participants. In the process, Fanfani himself was sacrificed. His hard-driving ways had aroused too much hostility on all sides. His heir as prime minister was a younger and more agreeable Christian Democrat, Aldo Moro.

The Moro government had rough going from the start. It was difficult at best to keep two such diverse parties working in harmony—and still harder when economic troubles arose. In the winter of 1963–1964, Italian prosperity got out of hand. With inflationary pressures mounting and a balance-of-payments crisis threatening, the government was torn apart by the contradictory remedies suggested. Two years later, when the economy returned to prosperity levels, the life had gone out of the opening to the Left. The result of the anti-inflationary struggle had been a postponement of the government's reform program. Its proposals for the regulation of urban growth, for massive aid to education, and for the industrialization of the south had not advanced beyond the preparatory stage.

When Italy went to the polls in the spring of 1968, the Socialists lost heavily to the Communists and to the fringe formations of the extreme Left. In the wake of the Socialist electoral losses, Moro, too, had to go, after having stayed in power longer than any prime minister since De Gasperi. His successors were routine Christian Democrats, who simply tried to muddle along as best they could. For by now it was becoming apparent that the Italian administrative machine was unable to cope with the problems of a modern industrial society. Underpaid, overstaffed, inefficient, and demoralized, the bureaucracy threatened to grind to a halt. Already in the autumn of 1966, when devastating floods hit such north Italian cities as Florence and Venice, the government had been bitterly criticized for its failure to foresee the danger and to take preventive action.

In these distressing circumstances, Italian political life sank into a bog of discouragement. Factional strife had reduced party organization to meaninglessness; parliamentary debate seemed more and more irrelevant to the real issues confronting the nation. Italians increasingly asked themselves whether electoral democracy itself could survive so dispiriting a state of affairs. Nothing seemed to be working; all the old remedies had been exhausted. Only the Italian economy—despite this political disarray—seemed capable of performing well.

The New Technicians and the Maladjustments of Prosperity

By 1960, nearly the whole of Western and Central Europe was enjoying the most sustained prosperity it had known since the outbreak of the First World War. In France, which earlier had lagged behind its neighbors but had now suddenly advanced into the lead, production increased by nearly two-thirds during the period 1952–1958. Elsewhere, an annual rise in productivity of approximately 4 percent had come to be taken for granted.

To operate this expanded industrial machine, a greatly increased staff of managers and technicians was required. These, like their counterparts in the Soviet Union, typified the changed society of the midcentury. They were realistic and matter-of-fact, and they admired the efficiency of American methods. As opposed to the old type of educated European, whose culture was literary and humanistic, these people were better trained in science and economics and reflected both the postwar changes in educational curricula and the new democratization of the technical schools and universities.

Indeed, there had emerged what the British called a "meritocracy"—a class of highly trained specialists coming from all strata of the population and closely attached to none. Such men and women, who more and more frequently derived from lower middle-class or working-class backgrounds, lost touch with their families and earlier associations as they rose in the social scale. They advanced *as individuals*, leaving their original class behind them. This was not at all what European Socialists had had in mind when they dreamed of the future society; they had thought of whole classes rising, and of the leaders of these classes remaining with their own people as directors of political parties or trade unions. Before the war, to rise out of one's class was considered treason to one's comrades.

With the postwar democratization of life and education, however, the American notion of an individual ascent became accepted. The result was an impoverishment of the Socialist parties and trade unions, which saw themselves deprived of their natural leaders. The new class of managers and technicians—and with them a great part of the population at large—was impatient of all forms of ideological debate, which, in the new Europe of the midcentury, sounded old-fashioned, stuffy, and irrelevant and seemed to have little to do with the real problems of the Continent's economy and society. By 1960, a mixed economy was everywhere the rule; the welfare state and a large measure of official intervention in economic life were universally accepted. West Germany, Belgium, and Switzerland leaned toward free enterprise; Britain, Scandinavia, and the Netherlands were more tinged with socialism; France and Italy were somewhere in between; but the differences between one nation and another were of degree rather than of kind. By mid-century, the pre-1945 debates over the merits of capitalism or collectivism seemed academic and tedious. On the one hand, people were convinced that state intervention and state planning were essential; on the other hand, they were skeptical of the traditional Socialist panacea of nationalization.

The result was widespread agreement on an implicit ideology that might be called "conservative socialism." As one skeptical but sympathetic critic put it, Socialist doctrines had "begun to wear a somewhat antiquated look" for the very reason that "so many of their predictions" had "come true."* But this had happened in a *form* that almost no one had predicted and that disoriented the parties of the Left. More particularly, the decline of the cult of revolution as an end in itself and the decreasing public interest in such old issues as anticlericalism deprived political debate of much of its earlier moral fervor. The great new questions were technical. Most of them did not lend themselves to impassioned advocacy and were dependent for intelligent discussion on the advice of experts.

Such was the outlook as the 1960s opened. As the decade progressed, however, and a new type of Socialist leader (like Harold Wilson) came to the fore, a second look at the newly emerging society suggested that matters were not quite so clearly on the road to a harmonious solution. Revolutionary spirit and class hatred might be greatly diminished, but status differences and large inequalities in wealth remained. A new generation of democratic left-wing leadership—men who themselves could lay claim to being technicians and experts—began to search out the social anomalies and the pockets of backwardness that belied the overall picture of a democratic and prosperous continent.

In a geographical sense, they found, the new prosperity was most unevenly distributed. It had attained its full development only in Europe's industrial heartland, stretching from Glasgow in Scotland to the north Italian city of Milan. Elsewhere—especially in Southern Europe—although the mid-century social changes had discredited the old ways of doing things, the standard of living had not risen proportionately. If Europe's own underdeveloped areas were more severely shaken by innovation than were the established industrial centers, they were still unable to keep up with the overall economic advance. In Italy, for example, although the south made more progress in the decade 1955–1965 than in any other such period of its history, *in comparative terms* the gap

*George Lichtheim, *The New Europe: Today—and Tomorrow* (New York: Praeger, 1963), 182.

between it and the north widened rather than diminished. Moreover, here, as in so many other backward parts of the Continent, job seekers increasingly found work either in the industrialized regions of its own nation or in more prosperous countries; by 1963, two and three-quarter million laborers were working in foreign lands. Almost necessarily, these people suffered from discrimination and difficulties in adjustment. And such social problems were compounded where, as in England, the immigrant workers were of another race. In the British election of 1964, the Labour party lost votes in more than one constituency for having championed the cause of nonwhites from the Commonwealth countries overseas who had been arriving in a steady stream since the Second World War.

In the 1950s, social criticism had focused on status differences. A decade later, economic questions had once more come into prominence. For if educational reform promised eventually to break down caste barriers, there was no corresponding technique at hand to reduce disparities in wealth. As the years of prosperity continued, it became apparent that the continuing gap between the rich and the poor regions of Europe had its exact parallel in the difference between rich and poor members of the various national populations. Although the latter were improving their lot, they were not doing so as rapidly as the wealthy. In comparison with America, the basic items (such as food) in the budgets of the poor remained expensive, whereas the luxury items, which the rich nearly monopolized, were relatively cheap. Moreover, the wealthy tended to come from the same families as they had earlier; the higher business leadership recruited itself within very narrow circles. In the Europe of the 1960s, as in the United States, it was easier for someone without family backing to make his way in politics than in the world of business.

Social and economic conflict had by no means simply been relegated to an unhappy past. Indeed, in certain respects the new availability of mass consumer goods made matters worse; it underscored the difference between those who had them and those who did not. Thus, after the comparative quiet of the 1950s, unexpected sources of class tension appeared, and trade unions began to regain their militancy. This, however, was no longer narrowly ideological; the working-class demands of the 1960s were directed toward concrete economic goals. The most important strikes of the decade were clearly inspired by the conviction that ordinary workers were not receiving their due share in the overall prosperity.

The Common Market

Most of these new social and economic questions crossed national frontiers. Both prosperity and the maladjustments it entailed were Western European in scope. Trade unionists and managers alike could agree that the strict separation of one economy from another by national boundaries no longer made sense. With the experience of the United States and the Soviet Union in mind, they argued that a wider market was required for maximum efficiency. Hence the pressure for "integration"—a tighter concept than alliance but a looser one than union—which as early as 1951 had manifested itself in the establishment of the European Coal and Steel community.

Despite the failure of the next move toward integration—the EDC—the six nations of "Little Europe" had proceeded to organize further economic "communities." In

1956 came the pooling of their resources of nuclear energy in "Euratom," and in the following year, the establishment of a Common Market, which would eventually mean the elimination of all tariff barriers among them. A year later, de Gaulle assumed power in France. Despite the turn toward national assertion under the Fifth Republic, the Gaullist regime continued to honor the commitments of its predecessor toward its European partners.

By January 1, 1958, all six nations had ratified the Treaty of Rome, establishing the Common Market, and the great experiment was launched. An area with a population of more than 170 million—comparable to that of the Soviet Union or the United States—was now associated in what was officially called the European Economic Community. From the start the new community aimed at something wider than a customs union. Like its predecessor, the Coal and Steel Community, the Common Market had a supranational executive responsible to an intergovernmental council of ministers. Its powers were theoretically weaker than those of the earlier community, but since it shared with it a joint international assembly and court of justice, the procedures of the two inevitably tended to merge.

Between 1958 and 1962, industrial production within the Common Market went up at an average annual rate of 7.6 percent—as opposed to 4 percent in the seven nations of the European Free Trade Association—which in itself gave eloquent evidence of the success of the venture. During the same years, trade among the six nearly doubled. The original idea had been to reduce tariffs among the member nations very gradually so as to give the individual economies time to adjust to the change. But once the experiment was launched, businesspeople began to lose their fears. Many argued that it was better to get the transition over with as rapidly as possible and to start immediately to meet the new competition that tariff reduction implied. As a result, by mid-1963, the Common Market was two and a half years ahead of schedule, with internal tariffs down to 40 percent of their previous level.

Five years later, on July 1, 1968, the full tariff union came into effect, as the last customs barriers fell. The great goal had apparently been achieved. Yet the Community still had not squarely faced the decision of what was to follow. Should political union succeed the customs union? And what of the requests to enlarge the Community made by other nations now anxious to join? Chief among these was Britain. After nearly three years of hesitation, in the summer of 1961 the Macmillan government applied for membership. This proposition placed "the Six" before a cruel dilemma. Most of them wanted Britain in. The governments of the Low Countries in particular were mindful of their long-standing cultural and commercial ties across the Channel and eager for a counterweight within the Common Market to offset the influence of France. At the same time, the British wanted to enter on terms of maximum benefit to themselves while retaining their favored position within the Commonwealth. Such conditions gave pause even to those who endorsed Britain's membership. It seemed a one-sided bargain, and it threatened the prospects of political federation by, in effect, giving the Community an open frontier.

In the end, de Gaulle settled the matter. After several months of a characteristic cryptic silence, he vetoed the British application in January 1963. Four years later, in May 1967, he repeated the performance, replying in similar terms to a second British bid for admission, this time coming from the Labour rather than the Conservative side, and attaching fewer conditions. Not until Britain had undergone a "profound economic and political transformation," de Gaulle maintained, would it be ready for partnership with its Continental neighbors. In effect, de Gaulle's twin vetoes served to restrict the scope of the Common Market's "integration" and to retain French dominance within that body. The so-called Luxemburg compromise of 1966 guaranteed that each member enjoyed the right to block unilaterally any Community decision if it should feel that the nation's vital interests were at stake. Jean Monnet and other founders of the Common Market ideal had assumed that economic cooperation would logically and inevitably bring with it a desire for political union among member nations as well. De Gaulle proved that the desire for unimpaired sovereignty was not so easily overcome.

The "affluent society" of the 1960s had brought with it a greater prosperity and optimism concerning the future than Europe had known for almost half a century. Not since the 1920s had there existed such general confidence in the prospects for continued growth and the possibility of a peaceful resolution to the conflicts among its states. The economic boom had now continued for so long that some Europeans began to take it for granted and to assume that the good times they now enjoyed would endure without a break for decades to come. They were soon to discover just how abruptly good times can end.

READINGS

An excellent introduction to the social and political changes that occurred during the 1960s is Stephen R. Graubard, ed., A New Europe?* (1964). Other general overviews are contained in Stanley Rothman's European Society and Politics (1970) and Anthony Sampson's The New Europeans, rev. ed. (1971). The new patterns of consumption made possible by growing affluence are explored in John Ardagh, The New French Revolution* (1968); in Arthur Marwick, British Society Since 1945* (1982); and in John Goldthorpe et al., The Affluent Worker* (1971). Richard Hoggart surveys the losses brought by the passing of traditional working-class culture in Britain in The Uses of Literacy* (1957).

Studies of the impact of change on a local level include Lawrence Wylie's classic portrait of a small town in the south of France, Village in the Vaucluse,* 3rd ed. (1974); Edgar Morin's The Red and the White: Report from a French Village (1970); Ronald Blythe's Akenfield: Portrait of an English Village* (1967); and Michael Young's and Peter Willmott's Family and Kinship in East London* (1957), a sensitive and sympathetic account of life in a lower-class housing project. Richard Kuisal, Seducing the French: The Dilemma of Americanization (1993), details the perceived dangers and attractions of American popular culture in France.

For similar changes in Eastern Europe, in addition to Hoskings and Nove (see readings for Chapter 10), consult Margaret Miller, The Rise of the Russian Consumer* (1965); George R. Feiwel's The Soviet Quest for Economic Efficiency (1972); and Peter A. Toma, The Changing Face of Communism in Eastern Europe (1970). The development of a

*Books available in paperback are marked with an asterisk.

bureaucratic middle class in the East bloc countries is analyzed by Milovan Djilas in *The New Class** (1957) and *The Unperfect Society: Beyond the New Class** (1969). Soviet domestic and foreign policy under Khrushchev is examined in Taubman (see readings for Chapter 19) and in Carl A. Linden, *Khrushchev and the Soviet Leadership, 1957–1964* (1966). A first-person account of life under Khrushchev is presented in Ludmilla Lexeyeva and Paul Goldberg, *The Thaw Generation: Coming of Age in the Post-Stalin Era* (1990). The checkered career of Trofim Lysenko, a symbol of Stalin's influence on Soviet science, is detailed in Zhores Medvedev, *The Rise and Fall of T. D. Lysenko* (1969), and Loren R. Graham, *Science and Philosophy in the Soviet Union* (1972).

On Germany in the years following Adenauer's departure, see Louis J. Edinger's *Politics in Germany** (1968), Kendall L. Baker et al., *Germany Transformed: Political Culture and the New Politics* (1981), and especially Ralf Dahrendorf's critical assessment of the weaknesses of German political culture in *Society and Democracy in Germany** (1968). Developments in France during the 1960s are discussed in Williams and Harrison (see readings for Chapter 19); Henry W. Ehrmann, *Politics in France,* 2nd ed. (1971); and Alfred Grosser, *French Foreign Policy Under de Gaulle* (1967). Michel Crozier analyzes French resistance to change in *The Bureaucratic Phenomenon** (1964) and *The Stalled Society** (1973).

For Britain in this period, see David McKie and Chris Cook, eds., *The Decade of Disillusion: British Politics in the 1960s* (1972); Bernard Levin, *The Pendulum Years* (1970), the acerbic but insightful observations of a British Conservative; Brian Lapping, *The Labour Government** (1971); and Samuel H. Beer, *Britain Against Itself: The Political Contradictions of Collectivism* (1982). For Italy and the failure of the "opening to the Left," besides Ginsborg and Kogan (see readings for Chapter 17), there is Donald Blackmer, *Unity in Diversity: Italian Communism and the Communist World* (1968).

On the rise of the new technicians, see Ezra Suleiman, *Politics, Power, and Bureaucracy in France* (1973); Philip Stanworth and Anthony Giddens, eds., *Elites and Power in British Society* (1974); and Ralf Dahrendorf's theoretical study *Class and Class Conflict in Industrial Society** (1959), which argues persuasively that an unequal distribution of power is unavoidable in industrial society.

The first decade of the Common Market is charted in Carl J. Friedrich, *Europe: An Emerging Nation?* (1969); James Marber and Bruce Reed, *The European Community: Vision and Reality* (1973); and F. Roy Willis, *Italy Chooses Europe* (1973). The misadventures of Britain's belated application to join the EEC are related in two studies by Uwe Kitzinger: *The Second Try: Labour and the E.E.C.* (1973) and *Diplomacy and Persuasion: How Britain Joined the Common Market* (1973).

A DECADE OF
DISILLUSIONMENT,
1968–1979

Italian students demonstrate in Rome in favor of school reform. The large banner at the rear reads: "Fascists Out of Our Schools." (*Courtesy AP/Wide World Photos*)

As the 1960s came to a close, Europeans—both in the East and in the West—sensed that something was fundamentally different about the historical situation in which they were living. It was now nearly a quarter century since the guns had fallen silent after the Second World War. More rapidly than anyone had dared hope in 1945, the Continent had recovered economically from the devastation and surpassed prewar levels of production and consumption. The war's spiritual and emotional scars were taking longer to heal, it is true; but with the passage of time, they too seemed close to disappearing.

It came as a surprise, therefore, that the decade following the affluent 1960s should have been so deeply marked by disillusionment. What accounted for this rapid change in mood? The first answer is that prosperity itself bred a sense of spiritual emptiness in daily life, especially among the young; sure of being able to meet their material needs, they turned their attention to demands for greater freedom in societies that seemed overly oppressive. There were parallels between their demands for personal liberty and the romantic stirrings that had led European youth on the eve of 1914 to a restless search for meaning beyond the self-satisfied prosperity of the times.

This was the first cause of disillusionment—a realization that material security did not in itself guarantee a fulfilled and fulfilling life. A second cause, especially evident in Eastern Europe, was the yearning for greater freedom and an impatience with the restraints and hypocrisies of life under Communist rule. There citizens felt trapped by a system that exploited their faith and talents while giving little in return. Again, the prosperity of the 1960s, which removed the most pressing problems of material want, made it possible to address more spiritual needs.

When in retrospect people tried to date both changes, they usually settled on 1968. In that year tumultuous events had shaken both Paris and Prague, as French students sparked massive demonstrations against the Gaullist government and Czechs called for a "socialism with a human face." The half decade after 1968 saw a number of challenges to the established order in a first wave of discontent. But in 1973 another, graver crisis appeared—the start of an economic recession that put Europe's recovery on both sides of the iron curtain at risk and threatened to plunge the Continent into the most serious slump that the Western world had known since the Great Depression of the 1930s.

I.   EASTERN EUROPE: THE BREZHNEV ERA

By 1968, First Party Secretary Leonid Brezhnev had begun to emerge as Khrushchev's chief successor, eclipsing his colleague Alexei Kosygin. Paradoxically, Brezhnev attained his status of *primus inter pares* by stressing the need for consensus and stability in high-level Soviet policymaking. After the Stalinist terror and the uncertainties of Khrushchev's impetuous style of leadership, a man who promised continuity and consultation, who believed in respecting the privileges of the *nomenklatura*, was a welcome change. Affable and tolerant in his dealings with other members of the Soviet leadership, Brezhnev refused to upset his colleagues with economic or political experiments. Instead, he oversaw the dismantling of many of Khrushchev's reforms in agriculture, education, and economic management, much to the leadership's collective relief. But while Brezhnev and the

Soviet Politburo worked to slow the pace of change, their aims were unexpectedly challenged by the new direction taken by their client state of Czechoslovakia.

The Occupation of Czechoslovakia and the "Brezhnev Doctrine"

In January 1968, there began a process of liberalization in Czechoslovakia that was to lead that country farther and faster than any Soviet had gone in the whole post-Stalin period. A new and untried leader, Alexander Dubček, became Czechoslovak Communist party head after the dismissal of his Stalinist predecessor, Antonín Novotny. Dubček's elevation to power came in the context not only of an almost universal longing for personal freedom, but of a languishing economy and a demand on the part of the Slovaks (among them Dubček himself) for full equality with the Czechs. The new leader, like many East European Communists, had spent the war years in Moscow. He was thus known to, and initially trusted by, Brezhnev and the Soviet Politburo. Had they known what his leadership would bring, they would certainly have blocked his appointment.

The new first party secretary was a pleasant, unassuming, and mild-mannered man, whose face seemed permanently to bear a sad smile. But Dubček was also a superb tactician, whose calm outward appearance belied his inner determination. Scarcely had he been raised to authority than he began to speak in tones of quiet eloquence an unfamiliar language that his people found both delightful and intoxicating. He talked of "socialism with a human face" and of democratization—that is, an irreversible process of returning power to the people, as opposed to the sort of liberalizing familiar in the rest of Eastern Europe, which was granted from above and could always be revoked. By the end of February, when the Czech party's censorship simply ceased to function, Dubček's had become the first truly *popular* Communist regime in European history.

Yet while Dubček altered in revolutionary fashion the whole style of Communist government, he at first took care to do nothing that might alarm the leaders of the Soviet Union. He engineered the election as the nation's president of Ludvik Svoboda, an elderly military hero esteemed in Moscow. He also saw to it that the Communist "Action Program" issued in April 1968, despite its permissive tone and its call for limited pluralism, should also declare the party's intention of continuing to act as the main motor force in Czechoslovak society and of allowing no rival parties to compete with it on an equal basis. Most important, Dubček constantly stressed his loyalty to the Warsaw Pact. Mindful of what had befallen the Hungarians in 1956, he drew a sharp distinction between his domestic reforms and his foreign policy, which remained irreproachably orthodox.

Perhaps this careful balancing act would have succeeded if the Soviet leaders had not been reduced to a state of extreme nervousness by the prospect of Czechoslovakia serving as a model for their own dissenters at home. The relaxation of censorship, the opening up of political life to new groups with their own independent aims (even if denied full equality with the Communist party), and provisions within the party for elections by secret ballot posed potential threats to the whole *nomenklatura* system that Brezhnev was pledged to protect. Now one of the disadvantages to the Soviets of possessing client states in Eastern Europe began to appear; for with the close links forged between Moscow and Prague, a victory of "counterrevolutionary forces" on the periphery threatened immediate infection of the Soviet heartland.

Still, Soviet leaders hesitated several months before bringing their superior military power to bear on their errant satellite. In May, Kosygin himself visited Czechoslovakia and apparently brought back a reassuring report. But the following month his government took the precaution of holding the staff exercises of the Warsaw Pact forces on Czech territory—an operation from which these troops were withdrawn with tantalizing slowness in the course of the summer. Almost simultaneously, at the end of June, a number of Czech intellectuals issued a manifesto entitled *Two Thousand Words*, which, in addition to pledging loyalty to Dubček's leadership, urged it to move even faster toward democracy and to resist Soviet pressure for a halt to reform. The hostility with which the Russian, Polish, and East German press greeted this manifesto suggested that Dubček's carefully contrived policy was coming unstuck and that a showdown with the USSR might be in the offing.

Dubček sought to forestall this potential crisis by offering a parley. Soviet leaders agreed to the Czech suggestion that they discuss their mutual differences on Czechoslovak soil, and at a meeting held at the end of July in a Slovak border town, Dubček was able to refute their charges point by point. Hence it came as an almost total surprise when in the early morning hours of August 21 the Soviet Union, supported by four Warsaw Pact countries, occupied Czechoslovakia with ruthless swiftness. What had apparently tipped the scales toward intervention was the publication on August 10 of draft statutes for the Czechoslovak Communists providing for an unprecedented range of freedom within the party itself, plus the announcement that an open party congress to ratify the changes that had occurred over the past seven months would take place in early September. The Soviets wished to ensure that no such congress could convene.

From a technical standpoint the invasion was a total success. Approximately 175,000 troops—predominantly Soviet, but with contingents from Bulgaria, Hungary, Poland, and East Germany (though notably *not* from Romania)—seized Prague and the other major Czechoslovak cities. It was the largest military operation that Europe had seen since the Second World War; by mid-September, perhaps half a million troops were occupying the country. Yet this military efficiency was matched by no corresponding political finesse. The almost total lack of advanced planning for an occupation regime suggested how late the Soviet leaders had made their decision and how bitterly the point had been contested in their inner councils. No "Quisling" emerged among the Czech Communists to collaborate with them. Faced with a spontaneous, improvised, nonviolent, but extraordinarily successful resistance among the civilian population, the Soviet occupying authorities had no idea what to do.

At first they imprisoned Dubček, threatened President Svoboda, and flew them both to Moscow. Within five days, the former was reinstated and brought to the Kremlin for negotiations. Dubček kept his nerve; Svoboda resorted to the extremely effective threat of suicide. Returning to Prague as national heroes, the two resumed the direction of their country. It initially seemed as if in fact they had conceded very little. They had merely undertaken to "normalize" the situation within Czechoslovakia and to dismiss a few prominent "liberals." In addition, however, they had called off the passive resistance, and this left them small leverage for withstanding further Soviet pressure. Month after month the process of wearing them down went on; piece by piece the structure of Czechoslovak democratization was dismantled. By April 1969, when Dubček himself was forced to retire, little was left of the brave reforms of the previous year. At least Dubček's

Defying the Warsaw Pact invasion of Czechoslovakia in August 1968, flag-waving
Czech patriots clamber aboard a Russian tank stalled beside a fiery barricade. (*Courtesy
H. Armstrong Roberts*)

successor, Gustav Husak, while compliant with Soviet wishes, was no Stalinist; the country had been federalized to give equality to the Slovaks; and in the smaller matters of life the memory of 1968 could not be erased from the consciousness and public procedures of a people that continued to cherish the memory of what might have been.

The Russians' invasion of Czechoslovakia naturally invited comparison with their suppression of the Hungarian revolt in 1956. Both produced the same shock of revulsion—with this time an almost total absence of bloodshed and a correspondingly mild response from the West. Yet from an ideological standpoint the events in Prague loomed larger than what had occurred in Budapest twelve years earlier. Imre Nagy had withdrawn from the Warsaw Pact; Dubček had not. That the same treatment was given to both suggested that the "sins" of the Czechoslovaks were not foreign but domestic; it was liberal or democratized Communism itself that was in question. In retrospect the Soviet occupation of Budapest had seemed episodic and uncharacteristic. It had not halted the process of liberalization in Eastern Europe. The takeover in Prague had done precisely that.

In November 1968, in a speech in Warsaw, the Soviet party secretary outlined what was subsequently called the "Brezhnev Doctrine." When "socialism" was threatened in any country, he declared, it became "not only a problem of the people of the country concerned, but a common problem and concern of all Socialist countries." In short, Brezhnev both justified the invasion of Czechoslovakia on ideological grounds and gave warning that any Communist regime that was tempted to pursue a similar course would meet a similar fate.

The New Stability at Home and Abroad

In the succeeding half-decade, tensions within the Soviet bloc did indeed become muted. And the change epitomized an increased self-confidence on the part of the Soviet rulers after the shocks and turmoil of the years 1967–1969. On balance, things did not go too badly for Brezhnev and his colleagues. For one thing, as had been true in the 1930s, their planned, collectivist society was to some extent proof against the economic storms that were beginning to batter the West. For another the Soviet leadership could profit from its own ripe experience as governments and leaders elsewhere came and went.

The decade following the fall of Khrushchev saw fewer changes in Russia's top personnel than had occurred in any previous such period since the Bolsheviks first seized power. In reaction to earlier upheavals, there now were no real purges—only minor shifts and retirements. And by the same token, the leadership grew older. By the mid-1970s, its average was sixty-five—the oldest in any major European country. This gerontocracy had naturally become cautious. Its prudence meant that even the most urgent reforms proceeded with glacial slowness. An entrenched bureaucracy, although it might sometimes work at cross purposes with the competing hierarchy of the Communist party, was in agreement with it on resistance to innovation.

Thus Brezhnev's younger and more imaginative coworkers found themselves constantly thwarted. But at least the leadership remained convinced, as Khrushchev had been, that Soviet consumers should be placated, and, more consistently than he, that the way to such satisfaction lay through increased industrial efficiency. In 1973, Kosygin's decentralizing reforms were extended, through the elimination of superfluous levels of management. Year after year, the ordinary citizen's standard of living rose perceptibly. This standard was difficult to measure by Western indexes. Clothing, for example, stayed expensive, whereas rents and public transport were relatively cheap; refrigerators and television sets were fairly accessible, whereas private cars, as in the past, were far beyond the means of the average Russian. Perhaps the clearest sign of the faint beginnings of affluence was the long waiting lists of those who could afford to buy their own automobiles.

Despite such modest signs of progress, the Soviet leaders realized full well that their own country's technology was lagging behind that of the West. Agriculture remained in so shaky a condition that a bad wheat harvest, as in 1972, could necessitate massive purchases abroad. On the industrial front, the Soviet Union had barely entered the computer age. The remedy Brezhnev proposed was to seek help from the most advanced Western nations—notably the United States and Germany. And here he had the good fortune to deal with governments that were prepared to meet him halfway.

The price, however, of trade and technological help was at least a token mitigation of the hard line that had marked the immediate post-Prague era. The American Congress wanted the Soviet Union to permit an increase in Jewish emigration; the Germans pressed for enlarged contact between the two parts of their divided country. And as though to prove to the West that they were no longer quite so heavy-handed as they had been in 1968 and 1969, the Soviet leaders explicitly recognized the practical necessity of letting other countries' Communist parties follow a variety of courses. At a meeting of the European parties held in Warsaw in the autumn of 1974—with Yugoslavia represented for the first time in a quarter century—the delegates noted with approval a new tolerance for ideological flexibility and adaptation to local circumstances.

Dissent in Eastern Europe

At the same time, however, the cultural options within the Soviet Union had narrowed. By the late 1960s, the familiar oscillation between thaw and refreeze was turning decisively in the latter direction as a result of Brezhnev's campaign for "stability." In 1966 the writers Andrei Sinyavsky and Yuli Daniel—whose heterodox work had for a long time been circulating clandestinely and under pen names—were brought to trial and sentenced to deportation. This time the pendulum swing from leniency to rigor went farther than it had done at any point since the death of Stalin, and a shudder of fear traversed the Soviet intellectual community. In countless small ways the pall of conformism descended once again. Conversation became less uninhibited, the secret police were more in evidence, and there were even signs of a partial rehabilitation of the fearsome tyrant whose name had apparently been discredited forever.

But the freer spirits refused to be terrorized. They would sometimes gather in the streets of Moscow and stage a tiny public protest—which the police would repress in a matter of minutes. Notable among those speaking out against the wave of conformity was Alexander Solzhenitsyn, who since Pasternak's death had emerged as Russia's greatest living writer. It had taken Khrushchev's personal intervention to ensure the publication of Solzhenitsyn's *One Day in the Life of Ivan Denisovich* two years before the former's fall from power. Solzhenitsyn's subsequent novels, *The Cancer Ward* (1966) and *The First Circle* (1968), enjoyed no such official protection; although they circulated underground among the Soviet intelligentsia, they could be published only abroad. The second of these created a literary sensation comparable to the appearance of *Doctor Zhivago* a decade earlier. An account of life at the end of the Stalinist era in an "institute" near Moscow, where highly gifted political prisoners worked on top secret projects, *The First Circle* recalled Tolstoy in its dense array of characters, its sweep of vision, and its warm humanity. The novel's success was more than the Soviet establishment could bear. In November 1969, Solzhenitsyn was expelled from the Russian Writer's Union, with the strong implication that it might be wise for him to leave the country.

Yet Solzhenitsyn continued to stand his ground, and a few of his literary peers such as Yevtushenko (who had described him as "our only living Russian classic") rallied to his support. For Solzhenitsyn was not a man who, like Pasternak, could be dismissed as a relic of the pre-Soviet period. He was a writer in the full vigor of maturity, a veteran both of war and of forced-labor camp, and an indomitable moral force. To the charge that he wrote in insufficiently positive terms about Soviet society, he replied with the countercharge that society itself was "seriously sick." Nor did his tribulations end with the official condemnation of his work. When in 1970, like Pasternak before him, he learned that he had been awarded the Nobel Prize for literature, Solzhenitsyn declined the risk of traveling to Sweden to accept it. But, unlike Pasternak, he acknowledged the honor by writing a stinging attack on the denial of freedom in his own country. A year later he turned his fire on the Russian Orthodox Church, accusing it of passivity and subservience to the regime. This latter gesture—which surprised many of his admirers abroad—suggested that Solzhenitsyn's views were closer to traditional Christianity than were those of other Russian dissidents.

Yet Solzhenitsyn's final rupture with the Soviet establishment did not come until the end of 1973 with the publication in Paris of a work that was no longer fictional, *The Gulag Archipelago*. "An experiment in literary investigation," as its author called it, it was a vast fresco, part history, part reminiscence, depicting the whole ramifying state-within-a-state, in all its frightfulness, that the secret police had been running ever since the consolidation of Bolshevik rule. Solzhenitsyn had not originally intended to publish the book. It had simply passed from hand to hand among the Soviet intelligentsia. But after the secret police had seized a copy from one of the author's associates—who subsequently committed suicide—Solzhenitsyn saw "no alternative but to publish it immediately." The result was doubtless what he expected: another literary sensation in the West, fury in the Kremlin. This time the Soviet authorities did not stop at half measures; after mounting a massive press campaign against the novelist and serving him repeated summonses to an interrogation with which he refused to comply, they finally arrested him and hustled him aboard a plane bound for West Germany, where he was welcomed by his fellow Nobel laureate, Heinrich Böll.

Paralleling Solzhenitsyn's struggle—and less well known in the West—came a worsening of the situation of the other dissidents. The post-Prague era saw a gradual tightening of intellectual control and a systematic effort to silence the opposition. Some had already been dealt with. Those like Sinyavsky who had served out their terms in Siberia had had their spirits broken and were not eager to begin again. Moreover, in addition to the familiar sentencing to prison or a forced-labor camp, the authorities had thought up the new and subtle technique of confinement to a mental institution; even the ostensibly humanitarian gesture of permitting increased Jewish emigration could serve the purposes of conformity, because a high proportion of the dissidents were Jews. Hence it was only rarely that the secret police needed to resort to the old Stalinist device of extorting a false confession by subjecting a prisoner to unbearable pressure.

After Solzhenitsyn's forced departure to the West, it was the physicist Andrei Sakharov who emerged as Russia's most outspoken oppositionist. And in the differences of opinion between the two, one could discern that Soviet dissent was far from being all of a piece. True to his moral absolutism, Solzhenitsyn condemned the notion of détente with the United States as the product of "cowardly self-deception" among Westerners who had "lost the will to live a life of deprivation, sacrifice, and firmness." Sakharov, while fully recognizing the peril of "détente without democratization" at home, nevertheless gave it his qualified support. Still a third position was that of the historian Roy Medvedev, who, skeptical of public demonstrations as almost invariably self-defeating, argued that the democratization of Soviet society could come only through gradual change in the governing personnel at the top.

Of this, however, there appeared little chance. Although the Soviet Union had signed the international convention on human rights agreed upon at the Finnish capital of Helsinki in 1975, it showed few if any signs of respecting its own treaty commitments (see Section II). Hence the new focus of dissident activity became an effort to monitor and publicize the lack of implementation of the Helsinki accords. Naturally those who did so got into trouble. The leaders of the "Helsinki group," Alexander Ginzburg and Anatoli Shcharansky, were tried and sentenced to prison terms. So too were their counterparts in Czechoslovakia, the drafters of the document known as "Charter 77," to which hundreds of Czech intellectuals and even industrial workers affixed their names. Such attempts were doomed from the start. But at the very least they proved that the advocacy of basic human rights could draw together the scattered voices of dissent and that protest in Russia was finding an echo elsewhere in Eastern Europe.

It was in Poland that such protest made the greatest headway. The economic discontent of the early and mid-1970s had produced a spontaneously formed Workers' Defense Committee, whose members had been jailed. In the summer of 1977, however, in a rare gesture of tolerance, the government released them. At the same time it began to adopt a hands-off policy toward comparably dissident groups—uncensored periodicals, variously estimated at from twenty-five to forty in number, an independent farmers' association, and a "Flying University," whose lectures were being held in private apartments. A visit to his homeland by the new Polish Pope, John Paul II, in June 1979, vividly demonstrated where the Poles' true allegiance lay. The joyous and tumultuous welcome he received from vast crowds of his compatriots left no doubt about how fervently Catholic the country had remained under Communist rule.

II.   WESTERN EUROPE: THE ERA OF DISCONTENT

In 1968, with the United States deeply involved in the Vietnam conflict, Europe found itself in a depressingly familiar situation. Once more, as in the early 1950s, the world's strongest power was at war; once more, as at the time of Korea, the military ally of half the Continent had embarked on a struggle to which it was impossible for Europeans, whether of the East or of the West, to remain indifferent. Moreover, the conflict in Vietnam recalled another set of painful post-1945 experiences. Unlike the Korean War, in which regular troops had fought each other along a recognizable front, the struggle in Southeast Asia was primarily of a guerrilla nature and one in which technological superiority failed to bring victory. Such had been the character of the two protracted and eventually hopeless wars that France had fought in its former overseas dependencies—Indochina and Algeria. Indeed, the Vietnam War in a number of respects was simply a continuation of the first of these; in the late 1960s the Americans were encountering on the same ground the same kind of agonizing difficulties with which the French had contended in vain a decade and a half earlier.

Under these circumstances it was understandable that Europeans should adopt an air of hard-learned wisdom and should advise their allies across the Atlantic to cut their losses and get out of Vietnam. Such, predictably enough, was the predominant view among the French—to which de Gaulle gave expression with his customary verve and irony. The Scandinavians were almost equally critical, but here the opposition to the Vietnam War sprang from humanitarian revulsion rather than injured national pride. In the countries that had close and crucial economic ties to the United States—Britain, Italy, West Germany—public criticism was muted by political realism, and the governments gave the American war effort their qualified support. It was only in the nations under authoritarian regimes of the Right—Spain, Portugal, and Greece—that the United

States found any enthusiastic backing. And in Eastern Europe, even the leaders most independent of the Soviet Union—such as those of Yugoslavia and Romania—found nothing good to say about America's Asian war. All in all, the struggle in Vietnam ranked throughout Europe as the most unpopular cause the United States had pursued for a quarter of a century.

Yet although the conflict in Southeast Asia loomed as the dominant event of the 1960s, overshadowing the whole second half of the decade, its effects on Europe were less devastating than those of Korea. For one thing, its financial repercussions were less profound. While it brought the same kind of inflationary pressures, the European economies were now more self-reliant and better protected against outside shocks than they had been in 1950. Moreover, this time the Europeans themselves were far less worried that the conflict would spread; very few thought that the Americans and the Russians would actually come to blows. The Soviet Union had enough trouble at home already, and the support it gave the Communist effort in Vietnam was undercut by its quarrel with China. The conflict in Korea had locked Europe into the frozen power relationships of the Cold War at its height; in contrast, the moral ambiguities of Vietnam merely intensified the Europeans' sense that they had entered an epoch of political fluidity in which the old guideposts were one by one being left behind. As the 1960s drew to a close, two substantial changes of power pointed the way to a new configuration—the end of de Gaulle's eleven-year rule in France and the passing of the Christian Democrats in Germany after a tenure of two full decades.

The End of de Gaulle's Rule

The first sign that de Gaulle's power was no longer what it once had been came with the French presidential election of December 1965. Riding the wave of confidence that had been bearing him aloft ever since he had settled the Algerian war, the general, despite the fact that he was turning seventy-five, decided to run for another seven-year term. At the start, the outcome seemed a foregone conclusion. Faced with the novel situation of a presidential campaign in which the entire electorate would be voting, the opposition was divided and lacked a clear issue on which to concentrate its fire. There were, however, sufficient miscellaneous discontents throughout the land to offer an opportunity to a politician who could weld them into a new political movement. Such a man was François Mitterrand. Supple, indefatigable, an experienced parliamentarian with a deceptively novel air about him, Mitterrand managed to rally behind him Socialists and Radicals and freelance politicians like himself; he also won the tacit support of the Communists. Still more, Mitterrand converted the electoral campaign into a nationwide personality contest, in which, as in the United States, public "images" counted for more than political labels. The result was a spectacular humiliation for de Gaulle. In a field of six candidates, Mitterrand polled 32 percent, to the general's 44 percent. Since no one had emerged with a majority, a second round of voting became necessary. This time, with only the two top candidates in the running, de Gaulle won—but with a margin of no more than 9 percentage points. France's first presidential election by direct popular vote had dispelled once and for all the myth of the general's indispensability.

Mitterrand's success in forcing de Gaulle into a runoff was matched fifteen months later in the parliamentary election of March 1967. For the first time since the

Popular Front campaign of 1936, Socialists and Communists regularly voted for each other's candidates on the second round, reducing the government's support in the Assembly to a razor-thin majority. This suggested that de Gaulle might eventually be succeeded by Mitterrand himself—and perhaps by a Popular Front government with Communist participation. Then the unexpected happened: An astounding series of events that made the month of May 1968 the strangest in France's postwar history both disoriented the Left and gave de Gaulle a year's reprieve.

It all started with student disturbances at Nanterre, a new, bleak, suburban branch of the University of Paris. From here the agitation spread to the Sorbonne, the center of the old university on the Left Bank. The grievances of French students were of long standing (see Chapter 16, IV). Overcrowded conditions and the rigidity of the examination system were perfectly legitimate targets of dissatisfaction, as was the school authorities' reluctance to offer courses in the newer disciplines of sociology and psychology. Between 1950 and 1965, the number of students enrolled in French universities had tripled, straining staff and library resources to the limit; at the Sorbonne, lectures were broadcast on the radio to student listeners because choked lecture halls could hold only a fraction of those who wished to attend them. For many, the universities seemed to mirror the impersonal, bureaucratic, oppressive face of the Gaullist state. To strike at the university, therefore, was to these students a symbolic blow directed against a regime whose monopoly of power, they felt, left little room for warmth, humanity, fantasy, or hope of change.

The student revolt of 1968—repeated with local variations in Germany, Italy, and the United States as well—might thus have been predicted. What came as a surprise was the breadth and explosive force of the May protest. By May 6, the students were fighting pitched battles with the police, who had forcibly entered the precincts of the Sorbonne (at the request of the rector) for the first time in almost two centuries. The following week a large part of the Left Bank was ringed with barricades, and public sentiment began to side with the students. A general strike of industrial workers began on May 13 and rapidly intensified when de Gaulle departed the next day for a previously scheduled state visit to Romania, leaving his government without clear directions for coping with the disturbances. Obliged by the unrest at home to cut short his journey, de Gaulle was still powerless to stem the force of a strike that soon idled ten million workers. By the end of the month, the government's authority had apparently collapsed, and Mitterrand was openly advancing his candidacy for the succession.

At that point, de Gaulle simply disappeared for the better part of a day. Having assured himself of the loyalty of his army commanders in a lightning visit to eastern France, he returned to Paris fortified by a new determination. He dissolved the Assembly, calling for elections within a month and summoning loyal citizens to rally behind him. In response, hundreds of thousands of conservative Parisians poured into the streets in a massive demonstration on the Right Bank. De Gaulle's declaration of May 30 marked the turning point. The initiative passed to the government, as the leaders of the democratic Left were caught unprepared for an election, and the Communists, who saw no profit to be gained from further agitation, urged moderation on their followers. By early June, both the student movement and the strike movement were subsiding. Workers were pacified by a pay increase, while student resistance ebbed and the police at last cleared the activists from the Sorbonne. At the end of the month, the elections gave de Gaulle's sup-

Protesters march in the heart of Paris during the "events" of May 1968. (*Courtesy Corbis-Bettmann*)

porters the biggest majority they had ever attained. The wily general, by allowing the pendulum of popular unrest to swing so far in the direction of anarchy, had ensured that a chastened electorate would vote for a return to order.

The "events of May"—as the French called them, at a loss to coin a more precise term—certainly fell short of being a revolution. This the Communists had early discerned and had taken their precautions by withholding their all-out support. But if it was not a revolution, what was it? An eruption of pent-up discontent, a season of street theater, an intoxicating moment of fraternity—it was all of these. But it lacked national leaders and a coherent program with which to replace what it perceived as the suffocating status quo. "Beneath the pavement lies the beach!" proclaimed one student slogan, alluding both to the use of paving stones as projectiles when attacking the police and to a more metaphorical vision of natural innocence waiting to be rediscovered beneath the artificial crust of civilization. In its impatience with convention, materialism, and the spiritual emptiness of postwar reconstruction, the inspiration behind the "events of May" was romantic and critical rather than rational and given to compromise. Its long-term effects in altering the social climate in France during the 1970s were to prove important and far reaching. For the moment, however, Gaullism had been given a new political lease on power.

De Gaulle himself survived in office for only a year. At the beginning of 1969, the general announced a referendum on a proposal to reorganize the administration of the country on a regional basis. The project had much to recommend it: Students of French government had long agreed that it suffered from overcentralization. But many vested interests felt threatened by the proposed change, and de Gaulle's enemies saw their opportunity when the general declared that he would treat the referendum as a vote of confidence. On April 27, when the French went to the polls for the third time in as many years, the regional project lost by the narrowest of margins. The general resigned, noting bitterly that his "contract with France" had been dissolved.

From Pompidou to Giscard d'Estaing

Yet the election of de Gaulle's former prime minister, Georges Pompidou, in June 1969, proved that Gaullism could continue without the general at the helm. It had been Pompidou, in fact, who had negotiated the return to labor peace the previous spring—a service for which de Gaulle, with the proverbial ingratitude of the powerful, had rewarded him with summary dismissal. Now, with the general gone and the Left divided, he grasped the chance for a political comeback. Pompidou's conservative instincts and desire for domestic order matched the general's; by training, however, he was a banker rather than a soldier, and by temperament a man who favored conciliation rather than the appeal to unbending principle. Sober, realistic, technically well staffed, the Pompidou government took up the unfinished task of liquidating the legacy of the month of near revolution.

Characteristically, the new president carried out this liquidation by meeting the protesters of May 1968 partway and acceding to some of their demands. Workers gained the right to representation through their unions on the governing boards of selected industries; students saw the number of French universities rise dramatically from twenty-two to sixty-five, thus alleviating the worst of the overcrowding. In foreign affairs as well, Pompidou proved a conciliator willing to acknowledge the validity of other claims besides those of French *grandeur*. Reversing de Gaulle's stand, he lifted the French veto on Britain's admission to the Common Market. At a meeting of the Six in early December at The Hague, he accepted the request of his five partners to open negotiations both with the British and with whatever other nations had requested entry.

If Pompidou displayed greater flexibility than his predecessor in accommodating dissent and the wishes of France's allies, he also showed greater appetite for innovation in the spheres of technology and the arts. At his insistence, Paris began a building program that included a new expressway along the Right Bank and the city's first skyscrapers—buildings not always, unfortunately, in the best taste. He also extended the state support of culture begun under de Gaulle's minister for the arts, André Malraux. It was therefore fitting that the new and strikingly modern museum of contemporary art inaugurated in Paris in early 1977 should have been christened the Pompidou Center, and should have pioneered attempts to make a broad spectrum of creative work accessible and understood.

Despite these successes, the Left gained ground during Pompidou's tenure in office. Gone were the doubts and divisions that had plagued it in 1968 and 1969; the ever-optimistic Mitterrand had taken over and enlarged the Socialist party and brought it back into alliance with the Communists. The outcome of the 1973 Assembly elections suggested that the "normal" French political attitudes were those of six years earlier—

that is, a fairly even balance between Right and Left. The conservative landslides at the end of the previous decade had been due to the near panic among moderate voters induced by the "events of May." Now, with double its previous total of seats, the French Left was once again ready to offer a credible opposition.

The last months of 1973 and the first of 1974 were dominated by agonized questioning about the health of Pompidou. As the president continued his round of official duties with ever-greater pain and difficulty, it became an open secret that he was ill—but how grave his malady was his entourage refused to disclose. Some found it courageous of Pompidou to carry on to the very end; others blamed him for not resigning or making provision for his succession. In any case, the public remained in the dark; one weekend in April, their president succumbed to cancer and left the nation's highest office vacant once again.

This time the presidency went to a dark horse: Valéry Giscard d'Estaing. Giscard was the leader of the Independents, a conservative grouping that antedated organized Gaullism and had even occasionally supplied a prime minister under the Fourth Republic. As a young man in his thirties, Giscard had revitalized this decrepit party and had delivered its support to Presidents de Gaulle and Pompidou. But Pompidou's death without a successor-designate gave him his chance. To the anger of loyal Gaullists—who feared that a division among conservatives would lead to a victory of the Left—he challenged their official candidate and emerged the leader of a Rightist coalition that won at the polls. A financial expert, aristocratic in origin and technocratic in education, Giscard brought to France's top leadership a new generation, a generation too young to have participated in their country's ordeal of war and occupation, collaboration and Resistance. A decade earlier, an unfamiliar type of pragmatist—like Pompidou—had come to the fore in French politics. The election of 1974 pushed this change a step further.

By 1976, Giscard felt secure enough to dismiss the Gaullist prime minister whom he had been obliged to appoint on the morrow of his election. As a replacement he chose the nonparty Raymond Barre, a portly economics professor who radiated calm and competence. Barre's policy stressed deflation and austerity—at the expense of the laboring classes. (And this in a country where the gap between the richest and the poorest segments of the population had grown wider than it was in Britain or Germany, or even Italy!) As the economic recession triggered by the Arab oil embargo three years before showed little signs of lessening, Giscard's claim that he had appointed "the foremost economist in France" to guide the country's fortunes encountered increasing skepticism. His attempt to steer a course between progressive social policies—appointing, for example, France's first Minister for the Status of Women—and an orthodox cure for the ailing economy gradually alienated his conservative supporters without attracting additional allies from the Left.

Added to this slow erosion of electoral support was the increasing disregard shown for the president himself. His alleged marital infidelities, the lavish presents received from an African head of state, frequent hunting trips, and a seeming disinclination to become too directly involved in managing the nation's affairs combined to tarnish the reputation for cool efficiency that had helped to ensure his election. While Barre doggedly continued to defend the politics of deflation, Giscard's critics became ever more vocal; those prepared to believe his assurances that France would soon recover its economic health dwindled in number. The president's party—enlarged and renamed the

Union for French Democracy—scored an impressive victory over its rivals in direct elections to the European parliament held in June 1979 (see Section IV). But Giscard's own bid for a second term in 1981 would subject his waning popularity to a more severe test.

The Advent of German Socialism

At the end of November 1966, fretting under Chancellor Erhard's weak leadership and the unpredictability of the parliamentary allies on whom it depended for its majority, Germany's Christian Democratic Union had decided on the long-untried expedient of a "Great Coalition," uniting it with the chief opposition party, the Social Democrats. For the latter, such a formula offered distinct advantages. Weary of an exclusion from power that had lasted for more than a generation, German Social Democracy was anxious to prove its responsibility and capacity to govern. The party had already taken the major step of abandoning its orthodox Marxist outlook in favor of support for a mixed economy and respect for the democratic process at its annual congress of 1959 held at Bad Godesberg near Bonn. The Bad Godesberg program committed German Social Democrats to become "a party of the whole people" rather than the advocates of the working class alone. With this shift, the chief impediment to its acceptance by the German middle-class public disappeared. Social Democrats knew how often in the past a coalition with a more conservative party had proved disastrous. But under the prompting of their chief political strategist, the astute Herbert Wehner, they now accepted the risk in order to convince the electorate that they deserved its trust.

The new chancellor, Kurt Georg Kiesinger, an urbane Christian Democrat in his middle years, was too young to have had a pre-Nazi political career. On the contrary, he was by his own admission a former member of the National Socialist party. This was a second innovation in postwar German politics, and it proved that a record of adherence to Nazism no longer posed an insuperable barrier to advancement. To German youth in particular, Hitler's era now seemed remote history. How was it possible, the young people asked, for their country to go on forever apologizing and atoning for the sins of the past? Along with such questions went a longing to "normalize" Germany's relations with the outside world—to be accepted as an ordinary European nation no different from the others.

Yet during Kiesinger's chancellorship, normalization proved unattainable. Although the Social Democratic leader Willy Brandt had taken over the foreign ministry and announced his intention of advancing by small steps toward better relations with the East, Germany's policy abroad changed very little; nothing substantial was accomplished to put the West Germans in closer contact with their eastern neighbors or to bring down the wall that divided Berlin in two. This near paralysis in foreign relations was matched by a lack of results at home. The collaboration of such dissimilar political parties made for a deadlock comparable to what the corresponding coalition in Italy had produced. The Social Democrats, as the weaker partners, naturally felt the greater frustration; but as the 1960s drew to an end, they began to sense that pressure for change was mounting and that it could be directed to their advantage.

In the spring of 1967, a year before the "events of May" in Paris, West Berlin students protested a visit by the Shah of Iran. One of the protesters was shot dead by police, causing students to redirect their anger against the city's governing senate and against school authorities more concerned with law and order than with civil rights. During the months that followed, as the wave of protest spread to other German universities, the "Great Coalition" was itself attacked. Many younger voters felt that the Social Democrats had deserted their principles by entering into a pact with the Right, and had robbed those opposed to the continuing domestic muddle of any chance to voice their concerns through elected representatives in parliament.

Thus when Brandt and his Social Democratic colleagues began a sharp and vigorous campaign against Kiesinger's Christian Democrats in the Bundestag elections of 1969, the end of the pragmatic truce that had governed German domestic politics for the previous three years was greeted by many with relief. When the electorate went to the polls on September 28, it was quite clear that Kiesinger's party would suffer losses and that Brandt's would make gains; all that was in doubt was the extent of the shift and the governmental formula that would result from it. With 46 percent of the vote and a loss of only three seats, the Christian Democrats still remained out in front; theoretically they might again have supplied the chancellor. But the third-ranking party that in Adenauer and Erhard's day had provided the margin they needed for a majority, the Free Democrats, was no longer interested in governing with its former partners. In the interval, it had evolved toward the left and now preferred to enter a coalition with Brandt's Social Democrats. The latter had gained twenty seats in the election; they could scarcely wait to assume power. On October 21, 1969, Willy Brandt became Germany's first Social Democratic chancellor in nearly forty years.

Once installed in authority, Brandt acted with the decisiveness his followers expected of him. Besides opening the way to Britain's entry into the Common Market, he revalued the mark at a higher rate—thereby underlining Germany's true financial strength as against the devalued British and French currencies. Most significant, he moved with speed and determination to carry out his pledge to improve relations with the East. To the Soviet, Polish, and East German governments, he offered the prospect of closer economic ties and an end to ideological polemics.

Ostpolitik and the Triumph of Schmidt

The hand stretched out to the East—*Ostpolitik,* as the Germans called it—was, then, the dominant feature of Brandt's four and a half years of power. It brought him his greatest triumphs, and eventually proved his undoing.

At the start, it all seemed clear sailing. Brandt's background and beliefs won him trust from Germany's former enemies abroad and from many at first inclined to question the aims of *Ostpolitik* at home. Unlike Kiesinger, Brandt had no Nazi past to defend or explain away; indeed, he was one of the few postwar West German politicians who could boast of having played an active role in the anti-Nazi Resistance during World War II. After joining the German Socialist youth movement in the late 1920s, Brandt had escaped from Germany in 1933 and sought refuge in Norway. When the Nazis invaded and occupied his adopted country seven years later, he became a leader of the Norwegian underground. His experiences during wartime both revealed to him the reality of German war crimes and led him to understand the legitimate grounds for a hatred and distrust of all things German that continued to color European attitudes toward Germany long after the war's end. Brandt was determined to act on these insights. He believed that Germany must reassure its eastern neighbors that it did not intend to recapture the territory lost in 1945, and he recognized the need for a moral, as well as a juridical, break with the past.

Capitalizing on his stature as an emissary from the "other Germany"—anti-Nazi and Socialist—Brandt journeyed to Moscow and to Warsaw soon after assuming power. In the summer of 1970, he negotiated a treaty with the Soviet Union in which both sides renounced the use of force in questions of European or international security. The following autumn, in an even more significant agreement with Poland, West Germany recognized at last the frontiers that the victorious Allies had imposed at Potsdam a quarter century before—in particular the eastern border along the Oder and Neisse rivers that in Adenauer's day had regularly (and ritualistically) been branded as unacceptable. Both these treaties were duly ratified by the Bundestag a year and a half later. Meanwhile, Brandt had been meeting with his East German counterpart, Chancellor Willi Stoph; in these encounters he had similarly tried to normalize an ambiguous situation of twenty-five years' standing. Although the treaty finally negotiated by the two German states bypassed the most difficult question of all—whether or not Germany should be considered a single nation that was only temporarily sundered—it notably improved communication between them and opened the way for the admission of both countries into the United Nations.

The culmination of Brandt's policy of *Ostpolitik*, however, came at the Helsinki Conference that began in 1972 and ended three years later with the signing of the Final Act on August 1, 1975. Brandt's desire for better relations with the East received broad support from thirty-four other nations who collectively endorsed the policy of détente. In effect, the Helsinki accords produced a first step toward a German peace settlement, some thirty years after the end of the Second World War.

By acknowledging the validity of the existing borders between East and West Germany, the Helsinki Final Act assured the Soviet Union that there would be no "revanchist" claims advanced by the West to upset the status quo. Moreover, since it guaranteed *all* European borders, the Final Act also accepted Soviet claims to those territories incorporated into the Soviet Union itself in 1945, including Estonia, Latvia, Lithuania, and parts of the former East Prussia. In return, the Russians and their Eastern European allies grudgingly accepted a series of provisions that called for a more liberal exchange of visitors and better cultural relations between the two blocs, as well as greater respect for human rights. Although these latter provisions were often disregarded by the Soviet authorities in succeeding years, the fact that they had been formally agreed upon gave both Eastern bloc dissidents and Western human rights organizations, such as Amnesty International, a legal basis upon which to protest their violation. Determined to keep its territorial gains of 1945, the Soviet Union had in the end traded a pledge to relax restrictions on freedoms within its borders for the West's official recognition of a legitimate Soviet sphere of influence in Eastern Europe—thus finally ratifying Churchill's unofficial agreement with Stalin three decades before.

Although Brandt's human qualities kindled respect wherever he went, people wondered whether he was tough enough for the era of economic recession that was beginning. The very gestures of national contrition that evoked admiration abroad—his kneeling on the site of the Warsaw ghetto, his recital in Jerusalem of a psalm imploring forgiveness—made Germans shake their heads at the "emotional" fashion in which he conducted foreign policy. The discovery of a spy in his immediate entourage gave his enemies precisely the ammunition they needed. Tired and discouraged, Brandt barely fought back. Forced out by his own supporters, he resigned the chancellorship in the spring of 1974.

A very different type of leader, a down-to-earth northerner from Hamburg, Helmut Schmidt, now took over. Brusque and self-confident, proclaiming that he was "skeptical of all visionaries," Schmidt seemed exactly the sort of hardheaded Social Democrat a gravely altered situation required. Under his leadership, Germany was to weather the economic slump of the 1970s in better shape than any other major Western nation. To counter the vertiginous rise in oil prices, domestic oil consumption was reduced by some 20 percent, while an increase in exports helped counter the loss in revenues paid out to members of the Organization of Petroleum Exporting Countries (OPEC). German rates both of inflation and of unemployment remained the lowest in the industrialized West. Its currency ranked as the strongest; it alone enjoyed an unbroken favorable balance of trade. Whatever economic criterion one chose, Germany came out first among the nations of Europe.

In this success story, socialist willingness to promote welfare policies alongside economic growth helped to preserve both social harmony and electoral support. But this concern for softening the rigors of pure market capitalism was by no means the same as doctrinaire socialism. The era was long since past when the term could appropriately be applied to Chancellor Schmidt's party. Schmidt himself was a pragmatist and a technocrat—like Giscard, a man more interested in efficient management than in ideology. Yet

Chancellor Willy Brandt (in office from 1969 to 1974) kneels before a memorial to the victims of the Warsaw Ghetto during a visit to Poland in 1970. This public act of contrition typified the conciliatory spirit of Brandt's *Ostpolitik*. (*Courtesy Corbis-Bettmann*)

the popularity that Schmidt's style of leadership brought him did not necessarily extend to his party. In the same year in which a new law gave workers broad new "codetermination" rights on supervisory boards within German industry, the Social Democrats and their allies sustained heavy electoral reverses and saw their parliamentary majority trimmed at a single stroke from forty-six to ten.

West Germany in the late 1970s was a country whose relative economic health did not prevent its citizens from falling prey to a host of other worries, ranging from the threat of urban terrorism to concern over relations with its neighbors to the East. By any objective standard, they had much to be thankful for. Yet their mood was morose. The Socialists under Brandt and Schmidt had brought about a historic change in the realm of *Ostpolitik* while simultaneously maintaining economic gains at home; the one thing they had not done was to make their fellow Germans happy and secure enough to appreciate their good fortune.

Tories, Labour, and Tories Again

Across the Channel, Britain's Labour party had lost one election and won two. The outcome of the first came as more of a surprise than it should have in view of the handicaps under which Harold Wilson's government was suffering after five and a half years of power. The trade unions were restive as Wilson tried—mostly without avail—to curb strikes and to hold wages in line. Intellectuals denounced the government's policy as unimaginative. Young people found it dispiriting and indulged in milder versions of the student disturbances that were simultaneously keeping the Continental universities in turmoil. In an obvious effort to win back Britain's youth, Wilson pressed through Parliament a bill lowering the voting age to eighteen, which went into effect on New Year's Day, 1970.

Under Labour, Britain continued to offer the Western world a model of personal decency and political fair play; in addition, it had acquired a reputation of being a fashion-setter in popular culture, with the youthful fashions of Carnaby Street and international rock stars such as the Beatles. But this sense that London was suddenly the center of a pop revolution did little to endear Wilson's government to the voters. If anything, the Labour government appeared all the more stodgy and fumbling in contrast to the energy and iconoclasm of the younger generation.

Nevertheless, Wilson gambled on success with the announcement of another early election in May, as he had in 1966. This time the gamble failed. In one of the greatest political reversals of the century, the election of June 18, 1970, swept the Conservatives into power, with 330 seats in the House of Commons to Labour's 287. The new prime minister was the Tory leader Edward Heath, who proceeded to appoint an experienced cabinet including Sir Alec Douglas-Home as foreign secretary. Its first order of business was to press on with the negotiations for Britain's entry into the Common Market (see Section IV).

Aside from its remarkable success in achieving this goal, however, the Heath government accomplished little. Its most conspicuous failure lay in the area of economic growth. Among advanced industrial nations, Britain had dropped from second place (after the United States) to next to last (just ahead of Italy). Heath's promised solution to this economic slide was to "stabilize" matters by curbing the power of the unions and reducing inflation through holding incomes in line. Goaded by this challenge, the trade unions reacted sharply. The coal miners in particular saw their chance in the autumn of 1973, when the world crisis in the supply of oil put them in an unexpectedly strong position. Heath refused concessions to their wage demands; confident that the country was behind him in his struggle with the miners, he called an unscheduled election in February 1974.

The results satisfied no one. Labour came out five seats ahead of the Conservatives, but still seventeen short of a majority. The balance of power rested not only with the Liberals (as had happened in the past) but now also with a miscellany of newly militant malcontents from the "Celtic fringe" of Scotland, Wales, and Northern Ireland. In these uncertain circumstances, both precedent and logic dictated that Wilson be invited to govern again. He was obliged, however, to proceed with extreme caution—once he had settled the miners' strike by granting them the 35 percent wage increase they wanted. No more major nationalizations were to follow the renationalization of steel (which he had accomplished tranquilly enough seven years earlier).

By the end of the summer, the prime minister and his colleagues decided that it was time to try for a real majority. The election of October—the first postwar election held in the same year as its predecessor—gave him at least this. But it was a bare majority of 21 seats, sufficient neither for comfort nor for experiment. The election also revealed a nation splitting apart at its ethnic seams; it had further reinforced Britain's local nationalists. The Welsh advocates of home rule might be dismissed as of little account. But their Scottish counterparts had replaced the Tories as Scotland's second party, had challenged Labour in some of its oldest strongholds, and had found in the discovery of North Sea oil the perfect economic issue to rally the Scots in defense of their "own" offshore resources.

Yet, as always in Britain, the economy remained Wilson's overriding concern. For government and people, 1974 and 1975 proved grim indeed. Inflation rose above 24 percent; the pound lost one-quarter its value. Facing up at last to the necessity of stern measures, Wilson cajoled the trade unions into a "social compact" limiting wage increases to 10 percent annually. Renewed for three successive years, this agreement was to rank as the prime minister's most substantial achievement. He himself, however, succumbed to discouragement. Alleging his age—which was not quite sixty—he retired in 1976, turning over Labour's leadership to an authentic son of the working class, "Sunny Jim" Callaghan, who was four years older than he!

Cheerful and well-liked, as his nickname implied, the new prime minister enjoyed a brief spell of good luck. In the "miraculous" year 1977, inflation fell by 10 percentage points; simultaneously the exploitation of North Sea oil began to pay off, as Britain found itself able to cover from its own resources nearly half its petroleum needs. Meanwhile, Callaghan was making ready to appease the Scots and the Welsh. He steered through Parliament a pair of bills "devolving" a number of the central government's powers on "assemblies" to be elected in the two regions. Had he called a parliamentary election in the autumn of 1978—as most of his advisers recommended—he might well have won. Instead he waited, while his prospects took a disastrous turn for the worse. First, the trade unions refused to renew the compact on wage restraint; there followed a "winter of discontent" with crippling strikes, more particularly in public services, which disgusted tens of thousands of ordinary citizens with both the unions themselves and the party that spoke for the laborer. Second, Callaghan's devolution strategy failed. In special referenda held late in the winter, the Scots endorsed by an insufficient margin the bill designed to satisfy their aspirations, while the Welsh overwhelmingly rejected theirs. For the time at least, devolution was dead—and with it Labour's ability to remain in power. Deserted now by the disillusioned Scottish nationalists, at the end of March 1979, Callaghan was swept from office by a no-confidence motion in the House of Commons, which carried by a single vote.

The ensuing election, not unexpectedly, was a triumph for the Conservatives. With a clear-cut majority of 339 seats—and with the Scottish nationalists losing most of theirs—they did not need to depend, as Labour had, on the whims of the "Celtic fringe." Their leader brought a novelty to European politics as Margaret Thatcher, who had replaced Edward Heath, became the first woman prime minister in any Western country. Energetic, self-assured, and with a biting tongue, she proposed to govern according to strict economic principles. But two virtually insoluble problems dogged her from the start—the sullen hostility of the trade unions to Tory rule and the long-festering sore in Northern Ireland.

The Tenacity of Ethnic Identity: Ireland and Belgium

Religion in Northern Ireland created a split dating back to the seventeenth century. The settlement of 1922 had left a large minority of Catholics in the Protestant-dominated North, which, after the liberation of the bulk of the country from British rule, had remained an integral, if self-governing, part of the United Kingdom. The Catholics of Northern Ireland had subsequently suffered discrimination of all sorts—in housing, in education, and in job opportunities; still more, a shameless gerrymandering of election districts had ensured the political preponderance of the Protestants. Meanwhile, the culturally subordinated element of the population had steadily grown in numbers. Yet not until a group of student leaders became active in their behalf did the northern Catholics find a voice for their discontents. The agitation that rocked the country in 1969 had originally been based on a labor ideology and had been directed at all the poor, regardless of religion. However, it quickly became a movement of Catholics, which by August had barricaded itself within the slums of the major cities and was engaged in an undeclared civil war with the Protestants. At this point Harold Wilson's government in London realized that it could no longer pursue the hands-off policy that had become customary in Britain's dealings with Northern Ireland. Instead it at last found itself obliged to exert the overriding authority that in theory it had always possessed. Wilson sent British troops to restore order, and he promised to see to it that the grievances of the Catholics were redressed.

Such undertakings had only begun to be carried out when Heath's Conservatives replaced Labour in London. Heath soon found himself trying to quell a civil war. In early 1972 in Londonderry, Northern Ireland's second city and its center of Catholic strength, British troops fired into a crowd of angry Catholic demonstrators, killing thirteen and wounding many more. "Bloody Sunday," as the event came to be called, made it impossible to carry on any longer under the old system of Protestant dominance. The following month, Heath suspended the government of Northern Ireland. To replace it, he subsequently proposed a new executive and a new assembly, in which the participation of Catholics in proportion to their population would be ensured; he also began to associate in the negotiating process the government of the Republic of Ireland to the south. By the end of 1973, Protestant and Catholic leaders were even agreeing to work together in the new executive for Northern Ireland.

Meanwhile, however, the killings on both sides went on; after a half decade of violence, the total had reached more than 1,000. By the time Harold Wilson returned to power, the tenuous compromise his predecessor had devised was already breaking down. In the late spring of 1974, a massive strike of Protestant workers forced their coreligionists in the executive to resign, leaving their compatriots and the Labour government in London with scant hope for the future. The following autumn, an almost solid phalanx of hard-core Protestants were returned to the British Parliament. By 1976, patience on all sides had run out. A desperately devised constitutional convention for Northern Ireland had ended in disorder. There remained no alternative to direct rule from London. Four years of devoted, painstaking effort at a settlement had produced little but further bitterness and distrust.

In Belgium, a similar, if less bloody, recrudescence of old antagonisms erupted over a question of language rather than religion. The hostility between Flemings and Walloons, which had lain quiescent for two decades following the abdication of Leopold III, broke out once more in bitter contention over the "linguistic frontier" that in the mid-1960s had been officially drawn across the country. The French-speaking Walloons, the erstwhile masters of Belgian business, culture, and politics, saw minority status threatening, as their birthrate remained significantly below that of the Flemings. The latter, conscious of their growing strength, were resolved to resist the quiet process of education and social advancement that in the past had converted so many of their number into French speakers. Thus it was not surprising that the focus of controversy should have been the old and distinguished University of Louvain, located a few miles on the Flemish side of the linguistic border, yet where the language of instruction had traditionally been French—a situation that militant Flemings found intolerable.

In February 1968, disputes over Louvain brought about the Belgian government's resignation. Splinter groups speaking for the two language elements made notable gains at the expense of the nationwide political parties in the ensuing elections. Finally, the only solution the Flemings would accept was to divide the university in two and to move the French-speaking part to a new location on the other side of the linguistic frontier. Still more, the country's constitution was revised in 1970 to provide political autonomy for its two language divisions and for the capital city of Brussels, which was officially declared bilingual. Not until the end of the decade, however, was this Belgian variety of "devolution" translated into legislation providing for the establishment of three self-governing regions.

More broadly, throughout the Continent, faced with the new uniformity of a predominantly urban culture, Western Europeans held on stubbornly to the traditional allegiances that continued to make them different from one another. Threatened with homogenization, they clung to the language or religion or customs that set them apart. Indeed, they sometimes stressed these distinctions more than ever or revived old ones that had almost vanished. The minor languages of Western Europe might be on their way to disappearing—both Breton and Welsh seemed doomed to eventual death, as many young people saw no point in speaking them—but the more robust allegiances shared by millions proved even hardier than before. Religion, language, and economic level continued to divide the Europeans into clearly marked nations and subgroupings. Thus there seemed no immediate danger that the infinite cultural variety which had given Europe its special charm might vanish forever.

Scandinavia and the Discontents of the Ordinary Citizen

After a generation of almost uninterrupted power, the Social Democratic governments of Denmark, Norway, and Sweden had begun to appear routine and antiquated. The welfare-state experiments that in the depression years of the 1930s had seemed so novel had been accepted at home by their political opponents and had been widely copied abroad. As a consequence, the Social Democrats were voted out of office in Norway in 1965, in Denmark in 1968, and in Sweden in 1976. By 1979, however, they had returned to power in two of these countries and had missed doing so in Sweden by the narrowest of margins. How could one account for such a reversal? The apparent explanation was that Scandinavian Social Democracy's experience in opposition had taught it lessons in political modernization. Once back in office, it began to apply a flexible economic policy that proved highly successful in resisting the Europe-wide slump. Along with Austria, Norway and Sweden alone managed to preserve full employment. Again in tandem with Austria, they proved far more adept than others in associating their trade unions in the process of economic planning and setting wage guidelines. Norway, in fact—profiting, like Britain, from the exploitation of North Sea oil—was on its way to achieving the highest standard of living in the Western world.

Yet dissatisfaction remained. The unpopularity of the high taxes that social welfare entailed encouraged political resistance, more particularly in Denmark, where a taxpayers' party for a while scored notably at the polls. Elsewhere in Western Europe, such "single issue" parties focused on the environment. "Green" movements of citizens strove to keep stretches of open countryside intact and to question the prevailing belief in economic growth at all costs; demonstrators—usually nonviolent—massed to block the construction of nuclear plants. Protests of this sort went on outside the orbit of the regular political parties. Indeed these latter, whether of the Left or of the Right, for the most part failed to understand or to capitalize on the new issues that were engaging the mind of the ordinary citizen. In common with most of those in authority, they were slow to realize that people like the ecologists had grown impatient with politics as usual, with rule by technocrats, with the state itself, and were prepared, on the local level at least, to take matters into their own hands.

III. SOUTHERN EUROPE: THE FRONTIER OF DEMOCRACY

Southern, or Mediterranean, Europe experienced the most profound political and social changes of the decade of the 1970s. The area where the old ways of doing things had lingered the longest was abruptly shaken out of lethargy or discouragement. With its agricultural labor force having fallen in a single generation from a half to less than a quarter the total, its social dislocations found expression in a resurgence of democratic vitality.

Italy: Protest and the "Historic Compromise"

At the turn of the decade, Italy stood isolated as Southern Europe's only political democracy. Even here, the continued functioning of such a regime was becoming increasingly doubtful. In Italy, as in Eastern Europe and France, 1968 had marked a watershed; after the elections of that year and the resulting demoralization of the Socialists, Italian politics had ceased to follow any recognizable pattern. Ministers and bureaucrats had merely lurched onward, improvising from month to month. In 1969, a "hot autumn" of discontent had brought a massive wave of strikes. The northern industrial centers had been shaken by sporadic but prolonged protests, sometimes violent in character, which had as their prime target the government's inability to provide adequate housing for hundreds of thousands of newly recruited workers from the depressed and overpopulated South.

The strikers were appeased by handsome raises in pay. But successive ministries had no idea how to deal with the inflationary pressures that followed. And when in the autumn of 1973, Europe's major economic crisis began, Italy quite naturally was the country that suffered most. As the nation that had risen last and most rapidly to the status of a first-rank industrial power, as the one whose prosperity had been most precarious and whose dependence on imports of oil had been greatest—in short, the nation that had lived farthest beyond its means—Italy was more exposed than any of its neighbors or competitors to a change in the international economic weather. By 1974, both its inflation and its unemployment rate were the highest in the Common Market.

Hence it was not surprising that Italians should desperately cast about for alternative political solutions and that military plots (real or imaginary) abounded. One possibility was neo-Fascism, whose organized movement, having absorbed the Monarchist party, was showing a new confidence. But neo-Fascism had two faces—one official and orderly, which it displayed at election time, one unofficial and terrorist, which was responsible for bloody and apparently senseless acts of violence. This second face was what the ordinary Italian saw, and for the most part it revolted him. In comparison, communism seemed tame and reassuring.

Some kind of Communist participation in the process of government was the other and more usual alternative suggestion. At the end of 1973, the Communist leaders themselves launched the formula of a "historic compromise" between their party and the ruling Christian Democrats. And even conservative Italians could find much to commend such a sharing of power. In the "swampy" situation of the 1970s, Italian communism could point with pride to its record of responsible behavior. Its substantial independence from Soviet direction was apparent in the stand it had taken on the occupation of Czechoslovakia; it had given honest government to a number of Italian cities, such as Bologna; it ran its cooperatives with quiet efficiency; its trade-union wing was striving to hold extremists in check and to direct labor agitation into constructive channels. Moreover, it was Italy's second largest party—Christian Democracy's only real competitor—and the strongest Communist party in the Western world. Along with the French, it was one of the two Western branches of communism that regularly made an impressive electoral showing. The Italian party not only held its ground; with each successive election it increased its vote.

But these electoral gains, far from demonstrating a rise in militancy, reflected a steady drift from revolutionary propaganda toward an emphasis on the party's "respectability." In the post-Stalin years, the Italian Communists had converted themselves into reformists who saw no reason why they should not share power in a reform-minded government. The profound change in Italian communism, plus its position as the country's sole untapped reservoir of competence and public spirit, suggested that it could not remain forever in the state of political quarantine to which it had been consigned for more than a quarter-century. At the very least, consultation with the Communists and their participation in legislative majorities seemed to be what the agony of Italy required.

From 1976 to 1979, precisely this occurred. At mid decade the prestige of Italian Communism reached its zenith. The gates to the "historic compromise" were swinging open. A new prime minister and Christian Democratic veteran, Giulio Andreotti, took on the ticklish assignment of persuading his own party to accept Communist parliamentary support, while inducing the Communists themselves to forego a claim to ministerial posts. For more than two years, the astute Andreotti kept up his balancing act. With the assurance of Communist backing, his government felt strong enough to deal firmly with the economy. Inflation and unemployment fell, as the trade unions adhered to a policy of wage restraint.

By 1978, however, this qualified version of "historic compromise" was showing signs of strain. Terrorism by groups both on the extreme Left and the neo-Fascist Right had become a major public concern, but the government seemed powerless to halt the wave of bombings and kidnappings. In March the abduction and murder by terrorists of the behind-the-scenes sponsor of the "historic compromise," Aldo Moro, deprived the policy of its most persuasive advocate. Communist losses in local elections suggested that the rank and file of the Left were growing impatient with an arrangement that was apparently bringing them few rewards. At the beginning of the following year, the Communist leaders endorsed this line of reasoning and ruptured their understanding with Christian Democracy. For the time being, the "historic compromise" was at an end. But it left behind it the memory of—or better, an aspiration toward—a social peace that most Italians had previously dismissed as beyond the realm of possibility.

Greece: From the Colonels to Karamanlis

In April 1967, a group of army colonels seized power in Greece. Faced with approaching elections that threatened to bring to power a center-left majority, the authoritarians of the Right had determined to forestall the popular vote. Democracy in postwar Greece had never functioned satisfactorily. Most of the time since 1949, when the struggle with the Communist guerrillas had come to an end, the country had been under conservative governments heavily dependent on support from the United States. The Right had been characterized by corruption and economic selfishness; the Left, by demagogic behavior and periodic flirtations with communism. Yet for all the weaknesses of the parliamentary system, the younger leaders of Greek democracy were beginning to devise coherent reform plans when the *coup d'état* came.

The rule of the colonels ended such hopes. A narrow, xenophobic, anti-intellectual tyranny descended on the country. The most prominent opposition leaders were jailed; some were later released under surveillance, and a few chose to go into exile. In December the king also fled abroad, after an abortive attempt at a countercoup. By the turn of the decade the new Greek regime had entrenched itself in power. Dissatisfaction was widespread, but no organized resistance had sprung to arms. Nor, despite a succession of promises, largely for American consumption, had the rule of the colonels been "liberalized" in any substantial fashion. While it might not be fascist in the strict interwar meaning of the term—it lacked both an explicit ideology and the support of a broadly based single party—it was unquestionably reactionary and suspicious of all forms of social and cultural innovation.

Seven years after their *coup d'état*, in July 1974, the colonels blundered into a colossal error that brought about their downfall. Lulled by the sense that they no longer had anything to fear at home, they plunged into adventure abroad. The scene was the island of Cyprus, in theory independent, in fact torn by unremitting strife between its Greek majority and its Turkish minority. By clandestinely intervening on the side of the Greeks, the colonels called down upon their heads the wrath of the Turkish government. And since Cyprus was a far shorter distance from Turkey than from Greece, it was immediately apparent both to the colonels and to those who opposed their rule that any further Greek military commitment on the island could end only in defeat. Thus publicly humiliated and exposed in all their foolhardiness, the colonels in effect abdicated. They let themselves be pushed from power with scarcely a show of resistance.

Freedom was restored to Greece as though by magic. The political exiles returned straightway, and the political prisoners were liberated almost as rapidly. By the end of the month, one of the exiles, Constantine Karamanlis, was firmly in power as prime minister. Karamanlis was an atypical opponent of the colonels in a number of respects. Of authoritarian temperament himself and a former prime minister, he had left his country of his own accord four years before the *coup d'état* and after a bitter disagreement with the king. A decade of solitary study and reflection in Paris had made him a wiser and more tolerant man; he came back to Greece convinced of the virtues of democratic procedures and almost universally respected for his integrity.

Karamanlis's program of an orderly, sober democracy, renouncing foreign adventures even in support of fellow Greeks, seemed to be what most of his people wanted after a generation of political uncertainty. In parliamentary elections held in November, they gave the prime minister a solid majority—which in an ideologically fragmented country like Greece was again something prodigious. A month later, an even greater majority voted out of existence what had become a shadow monarchy, and declared the nation a republic. For the next half decade, the Greeks were to enjoy political stability, but a stability unremittingly questioned by a Socialist opposition until its own candidate, Andreas Papandreou, finally succeeded Karamanlis as prime minister after new elections in 1981 (see Chapter 22, I).

Portugal's Return to Democracy

Three months before the astonishing overturn in Greece, freedom had returned to Portugal by quite a different route, and one that did not wholly take the country by surprise. Europe's longest-lived dictatorship of the Right had come to an end in two stages: a post-Salazar era of marking time, followed by an era of explosive innovation.

In September 1968, after a stroke had incapacitated the aged dictator (who was to die two years later), one of his erstwhile collaborators, Dr. Marcelo Caetano, became prime minister. Caetano's advent could not fail to mark a few changes. More cosmopolitan and modern-minded than his political mentor, he loosened up the censorship and gave slightly greater scope to the opposition parties. The broad outlines of Salazar's regime remained unaltered, nonetheless. More particularly, the costly effort to hold on to the Portuguese colonies in Africa continued as before.

The second stage of Portugal's liberation began with a book. Early in 1974, a popular and basically conservative general, Antonio de Spínola, who had himself helped to direct the repression in Africa, stunned his country's ruling elite by forthrightly declaring that Portugal's thirteen-year-old struggle to retain its African colonies could not be won. What Spínola's book expressed—and what evoked widespread sympathy for him—was the deep frustration felt by army officers, especially of the younger and more open-minded generation, at being condemned to fight a hopeless and apparently endless war. With the forces of discontent at home now having found a rallying point, events began to move swiftly. At the end of April, Spínola stepped forward to head a "junta of national salvation." As was to happen subsequently in Greece, the liberation of Portugal was virtually bloodless; the total lack of support the dictatorship could muster proved how shaky it had been and how much hatred for it had lain concealed under a façade of political apathy.

But in Portugal, as opposed to Greece, the road back to democracy was not clear or easy. In Greece, all that needed to be done was to restore a constitution that had been suspended for seven years. In Portugal, where democracy was no more than an aspiration or a dim memory, everything had to be improvised from scratch. Here, too, there was no strong conservative democratic movement, such as Karamanlis so successfully mobilized in Greece. The most visible political forces were the Socialists and Communists, who, despite smoldering disagreements between them, had emerged from clandestinity to push for some variety of Popular Front. And in this goal they were at one with the activist young army officers. Soon both types of leftists were finding Spínola too conservative. Although he had promised eventual independence to Portugal's African territories, his timetable for so doing was cautious and deliberate. In late September, disgusted with his colleagues of the Left and having proved unable to rally Portugal's "silent majority" behind him, Spínola resigned and a half a year later went into exile.

By the end of 1974, Portugal had ceased to be a colonial power. Mozambique was living under a transition regime, with full independence scheduled for the following summer; a similar pledge to Angola, delayed only by factional disagreements among the black insurgent forces, was to come into effect in the autumn. Meanwhile, at home, the country was groping its way toward democratic institutions. Prime ministers, first Socialist, then nonparty, succeeded each other with bewildering frequency. The discontent of those whose land had been nationalized in the period of revolutionary fervor reinforced the bitterness of the hundreds of thousands repatriated from the former colonies in Africa. By the end of the decade, unemployment stood at 25 percent; the inflation rate was the highest in Europe. Perhaps as a consequence, in further elections held in December 1979, the moderate parties won the first real (though slim) majority in the Portuguese parliament.

Spain after Franco

The ruler of Portugal's neighbor, Spain, Francisco Franco, although ailing and nearing eighty, had refused to relinquish power. Instead, in the summer of 1969 he had designated the young Bourbon prince Juan Carlos as his successor, passing over the prince's father, who was the legitimate pretender to the throne. If this solution was technically monarchist, it in fact gave encouragement to those who wanted to see the regime go on as it was; in his speech of acceptance, Juan Carlos pledged his loyalty to Spain's existing institutions. Indeed, one of the curious features of the succession settlement was that it disappointed so wide a variety of people. The democratic opposition of Socialists and Christian Democrats saw its hopes for a liberal regime postponed; the Falange viewed the designation of Juan Carlos as a further step in its gradual decline from the prominent part it had played in the Civil War.

Nor did this decision ease Franco's own lot. In the years immediately following 1969, both of Spain's irreconcilable minorities, the Catalans of Barcelona and the Basques, became even more stubborn, and their complaints found an echo among Spaniards at large. While the Catalans limited themselves to strikes and protest meetings, the Basques resorted to terrorism; they quickly admitted responsibility for the assassination of Franco's trusted prime minister in 1973. Moreover, by 1975 events in Portugal were threatening the Spanish dictator with an example too close for comfort. At the end of October of that year, illness obliged Franco to relinquish his powers to Juan Carlos. Three weeks later he was dead.

There followed a half decade of surprise and delight, both at home and abroad, at the dexterity with which the apparently inexperienced young king steered his country toward democracy. Step by step he dismantled the machinery of the dictatorship and converted himself into a constitutional monarch. Although Juan Carlos moved more swiftly than had been anticipated, he took care not to set so rapid a pace as to alienate political moderates and the crucially placed army. Indeed, his choice for prime minister—Adolfo Suarez, who had earlier been a follower of Franco—initially seemed too cautious. But once in power, Suarez ably seconded the king's policy. Still more, he built a loose coalition of middle-of-the-road politicians like himself into Spain's strongest party, which won a near-majority in the constitutional Cortes elected in 1977 and in the regular Cortes chosen two years later. With the country's second party—the Socialists—inclined to cooperate on fundamental reforms, Spain, although it had come to democracy later than Portugal, seemed in notably stabler condition.

Yet it was impossible to change so many things in so short a time and to satisfy everyone. Relations between church and state remained problematic, as the lifting of the censorship and a series of secularizing measures deprived Catholicism of the privileged position it had enjoyed under Franco. The Catalans were appeased with the restoration in 1977 of the local self-rule called their "Generality"; the Basques posed a graver dilemma. Not until a wave of terrorist violence had threatened the tourist trade did the government in midsummer 1979 grant them a measure of autonomy at least equal to what they had achieved under the Republic. In special referenda held the following October, a resounding majority of both Catalans and Basques ratified their newly won liberties—and thereby endorsed the idea of keeping Spain together as a single country.

The Yom Kippur War

On October 6, 1973, Yom Kippur, or the Jewish Day of Atonement, Arab forces from Syria and Egypt made a surprise attack on Israel as the nation was absorbed in celebrating the holiest ceremony of the religious year. While Egyptian troops crossed the Suez Canal on pontoon bridges and stormed the Bar-Lev defense line in the Sinai desert, massed Syrian tanks rumbled across the Golan Heights to threaten Israeli settlements in the valleys below. Caught unprepared, Israeli forces were at first unable to do more than parry these blows and plan for a counterattack. Only after ten days of fierce fighting did the tide of battle finally turn in Israel's favor, when its troops drove the Egyptians from the Sinai and crossed the Suez Canal in turn. The United Nations Security Council brought hostilities to an end when it imposed a cease-fire on October 22 and sent its own peace-keeping force into the area, with the support of both the United States and the Soviet Union.

The Yom Kippur War, as it came to be known, had an immediate effect on Europe through the oil embargo decreed by Arab oil producers against the Netherlands, which alone of all European countries had allowed American arms shipments to Israel to cross its borders. But the more general and long-lasting result of the war was the rapid increase in oil prices decreed on October 17 by OPEC*—first almost doubling in the fall of 1973, then reaching thirty dollars per barrel, or nearly ten times its former price, by 1979. The economy of Western Europe depended on oil far more now than it had in the past, when coal had supplied most of its energy needs, and the results of the price increase were correspondingly severe. First came a wave of inflation, as business raised their own prices to cover new energy costs; then, as these inflated prices slowed consumer demand for goods and services formerly available at a lower cost, factories began dismissing workers, and unemployment began to mount. Safeguards such as national unemployment insurance prevented a return to the catastrophic conditions of the Great Depression, to be sure. But the good times were over. The end of postwar reconstruction, increased competition from foreign industrial producers such as Japan, and the OPEC price squeeze combined to place unprecedented strains on the economic health of the Common Market at

---

*Founded in 1960 by Venezuela, OPEC counted among its thirteen members in 1973 seven Arab states: Algeria, Libya, Saudi Arabia, Kuwait, Qatar, the United Arab Emirates, and Iraq, plus Iran. From its wells came virtually all of Western Europe's oil.

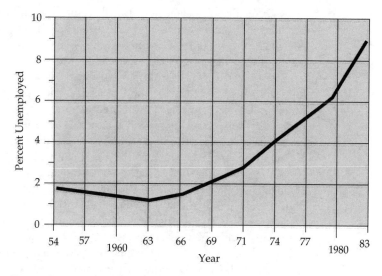

FIGURE 21.1   French unemployment 1954–1983. Note the rapid increase after the Arab oil embargo of 1973 began Europe's decade of recession.

the very moment when it was undergoing major political changes and expanding its membership (see Figure 21.1).

IV. THE EXPANDING COMMON MARKET AND THE ECONOMIC CRISIS

Britain's adherence to the Common Market, or European Economic Community, as it was increasingly called, had ranked as the decisive economic event at the start of the decade. The governments of the Low Countries had wanted it all along; the Germans had pushed for it. De Gaulle's successor, Pompidou, had dropped France's long-standing objection when Prime Minister Heath had assured him that Britain would no longer insist on a world role for the pound sterling—in return for which the French president had promised an understanding attitude toward Britain's special arrangements with the food-exporting countries of the Commonwealth. Once the French and the British had sunk their differences, matters proceeded without a hitch; in late June 1971, the six nations of the Community hammered out terms that Heath believed his Parliament would ratify. Negotiations subsequently went on with other countries, including former members of the nearly defunct Outer Seven. Only two followed Britain's example in joining the Common Market, however—Ireland, whose economy was closely linked to that of its larger island neighbor, and Denmark, where a hard-fought referendum produced a heavy majority for accession. A similar referendum in Norway gave the opposite verdict. The Six were becoming the Nine.

Yet Britain's agreement to adhere did not end the ten-year old controversy. It was now necessary to convince the British people that Heath's bold decision was correct. Age-old suspicions of the Continentals, pride in their own insularity, fear of a rise in food prices—these emotions reinforced each other to produce a deep-running reaction against the "marketeers." And Harold Wilson—alert, as always, to political stirrings—aligned himself with the majority of the Labour party in opposition. A large minority of pro-European Labour members of Parliament refused to follow his lead; a smaller minority of nationalist Tories broke loose from Heath. Thus the vote in the House of Commons crossed party lines. At the end of October, after a dramatic evening debate, nearly seventy Labour members finally provided the agreement with the margin needed for acceptance.

In their first two decades, the Community's institutions, although increasingly complex, had made little progress toward a true supranational authority. They functioned on three levels, only the last of which had any real power of decision. An executive commission of thirteen international civil servants (including a sprinkling of prominent politicians), with their headquarters in Brussels, drew up specific proposals. Such proposals were then discussed by a Community parliament, consisting mostly of pro-European members of the various national parliaments, which eventually passed them on to a council of ministers. This council was more a diplomatic than a ruling body. Those who attended it represented their governments at home, and all their important decisions had to be unanimous. It was only rarely, then, that the Nine could reach agreement on any major initiative—as, for example, at the end of 1974, when they voted appropriations for a regional development fund, of which, as the two poorest nations in the Community, Italy and Ireland were to be the chief beneficiaries.

In the mid-1970s, the advocates of European integration were lamenting that the impetus behind the Common Market idea had exhausted itself. By the end of the decade, however, the Community was showing new signs of life. Three innovations marked the last weeks of 1978 and the first half of 1979. First, the member nations (with the exception of Britain) linked their currencies in a tight arrangement for mutual support; under the procedures of the new European Monetary System, each participant undertook to buy up the currency of another when it sank below a specified point on the international exchanges. Second, the Community shifted to direct elections for the European parliament. After spirited campaigns in each country, 110 million voters—61 percent of those eligible—chose their representatives. Finally, in the same spring and early summer of 1979 in which the elections were held, the Community took the first step in enlarging its membership once more, to raise the eventual total from nine to twelve: Greece was admitted—with Portugal and Spain scheduled to follow within the next year or two (see Map 21.1). Now that these three Southern European countries had become democracies, there no longer remained an argument in justice or logic for keeping them out. Yet their relative poverty in comparison with the older members was bound to create grave difficulties for a Community already at grips with its own economic woes.

Double-digit inflation had begun in Europe several years before it reached the United States. By the early 1970s, it was becoming evident that the Western world's longest and most sustained economic boom was slowing down. An unprecedented phenomenon had appeared that left the experts at a loss—"stagflation," the unholy combination of inflation and a business slump. For two decades, "the Europeans had come to accept their economic miracle as a commonplace, as their due, which, with the inevitable

MAP 21.1 The European Common Market.

fluctuations, would continue indefinitely."* By the early 1970s, the more farsighted among them were starting to wonder; by 1980, even the most optimistic had lost their illusions. For by this time, unemployment had long ago joined inflation as a second major concern. In 1979, joblessness, except in Italy, was still below the American level; but the figures for inflation remained alarming. Both Italy and Britain still had inflation rates well above the 13.3 percent rise in consumer prices that had jolted the United States.

*Fritz Stern, "The End of the Postwar Era," *Commentary*, 57 (April 1974), 27.

The continuing strength of Germany's economy stood as an isolated phenomenon. By 1978, the European Economic Community might have overtaken the United States as the world's first trader—but the achievement owed more to the Germans than to anyone else. They accounted for a third of the Community's gross national product; they alone had heavier investments in the United States than the Americans had in their country. The time was long since past when the British could better afford household appliances and automobiles than the Germans. Now the reverse was true, as per capita income in Germany rose to more than twice the figure in Britain. Such a glaring discrepancy suggested the wider problem of the gap that had grown between the richer and the poorer members of the Community—a gap which would become more pronounced with the accession of the three Southern European nations. For most of Europe, economic progress had ground to a standstill; real net earnings were remaining stationary. This lesson labor leaders nearly everywhere except in Britain had learned from hard experience, and they had moderated their demands and adjusted to the status quo accordingly.

The decade of the 1970s had begun with a revolt of the young. It ended with men and women of all ages desperately seeking a way out of stubborn economic recession. If the prosperity of the late 1960s had given latitude to youth to cultivate a stance of alienation, the hard times of the 1970s brought young and old alike back to the bitter realities of existence. By mid decade, it was beside the point to thunder against the materialism of an unenlightened consumer society; the point was whether the individual could survive in a world suddenly turned hostile. By the decade's end, the answer to that question still remained open. Prosperity could no longer be taken for granted; once more, as in the 1930s, all such "givens" had been called into doubt.

In these new circumstances, the self-confidence of the Europeans cracked. Long-buried memories of the 1930s came flooding back. Europe had survived the loss of its colonies and its world preeminence. It had accepted its shrunken status with relative good grace. But how would it confront the end of the prosperity that had cushioned the change and compensated for the Continent's diminished pride?

READINGS

The "Prague spring" and Soviet intervention in Czechoslovakia are the subjects of Vojtech Mastny, *Czechoslovakia: Crisis in World Communism* (1972); Z. A. B. Zeman, *Prague Spring* (1969); William Shawcross, *Dubček* (1970); Jiri Valenta, *Soviet Intervention in Czechoslovakia, 1968: Anatomy of a Decision* (1979); and H. Gordon Skilling, *Czechoslovakia: Interrupted Revolution** (1979), which offers the best overall view of events. Dubček tells his own impressive story in *Hope Dies Last: The Autobiography of Alexander Dubček* (1993). The depressing aftermath of intervention is examined in Milan Simecka, *The Restoration of Order: The Normalization of Czechoslovakia, 1969–1976* (1984). For the Soviet Union under Brezhnev, see B. Kerblay, *Modern Soviet Society* (1983), and W. Morton and Rudolph L. Tökes, *Soviet Politics and Society since the Fall of*

*Books available in paperback are marked with an asterisk.

Khrushchev, 2nd ed. (1978). *An Insider's Life in Soviet Politics* (trans. 1992), the memoirs of Georgi Arbatov, a Central committee member and Soviet expert on relations with the West, is a revealing account of Khrushchev's fall and the beginnings of the Breshnev regime. Dissent and repression in the Soviet Union are analyzed in Rudolf L. Tökes, *Dissent in the USSR: Politics, Ideology, and People* (1975); while the views of the dissidents themselves are offered in Peter Reddaway, ed., *Uncensored Russia* (1972), and Zhores and Roy Medvedev, *A Question of Madness** (1971), which describes the use of forced confinement in psychiatric hospitals.

The French "events of May" 1968 and their aftershocks are detailed in Kristin Ross, *May '68 and its Afterlives* (2002), and by two eyewitness French observers, Raymond Aron, *The Elusive Revolution** (1969), and Alain Touraine, *The May Movement: Revolt and Reform* (1971). The former treats the student protesters with a skepticism verging on hostility, while the latter is far more sympathetic to their aims. For a general review of France in the 1970s, see William G. Andrews and Stanley Hoffmann, eds., *The Fifth Republic at Twenty** (1980). Germany in the era of *Ostpolitik* is assessed in Kendall L. Baker, Russell J. Dalton, and Kai Hildebrandt, *Germany Transformed* (1981); William E. Griffith, *The Ostpolitik of the Federal Republic of Germany* (1978); and R. Tilford, ed., *The Ostpolitik and Political Change in Germany* (1975).

For British affairs in the 1970s, besides Sked and Cook (see readings for Chapter 19) and Beer (see readings for Chapter 20), there is Andrew Gamble, *Britain in Decline* (1981), and the melancholy assessment in Isaac Kramnick, ed., *Is England Dying?* (1979). Martin J. Wiener, *English Culture and the Decline of the Industrial Spirit, 1850–1980** (1981), makes the argument that successful British entrepreneurs lost the will to compete internationally when they adopted the upper-class values of the landed aristocracy. The survival of ethnic identity in Wales is chornicled in Alan Butt Phillips, *The Welsh Question: Nationalism in Welsh Politics 1945–1970* (1975), and Ronald Frankenberg, *Village on the Border* (1957). The intractable politics of Ireland are discussed in Bruce Arnold, *What Kind of Country: Modern Irish Politics, 1968–1983* (1984) and Henry Patterson, *The Politics of Illusion: Republicanism and Socialism in Modern Ireland* (1989).

For Scandinavia and the problems of the welfare state, see M. Donald Hancock, *Sweden: The Politics of Postindustrial Change* (1972); Marquis Childs, *Sweden: The Middle Way on Trial* (1980); and the comprehensive survey of E. S. Einhorn and John Logue, *Welfare States in Hard Times** (1982). The byzantine workings of Italian politics during the 1970s are detailed in Alan S. Zuckerman, *The Politics of Faction: Christian Democratic Rule in Italy* (1979) and Joseph LaPalombara, *Democracy Italian Style* (1987). The new Iberian democracies are treated in Paul Preston, *The Triumph of Democracy in Spain** (1986); Raymond Carr and J. P. Fusi-Azpurúa, *Spain: Dictatorship to Democracy,** 2nd ed. (1981); Robert Graham, *Spain: A Nation Comes of Age* (1984); and Lawrence S. Graham and Douglas L. Wheeler, eds., *In Search of Modern Portugal* (1983). On the enlargement of the Common Market, see Helen Wallace et al., *Policy-Making in the European Community*, 2nd ed. (1983).

THE COLD WAR ENDS,

1980–1991

Sunday, November 12, 1989—the end of the "Wall of Shame" three days
earlier gave rise to new scenes of extraordinary fraternization between
Germans from the two sides of the Berlin Wall. (*Courtesy Corbis/Sygma*)

At the start of the 1980s, Europeans could detect few signs that the economic crisis of the 1970s was easing. The longest recession since the interwar period brought continuing un-employment, especially among the young, while it strained the capacity of governments to care for those in need. To add to these concerns, the Cold War, which perhaps a majority had been inclined to dismiss as a nightmare of the past, now appeared to be re-viving. At the end of 1979 the Soviet government jolted the West by occupying Afghanistan, which bordered on the Kremlin's own Asiatic republics; in early 1980 it banished from Moscow the leading dissident Andrei Sakharov, thereby climaxing a crackdown on dissent that had been in progress for several months. Détente seemed all but dead—and with it the hope that the ideological gulf between East and West could be bridged by a shared concern for "liberal" values.

Yet by the end of the 1980s, this picture of economic crisis and a revival of the Cold War had been radically transformed. While Western Europe revived economically, Eastern Europe experienced a series of dramatic political revolutions, bringing an end to Communist rule. In the course of a few months in late 1989, the East-West rivalry that had determined the balance of power in Europe since the end of World War Two yielded to a new political landscape, so swiftly and unexpectedly that even the most experienced political observers were caught by surprise. Suddenly it was possible to think of Europe as a united continent again, made up of many nations living in what Soviet President Mikhail Gorbachev, one of the principal architects of this transformation, referred to as "our common European home." When the Soviet Union itself disappeared in the course of 1991, it was clear that the Cold War was over, and a new phase of Europe's history had begun.

I. WESTERN EUROPE: THE RETURN TO PROSPERITY

The start of the 1980s saw new governments in most major countries of Western Europe. Yet aside from the face of change itself, there seemed to be little predictable pattern to these shifts, which favored neither the Right nor the Left in systematic fashion. Angry at the politicians in power for failing to solve problems of the late 1970s, the electorate sim-ply voted them out of office. No one could say whether their successors would be any more successful; but of the need for a fresh start there seemed little doubt. Most important, in the minds of the majority of voters, was the need to improve the dismal economic record of the preceding decade. Thus the new governments of the 1980s were all on notice. They must find a way to restore Western Europe's vanishing prosperity, or else face renewed voter anger and share the fate of the parties they had recently bested at the polls.

Britain: The Thatcher Decade, 1979–1990

Margaret Thatcher and the British Conservatives had won a convincing electoral victory in the general elections of May 1979 with the slogan "Labour isn't working." Inflation, industrial unrest, and the perception that the Labor party was too closely tied to the trade unions all played a part in Labour's downfall. So, too, did the political skills of the Conservatives' new leader. The daughter of a prosperous grocer from the British midlands, an Oxford graduate, and a successful tax lawyer before turning to politics, Thatcher combined a firm belief in her own merits with a most un-British disdain for compromise. Both her energy and her obstinacy earned her the nickname "the Iron Lady."

In the view of Thatcher and her advisors, what ailed Britain and the British was a debilitating dependence on the Welfare State. The system of social services put in place by the Labor government after 1945—the National Health Service, old-age pensions, scholarships for needy students, and public housing for the poor—seemed to Thatcher a crutch that Britain must discard if it wished to regain its old economic vigor. An ethic of individual initiative and self-reliance, she argued, should replace the old ethic of entitlement. If there was no longer a Welfare State to look after them, Thatcher reasoned, then the British would perforce learn to care for themselves.

Thatcher's election pledge to rescue Britain from industrial decline by rejecting the Welfare State met with initial public support; the failure of the Labour government to reverse the slide of the 1970s was so glaring that voters willingly accepted the need for stern measures from a Prime Minister who promised results. But the initial results of Thatcher's cure were worse than the disease. Her tight money policies prompted the bankruptcy of a number of small, inefficient firms, whose former employees now further swelled the unemployment rolls. Unemployment in turn spurred young rioters from Britain's racial minorities in London, Manchester, Liverpool, and other major cities to take to the streets in the summer of 1981, protesting their exclusion from hopes of prosperity with riots and looting. By January 1982, the Thatcher government's poll ratings had sunk to the lowest level recorded for any government since the war.

But then came an event in a distant part of the world that paradoxically strengthened Mrs. Thatcher's domestic position—the Falklands War. When an Argentine army force occupied the tiny and windswept Falkland Islands (settled by British subjects in the nineteenth century) off the South American coast in April 1982, Thatcher dispatched a hastily assembled battle fleet which, after more than a month at sea, landed British troops on the islands and routed the Argentines. Britain's victory provided a patri-

British Prime Minister Margaret Thatcher attacking the Labour party manifesto during an election rally at Cardiff, Wales, during the May 1983 general election campaign. (*Courtesy AP/Wide World Photos*)

otic uplift for its citizens and a public relations triumph for the Tories. After so many humiliations, the British now had a cause about which to feel proud; the returning troops received a heroes' welcome.

The "Falklands factor" contributed massively to the Conservatives' victory under Thatcher the following year. The 1983 general elections gave the Conservatives a parliamentary majority that came within two seats of equalling the massive Labor victory under Attlee in 1945. When the Conservatives went on and handily won the next general election in 1987, it became clear that the 1980s would be the "Thatcher decade" in Britain. No other British Prime Minister in this century had been twice reelected; of Europe's postwar leaders, only Konrad Andenauer and Charles de Gaulle had spent more years in office than she.

By now the painful deflationary cure Thatcher had imposed on the country seemed to be producing its hoped-for effects. Signs of prosperity increased. London, for example, after the genteel dinginess of the 1970s, began to sprout new building projects that promised to transform whole sections of the city, such as Covent Garden and the eastern docklands. The contentious trade unions had been humbled, business was "in," and the young executive with a Porsche in the driveway and a house in the country now spelled success in Britain as in the United States. When Lloyd's Bank advertised that "we're single-minded, hard-nosed and determined to make money," the slogan succinctly summed up the Thatcher ideal of a nation of shrewd and hungry entrepreneurs. Though they did not yet use the term, it is possible to see Margaret Thatcher and her Tory allies as early advocates of globalization. Their unsentimental embrace of free market policies would find even Labour disciples willing to follow their lead in the coming years.

Yet at the time a number of British observers wondered whether the price of refound prosperity was worth the gain. They noted other aspects of Thatcher's decade—a decline in traditional British civility, shoddy public services, universities starved for funds, the growing body of the homeless, urban decay in northern cities, a callous new materialism. The government had yet to develop a coherent policy for dealing with Northern Ireland's troubles, while Mrs. Thatcher's stiff-necked nationalism made collaboration with her Common Market colleagues difficult at best. But as long as the economy remained strong, most Britons seemed content to "vote their pocketbook" and to forgive Thatcher both the social costs of her programs and the abrasiveness of her personal style.

Violence in Northern Ireland continued throughout the decade, becoming so much a normal part of life as to evoke little outcry from the British public. Steps to defuse the conflict met with rejection by one side or the other. The Anglo-Irish Hillsborough Agreement, concluded between Thatcher and Irish head of government Garret Fitzgerald in the autumn of 1985, gave the Dublin government a limited voice in the administration of the North. Protestants from Ulster feared that this was the first step toward abandoning direct rule from London and that they would soon be absorbed, against their wishes, into Catholic Ireland. In the spring of 1986, as they had twelve years before, Protestants began a campaign of strikes (see Chapter 21, II). Here, at least, Thatcher's customary intransigence served her well. Refusing to be cowed by the politics of confrontation adopted by the Irish Protestants, she awaited further strikes and violence with the determination to oppose those who threatened to make Ulster "ungovernable."

But a decade after she entered office, Britain was again in economic difficulty and patience with Thatcherism was again wearing thin. By the spring of 1990, with an inflation rate bordering 8 percent and mortgage rates at twice that figure, the British saw both incomes and housing threatened by an overheated economy that the Tory government now seemed unable to control. For ten years, Thatcher had bullied, badgered, and cajoled the British into doing things her way. A prodigious appetite for work and a robust ego had allowed her to become the standard-bearer for middle-class British resentment against Labor, the unions, and foreigners. Now a combination of bad luck and poor judgment revealed her fallibility. For the first time, other politicians in her party were ignoring her lead and waiting for her to stumble, while the Labor party began to appear a credible alternative. As one Conservative member of Parliament noted after the Tory election losses in May, 1990, the "Iron Lady" might at last be "susceptible to metal fatigue." Indeed, as the year progressed, her leadership was challenged by rivals from within her own party—notably by the former defense minister, Michael Heseltine, who had quit the cabinet in 1986 in a dispute with Thatcher involving military contracting.

When Heseltine managed to poll a close second in the annual parliamentary vote for Conservative party leader in November 1990, the Prime Minister stunned the party and the British electorate by announcing her intention to resign. Her successor, finance minister John Major, was a Thatcher loyalist whose chief assets were youth and the promise of greater flexibility in dealing with Britain's mounting problems. The Tories were still in power; but the Thatcher era—dominated like few periods in modern British politics by a single, self-assured individual—was at an end.

Germany: The Turn to the Right

In Germany, as in England, the 1980s belonged to the conservative Right. In 1982, the Free Democrats announced their intention to leave the Socialists and rejoin forces with the Christian Democratic party, thereby forming a new center-right partnership. For the first time since the founding of the Federal Republic, a ruling government had lost its majority in parliament, not through elections, but through the defection of a coalition partner.

The elections of the following year gave the new Liberal-Christian Democratic coalition a clear victory at the polls. The German voters evidently felt disposed to continue the experiment under the leadership of the cautious but self-assured head of the Christian Democrats, Helmut Kohl. Kohl, unlike Thatcher, was a shrewd realist rather than an ideologue, a pragmatic tactician who avoided conflict rather than courting it. Kohl spoke confidently of the new *Wende*—the "turn" in German politics toward the Right—but in practice maintained continuity with both the foreign and domestic policy of the preceding coalition. A physically imposing figure whose bulk seemed an advertisement for German prosperity, Kohl radiated a calm, unruffled air of confidence. His avuncular manner, combined with an instinct for correctly guaging the public mood, made him a chancellor with unexpected staying power.

A new element in German political life in the early 1980s was the appearance of the Green party—so called because of its ties to the ecology movement—which won twenty-seven seats with slightly over 5 percent of the ballots and provided an alternative for disaffected voters. The Greens' candidates and constituency were largely drawn from the protest generation of the late 1960s, which felt that the German Socialists were too conservative to provide an effective opposition to Kohl, and remained suspicious of the parliament to which they had been elected on a platform of disarmament and environmental protection. Following new federal elections to the Bundestag in 1987, the Liberal-Christian Democratic coalition remained in power, but with the Liberals' position within it reinforced by a strong performance at the polls. The surprise winners in the election, however, were the Greens, who bolstered their previous showing and now appeared to constitute a permanent feature of the German political landscape rather than merely a single-issue aberration. At the same time, to the dismay of many, a growing fringe of right-wing voters turned toward the extreme nationalist "Republican" party. Thus at both ends of the traditional political spectrum a mood of protest was building against politics as usual.

Some of this voter discontent arose from political scandals that broke in the mid 1980s. Officials from both the CDU and FDP were accused of receiving money from the huge Flick industrial group in return for favorable tax treatment; Otto von Lambsdorff, the Liberal party's finance minister, was among those indicted and convicted (although he was cleared on charges of taking bribes for his personal gain). On the eve of the 1987 elections, the weekly newsmagazine *Der Spiegel* alleged that the Conservatives in the northern state of Schleswig-Holstein had engineered a dirty tricks campaign against the Socialists. The figure at the center of these accusations, state governor Uwe Barschel, at first protested his innocence, then committed suicide in a Swiss hotel. At the same time, the Socialists were hurt by the bankruptcy of a huge low-cost housing enterprise, financed by the trade unions that were among the party's principal supporters.

During the late 1980s, the German economy once again proved its strength, as it hauled the Common Market along the slow path to recovery. That it should assume this role was hardly surprising. As Western Europe's leading economic power, it produced a quarter of the European Community's steel, more than a third of its automobiles, and 30 percent of its total exports. Yet this very strength now became a source of worry to Germany's European neighbors, as East Germany and West Germany began to draw together. A united Germany, observers noted, would increase the Federal Republic's present population by a quarter and its gross domestic product by almost as much. Such an economic colossus, located in the strategic center of Europe, could prove destabilizing or expansionist, as had been the case during both world wars. Chancellor Kohl at first did little to allay these fears. Yet as the tempo of German unification intensified, he and other German leaders belatedly began to recognize their responsibility to the rest of the European community to treat its concerns seriously. Kohl now understood that he was in a position to achieve the prize that had eluded his predecessors, including Chancellor Adenauer, and make Germany one.

German reunification finally occurred in October 1990, as the German Democratic Republic (East Germany) formally became part of the Federal Republic of Germany. At Berlin's Brandenburg Gate, which had formerly lain just inside the East German border beyind the Berlin Wall, a mass of celebrants moved freely from one part of the city to the other, as search lights played on the crowd and all sung the (West) German national anthem. Václav Havel, in a congratulatory letter to Helmut Kohl, declared that "the war is over!" For many it appeared that one of the principal wounds left by the Second World War had at last been healed. Kohl himself won an overwhelming endorsement of his policy of rapid reunification that same December, when both halves of Germany joined to give the Christian Democrats the votes they needed to remain the senior coalition partners. This was Kohl's hour of triumph. He had gambled on the success of reunification, and won.

France: The Return of the Socialists

While Britain and Germany moved to the Right at the start of the decade, the French electorate made the opposite choice. At the polls in May 1981, the French chose the first Socialist head of state since the founding of the Fifth Republic. François Mitterrand, the perennial presidential candidate who had forced de Gaulle into a runoff in 1965 and almost defeated Giscard in 1974, saw his patience and tenacity rewarded at last. Mitterrand's personal victory was repeated and amplified on a broader scale the following month, when a coalition of Socialists and Communists won a comfortable majority in the French National Assembly elections.

Inevitably, the Mitterrand government that began work in the summer of 1981 invited comparison with Léon Blum's Popular Front government that had come to power forty-five years earlier. Indeed, the program the new president was pledged to implement reflected the Socialists' continuing loyalty to goals that Blum would have recognized as his own. Within a few months after taking power, Mitterrand carried out a series of nationalizations that more than doubled the state's ownership of major companies and financial institutions in France, from 15 percent to over 35 percent—including the acquisition of the venerable Rothschild Bank in Paris—at a cost of some $9 billion. In a second major initiative, the president took steps to reflate the economy through the classic Keynesian expedient of increasing purchasing power by raising wages and improving workers' social benefits. At a time when the European economy as a whole was contracting and when more conservative governments were preaching austerity, Mitterrand gambled on the opposite strategy of a direct stimulus administered by the state.

The atmosphere in which Mitterrand undertook this gamble was one of high expectation on the Left and foreboding on the Right. While Socialists and Communists celebrated an electoral victory so long delayed that they had begun to believe it impossible, business circles hurriedly explored ways of transferring their assets abroad, and property owners spoke darkly of a coming wave of expropriations. But although capital flight at first threatened to become a major problem for the regime—as it had been for Blum in 1936—it soon became apparent that the French Right had no real reason to take alarm. Within a year after assuming office, a combination of renewed inflation, growing trade deficits, and a weak franc forced Mitterrand to adopt austerity measures similar to those being applied in Britain and West Germany. Government spending was sharply curtailed, wages and prices were temporarily frozen, and some uneconomical steel mills and mines in the industrial northeast closed altogether. Although the Socialists argued that they were better able to implement these policies than a conservative government would ever have been, since they alone enjoyed the workers' trust, there was in fact little to distinguish Mitterrand's deflationary economic policy from that pursued earlier under Giscard and Barre (see Chapter 21, II). His Communist partners, who had secured four minor cabinet positions in the Mitterrand government, accused the president of betraying his working-class supporters by now tolerating the high rates of unemployment he had earlier sworn to oppose.

The 1980s saw many changes in traditional ruling coalitions, as voters attempted to solve Europe's economic problems through the election of new leaders. Here French President-elect François Mitterrand—the first Socialist head of government in over three decades—greets supporters and poses for the press near his home in Paris in May 1981. (*Courtesy Corbis-Bettmann*).

Despite these problems, however, after five years in office the Mitterrand government could point to a solid, if unspectacular, record. It had shortened the work week, lowered the retirement age, and raised social security benefits. It had loosened the government monopoly over the media by permitting the introduction of private radio and television programming. Its austerity measures were at last beginning to produce a healthier economy, and a program of decentralizing Parisian control over government at all levels was giving local regions more say in their own affairs. These achievements were not enough, however, to prevent the two main conservative parties from winning a narrow victory in the parliamentary elections of March 1986. For the first time since the founding of the Fifth Republic, a president from one party faced a majority in parliament and a prime minister belonging to the opposition. "Cohabitation," as the French termed this unaccustomed state of affairs, promised to introduce a new element of uncertainty into French politics.

In the end, President Mitterrand and the new conservative prime minister, Jacques Chirac, agreed to a pragmatic division of labor. Mitterrand retained control of defense and foreign affairs, while Chirac and his parliamentary backers assumed responsibility for domestic affairs. When presidential elections loomed in the spring of 1988, it seemed logical that the incumbent president should confront his prime minister for the nation's highest post. The result was a decisive reelection for Mitterrand, whose restraint and sense of fair play during the two years of "cohabitation" stood him in good stead with the voters. Mitterrand promptly dissolved the National Assembly, where the Right held a three-vote majority, and succeeded in uniting a Socialist-center coalition that gave him a narrow but workable parliamentary base from which to operate. This time there were none of the economic tremors that had accompanied the Socialists' first election victory in 1981; the sense of novelty and the economic fears inspired by the Left had since subsided.

Mediterranean Europe

The democratic transformation that had altered the politically repressive regimes of Spain, Portugal, and Greece during the 1970s brought them into closer harmony with those of Northern Europe. To many, the logical next step was the integration of all three countries into the economic and political structure of the Common Market (see Chapter 21, IV).

Greece was the first to be offered European Economic Community (EEC) membership in 1981. With a relatively modest population of 10 million and no commercial interests within the EEC contesting its admission, Greece's entry was readily agreed to by the other nine members. Spain and Portugal, however, posed problems on an entirely different scale. Their combined populations totaled 49 million; their relative poverty—per capita income in Spain was half the EEC average, that in Portugal a mere quarter—threatened to make them charity cases for the rest of the Community. In addition, the economies of both countries were still heavily agricultural, and farmers and wine growers in France and Italy protested fiercely against the threatened flood of Spanish citrus fruits and Portuguese wine and olive oil which, they feared, would swamp the Common Market should these two "poor cousins" gain entry. Nevertheless, after eight years of delicate negotiations, Portugal and Spain duly joined the EEC on New Year's Day, 1986. The complex treaty of accession, with its 403 separate articles, provided for a ten-year transition period, during which the economies of both nations would be gradually integrated into those of the Community as a whole.

Spain was governed throughout most of the decade by a young Socialist prime minister, Felipe González, whose moderate, reformist policies enjoyed broad popular support. González's Spanish Socialist Workers' Party (PSOE) received an absolute majority in the elections of October 1982, which reaffirmed Spain's return to democratic rule. Its commitment to democracy had been challenged the previous year, when a group of disaffected Civil Guard officers invaded the Cortes and held its parliamentary members hostage in an attempt to overthrow the regime. But the support that they had expected from their fellow officers failed to materialize. Instead, in a dramatic personal appeal, King Juan Carlos managed to secure pledges of loyalty from all but one regional military commander and ordered that no move be made to aid the rebels. The revolt soon collapsed. Despite the strains imposed on the Spanish economy by the European-wide recession and the fears provoked by Basque separatist terrorism, González's socialists again emerged victorious from the 1986 parliamentary elections, showing that a majority of Spaniards still felt committed to the path of moderate reform.

Greece, too, entered the 1980s under a Socialist government. Led by Andreas Papandreou, son of the former prime minister from whom the Greek colonels had seized power in 1967, it replaced the government of Constantine Karamanlis in the fall of 1981. Papandreou was an anomaly among the ruling politicians of the EC in several respects. He had behind him twenty years of life in the United States, where he had become a citizen, married an American wife, and enjoyed a distinguished academic career in the Berkeley Economics Department. A charismatic and dynamic leader, Papandreou promised his electorate to engineer a "transformation here and now" in the lackluster Greek economy. Yet during the next eight years, his vision of a revitalized, socialist Greece remained more rhetoric than reality. The generous raises he accorded to government workers were offset by continuing high inflation, which they helped to fuel; an ambitious program of investment in Greek industry brought few immediate results, while the country's external debt soared. The one sector of the economy that prospered was agriculture, due chiefly to the subsidies that Greek farmers received from membership in the Common Market (see Chapter 21, IV). Undeterred by these warning signs, Papandreou continued to court voters with generous government spending and to flatter Greek pride with anti-American speeches—tactics that helped to gain him reelection as Greek prime minister four years later in 1985.

But during the summer of 1989, campaigning for an unprecedented third term, the seventy-year-old Prime Minister's luck ran out. The bloated Greek economy was now sagging under a foreign debt of some $26 billion and suffering from 15 percent inflation—three times the EEC average. More serious for the fortunes of the Socialists was the corruption that pervaded the party after eight years in power. The head of the Bank of Crete was under indictment for embezzling millions from his institution and distributing funds lavishly within the Socialist party to buy influence. Papandreou himself was under indictment for accepting bribes. Scandal also touched the prime minister's personal life when he divorced his wife in favor of an airline hostess half his age. The elections were a defeat for the Socialists, but there was no clear winner; a second election that same year was equally undecisive. Faced with a worsening economic situation that threatened bankruptcy unless the EEC advanced a major loan, Papandreou and his Communist and Conservative rivals found nothing better to do than agree to new elections in the spring of 1990—the third national election in ten months. This time the weary electorate decided to end the stalemate and voted in the Conservative candidate, Konstantine Mitsotakis, by a narrow majority. The crisis of Greek democracy had ended, but mastering the country's economic crisis—with inflation now double that of the previous year—promised to be far more difficult.

II.   THE RIGHTS OF CITIZENS

The social strains of the 1960s—strains that had figured as no more than simple maladjustments in an overall context of prosperity and optimism—two decades later became a source of both far-reaching change and profound self-questioning. Particularly prominent among these issues was the plight of women, who for centuries had been denied what a new view of equality between the sexes had come to regard as basic human rights.

Indeed, a defense of human rights in the broadest sense increasingly replaced ideologies of the Left as the basis for analyzing the shortcomings of European society.

The Rights of Women: Divorce, Contraception, Abortion, and Careers

The women's movement was slower to develop in Europe than in the United States. And when it came in the early 1970s, it expressed itself chiefly in agitation for modern legislation in the field of sexuality and the family. Moreover, the situation that women confronted varied in both directions from the American norm. In Scandinavia, sexual permissiveness and equality went farther than in the United States; in Spain, an unyielding conservatism was long the rule. Between these northern and southern extremes lay an intermediate range of attitudes, with the major Continental countries, especially those in which Catholicism was strong, still inclining toward tradition.

With respect to sexual matters, however, the church was no longer monolithic. Although Pope Paul VI had resolutely opposed any change on the subject of contraception—a view reiterated by Pope John Paul II in 1988 on the twentieth anniversary of the encyclical *Humanae Vitae* (see Chapter 16, IV)—much of the clergy was only halfhearted in accepting this papal ban, and permissiveness in the realm of birth control gradually gained new adherents. The pill, first introduced in Europe in the early 1960s, facilitated the widespread use of contraception among younger women, while the AIDS epidemic of the 1980s led to more strenuous efforts at sex education. Yet for nearly a quarter century after the pill's appearance, progress toward more effective and hazard-free methods of birth control remained minimal. No male contraceptive was developed. And not until 1988 did a medical breakthrough occur which promised to affect the reproductive lives of women—the abortion-inducing drug RU 486, developed and marketed in France. For a time, antiabortion groups both in France and abroad succeeded in pressuring the drug's manufacturer, Roussel Uclaf, to withdraw RU 486 from the market. Only after the French Ministry of Health formally ordered it to resume production was the drug made available. By the following year, half of French doctors were recommending its use; by 1995, it was licensed for sale in Britain and Sweden as well.

As the storm over RU 486 demonstrated, contraception was easier to accept than abortion. For twenty years, European parliaments wrestled, often unwillingly, with an issue that pitted women's rights against the rights of the unborn. In 1971, 343 of France's outstanding women in the arts, literature, theater, and cinema launched a broadside attack against the country's antiquated legislation on abortion, which they claimed to have defied in person. This law, dating back to 1920 and reflecting the post–First World War concern over a decline in births, made it a criminal act to perform or to undergo virtually all such procedures. In the autumn of 1971, the trial of a teenage girl so accused aroused widespread indignation among women, intellectuals of both sexes, and several hundred outspoken members of the medical profession. Three years later in November 1974, after a prolonged and angry debate, the French National Assembly finally passed a bill legalizing abortion during the first ten weeks of pregnancy.

In Italy, the fight was over divorce. Alone among advanced Western European countries, Italy had no divorce law at all; indeed, the only effort to institute one had collapsed in the early years of the twentieth century. In these circumstances, the number of unwed couples who were living together, a great many of them with children, had increased to perhaps 2 million. By the late 1960s, such a bizarre social anomaly had become too much for the reformers in Italy's governing majority. In 1970 they pushed through a law—ultracautious by the standard of other nations—opening the possibility of divorce after a five-year waiting period. But even this went too far for the Christian Democratic rank and file and for the Catholic clergy. As the Italian constitution allowed, they gathered signatures for a petition calling for a referendum on the law. The petition campaign was a clear-cut success; the required number of signatures was far exceeded. Yet the results of the referendum itself, held in May 1974, came as a stunning shock to the opponents of divorce, who had counted on the conservatism of Italian women, particularly those in the South with husbands working abroad. The electorate defeated the move to repeal the divorce law by a majority of 60 percent. Even the southerners voted to maintain it. Italy was still below the general European level of permissiveness in sexual and family matters, but after 1974 it was impossible to class it any longer with the traditional Mediterranean lands of masculine and clerical dominance.

Even Spain, in many ways the most conservative European country, registered gains for women's rights after Franco's death in 1975. During the decade that followed, many of the legal disabilities under which women had suffered began to repealed. First to fall was the so-called *permiso marital* ("marital permission"), embodied in statutes which gave husbands the right to determine whether their wives could work outside the home, open bank accounts of their own, or even take an extended trip alone. A few months after Franco passed from the scene, the concept of *permiso marital* was abolished—56 years after it had been struck down in Italy and 37 years after its disappearance in France. A new divorce law followed in 1981, giving couples the possibility of obtaining a divorce by mutual consent after two years of separation, thus making it easier to obtain a divorce in Spain than in Italy. Finally, in 1985 a statute legalizing abortion passed both chambers of the *Cortes*; but abortions could still be refused by doctors and nurses on grounds of conscience, and frequently were.

By 1978, Italy had an abortion law too. Four years later, challenged as the divorce law had been earlier, the right to abortion was upheld by two-thirds of the electorate in a national referendum. Belgium waited until 1990 for similar legislation, which King Baudouin, a staunch Catholic, allowed to take effect over his personal protest. But such legalization did not settle the issue of unwanted pregnancies. Here, as elsewhere, women encountered humiliation and delay in surmounting administrative hurdles and in finding physicians willing to help them. Moreover, as the 1980s advanced, it became increasingly clear that women's rights to juridical and sexual equality with men would not automatically bring an improvement in women's lot. In countries such as the Soviet Union, where both divorce and abortion (but not contraception) were available on demand, systematic prejudice relegated most women to the less prestigious and poorer paying jobs and forced them to care for family and home with little support from their husbands. As a consequence, while they earned less, the working hours of women, especially those with children, were often far longer than those of men. For women who secured a divorce, this pattern of job discrimination, combined with men's reluctance to pay alimony to their former spouses, meant all too often that independence brought poverty.

In April 1986, the death of Simone de Beauvoir at age 78 was an occasion for the European women's movement to reflect on a record of uneven change. Since the publication of Beauvoir's *The Second Sex* in 1949, women in most Western European countries had gained divorce and abortion rights, and had also become an important part of the work force. In Sweden, they accounted for almost half of those regularly employed; in France and Italy, one third; and even in profoundly conservative Ireland, they were more than one quarter. (The Irish were to elect their first woman president in 1991.) Women could now be found among physicians, lawyers, and business executives in modest but increasing numbers. Yet they continued to face widespread if more subtle job discrimination. The "second wave" campaign for legal rights had now achieved the same success as the "first wave" campaign for women's suffrage between the wars. But it remained for a third and final wave of effort and achievement to ensure that women could at last move from basic rights to true equality.

Marxism and Human Rights

As the position of women was slowly improving, Marxism was rapidly declining in intellectual prestige throughout Europe. The belief in its analytical power and its visionary ideal of a classless society could no longer be sustained.

Marxism had enjoyed its greatest vogue in Europe during the 1930s and again in the years immediately following World War II, and varieties of Marxist thought continued to inspire much of the social protest of the 1960s. By the mid-1970s, however, Marxism had lost its reputation as a body of thought offering superior insights into the nature and ills of industrial society. In a book ironically titled *Barbarism with a Human Face* (1977), Bernard-Henri Lévy in France paid tribute to Solzhenitsyn for having helped veterans of the French "events" of May 1968 such as himself to recognize that "Marxism is not a science, but an ideology like any other, functioning as the others do to conceal and to shape the truth."* In Eastern Europe, too, faith in Marxism had all but vanished by the mid-1970s. It was seen as a façade from behind which the state exploited its citizens; the West, on the other hand, began to seem that part of Europe where the economy still functioned with some semblance of order and success. "What is socialism?" asked an Eastern European joke at the end of the decade. Answer: "The longest and most painful road from capitalism to capitalism."

The victory of the French Socialists in 1981 briefly revived the fortunes of Marxism. But when President Mitterrand's party retreated from their program of nationalizations and adopted economically conservative austerity measures to aid France's recovery, the ideology of the Left suffered a further blow. Thus unlike the Great Depression of the 1930s, the recession of 1973–1984 did not spur an interest in the solutions proposed by the Left; they had been tried and found wanting. Instead, some European observers turned to liberalism—the oldest of Europe's ideologies—whose demise had been heralded so often and so prematurely over the past century. In the name of liberalism, people longed for or strove to preserve a free society hospitable to individual needs and wishes. Interpreted as a belief in democracy, liberalism had inspired the return to freedom in Greece, Portugal, and Spain, as well as the founding of Solidarity in Poland, the revo-

---

*Bernard-Henri Lévy, *La Barbarie à visage humain* (Paris: Bernard Grasset, 1977), p. 182.

lutions of 1989 in Hungary, Czechoslovakia, and Romania, and the move toward a multi-party system in Gorbachev's Russia. Interpreted as an economic creed that stressed personal initiative and market forces with minimal state controls, liberalism also lay behind Margaret Thatcher's drive to reinvigorate the British economy and the faith in market forces professed by Helmut Kohl's governing coalition in Germany. The economic reforms introduced in much of Eastern Europe, with their stress on relinquishing centralized state control in favor of laissez-faire, seemed yet another sign of the pragmatic advantages of the liberal course.

The revival of liberalism in this double sense was accompanied by another response to the decline of Marxism: a renewed interest in the cause of human rights. In a sense this had always been a part of the program of social reform advocated by the Left, which professed to see in poor housing or inadequate health care a failure to provide for basic individual needs. Now, however, the concept of human rights served to guide a critique of socialist, as well as of Western, societies and to justify the attention paid to issues as diverse as protecting West German citizens against a system of computerized police records, providing famine relief for Africa, and challenging the right of the state to suppress free speech in Poland and Czechoslovakia. Just as the decline of formal religious faith in late-nineteenth-century Europe had left intact an independent belief in moral norms, so now the gradual disappearance of left-wing ideological faith left behind a commitment to human rights, expressed in a number of campaigns to improve the lot of victims of oppression and prejudice in Europe and abroad.

III. EASTERN EUROPE: THE COLLAPSE OF COMMUNISM

Twice in this century Europe had undergone a wave of sudden transformations—once in 1917–1919, and again in 1945–1947. In both cases, war was the catalyst of change. Now, in the late 1980s, a third major transformation occurred that was not imposed by force, but was instead largely achieved through peaceful means. In the Soviet Union, Hungary, and Bulgaria, the Communist party itself initiated change; in Poland, East Germany, Czechoslovakia, masses of men and women took to the streets to protest regimes that had held them in thrall for decades. Only in Romania (and later in the Soviet Union) did the revolution provoke bloodshed. Searching for historical precedents for a chain of events that both astonished and delighted them, European observers recalled the year 1848—the "springtime of peoples"—when a powerful but shortlived movement in favor of democracy had swept the continent. Yet remembering its untimely end, and the more recent crushing of the Chinese democracy movement in Tienanmen Square, these same observers were also forced to acknowledge the continuing fragility of the "peaceful revolutions" of 1989.

The Soviet Prelude: Gorbachev's Reforms

In November 1982, after eighteen years as leader of the Soviet Union, Leonid Brezhnev died. His longevity in office had been second only to Stalin's; yet there was little surprise and even less regret at his death. Since the mid-1970s, Brezhnev had been in poor health, while the question of who would succeed the aging General Secretary had become a staple topic of gossip both in the corridors of the Kremlin and abroad. The problems he bequeathed to his successor were enough to frighten the most stouthearted. The Soviet economy had slowed to the point that its growth was barely perceptible; corruption among both state officials and workers was widespread. Alcoholism, worker apathy, crime, environmental pollution, infant mortality—a host of attendant difficulties was steadily growing worse. At the same time, the economy of Western Europe was beginning to recover from the prolonged recession of the 1970s. The paths of the two Europes—one capitalist and dynamic, the other socialist and bankrupt—seemed to be diverging more dramatically than ever before.

What had brought the Soviet Union to this point of crisis? Why had it fallen so far behind the West after the early years of heroic industrialization under Stalin and Khrushchev? There were many reasons. One principal cause, paradoxically, was the success of Soviet elites in defending themselves against the powers of the state. After the erratic, unpredictable policies of Nikita Khrushchev, Soviet officialdom had understandably sought the calm and stability that were to become the hallmarks of Brezhnev's reign. Members of the Soviet *nomenklatura*—now assured of lifelong tenure—could expect to advance slowly but predictably up the career ladder. This group was large as well as powerful; in a country of 270 million inhabitants, the state employed over 17 million bureaucrats (not counting the army and the KGB). And their privileges were well worth defending. Assured of decent housing, good medical care, access to higher education for their children, and luxuries such as fine clothing and electronics imported from the West, it was this group, rather than the workers or the peasants, who had a genuine stake in the survival of the Soviet Union in its present form.

But while the Soviet bureaucracy flourished, the nation's economy stagnated. Agriculture—the perennially weak sector in the Soviet system—suffered continued neglect, and massive grain imports from the West were needed to compensate for a series of poor harvests. Raw materials on which industry depended, such as fossil fuels, became more difficult to extract in areas close to industrial centers, and more expensive when shipped in from afar. For this and other reasons, industrial productivity fell; indeed, there is evidence that by 1978 the Soviet economy had stopped growing altogether.

Overall, the decade of the 1970s seemed a time of paralysis and officially tolerated mediocrity. A contemporary Soviet joke defined Lenin's era as a period when the train of socialist revolution ran with the help of eager volunteers, while Stalin's era saw the train moving faster because the engineer had a gun held to his head. Under Brezhnev, however, the train had stopped completely; the passengers were lulled into thinking that they were still rolling toward their destination only because the curtains were drawn and Brezhnev's cronies rocked the cars from side to side to simulate movement.

The first two Soviet leaders to succeed Leonid Brezhnev spent such brief terms in office that neither was able to make headway in addressing these problems. Yuri Andropov, former head of the Soviet secret police (KGB) and a partisan of reform, was already sixty-eight when named General Secretary—the oldest man appointed to head the Soviet government since its founding. He died little more than a year after assuming his post, and was succeeded in turn by Konstantin Chernenko, a colorless member of the old guard who could be relied upon to change little during his tenure in office. Yet Chernenko's elevation to succeed Andropov was secured by his backers at a price. Andropov's own choice for a successor had been the Secretary for Agriculture, Mikhail Gorbachev, who now found himself promoted to the post of "second" secretary of the Politburo—in effect a stand-in for Chernenko. Thus younger members of the elite had reason to believe that the next Soviet leader would come from their own ranks rather than from those of the party's gerontocracy.

They did not have long to wait. In March 1985, barely a year after he had assumed the role of General Secretary, Chernenko in turn passed from the scene. Now the fourth Soviet leader in three years was installed as head of government. Michail Gorbachev, at age fifty-four, was a full generation younger than his three immediate predecessors. Intelligent, dynamic, and university educated (a rarity among Soviet leaders), Gorbachev was anxious to pursue the reformist initiatives of his former patron Andropov, yet at the same time well aware of the weight of inertia and self-interest that prevailed at all levels of the Soviet bureaucracy. At first the limits restricting his margin of maneuver appeared narrow indeed. There was no question of abandoning either the principle of a centrally controlled economy or of liberalizing the right of free expression. Nor was that what Soviet citizens expected. Their hopes rested instead on a strong and energetic leader who could arrest the drift of their country and instill a new discipline and idealism in both the governors and the governed. This was also the opinion of the spokesperson for the Kremlin old guard, Foreign Minister Andrei Gromyko, whose grudging support proved key for Gorbachev's election as party leader. "This man has a nice smile," Gromyko reassured his Politburo colleagues, "but he has iron teeth."

The new Soviet leader had been born and raised in Stavropol on the southern steppes—a rich agricultural region once home to the Cossacks. Following his graduation from Moscow University, Gorbachev had served successively as mayor of Stavropol and regional governor. There he paid special attention to local agriculture, and succeeded in increasing production by giving peasants a greater say in farming their own plots. His political apprenticeship in Stavropol contributed to Gorbachev's faith that change was possible within the Soviet system. Like Khrushchev, he did not want to bury communism, but rather to save it by imposing a new cure. A story circulated that after meeting a delegation of Western politicians in the Kremlin, Gorbachev continued to extoll Communist ideals to his aides. At first the aides were mystified; why continue to pretend now that the Westerners had left? Then they realized that Gorbachev actually *believed* in the virtues of communism.

By the summer of 1986, after some modest attempts to reduce alcohol consumption and improve worker discipline, the new General Secretary felt ready to embark on a more aggressive program of change. What were to be its principal elements? Gorbachev himself spoke of two primary aims: *glasnost* or "openness," and *perestroika* or "restructuring." Behind the first lay the wish to release the Soviet media and culture from the grip of censorship in order to bring the depth of the contemporary crisis home to the average Soviet citizen. *Glasnost* meant more truthful reporting on television news, the publication of more books and articles critical of the Communist party, an honest look at Soviet history, and a willingness to admit mistakes both past and present. In a sense, this was the easier reform to inaugurate, since it simply legitimized the voices of dissent that had tried for decades to make themselves heard (see Chapter 21, I). Its effect, however, was to create pressure for reform from below—pressure that Gorbachev intended to harness for other reforms.

A smiling Mikhail Gorbachev greets the signing of the Union Treaty in October 1991, three months before his departure from office. (*Courtesy AP/Wide World Photos*)

The meaning of *perestroika* could be seen most clearly in the political realm. Here Gorbachev aimed at a fundamental transformation of the Soviet political system by transferring the locus of power from the Communist party, where it had resided since Lenin's Bolshevik Revolution in 1917, to the federal government and to the republics. Over the next four years, he attempted to erect a second political system alongside the Soviet Communist party—a system that was in some important ways more democratic than its predecessor, but over which Gorbachev still hoped to maintain his influence. For Westerners used to a multiparty system where elected officials wielded the chief authority, the distinction between party and government might seem obscure. However, in Communist practice, the government had always been merely a front for the party which controlled it—a fact illustrated by the importance of Gorbachev's title as General Secretary of the Communist party. Without abandoning party control altogether, Gorbachev moved to give Soviet citizens a far greater say in their country's government through elections.

During this period of change, Gorbachev sought successfully to reduce Soviet military commitments and to distance his nation from the dangers and distractions of international conflict. Under his guidance the Soviet Union undertook major new arms control agreements with the United States that substantially reduced the number of nuclear missiles stationed in Europe, withdrew the Soviet troops from Afghanistan (first dispatched there by Leonid Brezhnev in 1979), and accorded a large measure of tolerance to regimes in Eastern Europe anxious to shake off Soviet tutelage. Addressing the United Nations in 1988, Gorbachev announced a unilateral withdrawal of some 500,000 Soviet troops from Eastern Europe. By 1989, as virtually all of the Soviet Union's former satellites declared their independence from Communist rule, it was clear that the Cold War had come to an end, and that the new Soviet leader was the principal architect of its demise. The following year the Nobel Peace Prize formally recognized his contributions in this domain.

Some fruits of Gorbachev's domestic political reforms appeared in that same year, when a new legislative body, the Congress of People's Deputies, was elected and in turn named Gorbachev its president. In February 1990, the Central Committee of the Soviet Communist party approved even more radical changes, including a revision of Article VI of the Soviet constitution, which had assured the party's "leading" position, thus opening the way for a multiparty sytem. The following month, after three days of stormy debate, the Congress of People's Deputies named Gorbachev to a new and powerful post as president of the Soviet Union with the ability to issue decrees and undertake a wide variety of other actions without the need to consult with and convince the Central Committee. In his acceptance speech, Gorbachev announced a "radicalisation" of the campaign for *perestroika*. As the economy continued to founder and serious shortages of bread and other foodstuffs strained the already thin patience of weary Soviet consumers, Gorbachev received a further strengthening of his powers in October from a Congress that preferred to defer difficult decisions to him. But with this new power came new responsibility. Having successfully outmaneuvered his political opponents among the Soviet old guard, Gorbachev now faced the greater test of subjecting the Soviet economy to genuine reform.

Poland: The Fortunes of Solidarity

In August 1980, thousands of striking Polish workers occupied the Lenin Shipyard in the port city of Gdánsk (formerly Danzig). Behind the closed gates of the huge industrial works—decorated with flowers and hung with portraits of the Pope—a strike committee formed under the leadership of a young electrician, Lech Walesa. Thus began the most significant social upheaval in Eastern Europe since the abortive Czech liberalization movement inaugurated by Alexander Dubček over a decade before. Unlike the "Prague Spring," however, where the impetus for reform had come from the top of the party hierarchy, the Polish labor movement that was to culminate that same year in the creation of the Solidarity union sprang from below. It was a popular movement in the broadest sense, an expression of pervasive discontent directed against a leadership whose corruption and lack of foresight had brought the nation's economy to the brink of collapse.

The characteristics that made Poland unique among the Soviet satellites of Eastern Europe—its extensive private agriculture and a strong Catholic church—had remained intact after the fall of Gomulka in 1970. His successor, Edward Gierek, sought to ensure the regime's stability by continuing to tolerate these vestiges of the old Poland, while at the same time attempting to create a new, industrially advanced nation whose

A triumphant Lech Walesa is borne aloft by solidarity members in Gdánsk in August 1980. (*Courtesy Getty Images, Inc./Hulton Archive Photos*)

rising standard of living would win the support of all. During the 1970s he was favored by the climate of détente. Loans from the West—including a credit of $200 million advanced by the United States in 1977—financed an ambitious program of industrial modernization. Gierek's policy of "socialist consumerism" mirrored similar policies undertaken in East Germany and Hungary, whose leaders had also concluded that a restive populace could best be controlled by giving it a material stake in the status quo. But a combination of bureaucratic rigidity and economic mismanagement defeated Gierek's ambitious plans. Having raised the hopes of his compatriots with promises he could not honor, Gierek now found his position as party leader increasingly undermined by disillusionment and mistrust. It took only the final push of the workers' strike in Gdánsk to provoke his fall on September 5, 1980.

After tense and prolonged negotiations between the government and the Workers' Interfactory Strike Committee in Gdánsk, the government conceded the fundamental right of workers to organize as they wished. With the Gdánsk Agreement of August 31, the Solidarity union was born. During the next fifteen months, Solidarity and its allies among the Polish intellectuals and the Catholic church attempted to improve the lot of Polish workers without provoking government reprisals or Soviet intervention. The example of Czechoslovakia and the brutal suppression of the "Prague spring" were a constant reminder of how little room they had for maneuver. Yet Solidarity's initial successes emboldened its leaders to press for further concessions from the Polish government. With a membership of nearly 10 million (half the adult population of Poland)—publishing its own newspapers, electing its own union representatives—Solidarity had become a state within a state, skilled in the art of brinksmanship. Meanwhile, a concerned Soviet Union and Warsaw Pact neighbors such as East Germany began to pressure the Polish party leadership to regain control of a situation that appeared to threaten both the stability of the Polish regime and their own security.

In December 1981, the Warsaw government finally moved decisively to meet Solidarity's challenge. In a nighttime operation the Polish army and security police proceeded, in effect, to occupy their own country. The Polish premier who had succeeded Giereck, General Wojciech Jaruzelski, declared a "state of war" and ordered his troops to seize radio and television stations, cut telephone lines, set up roadblocks, and arrest Solidarity's leaders. Jaruzelski's coup caught both the Poles and their many sympathizers in the West by surprise. The fact that no Russian troops participated in crushing the union movement was of little comfort. While Solidarity leaders went underground or languished in internment camps and Jaruzelski received congratulations from other Eastern bloc leaders, the majority of Poles adopted an attitude of sullen resignation to the new state of affairs. Spiritually the country remained nourished both by the Church and by a lively underground press. But politically and economically it was now effectively paralyzed.

During the 1980s Poland saw its living standards decline still further, its officials mired in corruption, its national debt swollen beyond the nation's ability to repay, and the majority of its citizens engaged in one form or another of passive resistance against a hated regime. In 1988 that passive resistance became active once again as workers struck in May and then in August in greater and greater numbers. By Christmas, Poland's economic woes had become so acute that General Jaruzelski at last felt obliged to undertake the unthinkable—open negotiations with the still officially banned Solidarity union. Roundtable discussions that began in January soon developed a momentum that led to yet more "unthinkable" steps. In April, the government agreed to legalize Solidarity after its eight-year ban, and to schedule elections for the Sejm (parliament) and the Polish senate. Though only a minority of the seats in parliament were eligible, the concession was momentous. On June 4 these elections—the first free vote in Poland since 1938— brought an overwhelming vote for Solidarity. In July, General Jaruzelski was elected by parliament to the newly created office of president. One month later he named Tadeusz Mazowiecki, a Catholic intellectual and Solidarity leader whom he had imprisoned in 1981, as prime minister. Mazoweicki's cabinet included other non-Communist officials in charge of social and economic policy, but Communists still controlled the key ministries of defense and internal security.

Such was the bloodless Polish revolution that returned Solidarity from official banishment to a position of political leadership within eight short months. Assuming leadership at this time, however, carried dangers as well as benefits. The government's decision to apply "shock tactics" to the Polish economy in an attempt to convert from socialism to capitalism in the shortest possible time meant that the price increases and a (temporarily) lower standard of living would be blamed on Solidarity rather than on the Communists. Within Solidarity itself, tensions grew between Prime Minister Mazowiecki and Lech Walesa, whose ambitions now centered on the presidency. Would the Poles maintain support for a government that asked them to suffer more than they already had? In a word, would the revolution last?

Change from the Top: Hungary and Bulgaria

In Hungary, unlike Poland, pressure for change during the 1980s came from within the Communist party itself. János Kádár, party chief since the failure of the 1956 revolution, had increasingly lost touch with the needs of his country as the decade advanced. A combination of poor economic growth and Kádár's declining popularity led to his ouster in May 1988, when he was replaced with the younger and more reform-minded Karoly Grosz.

Under the leadership of Grosz and a small circle of fellow reformers, the party began to undertake a series of major changes, culminating with its own dissolution a year later. In May 1989, the government decreed that the fortified border separating Hungary and Austria should be torn down; Hungarian troops dismantled miles of barbed wire and watchtowers, thereby creating a giant breach in the Iron Curtain separating East and West Europe. Then in June came the state funeral of Imre Nagy, Hungary's premier at the time of the 1956 revolution, whose courageous decision to call free elections had triggered the Soviet invasion of his homeland (see Chapter 19, IV), and who had subsequently been arrested, tried, and executed. In an act of great symbolic importance, the Hungarian leadership was deliberately reaching back to create a link with its own revolutionary past, bridging the thirty-three intervening years by rehabilitating the memory of a man the same party had earlier condemned to death. Finally, in an extraordinary congress held in October, the Hungarian Communists renamed themselves the Socialist party and voted to make the party's internal structures more democratic. For the first time in a Communist country, the ruling party had formally abandoned communism.

The following months brought a continuing erosion of Communist power in Hungary, despite the party's rebirth in Socialist guise. The nation's first free elections since 1945, held in the spring of 1990, gave victory to the Center Right and only ten percent of the vote to the ex-Communist party. But as in Poland, the political forces that emerged victorious from the election doubted that victory was an advantage if it meant presiding over unpopular measures required for economic recovery. With a foreign debt of some $21 billion, massive budget cuts would be needed in the public administration and defense sectors. Only with equally massive foreign investment in Hungary could the country continue to hope for a peaceful solution to its economic difficulties without a popular backlash.

In the four years that followed its first post-Communist elections, Hungary succeeded in attracting just such foreign investment. A stable government and aggressive efforts to find financial partners abroad helped it to capture more than half of all the Western funds invested in Eastern Europe (excluding Russia). The death of Prime Minister Joszef Antall in December 1993, marked the end of this first phase of Hungary's recovery. Though less economically robust than their neighbor Poland, the Hungarians still had reason for both pride and relief at the course taken by reform so far.

Bulgaria, too, introduced reforms from the top—though of a far more timid nature. On November 10, 1989, Todor Zhivkov, the longest serving leader in Eastern Europe, resigned after 35 years as President and Communist Party chief. His resignation was reported to have been influenced by Kádár's departure in Hungary; Zhivkov, it was said, wished to resign voluntarily rather than be forced out. The new Communist party General Secretary, Petar Mladenov, had been Foreign Minister under the Zhivkov regime.

Though younger and more open to innovation than his predecessor, Mladenov was by no means a radical reformer. "We have to turn Bulgaria into a modern, democratic, and lawful country," he stated upon assuming office. But both a sluggish economy and tensions with the country's million ethnic Turkish citizens presented immediate problems for Mladenov's attention. In June 1990, Mladenov's Communist party (now calling itself the Socialist party) won a convincing victory in Bulgaria's first free postwar elections—the only Communist party in Eastern Europe to receive popular backing after the revolutions of 1989. Whether it could revive the economy while maintaining its popularity remained an open question.

East Germany: Honecker's Heirs

The German Democratic Republic (GDR) was slow to accommodate to the mood of change being felt in Poland, the Soviet Union, Bulgaria, and Hungary. This delay was due partly to the country's relative economic prosperity—boasting the highest standard of living in the Eastern bloc—and partly to the stability of its leadership. Erich Honecker, the SED party chief, had succeeded Walter Ulbricht when the latter retired (voluntarily) in 1971. For eighteen years, the Honecker regime continued Ulbricht's policies of centrally planned economic development, internal political repression, and total loyalty to the Soviet Union. Projects that the regime made its chief priorities, such as the monumental new House of Peoples' Deputies in Berlin's city center or athletic performance at the Olympic Games, produced impressive results. But the price of such performance, in a small nation of 16 million, was the systematic neglect of its citizens' other needs.

The pressure for change in East Germany was not so much economic as demographic—the stream of thousands of emigrants which began in the summer of 1989. In June, East Germans eager to emigrate began gathering in the West German embassy compounds in Budapest and Prague, seeking permission to leave for the West; then when Hungary opened its border with Austria on September 10, thousands of East Germans vacationing there seized the chance and left without returning home. By November, the number of those who had fled through Hungary and Czechoslovakia had reached 200,000—mostly the young, skilled professionals and workers which the East German economy could least afford to lose. In the midst of this exodus, in early October, the GDR celebrated its fortieth anniversary, an event attended by other East bloc heads of state including Mikhail Gorbachev. Protests and police repression marred what was intended as a celebration of Communist achievement. Gorbachev pointedly reminded the East German leadership at the end of his visit that "History punishes those who wait." A week later, in the old university city of Leipzig, 100,000 East German citizens took to the streets for the first of what were to be many Monday evening marches protesting the current regime. "We are the people!" they chanted.

The combination of emigration and internal dissent were too much for the aging Erich Honecker. Shaken and perplexed, the 74-year-old leader resigned two days after the first Leipzig demonstration, to be replaced by the former head of the state security police, Egon Krenz. Krenz relaxed travel restrictions in an effort to stem the tide of emigrants, reasoning that many would now choose to remain at home in East Germany in the hope of further reforms. His decision, however, only accelerated the calls for sweeping change. On November 9, after the resignation of the entire Politburo, the Berlin Wall—symbol of the Cold War since its construction twenty-eight years earlier—was opened and East Berliners allowed contact with the western half of the city. The decision provoked a festival atmosphere: celebrating crowds sang, drank champagne, and perched atop the wall, waving to the East German border guards, who waved back.

Overnight, it seemed, the East German media was transformed from a docile government propaganda machine to a critical body given to Western-style investigative journalism. By late November, the press and television began reporting on massive corruption among highly placed government officials—secret sources of income, special airfields for private jets, vast hunting preserves, and a walled private residential compound in Wandlitz, near Berlin, stocked with fine food and the latest in Western consumer goods. These revelations delivered a final blow to the regime's moral authority. Krenz was booed by Communist party members when he appeared at a rally in Berlin in early December; when he promised to stamp out corruption, there were angry calls for his resignation. Krenz duly resigned the next day. In his place the party head became the young lawyer Gregor Gysi, who promised reform, yet also refused simply to liquidate the East German Communist party in Hungarian fashion.

However, the East Gerrman government's ability to control events was rapidly vanishing. Further emigration continued at the rate of 2,000 to 3,000 per day, while elections held in March 1990 became a referendum on the pace of reunification with the German Federal Republic. In the first free elections in the East for more than fifty years, the three-party Conservative coalition calling itself the Alliance for Germany was the principal winner. The Alliance cleverly played on East German resentment at being left behind by their prosperous West German neighbor, promising that a vote for the Alliance would bring "freedom and prosperity" through rapid unification. Chancellor Kohl responded to the Alliance's victory with a pledge that the West German mark would become the official currency of East Germany by July, 1990, and that "all-German elections" would follow in December of that year. The financial and political hurdles that must be overcome before the pledge could be implemented were considerable, but all now agreed that the two Germanies would be one.

The Winter Revolutions: Czechoslovakia and Romania

As the fog and frost of early winter settled on Central Europe in November 1989, it seemed that the wave of revolutions might end before it reached the two remaining hardline Communist states—Czechoslovakia and Romania. Yet such was not the case. In a climactic finale to this year of upheaval, a "velvet" revolution in Czechoslovakia and a bloody civil war in Romania brought down both governments within the short space of six weeks.

In Czechoslovakia, pressure for change began with the government's brutal and ultimately suicidal suppression of a student demonstration on November 17. Originally called to commemorate the death of a victim of Nazism fifty years before, the demonstration rapidly became a defiant call for freedom; police beat the unarmed students without provocation, creating rumors of a "massacre." In response, a small group of dissidents calling themselves Civic Forum mobilized around the playwright Václav Havel. They were supported by a far greater throng of ordinary Czech citizens who sensed that the time had come to shake off twenty years of passivity and stand up to the Communist regime at last. On November 24, only a week after the "massacre," Alexander Dubček arrived in Prague from his exile in the Slovak capital of Bratislava and was greeted by an ecstatic crowd, estimated at 350,000, in Wenceslas Square. The man who had embodied the hopes of the "Prague Spring" of 1968 had returned to offer his blessing on the new Czech revolution.

But the revolution itself was being shaped by a younger generation. After tense negotiations with the Communists backed by the threat of a general strike, Civic Forum succeeded in forcing adoption of a new government made up of opposition figures. The new president was Václav Havel himself, dissident and playwright, now leader of Czechoslovakia's transition to parliamentary government, duly elected by Parliament less than a year after his release from prison. In his New Year's address to Czechoslovakia, President Havel summed up the gains of the revolution this way: "Your government, my people, has been returned to you." Six months later, the people gave Civic Forum and its Slovak counterpart an absolute majority in parliament and gave President Havel a further two-year term. The Communists, however, surprised everyone with the second-strongest showing, leaving open the prospect that they might reap further benefits if Civic Forum's plans for a new Czechoslovakia faltered.

If the Czech revolution was gentle, cheerful, and crowned with success, the Romanian revolution was its opposite—brutal, tragic, with an outcome clouded with uncertainty. As in Czechoslovakia, it began with the repression of a popular demonstration. When Laszlo Tökés, an ethnic Hungarian pastor in the western Rumanian city of Timişoara, received a government order for deportation in mid-December, his parishioners gathered to prevent the police from arresting him. Gradually the crowd grew until some decided to march to the city center in protest, where they were met with savage police repression. To protest the deaths that followed, another demonstration took place on Sunday the 17th, which again was repressed by the feared Securitate police with more loss of life. Once the revolt in Timişoara became known to the rest of the country it spread rapidly and gained the ranks of the army, which turned against the secret police. The bloody cycle of repression and protest polarized the populace and drove many into open opposition.

On December 22, Romania's leader since 1965, Nicolae Ceausescu, and his wife fled the capital. They were captured and returned to Bucharest, where after a hasty military trial they were convicted of "genocide" and executed on Christmas Day 1989. That day and the next, pitched battles between heavily armed Securitate forces and the army and armed civilians continued, with thousands of dead and unknown numbers of wounded. In the end, however, a Council of National Salvation, which had assumed power after the Ceausescu's flight, declared itself the legal government of Romania pending free elections. When those elections were held in May, 1990, the Council of National Salvation and its leader, Ion Iliescu, won a resounding victory with over 80 percent of the vote. A number of Romanian observers, however, noted warily the large number of former Communists present in the government (including Iliescu himself) and wondered whether communism had really ended with Ceausescu's fall.

The Fate of Soviet Reform

At the start of the 1990s, the reforms initiated by Mikhail Gorbachev were encountering increasing resistance. Gorbachev had believed that *glasnost* and *perestroika* would work together in synergistic fashion to promote change. Yet in reality the two thrusts of reform, far from strengthening one another, frequently conflicted, with the result that by the summer of 1991, the entire reform process had slipped from the First Secretary's grasp. Gorbachev had invited citizens and journalists to voice their complaints about government. He calculated that by unleashing protest from below, he would be able to place additional pressure on those conservative leaders at the top whose obstruction and delaying tactics impeded change. Yet increasingly, the criticism Gorbachev had summoned up turned against *him*. With encouragement to speak their minds in the midst of a deteriorating eonomic situation, Soviet citizens did as one might have expected—they used the opportunities offered by *glasnost* to complain about the effects of *perestroika*.

The central failure of Gorbachev and his allies, however, lay in the lack of a coherent economic policy—a conceptual gap at the heart of *perestroika* that no amount of charisma or political finesse could replace. Since 1986, economic reforms had been promised, postponed, altered, rescinded, emended, and ignored in a zig-zag course that left even the government's warmest supporters perplexed. At times, Gorbachev seemed close to espousing a "reformed" version of the old Soviet economy, with central planning and state ownership intact; at other times he seemed poised to abandon the traditional planning system altogether in favor of private enterprise and private property. Each new initiative canceled out the previous one and produced an economic stalemate that disastrously weakened an already weak economy.

A second crucial failure was Gorbachev's blindness to the strength of nationalist sentiments within the Soviet Empire. It seems never to have occurred to the Soviet president that the peoples of the Caucasus or the Baltic republics would wish to leave the USSR for emotional reasons—ethnic pride and a thirst for independence. When he attempted to intervene militarily in order to stem the tide of secession of both regions, he acted clumsily, tardily, and ultimately without success.

Gorbachev sought a middle road between Soviet orthodoxy and radical reform. By temperament a moderate, accustomed to seeking comprimise, Gorbachev confronted a problem that could not be solved by half measures. His search for a gradual change in political institutions and economic policy ironically left the Soviet Union in the worst possible state—with neither the advantages of a centrally planned system nor with the strengths of free enterprise. "I want a stage-by-stage, step-by-step process that will not stimulate disintegration and chaos," he declared in *Pravda* in 1989. But his inconsistent approach to reform helped to precipatate the very chaos he sought to avoid.

In the summer of 1991, conservative forces at the summit of the Communist party made a decision to depose their president, as their predecessors had deposed Nikita Khrushchev twenty-five years earlier. Key leaders in the military, the KGB, and the Ministry of Internal Affairs felt themselves increasingly threatened by his reforms and the breakdown of party control. As had been the case with Khrushchev, they waited until their party leader was safely out of Moscow on a summer holiday, then acted in his absence. An eight-man State Committee on the Extraordinary Situation in the USSR proclaimed a state of emergency and declared that since Gorbachev was unable to continue in office for "reasons of health," they were assuming power.

The real surprise of the attempted coup was not the coup itself, but the strength of the opposition that met it. That opposition's leader was Boris Yeltsin, recently elected president of the Russian Republic. A former Politburo member whom Gorbachev had earlier forced to resign after a policy dispute, Yeltsin was widely regarded as a populist and a maverick of uncertain allegiance. Yet during the coup, Yeltsin proved himself a person of considerable courage, a master of political symbolism, and a highly effective organizer of resistance. From atop a tank in front of the Russian legislature (the "White House"), he preached defiance to a delighted crowd. Yeltsin and many of the elected members of the Congress of Peoples Deputies barricaded themselves within the White House and prepared to meet an attack by the troops the new masters of the Kremlin had ordered into Moscow.

After three days of seige, the coup plotters lost their nerve. Rather than order a full-scale assault on the "White House" and Yeltsin's supporters, they first tried to parley, then fled as evidence of the coup's failure mounted. When Gorbachev returned from house arrest, tired and shaken, it was clear that the coup had succeeded in at least one respect. He himself had been discredited, and a new leader had taken de facto control— Boris Yeltsin. But with the collapse of the coup, the days of the Soviet Union itself were numbered. Within months, many of the republics that comprised the Soviet Empire had declared their independence. Yeltsin, as the president of the largest and most populous of them—Russia—kept his post. But Gorbachev, with no Union left to govern, resigned.

The Balance Sheet

In many ways, the events at the end of the 1980s in Eastern Europe did not so much initiate as complete a process begun and then interrupted years or even decades before. Nowhere was this more apparent than in Czechoslovakia. Returning to Prague in triumph after a twenty-year absence, Alexander Dubcek symbolically linked the hopes of the "Prague spring" of 1968 with the achievements of the "velvet revolution" of 1989. In Poland, Lech Walesa and Solidarity similarly returned to center stage after an eight-year defeat. Even in East Germany, where the mass demonstrations in Leipzig and Berlin proved that the people possessed courage and convictions that few had suspected, there were memories of the first mass protest anywhere in the Eastern bloc against Communist rule—the workers' uprising of 1953 (see Chapter 14, IV). The passage of time, however, had imposed a degree of shared consensus on these differing national movements that had been absent ten, twenty, or thirty years before. Throughout Eastern Europe the revolutions of 1989 had brought forward the same triple demand for parliamentary democracy, the rule of law, and a market economy. All had demonstrated the astonishing power of the popular dissent that Communist rulers had sought to contain for so long.

At the same time, the collapse of corrupt and repressive Communist regimes was accompanied by demands for justice and full disclosure of past misdeeds that brought to mind the attempted purge of fascists and collaborationists after World War Two (see Chapter 15, I). Like the earlier purges, these new demands were prompted by moral

MAP 22.1 Eastern Europe in 1990.

indignation and a sense of national shame that so many crimes had occurred with widespread knowledge and tacit support. Like the earlier purges also, it seemed that a full reckoning might never be achieved. Germany began investigations into charges that some had spied for the hated *Stasi* (secret police) in the former German Democratic Republic, but the number of suspected cases and tons of salvaged files swamped attempts at a rapid reckoning. Elsewhere, as in Romania, Hungary, and Poland, the former Communist members of the *nomenklatura* staged a political comeback. As after the Second World War, the political and administrative elites whose skills were needed to rebuild the country was compromised by its past collaboration with a criminal government, but also indispensable for the future.

Hopes for the moral cleansing of Eastern Europe had therefore to be balanced against the needs of the present. At the very least, there was change at the top and the entry of a younger generation onto the political stage of Eastern Europe. Whereas Brezhnev, Honecker, Zhivkov, and Ceausescu had all been in their seventies when they died or departed office, a number of the new leaders such as Walesa and Havel were in their fifties. That in itself promised a fresh outlook on the old continent and its problems.

READINGS

The pessimistic mood of the early 1980s is reflected in two issues of the journal *Dædalus: Looking for Europe** (Winter 1979) and *The European Predicament** (Spring 1979).

For Britain under Thatcher, besides Sked and Cook (see readings for Chapter 19), see Dennis Kavanagh and Anthony Seldon, eds., *The Thatcher Effect** (1989), and Peter Riddell, *The Thatcher Decade: How Britain Has Changed During the 1980s* (1989). While the first two are generally critical of Thatcherism, the latter applauds the effects of Conservative rule on the British economy. Hugo Young, *The Iron Lady* (1990), is a splendid political biography of the country's dominant political figure in the past decade, while Lady Thatcher herself has weighed in with her detailed and unrepent political memoirs, *The Downing Street Years* (1993). On the Falklands War, see Max Hastings and Simon Jenkins, *The Battle for the Falklands* (1983).

The continuing troubles in Ulster are examined in two works by Padraig O'Malley, *The Uncivil Wars: Ireland Today** (1983) and *Biting at the Grave: The Irish Hunger Strikes and the Politics of Despair* (1990). Steve Bruch, in *God Save Ulster! The Religion and Politics of Paisleyism** (1986), argues that evangelical Protestantism has played a major role in blocking accommodation with Ulter's Catholic minority. For France under the Socialists, see John Ardagh, *France Today** (1987) and David S. Bell and Byron Criddle, *The French Socialist Party* (1984). Timothy Garton Ash, *In Europe's Name: Germany and the Divided Continent* (1993) presents a nuanced and thoughtful review of the concerns motivating the Federal Republic in a changing European order, while John Ardagh, *Germany and the Germans:* (rev. ed., 1991) presents a portrait of Germany immediately after reunification. A comprehensive survey of Spanish society after Franco is John

*Titles marked with an asterisk are available in paperback.

Hooper, *The Spaniards: A Portrait of the New Spain** (1987). See also Víctor M. Pérez-Díaz, *The Return of Civil Society: The Emergence of Democratic Spain* (1993). Joseph La-Palombara, *Democracy Italian Style* (1987), argues that the postwar Italian political system of the 1980s offered more stability than admitted by its detractors.

European women's issues are treated in Joni Lovenduski, *Women and European Politics: Contemporary Feminism and Public Policy** (1986), and Edith Hoshino Altbach et al., eds., *German Feminism: Readings in Politics and Literature** (1984). A sobering portrait of the condition of women in Brezhnev's Soviet Union is painted in Francine du Plessix Gray, *Soviet Women: Walking the Tightrope* (1989). Mary Buckley, ed., *Perestroika and Soviet Women** (1992) charts their progress under Gorbachev.

The literature on the revolutions in Eastern Europe is immense and still growing. An excellent short introduction to the subject is Misha Glenny, *The Rebirth of History: Eastern Europe in the Age of Democracy** (1990). An overview of the events of 1989 is presented in Bernard Gwertzman and Michael T. Kaufman, eds., *The Collapse of Communism** (1990)—a compilation of reports appearing in *The New York Times*—while a thoughtful appraisal of prerevolutionary thought and politics in the region is Timothy Garton Ash's *The Uses of Adversity: Essays on the Fate of Central Europe* (1989). The same author presents a splendid eyewitness account of the sequel in *The Magic Lantern: The Revolution of '89 Witnessed in Warsaw, Budapest, Berlin and Prague** (1990). Several excellent studies deal with Germany alone. Among them are Robert Darnton, *Berlin Journal, 1989–1990** (1991), which offers eyewitness testimony by a distinguished historian of eighteenth-century France; Konrad H. Jarausch, *The Rush to German Unity,** especially good on the complex negotiations leading to reunification; and Charles S. Maier, *Dissolution: The Crisis of Communism and the End of East Germany** (1997), a complex and balanced analysis of the decline and fall of the GDR based on extensive archival research. For a portrait of the leader of Czechoslovakia's "velvet revolution," see Edá Kriseová, *Václav Havel: The Authorized Biography* (1993). For events in Romania see Andrei Codrescu, *The Hole in the Flag: A Romanian Exile's Story of Return and Revolution** (1991). The social and cultural forces that helped to catalyze change are chronicled in lively fashion in Sabrina Petra Ramet, *Social Currents in Eastern Europe: The Sources and Consequences of the Great Transformation,** 2nd ed. (1995).

Literature offers an alternative and often revealing view of Eastern Europe. One of the most arresting portraits of East German life earlier under Erich Honecker is Rainer Kunze's ironic and understated chronicle *The Lovely Years* (1979). Václav Havel's best-known play, *Largo Desolato*, portrays the fears that immobilized opponents of the Czechoslovak Communist government after 1968. Ivan Klíma, *Judge on Trial* (1986, trans. 1991), offers an indictment of the moral compromises made by those who served that government, however unwillingly. Christa Wolf, *What Remains* (1996), is an autobiographical reflection on similar fears and compromises by a leading GDR author.

An excellent short introduction to the Soviet Union under Gorbachev, covering both politics and social change, is Geoffrey Hosking, *The Awakening of the Soviet Union* (1990). David Remnick, *Lenin's Tomb: The Last Days of the Soviet Empire* (1993), is an ambitious and fascinating portrait, and Michael Dobbs, *Down with Big Brother: The Fall of the Soviet Empire* (1996), offers snapshots of the empire in eclipse. The emergence of the new Soviet leadership is chronicled with rich detail in Mark Frankland, *The Sixth Continent: Mikhail Gorbachev and the Soviet Union** (1987). Gorbachev's own official platform is presented in Mikhail Gorbachev, *Perestroika: New Thinking for Our Country and the World** (1987). A retrospective analysis of his ideological itinerary emerges from Mikhail Gorbachev and Zdenek Mylnar, *Conversations with Gorbachev* (2002). Alec Nove's *Glasnost' in Action: Cultural Renaissance in Russia** (1989) examines the first effects of the liberation from press censorship. The social and political impact of Gorbachev's reforms in daily life is the subject of Roy Medvedev and Giulietto Chiesa, *Time Change: An Insider's View of Russia's Transformation* (1989). Gorbachev's eclipse and Boris Yeltsin's arrival in power are ably chronicled in John B. Dunlop, *The Rise of Russia and the Fall of the Soviet Empire* (1993). An excellent eyewitness account of the August 1991 coup is James H. Billington, *Russia Transformed: Breakthrough to Hope: Moscow, August, 1991* (1992). For a biography of Russia's first president, see John Morrison, *Boris Yeltsin: From Bolshevik to Democrat** (1991).

The best single analysis of the Soviet economy under Gorbachev is Anders Åslund, *Gorbachev's Struggle for Economic Reform** (1989). Other valuable studies include Abel Aganbegyan, *Inside Perestroika: The Future of the Soviet Economy* (1989), an apologia written by one of Gorbachev's principal economic advisors, and Marshall I. Goldman, *What Went Wrong with Perestroika** (1991). Grigori Medvedev, *The Truth about Chernobyl** (1989, trans. 1991) is a detailed reconstruction of the nuclear disaster by an expert called to the scene. For the Soviet Union's dismal ecological record, see Murray Feshbach, *Ecocide** (1992). Hedrick Smith, *The New Russians,** updated ed. (1991) also focuses on life beyond the Kremlin, though with far broader scope.

Events in Poland at the start of the decade—framed by the founding and suppression of Solidarity—are vividly chronicled in Timothy Garton Ash's *The Polish Revolution: Solidarity,** 2nd ed. (2000), Niel Ascherson's *The Polish August: The Self-Limiting Revolution** (1982), and Laurence Wechsler's *The Passion of Poland** (1984). The results of that suppression are the subject of Michael T. Kaufman, *Mad Dreams, Saving Graces, Poland: A Nation in Conspiracy* (1989). The Baltic states' struggle for liberation from the Soviet Union is recounted in Anatol Lieven, *The Baltic Revolution: Estonia, Latvia, Lithuania, and the Path to Independence* (1993).

On Western European relations with the East in the period leading up to the revolutions of 1989, see Lincoln Gordon, ed., *Eroding Empire: Western Relations with Eastern Europe* (1987) and William E. Griffith, ed., *Central and Eastern Europe and the West* (1989). Thoughtful attempts to link these changes with the emerging Europe in the 1990s, may be found in Ralf Dahrendorf, *Reflections on the Revolution in Europe* (1990), and Richard H. Ullman, *Securing Europe* (1991).

23

TOWARD A NEW
EUROPE, 1991–

A giant replica of the new one euro coin is displayed by the European commissioner for monetary affairs and the European Commission president at a news conference in 1998—a tangible sign of growing integration within the European Union. *(Courtesy AP/Wide World Photos)*

The end of the Cold War in Europe brought uncertainty as well as hope. Although the collapse of communism in the former Soviet Union and the former Eastern bloc opened a path for change, its shape and direction had yet to be determined. For those seeking the twin goals of democracy and prosperity in Eastern Europe, it became increasingly clear as the decade of the 1990s progressed that shaping the new Europe would prove an even greater challenge than ending the old.

Europe at the dawn of the twenty-first century counted ten more independent countries than a decade before. The break-up of the former Soviet Union in 1991 yielded the new states of Russia, Estonia, Latvia, Lithuania, Belarus, and Ukraine; the former Czechoslovakia split peacefully into the Czech Republic and Slovakia in 1993; and the former Yugoslavia devolved into Slovenia, Croatia, Bosnia, Serbia (federated with Montenegro), and Macedonia in a series of brutal and bloody civil wars that raged throughout the 1990s. These new states were often weak and untried. The trend of devolution into smaller political units further suggested the continuing power of ethnic and nationalist forces within the new Europe, repressed but not extinguished by the former Communist regimes.

The most significant change in Western Europe after 1991 was the strengthening of the European Union. It more than doubled its membership from twelve in 1993 to twenty-five in 2004, while at the same time successfully inaugurating an ambitious plan for monetary union. The divisive forces of nationalism were thus balanced by the opposite trend of integration within the structure of the European Union. At the same time, the globalization of markets and the overwhelming military superiority of the world's remaining superpower set limits to what even a united Europe could accomplish alone.

I. THE TRANSFORMATION OF EASTERN EUROPE

Among the nations of Eastern Europe, the end of communism brought increasing divergence. In a sense, there had always been something artificial about an "Eastern bloc" that united industrialized countries such as Czechoslovakia and East Germany with their more agrarian neighbors such as Romania or Bulgaria. But now, with the end of Soviet domination, these differences rapidly evolved into sharp contrasts in wealth and poverty, political innovation and lethargy, as the region began the dual transition from dictatorship toward democracy and from a state-controlled economy toward a free market system.

Three principal models emerged among the successor regimes in Eastern Europe. Democracy found strongest support in the tier of countries geographically closest to the West—Poland, the Czech Republic, Hungary, and the former East Germany, which had been formally incorporated into the (West) German Federal Republic in 1990—and in the three Baltic republics of Estonia, Latvia, and Lithuania, which had briefly tasted independence between the two world wars. In these two areas, political forces favoring reform were in the ascendant. In Romania, Bulgaria, Slovakia, Belarus, and most of the former Yugoslavia, in contrast, authoritarian regimes of a strongly nationalistic cast succeeded the Communists. There both economy and politics remained under state control. Finally, a third, mixed model emerged in Russia and the Ukraine. "Semiauthoritarian systems by consent" was a term used by some political analysts for this third model, pointing to the seeming contradiction of popular support for limited self-rule. At a time of economic and political uncertainty, "strong" government exercised an unmistakable appeal.

Even for those nations that managed the political transition to democracy most rapidly, however, the economic path from socialism to capitalism proved difficult. Economic conditions had deteriorated sharply in Eastern Europe during the 1980s; indeed, one of the principal spurs to the revolutions of 1989 had been the inability of the Communist economy to guarantee a tolerable standard of living. Budget deficits rose as governments struggled to maintain subsidized prices of food and housing, while at the same time repaying Western loans contracted in the 1970s, and inflation surged unchecked. Thus Eastern European economies began their post-Communist recovery from a position of weakness. Modern communication and transportation infrastructures were lacking, factories remained antiquated, and the work force apathetic. What is more, in a global economy the locus of economic expansion had increasingly shifted from manufacturing to information technology and the service sector, leaving Eastern Europe still further behind the West.

The practical question facing the non-Communist governments that assumed office in the early 1990s was how to make needed economic reforms while still retaining power. Ironically, the political reforms that brought an end to Communist rule also vested new electoral power in those most likely to suffer from the early stages of *economic* reform. Should those reforms cause too much pain, angry voters might well return the Communists to power. Their patience would be sorely tried in the months and years ahead.

Surviving "Shock Therapy"

The theory behind the attempt to restart the Eastern European economy was as simple in conception as it was brutal in its effects. Since decades of Communist rule had distorted the market—by planning production, controlling prices, and discouraging private enterprise—each of these three practices should now cease. The government would no longer tell managers what and how much to produce; prices would now be allowed to "find their natural level," and the legal impediments to creating small businesses would be removed. With the promise of freedom, profits, and respect for private property, entrepreneurs would be lured into providing the increased levels of goods and services that the public demanded, and with rising production, prices would fall again in due time. This theory was accepted by planners in Poland, the Czech Republic, Hungary, and the Baltic States as the basis for economic decontrol at the start of the 1990s. With the abolition of existing Communist constraints on the economy, the experiment had begun.

In the first few weeks under the new system, prices surged, but without triggering a corresponding increase in supply. Seeing that prices were still rising, those with something to sell (such as farmers) continued to hoard their produce, waiting for prices to rise still higher. This was indeed a rational response to the market; yet at the same time its overall effects were catastrophic. Critics wrote darkly of "shock without therapy." But as prices slowly started to level off, then dip after their initial surge, the hoarders reconsidered and released a flood of goods onto the market. Those who had previously held off selling, hoping that prices would increase further, now decided the time had come to liquidate their stocks. In Poland, where shock therapy began at the start of January 1990, convoys of farmers converged on major cities with livestock and vegetables for sale. The immediate crisis was past.

During the next four years, led by (now) President Walesa and a parliament dominated by the Solidarity movement, the Polish people endured a cruel period of economic adjustment. Prices still remained well above their prereform levels. Meanwhile employment plunged as huge state-owned plants (including the Lenin Shipyard in Gdánsk, Solidarity's birthplace) were either closed or downsized. Under communism, there had been money but nothing to buy; now shop windows were full, yet few could afford to go shopping. Shock therapy had in effect produced a depression. Only gradually did salaries begin to catch up with prices, as the private sector grew from a fifth to over half of the gross domestic product. Finally, by the start of the new millennium, despite pockets of unemployment and a widening gap between the richest and poorest Poles, the experiment was at last judged a success. The Polish economy had grown by 25 percent overall while avoiding the recessions and currency crises that visited Hungary and the Czech Republic—the best record in Eastern Europe.

This record was all the more impressive given Poland's political volatility. During the 1990s, the country saw nine prime ministers come and go, as the political center of gravity shifted from right to left of center then back again. Yet despite these frequent changes in political leadership, the policies of privatization, loosening state controls, and campaigning for EU membership remained consistent. In addition to progress toward a market economy, Poland could boast solid achievements in education, the strengthening of local government, and pension reform. In 1999, Poland became a member of NATO (see Section III) and was among the most prosperous of the ten candidates accepted in late 2002 for admission to the European Union.

Elsewhere in the more advanced regions of Eastern Europe, progress occurred at a slower pace. In the four years that followed its first post-Communist elections, Hungary had succeeded in attracting much-needed foreign investment. A stable government and aggressive efforts to find financial partners abroad helped it to capture more than half of all the Western funds invested in Eastern Europe (excluding Russia). Yet the pace of privatization and conversion from a state-run economy remained halting. The death of Prime Minister Joszef Antall in December 1993 marked the end of the first phase of Hungary's recovery. The succeeding economic downturn created the conditions for the return of the former communists, now calling themselves Socialists, as disappointed voters questioned the wisdom of Hungary's turn toward capitalism. In 1994, the Socialist party received an absolute parliamentary majority, and Hungary's neighbors watched to see which path the party would choose.

Surprisingly, the Socialists chose to back the most radical form of "shock therapy" that had yet been tried in Hungary. In a calculated gamble, they forged an alliance with the liberal Free Democrats and freed the economy from many of its remaining restrictions. The economic part of their gamble succeeded handsomely. The second half of the 1990s saw impressive economic gains in Hungary. Politically, however, the Socialists paid a price for the temporary hardships that were the inevitable result of such bold economic moves. In 1998, a conservative center-right coalition under Victor Orban replaced the Socialist-Free Democrat coalition. Still Hungary's conservative new leaders continued the shock therapy policies—even claiming to have originated them—thus giving the country an important measure of economic stability while reaping the political rewards that might more fairly have gone to their predecessors in office.

In Czechoslovakia, the most serious problem at the start of the 1990s was the deteriorating relations between the political leadership of the two dominant ethnic groups, Czechs and Slovaks. The Slovaks, led by the nationalist Vladimir Meciar, insisted that a democratic Czechoslovakia should accord greater autonomy to its eastern Slovak province. Václav Havel, though sympathetic to many of the Slovak demands, in the end lost the support of Meciar when Havel insisted that the country should remain united at all costs. In January 1993, the Slovak leadership had its way. Though opinion polls showed that a majority of both Czechs and Slovaks opposed partition, the country split in two. Havel, who had earlier been defeated in a reelection bid for the presidency of all of Czechoslovakia, was now confirmed as president of the new Czech Republic. Political power swung from right to left during the second half of the 1990s, as the conservative Civic Democratic Party lost power to the Socialists over corruption scandals and a slowing economy. Economic stagnation dogged the Czech Republic into the new millennium, with levels of unemployment rising into double digits. The massive floods of late summer 2002 submerged much of the old city of Prague and other population centers along the Vlatava River; relief and reconstruction placed a new burden on already strained state finances.

Slovakia, meanwhile, found the costs of independence heavy and pace of new investment disappointing. Prime Minister Meciar's attempts to control privatization of Slovakia's heavy industry reflected his reluctance to allow market forces full play and the continuing influence of old economic thinking in the new republic. His record on human rights—especially toward Slovakia's large Hungarian and Roma (gypsy) minorities—also reflected the police state methods of the past. But in 1998 Slovak voters defeated Meciar in his bid for the presidency, handing the office instead to his more liberal opponent, Rudolf Schuster. In April 2000, Meciar was arrested for corruption. Though he still remained a powerful political figure, the forces of both economic liberalization and political reform in Slovakia gained new strength and confidence.

Thus by the start of the new century, enough had changed for the better to allow for cautious optimism in Poland, Hungary, and the Czech Republic. Broadly speaking, those countries with the strongest democracies also boasted the strongest economies. This surprised those observers who had feared that electoral pressures might constrain new democratic regimes and keep them from taking steps that however necessary economically, remained deeply unpopular. In retrospect, it now appeared that the greater legitimacy of democratically elected governments, as well as their greater willingness to adopt Western models of economic reform, favored a successful transition to a market economy. It was no accident that these three former Communist countries led the list of those invited to join an expanded European Union in 2004.

Elsewhere in Eastern Europe—with the exception of the Baltic States and newly independent Slovenia—economic reform proceeded with agonizing slowness, as did the movement toward democratization. Ruling groups in Romania, Bulgaria, Ukraine, and Belarus alike all resisted the need for shock therapy. Parliaments heavily dominated by ex-Communists and nationalists insisted instead on a more gradual transition toward a market economy, reasoning that they could best safeguard their own political interests by shielding voters from the disruptive effects of economic transformation and widening income gaps. Indeed, what chiefly characterized both the political and economic landscape of this part of Eastern Europe in the mid-1990s was lack of change. With few democratic traditions, a tiny middle class, and little outside investment, entrenched elites in these countries found it relatively easy to weather the transition from communism to a post-Communist world without relaxing their grip on power. Newspapers and television remained under their control; so, too, did national education. Although the worse abuses of the Communist state had ended, the gap between these nations and their other Eastern European neighbors was widening.

Russia Reborn

On December 25, 1991, the red flag with a golden hammer and sickle was lowered above the Kremlin for the last time, ending nearly eighty years of Soviet rule. Boris Yeltsin and his new government lost no time in embarking on a more radical program of economic change than Gorbachev had ever contemplated. Advised by Western economic experts from the International Monetary Fund and a cadre of young Russian academics, Yeltsin attempted the same shock therapy that had been tried successfully in Poland. The Russian economy, they believed, could now be revived by an economic revolution that its enthusiastic proponents dubbed the "big bang."

For Russia's economic reforms to succeed, several major changes needed to occur in tandem. Former state property had to pass to private hands; private banks and a stock market needed to replace the state as the principal source of funding; and a legal system had to be created and laws enforced to prevent the first two changes from resulting in chaos. All three steps had occurred in Poland. But Russia posed a challenge of a different order than that of the rest of Eastern Europe. The vast scale of the world's largest country—with a population of 147 million spread over eleven time zones—made coordinated economic action difficult. Then again, Russia had lived under communism for seventy years, not forty, like Poland or Hungary, and thus had lost contact with the institutions and attitudes of its capitalist past. Unlike citizens of other former Communist countries further to the west, few Russians living in 1991 could remember their country before the revolution or the values of an earlier generation of bankers, bureaucrats, and entrepreneurs.

The most immediate result of the "big bang" in Russia was vertiginous inflation. For the year 1992 it reached an estimate 2,500 percent. Russians on fixed incomes, such as government employees and pensioners, suffered the most. But virtually the entire middle class lost its savings as the value of the ruble sank day by day. It was true that more goods were available for sale; but what did it matter if, just as in Poland, none could afford them? Economic shock in turn produced political paralysis. As the economy deteriorated, policy decisions were increasingly held hostage by the bitter standoff between Yeltsin and the Russian parliament, whose members feared that further reform would ruin what little functioning economy Russia still possessed. The brave hopes of the reformers quickly turned to recriminations, while those politicians nostalgic for the days of Communist rule began to feel the tide of public opinion shift in their favor. Russians who had cheered the end of the Soviet Union now wondered why they had supported a new regime that now brought them only economic misery. "All the good things the Communists said about communism were false," ran a popular joke at the time, "but all the bad things they said about capitalism were true."

In a country with no recent history of capitalist entrepreneurship, no independent banking system, and few laws governing business, a greedy few Russians managed to plunder the economy for their own private enrichment. Corruption extended well into Yeltsin's own circle. Government officials and businessmen with personal connections to the president (a group sometimes referred to as "the family") enjoyed lucrative state contracts and immunity from investigation. But others profited from the "big bang" as well. Under the guise of privatization, Soviet-era factory managers acquired controlling shares of their factories, paid off those who had helped them, and then stripped the assets.

As the gap between rich and poor widened, Russia was seeing a new class of so-called "oligarchs"—wealthy individuals who exercised virtual monopoly control over sectors of the economy such as energy or the media. These included not only ambitious entrepreneurs, like the bank director and media baron Vladimir Gusinsky, but also the so-called "Russian mafia," whose shadowy elements engaged in such classic criminal pursuits as extortion and prostitution. In Moscow opulent new homes surrounded by high walls were a sign of the times; so, too, were pizza parlors, billboards, and television advertisements for American-brand soft drinks and candy bars. But these pockets of prosperity could not hide the plunge in living standards that afflicted ordinary workers. In the new, "anything goes" atmosphere of Russia in the 1990s, there seemed little real hope that the average citizen would share in the material riches now suddenly available for a few.

The same global economy that brought McDonald's to Moscow also posed a threat to a country no longer insulated from world financial events. In 1997, when the economies of Thailand and Malaysia entered a severe recession, Russia soon felt the pressure of speculation against the ruble. Yeltsin appealed to the International Monetary Fund and the United States government for help, promising more vigorous economic reform in exchange for international aid. His plea was answered with assurances that help would be forthcoming. Few in the West wished to see Russia's economy fail. Despite these pledges, however, and the subsequent transfer of large sums to the Russian treasury, the economy remained weak and the ruble overvalued. Then in August 1998, the ruble finally collapsed; in consequence the Russian federal government defaulted on its sizeable international debt and the nation's economy entered a new phase of free fall. Yeltsin fired his newest prime minister after barely five months in office and appealed to the IMF once again. In the end, though still technically in default, Russia was allowed to reschedule its massive foreign debts. But no one could pretend that the "big bang" had brought prosperity.

From Yeltsin to Putin

Who ruled the new, post-Communist Russia? In theory, power was divided between the executive and legislative branches of government—between the president and his ministers on the one hand, and the parliament or Duma (a name revived from pre-Bolshevik times) on the other. Reformers dominated the executive during the early 1990s, while the Communist party (which had not been outlawed) retained significant power within the legislative branch. The precise limits of their respective spheres of influence, however, remained untested. When the leaders of the Duma tried to suspend President Yeltsin in 1993 for abuse of power, Yeltsin declared Parliament dissolved. The Duma leaders replied with an appeal for a popular uprising to topple the president in September, bringing an estimated 10,000 protesters onto the streets of Moscow, where they clashed with riot police. In a final escalation, Yeltsin ordered a military assault on the parliament building. After a day of shelling and over a hundred dead, the Russian president prevailed. But the cost of what his opponents denounced as Yeltsin's "coup d'état" was high.

His authority weakened by the violence he unleashed and by the abysmal state of the economy, Yeltsin now renewed a call for fresh elections. At the same time he proposed a vote on a new constitution (drafted the previous year) that would formally resolve the power struggle with Parliament by granting the president broad new powers. Once again Yeltsin achieved a partial victory. In 1994, Russian voters narrowly endorsed Yeltsin's constitution; at the same time, they elected a Duma packed with Yeltsin's foes. But parliamentary support now mattered less to the embattled president, since the new constitution significantly strengthened his hand. Like de Gaulle's French constitution of 1958—also adopted at a time when the country was deeply divided and sought decisive leadership (see Chapter 19, I)—it provided for an executive largely free from legislative control.

Yeltsin's other major domestic challenge lay in Chechnya. Situated in the mountainous north Caucasus and home to fiercely independent Muslim tribespeople, the region had been incorporated by force into the Russian Empire during the 1870s. Joseph Stalin, fearing that the Chechens might aid Nazi "liberators" during the Second World War, deported the region's entire population of half a million to Kazakhstan in 1944, where a quarter of them eventually died. The trauma of these events rendered the survivors particularly suspicious of Moscow, even after they were allowed to return to their homeland in 1957 following Stalin's death. Then in 1991, when other former Soviet republics with predominantly non-Russian populations such as Armenia, Georgia, and Azerbaijan declared independence by declining to join the new Russian Confederation, Chechen political leaders followed suit. Moscow first sent troops to reestablish control of the secessionist region, then accepted a de facto independent Chechnya while still attempting to ensure a pliant government. When these efforts failed, Yeltsin decided to intervene again. In late November 1994, persuaded of easy victory by his advisors, he dispatched 40,000 Russian troops to Chechnya with orders to end its bid for independence once and for all.

The Chechen war soon became Yeltsin's nightmare. Overconfident, poorly led, and badly supplied, Russian forces found themselves ambushed and outfought time and again by the Chechen guerillas. Stung and humiliated, the Russian military resorted to saturation bombing of the Chechen capital, Grozny, and the surrounding countryside. But even this brutal expedient produced no end to the conflict. Chechen fighters simply melted away into the Caucasus Mountains to continue the war on more favorable terrain, leaving their Russian adversaries as the hated conquerors of a capital city now reduced to a few square miles of rubble.

In April 1996, Yeltsin admitted that the Chechen war had been his "greatest mistake" and finally withdrew the troops he had sent to quell the rebels two years before. By now even his staunchest supporters had begun to question the wisdom of attempting to subdue the Chechens by force and welcomed the signing of a cease-fire that still left the contentious issue of independence unresolved. Yeltsin won reelection as president in 1996 after an energetic campaign, but failing health diminished his effectiveness thereafter. Many of the problems his government had failed to solve—a weak economy, an erratic legal system, nonpayment of taxes, widespread crime, and even more widespread corruption—now seemed truly beyond control. The term Russians now used to describe their country's condition was *bespredel*—a chaotic lawlessness for which they held Yeltsin largely responsible.

In the twilight of his reign, Yeltsin appointed a series of revolving-door prime ministers whose average tenure in office lasted less than four months. His fifth and final choice fell on a political unknown named Vladimir Putin. At first it seemed that Putin's tenure would be as brief as those of his predecessors; few guessed that Yeltsin had instead chosen his successor. Then on New Year's Day, 2001, Yeltsin abruptly resigned, leaving Putin acting president of Russia—as mandated by the new constitution—until early elections that March. When the time to vote arrived, Russians responded by electing Putin president in his own right by an overwhelming majority—the first democratic transfer of power in Russia's history. More than a year later, the 47-year-old former KGB officer and deputy mayor of Saint Petersburg still enjoyed a level of national popularity that exceeded Yeltsin's at its height.

What were the sources of Putin's appeal? In part it was the substance of his policies, in part their style. After nearly a decade of upheaval and uncertainty, Russian voters yearned for strong leadership. Putin's decision to renew the war in Chechnya soon after he became prime minister signaled decisiveness to them. Whereas Yeltsin had been an openly emotional politician—capable of both great warmth and volcanic anger—Putin appeared cool and controlled. Whereas Yeltsin's health had deteriorated steadily during the decade of the 1990s, Putin, a generation younger, boasted a black belt in karate. And whereas the Yeltsin regime had too often seemed like a series of hasty improvisations, lurching from crisis to crisis, Putin reimposed order from the top down. Thus after a decade and a half of disappointments and disruptions, it appeared that the worst of Russia's *bespredel* might be at an end.

Under Putin's watch, some aspects of Russian life indeed improved. The economy, buoyed by higher world gas and oil prices at the start of the new century, staged a modest recovery from the depths to which it had sunk in 1998, posting a healthy 8 percent growth rate in the year 2000. The federal government began at last to collect taxes; the legal system became less cumbersome and capricious; internal investment grew. Russia's international relations improved as well. In the wake of the September 11 terrorist attacks, Putin sided squarely with the United States and its antiterrorist coalition; the Russian president shrewdly used his support of the Bush administration to gain reciprocal support for his aim to subdue the rebels in Chechnya once and for all. As a "NATO partner," Russia now officially entered into cooperation with the military alliance created to curb Soviet expansion fifty years before.

At the same time, the Putin regime curbed civil rights and press freedom at home. Alarmed by aggressive media reporting on the Chechen war and on political corruption, the president and his ministers managed to annex or eliminate one independent newspaper and television station after another. Freedoms that had formed the core of Gorbachev's policy of *glasnost* now gave way to a more traditional Kremlin policy of media control. The respected weekly *Itogi* (*Summing-Up*) succumbed to pressure to adopt a more pro-government line, while the two most powerful figures in the media world, Vladimir Gusinsky and Boris Berezovsky, were driven into exile. But it was far easier to muzzle the press than to cure the problems it reported. While the renewed war in

Vladimir Putin, Russia's youthful president, poses for an official portrait shortly after his accession to office in 2001. (*Courtesy of the National Academy of Sciences*)

Chechnya festered, the country's infrastructure remained in disrepair; public servants such as teachers and doctors continued to be paid poorly, if at all; public health deteriorated further as clinics closed their doors to the poor and the rate of alcoholism soared. In one stark measure of health in the new Russia, life expectancy for men declined from 65 to 59 by 2001, that for women from 74 to 72.

The tenth anniversary of the fall of Soviet Union offered an occasion to assess the current state of Russia. The balance was somber. Former President Mikhail Gorbachev, interviewed on German television in the fall of 2001, concluded sadly that Russia had squandered many of the early opportunities offered by communism's collapse. His admission matched the country's bleak mood. Despite the spectacular fortunes amassed by the "oligarchs" and the upscale development in urban centers such as Moscow and Saint Petersburg, the decade of the 1990s had brought general impoverishment. Russian economic output now stood at a scant 60 percent of its level ten years before. It was telling that more than half of all Russians surveyed said they would prefer to return to life the way it had been in the Soviet Union. Despite Putin's continuing popularity, it was not clear whether Russia at last had a leader who would—or could—advance the process of reform to the point where the populace ceased to regret the past.

The Death of Yugoslavia

With the disappearance of the Soviet Union in 1991, Yugoslavia remained the last of the Communist multiethnic states in Eastern Europe. Greek Orthodox Serbs, Catholic Croatians, and Muslim Bosnians and Kosovars lived and worked together within a single

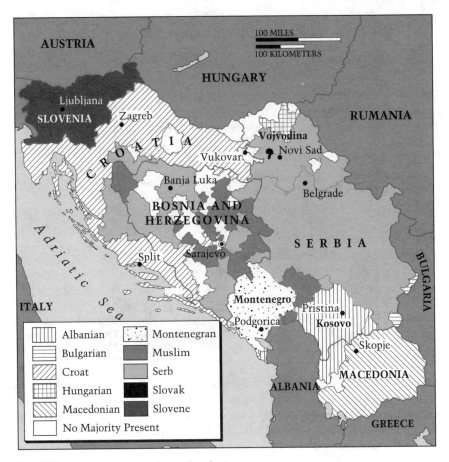

MAP 23.1 Ethnic groups in the former Yugoslavia.

federation. Yet the same forces of nationalism that had splintered the Soviet Union into fourteen states in 1991 now threatened to destroy Yugoslavia in turn, with far more tragic consequences.

The beginning of the end for Yugoslavia came with the death of Marshal Tito in 1980. Tito had well understood the explosive nature of Yugoslavia's ethnic rivalries and the ease with which nationalist demagogues could exploit them. He therefore sought to encompass the country's regions within the framework of a federal state—one that offered a measure of local autonomy, yet whose national army and police would check dissent. Tito's defiance of Moscow in the late 1940s and the courageous war record of his partisans against Hitler had helped to rally Yugoslavs of differing ethnic backgrounds to a common national cause. But his success in managing this difficult balancing act did not outlive him.

With Tito's passing, power in Yugoslavia devolved to an eight-person executive committee composed of representatives of the country's six provinces and two autonomous regions. Deep economic difficulties throughout the country and political ferment in the southern region of Kosovo gradually undermined an already fragile government. Interest on the massive international loans borrowed under Tito prompted the new authorities to squeeze Yugoslavia's standard of living in order to generate hard currency; this in turn bred anger and resentment toward the successor regime. When a young Serbian banker, Slobodan Milosevic, managed to unseat the aging leadership of the Serbian Communist League in 1988 by appealing to Serb nationalism, he accelerated the splintering of the one institution that held Yugoslavia together—the Communist party.

The struggle that now developed in Yugoslavia was essentially one between the Serbs and the Montenegrans—groups favoring a strong, unified Yugoslavia under Serbian control—and the Bosnians, Croats, Macedonians, and Slovenes, who preferred a loosening of the confederation of self-governing republics. But within each region there were minorities that sided with the opposite camp—the Serbs living in Croatia, who opposed the idea of a confederation, and the non-Serbs in Serbia, who welcomed it. When it was finally decided to hold multiparty elections in each republic in 1989, the ultimate winners were extreme nationalists on all sides.

Yugoslavia unraveled from the top down, starting with Slovenia in the north, then Croatia, then Bosnia-Herzegovina, and finally the enclave of Kosovo within Serbia itself. Each secession proved bloodier than the last. Slovenia and Croatia were the first to hold free elections in 1989. In both, the winners were non-Communist nationalists who favored greater independence from the Yugoslav state. Adjoining Italy and Austria, Slovenia was in many ways the most economically advanced among Yugoslavia's republics and thus best prepared for independence. It also enjoyed the inestimable advantage of a relatively homogeneous population, with few Croatian or Serbian minority citizens living within its borders. Its move toward independence was first blocked by the Serbs, then conceded after diplomatic intervention by the European Union, which finally offered it EU membership (alone of the Yugoslavian successor states) in 2002.

In 1991 Croatia, with a large Serbian minority, found itself plunged into a civil war pitting Croats against Serbs; hostilities ceased only after United Nations intervention following months of fierce combat. But the longest struggle raged in Bosnia. There Serbs, Croats, and Muslims confronted one another in a three-cornered conflict that dragged on for over three years and left the country partitioned. From Bosnia the Yugoslav civil war moved to Serbia, where Kosovo revolted in 1999, and where NATO imposed a UN-supervised peace settlement in 2000. In the end, a federation that had included six member states in 1989 was now reduced to two—Serbia and Montenegro—with the Kosovo region of Serbia under NATO control.

The wars that spelled an end to the old Yugoslavia were fought with stark savagery. Scenes that recalled the brutality of the Second World War—concentration camps, forced deportations, the shelling of cities, dynamiting of churches, and refugees desperate to escape these horrors—became commonplace once again. The term "ethnic cleansing" was coined by the combatants to signify forced expulsions from ethnically mixed villages in an attempt to make them entirely Serb or entirely Croat. Like the Nazi term "final solution," it was a verbal subterfuge used to disguise barbaric acts, including mass murder. Those Europeans who felt that such barbarism lay safely in the past were now forced to admit their naiveté. Indeed, by one grim statistic the conflict in the former Yugoslavia eclipsed the Second World War: The proportion of civilian casualties was far higher. During the Second World War, observers were shocked when equal numbers of soldiers and civilians were killed. But in Bosnia, more than 80 percent of the reported casualties were civilians. Put another way, soldiers shot unarmed women and children rather than each other. It was, as one commentator noted, a "war of cowards."

Almost as shocking as the atrocities committed in the Yugoslav civil war was the indifference of much of Europe and the United States to what transpired there. Despite clear evidence that the Serbian government intended to create a Greater Serbia and would be deterred by nothing short of force, European leaders preferred to believe (or at least to claim) that the Serbs fighting in Croatia and Bosnia received no military support from Serbia itself. When war crimes were reported to the United Nations, few of its officials seemed anxious to prosecute the criminals. Gradually, however, the Yugoslav wars became an embarrassment to the international community. Western Europe and the United States belatedly responded with humanitarian aid, peacekeeping troops, and earnest entreaties that the conflict end. Yet an arms embargo imposed on Bosnia simply ensured that the better-armed Serbian and Croat troops would prevail, while the European and Canadian UN peacekeepers became de facto hostages of the warring parties. Nor did the United States exercise leadership in the first two years of the war. Instead, the European capitals and Washington engaged in angry finger pointing, each protesting that its own inaction was the fault of its allies.

Nothing so well symbolized the impotence of the peacemakers as the siege of Sarajevo. For two years, from 1993 to 1995, the lovely capital of Bosnia was battered by Serbian guns placed in the mountains that overlooked the city and raked by snipers who hid in the ruins. Ten thousand of its inhabitants perished; many more were wounded in a combat that seemed to have no end. While United Nations flights kept the city minimally supplied with food, water and electricity were scarce, and citizens burned their furniture and books to keep from freezing during two long winters. A decade earlier, Sarajevo has hosted the Winter Olympics; now it lay smoking and wasted—a monument not to world peace but to the cost of local war.

By 1995, the conflict in Bosnia had claimed almost 200,000 dead and missing, and produced upward of 4 million refugees. But in that year the Croatian army finally drove occupying Serbs from their territory, while a Bosnian militia combining both Croats and Muslims inflicted heavy damage on the Bosnian Serbs. These losses (and fear of more to come) set the stage in turn for a provisional agreement. Peace accords signed in Dayton, Ohio, in 1996 created two separate entities in Bosnia—one, Muslim-Croat, holding 51 percent of the territory; the other, Serbian, holding the rest. Since Serbs made up barely 30 percent of the total population, some argued that they had still emerged as victors from the war. And although the signatories of the peace pledged to work toward reintegrating the two Bosnian ministates, most signs pointed toward a permanent partition. Nor did the Dayton agreement address the rights of another important minority—the ethnic Albanian Muslims living in the southern region of Kosovo, whose relative autonomy Slobodan Milosevic had abruptly ended in 1989, placing them under direct Serbian control.

The nonviolent resistance of the ethnic Albanian populace during much of the 1990s led nowhere. So in 1998, Kosovar Albanians changed their tactics. Grouped under the banner of the Kosovo Liberation Army (KLA), they began a series of terrorist attacks that directly challenged Serbian rule. In response, Milosevic launched a massive counterattack in the winter of 1999; as in Bosnia, civilians were the main targets. This exercise

A weeping Bosnian woman remembers the dead in a Muslim cemetery in Sarajevo in the spring of 1993; note the makeshift wooden markers and the tiny child's grave on the left. (*Courtesy AP/Wide World Photos*)

in "ethnic cleansing" produced an estimated 800,000 refugees, as ethnic Albanian families fled burning homes and systematic rape. This time NATO responded with new vigor. For the first time in the organization's fifty-year history (see Chapter 17, II), it launched a military offensive within Europe. After seventy-two days of ferocious bombing, during which NATO forces mistakenly destroyed the Chinese embassy in Belgrade, Milosevic sued for peace. Serbian troops withdrew from Kosovo, replaced by a United Nations force 50,000 strong. Now it was the local Serb population that feared ethnic cleansing; over 200,000 left to seek safety elsewhere. Late in 2001, however, the region's first democratic elections for a local assembly ended on a hopeful note. The winner was the most moderate of the ethnic Albanian parties, led by Ibrahim Rugova. In what was seen as a referendum on independence, most ethnic Albanians appeared to vote for autonomy within Serbia rather than outright secession. Yet support for independence remained high.

The war in Kosovo produced a ripple effect elsewhere in the Balkans. As the conflict intensified in 1999, Macedonia—a former part of Yugoslavia sharing borders with Albania and Greece—found itself a reluctant host to hundreds of thousands of ethnic Albanians fleeing Serb atrocities. With its own Albanian minority already numbering some 30 percent of the population, Macedonia's majority Slav leaders feared that the new arrivals would upset the fragile demographic balance in their fledgling state. Yet NATO success in defeating Yugoslavian troops in Kosovo, and the parallel success of the Kosovo Liberation Army in the months that followed, gave fresh heart to those ethnic Albanians in Macedonia who clamored for equal rights with the Slav majority. Then in the spring of 2001, armed ethnic insurgents seized territory within Macedonia as a step toward independence, only to be disarmed by NATO troops. A tense truce followed. But few observers believed that supporters of Kosovar independence or the Macedonian movement they inspired would soon abandon their dream.

The Struggle for Serbia

Serbia under Milosevic had never been a totalitarian state like Germany under Hitler, or Russia under Stalin. Instead it was an authoritarian regime with weak opponents. The opposition parties, divided by fierce rivalries and starved of state funds, found it difficult to mount an effective opposition. But there were independent journalists such as Veran Matic, who ran the fiercely independent radio station B92, and the student opposition movement Otpor (Resistance), founded in 1998. Otpor specialized in opposition spiced with humor. Its members stood in line for kitchen staples like cooking oil and sugar wearing T-shirts that read "Everything in Serbia is okay." Their critique sharpened after the loss of Kosovo, which Milosevic attempted to paint as a victory in the state-run media. By now it was clear to almost all that things in Serbia were anything but okay. But from what quarter would change come?

In the end, Milosevic engineered his own defeat. He amended the constitution to permit direct election of the president (rather than his election by parliament, as formerly), then called for elections in the fall of 2000. Some considered this a brilliant tactical stroke. In the face of international sanctions, Yugoslavia would defiantly reelect Milosevic and reject those who favored accommodation with the West. But almost as soon as the election date was announced, things began to go awry. For the first time, the majority of the opposition parties managed to unite behind a single candidate—a constitutional lawyer and leader of the tiny Democratic Party of Serbia named Vojislav Kostunica. And Serb voters began to back him.

Kostunica was that rarity in Serbia, a moderate. Modest in appearance, quiet and even dull in his public speeches, he had won acceptance as the candidate of a unified opposition in part precisely because he seemed so unthreatening. But his refusal to accept campaign funds from the West and his patriotic condemnation of NATO's bombing campaign also won him broad public support. In the voting of September 24, a majority of Serbians who cast their ballots chose Kostunica as their president. Milosevic refused to concede, arguing that his rival had not gained enough votes to win outright, and insisted that a second, runoff election was still needed. In the past such a delaying tactic might have overawed the opposition. But by now too many anti-Milosevic Serbians sensed vic-

tory. Buoyed by the refusal of their candidate, Kostunica, to concede, they resolutely rejected the need for another vote. Miners protested by striking, and were soon joined by
other workers. When anti-Milosevic demonstrators converged on Belgrade from throughout the country on October 6, they found the police on their side as well; crowds of Kostunica supporters occupied the Serbian parliament and state television unopposed. That
evening Kostunica proclaimed victory, greeting his supporters with the words "dear liberated Serbia." Milosevic conceded the following day.

After nine years of lies, corruption, military defeats, and disastrous misrule, his
fellow Serbs had finally voted Milosevic out of office. Politically, this outcome was preferable to foreign intervention, since it gave the Kostunica government internal legitimacy.
At the same time, however, no Serb could avoid the truth: Their country had become an
international pariah, its once healthy economy now in ruins. Years of effort would be required to repair the damage sustained by both infrastructure and institutions. Moreover,
the Serbian state government, separate from (and more powerful than) the largely ceremonial federal government, remained in the hands of Milosevic's lieutenants. This
changed in December 2000, when new elections returned the anti-Milosevic alliance Democratic Opposition of Serbia (DOS) to power under its leader, Zoran Djindjic, the new
Serbian prime minister. Despite their common stance against Milosevic, relations between
President Kostunica and Prime Minister Djindjic were those of rivals, not allies. Both had
pledged not to turn over Milosevic to the International Court of Justice in the Hague, yet
both came under increasing pressure to do just that. In its war-torn state, Yugoslavia
could not afford to antagonize the donors in which its economic future depended.

In March of 2001, Serbian police under orders from Djindjic finally arrested
Milosevic. Three months later, on the eve of an international conference considering aid
for Yugoslavia, Djindjic finally bowed to American and European pressure and extradited
Milosevic to the United Nations war crimes tribunal at the Hague—the highest ranking
defendant to face such proceedings since the Nuremberg Trials of 1946–1947. In return,
the aid conference voted $1.2 billion for reconstruction in Serbia. It was a humiliating
moment for a nation proud of its independence, which had faced down Stalin at the end
of World War II (see Chapter 14, IV), and did little to endear Djindjic to Serb nationalists, who soon engineered his assassination. As the anti-Milosevic alliance disintegrated
and the nationalists rallied, neither true democracy nor a flourishing market economy—
the twin goals of post-Communist Eastern Europe—seemed yet within Serbia's reach.

II. WESTERN EUROPE: THE CHALLENGES
OF COMMUNITY

Western Europe's democracies entered the 1990s against a background of economic
weakness and political drift, which left established institutions and politicians on the defensive. By early 1997, unemployment in Germany—the Continent's economic power-
house—had reached four and a half million. "Is Germany facing collapse?" the
mass-circulation weekly *Stern* asked rhetorically, while Chancellor Kohl (now Germany's
longest-serving modern head of government) proclaimed that reducing unemployment

would henceforth be the chief aim of his administration. Increased global competition and the high labor costs required by the welfare state combined to reduce European exports and placed governments in a quandary. If they attempted to fight unemployment by stimulating the economy, that increased state debt; if they refused to intervene, the number of jobless grew. Since the European Union set strict limits on deficits for countries sharing the new single currency, the euro, few were willing to borrow their way out of a slump.

The difficulties faced by Eastern Europe in adjusting to capitalism had been expected; the growing economic difficulties of the West during the 1990s came as an unwelcome surprise. Extreme nationalist or even fascist parties in France, Holland, Austria, and Italy attempted to profit from Western European fears of continuing unemployment, unchecked immigration, and imminent globalization. Though the solutions they proposed were hateful and simplistic, the support they received from voters highlighted the failure of the political mainstream to counter a pervasive public mood of worry and distrust.

Italy's Political Earthquake

During the decade of the 1980s, the Italian political system had remained essentially immobile. "Stalemate democracy," as Italians referred to this unhappy condition, had roots in a political tradition that prized accommodation over competition, and appeared impervious to change. For thirty years, an alliance between two parties, the Christian Democrats (DC) and Socialists (PSI), had dominated national politics, with Vatican and United States support. Their major rivals were the Communists, who, with the exception of the "historic compromise" of 1976–1979 (see Chapter 21, III), remained in permanent opposition. To many the Italian government seemed to exist primarily for the benefit of career politicians and their clients on the state payroll. The all too familiar ills of drift and corruption were tolerated by fatalistic voters who could see no hope of change. Yet the early 1990s were to challenge Italy's political elite in a dramatic manner that no one had foreseen.

The first shock came with the end of the Cold War. Fears of communism, which had ensured a reliable vote for the Christian Democrats, now melted away, and with them much of that party's support. Why, voters asked themselves, should they continue to reelect a corrupt party whose role as a conservative bastion against Italian communism was no longer needed? Then came a second, internal shock—the political scandal that Italians baptized *Tangentopoli*, or "Bribesville." Christian Democratic and Socialist politicians alike were found to have been involved in corruption on a massive scale. The first true power shift in Italian national politics in over thirty years resulted from revelations that left even cynical Italians astounded and ashamed.

Like the Watergate scandal in the United States, which began with a burglary and led eventually to the resignation of President Richard Nixon, *Tangentopoli* was ignited by a minor incident that sparked major repercussions. In the spring of 1992, a petty Milanese city official was indicted for accepting kickbacks when awarding city contracts to hospital cleaning services and funeral parlors. The accused official implicated other, more senior figures in the city administration, who implicated still higher figures in turn.

Like a spreading stain, evidence of corruption led from Milan's city hall to the Socialist party, the national government, and some of Italy's major corporations. Within months the examining magistrate, Antonio Di Pietro, and fellow judges were sifting through hundreds of cases in that would become known as the *Mani Pulite*, or "Clean Hands" campaign. By early 1994, 4,000 persons were under investigation, including half the members of Parliament, and Di Pietro had become a national hero.

As one political and industrial leader after another took his place among the accused, the breathtaking scale of Italy's political corruption began to emerge. One investigator calculated that the total of all bribes paid during the decade of the 1980s had amounted to as much as one trillion dollars. A sophisticated system of couriers ferried money among the principal beneficiaries, who hid their wealth in secret bank accounts in Switzerland, the Vatican, and offshore tax havens such as the Cayman Islands. An especially sinister aspect of the scandal was the light it shed on ties between the parties in power and the Italian mafia. When Giulio Andreotti, one of the leading figures of the Christian Democrats, was accused of protecting mafiosi in Sicily, it suggested that a major reason for the mafia's confined power was the complicity of the politicians. That complicity had long been suspected but never proved. Now the Italian police and judiciary, aided by mafia members who had turned state's evidence (the so-called *pentiti*), assembled solid evidence for the first time on which both the mafiosi and their political allies could be tried.

The combined impact of *Tangentopoli* and the end of the Cold War shook the Italian political landscape. Leading political parties, including the Christian Democrats, splintered or collapsed altogether. On the left, the Communists divided into the old-guard Rifondazione Comunista and the more moderate Democratic Party of the Left (PDS). The Right followed suit, with the former Christian Democrats splitting into the conservative Centro Cristiano-Democratico and the more moderate Partito Popolare (whose name recalled the earlier Catholic party of the 1920s). New parties, such as the regional Northern League and the conservative Forza Italia (Go Italy!) party of millionaire media tycoon Silvio Berlusconi, moved into the political vacuum.

When elections next occurred in early 1994, the winners were a Center-Right coalition grouping Italy's newest parties—Berlusconi's Forza Italia, the neofascist National Alliance, and the separatist Northern League. Yet within months, the Center-Right coalition collapsed, and the Italian President was forced to appoint a financial expert as interim prime minister. The next round of elections, in 1996, brought a Center-Left coalition to power. The so-called "Olive Tree" (Ulivo) group of parties, led initially by the economist Romano Prodi and then by the former Communist Massimo D'Alema, succeeded in helping Italy to meet the stringent requirements for participation in the European single currency by lowering inflation and drastically reducing state expenditures.

Maintaining fiscal discipline at a time of political uncertainty was an impressive achievement. Yet the Olive Tree's failure to complete the work of the Clean Hands campaign or to overhaul a bloated state government undermined hopes for further change. By the late 1990s, the energies liberated by *Tangentopoli* were largely spent. Many Italians seemed more comfortable with a modernized Right than with left-wing apostles of reform. When Berlusconi, despite being under multiple indictments for bribery, won the parliamentary elections at the head of his Forza Italia party in the summer of 2001, it was difficult to know whether this signaled a healthy *alternanza* in politics or a return to apathy and cynicism on the part of the Italian electorate. Berlusconi's call for more "liberty" and a reform of the judicial system were, at the very least, measures that stood to benefit him personally as well as Italy as a whole. His attack on judges for having overreached in the "Clean Hands" campaign, in particular, seemed an ominous sign that corruption would now be more readily tolerated than judicial independence.

Had Italy's political system changed in any basic way? Major issues that the Olive Tree had left untouched now demanded more attention than ever. But it seemed likely that reform would now more likely result from the pressures exerted by the European Union in Brussels, rather than by the politicians in Rome. Once again, as in the late 1940s, hopes that reform would automatically follow a political earthquake failed to anticipate the remarkable resiliency of Italian politics of the old school.

France and the Far Right

The popular support given Socialist President François Mitterrand and his party at the start of the 1980s dissipated as that decade advanced. Beset by scandal and fatigue, the Socialists maintained little of their old voter appeal. In his televised New Year's speech for 1992 the president, whose personal popularity had sunk to a meager 22 percent, spoke of the "atmosphere of discouragement" that had overtaken the country. Few were surprised the following year when a conservative alliance managed to win eighty per cent of the seats in parliamentary elections—the most lopsided legislative victory since the founding of the Fifth Republic thirty years before. Still Mitterrand refused to resign. Instead he insisted on his constitutional right to remain in office until the end of his term in 1995, preferring a return to the "cohabitation" with Prime Minister Jacques Chirac that had marked the end of his previous term (see Chapter 22, I). In 1995, it was finally Chirac's turn to enter the Elysée Palace as president. Exhausted by a long battle with cancer, Mitterrand died the following year.

Chirac promised change with a conservative flavor. Now that both the legislature and the president's office were controlled by the same party, he told French voters, projects such as tax cuts and the privatization of state-owned banks could be implemented at last. Yet just as Mitterrand had been obliged to temper his Socialist program in the early 1980s, Chirac soon found himself on the path to compromise. As had been true for Italy, the European Union's guidelines for a single currency required low inflation and low budget deficits for entry into the euro zone. France had neither. In addition, the country was plagued by stubborn unemployment, hovering between 11 and 12 percent— the third highest in the EU after Spain and Finland. High labor costs, rigid work rules, and generous worker benefits had all helped to create a system in which a tenth of the population was permanently out of work. With businesses failing at the rate of 6,000 a month, applying conservative doctrines of privatization and smaller government seemed likely further to increase unemployment in the short run, thereby pushing up government payments to those out of work at the very moment when deficit reduction was essential.

Faced with these unpalatable alternatives, Chirac and his prime minister, Alain Juppé, tried to engineer an electoral solution to France's economic problem. Convinced that they could catch the Socialists off guard, Chirac called a snap parliamentary election in April 1997. It was a mistake. The electorate that had overwhelmingly backed the

Right in 1993 now produced a parliamentary majority for the Left, while Lionel Jospin, the Socialist whom Chirac had defeated in the presidential election of 1995, now became prime minister. Once again France returned to the expedient of "cohabitation." Through budget cutting and aggressive accounting, Jospin's team massaged France's economy enough to satisfy the EU monetary union criteria. The most significant step toward reducing unemployment was the passage of a law requiring a 35-hour work week in 2000, intended to distribute work more broadly. Under Jospin's stewardship, unemployment finally fell from 12 to 9 percent.

French observers expected the first round of the presidential elections of 2002 to be a rematch of the Chirac-Jospin duel of 1995. Instead, record numbers of voters either opted for fringe candidates or boycotted the polls altogether. With sixteen aspiring candidates, there were choices to suit every taste. Three Trotskyite rivals competed for support on the far Left; there were also an ecologist and a free market liberal. But the real winner in the first round was the racist former French paratrooper and leader of the National Front, Jean-Marie Le Pen, who edged out Jospin for the number two spot by less than 1 percent of the vote. One government minister called the result a "political cataclysm," and he was correct. Suddenly voters found themselves facing not a normal run-off election, but a referendum on racism and French democracy. While President Chirac grimly warned that the Fifth Republic itself was in peril, millions of Socialist voters equally grimly cast their votes for him as the lesser of two evils. "Better a crook than a fascist" was their slogan. With more support from the Left than from his own party, Chirac won a resounding 82 percent of the vote in the second round. Still, almost a fifth of the French electorate had chosen a candidate of the far right.

In the aftermath, nearly every French political observer asked, How could this have happened here? It was not so much that the French people were racists, some argued, as that they were scared and angry—scared by rising crime, and angry that politicians seemed so oblivious to their concerns. By openly addressing fears concerning personal safety, Le Pen had forced his opponents belatedly to confront issues of law and order they would have preferred to ignore. The electoral results served as a warning, if one was needed, that despite the end of the Cold War, significant portions of the French population felt less safe than before. While the Russians had been a distant threat, the young North Africans who crowded into the suburbs of cities such as Toulon, Marseilles, and Paris stirred primal fears. Legislative elections in the summer of 2002 gave Chirac a solid parliamentary majority, and his choice for prime minister, Jean-Pierre Raffarin, radiated calm. Still, many concluded, there would have to be more than just words to avoid another "political cataclysm" in the near future.

Great Britain: From the Welfare State to the "Third Way"

Since the end of the Second World War, Western Europeans had become accustomed to government support from the so-called "welfare state" (see Chapter 15, IV). Government ministries administered programs of health insurance, old-age pensions, subsidized housing, family allowances, child care, and education as a matter of course. Farmers received price subsidies; industries received development grants; everyone received the assurance that in case of accident, illness, or unemployment, the state would be there to help. Now, in the early 1990s, a combination of renewed recession and growing global competition drove these same governments to reexamine their massive commitment to social programs and to ask whether they could still afford the cost.

Britain had already shown the way. Since Margaret Thatcher's electoral victory in 1979, Conservative governments in the United Kingdom had whittled away at entitlements and state ownership—reducing subsidies, selling off nationalized industries, and constricting social services. For those who depended on government assistance for unemployment insurance or health care, the results meant greater misery. But for the economy as a whole, the bitter Tory medicine yielded positive results. By the late 1990s, Britain had a lower rate of unemployment and a healthier overall economy than any of its EU partners on the Continent except Holland. Long the odd man out, Britain under the Conservatives could boast of being ahead of the pack in recognizing the need to reform the welfare state.

In the spring of 1997, Britain's Labour party—which under the leadership of forty-three-year-old Tony Blair had shed its image as a doctrinaire left-wing movement—swept into power with the largest electoral majority in a century. For the Conservatives, it was a humiliating defeat; their eighteen years of unbroken rule were at an end. For Labour, it was a lesson in compromise. Prime Minister Blair promised in effect to balance the Tory reliance on free market forces with Labour's traditional concern for the victims of untrammeled capitalism. One of the issues on which Labour successfully campaigned had been the "modernization" of the same welfare state that a previous Labour government under Clement Attlee had pioneered immediately following the Second World War (see Chapter 15, V). Education, national health care, and the needy were again to be priorities, but this time within an economic framework that even conservative Thatcherites might not disavow.

Blair termed his new Labour approach the "third way"—positioned between the orthodox Left and the doctrinaire Right. For many of his supporters, this pragmatic, flexible approach offered the perfect blend of fiscal prudence and social conscience. Yet applying the Blair formula to Britain's ossified and underfunded public services proved a major challenge. To "modernize" the public sector required both capital investment and government oversight. After eighteen years of Conservative neglect, Britain's hospitals, schools, and railways cried out for attention. Reforming health care proved the greatest challenge of all. More than a million patients (out of a total population of 59 million) awaited elective surgery in chronically understaffed hospitals. Despite promises to invest more funds in the health sector (hardly a novel remedy), Labour found itself hampered by a shortage of doctors and nurses and resistance from hospital administrators. To streamline the creaking National Health system erected a half century before now appeared a promise the party would come to regret.

After five years in office—following a second victory over the hapless Tories in 2001—Blair's government still not found the magic formula for "modernization." Despite creating government agencies with such promising names as the Forward Strategy Unit and the Performance and Innovation Unit, none of the government's initiatives seemed able to gain traction. Too little money was being spread over too many needs, with too little intelligent management. In pledging to improve public services, the Blair government had given voters a litmus test by which to judge its success. Every late train, poor teacher, and overbooked doctor gave them a chance to blame the politicians.

Aided by a strong economy and a weak opposition, the Blair government did its best to disguise its failures in reforming public services. "Teflon Tony" was a nickname given a prime minister who seemed remarkably impermeable to criticism. And not all news was bad. Even his critics conceded that New Labour's plan to devolve more power to representative bodies in Scotland and Wales (tried unsuccessfully by Harold Wilson) was a success, while the idea of restricting the House of Lords to life peers alone seemed sensible to many. And then there was the issue of the European Union. From the start, the prime minister skillfully sought to reassure pro-Europeanists that Britain would, indeed, eventually join the monetary union while at the same time insisting that it would be only "on our terms." Though not a tactic that could be infinitely prolonged, it bought New Labour time.

Blair's years as prime minister also saw significant developments in Northern Ireland, as both the British and Irish governments attempted to move beyond the bloody stalemate that had immobilized Protestants and Catholics for a quarter century (see Chapter 22, I). The so-called Good Friday Agreement of 1998, brokered by former United States Senator George Mitchell, offered both sides a way out. It proposed home rule and power sharing between Protestants and Catholics, in exchange for disarmament by Sinn Fein's military, the Irish Republican Army (IRA), and their Protestant paramilitary rivals. Yet despite wide support in both the Irish Republic and Northern Ireland for the Good Friday Agreement, hardliners in both camps found it hard to abandon the dream of total victory and the government found that it could not compel these groups to disarm. The IRA offered repeated promises to place its weapons "beyond use" yet seemed incapable of abandoning their use as a bargaining chip—a policy that galled the suspicious Protestant camp.

A final aspect of New Labour policy was the alliance with the United States. Following the terrorist attack of September 11, 2001, Tony Blair became the strongest defender among European heads of state of George Bush's energetic campaign against the Taliban and al-Qaeda in Afghanistan and Saddam al-Hussein's regime in Iraq. There was more than a hint of the old "special relationship" between the United States and Great Britain in these warm relations; at the same time, Britain's own assessment of security threats both domestic and foreign inclined Blair and his cabinet to accept the need for preventive action, despite strong antiwar sentiments among many Labour voters. When the United States invaded Iraq in the spring of 2003, Blair supported Washington with energy and determination, sending troops and risking a split within his own party and the EU for the sake of unity with Britain's most important ally.

Germany after Reunification

The German economy in the early 1990s was dominated by the enormous costs of reunification. Never in modern times had a European state willingly assumed such an economic burden—attempting to raise the standard of living of a neighbor one-third its size and many times poorer to match the high level enjoyed by its own citizens. Though united by a common language and memories of a shared prewar past, the Federal Republic and the former East Germany had followed markedly different paths since the end of World War II. Now two economies, two legal systems, two educational systems, and two cultures had to be made one again.

Reviving the economy proved less difficult in the end than overcoming the cultural divide. Yet the yearly expenditures required to renovate the infrastructure of the former East Germany, to transform its rusting factories into modern ones, and to ease the transition from a socialist to a capitalist economy for its citizens ran to billions of dollars. As the decade of the 1990s progressed, the strain on the West German economy began to tell, while the former East Germans, acutely aware of their dependency on their wealthier cousins, began to feel excluded or patronized in the new, united Germany. Their insecurities—as well as the Westerners' robust sense of self-worth—continued to create frictions and misunderstandings that resisted easy remedy.

Few were surprised when, in 1998, Helmut Kohl's sixteen-year tenure as chancellor finally ended. German voters had increasingly complained of being *"kanzlermüde"*— tired of the man whose conviction and commanding presence had helped to persuade both Germans and their neighbors of the wisdom of reunification. During his final years in office, Kohl's reputation had suffered when he steadfastly refused to reveal the sources of illegal contributions to his own Christian Democratic party. The so-called "Contribution Affair" pointed to widespread political corruption, while Kohl's silence suggested complicity. The new Socialist chancellor, Gerhard Schröder, headed a novel political pairing between his own and the ecology-minded Green party, which observers dubbed the "red-green" coalition. Like Tony Blair's New Labour, the Center-Left, red-green alliance promised to improve existing programs rather than strike out in bold new directions—in Schröder's words, to do "not everything differently, but many things better."

Like Blair again, Schröder's first term proved disappointing in its limited success at reform. But the chancellor still returned to power in 2002 after the closest election in Germany's postwar history, when both the Socialists and the Christian Democrats polled an identical 38.5 percent of the vote. What put Schröder over the top was the performance of the Greens, who now emerged as the third strongest party in Germany. Under the guidance of their charismatic elder statesman, Foreign Minister Joschka Fischer, the Greens had made the transition from critics outside the system to players within it, yet still retained enough of their idealism to appear both more principled and more innovative than either of the two established parties of the Left and Right. Yet as in France and Britain, the issues of unemployment and financing the welfare state refused to go away. The means for solving them required such politically unpopular measures as creating a more flexible labor market, offering fewer benefits, and imposing higher taxes. Here Western European politicians like Schröder confronted the same dilemma as their counterparts in the East: To impose needed economic reforms risked alienating the very voters who had brought them to power. But if "modernizing" the welfare state appeared costly, so did temporizing. In a forthright essay appearing in late 2002 in the weekly *Der Spiegel*, German author Bernhard Schlink taxed the current generation of leaders with timidity and "exhaustion." Kohl's successors, it seemed, feared reform and inaction in equal degrees.

The Promise of the European Union

In the Dutch city of Maastricht, the twelve members of the European Community met in December 1991 to conclude a historic agreement. It was of more than symbolic significance that the Maastricht meeting on Europe's future took place in the very same month and year that the Soviet Union existed from the European scene. With the end of the Cold War, European leaders—some uneasy at the potentially dominant role of a united Germany within the European Community, others at the now unchecked influence of the United States—sought to "deepen" integration. At the same time they planned to broaden Community membership to include several former Soviet bloc states to the East.

The twin goals of deepening and broadening were not always in harmony. Increasing EC membership, for example, ran the risk of lessening cooperation among members with divergent needs and agendas. Nevertheless, the signatories of the Maastricht Treaty pledged to create a European Union of 325 million individuals—larger in both population and gross national product than the United States—enjoying a single currency and divided by no internal borders. The treaty was to come into effect in 1992. By late 1993, a year later than expected, voters in all twelve EC countries had ratified its provisions, and Maastricht became law. The European Community was now reborn as the European Union.

Opinion surveys among citizens of member states, however, revealed a gap between the promise of European unity and popular skepticism about its price. One frequent target of criticism was the so-called "democratic deficit." Ordinary Europeans complained about the powers granted to faceless bureaucrats in Brussels, who often seemed far removed from the realities of everyday life. And they had a point. Few democratic institutions in fact existed within the European Union. The heart of the organization was the European Commission in Brussels—seventeen unelected officials charged with proposing EU policies and monitoring norms on everything from cheese production to labor laws. The one elected body, the European Parliament, located in Strasbourg, France, was correspondingly weak. Decisions at the highest level—including the Maastricht Treaty itself—were made by heads of government of the member states at periodic "summits," and then submitted to voters for ratification by referendum.

Yet in a very real sense, the lack of a strong legislative body within the EU reflected the power of existing democratic institutions in Britain, France, Germany, and other member states. Jealously defending their prerogatives, lawmakers in the individual EU nations resisted ceding power to any supranational parliament, however democratically elected. There was a tension in outlook between "federalists," such as Great Britain, who looked on the EU as a loose gathering of sovereign nations, and "integrationists," like Germany, who believed in the virtues of political as well as economic consolidation.

The need to address the "democratic deficit" within the European Union gained greater urgency as the plans to broaden its membership advanced. After three decades during which economics had been its prime focus, politics now demanded equal attention. In 1995, three members of the formerly rival European Free Trade Association—Austria, Finland, and Sweden—joined the EU. Ten more, including Poland, Hungary, and the Czech Republic, were accepted in late 2002 for inclusion in 2004 (subject to ratification by their electorates). In theory, a united Europe would now stretch from the Atlantic to the borders of Russia. How should decisions in such an enlarged European Union be reached? This crucial question resisted simple answers. Although a summit in Nice granted the president of the European Commission new powers, the EU member states remained deadlocked on how to assign individual countries new voting rights. A cartoon that appeared in the German weekly *Die Zeit* late in 2002 summed up the effects of this stalemate. An automobile labeled "EU Reform" is seen driven by the heads of state of the member countries. "The 15 brakes work wonderfully," Tony Blair is saying. "But where in heaven's name," Chancellor Schröder asks, "is the gas pedal?"

Despite these difficulties, the European Union scored one notable success during the 1990s with its project for monetary union. Not all EU members were eligible to join. By the terms of the Maastricht Treaty, the annual deficit of each candidate for admission could not exceed 3 percent of the gross national product, while the total public debt must remain below 60 percent of GDP. Set to ensure that "strong" currencies like the German mark were not diluted by "weak" currencies like the Greek drachma, the 3 percent limit also prevented governments from extending public assistance to citizens at the time of deepening recession and the highest unemployment in both France and Germany since the Second World War. Ironically, the very safeguards on which Germany's central bank had insisted now forced the Kohl government (and its successor under Schröder) to adopt deficit-cutting measures that reduced its ability to reflate the economy. At the same time, economically weaker members of the EU, such as Spain and Portugal, fought hard to be included in the Monetary Union as a matter of national pride.

When the euro was finally launched on New Year's Day 2002, displacing the French franc and German mark (among other national currencies) as legal tender, a surprising total of eleven nations among the fifteen members of the newly enlarged EU had adopted the euro. Though qualified, Great Britain, Denmark, and Sweden still refused to join in what they saw as a risky experiment; Greece remained the sole EU country unable to meet the economic criteria for inclusion (though it belatedly qualified in early 2001). A new European Central Bank headquartered in the German city of Frankfurt assumed responsibility for setting interest rates and regulating the money supply. Yet despite initial difficulties (including attempts at counterfeiting), the new currency found acceptance in the major markets of Germany, France, and Italy, as well as eight smaller EU states. From the common Coal and Steel Community foreseen in the Schuman Plan of 1951 (see Chapter 17, II) to a common currency a half century later was no small achievement.

Even before that Shuman Plan, Winston Churchill had invoked the vision of "a kind of United States of Europe." The aim of the survivors of World War II, he declared, should be "to recreate the European Family, or as much of it as we can, and provide it with a structure under which it can dwell in peace, in safety, and in freedom." That vision at last seemed within reach. "In 1989," the Danish prime minister told the prospective new EU members in Copenhagen in 2002, "brave and visionary people brought about the collapse of the Berlin Wall. They could no longer tolerate the forced division of Europe. Today we are giving life to their hopes."

III. A NEW EUROPE?

The Cold War had allowed Europeans to view their continent through the lens of dual and opposing definitions: the Free World and the Soviet Bloc, capitalism and communism, East and West. Now the prospect of reuniting that continent after fifty years of enforced separation challenged them to ponder their identity anew. "Europe" might mean parliamentary democracy, human rights, capitalism, and free trade. It also meant nationalism, anti-Semitism, xenophobia, corruption, and a controlled economy. As both the European Union and NATO expanded eastwards, some voiced fears that the Western European consensus of democracy and a free economy would become diluted by the post-Communist residue of the newly joining member states, while others speculated on the increased dangers posed by immigration and globalization. Who would define the new Europe? And what would that definition be?

The Specter of Immigration

In the Communist Manifesto of 1848, Karl Marx boasted that communism had become a "specter haunting Europe." A century and a half later, with that specter seemingly laid to rest, Western Europe appeared far more troubled by another specter: immigration. Just how many immigrants now resided in the European Union was impossible to determine with accuracy, since some arrived illegally or overstayed their visas. But at the beginning of the new millennium, their numbers amounted to at least 19 million individuals—among them, almost 13 million Muslims—or some six per cent of the total EU population.

Although this number was modest by U.S. standards, it represented a demographic revolution for Western Europe. Unlike the United States, Europe as a whole had no history of sustained immigration. Indeed, many Europeans of an earlier generation had themselves sought to escape poverty by emigrating abroad—Irish, Poles, Germans, Italians, and Jews from Eastern Europe had been among the many groups seeking a new life abroad. But now the trend was reversed. During the decade of the 1960s—a time of economic expansion—thousands of immigrants from former British colonies of Pakistan and India on the Indian subcontinent had first arrived to work in the mills. A decade later, their jobs began to vanish as British manufacturing declined, a victim of globalization. Yet the immigrants remained. Germany had similarly encouraged Turkish "guest workers" to take jobs in German factories in the 1960s, while France had accepted migrants from former French colonies in North Africa, especially Morocco and Algeria.

To what degree were Europeans prepared to tolerate cultural and religious diversity within their own countries? The second generation of native-born Europeans of Turkish or North African origin asked for civic rights but rejected total assimilation. Indeed, by 2000 Islam had become the second most important religion in France after Roman Catholicism, with more adherents than Protestantism and Judaism combined. Arabic-language radio programs could be heard in major French metropolitan centers, while Turks in Germany insisted on maintaining their own separate religious and cultural institutions. To admit difference without inferiority—this was the difficult challenge posed to the European conscience by the newest of the Continent's many minorities.

The most sensitive issue for EU public opinion was not the presence of established minorities, however, but the specter of continuing and future immigration. By 2001, legal migration into Western Europe was estimated at 400,000 persons annually. But illegal migration posed a far greater threat. Fears of unchecked immigration helped to fuel the political fortunes of right-wing parties such as Jean-Marie Le Pen's National Front in France and Jörg Haider's Freedom Party in Austria, which shrewdly linked immigration with unemployment, arguing that immigrants took jobs from the native born.

Similar fears also led more mainstream conservative parties like Britain's Tories to propose (and enact) severe restrictions on immigration. "Passengers seeking political asylum," read a sign at London's Heathrow Airport, the busiest in Europe, "are urged to apply immediately in order to avoid future problems."

By the turn of the century, the chance of receiving legal permission to enter the EU as an immigrant from Africa or Asia was close to zero. In such a climate, illegal immigration soared. Some estimates placed the number of such illegal immigrants entering Italy (whose borders were notoriously porous) at 700,000 in 1999 alone. Smuggling immigrants became a lucrative trade for organized crime, while bodies of those who had starved as stowaways or been drowned and washed up on beaches bore testimony to the dangers of clandestine entry. In addition, there was the issue of Albania. Barely forty miles of ocean separated the poorest of the countries of formerly Communist Eastern Europe from the Italian port city of Brindisi. A first wave of Albanian refugees reached the Italian shore in 1992 after the fall of communism; a second arrived in early 1997 as a civil war flared in their unhappy homeland.

Into this unstable mixture of distrust and hard-won tolerance came the shock of the terrorist attacks of September 11, 2001, in the United States. Not only did Europeans grieve for their countrymen lost in the World Trade Center; they also confronted the unsettling fact that Islamic terrorist groups now operated in Europe itself. Hamburg, Germany, had sheltered an al-Qaeda cell and one of the leaders of the September 11 attacks, Mohammed Atta; Richard Reed, the so-called "shoe bomber" apprehended attempting to blow up a transatlantic flight on route to Miami, had worshiped in a mosque in London.

Young German skinheads defiantly give the Nazi salute at a right-wing demonstration in Leipzig in February, 1990. (*Courtesy Andree Kaiser/Reuter/Corbis-Bettmann*)

Among Western Europe's nearly eight million Muslims, it was logical to assume that at least a some sympathized with Islamic extremists.

There were, however, some encouraging signs that Europeans were becoming more ready to differentiate between the benefits of a diverse population and the threat of terrorism—to accept multiculturalism while opposing religiously inspired violence of all kinds. Major cities like London, Paris, and Berlin had a truly international feel by the start of the new millennium; while one Indian observer noted that the favorite food of the British was now curry. But beyond the attractions of world music and ethnic cuisine, there was a more practical reason to continue to welcome immigrants from abroad. Europe's birth rate was in sharp decline. With the exception of France, no member state of the EU now succeeded in replacing its population by natural means. Germany, for example, registered annually an excess of 200,000 deaths over births. The long-term consequences for the economy and tax revenues were dramatic; as the working-age population contracted, fewer and fewer tax-payers would be obliged to support more and more retirees. Economists predicted that the European welfare state—already under severe financial strain—would be bankrupt by 2025 at the latest. Like it or not, western Europe was now increasingly dependent on immigration to maintain its standard of living.

NATO and European Security

NATO at first seemed an anomaly in the new Europe. Created in 1949 as a defensive alliance against the Soviet Union and its client states (see Chapter 17, II), it found itself forty years later without a clear mission. The collaboration among Western European countries that it fostered early in its history—especially the reconciliation between France and the Federal Republic of Germany—was now enshrined within the European Union. Meanwhile the military threat posed by Eastern Europe had disappeared along with the old Soviet Union. NATO's military preparedness and the threat of an escalating arms race helped ensure a peaceful conclusion to the revolutions of 1989; in the end, the Red Army had neither invaded Western Europe nor tried to shore up regimes in Eastern Europe, as it had in 1956 and 1968. Instead, between 1989 and 1992 it had retreated from its garrisons in Poland, East Germany, and Czechoslovakia and returned to Russia. Surely NATO could now disband.

NATO's leaders chose otherwise. At a summit meeting held in the Belgian capital, Brussels, in January 1994, the decision was made for NATO to expand eastward into territory once dominated by the Warsaw Pact by admitting Poland, the Czech Republic, and Hungary, with further expansion possible in the new millennium. Against the argument that no current security threat justified a military alliance, NATO's defenders replied that while communism itself had vanished, other military threats to European security had not. But in fact the real arguments for NATO expansion had little to do with an immediate military threat. For the United States, the prospect of an enlarged NATO ensured a continuing American presence in Europe; for the prospective new NATO members, it both meant the satisfaction of joining the likes of Britain and France in an international "club" and served as a counterweight against a resurgent Russia.

Would NATO retain a military role in Europe? Its early post–Cold War record was not reassuring. During the 1992–1995 Bosnian war, where the bloodiest fighting in

Europe since World War II occurred close to the borders of a NATO member (Italy), the alliance failed to agree on a coherent strategy. While the United States called for bombing against the Serbs, the British and French refused to place their ground troops in danger. Not until August 1995, did the alliance manage to resolve its differences and apply pressure on the Bosnian Serbs, forcing them to the peace talks that culminated in the Dayton Agreement. At best, then, the advantages of NATO membership might be said to be psychological rather than military. Hungarians might not expect American troops to fight to safeguard their eastern borders, but they could still take pride in belonging to an organization that symbolized victory in the cold War and through whose membership they could demonstrate that they now belonged to the winning side. The prospect of membership also created leverage for further change in Eastern Europe—inducing Hungary to resolve historical claims against neighbors (such as Slovakia and Romania) with large Hungarian minorities, for example, or helping the civilian government in Poland to assert greater authority over the nation's armed forces.

The most negative reaction to NATO's planned expansion occurred, not surprisingly, in Russia. Former President Gorbachev had earlier been criticized for permitting a reunited Germany to remain in NATO; few Russians were prepared to see NATO's eastern border creep closer still. With rare unanimity, politicians from across the political spectrum denounced the prospect that former Warsaw Pact countries would now shift their allegiance to an organization that had been their principal during in the Cold War. In addition to the perceived military threat of American forces stationed near Russia's borders, there were other reasons for the Kremlin's displeasure. NATO expansion brought home the humiliating fact that Russia was no longer a superpower, that it no longer possessed the military strength to prevent NATO and the United States from moving into that part of Europe that the Soviet Union had regarded as its own private sphere of influence.

Despite deep misgivings, Russian leaders at length decided that they had little choice but to acquiesce and then demand as much as possible in return. At a meeting with President Bill Clinton in the Finnish capital Helsinki in 1997, Boris Yeltsin agreed to NATO's eastward expansion in return for a pledge that no nuclear weapons would be stationed on the territory of new members. This concession allowed Moscow to preserve some measure of national pride, and at the same time to be named a "NATO partner." Then came September 11, 2001, and the al Qaeda terrorist attack on the World Trade Center and the Pentagon in the United States. Invoking Article V of the North Atlantic Treaty, which declared that an attack on one member constituted an attack on the alliance as a whole, the United States requested the support of its fellow NATO members in Operation Enduring Freedom in Afghanistan. Although the United States performed most of the military operations in Afghanistan either alone or in partnership with the Afghan Northern Alliance, NATO played an essential role in naval support and post-combat peacekeeping. Its declared enemy was no longer Communist aggression, but world terrorism.

Poland, Hungary, and the Czech Republic were the first former Warsaw Pact members inducted into the NATO alliance in 1999. Then at a summit meeting held in the Czech capital, Prague, in November, 2002, seven additional Eastern European states—Bulgaria, Estonia, Latvia, Lithuania, Romania, Slovakia, and Slovenia—gained formal admission. The term "North Atlantic," which had already ceased to be an accu-

MAP 23.2 NATO expansion.

rate description of alliance geography after the admission of Turkey, now became even more of an anachronism. Having expanded well into Eastern Europe, however, NATO leaders were now faced with the same challenges of governance as the leaders of the EU. Indeed, because NATO decisions required unanimity, the potential for new members to block initiatives was now greater even than in the European Union. How could NATO function as an effective military organization with twenty-five members whose interests often diverged? Outgoing president Václav Havel, the host of the Prague summit, observed that an expanded NATO now resembled "a large, but somewhat empty structure." Filling that structure with a common vision was a task that could not long be delayed.

Europe's Cultural Identity

Was there a single standard that defined what it meant to be "European" in the early twenty-first century? To some observers, the community of nations grouped within the European Union held the keys to prosperity and political stability. To be European, in their eyes, meant to meet the admissions criteria of the EU or of NATO. With the collapse of the Soviet Union and the alternative form of modernism that it represented, only one way to be European apparently remained. Democratic institutions, a market economy, a wealth of consumer goods, and assertive individualism now seemed to define not just Western Europe, but the continent as a whole.

Yet the desire to emulate Western Europe was not without its critics. In Russia and other parts of Eastern Europe, voices defended a special national mission—spiritual rather than material, authoritarian rather than democratic, communitarian rather than individualistic. Such voices gained in strength as Russia itself lost political power within Europe. Many there feared that becoming more European simply meant becoming less Russian. They pointed to the soaring crime rate, growing disparity between rich and poor, and rampant materialism that followed the transformation of 1989–1991 as evidence that the new, Western model did not work for them. At the same time, some attempted to demonstrate the distinctiveness of Eastern Europe and its separation from the West by evoking the past. Urged on by their respective governments, historians wrote to illustrate parochial, patriotic themes. In Slovakia, for example, new history textbooks now praised the very politicians who had collaborated with Hitler during the Second World War in return for the Nazi dictator's willingness to grant Slovakia independence from its Czech neighbor. No mention was made of their anti-Semitism or suppression of civil rights.

But even those who accepted the overall framework of democracy and capitalism often defended Europe's rich and varied mosaic of regional cultures as a resource to be protected against the leveling influences of globalization. Indeed, one of the most frequent criticisms of the European Union itself was that its rules were too restrictive, tending toward a bland uniformity at odds with Europe's past. Perhaps, these observers suggested, what was most distinctly European could not be reduced to a single model—certainly not the model of a consumer society addicted to American products, or controlled by multinational corporations. In fact, the supposed perils of American dominance were often conflated with those of globalization. The French farmer José Bové won widespread sympathy when he set fire to a McDonald's restaurant in protest, later declaring "the world is not for sale."

The collapse of the Soviet Union and the disrepute into which planned economies had fallen did not in fact prevent thousands of protesters—mostly young—from voicing their opposition to globalization. The movement that demonstrated at meetings such as the G-8 summit in Genoa in 2001 had no patience for the World Trade Organization and the World Bank, whom they accused of putting profits before human welfare or environmental concerns. Though their indictment was rejected by both politicians and business leaders, the fact remained that Europe was vulnerable to many transcontinental forces, ranging from genetically altered foods to global warming, that had replaced the Cold War as a source of popular anxiety.

Many Europeans also wished to preserve what remained of traditional local patterns of landscape and architecture—Europe's "patrimony," as the French termed it. As the globalizing pressures for change and the threat from environmental pollution grew, so did efforts to preserve monuments throughout the Continent, from the Parthenon in Athens to wooden churches in Norway, while the Green parties pressed for the creation of more national parks. Reminders of the old Europe were more numerous in the East and South, where industrialization was less advanced. One of the attractions of the newly liberated countries of Eastern Europe for Eastern European visitors was the sense that there time had stood still, that the charm of the past has better resisted the destructive effects of technological change because of the continuing poverty of the East. Prague—one of the most beautiful cities in Europe—remained for a time unspoiled by the neon displays that marred Vienna; the Spree Forest near Berlin still looked much as it had in the time of Bismarck and Fontane, a century and a half ago; monasteries in Romania's Carpathian Mountains were spared from Ceausescu's fantasies of urban renewal. But to maintain them in this state, or to restore what had fallen into decay, represented a major challenge.

Thus the search for European cultural identity pulled in contrary directions. Against the centripetal force of European unification, national and regional loyalties gained a new prominence. The same Western European governments that sent representatives to the EU Commission in Brussels also ceded autonomy to their own regions, such as Catalonia and the Basque provinces in Spain or to Scotland and Wales in Great Britain, where "devolution" finally won the day. The new Europe, it seemed, would include both a supranational and a local dimension, both common institutions and a sense of separateness. Significantly, of the approximately 15,000 EU bureaucrats whose presence in Brussels attracted such criticism, fully one-fifth were engaged simply in translating documents from one to another of the EU's eleven official languages. More would be needed to cope with ten additional official languages in 2004.

Thus the drive for increased European unity paradoxically fostered awareness of the impressive breadth of existing European cultures, languages, literatures, religions, and beliefs. Advertising campaigns—a good barometer for assessing cultural differences—received sharply contrasting emphases in different of regions of Europe. A prize-winning ad for a fruit drink in Britain, for example, showed an Englishman taunting the French for being unable to appreciate its taste—hardly a strategy that would sell in Paris. The same automobile that was praised for its speed and handling in Italy was promoted for its safety in Sweden. In place of a Europe sharply divided in two by the Iron Curtain, what was now appearing were multiple, overlapping Europes. But there were also constants that underlay these differences—a growing belief in democracy, relative affluence, and a sense of belonging to a cultural tradition that valued the quality of life as well as financial success.

A century earlier on the eve of the First World War, Europe had been the world's preeminent power—its wealth, military strength, and artistic brilliance beyond challenge (see Chapter 1, I). Now that preeminence had vanished—the victim of two world wars, a global economy, and the emergence of the United States as the world's sole superpower. But though it could no longer lay claim to its old, unquestioned hegemony, Europe remained potent in its new guise as the European Union. The challenge was to agree on just what "Europe" meant and to balance that definition and the need for roots with the broader obligations and opportunities of the new, post–Cold War era.

READINGS

For an introduction to the problems faced by Eastern Europe in the immediate post-Communist era, see Tina Rosenberg, *The Haunted Land: Facing Europe's Ghosts after Communism** (1995) as well as the issue of *Daedalus* entitled *Eastern Europe . . . Central Europe . . . Europe* (Winter 1990). On the introduction of shock therapy in Poland, seen through the eyes of a key American advisor, see Jeffrey Sachs, *Poland's Jump to the Market Economy* (1992). Rudolf L. Tőkés, *Hungary's Negotiated Revolution: Economic Reform, Social Change, and Political Succession** (1996), details the twin transitions toward democracy and a market economy.

David Remnick, *Resurrection: The Struggle for a New Russia** (1997), captures both the disorder and the promise of post-Communist Russia, as seen by a gifted journalist. Michael McFaul, *Russia's Unfinished Revolution: Political Change from Gorbachev to Putin* (2001) offers a detailed look at the political twists and turns of the 1990s, while Nicolai N. Petro, *The Rebirth of Russian Democracy: An Interpretation of Political Culture* (1995), makes the case for an indigenous Russian political tradition balancing a strong executive with decentralized control over local issues. Roy Medvedev, *Post-Soviet Russia: A Journey through the Yeltsin Era** (2000) offers a rich and detailed account by a major Russian historian. Luke March, *The Communist Party in Post-Soviet Russia** (2002) examines the party's efforts to adapt to a radically altered political landscape. On Yeltsin's fateful incursion into Chechnya, see Carlota Gall and Thomas de Waal, *Chechnya: A Small Victorious War** (1997).

An analysis of Russia's economic prospects following Gorbachev's departure can be found in Andrei Schleifer and Daniel Treisman, *Without a Map: Political Tactics and Economic Reform in Russia* (2000), where the authors (who themselves consulted for the Yeltsin government) argue that many economic setbacks were unavoidable. Broader social responses to reform in post-Communist Russia are explored in Richard Sakwa, *Russian Politics and Society,** 2nd ed. (1996), and Mary Buckley, *Redefining Russian Society and Polity** (1993). Russian efforts to clarify the historical record of the Soviet years are the subject of Andrew Baruch Wachtel, *An Obsession with History: Russian Writers Confront the Past** (1994).

The best single analysis of the death of Yugoslavia is Misha Glenny, *The Fall of Yugoslavia: The Third Balkan War,** 3rd rev. ed. (1996). See also John B. Allcock's detailed *Explaining Yugoslavia* (2002), the work of a well-informed British sociologist. Norman M. Naimark, *Fires of Hatred: Ethnic Cleansing in Twentieth-Century Europe** (2001), contains a chilling account of the civilian losses during Yugoslavia's civil wars of the 1990s (as well as treating the Soviet deportation of Chechens during World War II).

*Books marked with an asterisk are available in paperback.

Other studies, written from a variety of individual standpoints, include Paul Harris, *Somebody Else's War: Frontline Reports from the Balkan Wars, 1991–1992** (1992); and Christopher Merrill, *Only the Nails Remain: Scenes from the Balkan Wars* (1999). Zlatko Dizdarevic, *Sarajevo: A War Journal* (1993), is the story of the siege and destruction of the Bosnian capital as experienced by a brave journalist and native Sarajevan. Tim Judah, *Kosovo: War and Revenge,** 2nd ed. (2002) provides the best introduction to that conflict; Wesley K. Clark, *Waging Modern War** (2001), by the NATO supreme commander in Kosovo, describes the intricacies and frustrations of leading a military campaign subject to design by committee. The case against Milosevic is detailed in Norman Cigar and Paul Williams, *Indictment at the Hague: The Milosevic Regime and the Crimes of the Balkan Wars* (2002). His political career is the subject of Leonard J. Cohen, *Serpent in the Bosom: The Rise and Fall of Slobodan Milosevic* (2001).

An outstanding introduction to contemporary Italy is Paul Ginsborg, *Italy and Its Discontents: Family, Civil Society, State, 1980–2001* (2003). The political earthquake that began in Italy in 1992 is explored in Mark Gilbert, *The Italian Revolution: The End of Politics Italian Style?** (1995) and in Matt Frei, *Getting the Boot: Italy's Unfinished Revolution* (1995). The former author is a political scientist with first-hand knowledge of Italy, the latter a gifted BBC correspondent stationed in Rome. Alexander Stille, *Excellent Cadavers: The Mafia and the Death of the First Italian Republic* (1995) explores ties between the mafia and the Christian Democrats as well as the courageous anti-mafia campaign waged against them by Giovanni Falcone and Paolo Borselino. Twin issues of *Daedalus* offer a balance sheet after *Tangentopoli*: "Italy: Resilient and Vulnerable, Volume 1: The European Challenge" (Spring 2001) and "Italy: Resilient and Vulnerable, Volume 2: Politics and Society" (Summer 2001).

On contemporary France, see John Ardagh, *France in the New Century: Portrait of a Changing Society** (2000). On Ireland, see Tim Pat Coogan, *The Troubles: Ireland's Ordeal and the Search for Peace** (1996). Germany after reunification is the subject of Michael Mertes, Steven Muller, and Heinrich August Winkler, eds., *In Search of Germany** (1996), which first appeared (in abbreviated form) as an issue of the journal *Daedalus*. Stanley Hoffmann, *The European Sisyphus: Essays on Europe, 1964–1994** (1995), traces the project to unify Europe over three decades, as analyzed by a master observer. Equally rewarding is the same author's *World Disorders: Troubled Peace in the Post-Cold War Era* (1998). The successes and remaining problems of an expanded European Union are detailed in John Pinder, *The European Union: A Very Short Introduction** (2001) and Loukas Tsoukalis, *The New European Economy: the Politics and Economics of Integration,** 2nd rev. ed. (1993).

On the problems of immigrants, see Riva Kastoryano, *Negotiating Identities: States and Immigrants in France and Germany** (2002) as well as the older study of S. Castles, *Here For Good: Western Europe's New Ethnic Minorities* (1984). A sensitive and fascinating portrait of Britain's black and Asian population can be found in Dervla Murphy, *Tales from Two Cities: Travels of Another Sort** (1987). How multiculturalism has and will transform Britain's self-image is explored in Yasmin Alibhai-Brown, *Who Do We Think We Are? Imagining the New Britain** (2000). Ingo Hasselbach, *Führer-Ex: Memoirs of a former Neo-Nazi* (1996), describes the seduction and subsequent disillusionment of a young German on the radical Right, while Françoise Gaspard, *A Small City in France** (1995), recounts the struggle of a Socialist mayor to combat racist extremism in the northern French city of Dreux. For the rationale of French opposition to globalization by a militant, see José Bové and François Dufour, *The World is not for Sale: Farmers against Junk Food* (trans. 2001). On the attractions and frustrations generated by the concept of Europe itself, especially within the EU, see Tony Judt, *A Grand Illusion? An Essay on Europe* (1996). Russian ambivalence toward its European neighbors is explored in Iver B. Neumann, *Russia and the Idea of Europe** (1996).

Index

Hiroshima, 340
Hitler, Adolf, 238. *see also* Nazi
    Party/Regime
    anti-Semitism, 220, 235
    chancellor, appointment as, 223
    during Great Depression, 197
    Mein Kampf, 221, 280, 312, 318
    and Mussolini, compared, 219–20
    as Nazi Party chief, 220
    and Pan-Germanism, 27, 220
    power of, intentionalists versus
        structuralists, 224–25
    rise to power, 220–23
Ho Chi Minh, 435–36
Holocaust, 320–21
Homage to Catalonia (Orwell), 269
Honecker, Erich, 557, 563
Honegger, Arthur, 186
Horkheimer, Max, 404
Horthy, Miklós, 99
House, Edward M., 113, 115
Hugenberg, Alfred, 163, 197, 221
Hungarian Revolution (1956),
    466–69, 469
Hungary
    and Bolshevism, 98–99
    Catholic Church in, 358
    collapse of communism, 556
    Communist rule, imposition of,
        356–57
    and the European Union, 589
    fascism, 234
    and NATO, 594
    "Red Terror" (1919), 99
    shock therapy, 569–70
    Trianon, Treaty of (1919), 118
    "White Terror" (1919–1921), 99
Husak, Gustav, 506
al-Hussein, Saddam, 587

I

I. G. Farben, 58, 131, 138
Ideology. *see also* Conservatism;
        Democracy; Liberalism; Radical-
        ism; Socialism
    defined, 15–16
    First World War, 77
    imperialistic, 26–27
    syndicalism, 28–29
Iliescu, Ion, 559
Immigration, 132–33, 591–93
Imperialism (1880–1914)
    Africa, 24–26
    China, 24
    colonial rule versus democracy,
        25–26
    economic need for, 25
    Ottoman Empire, 24
    superiority, ethnic and racial, 26–27
Indeterminacy principle, 174–75

India, 166–67, 433
Indochina, 435–36
Indonesia, 432–33, 435
Industrial Revolution
    class distinctions, diminishing, 10
    creation of the proletariat, 18
    rural versus urban effects, 10
    scientific thinking, 10–11
    twentieth century sequel, 10, 127
    urbanization, 8, 9, 10
Inflation of 1923, Germany, 131,
    135–37
International Monetary Fund (IMF),
    572
"International Style" architecture,
    164, 188–91, 209
Ionesco, Eugène, 398–99
Iraq, 587
Ireland, 155–57, 522–23, 539, 548, 587
Irish Free State, 156, 167
Irish Republican Army (IRA), 587
Iron Guard, 234, 351–52
Israel, 406, 530
Italian Mafia, 583
Italy. *see also* Fascism; Mussolini, Ben-
        ito
    abortion, 547
    agrarian poverty, 421
    Albania, annexation of, 299
    Albanian refugees, 592
    and Bolshevism, 98
    Christian Democracy, post De
        Gasperi, 453–55
    constitution, 387
    currency inflation, 134
    democracy, progress of, 22
    divorce, 546–47
    and Ethiopia, 25, 282
    fascism, 167–68
    First World War, 51–52, 57, 71
    Fiume, quarrels with Yugoslavia
        over, 123, 214
    Four-Power Pact (1933), 280
    the "historic compromise," 525–26
    immigrants, illegal, 592
    Mani Pulite campaign, 583
    marriage law, 218
    Maximalism, 98, 100, 215
    and militarism, 28
    as a nation-state, 6
    Olive Tree, 583–84
    "opening to the left," 495–96
    Paris Peace Settlement, 113, 116
    parliamentary government, 21
    Party of Action, 380
    People's Bloc, 417
    the Resistance, 330, 339–40
    Risorgimento, 22
    Rome-Berlin Axis, 283–84, 294
    Second World War, 310–11, 328,
        329, 368–69

and the Spanish Civil War, 288–89
syndicalism, 28, 29
Tangentopoli, 582–83
and Trieste, 414
tripartism, 380–82, 417
women in the workforce, 548
women's suffrage, 143–44
Ivan the Terrible, Tsar of Russia, 255

J

Jannings, Emil, 275
Japan
    atomic bombs, dropping of (1945),
        340
    Paris Peace Settlement, 113,
        114–15
    Russo-Japanese War (1904), 9, 14,
        42
    Second World War, 314, 315, 340
Jaruzelski, Wojciech, 555
Jellicoe, Sir John, 55
Jodl, Friedrich, 330
Joffre, Joseph, 45, 48, 51, 60, 61, 64,
        71
John XXIII, Pope, 407–08
John Paul I, Pope, 409
John Paul II, Pope, 409, 510, 546
Joplin, Scott, 130
Jospin, Lionel, 585
Joyce, James, 183–84
Juan Carlos, King of Spain, 462, 529
July Monarchy (1830–1848), 17
July Revolution of 1830, 17
Jung, Carl G., 178
Juppé, Alain, 584
Jutland, Battle of (1916), 55

K

Kádár, János, 556
Kafka, Franz, 182, 183
Kaledin, Alexei, 90
Kamenev, Leo, 244, 245, 254
Kandinsky, Wassily, 187, 188, 189
Kapp Putsch (1920), 124, 198, 221
Karageorgevich dynasty, 31
Karamanlis, Constantine, 527–28,
        528, 545
Károlyi, Count Mihályi, 98–99
Kazakhstan, 573
Kemal, Mustapha. *see* Atatürk
Kennedy, John F., 493
Kenya, 437, 439
Kerensky, Alexander, 70, 86
Keynes, John Maynard, 120, 197,
        266–68
Khrushchev, Nikita, 450, 462, 465,
        466, 467, 471, 480, 481, 483,
        484–86, 503, 549, 551, 560
Kiel mutiny (1918), 72

Weber, Max, 176, 178–79
Webern, Anton, 185
Wehner, Herbert, 516
Weill, Kurt, 275–76
Wells, H. G., 181
Wenceslas Square, 559
Werkbund Exhibition, 144
Whitehead, Alfred North, 180
Wiechert, Ernst, 393
William II, Emperor of Germany, 6, 31, 58
Wilson, Harold, 494, 520, 521
Wilson, Woodrow, 42, 56–57, 65, 67, 78, 85, 99, 105, 106–07, 111–17, 120, 149, 159
Wittgenstein, Ludwig, 180, 181, 266
Women
    abortion and birth control, 145
    emancipation of (1920s), 143–45
    family size, reduction in, 13–14
    in homemaker role, 145
    position of, prewar (1914), 12–13
    professions and politics, entry into, 143
    suffragette campaign, 13
    and Victorian codes of behavior, 13

Woolf, Virginia, 13, 181, 183–84
Wrangel, Baron Peter, 91
Wright, Frank Lloyd, 188–91, 189
Wyszynski, Cardinal Stefan, 358, 470

Y

Yalta Conference (1945), 337–38
Yeltsin, Boris, 561, 571, 572–74, 594
Yevtushenko, Yevgeny, 482, 508
Yom Kippur War, 530
Young, Owen D., 152–53
Young Plan of June 1929, 153, 163, 221
Ypres, Second Battle of (1915), 48
Yudenich, Nicholai, 89
Yugoslavia
    Catholic Church in, 358
    Chetniks, 323
    civil wars, 575–80
    and communism, 349, 352
    conquest of, by Hitler, 312
    "ethnic cleansing," 577
    ethnic rivalries, 576
    expulsion by the Cominform, 359
    Fiume, quarrels with Italy over, 123, 214

independence, 110
and the Little Entente, 150
Neuilly, Treaty of (1919), 118
Paris Peace Settlement, 116
the Resistance, 323–24, 333–34
royal dictatorship, of King Alexander, 168
Tito, death of, 576
Tito regime, 359–60, 469–70
Trianon, Treaty of (1919), 118
and Trieste, 414
unification versus confederation, 577
and the U.S.S.R., 466

Z

Zhdanov, Andrei, 355, 360, 402, 417, 427, 462
Zhivkov, Todor, 556, 563
Zhukov, Grigori, 314, 326, 340, 354, 372, 465, 471
Zinoviev, Grigori, 158, 243–44, 245, 253, 254, 255
Zinoviev letter, 158, 203

EUROPE TODAY

ATLANTIC OCEAN

60°   30°   15°

Reykjavik   **ICELAND**

FAEROE ISLANDS

SHETLAND ISLANDS

Berg

HEBRIDES   *ORKNEY ISLANDS*

NOR SEA

Glasgow
• Edinburgh

Belfast

IRELAND   **Dublin** ★
Liverpool
Cork

GREAT BRITAIN

NETHERLAND

London ★   Amsterdam
Southhampton

Brussels ★
BELGIUM

Cherbourg   • Le Havre   Fra
Brest •
LUXEMBOURG
Paris ★ Seine Strasbo
Nantes   Loire River

FRANCE

SWITZER

Clemont- • Geneva
Ferrand
Bordeaux •   Lyon   Tu

Ger

Santander
Rhône River

Porto •   *Douro River*

Marseille   **Mo**

PORTUGAL   **SPAIN**
Tagus River
Madrid ★
Lisbon •

Valencia

• Barcelona

BALEARIC ISLANDS

MAJORCA

CO
SAR

Guadalquivir River

Sevilla •
Malaga

MADEIRA

Tangier   • **Gibraltar**

Algers ★

Rabat ★
Casablanca •
•Oran

CANARY ISLANDS

MOROCCO

ALGERIA   **TUN**

WESTERN SAHARA   **MAURITANIA**

45°

30°

0   250   500 Miles

0   250   500 Kilometers